Readings in
POPULATION

Readings in
POPULATION

EDITED BY

WILLIAM PETERSEN

ROBERT LAZARUS PROFESSOR OF SOCIAL DEMOGRAPHY

THE OHIO STATE UNIVERSITY

THE MACMILLAN COMPANY, NEW YORK

COLLIER-MACMILLAN LIMITED, LONDON

The Macmillan Company
866 Third Avenue, New York, New York 10022

Collier-Macmillan Canada, Ltd., Toronto, Ontario

Library of Congress catalog card number: 78–169981

Printing: 1 2 3 4 5 6 7 8   Year: 2 3 4 5 6 7 8

PREFACE

In any academic discipline, a student's understanding of the subject matter is improved if, on occasion, he supplements his basic studies with journal articles that report in detail the research that is only briefly summarized in his textbook. No library, however, has enough sets of such journals, and of course no student can afford to buy the volumes in order to read only one article in each. To resolve this dilemma, publishing firms have issued so-called "readers" in almost every field. In their most modest form, these are collections of articles in their original type font, photocopied and bound as a unit. Or the various papers are reset in all of their variety of literary style, with their overlap and repetition. There are several such readers in the discipline of population, and it would serve little purpose to offer yet another.

This book differs from the usual anthology in several important respects. I hope that it will both serve the usual function of supplementing a textbook and go well beyond that minimum.

A field such as demography has, at any one time, about a hundred articles deemed to be of the greatest importance, and the particular taste of any editor is likely to reduce this total by perhaps half. In many of this book's selections, I have followed this kind of criterion. I do not believe, for example, that the current emphasis on population policy and the control of fertility is merely transitory, and the heavy representation here under these headings reflects this judgment. Nor, along another dimension, is a presidential address to the Population Association of America an esoteric choice. A number of papers are reprinted from such journals as *Demography* and the *Milbank Memorial Fund Quarterly*, which because of their general excellence are obvious sources. On the other hand, three of the articles printed here have not appeared elsewhere. Three or four others have been revised so much from their first presentation that they can reasonably be denoted as original papers. Three others have been translated from other languages and, for those who do not know them, are the equivalent of new analyses. The range of sources, over all, is far wider than the five or six journals to which American demographers generally subscribe.

Whenever this could be done with no sacrifice of quality, an effort was made to add another dimension to the usual discussion of a topic. On international migration, for instance, the well-established American bibliographies list several hundred papers concerning the impetus to leave Europe, the settlement in the United States, the process of assimilation, the adequacy of the statistics, and so on. I chose rather to offer an analysis in the framework of two other countries: Argentina in historical depth and Switzerland for the recent past. And two other papers, on Palestinian refugees and tourism, are concerned with types of migration that many demographers prefer to ignore. Or, on the over-all topic of population data, several articles could have been chosen to round out the single one on the United States census. Instead there is one each on the garbled historical record in the South Seas (not remarkably improved, according to another report, in Papua's first census) and on the techniques involved in counting the populations of China and the Soviet Union. I find these not only interesting in themselves but an aid to someone who wants to understand, apart from the specifics of a particular locale, some of the general limits to collecting full and accurate statistics.

Chosen for a variety of reasons from a wide range of sources, the articles were then shaped into sufficient uniformity really to constitute a book. The conventions governing table headings, citations, footnoting, and so on were adapted to the style set for all the contributions. But the editor's control of form stopped well short of any interference with the substance of the individual pieces, which have remained the idiosyncratic products of their distinguished (in both senses of that word) authors. No anthology can be as unified as a book by a single writer, and to attempt to make it so would be both presumptuous and foolhardy. But by interpolating a commentary between papers, rather than in longer introductions to each of the several sections, I have tried to tie the pieces together and provide continuity. By walking across the bridges so constructed, the reader will be saved the sometimes almost painful leaps required when only a heading introduces another topic, analyzed in a new manner and presented in a different style.

Compiling this volume has been, among other things, an enjoyable intellectual jaunt through some unfamiliar corners of our discipline. I hope that some of the joy will be shared, that those who read this book will also find that learning need not be entirely a solemn enterprise.

WILLIAM PETERSEN

Columbus, Ohio

CONTENTS

1 Population Growth, Past and Future   1

The Equilibrium Population, *by Edward S. Deevey*   2

The Population of Norway during the Past Two Centuries, *by
Louis Henry*   17

From the Traditional to the "Tertiary" Life Cycle, *by Jean
Fourastié*   29

2 Population Theories   39

Population Theory and Doctrine: A Historical Survey, *by
Nathan Keyfitz*   41

3 Concepts and Data   70

Garbled Population Estimates of Central Polynesia, *by
Robert C. Schmitt*   71

On Coming to One's Census, *by Edward P. Wolfers*   77
China's Population Statistics: An Illusion? *by Leo A. Orleans*   86
Observations on the Soviet Census, *by Murray Feshbach*   97
Changes in Census Methods, *by Joseph Waksberg and Leon Pritzker*   108

4 Age and Sex   114

How a Population Ages or Grows Younger, *by Ansley J. Coale*   115
The Social Status of the Sexes and Their Relative Mortality in Ireland, *by Robert E. Kennedy, Jr.*   121
The Sex Labeling of Jobs, *by Valerie Kincade Oppenheimer*   136

5 Subnations   146

Population Trends and Residential Segregation since 1960, *by Reynolds Farley and Karl E. Taeuber*   148
Inequality and Opportunity, *by Otis Dudley Duncan*   158
What to Do about the Palestinian Refugees, *by James A. Michener*   165

6 Classification by Residence   176

The Limits of Metropolitan Dominance in Contemporary Latin America, *by Richard M. Morse*   177
Urbanization and Fertility: The Non-Western Experience, *by Warren C. Robinson*   188
Urbanization and Social Change in Africa, *by A. L. Epstein*   199

7 Migration   214

On Measuring Geographic Mobility, *by Larry H. Long*   215
Mass Immigration and Modernization in Argentina, *by Gino Germani*   223
Postwar Immigration and Switzerland's Demographic and Social Structure, *by Kurt B. Mayer*   241
The American Tourist, *by Somerset R. Waters*   256

8 Health and Mortality   263

Social Correlates of Weight in an Aging Population, *by Robert G. Burnight and Parker G. Marden*   264

Some Remarks on Contemporary British Medical Statistics, *by E. D. Acheson* 276

Two Articles from *China's Medicine* 283

9 The Analysis of Fertility 289

Migration and Place of Work as a Cause of Male Sterility, *by Aleksandar D. Milojković, Serćo F. Šimić, and Mehmed S. Džumhur* 290

The Effect of the Great Blackout of 1965 on Births in New York City, *by J. Richard Udry* 293

The Character of Modern Fertility, *by Norman B. Ryder* 296

Economic Development and Fertility, *by David M. Heer* 307

Extended Family Structure and Fertility: Some Conceptual and Methodological Issues, *by Thomas K. Burch and Murray Gendell* 329

Roman Catholic Fertility in Tudderen: An Analysis of One Factor, *by Anthon J. van 't Veer* 342

Ideology, Faith, and Population Growth in Latin America, *by J. Mayone Stycos* 347

Genetic Implications of Demographic Trends, *by Dudley Kirk* 356

10 Population Policy 366

Sociological Aspects of Genetic Control, *by Kingsley Davis* 367

Birth Control for Economic Development, *by Stephen Enke* 381

The Development of India's Policy of Population Control, *by T. J. Samuel* 391

120 Children Born after Their Mothers' Application for Therapeutic Abortion Had Been Refused, *by Hans Forssman and Inga Thuwe* 401

Population Control: More than Family Planning, *by Philip M. Hauser* 413

Population Policy for Americans: Is the Government Being Misled? *by Judith Blake* 424

Family Planning and Public Policy: Who Is Misleading Whom? *by Oscar Harkavy, Frederick S. Jaffe, and Samuel M. Wishik* 444

A Reply, *by Judith Blake* 459

Index 471

1 POPULATION GROWTH, PAST AND FUTURE

Most demographic analyses concentrate on man as a cultural being, for during the period studied in virtually all works the major determinant of population trends has been that congeries of artifacts, institutions, and beliefs that we term modernization. *The power of modern science and the force of modern ideology are so great that we typically pass over the fact that the species being shaped by them is, like any other, fundamentally subject to biological controls.*

Man's biological limitations are especially pertinent to a discussion of long-term trends, from the remote past to the possible future. Since paleolithic hominids—a total on the whole earth of perhaps a million—lived from hunting and gathering, they had hardly any more control over their food supply, or their way of life generally, than any other intelligently adaptable omnivorous mammal. The scant archeological data from which we reconstruct their pattern of life can be usefully rounded out with the much fuller record, whether fossil, field, or experimental, on other species. And at the other end of a long time scale, the more or less remote future, we revert again to the physiological demands of Homo sapiens *in trying to assess the upper limit of the present population growth. Whether means will be found*

1

to increase the food supply fast enough to keep up with the demand must be a factor in any extrapolation.

Even in analyses of the modern period, it may be that greater understanding can be achieved by paying more attention to the biological animal almost hidden under his culture. The survey of population theory and doctrine in Chapter 2 includes, as it probably would not have done some years ago, sections on the biological perspective and the environment, topics that have become important as public issues if not yet as areas of sociological analysis. The large literature on the links between overcrowding, psychological stress, and reduced population growth pertains mostly to other species; but some data suggest that man's physiology responds in a similar way. In short, social scientists should at least keep aware of biologists' studies on the population and ecology of other species, for the interdisciplinary stimulation can be highly significant.

Dr. Deevey, the author of the first essay in this book, is a biologist. His expertise ranges from his narrower specialty of limnology (the scientific study of fresh waters) to historical ecology. Presently associated with the Florida State Museum in Gainesville, he spent most of his career at Yale, rising from a Sterling Fellow to professor and director of the Geochronometric Laboratory. He is the author of some eighty papers. Professional societies and government boards have bestowed honors on him; he has served, for instance, on the editorial boards of five professional journals. The article we have chosen, written for an audience of social scientists, is informed by the background of an impressive career in biology.

THE EQUILIBRIUM POPULATION

Edward S. Deevey

Man's objective is that of all species: to maintain the population, that is, to exist. Our old friend, the "struggle for existence," is nowadays called equilibrium, a balance between opposing forces. In Darwin's time the emphasis was ordinarily placed on downward displacements from equilibrium. Today, and particularly with regard to our own species, we are more conscious of the force of procreation that opposes and may temporarily outrun the forces of destruction. Unlike the demographer, the biologist is accustomed to populations at and above as well as below equilibrium; hence, his viewpoint may be useful in considering these questions.

I propose first to deal with statics, and then to move closer to some popu-

SOURCE: Slightly edited from Edward S. Deevey, "The Equilibrium Population," in *The Population Ahead*, edited by Roy G. Francis, Minneapolis: University of Minnesota Press. © copyright 1958 by the University of Minnesota.

lations in an effort to see their kinetics, or what makes them tick without exploding. Finally I shall return to the advantages and disadvantages of an oscillatory equilibrium.

ECONOMIC DENSITY AS A FUNCTION OF PRODUCTIVITY

The ecologist's model of community equilibrium was first sketched in some detail by a Minnesota biologist, the late Raymond Lindeman (1942). In a four-year study of Cedar Log Lake, surely one of the most valuable doctoral theses ever done in ecology, Lindeman measured with great care the standing crops of algae, pondweeds, rotifers, copepods, insects, fish, and the like, and then proceeded with great insight to estimate their various rates of turnover in order to compute the input and use of energy of the whole aquatic community. It had been axiomatic in ecology that the *numbers* of animals at different levels in a food chain should stand in roughly pyramidal relation to each other—many springtails, fewer spiders, still fewer mud-daubers, still fewer birds that eat muddaubers. What Lindeman did was to convert such numbers into *masses,* so that the plants could be included, then to turn these masses into rates of production, and then to express them in units of the chemical energy fixed by one level and handed on to the next higher level. This led him to the discovery of a fairly systematic relation, which had been suspected before but never made quantitative: while the plants on a given area used solar energy with an efficiency of the order of 0.1 percent, the herbivores were about 10 percent efficient in utilizing plants, and the carnivores in turn were about 10 percent efficient in utilizing herbivores. So the theoretical figure for the growth of all carnivores on an area is 10 percent of 10 percent, or 1 percent; it will not be very different if carnivores are 20 percent efficient, as Lindeman's seemed to be, for 20 percent of 10 percent is only 2 percent. We see at once why meat costs more than corn.

The energetics of a land community are more difficult to work out, and in applying Lindeman's scheme to the production of human substance we have to make a number of guesses. To determine the cost in energy for population growth we need to know the following: How many people are added each year, at least approximately? How much do they weigh? How many calories are needed to enable a person to weigh this much? How much energy must be produced to obtain this much food? These calculations require very large numbers. A shorthand way of writing big numbers is to write them as a product of a number times 10 raised to a *power.* Thus, $10^9 = 1,000,000,000 = 1$ billion. Hence 2½ billion may be written as $(2.5)(10^9)$; 250 as $(2.5)(10^2)$; and so on.

The standing crop of human beings (those living in 1950) was about $(2.6)(10^9)$ persons, on an average weighing 60 kilograms "fresh," or 21 kilograms "dry" (the difference being essentially the amount of water which man need not produce). The rate of production of new substance by the crop is about

4 percent of the crop, since the mean life span of humans was about 25 years; here we write down at once the figure that is most uncertain and difficult to obtain for nonhuman species. The dry matter can be taken to be all protein, with an energy content of 5,650 calories per gram. Multiplying these factors together, we find that the new growth, what ecologists call the net productivity, represents $(1.23)(10^{13})$ kilocalories per day. Now in order to produce this net the crop consumes a great deal of energy and spends it to maintain its bodies intact and functional; that is, most of the fuel intake is respired away and does not appear as output. Allowing 1,690 kilocalories per day as the metabolism of a working man of 60 kilograms average weight, the respiratory loss amounts to $(1.6)(10^{15})$ kilocalories per year, or 130 times the energy remaining as net production. Disregarding the net output as too small to affect the figures, we can consider $(1.6)(10^{15})$ kilocalories per year as the gross productivity, and this can be compared to the gross productivity of all plants on the terrestrial earth. The plants' net production was estimated by Schroeder in 1919 as about $(1.6)(10^{17})$ kilocalories per year; to this we must add the 25 percent or so that the plants spend for their own vegetable purposes, giving a gross productivity of $(2.0)(10^{17})$ kilocalories per year. The fraction 1.6/200 gives the efficiency of human gross production as 0.8 percent. Let us call this about 1 percent, and remember that 1 percent is the theoretical figure for all carnivores referred to the plants at the base of their food chains. The calculation implies that if man were entirely a carnivore he would require essentially all the carnivory there is or can be on land.

Recent, direct estimates of the net productivity of terrestrial vegetation converge on a figure of $(56)(10^9)$ tons of carbon per year—that is, roughly $(5.6)(10^{17})$ kilocalories per year or 3.5 times Schroeder's indirect estimate (Deevey 1960, 1970; SCEP 1970). Gross productivity would then be $(7.3)(10^{17})$ kilocalories per year. Meanwhile, the human population has nearly doubled, increasing from $(2.6)(10^9)$ to about $(4.0)(10^9)$ persons, who respire not $(1.6)(10^{15})$ but $(3)(10^{15})$ kilocalories per year. The ratio of gross productivities thus seems to have fallen from 0.8 to 0.4 percent. Of course, this ratio is not a true efficiency, for man's dependence on the biosphere is less for food than for efficient conversion of pollutants into resources. Still, as an efficiency ratio, the figure is close enough to 1 percent as not to affect the argument.

This result is worth some thought in the light of what we know of plant production generally. About 5,000 kilocalories per square meter per year is the production of a good forest, of which about two-thirds goes into wood and one-third falls down as leaves and twigs. Lakes and the ocean in temperate latitudes are about as productive as land. The average agricultural land under conditions in the United States produces about half as much as forest, or only about one-fourth as much in harvestable grain (because these figures include the whole corn and rice plant above ground). The worldwide terrestrial average, including deserts and the arctic tundra, is about one-fifth as much as a good forest. Yet it is this last figure we used in computing human efficiency, and it is arithmetically convenient that agricultural products yield a like amount—about 1,000 kilocalories per square meter per year of edible carbohydrate.

What, then, would be the consequence of increasing the human crop by ten times? Not only would meat eating become impossible, but human productive efficiency would have to increase to 10 percent, that of all the herbivory on earth. I think I am not wrong in suggesting, therefore, that a factor of 10 is beyond the margin of safety; yet at the rate of increase of 1 percent per year the human population will grow tenfold in 230 years.

In considering man as a carnivore, it is amusing to deal with the simplest imaginable stage, that of naked, acultural men dependent on the animal food produced by a temperate forest. The requisite data do not exist for any one forest community, but by piecing information together we can arrive at some estimates of the productivity of herbivorous animals.

If we take the ratio of gross productivities as 10 percent, 16,000 calories of animals support 1,600 calories of hunter, all but 1/130th of which goes for respiration, leaving 12.3 calories for growth. The standing crop would be about 25 times this, making the surprising total of 2.6 persons per square kilometer. But then we remember that this assumes that all the yield of catchable animals goes into human substance, leaving none for other carnivores. It seems safer to calculate from the net production of animals, and assume a physiologic conversion rate of less than 1 to 1, say 50 percent. Then 700 calories of food support 350 calories of hunter, 2.7 calories of which go for growth. The standing crop then comes out at 0.57 persons per square kilometer, which is only about fifteen times the average density of 18th-century American plains Indians.

A comparable average density of aboriginal hunters and gatherers is given for Australia by Birdsell (1953), 0.03 per square kilometer as compared to the American 0.04. Presumably the factor-of-15 discrepancy between the computed and the actual human crops means that they were usually limited by some component of the environment other than food. It may have been "social forces"; it may merely have been the unequal distribution of water or of salt. But we should note that a 15-fold margin of safety is not a serious discrepancy, since the figures are based on averages.

Let me summarize the statics of energy balance:

1. For a hunting and gathering economy, average density is about 0.04 person per square kilometer; the energy balance suggests that this figure can be increased locally by about twenty times, say to 1 per square kilometer, or even higher if much plant food is gathered.

2. For an agricultural economy, optimal density, considering increased productivity of land and increased efficiency of exploitation of vegetable food, is about 100–300 per square kilometer. Typical densities at this stage, however, are 400 per square kilometer (Java) or 600 per square kilometer

(Egypt). At this level human productivity is maximal, but the standard of living is low.

3. For an industrial-agricultural economy, such as the United States, density is 20 per square kilometer; the worldwide average is also 20 per square kilometer. A slight increase in productivity of agricultural land does not compensate for the proportion of land removed for other purposes or simply not exploited.

4. After a tenfold increase, the worldwide population density would be 200 per square kilometer. Population needs for food alone require either that all men become exclusively herbivorous, dependent on worldwide plant production at its present value, or that the average production of agricultural land be increased by ten times.

INCREASE AND LONGEVITY

It is customary to begin discussions of population dynamics in general by writing down the Pearl-Verhulst logistic equation for population growth:

$$\frac{dN}{dt} = bN \left(\frac{K - N}{K} \right)$$

where dN/dt is the rate of change of numbers (N) with respect to time (t), b is the constant of maximal potential increase, and ($K - N$)/K is a density corrective, expressing the fact that growth is slowed increasingly as N approaches saturation, K (Pearl 1940). As commonly used to describe growth, this equation is often sterile. The trouble is that an "S" curve of this kind "fits," or describes, one set of data but does so no better than does a mathematically different "S" curve. We make progress faster by studying births and deaths separately, first as related to population density and then as related to each other.

Although no sociologist can do likewise, the biologist can create a situation of "unlimited food supply." Removing the effects of having to search

Table 1. Reproductive Potentiality of Several Animals

ANIMAL	INTRINSIC RATE OF NATURAL INCREASE (r)		MEAN LENGTH OF A GENERATION (T)		RATE OF MULTIPLICATION PER GENERATION (R_0)
Daphnia	0.8	per day	6.8	days	221.5
Pond snail	0.02–0.04	per day	124–246	days	ca. 450.0
Body louse	0.111	per day	30.92	days	30.93
Flour beetle	0.707	per week	7.9	weeks	275.0
Rice weevil	0.76	per week	6.2	weeks	113.6
Rat	0.103	per week	31.0	weeks	25.66
Vole	0.088	per week	20.2	weeks	5.90
Man (Egypt)	ca. 0.012	per year	28	years	ca. 1.4

for food is a way of removing from consideration one effect of *density* of population as such. In such a situation, the population grows as what may be termed a "snowball"—each succeeding period being dependent upon the size of the preceding population. To use mathematical symbols, $dN/dt = rN$, where N refers to "Numbers," "t" refers to "time," and "r" refers to "rate." This "r" turns out to be the rate of growth that Malthus talked about, for the geometric growth that disturbed him is simply a snowballing.

In Table 1, the constant r gives the instantaneous rate of increase, what Lotka (1945) calls the *intrinsic rate of natural increase*. To find out what this means in terms of a finite rate of multiplication we need the mean length of a generation, shown in the next column; the last column shows R_0, the rate of multiplication per head per generation. All these figures are to be found in the literature except those for the water flea Daphnia, which I have computed from some rough figures of my own to show what an animal can do. These values are possible because the population consists entirely of parthenogenetic females that bring forth 10 to 30 live young every time they moult, which is about every second day through adult life.

These figures, of course, show potentialities only; r represents maximum births minus minimum deaths. For real populations living in real environments the effect of increasing N is to make the death rate increase and the birth rate decrease until, at equilibrium, $dN/dt = 0$. We can infer, then, that deaths vary as some positive function of N, while births vary as a negative function of N. When these relations are examined empirically they prove invariably to be nonlinear, to require a curved rather than a straight line. The most interesting cases are those where the effect of density is not even monotonic; that is, the natality (or mortality) may both increase and decrease with density.

As an example that is reasonably well understood, we may take the case of Tribolium, the flour beetle. Two pairs per 32 grams of flour increase faster than one pair, and four pairs increase faster than two pairs. Above a density of four pairs the natality falls again. The explanation is that fertility increases with repeated matings, at least up to a point; one or two pairs per 32 grams of flour is too rarefied a population for females to meet males often enough for adequate insemination. But as the opportunity for encounters increases, there is also opportunity for the adults and larvae to meet the defenseless eggs and pupae, which they do not distinguish from bits of flour. So we find that there is an optimum density for effective fertility, both lower and higher densities being deleterious.

We do not know what the optimum density is for man today; at times in the past it clearly lay at some value below that found in cities. If one takes the archeologic data for deaths at particular ages, and uses them (swallowing some outrageous assumptions) to compute life tables, one finds that mean longevity in Bronze Age Anatolia was markedly greater than for urban classical Greece or Rome. The downward trend of mean longevity with urbanization is something that has begun to be corrected only recently, and in Western cities; Calcutta must be as unlikely a place in which to live a long life as ancient Rome was.

LONGEVITY OF ANIMALS IN NATURE

This brings me to life tables for natural populations of animals. Because we seldom want to insure the life of a robin or a vole, it is not worth while to compute their life tables with rigor. Moreover, it is obvious that mean longevity depends heavily on density, so survivorship curves showing death rates for specified ages can vary enormously, even in theory. But the pattern of survival probably varies less than do the values of its constants, and inasmuch as we deal with populations at or near equilibrium densities, we can learn much from the changing force of mortality with age.

If every age group is as likely to suffer death as every other, a graph of logarithm of survivors against age produces a straight diagonal line. Oversimplifying the situation considerably, we can say that secure laboratory populations of most invertebrates—Hydra, rotifers, Daphnia, insects—display little variation from this diagonal straight-line form. And there is no good reason why such animals should do so: they have little or no power to learn, and so to avoid death, and their life span in typical environments is never more than a small fraction of their physiologic maximum.

When we come to birds and mammals we expect the interplay between life and death to wear a different aspect, for the higher animals are more capable of learning, and many of them are at least incipiently social. But oddly enough, in adult birds at any rate, experience of life seems not to teach ways of avoiding death. Of the great variety of species studied, all prove to have essentially constant mortality rates from the first year onward. And in one social species, the herring gull, Paynter's (1949) studies of juvenile mortality suggest that sociality is not an unmixed blessing. In a large gullery the chief destroyers of eggs and chicks appear to be other gulls. The parents defend their own territories and nests with vigor, but they cannot be everywhere at once, and when the chicks begin to wander they suffer heavy losses from their neighbors. The gull data imply that the overall form of the survivorship curve is J-shaped, the heaviest mortality falling on the young of pre-reproductive ages. Plainly, not all birds give quite so steep J-shapes as does the gull: for passerine birds that build protected nests, especially in nest boxes, typical hatching rates are above 80 percent and fledging rates are also typically 80 percent, so that the proportion of fledged young from complete clutches averages 67 percent in hole-nesting species. Now the average number of eggs laid by a bird varies somewhat within the species, with environmental, hereditary, and psychologic factors all playing complicated roles. In some species, such as the Great Tit, it has been found that the number of eggs laid is slightly lower at higher population densities. But the variability in fecundity is not nearly enough to account for the variable rates at which the populations increase according to circumstances. What varies much more systematically is the proportion of survival to fledging; that is, the net natality is heavily influenced by mortality of the young. And this in turn not only varies with the clutch size but does so in remarkably different ways.

Among the factors governing population equilibria in nature, juvenile survival is of critical importance. Parental care is minimal in marine invertebrates and fishes; clouds of eggs and sperm cost little metabolically, and presumably a sessile species like the oyster gains enough advantage from the pelagic dispersal of its larvae to offset the colossal loss of gametes, larvae, and spat. But such a reproductive system, though possible for higher plants, is altogether too wasteful to be practiced by a mammal. The price that mammals have paid for being both terrestrial and successful includes the expense of elaborate devices to protect the embryos from loss of water, and these devices are designed for high efficiency, not for high productivity. So we do not expect to find mammalian survivorship so markedly J-shaped as is that of an oyster, or even of a gull. Moreover, although the advantage conferred by ability to learn does not show up in wild birds' patterns of mortality, perhaps it will show up in those of mammals.

The available studies confirm both deductions. For example, many life tables have been computed from skeletons, the age at death being estimated from growth rings on horns or from less reliable criteria. The data are then reasonably satisfactory for adults, but the fragile skeletons of the young are underrepresented in the sample. Fortunately we usually know or can guess at the reproduction rate of a mammal species, so the loss of young before they enter our sample can be estimated. Guesses approximating 70 percent mortality between birth and maturity have been made for several large ungulates, living and extinct (Kurtén 1953); if we add to this an adult mortality approximating 30 percent per year in middle life, the result is a curve that dips sharply in the youngest ages, but not nearly so sharply as that of the herring gull. Some modern human populations, India's for example, suffer 55 percent mortality between birth and maturity; thus, we can say that juvenile mortality of wild mammals, though heavier than that of adults, is not necessarily more severe than that of civilized man.

It is even more interesting to find that mammalian mortality rates decrease with age and experience, so that the survivorship curves, from maturity onward to old age, are convex upward exactly like that of man. When I first found this for the Dall mountain sheep of Mt. McKinley (Deevey 1947), I thought it might be an artifact, but the fact has been abundantly confirmed for other ungulates. The Dall sheep has a single important predator, the timber wolf. Death by predation can be avoided by at least two kinds of activity: group defense of the young by a circle of horned heads and systematic flight to altitudes so high that wolves cannot pursue. Both kinds of behavior are presumably learned by communication in a social context; they therefore are indistinguishable from *culture*. Cultural transmission of learned behavior in nonhuman mammals has been most convincingly demonstrated in a social rodent, the prairie dog. King (1955) has shown that the social unit, or coterie, not all of whose members are related by blood, defends its common territory against members of other coteries. The boundaries of the territory are arbitrary, and have to be learned, yet they may remain stable while the personnel of the groups undergoes complete turnover.

AGGRESSION, ANXIETY, AND NATALITY

House mice live wild in many parts of the world, having been spread by man from their ancestral home on the steppes of Russia. Even in northern countries, like Great Britain, they may live wild throughout the year, competing with and sometimes displacing the native rodents; as opportunity arises they display their superior ability to become commensal with man, the ability that brought them to such countries in the first place. As wild animals they are distinguished by what is probably the smallest home range of any rodent; in one study on Guam the maximum distance over which mice moved for many weeks was 36 yards for males, 30 yards for females (Baker 1946). In barns near Baltimore, Brown (1953) found that 98 percent of the population moved less than 16 yards between successive points of capture. When the environment is three-dimensional, densities can vary from less than two to nearly fourteen mice per cubic meter (Laurie 1946). In an elaborate study of the utilization of space by mice, Calhoun (1956) found that the probability of their stopping in unstructured space is very small; when highly motivated, as in the search for shelter or nesting material, mice quickly learn to select the shortest route to a goal.

These facts imply a low degree of dispersal from a desired habitat, and intense competition for goals within one. Mice habitually live close to other mice; if threatened, they would rather stay and fight than run away. Moreover, as in all other vertebrates when crowded, a dominance hierarchy (called "peck order" in flocks of chickens) is readily established as a consequence of fighting, so that mice respond to each other as individuals; but their individual lives are short as well as brutish, and upward social mobility poses a constant threat to the status of the higher-ranking individuals.

Laurie (1946) studied British mice in four environments: the ordinary urban one in the back streets of Oxford, a cold-storage plant, a flour depot, and a country habitat of ricks and grain fields. Judged by the incidence of pregnancy and the annual litter production, the four environments were increasingly favorable in that order: urban, cold-storage plant, flour depot, and ricks. The country mouse has it all over the city mouse; urbanization, for mice as well as men, brings declining fertility. That it brings social problems as well I can best demonstrate by describing some laboratory studies. Strecker (1954) established mouse populations in a junkroom in the basement of a building at the University of Wisconsin, fed them on controlled amounts of food, and set traps in the neighboring offices and laboratories. When the food was limited to 250 grams per day, the population grew slowly but regularly until its food consumption leveled off at 250 grams per day. While the mice were increasing they saw no reason to leave home, but when the food supply became limiting the surplus mice began to leave the room in trickles, and then in droves. Next, populations were set up in two large pens from which escape was impossible, and fed 250 grams of food per day. Each population increased in time to a peak, but the larger initial population increased to a very high peak of more than 100 mice, whereupon reproduction stopped abruptly, the gonads of the adult females regressed, and the population declined to the original level. The smaller initial population increased to about 40, declined to 30, and rose again to 40; reproduction was more or less normal at all times.

The question that arises is, why should one population level off at 40 when another goes on to reach more than 100? Southwick's studies (1955a, 1955b) confirm this remarkable variability, and also give us some insight into its causes. Aware that the social structure of the pens might have some bearing on the kinetics, Southwick set up three identical populations in pens with concentrated areas of shelter, food, and water, and another three in pens where the essential needs of mice were spatially dispersed. At first sight the results seemed puzzling and inconclusive, but closer observation showed that the social structure explained the variable results—though in unpredictable ways, being unrelated to the geometric structure of the feeding and nesting arrangements. The one consistent result that emerges is that successful reproduction, and especially the survival of litters, are sharply inhibited by fighting; litter mortality was greatest when the observed number of fights exceeded one per mouse per hour. But whereas most of the fights are initiated by males, the psychology of the females is equally affected; cannibalism and desertion are the chief causes of loss of litters, but underlying these forms of behavior is the failure of maternal drive.

Now fighting is a learned response in rats and mice; frustration leads to aggression only so long as aggression is rewarding (Scott and Fredericson 1951). And there is a critical period, between twenty and thirty days of age in a mouse, in which fighting is either learned or is not, according to its reward value (King and Gurney 1954). Play and social contact normally teach a young mouse to fight during the socialization process. Fighting, then, is apparently a cultural trait. Evidently this is the explanation for the relative unpredictability of population responses in Southwick's experiments.

Once learned, however, intense fighting has some predictable consequences for natality. The guiding principle here is Selye's General Adaptation Syndrome (GAS), a suite of largely endocrine responses to various forms of shock or stress, in which the adrenal cortex plays a central role. According to Selye's massively documented theory, the reaction to stress is first given by the pituitary gland, which secretes adrenocorticotropic hormone (ACTH). The adrenal hormones then mobilize the resources of the body to resist—the blood sugar increases to provide ready energy for flight or tension, the kidney becomes an endocrine gland, with resulting effects on salt and protein balance, etc. Under conditions of chronic stress the adrenal cortex is hypertrophied, and its hyperactivity inhibits the production of other pituitary hormones, notably the gonadotropins, for reproduction is a luxury when stress is severe and chronic. Increased stress may then cause death from "shock," the resources of the body already being mobilized to the full; the proximate cause of death is hypoglycemia, or lack of sufficient sugar in the blood. Anxiety is a form of stress and, when chronic, decreases resistance to other stresses (Selye 1950). There is no doubt that anxiety is communicable, in mice as well as men, and so we see again the essential kinship between man and the vertebrates.

The view that Selye's GAS plays a major role in the population dynamics of mammals is exceedingly persuasive. Christian (1956) has found that crowding of mice leads to hypertrophy of the adrenal cortex, along with the ramifying effects that Selye predicts: delayed puberty, delayed involution of the thymus, regression of secondary sex characteristics, depression of fecundity; the weight of the adrenal glands in Christian's mice was a direct function of the population size. Similar results were obtained with crowded meadow voles by Louch (1956), who lays special emphasis on reduced production of prolactin as the probable proximate cause of reduced maternal drive. And the notion that shock disease is a consequence of excessive density, and therefore of excessive stress by fighting, is well supported by the studies of the snowshoe hare. The peak of the population cycle is followed by a crash; seemingly healthy hares may die when trapped or when merely chased, and elaborate studies of the incidence of disease show no obvious reason for the mortality other than hypoglycemia.

So we are beginning at last to glimpse the mechanisms of the remarkable cyclic fluctuations in animal abundance. The three- or four-year cycle of mice, voles, and lemmings, and the ten-year cycle of snowshoe hares, seem to be generated internally by psychic and endocrine responses to population density.

The experimental studies, with their cannibalism and other deranged behavior, their "shock disease," and their heartless records of "one fight per mouse per hour," probably emphasize unduly what Malthus called the positive checks to increase—pestilence and warfare. The situations are of course abnormal. Still, field ecologists have long known that periodic disturbances of equilibrium are the rule, and have devoted much fruitless effort to the search for extrinsic causes. Are these fluctuations to be expected in animals that have culture but no ethics? Are they part of the price the mammals pay for being, successfully, sentient, thinking, social beings like ourselves? Or are they, perhaps, fundamentally adaptive?

OSCILLATING EQUILIBRIA

When Hutchinson and I (1949) wanted to make the point that an animal population can fluctuate regularly for reasons intrinsic to the system, these facts about small mammals were undiscovered and we were forced to rely on the case of Daphnia. To return to Daphnia now is something of an anticlimax, because while it is still true that Daphnia populations oscillate without external cause, Daphnia is so unlike a vertebrate biologically that its relevance to the classic cycles is remote. Nevertheless it is useful in constructing a mathematical model of population equilibrium to think in terms of this delightfully simple and prolific animal.

What draws our attention is the delayed reaction, first clearly shown by Pratt (1943), between population density and the attainment of appropriate birth and death rates. Certainly, as numbers increase, the birth rate slows down and the death rate rises, but each reaction takes a little time. On the rising curve of population growth most of the animals have spent most of their lives at lower densities, and they reproduce too rapidly for the conditions of the moment—so the numbers overshoot equilibrium. Then, with births minimal and deaths maximal, the population declines; but now most of the animals have spent most of their lives at higher densities, and they die too rapidly for conditions of the moment. Undershooting is the result, and so the oscillation continues, though in time it progressively diminishes. An appropriate equation for the corresponding growth process starts with the logistic equation

$$\frac{dN}{dt} = bN \left(\frac{K - N}{K} \right)$$

Two kinds of time lag can be allowed to start with: the time needed for an animal to start reproduction when conditions are favorable, and the time required for the individuals to react to changing density by altering their birth and death rates. Letting these time lags be $t - t_1$ and $t - t_2$, respectively, Wangersky and Cunningham (1956, 1957) give

$$\frac{dN(t)}{dt} = bN_{(t - t_1)} \left(\frac{K - N(t - t_2)}{K} \right)$$

Such equations rapidly become intractable, but they can be studied with profit by use of an analogue computer of modest design. They are much easier to study in this way, in fact, than to provide with empirical data from real populations, yet in principle all constants and variables in such equations can be evaluated experimentally. By assuming reasonable values for birth rates, equilibrium densities, and time lags it is a simple matter to test out whether the resulting population oscillates indefinitely, shows damped oscillations, or approaches saturation in the orthodox way. The same procedure can be used to study interaction between two populations, whether in a predator-prey or a competition situation, but these situations, if realistically formulated, exceeded the capacity of the computer in the 1950s. What emerges from this admittedly abstract approach is, first, that almost anything that populations have ever been observed to do can be duplicated by the computer and, second, that damped oscillations should be more frequent than any other kind of equilibrium.

This last appears to be a conclusion of first-rate importance. Its basis is probably twofold: a species that approaches equilibrium slowly and steadily in the classic way supposed by Pearl and other early students is insufficiently reactive to take advantage of changing environments, whether they change seasonally or randomly. But to generate an infinite series of oscillations requires a very careful balance of birth rates and time lags, and if the amplitude of the oscillations is great the chances are good that one of them will take the population too close to zero. What seems to be built into living systems, then, is an adaptive ability to undergo damped oscillations.

Has all this any relevance for demography? I think it has. Man's power of increase, though low for an animal, is adequate to produce great changes in the lifetimes of individual members. So the time lags, though also very long, are finite. A certain amount of overshooting would not be fatal, and might even be salutary, as well as biologically inevitable. The hope, and the challenge, lie in the fact that the world is now more unified than it used to be. What happens in Timbuktu affects us all, and the equilibrium that I think is near, whatever form it takes, will apply to the whole world. Self-regulation of numbers may be nearer than we are accustomed to thinking, and one can expect that the process will in the long run be less painful than it is for mice, or even for Daphnia.

References

BAKER, R. H. 1946. "A Study of Rodent Populations on Guam, Mariana Islands," *Ecological Monographs,* **16,** 393–408.

BIRDSELL, J. B. 1953. "Some Environmental and Cultural Factors Influencing the Structuring of Australian Aboriginal Populations," *American Naturalist,* **87,** 169–207.

BROWN, R. Z. 1953. "Social Behavior, Reproduction, and Population Changes in the House Mouse (*Mus musculus* L.)," *Ecological Monographs,* **23,** 217–240.

CALHOUN, J. B. 1956. "Behavior of House Mice with Reference to Fixed Points of Orientation," *Ecology,* **37,** 287–301.

CHRISTIAN, J. J. 1956. "Adrenal and Reproductive Responses to Population Size in Mice from Freely Growing Populations," *Ecology,* **37,** 258–273.

DEEVEY, EDWARD S. 1947. "Life Tables for Natural Populations of Animals," *Quarterly Review of Biology*, 22, 283–314.

———. 1960. "Human Populations," *Scientific American*, 203, 194–204.

———. 1970. "Mineral Cycles," *Scientific American*, 223, 148–158.

HUTCHINSON, G. E., and E. S. DEEVEY. 1949. "Ecological Studies on Populations," in G. S. Avery, ed., *Survey of Biological Progress*, Vol. 1. New York: Academic Press.

KING, J. A. 1955. "Social Behavior, Social Organization, and Population Dynamics in a Black-Tailed Prairiedog Town in the Black Hills of South Dakota," *Contributions from the Laboratory of Vertebrate Biology of the University of Michigan*, No. 67, 1–123.

———, and N. GURNEY. 1954. "Effects of Early Social Experiences on Adult Aggressive Behavior in C57BL/10 Mice," *Journal of Comparative and Physiological Psychology*, 47, 326–330.

KURTÉN, BJÖRN. 1953. "On the Variation and Population Dynamics of Fossil and Recent Mammal Populations," *Acta Zoologica Fennica*, No. 76, 1–122.

LAURIE, E. M. O. 1946. "The Reproduction of the House Mouse (*Mus musculus*) Living in Different Environments," *Proceedings of the Royal Society of London*, Series B, 133, 248–281.

LINDEMAN, RAYMOND L. 1942. "The Trophic-Dynamic Aspect of Ecology," *Ecology*, 23, 399–418.

LOTKA, A. J. 1945. "Population Analysis as a Chapter in the Mathematical Theory of Evolution," in W. E. LeGros Clark and P. B. Medawar, eds., *Essays on Growth and Form Presented to D'Arcy Wentworth Thompson*. Oxford: Clarendon Press.

LOUCH, C. D. 1956. "Adrenocortical Activity in Relation to the Density and Dynamics of Three Confined Populations of *Microtus pennsylvanicus*," *Ecology*, 37, 701–713.

PAYNTER, R. A. 1949. "Clutch-Size and the Egg and Chick Mortality of Kent Island Herring Gulls," *Ecology*, 30, 146–166.

PEARL, RAYMOND. 1940. *Introduction to Medical Biometry and Statistics*, 3rd ed. Philadelphia: Saunders.

PRATT, D. M. 1943. "Analysis of Population Development in Daphnia at Different Temperatures," *Biological Bulletin*, 85, 116–140.

SCEP (Study of Critical Environmental Problems). 1970. *Man's Impact on the Global Environment*. Cambridge, Mass.: M.I.T. Press.

SCOTT, J. P., and EMIL FREDERICSON. 1951. "The Causes of Fighting in Mice and Rats," *Physiological Zoology*, 24, 273–309.

SELYE, HANS. 1950. *The Physiology and Pathology of Exposure to Stress*. Montreal: Acta.

SOUTHWICK, C. H. 1955a. "The Population Dynamics of Confined House Mice Supplied with Unlimited Food," *Ecology*, 36, 212–225.

———. 1955b. "Regulatory Mechanisms of House Mouse Populations: Social Behavior Affecting Litter Survival," *Ecology*, 36, 627–634.

STRECKER, R. L. 1954. "Regulatory Mechanisms of House Mouse Populations: The Effect of Limited Food Supply on an Unconfined Population," *Ecology*, 35, 249–253.

WANGERSKY, P. J., and W. J. CUNNINGHAM. 1956. "On Time Lags in Equations of Growth," *Proceedings of the National Academy of Science*, 42, 699–702.

————, and ————. 1957. "Time Lag in Prey-Predator Population Models," *Ecology*, 38, 136–139.

The grand transformation from prehistory to history was less fundamental for demographic analysis than one might suppose. Whether one studies a population living before or after the invention of writing, for some centuries the problem remained essentially the same: how to infer evidence from records more or less remotely associated with population number and structure. For paleontologists, these primary data might be potsherds or bones; for historians of the ancient or medieval world, tax rolls or conscription lists. Sometimes identical techniques are used in both disciplines—as an example, in estimating the number of inhabitants from the area covered by a settlement. For demography, the basic change came when vital events themselves began to be recorded: the numbers and characteristics of all persons rather than of particular categories, as well as their marriages, births, and deaths. This happened not at the dawn of history but at the beginning of the modern epoch.

Historical demography, or the study of these early population records, has benefited from an enormous and quite sudden spurt of interest, especially in England and France but also in the Low Countries, Italy, and— with a few faint glimmers—the United States. Today one center of these studies is Scandinavia, where records of vital events were first established on a national scale and where quite early they attained a respectable level of completeness and accuracy. The English reader can learn about the early growth of the Swedish population from such scholars as, among others, Dorothy Swaine Thomas, Eli Heckscher, and H. Gille. But the comparable record in Norway (not to say Denmark, Iceland, and Finland) has been analyzed far less in the major European languages.

The next paper combines two elements of historical demography in a most satisfying manner. A volume commemorating two centuries of Norwegian population statistics is analyzed by Louis Henry, who has contributed to this subdiscipline as much as any other one person. Professor Henry's first degree was in engineering, and during the Second World War he was an artillery officer in the French army. Only after the war did he concentrate on population analysis, studying at the Statistical Institute of the University of Paris and joining the staff of the National Institute of Demographic Studies (INED), with which he is still associated. He has been professor of demography at the University of Paris, president of the Commission on Historical Demography (since 1963), and president of the Society of Historical Demography (since 1969). The author of several monographs and numerous shorter articles on various demographic topics, Professor Henry has concentrated on adapting modern techniques to the analysis of defective historical data.

Parallel analyses in English discuss the development of population statistics in Norway (Backer 1947), the social and economic developments associated with the growth of population (Drake 1965), and emigration from Norway (Backer 1966). The specific quality of the article chosen here is its focus on a demographic analysis of the available population data. With expertise developed to Professor Henry's high level, one need not acquire a full background of a country's history to make a significant contribution to its historiography.

THE POPULATION OF NORWAY
DURING THE PAST TWO CENTURIES

LOUIS HENRY

From the beginning of the modern period, the quality of Scandinavian population statistics has been good enough to lay the basis for demographic studies whose importance transgresses the limits of those countries. Unfortunately, the older statistical data are not always easy to come by. Several recent publications about Norway now make it possible to fill in gaps in our knowledge and to throw new light on this country. This paper was stimulated in particular by a retrospective yearbook recently published by Norway's official statistical bureau (Norway 1969), supplemented by two recent books (Jahn 1957; Backer 1965) and the census volumes dealing with marital fertility.

Let us begin with Norway's population (Table 1), which increased by five times in two centuries. The growth was particularly rapid from 1815 to 1865, during which period the numbers almost doubled. Population density rose from 2.3 persons per square kilometer in 1769 to the still very low figure of 11.6 in 1960 (or from 0.89 to 4.48 persons per square mile). Over the same period the urban sector increased from 9 to 32 percent of the population.

The age structure, as it developed from the beginning of the 19th century (Table 2), is characteristic of a country whose fertility declined late. The initial increase in the proportion of youth was a result of the decline in

SOURCE: Translated by William Petersen from "La Population de la Norvège depuis deux siècles," *Population*, **25** (1970), 544–557, and reprinted in this slightly abridged form with permission of the author and the journal.

Table 1. The Population of Norway, 1769–1960

CENSUS DATE	POPULATION (-000)
1769	723
1825	1,051
1875	1,807
1900	2,240
1930	2,814
1950	3,278
1960	3,591

mortality and, perhaps also, a rise in fertility; then the fall in fertility brought about an aging of the population.

Table 2. Percentage Distribution of Three Main Age Categories, Norway, 1801–1960

AGE CATEGORY	1801	1875	1900	1930	1960
0–19 years	42.9	44.5	44.8	38.1	33.2
20–59 years	48.2	46.6	44.4	50.3	50.6
60+ years	8.9	8.9	10.8	11.6	16.2
Total	100.0	100.0	100.0	100.0	100.0

CRUDE RATES

A graph of the crude rates of marriages, births, deaths, and overseas emigration (Figure 1) shows the following broad characteristics:

The marriage rate was stable, though with wide short-term fluctuations, until the middle of the 19th century. It then declined and, from the end of the century to 1930, leveled off. It rose very sharply during the 1930s, reaching a peak in the 1950s, and subsequently declined until 1965, with a revival visible in 1966 and 1967.

The birth rate remained stable, though again with wide short-term fluctuations, until the end of the 19th century. Thereafter it fell very rapidly to less than 15 per 1,000 in 1933–36, when the economic crisis intensified the secular decline. After a revival during and after the Second World War, the rate returned to the same level as in 1927.

The death rate evolved in four stages: a slow and irregular decline until the beginning of the 19th century; a very rapid fall in the decade following the end of the Napoleonic wars; a slower decline, but this time without interruption, until the end of the 19th century; and thereafter again a fall at first much more rapid and then, for the past 10 years or so, somewhat slackened.

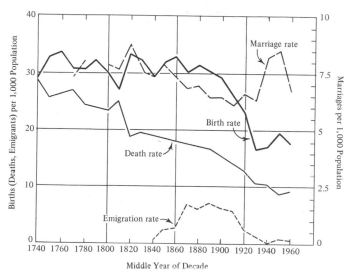

Figure 1. Ten-year Averages of Crude Rates of Marriages, Births, Deaths, and Overseas Emigration, Norway, 1736–1965

From 1865 to the First World War, overseas emigration amounted to almost half the natural increase, so that the rate of growth was 7 rather than 13 per 1,000. It was for this reason that the population grew fastest from 1815 to 1865—when the birth rate was about 31 and the death rate less than 20 per 1,000, while emigration was negligible. Of the 632,000 who emigrated overseas from 1866 to 1910, 616,000 (or 97.5 percent) went to the United States and most of the rest to Canada. Their sex ratio was a bit higher than 140 males per 100 females. The emigrants since 1930, very much smaller in number, have comprised a few more females than males. An estimated 25 percent of the overseas emigrants returned to Norway.

MARRIAGE AND DIVORCE

Putting aside the crude rate, one could measure marriages more precisely with such other indices as the proportion single among persons aged 50 (Table 3) and the mean age at first marriage, both of which refer to cohorts. Lacking the data needed for the latter, we can make do with the mean age of the newly married in specified time periods (Table 4). A wave of emigration was associated with a low point in the crude rate of marriage and a greater proportion of single females. It would seem that the mean age of the newly married, males as well as females, rose to about 1860, thereafter declining more or less regularly except for one temporary rise, undoubtedly due to the subsequent accumulation of marriages that had been deferred during the depression of the 1930s.

Table 3. Percent Single Among Persons Aged 50, by Sex, Norway, 1750–1920

CENSUS YEAR	MALE	FEMALE
1750	7.3	14.1
1805	10.4	13.5
1825	11.0	15.2
1850	10.7	17.7
1880	13.8	21.8
1910	13.6	14.4
1920		>11.0

Table 4. Mean Age of the Newly Married, Norway, First Marriages during Specified Periods

PERIOD	MALE	FEMALE
1851–1855	28.7	27.1
1861–1865	29.2	27.2
1871–1875	28.7	26.6
1876–1885	28.2	26.3
1886–1895	28.2	26.4
1896–1905	27.7	25.8
1906–1915	27.9	25.6
1916–1925	27.8	25.5
1926–1935	28.9	26.1
1936–1945	29.2	26.4
1946–1955	28.8	25.9
1956–1965	26.8	23.7

These developments can be interpreted thus: The rapid growth of population from 1815 to 1865 generated economic difficulties and thus a postponement of some marriages, but without any appreciable increase in the proportion who remained single all their lives. Emigration, by creating an imbalance between the sexes, resulted in a marked rise in permanent spinsterhood. This could have been accompanied by a fall in permanent bachelorhood, but it was not: The proportion single among persons aged 50 also increased among males, but at a later date, thus resulting in another rise in the proportion single among females. After the end of emigration and the fall in mortality, the excess of females was replaced by an excess of males, with a consequent sizable decline in the proportion single among females and an only slight change among males.

The divorce rate, negligible until around 1910, rose appreciably during the years that divorce was becoming accepted as part of the mores, but it then leveled off after 1945. With the present rate, about one marriage in ten ends in a divorce.

FERTILITY

The study of Norway's fertility is especially interesting, for birth control was not widely used there until the end of the 19th century. With the early data available, it is probably the European country where one can best follow the transformation from the primitive situation, with almost no limitation of births by contraception, to the present state of affairs.

The birth rate before 1900, a bit above 30 per 1,000, is well below the physiological limit. Girls married late, the proportion of single persons was relatively high, and, moreover, marital fertility was rather moderate. Illegitimate births, around 7 percent of the total during the first half of the 19th century, rose to a high point of 9 percent in 1871–75, fell again to 7 percent from around 1890 to 1945, thereafter declined to less than 4 percent in 1950–62, and in the most recent period went up again. That in spite of the decline in nuptiality the birth rate in the second half of the 19th century remained at the same level as before cannot be explained, therefore, by a rise in the proportion of illegitimate births. The fall in mortality, by prolonging marriages, played a part. There was also a rise of marital fertility among young women under 25 years and especially under 20, undoubtedly due to an appreciable increase in premarital conceptions.

Figure 2 shows the contrasts among age-specific fertility rates. The rates of younger females, especially those aged 15 to 19, rose to a high point and then fell off. At higher ages, the rates were more or less stable until the

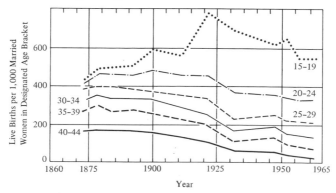

Figure 2. Age-specific Marital Fertility Rates, Norway, 1871–1962

end of the 19th century, thereafter declining the more the higher the age category. This great decline in fertility at advanced ages is not specific to Norway. The limitation of births has been brought about everywhere in a similar pattern: fewer children than are physiologically possible, but also with confinements concentrated at the start of conjugal life rather than spaced out up to age 40 and above. A study of the age at the last confinement would be appropriate here, but unfortunately the data do not permit it.

Let us compare the two extreme situations, in 1871–75 and in 1959–62 (Figure 3). The age-specific fertility rates of the first period describe a

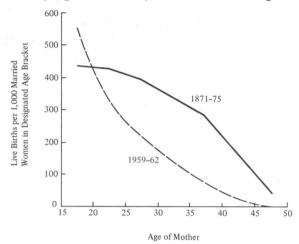

Figure 3. Age-specific Marital Fertility Rates, Norway, 1871–75 and 1959–62

convex curve as seen from above, since the decline in the rates accelerates as the mothers' ages rise. The curve for the second period is clearly concave: the decline in fertility is the greater, the lower the age. The differentiation followed from the diffusion of birth control, but it was also reinforced by a rise in the frequency of premarital conceptions among very young girls.

No data exist on marital fertility before 1871–75, but we can compare the legitimate births to be expected from the general fertility of that period with that recorded from 1806–15 to 1861–65. Such a comparison suggests that marital fertility during the first two-thirds of the 19th century was somewhat lower than in 1871–75.

For females married at ages 24 to 25, the number of children born to a couple married at the time of a census (omitting, thus, infants born before the marriage, irrespective of who the father was) is shown in Table 5. These figures represent completed, or (in the case of women who were married by 1940 and enumerated in 1960) almost completed, fertility. At the beginning of this record, three-quarters of the families had five or more children, but among the women married in 1940, 90 percent had fewer than five. Between these two extremes, the division is less clear, whether at the

Table 5. Proportional Distribution of Completed Family Sizes,
Females Married in 1876–1940 at Ages 24 to 25, Norway

LIVE BIRTHS	YEAR OF MARRIAGE						
	1876–85	1890	1900	1910	1920	1930	1940
0	41	48	46	69	63	73	56
1	33	41	46	81	121	186	149
2	39	63	80	124	226	291	319
3	65	76	102	148	195	203	238
4	72	100	118	129	140	114	134
5	93	95	111	123	105	58	57
6	115	104	117	98	56	34	27
7	126	112	107	73	43	18	11
8	146	118	108	71	22	11	4
9	117	105	70	46	15	5	3
10+	153	138	86	38	14	7	2
Total	1,000	1,000	1,000	1,000	1,000	1,000	1,000
Mean Number of Children	6.52	6.03	5.49	4.39	3.34	2.66	2.64

lower or the upper end of the distribution. Particularly at the beginning of the secular change, some couples retained traditional family norms and others—an increasing proportion of the total—took steps to reduce their fertility.

It is thought that birth control is diffused first among the wealthier and better educated. Females married at ages 20 to 29 in 1913, 1933, and 1943 were classified by their husbands' occupations and the average number of children after 17 years of marriage. In Figure 4 these occupations are ranked from high to low according to the average number of children to the 1913 marriages, as follows:

1. Fishermen
2. Agricultural workers
3. Farmers
4. Construction and kindred workers
5. Merchant seamen
6. Factory workers
7. Artisans
8. Small businessmen
9. Civil servants and kindred workers
10. Owners of industrial or commercial firms
11. Merchant marine officers
12. White-collar workers
13. Higher professionals and intellectuals

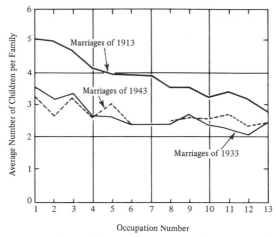

Figure 4. Average Size of Family after 17 Years of Marriage, by the Husband's Occupation

For some occupations, the definition is not entirely the same in the 1960 census as in the censuses of 1950 and 1930; "artisans," for example, are not a consistent category. But this does not alter any of the conclusions.

Clearly fertility is lowest at the top of the social scale, but with certain nuances: white-collar workers in commercial firms and banks (12) had a slightly smaller family than their bosses (10) or civil servants (9). From 1913 to 1933, the number of children fell off most among the occupations with the largest families initially, so that the differences were reduced substantially. From 1933 to 1943, no great changes occurred, except among agricultural workers.

The farmers, the fishermen, the merchant seamen, and—toward the upper end of the scale—the officers of the merchant marine retained a higher fertility than those in the other occupations. The long-term evolution thus varied slightly from what might have been anticipated. At the end, or almost the end, of the secular decline, differences in fertility persist, no doubt reflecting differences in the way of life and of thinking. From this point of view, the higher fertility of those who live from the sea is noteworthy.

MORTALITY

A rapid survey is usually limited to data on the expectation of life at birth, as an indication of the over-all state of health, and on infant mortality. We add some recent statistics on deaths at mature and advanced ages.

The arithmetic mean of the expectations of life at birth of the two sexes, and the excess mortality of males, evolved differently in Norway and France (Table 6). Of the two, Norway has always had the better state of health. In the second half of the 19th century, the difference increased to Norway's

Table 6. Expectation of Life from Birth, Norway and France,
1820s to 1960s

| | NORWAY | | | FRANCE | | |
| | EXPECTATION OF LIFE FROM BIRTH | | | EXPECTATION OF LIFE FROM BIRTH | | |
PERIOD	ARITHMETIC MEAN OF TWO SEXES	EXCESS MORTALITY OF MALES	PERIOD	ARITHMETIC MEAN OF TWO SEXES	EXCESS MORTALITY OF MALES
1821–1830	46.5	3	1825–1827	38.4	1.2
1831–1840	43.7	3.8	1835–1837	40.0	1.5
1841–1850	45.2	3.4	1845–1847	41.3	1.2
1846–1855	46.4	3	1850–1852	32.3	0.9
1856–1865	48.7	2.6	1860–1862	41.9	1.5
1871–1880	49.8	3	1875–1877	43.2	2.1
1881–1890	50.0	2.5	1885–1887	43.3	2.8
1891–1900	52.3	3.7	1895–1897	46.2	3.3
1901–1910	56.2	2.9	1898–1903	47.0	3.4
1911–1920	57.2	3.1	1908–1913	50.5	3.9
1921–1930	62.4	2.9	1920–1923	54.1	3.7
1931–1940	65.8	3.5	1933–1938	58.7	5.7
1946–1955 [a]	71.9	3.5	1952–1956	68.1	6.2
1956–1965 [b]	73.4	4.6	1960–1964	71.1	6.6

[a] Arithmetic mean of two periods, 1946–50 and 1951–55.
[b] Arithmetic mean of two periods, 1956–60 and 1961–65.
SOURCES: For the French data up to 1895–97, Jean Bourgeois-Pichat, "Evolution générale de la population française depuis le XVIII siècle," *Population*, 7 (1952), 318–329; thereafter, Institut National de la Statistique et des Etudes Economiques, *Annuaire statistique de la France, 1961 (rétrospectif).*

advantage; and since 1900 it has been reduced, gradually at first but faster for the last ten or twenty years. The excess mortality of males, larger at first in Norway, is now so in France.

The most notable fact of the recent period is that, from about age 40 on, male mortality has risen. Age-specific death rates are higher for 1961–65 than for 1956–60, 1951–55, and even, beginning with age 60, than for 1946–50 and 1941–45. Female mortality showed only a lack of change from 1956–60 to 1961–65, and that only beginning with age 60 (Table 7). This recent development in the mortality of adult and aged males is not specific to Norway. It can be seen—more or less conspicuously—in Denmark, Sweden, the Netherlands, and Germany, but not in France or Italy, even though the state of health at these ages is not worse there than in some of the countries listed earlier. No explanation would appear to be fully satisfactory. If it were an excess mortality of veterans, one would not find the

Table 7. Expectations of Life of Mature
and Aged Persons, by Sex, Norway, 1901–65

PERIOD	MALES e_{40}	MALES e_{60}	FEMALES e_{60}
1901–10	31.5	16.8	17.9
1921–30	32.4	17.0	18.2
1931–40	33.2	17.2	18.4
1946–50	35.2	18.4	19.4
1951–55	35.5	18.5	19.9
1956–60	35.2	18.1	20.1
1961–65	34.6	17.6	20.1

same situation in countries whose experience of war had been very different. If automobile accidents were the cause, France ought to be included among the countries with a rising mortality; moreover, these accidents affect least men of advanced ages.

The stagnation of the female rate from 1951–55 to 1961–65 is not found elsewhere. In the Netherlands, in particular, the expectation of life of females from age 60 went from 18.8 years in 1951–55 to 20.1 in 1961–65. Norway and the Netherlands now have more or less the same female expectation of life at age 60, the highest in the world; but progress has slowed down in one of these countries and not in the other. Thus, one cannot argue that the lesser present progress in Norway is the price of the great earlier advances, even if it is reasonable to suppose that, lacking such innovations as an effective therapy for cancer, the decline in mortality must slow down.

Table 8. Infant Mortality Rates, with Their Endogenous
and Exogenous Components, Norway, 1876–1965

PERIOD	INFANT DEATHS PER 1,000 LIVE BIRTHS		
	TOTAL	ENDOGENOUS	EXOGENOUS
1876–1885	99.8	20.8	79.0
1886–1895	97.0	18.9	78.1
1896–1905	87.9	19.3	68.6
1906–1915	67.6	16.4	51.2
1916–1925	57.0	16.7	40.3
1926–1935	47.2	18.3	28.9
1936–1945	38.3	15.8	22.5
1946–1955	26.8	11.9	14.9
1956–1965	18.5	10.9	7.6

The infant mortality rates shown in Table 8 are divided into *endogenous* and *exogenous,* which are not quite the equivalent of the usual terms in the United States: *neonatal* and *postneonatal.* As exogenous are taken 1.22 times the number of deaths from four weeks of age to one year; the remainder are termed endogenous.

Around 1880, the infant mortality of Norway, as of Denmark and Sweden, was already low compared to the other countries of Western Europe (around 200 per 1,000 in Italy and the Netherlands, 170 in France, 160 in Belgium, and 150 in England and Wales). It changed little until the end of the 19th century; thereafter, the absolute decline was most notable at the beginning of the 20th century, though the proportionate decline was greater. Exogenous mortality has followed essentially the same course, but with a still more notable relative decline in recent years. The endogenous component changed little until the Second World War, thereafter definitely falling.

The absolute difference in infant mortality between France and Norway decreased greatly, but the relative decline was much smaller. In Norway the 1960 rate was equal to 18 percent of that in 1880, and in France to 16 percent. But in the case of the Netherlands the difference was very marked: its rate was double that of Norway around 1880 but in 1960 was slightly under it (17.2 as against 18.5 in 1956–65).

Broadly speaking, the principal features of the demographic history of Norway over the past two centuries have been precocity in the control of deaths and retardation in the control of births. It is therefore one of the countries where the lag between the decline of mortality and that of fertility has been most marked—in particular contrast to France, where this lag was nonexistent or slight, depending on whether one considers the fall in mortality during the second half of the 18th century a happy accident or the beginning of a since uninterrupted evolution.

References

BACKER, JULIE E. 1947. "Population Statistics and Population Registration in Norway," *Population Studies,* 2, 318–338.

———. 1965. *Ekteskap, fødsler og vandringer i Norge, 1856–1960.* Oslo: Statistisk Sentralbyrå.

———. 1966. "Norwegian Migration, 1856–1960," *International Migration,* 4, 172–182.

DRAKE, MICHAEL. 1965. "The Growth of Population in Norway, 1735–1855," *Scandinavian Economic History Review,* 13, 97–142.

JAHN, GUNNAR. 1957. *Barnetallet i norske ekteskap.* Oslo: Grøndahl.

NORWAY. STATISTISK SENTRALBYRÅ. 1969. *Historisk statistikk, 1968.* Oslo.

When a historical analysis is based on the few data still extant, how much of it can one legitimately extrapolate to portions of the same world about which we have no statistics at all? This problem of representativeness is central to historical demography. Any parish, or town, or nation, that first developed good data, we can reasonably assume, was probably atypical also in some of the phenomena that the data measured. Paradoxically, Scandinavia's relatively excellent statistical record—the very reason that historical demography has flourished there—reduces some of the general importance of these studies.

In that respect, early-modern France was much more representative, but it is of course much harder to make sense out of the bits and pieces of evidence that have come down to us. It was in this more difficult terrain that Professor Henry trained himself, sufficiently well to write a technical manual on the subject (1967), which he later summarized in English (1968). The next article brings together some of the best work of the French school, borrowing the expertise of demographers and translating their findings into an imaginative reconstruction of the day-to-day life that the figures connote.

Jean Fourastié, the author of our next paper, is a professor at the Institute of Political Studies and holds a chair in economics and industrial statistics at the Conservatoire National des Arts et Métiers. Since 1946, he has been a member of France's General Planning Commission, serving in various executive functions and introducing to his country and, through the European Organization for Economic Cooperation, to continental Europe some modern ideas on how to raise productivity.

In their very titles, some of his principal works suggest his recurrent interest in the future: The Civilization of 1975, Economic Forecasting, and Economics—Work—The Future. One book that has been translated into English, The Causes of Wealth (Glencoe, Ill.: Free Press, 1960), illustrates very well his extraordinary ability to round out macro-economics, not with a yet more abstract micro-analysis, but with a discussion of housing, family budgets, and similarly personal dimensions of the national economy.

The title of the article, "From the Traditional to the 'Tertiary' Life Cycle," derives, of course, from the classification of economic functions that Colin Clark devised several decades ago: primary—agriculture; secondary—manufacturing; and tertiary—services. Over the several centuries that Professor Fourastié surveys, France passed from an economy based mainly on agriculture to one in which most workers were engaged in service industries; and over the same period its fertility and mortality fell dramatically. The author uses two measures of mortality, the average expectation of life from birth (symbolized by e_0) and median, using sometimes one, sometimes the other, and often both. What does it mean in relation to one's family that $e_0 = 25$, and what in relation to the advance of knowledge when $e_0 = 70$? It is questions of this order that the paper answers.

FROM THE TRADITIONAL TO THE "TERTIARY" LIFE CYCLE

JEAN FOURASTIÉ

Scientific and technical progress, particularly in hygiene and medicine, has raised the level of life and uninterruptedly altered the demographic dimensions of human existence. For the early-modern period, data are available on the average duration of life and the age at death, on the age at marriage and the duration of marriages, on the number of children per family, and even on the age at which the heir takes over the family property. With such statistics and the less well known advances in techniques, it is now possible to construct a demographic history of the average person. In this essay a first attempt is made to contrast the precise life cycles of the average Frenchman at the beginning of the 18th century and at the present time.

At first we thought it would take only a few days to compose a life cycle of the average man, based for the early period on the good analyses of Crulai (Gautier and Henry 1958), Beauvais (Goubert 1952; 1960), and Thezels (Valmary 1965). But from the beginning, the work was complicated by the problem that population growth during the 17th and 18th centuries was most irregular, so that data vary greatly not only from one period to another but even from village to village. One can try to overcome these irregularities and the gaps in registration statistics of a particular township (*commune*) by having recourse to the large number of studies about many different townships. But studies of scientific value are extremely rare, limited in effect to those already noted.[1]

Everything we know of demographic conditions at the end of the 17th and the beginning of the 18th century seems more or less to confirm the data from Auneuil in 1635–1756 (Goubert 1960). France's last great famine was in 1709, and from the 1740s on, even local food shortages were less severe. Because of this fact, mortality began its modern phase around that time. For the beginning of the 19th century, finally, official statistics are available. The expectations of life from birth (conventionally represented by $^0e_0$, but here simply by e_0) for these three periods can be estimated as follows:

SOURCE: Translated by William Petersen from "De la vie traditionnelle à la vie 'tertiaire,' " *Population,* 14 (1959), 417–432. Reprinted in a slightly abridged form with permission of the author and the journal.

[1] Such works, moreover, are full of snares for the nondemographer. In order to recognize these traps and to know the means (often subtle) needed to avoid them, one should consult the works especially of Louis Henry, whom the author thanks especially. Though this remains an intuitive and conjectural article, it is based on the technical advice and assistance of several of the author's colleagues at the Institut National d'Etudes Démographiques. Françoise Leridon did most of the calculations summarized herein.

$$1680\text{--}1720 \qquad e_0 = 25$$
$$1770\text{--}1790 \qquad e_0 = 29$$
$$1800\text{--}1820 \qquad e_0 = 35$$

PROLONGATION OF LIFE AND ITS DIRECT CONSEQUENCES

With the prolongation of life over the past several centuries, the average man can now complete the full biological span of infancy, adolescence, adulthood, and old age, a complete life that in the traditional era had been vouchsafed to only a very small minority. A population more than half of which attains the age of 75 years ($e_0 = 73.0$) differs vastly from one of which one person in two dies before his 21st birthday ($e_0 = 27.5$) or even before his 16th ($e_0 = 25$). Conscious intellectual life hardly begins before age 12 and personal independence hardly before age 20. Most humans used to exist in a sort of vegetative state, whose dead weight strongly influenced even that small minority responsible for sustaining and guiding the whole.

But can a population with an expectation of life of only 25 years reproduce itself? With 25 as the average age at a woman's first marriage, it appears that such a population declines by about 10 percent per generation; but if the life expectation rises to 30 years, with the same marital pattern it increases by about 10 percent per generation. Thus, in a population with traditional fertility and mortality oscillating between these two figures, the numbers would remain essentially static.

The reproduction rate, one should note, is extremely responsive to changes in the age at marriage. With $e_0 = 25$, the average age at marriage need fall by only 2.5 years for the population to grow by 6 percent per generation. But in fact we know very little about ages at marriage, for the number of observations is tiny relative to France's population. For a few generations the average age for females might easily have gone as low as 22 or 23 years, and in that case one can conceive that—for several generations of population decline in the 17th or earlier centuries—the expectation of life may have fallen to 20 years.

Of 317 marriages in Auneuil from 1656 to 1735 (Goubert 1960), the median duration was 19 years, the average 21 years. But one cannot be sure whether these data were not somewhat falsified by the absence of families that had left the township, either temporarily or permanently. It would seem to be preferable to calculate the duration of marriages from life tables rather than from the vital statistics of a parish. Combining both types of data gives the results shown in Table 1.

This summary can be usefully supplemented with other data, based on the study of Crulai village, supplemented by the schematic life tables prepared by the United Nations. The figures in Table 1 pertain to first marriages only, but the high mortality made remarriages very common. Table 2 shows the age at marriage according to the prior marital status of the bride and

Table 1. Demographic Data on Mortality and Marriage, France at Various Periods and Comparative Figures

LOCALITY	OF 1,000 BORN ALIVE, NUMBER SURVIVING TO AGE—		AVERAGE AGE AT FIRST MARRIAGE		OF PERSONS WHO REACHED THE AVERAGE AGE AT MARRIAGE, AVERAGE AGE AT DEATH		DURATION OF MARRIAGE	
	1 YEAR	20 YEARS	MALE	FEMALE	MALE	FEMALE	MEDIAN	MEAN
Crulai ($N = 297$), 1675–1750			27	25	53	52		17 (?)
Life table, Crulai, 1675–1775	780	587		25	57	56	19.2	20.7
Life table, Duvillard, c. 1770–90 ($e_0 = 29$)	767	502	27	25	58	58	19.9	21.4
Auneuil 1656–1735	712	489	27	25				21
Auneuil 1737–1756	720	460						
Auneuil 1757–1790	800	620						
France 1805–1807	808	604	27	25	61	62	24.6	25
France 1952–1956	964	948	26	24	71	77	41.1	39
Life table, Sweden, 1951–55 ($e_0 = 71.7$)	980	968	26	24	76	79	44.8	42.5
Life table based on the assumed ultimate decline in mortality, France, 1980–90? ($e_0 = 77$)	989	987	26	24	79	81	47.8	46.4
Schematic life tables calculated by United Nations $e_0 = 20$	680	393	27	25	48	47	15	17
$e_0 = 25$	720	474	27	25	51	51	16.5	18.5
$e_0 = 27.5$	738	511	27	25	53	53	18.1	19.6
$e_0 = 30$	755	545	27	25	55	55		

Table 2. Mean Age at Marriage, Crulai, 1674–1742

PRIOR MARITAL STATUS OF SPOUSE	PRIOR MARITAL STATUS				TOTAL	
	SINGLE MALE	SINGLE FEMALE	WIDOWER	WIDOW	MALE	FEMALE
Single	27.2	24.6	40.6	35.6	29.5	25.5
Widower or widow	31.3	28.9	46.7	39.5	36.8	31.0
Total	27.5	25.3	41.8	37.0	30.3	26.6

groom. The average duration of marriage depended, of course, on the life expectations of persons at the ages at marriage. Consider the first case given in Table 2, a bachelor of 27 marrying a spinster of 25. Given a life table with $e_0 = 25$, this marriage would last 17 years; given one with $e_0 = 30$, it would last 19.6 years. But second and subsequent marriages are at considerably higher ages and last a much shorter period—only 5 years for the marriage of a widow, only 1.5 to 2 years for that of a widower.

In a population with little or no deliberate control of conception, family size depends on the duration of marriage, which in turn depends on the average age at marriage and the death rate (Table 3). Note that only the last of the four combinations provides a margin for sustained growth.

Table 3. Fertility under Postulated Conditions of Marriage
Formation and Mortality, Crulai, 1675–1742

POSTULATE	NUMBER OF (RE) MARRIAGES	NUMBER OF LIVE BIRTHS	AVERAGE NUMBER OF CHILDREN PER MARRIAGE	NET REPRO-DUCTION RATE
1,000 spinsters of 25 marry men of 29				
Life table with $e_0 = 25$	1,126	4,620	4.10	0.89
Life table with $e_0 = 30$	1,110	4,870	4.38	1.09
1,000 spinsters of 22.5 marry men of 26.5				
Life table with $e_0 = 25$		5,270		1.06
Life table with $e_0 = 30$		5,675		1.34

When children were born under the conditions prevailing in Crulai, the average age of the mother was 32, of the father 36. Given a life table with $e_0 = 30$, a female of 32 survives on the average to age 58, a male of 36 to age 58.5. One can represent the effect of mortality on the succession of two generations either by calculating the age of children when one or the other of their parents dies or, vice versa, by calculating the percentage of families with one or the other parent surviving when children reach 18, taken as the age marking readiness for mature roles. Both calculations are given under various designated assumptions in Table 4.

Table 4. The Effect of Mortality on the Succession of Two Generations, Crulai, 1674–1742

INTERGENERATIONAL EFFECTS	LIFE TABLE WITH—			
	$e_0 = 25$		$e_0 = 30$	
Average age of surviving children				
At death of father	20.2		22.5	
At death of mother	23.3		26.0	
At death of either parent	14.0		16.2	
At death of the second parent	29.5		32.5	
	MALE	FEMALE	MALE	FEMALE
Of persons reaching age 18, percent with ——— still alive				
Only their father	13.6	14.7	14.7	15.3
Only their mother	20.9	22.0	22.8	23.2
Both parents	11.0	14.4	16.6	20.6
Neither parent	33.1	28.3	26.9	22.3

THE TWO LIFE CYCLES

At the end of the 17th century, the life of the average family head, who had married for the first time at age 27, could be represented schematically thus: Born into a family of five children, of whom only half reached the age of 15, he also, like his father, had five children, of whom again only two or three were still alive when he died ($e_0 = 25$). This man, living to an average age of 52—which placed him among the venerable aged (for with $e_0 = 25$, only 205 of every 1,000 males born reach 52 years)—survived in his immediate family (not to speak of uncles and aunts, nephews and nieces, and first cousins) an average of nine persons: one of his grandparents (the other three having died before his birth), his two parents, three siblings, and three of his children. He had lived through two or three famines as well as three or four periods of high-priced grain, which were tied to the poor harvests that on the average recurred every ten years. Moreover, he had lived through sicknesses of his brothers and sisters, his children, his wife (or wives), his parents, and himself, having survived two or three epidemics as well as the more or less endemic whooping cough, scarlet fever, diphtheria, and so on, which each year claimed their victims. He had often suffered from such physical ailments as toothaches and wounds that took long to heal. Poverty, disabilities, suffering were constantly before his eyes.

Today, the average man reaches not 60 years but 65, 70, and even 75 (depending on the region of France); and according to the current life table (Bourgeois-Pichat 1951–52), half of the children born alive can be expected to live to 80 years. If our average man reached age 50 in 1959, his past is easy to summarize: Born into a family with three children, he married at age 26 a girl of 24, and they had two or three children. Sicknesses were mild, hardly one having been worrisome. The only deaths in his family, of his four grandparents, were less dramatic departures than long awaited deliverances. Physical pain had almost disappeared. And this man of 50 had still one chance in two of living 26 years more.

With even a slight knowledge of the human condition, we can understand how the prolongation of life by this proportion must have changed the average person's way of thinking. In the traditionalist era, death was in the center of life, just as the cemetery was in the center of the village. Since then death, poverty, and physical pain have retreated. Viewed no longer as man's rough companions, who force him toward spirituality and moral progress, they are now seen as accidents, deformations, and bad luck that contradict the true nature of human life, to be not only fought but minimized and camouflaged.

Yesterday one child in two died before his father, and half of the rest saw their father die before they attained their majority. A child's average age when the first of his parents died was 14 years ($e_0 = 25$). Tomorrow the average son will be 55 or 60 when his father dies; he will first have watched him waste away into senility. Hereditary family property will almost always belong to persons over 60, and almost half of France's private fortunes will be owned by men and women over 70.

Changes in the marital pattern have been even sharper. Yesterday men of 25 to 30—already scarred by harsh experience (having in almost every case lost at least one parent) and motivated much more by enduring family needs than by the superficial attraction of physique or intellect—contracted unions that, though broken only by death, lasted on the average less than 20 years. For the period 1680–1720, the average duration of a French marriage was about 17 years, the median 15 years; for the period 1750–80 these values were, respectively, 19.5 and 18 years. Today boys not much younger in years but far less marked by life, relying thus only on the physical drives of their age, still in principle marry for life but this time for close to 50 years. Traditionally parents died before the education of their youngest children had been completed. Tomorrow a typical couple will survive the marriage of their youngest child by 15 to 20 years.

THE EVOLUTION OF INTELLECTUAL LIFE

With the mortality prevailing in Crulai, approximately half the males born alive survived to age 27, which we can take as their usual age at first marriage. Of 1,000 bachelors married at that age, between 530 ($e_0 = 25$) and 604 ($e_0 = 30$) lived to age 50. A summary of their lives up to that point is given in Table 5.

Table 5. The Demographic Situation of a Man of 50, Crulai, 1674–1742

OF 1,000 MALES WHO REACHED AGE 50—	LIFE TABLE WITH—	
	$e_0 = 25$	$e_0 = 30$
Number of marriages	1,360	1,293
Number of children born	5,940	6,035
Of whom, number surviving	3,020	3,455
Number of deaths in immediate family		
Grandparents [a]	850	1,120
Parents	1,970	1,942
Siblings [b]	3,045	2,780
Wives	540	435
Children	2,920	2,580

[a] In each case, of 4,000 grandparents still alive when their grandchildren surviving to age 50 were born.
[b] Assuming the survivors were the third of five children.

Once upon a time, old age was the culmination of an exceptional career. Having triumphed over a thousand dangers and cheated death many times, the old man was recognized as a sage—and so he considered himself—the holder of a magic power that benefited his village and his family. In a word, he was a patriarch. In spite of the fact that part of the high fertility was undercut by high infant and child mortality, a grandfather of 65, though often having lost all his children and nephews and nieces, was nevertheless surrounded by five or six living grandchildren and as many grandnephews or grandnieces. Today old age is no more than a commonplace and pitiful decay of a body already used up, which returns to death by way of a supine life.

This relation is shown by the age structure. Population pyramids for past periods are broad at the base and sharply pointed at the top, where only chiefs and leaders are represented. The pyramids of tomorrow's world will be rectangles; the traditional hierarchy of age categories will have disappeared.

Thus it is that the traditional base of social life started to founder during the first centuries of technical progress. By these facts we see how profound were the several evolutions imposed on mankind by technical progress, however much it seemed to focus only on the improvement of technology. And the prolongation of intellectual life has had even more influence on the usual objects of conscience, on constructive thought, and on civilization.

Through the progressive extension of schooling, the average man's access to intellectual life has reached the limit of what might be termed intellectual adolescence. Aptitudes at the highest level no longer seem to be improving; in concrete terms, the difficulty of studies and the scholarly achievement in the students' major studies at France's top schools (the Ecole Normale, the Ecole Polytechnique) have leveled off. In contrast, the base keeps broadening and will continue to broaden until, already foreseeably, every adolescent, no longer constrained by the traditional rationing of the economy and society, will be educated to the physiological limit of his brain power.

On a broad scale little is yet known about this limit. It may be that intellectual ability is apportioned the same way as physical, of which we know the mass to be very inferior to the elite. But the fact of mankind's intellectualization is nevertheless clear. Traditional humanity as a whole was vegetal, with its intellectual faculties fallow; men of the future, on the contrary, will generally derive as much as possible from their power to think, no matter how limited it may be. It is useful, therefore, to try to add an intellectual component to the life cycle of the average man.

With the mortality of 17th-century France, of 1,000 males born alive only 475 survived to 20—that is to say, to the age when one begins to think independently—only 318 to age 40, and only 130 to age 60 ($e_0 = 25$). Consider the case of well-to-do intellectuals, recognized as able to teach in higher education and themselves desirous of success. On the assumption that their mortality was the same as the whole country's, out of 1,000 intellectuals born alive, 960 today acquire a complete secondary education, as against 475 formerly; 955 finish their higher education, as against 437 in the 17th century. But of these 437, 120 died before 40 (the age of maturity, after which creativity generally begins in the social sciences, in philosophy, in the sciences of man), and only 130 reached 60.

In today's average life, the young man of 25 who finishes his higher education has before him an average of 50 years of life, 18 of which will on the average fall between ages 40 and 60—whereas at one time he could look forward to only 25 years, of which 8 were between ages 40 and 60. Taking the two decades between 40 and 60 as intellectually the most creative period, and adjusting these figures to allow for illness, suffering, mourning, and various other interruptions, we come to orders of magnitude something like the following:

—of 1,000 intellectuals born alive and into a family sufficiently affluent to afford them access to culture:

17,000 creative years today,

2,500 creative years formerly

—of 1,000 young people who at age 25 have completed their higher education:

18,000 creative years today,

6,000 creative years formerly

To this increase in the expectation of creative intellectual life one must add, of course, the effects of progress in techniques of documenting and disseminating information.

And if the base population is not 1,000 children socially destined to teach in higher education but rather 1,000 children taken randomly from the entire nation, the contrasts are still greater between their expected intellectual life in 1700 and in 1960. For the low level of life, the social sclerosis, and the lack of basic schooling effectively closed the university to all but a very small fraction of gifted men and to almost all women.

Bibliography

BOURGEOIS-PICHAT, JEAN. 1951–52. "Evolution générale de la population française depuis le XVIIIᵉ siècle," *Population,* **6**, 635–662; 7, 318–329.

———. 1952. "Essai sur la mortalité 'biologique' de l'homme," *Population,* **7**, 381–394.

GAUTIER, ETIENNE, and LOUIS HENRY. 1958. *La population de Crulai, paroisse normande: Etude historique.* Cahier No. 33, Institut National d'Etudes Démographiques. Paris: Presses Universitaires de France.

GOUBERT, PIERRE. 1952. "En Beauvaisis: Problèmes démographiques du XVIIᵉ siècle," *Annales: Economies, Sociétés, Civilisations,* **7**, 452–468.

———. 1960. *Beauvais et le Beauvaisis de 1600 à 1730: Contribution à l'histoire sociale de la France du XVIIᵉ siècle.* Collection "Economies et Sociétés," Ecole Pratique des Hautes Etudes. Paris.

HENRY, LOUIS. 1952. "Mesure de la fréquence des divorces," *Population,* **7**, 267–282.

———. 1953. "Vues sur la statistique des familles," *Population,* **8**, 473–490.

———. 1954a. "Mise au point sur la natalité française," *Population,* **9**, 197–226.

———. 1954b. "La nuptialité à la fin de l'Ancien Régime" (review of G. Duplessis-Le Guélinel, *Les mariages en France*), *Population,* **9**, 542–546.

———. 1956. *Anciennes familles genevoises: Etudes démographiques, XVIᵉ–XXᵉ siècles.* Cahier No. 26, Institut National d'Etudes Démographiques. Paris: Presses Universitaires de France.

———. 1967. *Manuel de démographie historique.* Geneva: Librairie Droz.

———. 1968. "The Verification of Data in Historical Demography," *Population Studies,* **22**, 61–81.

JACCARD, PIERRE. 1957. *Politique de l'emploi et de l'éducation.* Paris: Payot.

PRESSAT, ROLAND. 1956. "Le remariage des veufs et des veuves," *Population*, 11, 46–58.

REINHARD, MARCEL. 1949. *Histoire de la population mondiale de 1700 à 1948*. Paris: Editions Domat-Montchrestien.

UNITED NATIONS. 1956. *Methods for Population Projections by Sex and Age*. Population Study No. 25. New York.

VALMARY, PIERRE. 1965. *Familles paysannes au XVIIIᵉ siècle en Bas-Guercy: Etude démographique*. Cahier No. 45, Institut National d'Etudes Démographiques. Paris: Presses Universitaires de France.

2 POPULATION THEORIES

What set of linked propositions in the natural or social sciences might not be termed a "population theory"? Any broad statement about the biological determinants of fertility or mortality (or, in recent years, migration), any about the consistent differentiation among human groups or the influence of social institutions, as well as any religious-ethical tenets on the meaning of the good life and the proper way to attain it—all these and more have been included under this rubric. At one time, it is true, students of population focused their expertise more narrowly, communicating mainly to relatively small coteries in the code language of professional jargon through journals whose very names no one else knew. Geneticists discussed with other geneticists, economists with other economists, Catholic theologians with other Catholic theologians; and if on rare occasions the twain met it was as much an anomaly as in Kipling's poem, "when two strong men stand face to face, though they come from the ends of the earth."

Today little of this protective insulation remains. The problems associated with population size, growth, and composition have become public issues; and from all the reservoirs of facts, concepts, and learned opinions, these are marshaled to debate policy. We seem to be moving back to the period before the separation of disciplines, when all knowledge and beliefs were fitted into "political economy" or "moral philosophy," when a Herbert Spencer could write compendia on both biology and the social system. The difference, of course, is that in the interim each science has developed its own techniques of research and understanding, its own vast accumulation of data. On a complex issue like "the environment," no one person can acquire a just appreciation of all that is pertinent to making policy, which is why on such matters most discussion is by the terrible simplifiers.

On so wide-ranging a topic as population theory, we offer in place of several shorter articles one long paper, which was written specially for this book. It welds its diverse elements into a degree of unity by structuring them according to three principles:

1. The current concentration on policy making echoes one recurrent theme in population analysis, from the ancient Greeks through the mercantilists and Malthus to those who have tried to define the optimum. And when this was not the case originally, the author shows how often moderns have converted ancient doctrines into present-day concerns.

2. Very often, thus, the same questions recur in quite different social settings—the population-resources ratio, for instance, or how to define legitimate sexuality. On some crucial issues thinkers as diverse as Augustine, Malthus, and Gandhi held similar views. In a review of population theories, then, the variation in cultures can be reduced to a manageable size by emphasizing the much smaller number of answers to such basic questions.

3. And the diversity that is thus highlighted in basic policies is not merely recorded. What is likely to be the population doctrine, the author asks, of a small city-state as contrasted with a vast empire; what is the optimum population of a totalitarian state as against that of a democracy? In short, the variation in attitude and policy is not random but, it is suggested, is shaped by social-economic-political conditions.

It would take a book to work out these organizing principles in detail, but even in a chapter they help guide the reader through a mass of detail.

The author of the paper, Nathan Keyfitz, has taught at the Universities of Toronto and Chicago and is presently a professor of demography at the University of California in Berkeley. His international reputation is based first of all on his preeminence in statistical and mathematical analysis; he is the author of perhaps the best book in the field—Introduction to the Mathematics of Population *(Addison-Wesley, 1968). Others who know his work might recall his extraordinarily wide experience all over the world— as senior research statistician in the Dominion Bureau of Statistics in Ottawa; as consultant, teacher, or researcher in Ceylon, India, Argentina, Chile, Germany, Hawaii, and especially Indonesia (of whose vast population he has been one of the few Western analysts). Most of his several books and some fifty papers reflect this statistical competence and cosmopolitan background. This paper represents something of a new departure for him.*

POPULATION THEORY AND DOCTRINE:
A HISTORICAL SURVEY

NATHAN KEYFITZ

The number of people in the city, the nation, or the world—what determines that number and how in turn it affects power and welfare—has always been a persistent theme of social science, whose topicality shows no sign of diminishing in the last decades of the 20th century. Philosophers, counselors to princes, theologians, and legislators have elaborated population doctrines and promoted policies based on them, or else promoted policies and created doctrines to buttress them. Views of population are linked to views of the state and of society as a whole, as well as to the objective facts of population, technology, and social organization at the time of their enunciation.

ANTIQUITY

As early as the time of Confucius, Chinese writers saw that when the population was too small the land was idle and taxes were not paid, when it was too large hardship ensued. A primitive notion of optimum is implicit in their thought. A land empire, in which periods of local prosperity alternated with famines, floods, and epidemics, could usefully shift people from overpopulated to underpopulated regions. Voluntary movements were seen as being in the right direction but sometimes too small, and hence to be reinforced by administered transfers (Chen 1911; Lee 1921; Pan 1950: 61, 126–27, 302). Rapid growth took place twice in Chinese history—after 1000 A.D. and in the 18th century, with the introduction, respectively, of fast-growing crops from Southeast Asia and of maize, potatoes, and peanuts from America (Ho 1959; McNeill 1963: 176, 581). In both instances scholars were conscious that expanded food supplies brought about the increase of population.

Greek thought on population developed in city-states with constitutional rule by the minority who were citizens. According to Plato (*Laws*, Book V, para. 637), a population must be sufficient to defend itself against its neighbors, and the optimum thus depends partly on the strength of these neighbors; but no city should exceed its capacity to provide materially for its

SOURCE: This article is in large part due to William Petersen. He rewrote it completely at one point in the succession of drafts and edited it drastically at two other points, in each instance contributing many clarifications and corrections. I have also incorporated suggestions by Diana Dixon, James Dobbins, Robert Lunde, Geoffrey McNicoll, and Gordon Praeger. Acknowledgment is made of NSF grant GZ995, NIH research contract 69–2200, and teaching grants to the department of demography, University of California at Berkeley, from the National Institutes of General Medical Sciences (5 TO1 GM01240) and the Ford Foundation.—N.K.

citizens. Effective rule and civil order depend on whether the citizens know one another, which sets another limit to size. In his discussion he used the arbitrary figure of 5,040 landholders, a number sufficient for the various specialties the state requires. This total is divisible by 59 numbers, and so would facilitate the allocation of tasks and the division of property. When more or fewer children were needed to attain the ideal, the change in fertility could be realized by appropriate honors or negative sanctions; fostering immigration or dispatching citizens to the colonies were also acceptable policies for influencing the total. Aristotle was especially concerned that the city not be too large; he advocated abortion, rejecting infanticide except as a eugenic measure (*Politics*, Book I, para. 1; Book VII, para. 4; see Barker 1959: 407–8; United Nations 1953).

In India not long after Plato—around 300 B.C.—Kautilya wrote *Arthasastra* (Book VII, chaps. 1, 11; Book VIII, chap. 3; Book XIII, chap. 4; cf. Spengler 1963), which discussed population as a source of political, economic, and military strength, the necessary complement of land and mines. Though a given territory can hold too many or too few people, the latter is the greater evil. Kautilya restricted asceticism to the aged, favored the remarriage of widows, opposed taxes so high as to provoke emigration. The optimum village consisted of 100 to 500 agricultural families on a square mile or two (Book II, chap. 1).

With their tightly administered land empire and ceaseless wars on their borders, the Romans needed men even more than China or India. Any excess of men could go forth as an army and conquer the lands that would sustain them. Roman writers condemned celibacy and advocated monogamous marriage as the type that would produce the most offspring. Vice leads not only to individual ruin but to collective depopulation (Cicero, *De republica*, Book IV, para. 5). The literary emphasis on virtue and on Rome's need for men did not prevent small families, especially in the upper and middle classes, or an increasing dependence on hired barbarians.

CHRISTIAN THOUGHT

Christian thought developed in the declining Roman Empire, but encouraging population growth to meet the secular needs of the Empire formed very little part of it (Noonan 1965). To the Church Fathers virginity was the ideal; only for those too weak to abstain from temptation of the flesh was marriage recommended. Augustine reacted against the pessimistic heresies of Gnosticism and Manicheism, which condemned marriage and procreation as producing material human bodies in which the Light would be imprisoned. He sought a justification for marriage, and found it above all in procreation. His doctrine of the marital goods—offspring, fidelity, symbolic stability—dominated Christian thought for a thousand years, during which marriage remained the second-best state. "I am aware," Augustine wrote, "of some that murmur, 'What if all men should abstain from sexual relations, whence will the human race subsist?' . . . I answer, so much more speedily would the City of God be fulfilled and the end of the world hastened."

The contrast to the prior Hebrew teaching is striking. The early Christian theologian did not refer to the injunction of Genesis to increase and multiply, nor did he speak of spreading Christianity by having children. The less austere Thomas Aquinas reintroduced the Aristotelian concept of nature; just as it is the nature of the eye to see, so it is the nature of the genitalia to procreate—the very word tells that. It is right and pleasurable to do what is according to nature.

In 1930, the encyclical *Casti Connubii* synthesized a variety of themes from many historical epochs. It condemned contraception on the grounds of the need to propagate the human race and to bear children for the Church of Christ, as well as on Augustine's three goods of marriage. It recalled Aristotle and Aquinas in arguing that "no reason can make congruent with nature what is intrinsically against nature." It used 19th-century theology to condemn the sin of Onan (Noonan 1965: 508). Following the lead of the Lambeth Conference, which in 1930 opened the door to contraception in the Anglican Church, most other Protestant groups have found little difficulty in reversing their previous stand against birth control. But Catholic doctrine up to this writing has yielded only the theologically confusing concession of the rhythm method, sanctioned by Pius XII in 1950 after much debate within the Church, which seemingly shifted from the intention of contraception to the method.

THE CYCLE OF POPULATION AND EMPIRE

Ibn Khaldun, who lived before the 18th century invented the idea of progress, saw history as the rise, prospering, and fall of states and civilizations (Mahdi 1957: Part 4). When a tribe becomes numerous under an aggressive chief, it enters on a career of conquest, builds or captures a capital city, and adapts its tribal religion in order to strengthen loyalty to the chief. The tribal chief's successors make themselves absolute rulers of an expanding state, build palaces and temples, and sponsor the arts and the sciences. Rule comes to depend less on the respect for a senior kinsman and more on a tightly organized bureaucracy and army. The city expands with the expansion of the hinterland supplying its food.

Later generations of rulers, attracted to luxury, lose their martial virtues. The original population declines; foreign mercenaries are hired for the army, and foreign officials for the administration. These can only be paid by high taxes, levied on both the artisans and the surrounding peasantry. The absorption of the rulers in luxury, the decline of the native population, and the spread of intrigue in the bureaucracy and army lead to the loss of the provinces on whose food and other raw materials the state depends. Having broken the original bonds of kinship and perverted religion to the service of the state, the rulers are helpless when the artificial military and civil structure dissolves. In the last phase the provinces have fallen away, commerce is undercut by taxes and insecurity, and the birth rate declines further. If it is not conquered by a newly rising population, the state burns out like a lamp wick when the oil is exhausted.

Machiavelli, also a counselor to princes and a political realist, lived about a century after Ibn Khaldun, and like him saw population growth as initiating new cycles of history. He gave as an example the demographic expansion of the barbarians beyond the Rhine and the Danube. A community that became numerous would divide into three parts, each containing the same proportions of nobles and people, rich and poor, and draw lots to see which third would move out of their native country, generally toward the south. The migrating masses destroyed the Roman Empire. Population was indeed a matter for the ruler to be concerned about: "I think those princes capable of ruling," said Machiavelli, "who are capable, either by the numbers of their men or by the greatness of their wealth, to raise a complete army and bid battle to any enemy that shall invade them" (*History of Florence*, quoted by Malthus 1960b: 195).

In Europe of the 16th to 18th centuries, states competed ceaselessly for military, political, and economic power. Absolute rulers had an interest in maximizing their territories' populations, from which both armies and manual workers could be recruited. The monarch's wealth was seen as a function of the total value produced by his kingdom less whatever was paid in wages. Since the wage per worker would always diminish as the number of workers increased, people were an unqualified asset to their masters. A king could no more have too many subjects than a modern farmer can have too many cattle. "One should never fear there being too many subjects or too many citizens," wrote Jean Bodin, "seeing that there is no wealth nor strength but in men" (*La République*, Book V, chap. 2). The goods they produced could be exported for gold or silver, and so people were money. For Frederick the Great it was a certain axiom that "the number of the people makes the wealth of states" (Stangeland 1904: 131). For Süssmilch (1788, 1: 17ff), a chaplain in Frederick's army, the interests of the sovereign coincided with the divine order, and both would be furthered by more Germans (Mackenroth 1953: 301–2). With minor exceptions, other French, Italian, and Spanish mercantilists favored population growth unanimously. Botero (1956) offered advice on how larger populations might be attained: Agricultural and especially industrial production should be encouraged; the export of raw materials should be forbidden and that of manufactured goods fostered. The English writers were more qualified in their populationism; Petty, as a prime example, both accepted the thesis that men create wealth and feared the poverty and social turmoil consequent on too great numbers.

POLITICAL ARITHMETIC AND THE PHYSIOCRATS

The numerical study of population starting in the 17th century, rather than earlier speculations, marked the beginning of demography. When John Graunt worked up bills of mortality, he observed many constant features of deaths and births. Estimating that the ratio of deaths to births was 14 to 13 in London, as against 52 to 63 in the countryside, he calculated the in-migration from the countryside needed to maintain and increase London's population. The statistics were poor, but Graunt made what reasoned adjustments he could and did not hesitate to draw conclusions. The concept of a cohort that is diminished by death as it goes through successive ages was clear to him, though his estimates of its diminution were too high. (The life table implied in his calculations has an expectation of life at birth of about 17.5 years, as against the 27.5 years of Halley's [1693] table for Breslau. The European urban average of the time was probably between these two figures.) He calculated age distributions from the life table, although he did not quite understand the notion of a stable as against a stationary age distribution, apparently first stated precisely by Euler (1970) in 1760. He made some corrections for misstatement in the bills' totals by cause of death, and noted that aside from the plague, the distribution by cause did not change greatly from year to year. The records of baptisms, which he also analyzed, showed a slight but constant excess of males over females at birth, and he considered that this excess held in the population as a whole. Childbearing women "one with another, have scarce more than one childe in two years," a birth interval close to that computed by present-day scholars from data on 17th-century Europe.

It is not clear, however, whether the credit for initiating demography goes to Graunt or to his more imaginative younger contemporary, Sir William Petty. Even the original authorship of the *Observations on the Bills of Mortality* has been attributed to Petty. At least "Petty may have stimulated Graunt's initial interest in this sort of enquiry; he later carried through somewhat similar, but more superficial, observations on the Dublin bills of mortality; and he edited a posthumous edition of Graunt's *Observations*, published by the Royal Society" (Lorimer 1959: 126; Glass 1963).

Petty's new science of Political Arithmetic (1691), based on empirical work by Graunt among others, raised exciting perspectives in the Royal Society of London. Toward the end of the 17th century, Gregory King assembled enough data to produce a realistic estimate of England's population—5.5 million. Such work as that of Graunt, Petty, Halley, and King, who made good use of the crude data at hand, when combined with later theorizing on population convinced legislators of the need for censuses and vital statistics.

By the 18th century the mercantilists' emphasis on numbers was tempered by the recognition of poverty. Cantillon, standing between the mercantilists and the physiocrats, saw that an overcrowded state could acquire some relief by exporting manufactured goods and importing food—a frequent mercantilist theme (Hoselitz 1960: 26–42; Spengler 1942). Cantillon's masterpiece, *Essai sur la nature du commerce en général* (1952: 1), made land or nature the source of all wealth. Population is created by the means of subsistence, which depend not only on nature and such institutions as property rights in land but also on the decisions that princes and landowners make. If those who control the land want horses for hunting and war, the human population will be smaller than if they prefer domestic retainers. That French landowners preferred Dutch cloth reduced France's population and increased Holland's. The prince's way of living sets the style for smaller landholders. Cantillon does not moralize, but by implication he tells the rulers by what personal sacrifices they could increase population. That in China bearers carry travelers on litter-chairs, he says, explains why compared with Europe the human population is larger, the horse population smaller.

François Quesnay (Sauvy 1958; Landry 1909), in opposition to the mercantilists, held that men must not be encouraged to multiply beyond the point of comfort. Inadequate opportunity to work generates laziness, misery, and other social costs. Quesnay, a physician, was interested in social reforms that would heal the body politic; his way to a healthy society was to increase capital, especially in agriculture, in order to make labor more productive and so bring more men into existence. Government should not interfere with nature or with markets, but provide an institutional framework within which the sum of men's natural individual acts will serve the common interest. Rules governing property and marriage are essential to avoid irresponsible procreation (Quesnay 1908; Vialatoux 1959, 2: 175), but generally physiocrats (the word means "rule by nature") wanted as little regulation as possible.

Less concerned than the mercantilists with foreign trade, the physiocrats emphasized the circulation of wealth within the state. The way in which the costs of one class become the income of another was formalized in a *Tableau Economique* that analyzed the gross product, so that physiocracy anticipated the macro-economics of the 20th century as well as the liberalism of the 19th. In showing how the growth of agriculture underlay economic advance, it even anticipated one 20th-century school of economic development. Labor produced only enough for its own subsistence and for population replacement; all surplus was attributable to land. We shall see how Marx reversed this with his better known imputation of all surplus to labor.

THE ENLIGHTENMENT AND MALTHUS

Some mercantilists feared a growth of population beyond the subsistence already in sight, but most expressed confidence that any number of new subjects could produce their own subsistence. The latter view was incorporated in the very different framework of the 18th century's new theory of progress and human perfectibility. Among others, Condorcet, Godwin, and Daniel Malthus held that the numbers of men determine available resources, rather than vice versa. In the era that they saw dawning, such past coercive institutions as property, the family, and the punishment of criminals would disappear, their objectives to be realized through the individual consciences of perfected men. No growth of population in an adequately organized society could conflict with progress, in Godwin's view, for the new City of Man (like Augustine's City of God) would harmonize all social classes and the whole of society with its material base. "There is in human society a principle whereby population is constantly maintained at the level of the means of subsistence," for "the goods of the world are a common fund from which all men can satisfy their needs" (Godwin 1793: 466, 520; Hutchinson 1967).

These views, which he heard first from his father, stimulated Thomas Robert Malthus (1960b) to seek a more realistic analysis of how population relates to resources. By his famous "principle of population," the number of people, if unchecked, grows in geometric progression, while the resources on which they depend at best increase arithmetically. Moreover, the capacity of men to multiply, and through their multiplying to make themselves miserable, would be accentuated by the very changes in institutions designed to attain an earthly paradise. Malthus's persistence in opposing this thesis to the optimism of the *philosophes* established him as the central figure of population doctrine. For his immediate predecessors—Hume, Wallace, Adam Smith, and Quesnay—population growth was primarily a sequel to an increase in produce; demand for labor (as for shoes) produces the supply in a self-regulating system (Coontz 1957; Smith 1921, 1: 82–83). Malthus opposed to this natural harmony the conflict between population and its means of subsistence.

To ascertain the power of population one had to look at a territory where good land was plentiful. America showed a doubling in less than 25 years. In countries settled longer the pace was much slower, and most of Malthus's writing and research concerned the nature of the checks by which the rate of growth is held down. He found that in Europe late marriages made for small families. This moral restraint, incorporated in custom and in individual responsibility, he termed a *preventive* check. Also included under preventive checks were vices such as homosexuality, adultery, birth control, and abortion, and these Malthus certainly did not recommend (Petersen 1969: 149). When preventive checks were inadequate, such *positive* checks as wars and epidemics would supplement them. The ultimate positive check, standing behind all the others, was famine, but this did not often come into operation.

Malthus was part moralist, part scholar; his system was inductive and deductive as it developed in different writings; he incorporated both biological and social causes (Petersen 1969: 155–59). Davis (1955) has helped disentangle some of the diverse strands in Malthus's thought. Boulding (1955), Peacock (1952–54), Nelson (1956), and others have translated Malthus into graphical and mathematical models, using in particular his view that resources determine numbers of people, as the physiocrats had thought, and not vice versa, as most mercantilists held. This view can be traced through numerous predecessors, even with resemblances in the phrasing. Malthus's "Population does invariably increase when the means of subsistence increase" (1960b: 52) recalls Cantillon's "Men increase like mice in a barn if they have access to unlimited subsistence" (1952: 47). And one can go back through Mirabeau and others, ultimately to the succinct "When goods increase, they are increased that eat them" of Ecclesiastes 5:11.

It was for Malthus to derive from this proposition an entire philosophy of history and a theory of society, as well as an inexhaustible source of policy recommendations. All poor laws and personal charity must be so arranged that those receiving doles do not respond by increasing the number of their offspring. For those individuals and nations failing to exercise the preventive check of moral restraint—through chaste postponement of marriage until prospective parents could care for their children—the more severe positive checks of war, pestilence, and famine would become operative. Avoidance of these must be the central aim of policy.

Malthus's intentions were liberal and humane. "There never was a more singular delusion than the common belief in the hardheartedness of Malthus" (Bonar 1885: 57; also Keynes 1963). He advocated the conversion of hunting estates that could be used for agricultural production, the more efficient use of land already occupied, the development of industry. While education of the masses was feared by Godwin, Malthus favored universal literacy. He promoted medical assistance for the poor and a wider democracy, all in terms consistent with the mature version of his population theory (Petersen 1971). From the second edition of the *Essay* on, Malthus stressed that progress was possible, that "on the whole the power of civilization is greater than the power of population" (Malthus 1960b: 593). By the organization of property, individuals can be encouraged to discipline themselves to adapt without pain, indeed with personal gain, to forces that ineluctably control society as a whole. The population dilemma can be resolved by an ethic of individual responsibility, and the standard of living can accordingly rise. This was Malthus's answer to the French revolution.

Malthus remains one of the most controversial figures in social thought. Regarded as a reactionary by those who dreamed of an earthly paradise, he in fact helped develop the economic theories that propelled the revolutionary social changes of the 19th century. The traditionally pious accused him of blasphemy for urging men to take responsibility for the size of their families; had not the Creator himself enjoined all to be fruitful and multiply? Had not Luther declared that any man hesitating to start a family because he lacked property or a job showed a want of faith? One of the most vigorous attacks came from Proudhon, who held that early marriage is the surest guarantee of good morals. To defer love in the name of moral restraint would restrict marriage to superannuated spinsters and aging satyrs. Like other socialists, Proudhon argued that the imprudence of the working classes was not the cause of their misery but a consequence; with the institution of a society based on justice people would not want more children than could be provided for (Vialatoux 1959, 2: 375–98).

That Malthus's ideas were simple has not saved him from misinterpretation, much of it based on the first edition of the *Essay*, a hastily written pamphlet, and in disregard of the carefully researched later editions and other works. Writers pointed to the absurdity of geometric increase, as though Malthus was so dull as to think that population actually does grow geometrically. He is regarded as against population, rather than against misery. In France "*malthusien*" denotes a narrow, pessimistic view of resources, with a consequent acceptance of parsimony. In England and elsewhere, "Malthusian" or "neo-Malthusian" came to designate a proponent of contraception.

In fact, Malthus explicitly disavowed birth control. In an appendix to the *Essay*'s fifth edition he wrote: "Indeed I should always particularly reprobate any artificial and unnatural modes of checking population, both on account of their immorality and their tendency to remove a necessary stimulus to industry. If it were possible for each married couple to limit by a wish the number of their children, there is certainly reason to fear that the indolence of the human race would be very greatly increased." In recent years a similar opposition to contraception was expressed by Gandhi: "If Indians made the necessary effort, they could grow all the food they need; but without the stimulus of population pressure and economic need they will not make the effort" (Clark 1964: 283).

Contraception goes back to the beginning of human history, with references to it in the Kahun Papyrus, the Bible, the writings of Charaka (an Indian physician of the first century B.C.), Herodotus, al-Razi (900 A.D.) and other Islamic scholars (McCleary 1953: 83; Himes 1936). Nearly all known human cultures have had sufficient knowledge of the facts of human reproduction to be able to use at least coitus interruptus, and most have had other devices as well. Among moderns it appeared in the writings of Moheau,

Condorcet, and especially Francis Place (1822), who was followed by Richard Carlile, Charles Bradlaugh, and Annie Besant. These did not share the puritanical view that hunger and sex were the stick and carrot without which men would be slothful, and they found in contraception the full answer to the problem Malthus had posed. "Contraception . . . is both old and new; old in the sense that the *desire* dates back half a million years and some *practice* nearly as long; . . . new in the sense that democratized knowledge is an ultramodern phenomenon . . . that we have been able, more effectively than our ancestors . . . to winnow out the reliable, the harmless" (Himes 1936: 422).

In one of his last statements on the matter, a "summary view" published in 1830, Malthus (1960a: 13) went one step toward applying his principle to nonhuman populations, but he never developed this farther. Even so, the principle of population was a direct forebear of the theory of evolution. "I happened to read for amusement Malthus on *Population*," Darwin (1961: 58) noted in his autobiography, "and being well prepared to appreciate the struggle for existence which everywhere goes on from long continued observation of the habits of animals and plants, it at once struck me that under these circumstances favorable variations would tend to be preserved, and unfavorable ones to be destroyed. The result of this would be the formation of new species. Here then I had at last got a theory by which to work." Wallace, who developed an evolutionary theory independently of Darwin, also acknowledged a debt to Malthus. The relation seems to have been no accident.

THE BIOLOGICAL PERSPECTIVE

The tendency of species to out-reproduce their means of support exerts a constant pressure toward differentiation. Each species seeks to adapt to a niche in which it will have some degree of shelter from competition. Some species become complementary to others and enter into symbiotic relations with them. "We can dimly see why the competition should be most severe between allied forms, which fill nearly the same place in the economy of nature" (Darwin 1962: 88). In Spencer (1867, 2: 406–10, 479–508) this leads to an escape from the original Malthusian predicament by way of biology: organisms become more complex in the process of adaptation, and complexity reduces the animal's drive to reproduce. Human individuation is a continuation of animal evolution: the nervous system becomes more active, with a consequent further reduction in reproductive activity. The theory has been used to explain why bacteria are more prolific than mice, why men are among the least prolific of the higher animals, why the Victorian upper classes had fewer children than the lower classes. In every case the group comprising more differentiated, more elaborately adapted individuals has a lower reproduction combined with a more efficient sustenance. In Spencer's optimistic view, the evolutionary process that population growth initiated would persist until both fertility and mortality had reached a low-level harmony.

More immediately suggestive for our subject is the recent observation of ecologists and ethologists that fertility in many species of birds and animals depends on density. We all know that beyond a certain point mortality is density-dependent through the ultimate check of starvation. But starvation is not very often seen in nature and, even combined with predators, disease, harsh weather, and other disasters, does not seem to exercise the continuous control that would explain the relative constancy of numbers in most species of higher animals. Rather the constancy is explained by a territorial mechanism of reproductive control, to accord with long-term food supplies. Among some species of birds, at the beginning of the breeding season each male lays claim to an area of suitable size and keeps out other males; all of the available ground is thus parceled out as individual territories. The often furious competition for an adequate piece of ground takes the place of direct competition for food. This territoriality is a special case: some species compete merely for membership in a hunting group, and only so many are accepted. Those without territory, or left out of the hunting group, have no opportunity to reproduce. The peck-order among birds has the same function: those low on the scale are a reserve that can fill in for casualties among the established members or be dropped, as circumstances require.

By such territorial and analogous mechanisms population is maintained comfortably below the ceiling imposed by resources. The analogy to Malthus's preventive check comes as close as is conceivable for species lacking human foresight. Man has indeed the possibility of foresight, yet he offends more than most species in overgrazing, overfishing, and generally overexploiting his habitat (Wynne-Edwards 1962).

POPULATION AND THE GIFTS OF NATURE

The classical school of economics developed from Malthus the law of diminishing returns: more work applied to given land produces less than proportional returns, and indeed increments of any one factor of production eventually generate lessening amounts of income. The doctrine was given mature expression in Mill: (1876, Book I, chap. 13, §2): "The niggardliness of nature, not the injustice of society, is the cause of the penalty attached to overpopulation. An unjust distribution of wealth does not even aggravate the evil, but, at most, causes it to be somewhat earlier felt. It is vain to say that all mouths which the increase of mankind calls into existence bring with them hands. The new mouths require as much food as the old ones, and the hands do not produce as much." The operation of the law may be long postponed if there is vacant land to which people may move and, subsequently, if technical improvements are developed, but over the longer run its course is seen as inexorable. The law is applied to an increase in the land under cultivation through the presumed fact that rational men would start to till the most fertile and accessible portions first, so that any new lands added to the nation's agriculture would be less and less productive. As population grows in any country closed to trade, poorer lands will necessarily be brought into use, and any excess over the return to labor on marginal land will be taken as rent by landowners in the natural operation of the market. Population growth beyond a certain point would provide landlords with an increasing proportion of the national product. The model requires an agricultural community of fixed land and techniques with a growing population.

But quite different conditions apply in industry, where the factors of production are extensible and the division of labor advantageous. True, industry depends on a finite supply of raw materials, but the limits of these are more distant than the coming shortage of agricultural land. If in some sectors of the economy returns increase with added effort while they diminish in others, then there will be a certain size of population at which over-all production per head will be at a maximum (Cannan 1895). It is useful to consider production a function of population whenever the economy is relatively static while population grows—the situation of many countries today. In Figure 1 the three curves represent, respectively, total,

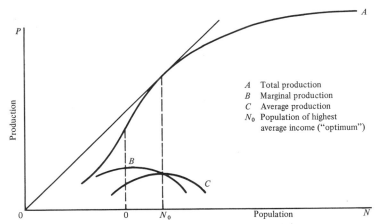

Figure 1. Production as a Function of Population, and Location of the Welfare Optimum of Population

A; marginal, B; and average production, C. The maximum point on B is at the inflection point along A, where the slope of total production ceases to increase and begins to decrease, the maximum on C at the point on A tangent to a line drawn from the origin. The curve B can be shown to cut C at its maximum point; where the marginal product equals the average, the latter is at its peak. This is demonstrated by considering the output of the last man; if it is greater than the average, the average will be raised by the presence of this last man. The reverse is true if the last man's output is lower than the average. Only if the last man's output is equal to the average will the average be at its peak and the population optimum from a welfare viewpoint.

Consider now the curve of marginal production B along with line D, representing the minimum that will keep individuals alive, assumed to be equal for all sizes of population (Figure 2). The area below B and above D

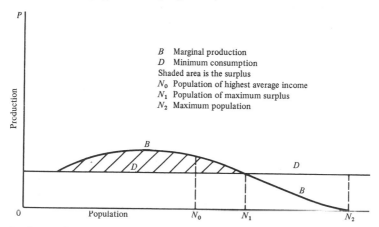

Figure 2. Optimum Population and the Surplus

can be called a surplus, which is at a maximum for the population where B and D cross, or N_1. A technically primitive and static state that wants to maximize its armed strength or any other entity not dependent on immediate consumption will aim at population N_1 in its countryside. The surplus will be drained off and used to support an urban court, artisans, and armed forces, including the police and tax collectors who remove the surplus. The mechanism for this removal will vary and may include resident or absentee landholders taking rents. In modern times, a well entrenched development-minded government determined on heavy investment for industrial growth will appropriate the surplus for that purpose; it will be inclined to favor a population N_1, larger than the optimum N_0. But any diminution in the authority of government, reflected in a rise of the level D regarded as subsistence, lowers N_1 and moves it closer to N_0.

A state seeking the maximum population will aim at N_2—set where the areas between curves B and D are equal in the intervals $0N_1$ and N_1N_2. Under mild assumptions the welfare optimum N_0 is smaller than the power optimum N_1, which in turn is smaller than the maximum population N_2 (Sauvy 1956, 1: 60). Fixed costs raise the optimum population, while lowering average income.

Inevitably 19th-century English economists tried to adapt these arguments, which apply to a closed economy, to one heavily based on foreign trade. Some thought that Britain could increase per capita production indefinitely, since any excess population could emigrate to distant lands, there to grow food that would be exchanged for British manufactured goods. But since that time freely available lands have been appropriated by population growth elsewhere, and agricultural countries want to develop their own industry.

In the 1920s England and some other advanced countries seemed to have passed their optimum and arrived at the point of rapidly diminishing returns (Keynes 1920; Wright 1923; Overbeek 1970: 141–63). The best coal deposits were being exhausted, cotton was attacked by the boll weevil, and for these and other commodities prices could only rise in response to increasing scarcity, with a resultant fall in the standard of living. Population control was an important part of the answer.

The optimum depends on the criterion used and will be very different if it is national power or real income per capita. Even with the best of statistics on the present and past, the optimum is not readily calculable; it can be determined only if we know what income would accord with various levels of population. This lack of empirical applicability contrasts with the sharply defined theory. Any curve relating population and production may "for large spaces have a very level course" (Myrdal 1940: 142). Even if one proved that, for instance, a given country has double its optimum population and has also the power to reduce it by emigration, a sharp reduction might be a disaster; for the disadvantages of the change—particularly since most emigrants would be young adults, whose rearing their native country had paid for up to the age when they began to produce—could more than offset any advantages of arriving at the optimum level. Despite these drawbacks, Sauvy (1968) regards it as the core of population theory.

THE ENVIRONMENT

Contemporary ecologists are interested in optimum population, but they sharply reject the gradually diminishing returns and continuous changes of classical economics. Their writings constitute a radical attack on the modern system of production and consumption (Ehrlich and Ehrlich 1970). At best, the kinds of damage not now entered in private or national accounting schemes must be deducted from our calculation of national product and income. At worst, the word *production* itself is seen as an ironic misnomer for such a process as depleting supplies of invaluable crude oil (that ought to be saved for lubrication), destroying it in an inefficient way of moving people from place to place, and creating unbreathable air that may well be raising mortality rates. If the population of Malthus's time was pushing against a food ceiling, that of today seems to be pushing against a ceiling of space, air, water, and mineral resources (Wright 1923; Brown 1954).

The problem for us is whether such complaints really have a bearing on population. Parking space is short not because there are too many people in the country, or even too many automobiles, but because people want to live in large cities, or because they all want to go to the same place at the same time. The air is polluted either because automobiles are badly designed, or because some other solution to the transport problem should replace them. The present system of production would quickly direct itself along lines that preserve the environment and enable it to take care of far more people if manufacturers were charged for the damage their products cause. They receive income for their goods and should pay for their bads, as Kenneth Boulding says. He proposes (1966: 9) to rescue national-income accounting by distinguishing "that part of the Gross National Product which is derived from exhaustible and that which is derived from reproducible resources, as well as that part of consumption which represents effluvia and that which represents input into the productive system again."

At least up to now technology has year by year enabled more people to live better. Most economists believe that future technology can remedy the defects that present technology is bringing about; that we can continue, for instance, to secure the larger crops that fertilizers provide and escape the accompanying water pollution. Any approach to exhaustion of one mineral will cause price changes and so force substitution by other minerals or nonmineral products. The productive system is flexible enough to cope with the disturbances in the environment that it creates. The process is not entirely automatic, however, and ecologists deserve credit for having brought such matters to public attention, and for having agitated for reforms at some immediate danger points (Coale 1970b).

On their side ecologists stress how tenuous and potentially unstable man-habitat relations are, and how ignorant science is of the operation of atmospheric, oceanic, and other systems, especially of their disequilibria and discontinuities. We use DDT to eradicate malaria and to save crops from insects; both uses have the effect of building population on DDT. What happens to the population when DDT-resistant strains of insects develop, and when contamination of the environment by DDT rises to intolerable levels? If such dangers are real, then the present world population of about 3.7 billion may be much above the long-term carrying capacity of the planet. This especially affects the underdeveloped world, which lives so close to the hunger margin; but developed countries have little basis for complacency. Smog is not proportional to the number of automobiles in an area, but in a given local configuration of the landscape suddenly comes into existence at a certain point in the increase of automobile density. Moreover, any simplification of ecological systems (as from intensive agriculture, which reduces the number of species present, or from the so-called "green revolution," which reduces the number of subspecies or strains) aggravates their instability, exposing population to sudden adverse changes.

Ecologists have contributed a justified apprehension of instability in the systems on which our lives depend, and they have shown how much mankind is gambling on the further progress of science. This negative contribution is important. We now badly need the positive contribution of further facts and a model that will take simultaneous account of population numbers, technology and human behavior, and the environment, and allow for instabilities and disequilibria in the many variables.

SOCIALIST WRITERS ON POPULATION

Marx was generally well disposed toward the classical economists, of whose school he was a wayward member. But he repeatedly attacked not only Malthus's doctrines but also his motives and personality:

> Malthus . . . asserts that population constantly exerts pressure on the means of subsistence. . . . If there are too many people, then in one way or another they must be eliminated. . . . Now the consequence of this theory is that since it is precisely the poor who constitute this surplus population, nothing ought to be done for them, except to make it as easy as possible for them to starve to death. . . . The giving of alms would be a crime, since it would encourage the growth of surplus population (Meek 1953: 59).

Malthus had propagated a "vile and infamous doctrine, this repulsive blasphemy against man and nature." No general law of population could be valid for all societies; each had its own law. The irreducible opposition between population and welfare, far from being universal, was in Marx's view the special predicament of capitalism, with its impoverishment of the proletariat. The reproduction of the working class made new workers cheap and so permitted the bourgeoisie to extract surplus value from their work. But to ask the proletariat to be more responsible was futile, for the very degradation inherent in capitalism ruled out an appeal to their highest natures. The transformation of capitalist to socialist institutions would eliminate the Malthusian dilemma. As on other points, Marx started with the classical premises and reached a conclusion very different from the classical harmony.

The history of capitalist society, as he viewed it, is divided between a period of original accumulation and one of maturity and imperialism. In the period of original accumulation all the conclusions of Adam Smith and Ricardo are valid, with only a change of terms and some simplification. Marx divided capital into constant, C (for example, buildings and machinery), and variable, V (comprising consumer goods such as food bought with workers' wages). Constant capital is so called because it is merely reproduced without a quantitative change in the product; all surplus is earned on labor. The capitalist tries to use all the labor he can employ, for thus he makes the largest profit. If it costs six hours per day to produce labor—the amount of time the average worker requires to feed, clothe, and house himself and his family at a subsistence level—and if the goods he produces sell for the equivalent of twelve hours' time, then the capitalist's surplus value is six hours multiplied by the number of workers he employs. The rapid increase of population in early capitalism was due to the demand for labor, just as Adam Smith had said.

For the second or "imperialist" period, however, Marx diverged sharply from the classical economists. The wage rate is V/P, variable capital divided by population, as before. But now as technical progress and competition force capitalists to substitute machines for men, the "reserve army" of the unemployed grows continually. Workers respond by lowering their birth rate as less labor is demanded, and Marx pictured a struggle around the ratio V/P, with the capitalists trying to shift the resources they control from V to C, and the workers seeking to counter this effort by reducing P. Unfortunately for the system as a whole, the birth rate cannot fall fast enough to prevent capitalism from producing the surplus workers that are its grave-diggers.

That labor-saving methods of production make an increasing fraction of the population redundant has been a popular fear before and since Marx. Today the identification of surplus population with unemployment is found in underdeveloped countries, while the countries with the largest stock of capital have more often encountered a labor shortage.

The world at large sees Malthus and Marx as "the two great antagonists, battling eternally" (Sauvy 1963: 13). But the very vehemence of Marx's attack stemmed from the lack of a substantive rebuttal, as his *Critique of the Gotha Program* pointed out: "If [Malthus's] theory of population is correct, then I can *not* abolish this [iron law of wages] even if I abolish wage-labor a hundred times, because this law is not only paramount over the system of wage-labor but also over every social system" (Marx and Engels 1959: 124). Marx and Malthus agreed that the condition of the proletariat was miserable and that its misery should be alleviated (Petersen 1964: 72–89). For Malthus the solution was to increase individual responsibility, for Marx to attain a collective condition called socialism; but in the analytically better part both concentrated on posing the problem.

Marx and Malthus agreed profoundly on the material base of social existence. At Marx's graveside Engels summed up his collaborator's contribution: "Marx discovered the law of evolution in human history: the simple fact, previously hidden under ideological growths, that human beings must first of all eat, drink, shelter, and clothe themselves, before they can turn their attention to politics, science, art, and religion" (*ibid.*). Malthus (1960a) made the same point with equal clarity in his own summing up, published four years before his death: "Elevated as man is above all other animals by his intellectual faculties, it is not to be supposed that the physical laws to which he is subjected should be essentially different from those which are observed to prevail in other parts of animated nature." Says Mehring (1962: 149) of the Marxist view:

> This theory, the contention that the capitalist mode of production impoverishes the masses wherever it prevails, was put forward long before the *Communist Manifesto* was published, even before either Marx or Engels put pen to paper, . . . first of all by bourgeois economists. The *Essay on Population* written by Malthus was an attempt to refine this "theory of increasing misery" and turn it into an eternal natural law.

That the workingman can avoid increasing misery, both collectively and individually, by restricting his family, that mothers should in effect become a trade union and declare a childbearing strike, was a theme of Leftist social reform in the writings of John Stuart Mill, Bernstein, and others. But Marxists insisted that advanced capitalism could always undercut the workingman with more efficient equipment; in the race between voluntary reduction of the work force and substitution of labor-saving devices, the latter would necessarily win. Relief must be sought in revolution rather than in contraception.

Marx bequeathed his opposition to Malthus to succeeding Marxist thinkers. Lenin in particular stressed that evolving technique would undercut the law of diminishing returns. Much of Stalin's argument has the tone of the mercantilists: the growth of population facilitates economic advance. Recent Soviet writings on population include a study of Europe's population increase during the past century (Urlanis 1941; cf. Valenti 1963). The increasing growth under industrial capitalism was followed by a slower rate during the "imperialist" stage; and since private property in land or other means of production in itself diminishes fertility, Western birth rates will continue to fall. Although Soviet society was supposedly immune to these pressures, its birth rate over the past two decades has followed very closely that of the United States. Hungary's birth rate fell to 14 per thousand, well below that of the capitalist countries of Western Europe. Evidently fertility differs less between socialist and capitalist than between industrial and traditional societies. However, it is true that the optimum population of a directed economy is greater than of a free one, insofar as individuals will accept a lower standard of consumption in the former.

The population problem of the developing countries has now become a topic of public discussion in the USSR (Brackett 1968). By the dominant view, industrialization is the solution in those countries, just as it was in the Soviet Union, where the growth of cities, the development of culture, and the involvement of women in public activity cut the birth rate by more than half (*ibid.*: 168). And if high growth rates continue in developing countries, the infinite power of science and technology can overcome any shortages of food and materials that may arise. Billions and billions of people will be required to master the earth and the solar system. Birth-control propaganda is unnecessary on the one hand and useless on the other, since people will not heed it before their societies are industrialized.

But less orthodox Soviet writers, less confident that even socialist industry will solve the population problem, would encourage family planning before the advent of industry. Merely maximizing the number of inhabitants is hardly a worthy goal for humanity, and as a goal of individual countries it recalls the feudal rulers who boasted of the number of their subjects (*ibid.:* 170). A policy choice must be made between doubling the prosperity of a fixed number of people every 20 years and doubling the population instead, leaving the standard of living unchanged. Better than a choice between the two investment policies would be an optimum combination. While reiterating the obvious truth that birth control is no substitute for industrialization, Soviet writers are now coming to concede that more resources will be available for investment if dependency ratios can be reduced.

DENSITY AND THE DIVISION OF LABOR

Durkheim (1960) marked society's change from a small undifferentiated clan or tribe to the complexity of his day, noting that interdependence increases with the greater specialization of societal sectors. The complex society, he concluded, comes with population growth. As a tribe increases in volume and density, individuals and groups compete more and more intensely; only by specialization can they find shelter from competition. "In the same city the different professions can coexist without having to harm each other, for they pursue different objectives. The soldier seeks military glory, the priest moral authority, the statesman power, the industrialist wealth . . . ; each can thus reach his goal without preventing the others from reaching theirs" (*ibid.:* 249–50). For Durkheim population growth, through the "moral density" that arises from it, is responsible for the advance from a simple segmented society to a complex organic one.

Among peasant populations, one that is small and stationary is more likely to stay with slash-and-burn agriculture, which under many circumstances of low density produces more with less labor. Higher density forces a shorter fallow and ultimately annual crops, even though these mean more work. A "gradual adaptation to harder and more regular work is likely to raise the efficiency of labor in both agricultural and nonagricultural activities; the increasing density of population opens up opportunities for a more intricate division of labor" (Boserup 1965: 75). Note how this paraphrases Durkheim's thesis.

POPULATION AND DEVELOPMENT

If a poor country somehow does manage to cut its birth rate, this improves its development prospects, in the theory worked out by Coale and

Hoover (1958) and others. From alternative projections for India and other countries Coale (1969) concluded:

Any low-income country that succeeds in initiating an immediate reduction in fertility would in the short run enjoy a reduction in the burden of child dependency that would permit a higher level of investment and more immediately productive uses of investment.

After 25 or 30 years the advantage of reduced dependency would be enhanced by a markedly slower growth of the labor force, making it possible to achieve a faster growth in capital per worker from any given investment, and making it easier to approach the goal of productive employment for all who need it. . . . In sum, a reduction in fertility would make the process of modernization more rapid and more certain.

Between two countries with different birth rates, the one growing faster will initially be at a disadvantage by its lack of industrial capital rather than of food. For economists in the underdeveloped countries, the choice is whether to use resources in order to produce more capital rather than more labor, so that each unit of labor will be better equipped in the next generation. This concentration on capital accumulation dominates professional thinking on population and development (Ohlin 1967).

And yet it is far from universal. Latin Americans argue that their empty spaces can hold many millions, and that the internal migrants to those spaces can construct their own agricultural and other capital. According to Nurkse (1953), a dense rural population positively helps the development of a country with a sufficiently strong and single-minded government. Everyone in the countryside may appear to be working, at least for part of the year, yet some of the rural population constitutes disguised unemployment in the pertinent sense that it could be removed, even with no substituted technical improvements, without a loss in production. Such persons could engage in the construction of buildings, roads, and urban industrial projects that do not require much capital. Since they all somehow obtained a minimal diet before, the shift would entail merely transporting their food to the city. But it is not clear that fewer agriculturists can produce the crop merely by reorganizing the task and without major technical improvements (Schultz 1964). If there was a genuine surplus of labor, moreover, it would not be easy to hold per-capita consumption fixed in a half-starving countryside; and if those remaining on the land simply eat better, the expected surplus from the land disappears with the out-migrants. This was the famous "scissors" problem in the Soviet Union of the 1920s; it has never been solved, for the punitive measures used to mitigate it generated new troubles.

Global development may be prevented by too many people, not through the difficulty of accumulating capital but by the absolute shortage of raw materials. After showing what large quantities of metals and fuels are now required to keep the advanced economies in operation, and noting the rate of increase in world population, Harrison Brown (1954: 226) considers it unlikely that the agrarian underdeveloped regions of the world will be able to attain their goal of industrialization. "The picture would change considerably if Western machine civilization were to collapse, thus giving the present agrarian cultures room into which they could expand. But the collapse of Western culture would have to come well in advance of the time when high-grade ore and fuel deposits disappear." The raw materials in the earth's crust set a limit on the volume of development, on the number of people—or more exactly the number of person-years—that can exist in the developed condition, as that condition is understood today in the United States. How the volume of development will be apportioned among peoples, and over time, could well be the major question of national and international politics in the next generation.

For the advanced countries population has often been seen as an aid to growth. Writing in the 1930s, Keynes and Hansen saw an increasing population as a guarantee of markets. Housing demand, for example, varies with the rate of growth of a population. Investors know that even a product that does not quite fit consumers' tastes still finds buyers in an expanding economy. But in recent decades it has been noted that an expanding economy could be arranged more easily by an increase of purchasing power than of population.

The basic prerequisite to expanding the economy is a high level of investment, and the chief argument against rapid population growth has been that it diminishes savings and hence investment. But expenditures on children do not necessarily reduce savings, for at least in advanced countries expenditures on children may be a substitute not for savings but for more consumer goods or more leisure (Kuznets 1960: 332). Looking into the past, Hicks (1939) asked whether the whole industrial revolution of the last two centuries has been nothing but a vast secular boom, largely induced by the unparalleled rise in population (Bladen 1956: 115). Myrdal (1940: 161–66) held that the cessation of population increase "will have a restrictive effect upon young people's opportunities for advancement," and Coale (1968) also opposed any immediate policy to bring about a zero population growth in the United States.

These theories relating population and the economy in a macro-economic model say nothing about how individual parents are motivated. The route from micro-models that describe individual behavior to an explanation of aggregates was traveled at least as far back as Adam Smith. In his view, the demand for labor increases population by permitting individuals to marry earlier and to raise a larger proportion of the children born to them (Coontz 1957: chap. 4). But quite different mechanisms have been proposed in recent years to account for the quite different phenomena now observed.

THE ECONOMIC THEORY OF FERTILITY

In a micro-economic framework the decline of the birth rate with economic development can be analyzed in relation to the utilities and costs of children to their parents (Leibenstein 1963). With increasing income the cost of a child of a given order rises, let us say in proportion to the family income. The consumption utility—that is, the pleasure of having the child in the house—is difficult to assess and can be estimated as fixed independently of income. The utility of the child as a source of security certainly declines: parents with more income can provide for their own security, or a wealthier state provides it for them; and if increased income is accompanied by weakening of family discipline, parents are less likely to be able to exercise claims on their children even if they need to. The child is less valuable as a producer as income increases, because schooling is extended and the household ceases to be the unit of production (Figure 3). If these

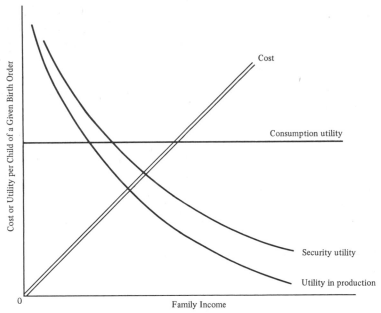

Figure 3. Cost and Utility Curves for a Child of a Given Birth Order (after Leibenstein 1963: 162)

four elements (one of cost and three of utility) are exhaustive and correctly portrayed, then the individual family is likely to have fewer children as per-capita income increases and as development proceeds. At any given stage, moreover, richer families would be inclined to have fewer children than poorer ones.

One can start with the opposite view, that the price per child does not go up with the parents' income. The rich could spend as little on their children as the poor, but choose to dress them better, send them to better schools, and so on; in effect, they purchase higher-quality children (Becker 1960). By this view the cost curve in Figure 3 for a given quality of child becomes horizontal. Thus, Becker comes to the opposite conclusion from Leibenstein: people have more children as they become richer, just as the well-to-do have not only better cars than the poor but more per household. In any large population the relation is hidden by the fact that the rich practice contraception more effectively; and among contraceptive couples, according to data that Becker cites, income is related directly with family size, as his theory demands. Duesenberry (1960), Leibenstein (1963), and Okun (1960) reject Becker's distinction between price and cost, on the grounds that each family is constrained to house, clothe, and feed its children in accordance with the norms of its income group. If custom requires richer families to spend more on each of their children, one cannot conclude from their larger income that they will also want more children. If one controls for the differential knowledge of contraception, not by comparing the family sizes of birth-control users but by using surveys of ideal family size, the correlation with income is reversed. From such data the poor *want* more children than the better off (Blake 1967).

These are micro-explanations in that they reason from individual behavior to certain aggregate phenomena of the community or country taken as a unit. Economics (like physics) tries to explain the mass in terms of the atoms, but explanations of this type are not wholly convincing in population analysis.

SOCIAL CAPILLARITY AND FAMILY STRUCTURE

The decline of the birth rate in industrial countries has followed a decline of the death rate. The populations involved have undergone a more or less uniform change: first a slow and accelerating fall in mortality, followed at some interval by a corresponding fall in fertility. The pace varies from country to country; the later the fall in the death rate, the more rapid it is. In one country, France, the fall of births followed very closely on the fall of deaths; elsewhere there has been a considerable lag. Whatever its local variation, the phenomenon has been so widespread, and commented on by so many writers, that it has acquired a name: the demographic transition (Notestein 1945; Taeuber 1960; and others).

Both the fall in deaths and the slower fall in births may be a concomitant of modernization (Notestein 1945), or the decline of fertility may be a response to the earlier decline of mortality (Davis 1963). In either case, the literature is incomplete concerning the causal mechanisms operating. In particular, there is no answer to the big question: Will the fall in mortality that by now has taken place in the underdeveloped countries by itself produce a fall in fertility, or will it do so only in the presence of development? Must poor countries wait for development before their birth rates can fall? If high fertility prevents capital accumulation and so development, then they will have to wait a long time.

A French social scientist, Arsène Dumont (1890), tied declining fertility to the structure of society and to the individual's desire to rise in the world. Trained as an anthropologist, Dumont was a passionate nationalist who saw in France's depopulation a harbinger of her downfall and devoted his life to analyzing the familial conduct of his countrymen. Paradoxically, he never married, and at the age of 53 took his own life. "All men," he wrote, "tend to raise themselves from the lower functions of society to higher ones. . . . Guided by an unerring and inescapable instinct, each social molecule strains with all the energy at its command . . . to rise unceasingly toward a luminous ideal which charms and attracts it" (*ibid.*: 106). This ascent is not by income alone, but in every field of manual work, of intellect, and of art (Sutter 1953). In the competition for higher places, the man with few or no children has as certain an advantage over the father of many as the liquid in a narrow tube has over that in a wide one. This is the law of social capillarity.

The impulse to rise, though in principle universal, is manifested most in societies with both a great inequality of conditions, giving a long scale through which to rise, and a good chance that individuals can realize this aspiration. In modern societies political equality—the abolition of hereditary orders—is combined with great economic inequality; and individuals believe it a right, indeed a duty, to advance themselves. The markers of social status are numerous and conspicuous enough to provide a constant challenge.

The denatalist effect does not eliminate the family: those who fail to rise, or rise only part of the way, continue the upward struggle through their children, and those who succeed perpetuate their success through their descendants. But families of few children, two at most, can grasp the very best opportunities. For Dumont the decline of the birth rate was a symptom of the burning ambition of the French middle classes. We have no way of determining whether indeed the Swedish and English middle classes were less ambitious; we know only that their fertility was higher than in France.

Social mobility gradually intensified over a century or more in Europe and America. It was functional for economic development, but signs of change are appearing:

One does not have to be a prophet to foresee that our present passion for demographic and economic growth will some day be superseded by a concern for population quality and ecological balance. When this inevitable adaptation is effected—inevitable, that is, barring the catastrophe that will forestall all adaptation—perhaps it will seem more natural to espouse a hierarchy of values in which our assessment of men will not depend so heavily on their ability to "get ahead" (Duncan 1969: 365; see below, pp. 158–64).

The drive for social mobility can be expected to run its course at different times in different countries, and one can suppose with Dumont an association with a fall in the birth rate whenever and wherever it takes place.

Other features of modern life affect the conjugal family (Ogburn 1964: 175–86). The family is less often than in earlier times the unit of production, education, and security. These functions are performed by specialized agencies of government and of business, to whom the family provides recruits. A functional congruence seems to exist between family structure and societal type, and in the modern organization of the family,

since couples are free to set up their households independently, they may move physically to wherever the demands of the industrial system call them. The individual with talent can move upward occupationally, without having obligation to all of his extended family. . . . The young man who must make decisions in his job need no longer be subject to the traditional thinking of family elders. . . . The system can use the talents of women, without needing the permission of husbands or fathers. An industrial system, based as it is on impersonal individual achievement, creates much psychological tension; the conjugal system lays great stress on individual, emotional ties within the family, and especially on the emotional solace which its members gives to one another (Goode 1963).

The family becomes a private relation centered on the affectionate companionship of husband and wife; as economic, educational, security, and other traditional functions fall away, so does the interest of the community in its formation and continuance. Arranged marriages disappear and divorces become frequent. Contrary to what biology might suggest, the focus on privacy and affection does not lead to children, but rather to restrictions on their number. The small and independent nuclear family is not only functional for modern industry, but industry helps to bring it into existence by giving women status outside the home, so that their importance is less dependent on producing and raising children.

References

BARKER, ERNEST. 1959. *The Political Thought of Plato and Aristotle.* New York: Dover.

BECKER, GARY S. 1960. "An Economic Analysis of Fertility," in National Bureau of Economic Research, *Demographic and Economic Change in Developed Countries.* Princeton, N. J.: Princeton University Press.

BLADEN, VINCENT W. 1956. *An Introduction to Political Economy,* rev. ed. Toronto: University of Toronto Press.

BLAKE, JUDITH. 1967. "Income and Reproductive Motivation," *Population Studies,* 21, 185–206.

BONAR, JAMES. 1885. *Malthus and His Work.* London: Macmillan.

BOSERUP, ESTER. 1965. *The Conditions of Agricultural Growth: The Economics of Agrarian Change under Population Pressure.* Chicago: Aldine.

BOTERO, GIOVANNI. 1956 (1589). *The Reason of State,* edited by D. P. Waley. New Haven: Yale University Press.

BOULDING, KENNETH E. 1955. "The Malthusian Model as a General System," *Social and Economic Studies,* 4, 195–205.

———. 1966. "The Economics of the Coming Spaceship Earth," in Henry Jarrett, ed., *Environmental Quality in a Growing Economy.* Baltimore: Johns Hopkins Press.

BRACKETT, JAMES W. 1968. "The Evolution of Marxist Theories of Population: Marxism Recognizes the Population Problem," *Demography,* 5, 158–173.

BROWN, HARRISON. 1954. *The Challenge of Man's Future.* New York: Viking.

CANNAN, EDWIN. 1895. "The Probability of a Cessation of the Growth of Population in England and Wales," *Economic Journal,* 5, 505–515.

CANTILLON, RICHARD. 1952 (1755). *Essai sur la nature du commerce en général.* Paris: Institut National d'Etudes Démographiques.

CHEN HUAN-CHANG. 1911. *The Economic Principles of Confucius and His School,* 2 Vols. New York: Columbia University Press.

CLARK, COLIN. 1964. "Overpopulation—Is Birth Control the Answer?" in Garrett Hardin, ed., *Population, Evolution, Birth Control.* San Francisco: Freeman.

COALE, ANSLEY J. 1968. "Should the United States Start a Campaign for Fewer Births?" *Population Index,* 34, 467–479.

———. 1969. "Population and Economic Development," in Philip M. Hauser, ed., *The Population Dilemma,* 2nd ed. Englewood Cliffs, N. J.: Prentice-Hall.

———. 1970a. "Man and His Environment," *Science,* 170, 132–136.

———. 1970b. Review of Ehrlich and Ehrlich, *Population, Resources, Environment* in *Science,* 170, 428–429.

———, and EDGAR M. HOOVER. 1958. *Population Growth and Economic Development in Low-Income Countries.* Princeton, N. J.: Princeton University Press.

COONTZ, SYDNEY H. 1957. *Population Theories and the Economic Interpretation.* London: Routledge and Kegan Paul.

DARWIN, CHARLES. 1961 (1876). *Autobiography,* edited by Sir Francis Darwin. New York: Collier.

———. 1962 (1859). *The Origin of Species.* New York: Collier.

DAVIS, KINGSLEY. 1955. "Malthus and the Theory of Population," in Paul F. Lazarsfeld and Morris Rosenberg, eds., *The Language of Social Research.* Glencoe, Ill.: Free Press.

———. 1963. "The Theory of Change and Response in Modern Demographic History," *Population Index,* 29, 345–366.

DUESENBERRY, JAMES. 1960. Comment on Becker, *op. cit.,* pp. 231–234.

DUMONT, ARSÈNE. 1890. *Dépopulation et civilisation: Etudes démographiques.* Paris: Lecrosnier et Babé.

DUNCAN, OTIS DUDLEY. 1969. "Inequality and Opportunity," *Population Index,* 35, 361–366.

DURKHEIM, EMILE. 1960 (1902). *De la division du travail social.* Paris: Presses Universitaires de France.

EHRLICH, PAUL R., and ANNE H. EHRLICH. 1970. *Population, Resources, Environment.* San Francisco: Freeman.

EULER, LEONHARD. 1970 (1760). "A General Investigation into the Mortality and Multiplication of the Human Species" (translated by Nathan and Beatrice Keyfitz), *Theoretical Population Biology*, 1, 307–314.

GLASS, DAVID V. 1963. "John Graunt and His *Natural and Political Observations*," *Proceedings of the Royal Society*, Series B, 159, 2–37.

GODWIN, WILLIAM. 1793. *An Enquiry Concerning Political Justice and Its Influence on General Virtue and Happiness.* London: G. G. J. and J. Robinson.

GOODE, WILLIAM J. 1963. "The Role of the Family in Industrialization," in United Nations, Conference on the Application of Science and Technology for the Benefit of the Less Developed Areas, *Social Problems of Development and Urbanization*, Washington, D. C.: U. S. Government Printing Office, 7, 32–38.

HALLEY, EDMUND. 1693. "An Estimate of the Degree of the Mortality of Mankind," *Philosophical Transactions of the Royal Society of London*, 17, 596–610.

HICKS, JOHN R. 1939. *Value and Capital.* Oxford: Oxford University Press.

HIMES, NORMAN E. 1936. *Medical History of Contraception.* Baltimore: Williams & Wilkins.

Ho PING-TI. 1959. *Studies on the Population of China, 1368–1953.* Cambridge, Mass.: Harvard University Press.

HOSELITZ, BERT F., ed. 1960. *Theories of Economic Growth.* Glencoe, Ill.: Free Press.

HUTCHINSON, EDWARD P. 1967. *The Population Debate.* Boston: Houghton Mifflin.

KEYNES, JOHN M. 1920. *The Economic Consequences of the Peace.* London: Macmillan.

———. 1963 (1933). *Essays in Biography.* New York: Norton.

KUZNETS, SIMON. 1960. "Population and Aggregate Output," in National Bureau of Economic Research, *Demographic and Economic Change in Developed Countries.* Princeton, N. J.: Princeton University Press.

LANDRY, ALPHONSE. 1909. "Les Idées de Quesnay sur la population," *Revue d'Histoire des Doctrines Economiques*, 2, 41–87.

LEE, MABEL PING-HUA. 1921. *The Economic History of China, with Special Reference to Agriculture.* New York: Columbia University Press.

LEIBENSTEIN, HARVEY. 1963. *Economic Backwardness and Economic Growth.* New York: Wiley.

LORIMER, FRANK. 1959. "The Development of Demography," in Philip M. Hauser and Otis Dudley Duncan, eds., *The Study of Population.* Chicago: University of Chicago Press.

MACKENROTH, GERHARD. 1953. *Bevölkerungslehre.* Berlin: Springer.

MAHDI, MUHSIN. 1957. *Ibn Khaldûn's Philosophy of History.* Chicago: University of Chicago Press.

MALTHUS, THOMAS ROBERT. 1960a (1830). "A Summary View of the Principle of Population," in Malthus *et al.*, *Three Essays on Population.* New York: Mentor.

———. 1960b. *On Population.* New York: Modern Library.

MARX, KARL, and FRIEDRICH ENGELS. 1959. *Basic Writings on Politics and Philosophy*, edited by Lewis S. Feuer. New York: Doubleday.

McCLEARY, G. F. 1953. *The Malthusian Population Theory.* London: Faber and Faber.

McNEILL, WILLIAM H. 1963. *The Rise of the West.* Chicago: University of Chicago Press.

MEEK, RONALD L. 1953. *Marx and Engels on Malthus*. London: Lawrence and Wishart.

MEHRING, FRANZ. 1962. *Karl Marx, The Story of His Life*. Ann Arbor: University of Michigan Press.

MILL, JOHN STUART. 1876. *Principles of Political Economy*, 5th ed. New York: Appleton.

MYRDAL, GUNNAR. 1940. *Population, A Problem for Democracy*. Cambridge, Mass.: Harvard University Press.

NELSON, RICHARD R. 1956. "A Theory of the Low Level Equilibrium Trap in Underdeveloped Economies," *American Economic Review*, 46, 894–908.

NOONAN, JOHN T., JR. 1965. *Contraception: A History of Its Treatment by the Catholic Theologians and Canonists*. Cambridge, Mass.: Belknap-Harvard University Press.

NOTESTEIN, FRANK. 1945. "Population—The Long View," in Theodore W. Schultz, ed., *Food for the World*. Chicago: University of Chicago Press.

NURKSE, RAGNAR. 1953. "Population and the Supply of Capital," in *Problems of Capital Formation*. Oxford: Basil Blackwell.

OGBURN, WILLIAM F. 1964. "Why the Family Is Changing," in Otis Dudley Duncan, ed., *William F. Ogburn on Culture and Social Change*. Chicago: University of Chicago Press.

OHLIN, GORAN. 1967. *Population Control and Economic Development*. Paris: Development Centre of the Organisation for Economic Co-operation and Development.

OKUN, BERNARD. 1960. Comment on Becker, *op. cit.*, pp. 235–240.

OVERBEEK, JOHANNES. 1970. *Comparative Thoughts on Overpopulation between the Two Wars*. Rotterdam: Drukkerij Princo.

PAN KU. 1950. *Food and Money in Ancient China*, translated by Nancy L. Swann. Princeton, N. J.: Princeton University Press.

PEACOCK, ALAN T. 1952–54. "Theory of Population and Modern Economic Analysis," *Population Studies*, 6, 114–122; 7, 227–234.

PETERSEN, WILLIAM. 1964. *The Politics of Population*. New York: Doubleday.

———. 1969. *Population*, 2nd ed. New York: Macmillan.

———. 1971. "The Malthus-Godwin Debate, Then and Now," *Demography*, 8, 13–26.

PETTY, WILLIAM. 1691. *Political Arithmetick*. London: Clavel.

PLACE, FRANCIS. 1822. *Illustrations and Proofs of the Principle of Population*. London: Longman, Hurst, Rees, Orme, and Brown.

QUESNAY, FRANÇOIS. 1908. "Hommes," *Revue d'Histoire des Doctrines Economiques*, 1, 14ff.

SAUVY, ALFRED. 1956. *Théorie générale de la population*, 2 Vols. Paris: Presses Universitaires de France.

———. 1958. *François Quesnay et la Physiocratie*. Paris: Institut National d'Etudes Démographiques.

———. 1963. *Malthus et les deux Marx*. Paris: Denoel.

———. 1968. "Population Theories," *International Encyclopedia of the Social Sciences*. New York: Macmillan and Free Press, 12, 349–358.

SCHULTZ, THEODORE W. 1964. *Transforming Traditional Agriculture*. New Haven: Yale University Press.

SMITH, ADAM. 1921 (1776). *The Wealth of Nations,* 2 Vols. London: G. Bell.

SPENCER, HERBERT. 1867. *The Principles of Biology,* 2 Vols. New York: Appleton.

SPENGLER, JOSEPH J. 1942. *French Predecessors of Malthus: A Study in Eighteenth-Century Wage and Population Theory.* Durham, N. C.: Duke University Press.

———. 1963. "Arthasastra Economics," in Ralph J. D. Braibanti and Joseph J. Spengler, eds., *Administration and Economic Development in India.* Durham, N. C.: Duke University Press.

STANGELAND, CHARLES E. 1904. *Pre-Malthusian Doctrines of Population.* New York: Columbia University Press.

SÜSSMILCH, JOHANN PETER. 1788 (1741). *Die göttliche Ordnung in den Veränderungen des menschlichen Geschlechts, aus der Geburt, dem Tode und der Fortpflanzung desselben erwiesen,* 3 Vols. Berlin: Verlag der Buchhandlung der Realschule.

SUTTER, JEAN. 1953. "Un démographe engagé: Arsène Dumont (1849–1902)," *Population,* 8, 79–92.

TAEUBER, IRENE B. 1960. "Japan's Demographic Transition Re-examined," *Population Studies,* 14, 28–39.

UNITED NATIONS. 1953. *The Determinants and Consequences of Population Trends.* Population Studies No. 17. New York. Chap. 3: "History of Population Theories," pp. 21–44.

URLANIS, B. T. 1941. *Opyt izchisleniya* [The growth of population in Europe]. Moscow: Ogiz-Gospolitizdat.

VALENTI, D. I. 1963. *Reaktsionnye teorii narodonaseleniia perioda obshchego krizisa kapitalizma* [Reactionary population theories of the period of the general capitalist crisis]. Moscow: Izd-vo sotsial'no-ekonomicheskoi literatury.

VIALATOUX, JOSEPH. 1959. *Le Peuplement humain,* 2 Vols. Paris: Editions Ouvrières.

WRIGHT, HAROLD. 1923. *Population.* New York: Harcourt, Brace.

WRIGLEY, E. A. 1969. *Population and History.* New York: McGraw-Hill.

WYNNE-EDWARDS, V. C. 1962. *Animal Dispersion in Relation to Social Behaviour.* Edinburgh: Oliver and Boyd.

3
CONCEPTS AND DATA

Nothing marks the stance of a professional more clearly than his attitude toward the data he uses. Very often the general public both overestimates the accuracy and completeness of census returns and then, when by some test they prove to be fallible, overreacts in a spirit of general derogation. Demographic statistics are at once the best in the social disciplines and far from perfect. A just appreciation of their uses and limitations demands that we keep in mind both their solid worth and their lacks.

By and large the quality of population statistics has improved over time and, for any period, is best in the countries of Western Europe and their overseas extensions. We begin with a paper discussing an area remote from the Western world, Central Polynesia, and population estimates made mostly in the past. It would have been no startling contribution to demonstrate the obvious fact that these early guesses about the number of the islands' inhabitants were extremely rough. The point of the article is rather that Western scholars reporting these estimates from one monograph or journal article to the next showed themselves unable to copy the figures accurately. From this almost comic performance we can understand why every historian is enjoined to go to original sources.

Robert C. Schmitt, the author of the paper, is the State Statistician of

Hawaii. He is the author of Demographic Statistics of Hawaii, 1778–1965 *(Honolulu: University of Hawaii Press, 1968), the definitive work on its topic, and of seven monographs and over a hundred articles in professional and technical journals, as well as numerous, usually unsigned government reports.*

GARBLED POPULATION ESTIMATES OF CENTRAL POLYNESIA

ROBERT C. SCHMITT

A major problem in Polynesian demography is the wide range and dubious accuracy of population estimates made by early white visitors and residents. Even more disturbing, however, is the extent to which these estimates have been mistranslated, misquoted, misinterpreted, and otherwise garbled by later writers.

One authority, for example, states that when "Cook discovered Tahiti in 1769, . . . he estimated the population of Tahiti at 240,000 souls" (Huguenin 1902: 60, 97). Yet Wallis, not Cook, discovered Tahiti; Cook made his estimate in 1774, not 1769; and his figure was 204,000, not 240,000. This example is not an isolated one. Many historians have quoted Cook's estimate incorrectly. Similar errors have been made in citing estimates for other islands and island groups in Central Polynesia.

Cook's original estimate is unmistakable. On May 14, 1774, viewing an enormous fleet of war canoes, he concluded that a similar fleet representing all of the districts of Tahiti would "require Sixty eight Thousand able bodied men and as these cannot amount to One third part the number of both Sex the whole Island cannot contain less than two hundred and four thousand inhabitants" (Beaglehole 1961: 409; cf. Cook 1777: 349). Unfortunately, Cook's figure was immediately mistranslated in its first French edition, which rendered the crucial sentence as *"toute l'isle contient au moins deux cent quarante mille habitans"* (Cook 1778: 389).

Among later writers, few if any checked Cook's arithmetic or the original English source. The erroneous figure of 240,000 has been unsuspectedly quoted by Taitbout (1779: 2–3), Vincendon-Dumoulin and Desgraz (1844: 279–80), Ribourt (1863: 313), Cuzent (1860: 35), Quatrefages (1864: 69), Huguenin (1902: 97–98), Saint-Yves (1902: 303), Caillot (1909: 71), Vernier (1948: 46), Teissier (1953: 16, 23), and Lescure (1957: 18–19). Only three of these authors—Taitbout, Vincendon-Dumoulin and Desgraz,

SOURCE: Reprinted from the *Journal of the Polynesian Society*, 74 (1965), 57–62, with permission of the author and the journal.

and Cuzent—footnoted their source, citing Volume II, p. 367 of the 1778 Paris edition, rather than the correct location, Volume III, p. 389. At least two, Huguenin and Teissier, misdated the estimate.

Others even misquoted the mistranslation. Cook's figure was given as 140,000 by Nordmann (1939: 88), 130,000 by Sasportas (1931: 63; cf. Commissariat des EFO 1931: 63), 100,000 by Seurat (1906: 10), and 30,000 by Lesson (1838: 258). Three of these authors (all but Seurat) dated Cook's estimate as 1769.

Several writers have reported a second population estimate by Cook, allegedly made on his third voyage to Tahiti. Lt. E. de Bovis (1855: 10) stated that Cook spoke of *"soixante-dix à quatre-vingt mille âmes"* at the time of his last visit. The same range of 70,000 to 80,000 was later attributed to Cook by H. Le Chartier (1887: 47), who left it undated; and by Caillot (1909: 71), who dated it 1777. Huguenin (1902: 98) and Teissier (1953: 16, 23) showed only a single figure, 70,000, and assigned it to 1776. A careful reading of the original English edition (Cook and King 1785) fails, however, to reveal any such estimate. Perhaps these writers were confused by an earlier estimate of the same size, made by an anonymous "gentleman and scholar, who made the voyage" with Cook on HMS *Endeavour* in 1769 (McArthur 1970).

Although Cook's 1774 estimate for Tahiti is but one of many made for the island during the 1760s and 1770s, it is virtually the only one to be either quoted or misquoted. At least seven others were reported by early visitors (Beaglehole 1955: clxxiv–vii), and many more were offered by later authorities (for example, Lesson 1838: 260–61; Adams 1947: 6; and Beaglehole 1955: clxxvi–vii).

The confusion over Cook's 1774 Tahiti estimate is almost equaled by the mix-up regarding his nonexistent estimate for the Marquesas in the same year. Cook ventured no such figure for the Marquesas (see Beaglehole 1961: 362–76), but a casual reading of the 1778 French translation may leave the impression that he did. The estimates sometimes attributed to Cook were actually made and published by the Forsters, father and son, who accompanied Cook to the southeastern Marquesas when he visited that group between April 6 and 10, 1774. George Forster (1777: 34) wrote that "it is to be doubted whether the whole population of this group amounts to fifty thousand persons." John Reinold (or Johann Reinhold) Forster (1778: 223, 225) reported 100,000 for the Marquesas, excluding, of course, the as yet undiscovered northwestern group but including the "Low Isles." George Forster's remarks were interpolated into Cook's narrative by the French translator, who used quotation marks to set the added material apart (Cook 1778: 226; cf. Public Library of New South Wales 1928: 52, n. 1). Some readers have unfortunately not noticed the quotation marks.

A surprisingly large number of later writers have ascribed the Forsters' estimates to Cook, often showing confusion over the actual number, geographic coverage, or date of the figure. Clavel (1885: 74), Rollin (1929: 63), Roberts (1927: 92), Teissier (1953: 19, 24), Lescure (1957: 93), Suggs (1962: 53), and Voisin (1962: 171) have been among the authors incorrectly crediting the estimates to Cook. Suggs erroneously gave their date as 1767, Teissier as 1769, Voisin as 1772, and Clavel and Roberts as 1773. Only Clavel, Rollin, and Teissier correctly gave the total as 50,000 and its scope as limited to the southeastern group. Suggs thought that Cook had estimated between 50,000 and 100,000 for the southeastern Marquesas. Roberts and Lescure reported that Cook had given the population of the entire archipelago, northwestern and southeastern groups combined, as 100,000. Voisin somehow misread this total as 220,000. It thus appears that at least seven authorities have wrongly ascribed authorship of the Marquesas estimates, five have misdated them, three have incorrectly reported their geographic coverage, and four have shown the wrong population figures.

Similar confusion surrounds Krusenstern's 1804 estimate for Nuku Hiva (1813: 177–78). An English resident, Roberts, told Krusenstern that the warriors of Nuku Hiva numbered 5,900, suggesting to the latter that so many warriors implied a total population of about 18,000. Deeming this total too large, however, Krusenstern arbitrarily reduced it by one-third and concluded that the actual population was only about 12,000.

These straightforward figures have been consistently misquoted by later writers. Clavel (1885: 75–76), giving Krusenstern's Nuku Hiva estimate as 16,000, said that it implied a total of 50,000 for the entire archipelago. Jouan thought that Krusenstern had estimated 9,000 warriors and 50,000 inhabitants, and that his data referred to all the Marquesas, not just Nuku Hiva (Quatrefages 1864: 70). Roberts (1927: 92), Rollin (1929: 63), and Teissier (1953: 20, 24) were similarly under the impression that Krusenstern had made a population estimate of 50,000 for the entire archipelago. Voisin (1962: 171) misread this total as 70,000.

In 1813, nine years after Krusenstern's visit, Captain David Porter landed at Nuku Hiva. Although Porter did not offer any population estimates for the island, he noted (1815: 35) that the eight "tribes" living there could send as many as 19,200 warriors into the field. Vincendon-Dumoulin and Desgraz (1843: 184) wrote that Porter's military figure implied 80,000 to 100,000 inhabitants on Nuku Hiva and was probably "exaggerated." Eyriaud des Vergnes (1877: 37) contended that Porter's data indicated at least 25,000 warriors on the island and perhaps 75,000 or 80,000 inhabitants.

Later writers were less cautious in quoting Porter. Quatrefages (1864: 70), who observed that 19,000 warriors implied a population of 60,000 to 80,000, seemed to think that Porter's military figure referred to all of the Marquesas, not just Nuku Hiva. Clavel (1885: 75) and Caillot (1909: 71) erroneously ascribed the figure of 80,000 to Porter instead of to his critics.

Voisin (1962: 171) quoted Porter as estimating the population of the entire archipelago at 200,000. Unfortunately, none of these authorities reported the sources for their mysterious figures.

Many other examples of garbled population estimates could be cited. For instance, Vancouver's 1791 estimate (1801: 216–17) of 1,500 Rapanese was quoted as 1,200 by Garnier (1871: 324) and as 2,000 by Caillot (1909: 71). The population estimate made of Tahiti by Wilson (1799: 215) in 1797 was incorrectly dated 1807 by Huguenin (1902: 98) and Teissier (1953: 16). An 1872 census of the Marquesas conducted by Eyriaud des Vergnes (1877: 37) showed a population of 6,045, but was quoted as 6,246 by Rollin (1929: 64) and by Teissier (1953: 20), who gave its date as 1867, and as 6,000 by Roberts (1927: 92), who gave the year as 1877.

The original estimates of the population of Central Polynesia by early visitors are regarded by many authorities as inconsistent, unrealistic, and misleading (for example, Lesson 1838: 261; Ellis 1844: 113; Clavel 1885: 75–76; Beaglehole 1955: clxxiv–vii; Beaglehole 1961: 409). It is thus doubly regrettable that they should be made more so by subsequent mistranslation, incorrect ascription, and misinterpretation.

References

ADAMS, HENRY. 1947. *Tahiti. Memoirs of Arii Taimai e Marama of Eimeo, Teriirere of Tooarai, Terrinui of Tahiti, Tauraatua i Amo*, edited with an introduction by Robert E. Spiller. New York: Scholars' Facsimiles and Reprints.

BEAGLEHOLE, J. C., ed. 1955, 1961. *The Journals of Captain James Cook on His Voyages of Discovery*, Vols. 1 and 2. Cambridge: Hakluyt Society.

CAILLOT, A. C. EUGÈNE. 1909. *Les Polynésiens orientaux au contact de la civilisation*. Paris: Ernest Leroux.

CLAVEL, A. 1885. *Les Marquisiens*. Paris: Octave Doin.

COMMISSARIAT DES ETABLISSEMENTS FRANÇAIS DE L'OCÉANIE. 1931. *Dans les eaux du Pacifique: Tahiti et ses archipels*. Paris.

COOK, JAMES. 1777. *A Voyage Towards the South Pole and Round the World. . . .* , Vol. 1. London: Strahan and Cadell.

COOK, JACQUES. 1778. *Voyage dans l'hémisphere Austral, et autour du monde. . . .* , Vol. 3. Paris: Hôtel de Thou.

COOK, JAMES, and JAMES KING. 1785. *A Voyage to the Pacific Ocean. . . .* , 3 Vols. London: Nicol and Cadell.

CUZENT, G. 1860. *Iles de la Société: Tahiti*. Rochefort: Ch. Thèze.

DE BOVIS, LT. E. 1855. "Etat de la société taïtienne à l'arrivée des Européens," *Revue Coloniale* (reprint).

ELLIS, WILLIAM. 1844. *The History of the London Missionary Society*, Vol. 1. London: John Snow.

EYRIAUD DES VERGNES, P.-E. 1877. *L'Archipel des Iles Marquises*. Paris: Berger-Levrault.

FORSTER, GEORGE. 1777. *A Voyage Round the World in His Britannic Majesty's Sloop, Resolution . . .* , Vol. 2. London: White, Robson, Elmsly, and Robinson.

FORSTER, JOHN REINOLD. 1778. *Observations Made during a Voyage Round the World* . . . London: Robinson.

GARNIER, JULES. 1871. *Voyage autour du monde: Océanie.* Paris: Henry Plon.

HUGUENIN, PAUL. 1902. *Raiatea la sacrée.* Neuchâtel: Imprimerie Paul Attinger.

KRUSENSTERN, A. J. VON. 1813. *Voyage Round the World in the Years 1803, 1804, 1805, & 1806.* . . , translated by Richard Belgrave Hoppner. London: John Murray.

LECHARTIER, H. 1887. *Tahiti et les colonies françaises de la Polynésie.* Paris: Jouvet.

LESCURE, PH. REY. 1957. *Abrégé d'histoire de la Polynésie Française.* Papeete: The author.

LESSON, P. 1838. *Voyage autour du monde.* . . , Vol. 1. Paris: P. Pourrat.

MCARTHUR, NORMA. 1970. "The Demography of Primitive Populations," *Science,* **167**: 1097–1101.

NORDMANN, P. I. 1939. *Tahiti.* Paris: Fernand Nathan.

PORTER, DAVID. 1815. *Journal of a Cruise Made to the Pacific Ocean.* . . , Vol. 2. Philadelphia: Bradford and Inskeep.

PUBLIC LIBRARY OF NEW SOUTH WALES, MITCHELL LIBRARY. 1928. *Bibliography of Captain James Cook, R.N., F.R.S., Circumnavigator.* Sydney: Government Printer.

QUATREFAGES, A. DE. 1864. *Les Polynésiens et leurs migrations.* Paris: Arthus Bertrand.

RIBOURT, PIERRE FRANÇOIS. 1863. "Etat de l'île Taiti pendant les années 1847, 1848," *Annuaire des Etablissements Français de l'Océanie et du Protectorat des Iles de la Société et Dépendances pour l'Année Commune 1863.* Papeete: Imprimerie du Gouvernement. Reprinted from *Revue Coloniale,* 1850.

ROBERTS, STEPHEN H. 1927. *Population Problems of the Pacific.* London: Routledge.

ROLLIN, LOUIS. 1929. *Les Iles Marquises.* Paris: Société d'Editions Géographiques, Maritimes et Coloniales.

SAINT-YVES, G. 1902. *L'Océanie.* Tours: Alfred Mame.

SASPORTAS, L. 1931. *Les Etablissements français de l'Océanie. Extraits des Bulletins de l'Agence Générale des Colonies,* Nos. 267, 268, 270. [Paris?] Imprimerie Administrative.

SEURAT, L. G. 1906. *Tahiti et les établissements français de l'Océanie.* Paris: Librairie Maritime et Coloniale.

SUGGS, ROBERT C. 1962. *The Hidden Worlds of Polynesia.* New York: Harcourt, Brace & World.

[TAITBOUT]. 1779. *Essai sur l'isle d'Otahiti.* . . . Avignon: Chez Froullé.

TEISSIER, RAOUL. 1953. "Etude démographique sur les établissements français de l'Océanie de Cook au recensement des 17/18 Septembre 1951," *Bulletin de la Société des Etudes Océaniennes,* 9, 6–31.

VANCOUVER, GEORGE. 1801. *A Voyage of Discovery to the North Pacific Ocean, and Round the World.* . . , Vol. 1. London: John Stockdale.

VERNIER, C. 1948. *Tahitiens d'hier et d'aujourd'hui.* Paris: Société des Missions Evangéliques.

VINCENDON-DUMOULIN, C. A. and C. DESGRAZ. 1843. *Iles Marquises ou Nouka-Hiva.* Paris: Arthus Bertrand.

———— and ————. 1844. *Iles Taiti*, Vol. 1. Paris: Arthus Bertrand.

VOISIN, HUBERT. 1962. "Contribution à l'étude de la démographie des Iles Marquises," *Bulletin de la Société des Etudes Océaniennes*, **12**, 171–186.

WILSON, WILLIAM. 1799. *A Missionary Voyage to the Southern Pacific Ocean. . . .* London: Missionary Society.

Under the auspices of its Population Commission, the United Nations has developed and promoted a "1970 World Population Program," whose purpose it has been to induce as many nations as possible to conduct a census during the decade centering on 1970 and, if convenient, in that year itself. In order to establish uniform professional procedures, the commission arranged for the publication in four languages of a manual, Principles and Recommendations for the Population Censuses. *It noted that 47 nations had counted their populations during the first three years of the target decade (1965–67), that 128 had confirmed their intention of carrying out complete enumerations before 1975, and that 22 more had expressed hopes of doing so. With the encouragement and assistance given them, more countries are holding censuses than ever before in history.*

However great this progress may seem to be, it does not mean that the world is on the verge of knowing precisely what its population is. The underdeveloped countries now having their first or second censuses constitute in aggregate a sizable portion of the total. The difficulties specific to these efforts could be illustrated from almost any one of them; the choice of the first census of Papua and New Guinea was made partly to provide a certain continuity with the previous article (though these peoples, of course, are not Polynesians).

Many of the observations about this census apply so widely that one can offer them as generalizations. Getting a complete count of a people widely scattered over a difficult terrain with poor communications, who are often suspicious of the motives behind such official attention, is itself a task beyond the capacity of most colonial administrations or underdeveloped countries. And any classifications are likely to be far less reliable than the head count, either because questions relate to elements absent from that culture (such as, in this case, chronological age or usual occupation) or because large proportions find it expedient to stretch the truth (as on their religion).

Edward P. Wolfers, the author of the article, is an Australian, a graduate of the University of Sydney with first-class honors in Government and Public Administration. As a Fellow of the Institute of Current World Affairs, New York, he presently resides in Port Moresby, Papua. His many articles for scholarly journals or general audiences have dealt mainly with politics in Papua and New Guinea.

ON COMING TO ONE'S CENSUS

EDWARD P. WOLFERS

Melanesia is one of the last great areas of the world for the speculative demographer. The student of the decline of populations through starvation, warfare, or the collective loss of the will to live, and—more rarely, if more accurately—of sudden and dramatic rises in population, can still practice his art here relatively unhampered by the presence of "hard data." As Sir Hubert Murray lamented in 1925, when psychologically based explanations of a suspected decline in the population of Melanesia had some currency, "this question of the decrease in population has been made a happy hunting-ground for all the faddists of the Pacific":

> One is continually being told that the natives dance too much and that dancing should be forbidden; that they do not dance enough and that dancing should be encouraged; that feasts should be approved as a means of assisting and improving native agriculture; and that they should be disapproved as encouraging waste, gluttony, and sickness; that the natives eat too much and work too little; and that they eat too little and work too much. The advice is sometimes rendered more impressive and obscure by being clothed in the language of psychoanalysis, or some other philosophical system with which few of us are familiar (Murray 1925: 203).

Some years earlier, he had himself inclined to the view that "so far as one can form an opinion in the complete absence of statistics . . . the population was probably stationary; that is, I think that in some places it increased while in others it diminished, and that very probably the increase and decrease about balanced one another" (Murray 1912: 374). Today, the problem is no longer depopulation, but an unduly rapid, if not dangerous, tendency toward population growth in some areas, analyzed in terms of only the crudest statistical data.

I have been using the results contained in the Papua and New Guinea *Population Census, 1966* (1969a) for a variety of purposes since they first began to be published. Even now, however, many important data have still not been decoded, or at least have not been made public, and a second census is already scheduled for the middle of 1971. Nonetheless, a great deal of useful to amusing information is available, and quite worthy of pondering. All too few people read rather than refer to the hard-won findings of the census takers.

The Australian administrative style in Papua and New Guinea has long had something of a quantitative bias. Almost since the beginnings of Aus-

SOURCE: Reprinted from Newsletter EPW-26, October 20, 1970, of the Institute of Current World Affairs, with permission of the author and Richard H. Nolte for the Institute.

tralian rule in the Territory, patrol officers have toured the countryside to record names (and sometimes quite offensive comments on the illiterate villagers) in the village books that were kept on their behalf by New Guinea's *luluais* and Papua's village constables. In fact, it has been illegal since 1924 in New Guinea and since 1948 in Papua not to appear to be counted or to conceal another person from an enumerator, on pain of a fine or a jail sentence. As the same village books were used as the primary source for the collection of head-taxes and for estimates of the number of people a village could spare for recruitment as plantation laborers, it is perhaps understandable that many Papuans and New Guineans were quite careful not to come to their census.

In this respect, then, Australian rule has been crudely interventionist and quite openly paternalistic toward village life. The successive Australian administrations of Papua and New Guinea have always insisted on knowing how many Papuans and New Guineans there were living at the time of each patrol even when they lacked the financial resources to provide the indigenes with even minimally useful long-term medical attention. The Australian government was able to report to the UN Trusteeship Council some time ago that, as of June 30, 1966, the population of New Guinea (exclusive of Papua) totaled 1,600,814, including both the estimated and enumerated totals. In the Kainantu Subdistrict, there were an "estimated" 901 uncounted people (Australia 1967: 190–91).

But enough of frivolity and speculation. The truly censitive social scientist can learn much of benefit from a good census book.

THE CONDUCT OF THE 1966 CENSUS

The 1966 count was the first nationwide census to be held in Papua and New Guinea, except for the crude cumulative totals which could be calculated in the course of the numerous, episodic patrol officers' tax-collecting and other routine tours, which together covered most of the Territory's village population perhaps once in every two years Until 1966, the Territory's expatriate population was habitually counted concurrently with the Australian census.

In the words of the Director of Public Health, the 1966 census was "a milestone in statistical development." It was designed to provide the kinds of demographic, economic, and social information suggested as appropriate for developing countries by the UN Statistical Office, and penalties were provided for those not cooperating in its conduct. To add to the popular impact of the census, special school holidays were declared for its duration, so that teachers could be made available for its administration and as many people as possible would be at home on census day, June 30. To that extent, the very conduct of the census distorted the normal distribution of population in the Territory, and some adjustments in the definition of a person's "normal place of residence" therefore had to be made.

Given the dispersion of the Territory's settlements and the lack of adequate communications and of personnel who could be trained as enumerators and supervisors, the census was neither complete nor simultaneous. The total non-indigenous population and the indigenous inhabitants of urban areas, plantations and other commercial establishments, missions, and government posts were completely enumerated on census day. But only a 10-percent sample of the village population was enumerated, stratified on the basis of 102 strata, including geographical location, tribal groups, staple foods, and religion, with the total population estimated from the old patrol "censuses." The anticipated standard error for the entire Territory population was about 0.5 percent, but about 3 percent for any given district. The District reports warn that "for very small numbers, the error will be very great":

Such figures should be used only with extreme caution and a thorough understanding of their limitations. . . .

Further minor errors arise from incorrect replies, incorrect coding of replies, and other processing errors. These are virtually all detected and rectified. However, because of the complexity and magnitude of the Census, a very small number remain uncorrected, but these do not affect the general validity of the results.

However, these uncorrected errors in the sample grid would be expanded by the sample-raising factor. Thus, for example, if one accountant were incorrectly recorded in a sample area in which there were in fact no accountants, this would be expanded and appear in publications as perhaps 10 or as high as 14 accountants. This emphasizes the need to be cautious in using the sample data for small cells (Papua and New Guinea 1969b: 5).

Because of the need to conduct much of the census on patrol, the data collected in some areas had also to be corrected to the ostensible census date, June 30. Finally, as most of the people were thought to be illiterate, inquiries were generally conducted through a verbal rather than a written interrogation.

DISTRIBUTION OF THE POPULATION—GEOGRAPHICAL AND "RACIAL"

The total population of Papua and New Guinea on the day of the census was estimated to be 2,184,986. The population density, 11.91 persons per square mile over all, ranged from 1.55 in the swamplands of Papua's Western District to 59.73 in the mountainous, land-short Chimbu District of the New Guinea Highlands. Almost 1.6 percent of the Territory's total population was not indigenous.

In all, 87.05 percent of the population lived in rural villages, 7.09 on a plantation, mission, or government station in a rural area, and 5.86 in one of the Territory's 34 designated "towns" (that is, centers with a population of at least 500, excluding separately located schools, hospitals, missions, plantations, rural settlements, and villages of whatever size). Some 251 expatriates purportedly lived in a "rural village"—presumably mainly anthropologists, missionaries, and other members of that small band who have eschewed the benefits and pleasures of urban colonial society for real contact with the people of the country. Almost 40 percent of the non-indigenous village dwellers worked mainly within the subsistence sector of the economy: 66 as gardeners, 4 females as fishermen, and 15 more as sago processors, plus a handful whose specialties were not given. The villagers constituted rather less than 1 percent of the non-indigenous population, while just on two-thirds of all expatriates lived in "town." The out-stations no longer account for as great a proportion of the expatriate population as they did in the pioneering days of Australia's administration of Papua and New Guinea.

The "towns" varied in size from Kerowagi, with a population of 506, to Port Moresby, with 41,848. Every town was predominantly indigenous, with at least twice as many males as females. There is surely food for thought in these figures for students of the putative relation between urbanization, crime, and other social disorders. It seems clear, for example, that most urban employers provide, at best, only all-male barracks for the accommodation of their indigenous employees rather than family quarters, though insofar as urban employment and youth overlap it may be that many of the indigenous employed are not married.

For the student of "race," the census provides some fascinating data on the mixtures to be found in the Territory, calculated in many cases down to the nearest full half. The 312 persons of more complex mixture (that is, those of less than 50 percent European or indigenous descent and 50 percent or less of any other race) were relegated to "Other Mixed Race." There were, in sum, 2,150,419 varyingly "indigenous" inhabitants of Papua and New Guinea, defined with magnificent disregard for detail in this case as comprising "the aboriginal people of the Territory of Papua and New Guinea, Australia, New Zealand, and other islands of Polynesia, Melanesia, and Micronesia," and anyone else who was "descended from these aboriginal peoples to the extent of more than one half." There were also 29,350 ("more than 50 percent") Europeans and 2,749 others, including 2,455 Chinese, a solitary Afghan, and 3 persons who were "more than 50 percent" of "Other and Indefinite Race." The Territory's total population of mixed racial origins (not counting those more than 50 percent of one race) was 2,484, of whom more than half were part-European, including 2 partly of European and partly of "Sinhalese Burgher" extraction.

Just under one-quarter of the non-indigenous population of Papua and New Guinea were born in the Territory, and slightly more than half (17,847 persons in all) were Australian-born. The next largest group were English-born (2,151), followed by a long list of birthplaces down to Syria, whence came a single migrant, and 2 persons who were evidently born "at sea." More than 85 percent of the non-indigenous population held British citizenship, a category that still includes Australian nationals.

Apart from New Guinea's Chinese (the relatives and descendants of the coolies brought there by the Germans) and 618 other Pacific Islanders (probably mission employees in the main), there were almost no other non-European non-indigenes in Papua and New Guinea. This last datum has probably been mildly modified since the census was taken in that a handful of carefully selected, highly skilled Asians have recently been admitted into the Territory to work for the University of Papua and New Guinea and for various large Japanese firms.

AGE, MARITAL STATUS, AND LENGTH OF STAY

The estimation of a person's age can be a source of considerable amusement and education in Papua and New Guinea. In the absence of documentary information, the enumerators were instructed to estimate ages by reference to locally significant historical events:

From a list of notable events the informant was asked to identify an event which he remembered during his childhood. He was then asked to point out a child the same size as he remembered himself to be at the time of this event. The child's age was then subtracted from the date of this event to give an estimate of the date of birth of the informant (Papua and New Guinea 1969a: 9).

If the procedure could not be made to yield a satisfactory result, a person's age was calculated in terms of the age of someone else who could remember an identifiable event which could be dated with some accuracy.

The lists of dates were usually catalogues of natural disasters and administration-centered ethnohistory, as if nothing (at least nothing to which a specific date could be attached) had ever occurred that was an act neither of god nor of government. In some cases, such a list had to be produced separately for each small island in a district, and for many small areas which had a "contact" history all of their own. The age estimates were probably no more accurate than those of the harassed patrol officer who (in 1967) suddenly began to hope quite feverishly that a certain candidate would lose an election because he had now re-estimated him to be less than 21 years of age, or than those which led a prominent member of the House of Assembly to be listed officially as 44 in 1964 and 57 in 1968. One can grow old very quickly in the tropics, it would seem.

For students of the revolution to be wrought by the young, they (that is, those under 21) represented 53.28 percent of the indigenous population in 1966. Only 1 percent of Papuans and New Guineans were aged 65 or

over—an indication of the relatively low life expectancy of most Melane-
sians. The expatriate population consisted predominantly of the young-but-
not-youthful on the make, with 64.87 percent between 21 and 65 and more
than 40 percent between 20 and 39. Old-age pensions, not provided in Papua
and New Guinea, are universally available to those who need them in
Australia at age 65; only 1.88 percent of the expatriate population had
reached retirement age.

Insofar as the age distribution of the indigenous population reflected
a rising birth rate, it served to highlight a growing clash of values in the
Territory. Under the Native Regulations and the Native Administration
Regulations, the administrations of both Papua and New Guinea have consistently striven to outlaw abortion and to discourage such other forms of
population control as warfare, sorcery, and the use of traditional medicines.
In this case, official policy accorded with at least one important aspect of
traditional custom, in that throughout most of Melanesia a large family
was a source of prestige, wealth, and security in old age. However, now
that the indigenous population has begun to increase—rather dramatically
in some areas—the administration has begun to try to extend its public-
health programs into population control, a policy which offends many
Papuans and New Guineans on religious grounds, and even more on the
same traditional grounds which underlay the comparative success of the
earlier laws. Among some sophisticates, the very mention of population
control can stimulate a lecture on the evils of colonialist plotters who seek
to keep their subjects' numbers down. The fuel of proof is added to the fire
of suspicion by the seemingly prolific breeding of the Territory's expatriate
population. The latter group would argue, of course, that they seem to have
so many children only because they are on the average quite young; and,
anyway, what else is there to do amid the boredom of the tropics?

The questions pertaining to the marital status of the population yielded
a perhaps unique word of advice for the census taker: "Where it [is] established that a man [has] been married to more than one wife and [has] lost
them all, the way he lost his last surviving wife [determines] his marital
status"—that is, whether he has been widowed or divorced (Papua and New
Guinea 1969a: 17). In all, almost 10 percent of Papua and New Guinea's
married males had more than one wife, and nearly 2 percent had more than
two, the traditional symbol of wealth and status in many parts of the Territory. There were no publicly recorded practitioners of polyandry.

The marriage figures also revealed something important about the structure of colonial society: there were nearly 1,500 more married expatriate
males than married females in the Territory. Even after a generous allowance has been made for interracial liaisons, it would still seem quite likely
that Papua and New Guinea serves as a refuge for Australia's unhappily
married males.

Certainly, very few expatriates seem to commit more than a few years
of their lives to the Territory. Of the non-indigenous population of Papua

and New Guinea at the time of the census, almost one-quarter had been born in the Territory. Of those born elsewhere, fully a quarter had been resident in the Territory for less than one year, and only a little more than a third for five years or more. The median term of residence was just over three years—a measure of the expatriate population's generally transitory connection with the Territory and, perhaps too, of the increasing recruitment of overseas personnel as development has proceeded.

RELIGION

Probably the most questionable results produced by the census were those concerning religious affiliations. Few missionaries would claim that more than half of the people in their areas were even nominally Christians, much less complete converts. Even among the "Christians," there have been many who were not rational believers but seekers after a materialistic millennium, or who have not been finally baptised because they could not demonstrate the requisite knowledge of the rituals and beliefs of the church, or were polygamists. However, fully 92.27 percent of the indigenous population thought it desirable to tell the enumerators that they were Christians. Only two denominations accounted for at least a tenth of the indigenous population, the Catholics (31.23 percent) and the Lutherans (27.63 percent). One is tempted to ponder to what degree the census itself seemed to hold out the threat of divine retribution to those who would deny the church, and to what degree the original specification of the sample to be questioned was inaccurate. Certainly, the indigenes' religiosity outshone that of their expatriate mentors, only 86.31 percent of whom professed to be of either the Christian or what the census called the "Hebrew" faith. However, 13 expatriates claimed to have moved in the opposite direction and now adhered to an "Indigenous Religion."

Probably the most remarkable finding of the religious survey was the revelation that there were 37 Papuans and New Guineans of "Hebrew" religious affiliation—14 of them, all females, resident in the Southern Highlands of Papua (Papua and New Guinea 1969b: 16). Now, it has often been pointed out by those explorers and travel-writers who have penetrated the mud of Papua's Western District and the mountain fastnesses of the remote and newly pacified Southern Highlands that many of the people there have a very distinctively Semitic appearance. Perhaps these are the last remaining members of those "lost tribes" of Israel whom so many explorers have sought in New Guinea.

LANGUAGE, EDUCATION, OCCUPATION

Fluency in one or more of the three principal *lingue franche*, some schooling, and a history of paid employment are the hallmarks of the modern man in Papua and New Guinea. Indeed, the first attribute is virtually a prerequisite for the achievement of the other two. However, apart from a very small elite, the attainment of even a modicum of "modernity" among the indigenous population is still an aspiration rather than a reality.

To take language first: only 13.26 percent of the indigenous population aged 10 or over could say, and 11.41 percent could read and write, a simple sentence in English, proportionately more in Papua than in New Guinea, and twice as many males as females. For Pidgin, the comparable figures were 36.46 percent who could speak and 12.23 percent who could read and write in the language (both mainly New Guineans), and for Motu 8.13 and 3.38 percent, respectively (mainly Papuans). All but 3 percent of the Territory's expatriates spoke English, two-thirds claimed to speak Pidgin (although only about three-quarters of these claimed to be literate in this phonetically written language), and only three-quarters of the Territory's 8 percent who spoke Police Motu could also read and write in that language (which, again, is phonetic).

In short, the linguistic basis for interracial communication was not very broad, quite apart from the social barriers in the very structure of colonial society.

Possibly a quarter of the indigenous population had undergone some formal education. Only 2 individuals were university graduates, some 14,546 had undergone at least part of a secondary education, and at least 6,333 more had some kind of postprimary qualification. There were, by comparison, 1,555 expatriate university graduates in the Territory and 7,492 with other postprimary qualifications, while the rest either were still at school or had no specific skills to further the Territory's development.

Of a total indigenous work force of just over 1,250,000, only 20 percent worked wholly or mainly in the money sector of the economy, more than a third mainly in the subsistence sector (supplemented by a small income to pay for their clothes, medical and school fees, and taxes), and the rest wholly in subsistence production.

The census analysts were particularly dubious about the value of their findings on occupation. Many Papuans and New Guineans seem to work for varying periods at quite different jobs, which are called by a multitude of similar names, all within an economy in which the number and kinds of jobs available are rapidly increasing. However, according to the census about 85 percent of the Territory's indigenous money earners were farmers, fishermen, hunters, or lumber workers; some 6 percent were craftsmen, production-process workers, or laborers; and the remaining 9 percent were skilled, semiskilled, or marginally trained workers.

A quarter of the expatriate work force consisted of professional and technical workers, and nearly 20 percent were engaged in clerical duties. There were enough Papuan and New Guinean domestics to provide one in every four non-indigenes (man, woman, and child) with a personal servant, but even with this tremendous national reservoir of those seeking low-paid employment, 38 non-indigenes were in domestic employment in private households.

While only about 15 percent of the indigenous work force was in government employ, 39.55 percent of the Territory's non-indigenous population worked for the Australian or Territory government. The figure reflects Papua and New Guinea's contemporary social status, midway between a "settler" and a purely administrative colony.

Of the many inferences to be drawn on the nature of census taking in Papua and New Guinea, one important one can be illustrated by a single episode in the life of the Tari people of the Southern Highlands. At the time of the great influenza epidemic which swept through the Highlands in October and November of 1969, when Australian troops were hurriedly airlifted to the Territory to take part in a massive effort to treat and inoculate the people, more than 100 percent of the known population of the Tari Subdistrict received an injection of vaccine. The process seemed clearly to indicate that care and consideration for others is an important part of efficient colonial administration and development. "If you want to be able to count on us," the Tari people seemed to be saying, "then we must be able to count on you."

References

AUSTRALIA. 1967. *Report to the General Assembly of the United Nations: Administration of the Territory of New Guinea, 1 July 1965–30 June 1966.* Canberra.

MURRAY, J. H. P. 1912. *Papua or British New Guinea.* London: T. Fisher Unwin.

———. 1925. *Papua of To-Day, or an Australian Colony in the Making.* London: P. S. King.

PAPAU AND NEW GUINEA. BUREAU OF STATISTICS. 1969a. *Population Census, 1966. Preliminary Bulletin No. 20:* "Summary of Population." Konedobu.

———. ———. 1969b. *Population Census, 1966. Preliminary Bulletin No. 26:* "Southern Highlands District." Konedobu.

Gaps in the data about world population relate to two types of countries: those whose counts are so inadequate that they must be regarded only as rough estimates—which we have exemplified in the previous article—and those that will not conduct a census in the foreseeable future. The outstanding example of this second category is the most populous country of the world, Mainland China. Whatever it may be, its population is so enormous that our relative ignorance concerning it greatly affects any estimate of the world total.

Leo Orleans, the author of the following paper, is China Research Specialist of the Library of Congress, where except for two years with the

National Science Foundation he has worked since 1951. Born in Russia, he spent the early years of his life in China, about which he has written numerous articles, primarily on its population and manpower, and one book, Professional Manpower and Education in Communist China.

The most important assertion in this paper is not that Western sinologists know nothing of China's population trends since 1953, a fact that they at least are well aware of, but that the Communist regime knows no more. According to the author's well buttressed thesis, the lack of statistics abroad cannot be explained merely by the fear of what these might reveal, as in the case of some Soviet data. Since even those Americans who abhor totalitarianism often believe that a planned society is possessed of an almost magical efficiency, it comes as a salutary shock to learn that the largest totalitarian state is incapable of preparing the most essential prerequisite to economic and social planning, a count and classification of its own people.

CHINA'S POPULATION STATISTICS: AN ILLUSION?

LEO A. ORLEANS

Whether one agrees or disagrees with a particular evaluation or interpretation of the 1953 census-registration—"the first modern census of China" —one must admit that the few published statistics have been thoroughly covered and analyzed. Not enough attention, however, has been given to the system that was established to produce the population data published since 1953. Most of the analysis has naturally focused on acceptability of the figures themselves and reasonableness of the indicated rates of growth rather than on the capabilities of the responsible institutions and individuals to collect the necessary data for current population statistics—the only means of determining a nation's population and its rate of growth during the intercensal period (cf. Aird 1961).

To comprehend the problems that Communist China faces in producing population figures, it is important to understand that most of the prerequisites for the maintenance and reporting of all types of statistics are admittedly in short supply on the mainland (Li 1962). The statistical system is poorly organized and poorly directed. There is a serious shortage of personnel capable of collecting, processing, and analyzing statistical data, as well as an inadequate program for training and educating statistical workers. At the same time there is great inefficiency in the use of personnel who are

SOURCE: Reprinted from *China Quarterly*, No. 1 (1965), pp. 168–178, with permission of the author and journal.

available for the work. Most serious, however, are the lack of motivation and the indifference of most of the individuals involved in statistical work.

Although such shortcomings are frequently admitted or implied by official Communist sources concerning statistics in general and economic statistics in particular, any critical self-evaluation of the problems faced in the collection and analysis of population statistics is rare indeed. And yet many of the same difficulties that preclude accurate economic statistics must be just as evident in demographic data. It may be argued that expert statisticians are not needed to "count noses." Registering births should be considerably simpler than estimating coal production or the number of tons of grain gathered in a particular *hsien*. The registration of an individual's death should offer less possibility for confusion than accounting for a stalk of corn, which can be hidden, stored, paid as a tax, lost, spoiled, or eaten. Economic statistics can be much more involved and detailed, more difficult to obtain, and more easily subject to accidental or intentional error, and can require greater sophistication on the part of the collector, compiler, and analyst. Nevertheless, it has been proven that even an accurate "nose count" requires proper training and motivation of enumerators and considerable sophistication at the higher levels of responsibility.

EFFORTS AT DATA COLLECTION

Before 1953 there was no uniform registration system in Communist China. The efforts of the Ministry of Public Security to maintain a register of the population were limited primarily to the urban areas, and even there coverage was incomplete and the figures were unavailable. In 1954, some provinces drew up plans for a registration system, but implementation was extremely spotty. It was not until 1955, almost two years after the official date of the 1953 census-registration and five months after the results were released, that a newspaper editorial proclaimed the need for a regular system of population registers. The editorial pointed out that the data from the census were already outdated and that continuous registration should be instituted, because "if census records are not verified as early as possible, there will be many difficulties in clearing up the changes of population since the last census." An overlap in functions among the various civil administration and public security departments was also noted. "Only when the civil administration and public security departments coordinate their work and take uniform steps can the system of registration of persons be instituted in an orderly manner in cities and rural areas." The editorial concluded by urging close supervision over registration and by stressing the need to "teach the people to observe and carry out the system." [1]

[1] *Kuang-ming Jih-pao*, April 2, 1955. *Survey of China Mainland Press (SCMP)*, Hong Kong: United States Consulate General, No. 1040.

The criticism of the divided responsibilities of the Ministries of Interior and Public Security was resolved in a directive of the State Council dated January 13, 1956: "To standardize household-control work in cities and villages, it has been decided that all work connected with rural household registration, statistical work, and the adjudication of questions of nationality administered by the Ministry of Interior and civil administrations of all levels will be transferred to and administered by the Ministry of Public Security and security offices of all levels." [2]

In actual fact, much of the system at the lowest administrative levels remained unchanged in that household registration in the villages and towns was to be carried out by "village or town people's council secretariats or original responsible personnel," although all civil administrative committees were made responsible to the peace and security committees and were to report on all their activities with regard to registration work. The civil affairs sections and departments of *hsien*, autonomous *chous*, cities, provinces, and autonomous regions, however, were required to transfer to the appropriate officers or departments of public security their reports on household registers, rolls, and statistical forms from the 1953 census, and all other materials pertaining to population registration. This transfer was to be accompanied by a shift of all full-time personnel of the civil-affairs departments engaged in registration and statistical work to the public-security departments at their respective levels. Thus, although some registration responsibilities were maintained within the civil-affairs offices under the Ministry of Interior, primary nationwide responsibilities for population registers were vested in the Ministry of Public Security.

On January 9, 1958, the Standing Committee of the National People's Council adopted a new set of regulations governing household registration. In explaining these regulations, Lo Jui-ch'ing, Minister of Public Security, pointed out that they were necessary to "perfect the system of household registration," since "the existing system is still far from perfect." He listed three main defects in household registers: (1) lack of uniformity in the system, not only between urban and rural registration procedures but among individual cities; (2) "certain systems to be instituted have either not been instituted at all or have not been instituted properly"; (3) changed conditions, making it necessary to revise or do away with systems that are obsolete. [3]

Although special provisions were included in the new regulations covering persons in the armed services, convicts, temporary absence, marriage, and so forth, population registers were relatively simple to maintain, particularly in comparison with the complicated and lengthy forms required for economic data. Usually maintained on the basis of traditional house-

---

[2] *Chung-hua Jen-min Kung-ho-kuo Fa-kuei Hui-pien* [Digest of Laws and Regulations of the People's Republic of China] (Peking, 1956).

[3] NCNA, January 9, 1958. *SCMP*, No. 1695.

holds, registration books were to contain basic information on the number of permanent residents, as well as current information on births and deaths. Before moving, a person was to obtain a "removal certificate" in order to be taken off the local register, and re-register immediately (within three days in urban areas and ten days in rural localities) upon arrival at his new place of residence. Births and deaths were to be reported within one month in the country and, in the case of deaths, before the funeral in the city. This is the registration system, with relatively minor variations over the years, that presumably has provided the Communist regime in Peking with all its population data since the 1953 census. Has the system measured up to the requirements placed upon it? Do the published figures provide an accurate reflection of Communist China's population?

Intent is an important aspect of any endeavor. It is very significant, therefore, that the primary purpose in establishing the registration system apparently was not to maintain population records but to maintain control over the population. This is evident not only from the emphasis in the various proclamations, but from the fact that the responsibility for population registers lay not with the State Statistical Bureau or even the Ministry of Interior. The records were maintained by the Ministry of Public Security and its various branches and offices, which reach down to every administrative level. The first article of the 1958 regulations governing registration states: "These regulations are enacted to maintain social order, to protect the rights and interests of the citizens, and to serve Socialist construction." [4] All the country's requirements for population statistics are included under the need to "serve Socialist construction." An editorial on this subject in the *People's Daily* only mentioned the need for population data and concentrated on the security aspects of population registers:

As we all know, one of the characteristics in the development of sabotage activities by counterrevolutionaries and other bad elements is the adoption of all measures to change their real names, to assume false identities, to fake evidence, and to make false reports to the registration authorities in their attempt to masquerade as other persons. The perfection of the work of household registration will further restrict and expose the attempts at imposture on the part of these counterrevolutionaries and other bad elements, and better protect national construction and the personal safety of the people.[5]

It is not surprising that the Minister of Public Security would accuse these same "undesirable elements in the population" of sabotaging the registration system:

A small number of people still have not observed this system. This may have been due to their ignorance of the contents and meaning of the system, or to their

---

[4] *Ibid.*
[5] *Jen-min Jih-pao* [People's Daily], January 10, 1958.

selfishness and laziness. In addition, some counterrevolutionaries and other bad elements have purposely sabotaged this system.[6]

It could be argued that, although the Ministry of Public Security may not be the most appropriate agency for maintaining population registers, at least it has the necessary authority to ensure compliance. This may be so, but it is also a factor against the complete reporting of arrivals, departures, and vital events. Most Chinese have a well founded apprehension and even fear of any contact with authority, usually represented by the local constable or the district police station. Usually of local origin and with little education, the policeman traditionally has wielded his power with a vengeance only a Chinese peasant can fully appreciate. It is easy to imagine, for example, that many individuals would chance breaking the regulations, the importance of which are difficult for them to comprehend, rather than voluntarily step inside a police station to report a death that may have occurred a month earlier. In other words, leave well enough alone.

Population registration was often integrated with other types of surveys, referred to as "central tasks." It seemed convenient for the local authorities who were required to supply the people in the *hsiang* center with a population count to combine this effort with another activity. For example:

In many *hsiang* of Luang *hsien*, Anhwei, the registration system was instituted in coordination with planned purchase and planned marketing of grain. . . . When the number of households involved in the planned purchase and planned marketing program was calculated, the census records were completed. Thus upon completion of such central tasks as planned purchase and planned marketing, the system of registration of persons was instituted.[7]

Population data derived in this manner had to be of dubious quality and, more important, did little toward a continuing operating system of population registers that would reflect current conditions.

FROM COLLECTION TO PUBLICATION

The steps through which population data move up the administrative ladder are not known. What follows is a somewhat speculative description, based on interpretation of available material, of how population figures are collected, how they are reviewed and passed on, and what may be some of the considerations of individuals responsible for these figures.

Let us take, as an example, Kuo Hsiang commune in Ch'ang-li *hsiang*, located in the eastern part of Hopeh Province, and try to follow a set of figures from the lowest level to their final destination in Peking. This commune was created in September 1958 from six *hsiang*, one town, 75 villages,

[6] *Ibid.,* June 29, 1956.
[7] *Kuang-ming Jih-pao* [Kuang-ming Daily], April 2, 1955. *SCMP,* No. 1040.

and 38 high-level cooperatives. In 1960 it was reported to consist of 11,098 households, with a total population of 52,700, of whom 23,786 were in the labor force. The commune was subdivided into 10 production administrative areas, subdivided into 29 production brigades and 156 production teams.[8]

It is safe to assume that despite the absence of a full-time statistical worker at the production-team level, the team leader, with approximately 70 families and 350 persons under his jurisdiction, has a fairly good idea of how many persons he controls. It is true that he is much more concerned with production statistics, with the inventory of hoes, plows, and wheelbarrows, or perhaps with the procurement of supplies for the messhall; but he must also know the number of mouths that these messhalls have to feed and the number of hands available for work in the field, for manure collection, or for some of the subsidiary projects and miscellaneous activities.

The team leader is undoubtedly aware of the requirement to report births and deaths to the commune center, but since neither the old people nor the newborn figure in his labor allocation, these records are probably kept hit-or-miss. Besides, since this information need not be reported for a month after the occurrence of the event, "there is time enough." The team leader knows that he will be accountable for the statistics he reports on the production of grain, some of which will be taken by the state and some to feed the members of the team. He knows equally well that it would be most unusual for anyone to check on the population figures he reports. Thus, if the figures he passes on correspond to within ten, or maybe twenty-five, persons of the actual number in the production team, he feels he has satisfactorily accomplished his duties as an "enumerator."

It is not known whether the team reports are sent for review to the ten production administration area centers in Kuo Hsiang commune before being passed on to the commune center, but the reports from the 156 production teams covering over 11,000 households and over 50,000 persons eventually do reach the administrative office in the commune. The population data in these reports are probably included among a mass of other statistics. Descriptions of communes show that although some may have two full-time statistical workers, most have only one and others none. The assistance that the commune statistical worker may have in maintaining records and in compiling the numerous reports required of all communes is not known and may vary from one location to another. It can be assumed, however, that population data would not have the same priority as certain other quantitative records. That population figures are left until the last moment and assembled "if time permits" is therefore quite conceivable.

How much change can there be in the population of a commune during a period of several months? With a slight adjustment the old figures can always be used again. Manual addition of population figures for 156 produc-

---

[8] *Ching-chi Yen-chiu* [Statistical Research], No. 1, January 17, 1960.

tion teams takes time and it is, of course, even more time-consuming to check the sums done at the team level. One check is sure to be made, however. The commune statistician must be certain that the new total does not deviate too much from the population figures he has on hand, for a different figure will undoubtedly result in inquiries, in checking of individual reports, and may even reveal some factual or procedural errors. It is much safer to report a figure that does not differ much from the previous total.

By the time the population figures reach the *hsien* seat of Ch'ang-li, they are at least two or three times removed from their original source. It is also the first administrative center with a public-security office, which has a direct responsibility for maintaining population records. This responsibility of the *hsien* officials is not new. The *hsien* magistrate, as far back as the 18th century, was responsible for the *pao chia* system of population records, and the basic tabulations under the Republic of China were also assembled at the *hsien* level. Although in most cases the intent and efforts of the officials were commendable, the accuracy of the data was not. To quote from a 1928 statement by the chief of the Department of Statistics: "Our country never had an accurate investigation of the population of each province. Whenever the *hsien* were ordered to make household investigations, they either made arbitrary false reports with no reality in them or copied from old figures without due inquiry." [9] Has there been a change in this traditional attitude towards population statistics? That the control mechanism under the Communist regime is much more pervasive and effective at all levels of the administrative structure cannot be denied. However, the important question is not so much the effectiveness of control as the training and integrity of those responsible for population statistics.

At the *hsien* center, at least one individual should have as his principal responsibility the maintenance of population data. Although it may be too much to expect this person to be trained in population work as such, he probably has had some training in statistics, sufficient for a post that probably requires little more than what may be termed "population bookkeeping."

Let us assume that the statistical worker in the public security office in Ch'ang-li *hsien* has had a junior middle education, has had some training in basic statistics, and is a responsible and well intentioned cadre. He receives population figures from approximately ten communes located in the *hsien*, covering about half a million persons. The only basis on which he can judge the validity of these figures is the data he already has. With respect to the nature of the count, the number of people involved, and the limitations of a manual operation, the new figures could correspond to those he already has

[9] *Min-kuo Shih-ch'i-nien Ko Sheng Shih Hu-k'ou T'iao-ch'a T'ung-chi Pao-kao* [Statistical Report on Household Investigation in Various Provinces and Municipalities, 1928] (Nanking: Ministry of the Interior, Department of Statistics, 1931); quoted by Taeuber and Wang 1960.

only by coincidence, or because those responsible at the team, brigade, and commune levels made them correspond.

In the event that the population figures in the latest reports deviate significantly from the records of the *hsien* statistical worker, what course of action is open to him? As far as is known, there is no provision for a recheck of the data—a formidable job under any circumstances. Thus, he has two alternatives: (1) to send the figures up as reported to him, or (2) to adjust the new data to his own records before sending them to the appropriate officials in the provincial capital of Tientsin. In most cases the latter alternative would surely be selected. It would be dangerous indeed to send figures to the provincial capital that deviate by ten, twenty, or more percent from the population that is currently carried.

When the population statistics from Kuo Hsiang commune in Ch'ang-li *hsien* finally reach Tientsin, the capital of Hopei Province, they constitute only a small segment of the data that filters up from about 20,000 production brigades, via 1,000 communes and some 130 *hsien*, covering a rural population of between 35 and 40 million. When these data reach the State Statistical Bureau in Peking, they cover about 3 million production teams, about 500,000 production brigades, over 30,000 communes and over 2,000 *hsien* spread out over 26 provinces and autonomous regions and incorporating a total rural population that may exceed 550 million.

The State Statistical Bureau in Peking undoubtedly has specialists trained in statistics and population registers, and some even in demographic theory. Because they have this knowledge, they must be aware of the nature of the data that reach them. Thus, it is probable that these data are, at best, extensively adjusted or, at worst, completely ignored in preparing national estimates of population and rates of growth—which must show consistency not only over time but also with current policies as established by the leaders of the Communist Party.

SOME PUBLISHED FIGURES

It is not surprising that there are many questions concerning the validity of the population figures released officially or cited by various agencies or officials of Communist China:

1. The only series of population figures officially released by Peking was published in the journal of the Statistical Bureau in June 1957 and covers the years 1949 through 1956.[10] The populations for 1949, 1950, and 1951 were based on "the trend of natural increase of our population in the past." Since the natural increase of the past can only be surmised, is there any validity in the rates used?

[10] *T'ung-chi Kung-Tso* [Statistical Work], No. 11, June 14, 1957.

The year-end figure for 1953 was "inferred from the 1953 census," but the figures for 1952, 1954, and 1955 were based primarily on "reports of provinces and municipalities." Since the registration was incomplete, are the figures for 1952, 1954, and 1955 then admittedly erroneous? Were the provincial reports adjusted? If adjusted, how?

2. If the figures in the series for years up to and including 1955 were obtained from population registers, did these registers suddenly cease to function after 1957? Does the virtual absence of population data since 1957 reflect a statistical dislocation produced by the "great leap"? Is this why a population of 650 million has been used almost exclusively for some half-dozen years now?

3. If population data exist, they should be available to an official of ministerial rank. Why then was the Minister of Food forced to admit at the end of 1959 that "there has been no new statistical material yet regarding the population for 1958 and 1959"? [11]

If the official population data released by the State Statistical Bureau are reliable, why would Premier Chou En-lai, in an interview by a British correspondent in September 1960, respond to questions concerning China's population growth by giving an annual increase for 1949–59 of "over 10 million," implying a difference of over 30 million between his data and those of the Statistical Bureau? Since the questions were submitted to Chou prior to the interview, he could have used the best data available.

4. If the national populations that were reported were summations of provincial populations, as suggested, why were the latter not published? Only two provincial series have been published since the results of the 1953 census-registration were released—one for 1955 and one for 1957.[12] It may be argued that provincial populations are state secrets, but state secrets would not have been published for any year. Provincial populations should be available at least for the years in which national totals were made public.

5. If the household registration could not provide the government with accurate reports on total population, could the few figures that were published have been derived from the reports of natural increase? Was the registration of births and deaths so complete that yearly changes in China's total population could be computed solely by adding births and subtracting deaths? According to Fei Hsiao-t'ung, one of China's foremost anthropologists and chairman of the Minorities Institute in Peking, "The registration of vital rates has not been established in China as yet. Only a few large cities have been practicing registration, but their data are very doubtful from a scientific point of view." [13] Ta Ch'en, the author of a number of studies on China's population, noted that the registration of vital statistics should be

[11] *Jen-min Jih-pao* [People's Daily], October 25, 1959.

[12] *Ten Great Years* (Peking, 1960); *Ti-li Chih-shih* [Geographical Knowledge], September 1957.

[13] *Hsin Chien-she* [New Construction], No. 4, 1957.

handled by qualified personnel and concluded rather cautiously, "I am not satisfied with the present work in registering vital statistics, which is not scientific." [14] T'ien Feng-t'iao, a member of the Teaching and Research Office of the Academy of Advanced Study for Cadres of the Ministry of Public Health, indicated that the situation had not improved during the following years; China still lacks data on birth and death rates for the entire nation, he pointed out, and can only furnish these rates for selected cities. [15] How then was it possible to report precisely that the natural increase per 1,000 population was 23.4 in 1954 and 21.4 in 1955? Perhaps the patently unrealistic character of these high rates for the whole of China in 1954 and 1955 is sufficient to challenge their validity.

The conclusions seem fairly obvious. Lacking trained and reliable personnel and at all times under pressure to reflect the current political line, the State Statistical Bureau in Peking has been unable to establish a system that would produce reliable population figures. Using an entirely different approach, Taeuber and Wang (1960) reached essentially the same conclusion:

> There has never been either a field enumeration or a controlled registration of the population of China. There has never been a record or reporting system that yielded accurate data on births, deaths, and migration in all China. Hence there can be no objective knowledge of the size of the population of China and its rate of change over time. China remains "the country without statistics."

The State Statistical Bureau did, however, supply figures to support Communist China's internal policies and to present the desired image to the outside world. In other words, statistical failures have not prevented an extensive use of political arithmetic.

The reason that population data have not been published since 1957 is that the regime lost count of the numbers of people inhabiting the Chinese mainland. It is difficult to believe that the present registration system will supply the regime with anything more than a rough approximation. A full-fledged scientific census in Communist China would be almost as difficult now as it was 10, 20, or 100 years ago, and it seems safe to predict that for many decades to come China's population will continue to be an enigma and a subject for academic guessing games.

References

AIRD, JOHN S. 1961. *The Size, Composition, and Growth of the Population of Mainland China.* U. S. Bureau of the Census, International Population Statistics Reports, Series P-90, No. 15. Washington, D. C.: U. S. Government Printing Office.

LI CHOH-MING. 1962. *The Statistical System of China.* Berkeley: University of California Press.

[14] *T'ung-chi Kung-Tso* [Statistical Work], No. 12, 1957.
[15] *Jen-min Pao-chien* [People's Health], Vol. 1, No. 5, 1959.

TAEUBER, IRENE B., and NAI-CHI WANG. 1960. "Questions on Population Growth in China," in Milbank Memorial Fund, *Proceedings of the 36th Annual Conference.* New York.

Among the countries that counted their populations in 1970, two of the most important were the Soviet Union and the United States, the subjects of the next two articles. With these reports, it is possible to compare the techniques of enumeration, preliminary results of the count, and implications for long-term trends.

Population Trends, Soviet Union (1913–70) and
United States (1910–70)

	SOVIET UNION			UNITED STATES		
DATE	POPULA-TION WITHIN PRES-ENT BORDERS (MIL-LIONS)	AVERAGE ANNUAL INCREASE DURING PRE-CEDING PERIOD (PER-CENT)	PER-CENT URBAN	CENSUS DATE	RESI-DENT POPULA-TION (MIL-LIONS)	AVERAGE ANNUAL INCREASE DURING PRE-CEDING PERIOD (PER-CENT)	PERCENT URBAN
1913 [a]	159.2		18	1910	92.0		45.7
1940 [a]	194.1	0.8	33	1940	131.7	1.4	56.5
1959	208.8	0.4	48	1960	178.5	1.8	69.9 [c]
1970 [b]	241.7	1.4	56	1970 [b]	204.8	1.4	73.5 [c]

[a] Estimate.   [b] Preliminary.   [c] Current definition.

Some over-all contrasts are evident from the accompanying table. During the eleven intercensal years, the rural population of the Soviet Union underwent an estimated natural increase of more than 18 million, but the enumerated rural population declined by 3 million. In contrast, the urban population grew by about 36 million, of which 14.6 million was due to natural increase, 5 million to the reclassification of previously rural districts, and the balance to rural-urban migration (Pravda, August 22, 1970). That this shift is regarded as a major social problem is indicated by not only the extra questions in the census but numerous articles in the Soviet press. An editorial denounced the low rate of urban construction (Pravda, February 24, 1970); an article noted that cities were encroaching on rich agricultural land in the Ukraine (Pravda, March 2, 1970). In 1964, 430 questionnaires had been completed by recent graduates from five rural schools in Smolensk

Province on why young people want to leave the village; and a follow-up in 1970 traced most of the original respondents and compared them with current graduates from the same district. In 1964 only 20 percent, and in 1970 still only 22 percent, wanted either to work in the village or to continue their studies in an agricultural school (Izvestia, July 12, 1970).

In the United States, on the contrary, the first results of the 1970 census showed that the period of rapid urbanization had passed. The major movement was to the suburbs, which in sum constituted the largest component of America's population, about 71 million out of the total of about 205 million. This trend will affect, in ways that are not always entirely clear, the country's economy, politics, and social structure.

Murray Feshbach, author of the paper on the Soviet census, is chief of the USSR/East Europe Branch, Foreign Demographic Analysis Division, of the U. S. Bureau of the Census. He has undergraduate and master's degrees in history and is a candidate for a doctorate in economics at the American University. His special interest is Soviet labor statistics, on which he has written two monographs and a number of articles.

OBSERVATIONS ON THE SOVIET CENSUS

MURRAY FESHBACH

Climaxing four years of advance preparation and publicity, a nationwide census was taken in the Soviet Union during the week of January 15–22, 1970. The primary purpose of the census was to collect the data necessary to make a detailed assessment of the population and manpower resources of the USSR—information that is perhaps especially crucial in a country whose economic system is based on central planning. But as in other countries, census data can also yield a wide range of other information on the state of the nation. While the results of the Soviet census will only become known at scheduled intervals over a three-year period, a number of preliminary insights can be gained from an examination of how the census was conducted, what questions were asked, and what kinds of studies are planned through correlations of the data collected. This paper is intended to provide some brief background to help assess the significance of forthcoming census reports as they become available.

For the first time in the Soviet experience, the 1970 count marks an intercensal interval not characterized by major losses of life from either internal or external factors. Soviet history has witnessed one demographic

SOURCE: Reprinted from *Problems of Communism*, 19 (May–June 1970), 58–64, with the author's permission. Unless otherwise stated, all information on the Soviet census in this article is from four sources: Podiachikh 1969, 1970; USSR 1969a, 1969b. For additional details, see also Leedy 1969.

catastrophe after another. Dating from the last year of peace in Tsarist Russia (and counting only territories that initially came under Soviet rule), the combined devastation of the First World War, the revolution, the civil war, foreign intervention, famine, and epidemics reduced the 1914 population of 142.4 million to 136.1 million by the beginning of 1923—a net loss of 6.3 million (Lorimer 1946: 30). In the 1930s collectivization cost an estimated 5 million lives; the purges and labor camps cost untold millions more (*ibid.*: 133–34; also see Conquest 1968: 365, 525–35). Then came the Second World War, in which Soviet male military losses alone have been calculated at 15 million—almost 3 million more than the entire strength of the United States armed forces at their peak level of 12.1 million in 1945 (Brackett 1962: 510; U. S. Bureau of the Census 1968: 257). Had the 1917 population on what is now Soviet territory increased at the rate of 2 percent a year, which was then the normal rate for a rural country, there would have been 325 million Soviet citizens by 1950; instead there were 178.5 million—representing a real increase of only 15.5 million persons over the 33-year period, or a deficit of some 147 million lives (USSR 1963: 7–8).

This history has had a demonstrable effect on the timing and utilization of past Soviet censuses, more than once creating a conflict between the regime's urge to conceal demographic trends and its need to collect and disseminate reliable data on which to base economic planning. The five previous censuses in Soviet history were conducted at irregular intervals, and for specific purposes. The first, in 1920, was to make a count in the wake of the enormous disruptions of the revolutionary years. The second, in 1926, was intended to supply vital information for the preparation of the first five-year plan (1928–32). The third, in 1937, was supposed to show the results of the first two five-year plans and also to measure the impact of collectivization. However, Stalin repudiated this census and ordered that its findings be discarded, presumably because of what they implied about the millions of Soviet citizens who had been lost during the collectivization drive and who were still disappearing in the purges. The fourth census, in 1939, was designed to produce a more favorable accounting of the population, and at the same time to take stock as mobilization got under way on the eve of Soviet involvement in the Second World War. Twenty years went by before the next census. Given Stalin's reaction in 1937, it seems fair to surmise that he had no wish to engage in a postwar tally that would have revealed the war's devastating effects on the Soviet population. The fifth census was finally held in 1959, in time to be used as the basis for preparing the annual plans of the subsequent seven-year plan (1959–65).

ADMINISTRATION OF THE 1970 CENSUS

Originally scheduled for January 1969, the most recent census was timed to cover a convenient ten-year interval since the 1959 census and also to provide data in the preparation of the 1971–75 plan. In 1967, however, the Soviet regime suddenly announced that the census would be postponed for one year, without offering any explanation for the delay (*Izvestia*, April 9, 1967). Later, Soviet sources came up with at least two reasonable—and also face-saving—explanations for waiting until 1970: that the United Nations had advocated a universal practice of holding decennial censuses at the start of each decade and that the hundredth anniversary of Lenin's birth, 1970, would make a fitting date for this part of the nation's stock taking. Much evidence suggested incomplete preparations—in particular a lack of data-processing equipment—were at least partly responsible for the delay. In any event, the postponement meant that Gosplan (*Gosudarstvennyi planovyi komitet*—the State Planning Committee) was denied the fully processed data from the census in time to apply them in over-all planning decisions for 1971–75.

The census count eventually taken in the third week of January 1970 was intended to record the status of the population at the hour of midnight between January 14 and January 15. (In regions of the Far North and other areas where access would have been difficult in the middle of winter, an enumeration of the population was made in the fall of 1969.) Well in advance, it was announced that a vast army of census takers would be needed in addition to the regular staff of the Central Statistical Administration (*Tsentralnoe statisticheskoe upravlenie*—hereafter TsSU); about 670,000 personnel were to be recruited, including 540,000 enumerators, about 100,000 instructors, over 26,000 census "chiefs" and assistants at the district level, and about 4,000 assistants, added to the full-time statistical inspectors at the county (*raion*) level (USSR 1969b: 197). The number of enumerators—that is, of those responsible for the initial collection of data—was calculated to give each of them an average workload of 675 persons in urban areas and 575 persons in rural areas. The corps of temporary census workers included schoolteachers, instructors and students of higher and specialized secondary educational institutions, and employees of enterprises, institutions, and collective and state farms. Employed persons received their regular salaries during the time they worked on the census, ranging from 17 days for enumerators to three and a half months for the assistants to the state statistical inspectors (Kolpakov 1969: 47). In addition, all census workers were paid an "enumeration bonus," presumably prorated on the basis of their time and the type of work they performed.

Under the procedures adopted for the 1970 census, the enumerators visited all dwelling units twice, and half of them a third time. During the days January 11–14, each enumerator was required to make a preliminary visit to all households in his assigned district in order (1) to establish the address and location of each household, the name of its head, and the number of persons in it; (2) to arrange an appointment during the week of the official census (January 15–22); and (3) to leave census forms to be filled out if, in an exceptional case, he concluded that members of the household were capable of answering the queries. On his second visit, the enumerator checked over, helped complete, and collected forms for every household. Finally, in the week following the census, the enumerator and his immediate superior, or "instructor," revisited half the households in his district to doublecheck the accuracy of the information.

The basic census form delivered to all households contained eleven questions. In addition, seven supplementary questions were posed to every fourth household. This was the first time sampling had been permitted in a Soviet census. Interestingly, much of the original theoretical work on sampling was performed by Russians, but it was applied in other countries long before its wide use was allowed in the USSR. For many years the Soviet authorities clung to a preference for direct statistical reporting by all economic units. Their reluctance to use sampling retarded the development of analytical procedures, since data collected by total coverage had to be much simpler and less detailed than those possible in a sample.

Two special questionnaires were also distributed on a selective basis. The first was left to be completed in any case where the enumerator discovered a person in the so-called "able-bodied" age group (males 16 to 59 and females 16 to 54 years of age) who did not work in an enterprise, in a public institution, on a state farm or in the public sector of a collective farm, or as a full-time student—in other words, a person who worked solely in a household or (with respect to the rural population) only in the private sector of agriculture. The other special questionnaire was distributed in 34 cities with estimated populations of 500,000 or more and in their surrounding *raions;* its purpose was to determine commuting patterns on the part of workers, employees, and students of higher and specialized secondary schools.

QUESTIONS IN THE SCHEDULE

The potential significance of the data collected in the census can best be shown by reviewing what questions were asked and then discussing how the information is to be used.

The eleven basic questions of the census schedule completed for the entire population covered the following items:

1. Relationship of each individual to the head of the household.

2. In the case of permanent residents who were temporarily absent: (a) the reason for the absence; (b) the length of time absent from the permanent residence.

3. In the case of temporary residents: (a) the place of permanent (usual) residence; (b) the length of time absent from the permanent residence.

4. Sex.

5. Age (as of last birthday).

6. Marital status at the present time.

7. Nationality.

8. Native language (and any other language spoken by Soviet peoples in which the person is fluent).

9. Level of education attained: higher; incomplete higher; specialized secondary; general secondary; incomplete secondary; primary; less than primary.

10. In the case of students, the type of course and educational institution in which the person was studying: higher; specialized secondary; general secondary; vocational or technical; other.

11. Source of livelihood or means of existence: work in an enterprise or other institution; work on a collective farm; work in one's own "economy" or *khoziaistvo* (that is, as an individual peasant outside the system of collective or state farms or as an independent artisan producing salable goods at home—the 1959 census had listed only 266,000 such persons, a minuscule portion of the population); work for other individuals, for example, as a maid or chauffeur; work in private subsidiary agriculture (that is, as a family member on a collective or state farm solely engaged in production on the household's small private plot); pension; stipend; dependent status; other source.

The 25-percent sample of the population was asked the following seven additional questions:

12. Place of work: name of enterprise, institution, or collective farm, or place where the respondent engaged in his own "economy."

13. Occupation at this place of work (position or work performed); in the case of pensioners, previous basic occupation.

14. In the case of any person who worked only part of the year in 1969, (a) whether the job was permanent, seasonal, or temporary; (b) number of months he worked.

15. Classification by socio-economic group: wage earner (*rabochii*, or blue-collar worker); salaried employee (*sluzhashchii*, or white-collar worker); collective farmer; craftsman; wage earner who is also a member of a collective farm; salaried employee who is also a member of a collective farm; individual peasant; minister or church official.

16. Length of time in years and months that the person has resided continuously in the town, city, or other local geographic unit.

17. In the case of a person with less than two years' local residence, former permanent residence (including by name the republic, *oblast, raion,* and city or city-type settlement or rural administrative unit).

18. Reason for changing place of residence: enrollment in school at a new location; graduation from school; "social mobilization"—that is, a voluntary change of job and residence undertaken with approval, as expressed by a Party or Komsomol travel pass; organized recruitment; work transfer made

for the government's convenience; or personal motives, covering unplanned and unofficial moves.

The first six of these items are basic demographic questions designed to determine general population characteristics and to give information (in combination with responses to other questions) on the number and size of families as categorized according to particular urban and rural areas, socioeconomic groups, nationalities, and so on. The data on age and sex can be used to project the future population and labor resources of the country, as well as to determine the potential demand for a great variety of goods, services, and such public facilities as child-care institutions and schools.

The responses to the two questions on nationality and language (7 and 8) are to be analyzed on the basis of a list of 122 nationalities in the USSR. The nationality data will be coordinated with the data on language, area of residence (at the *raion* level), age, marital status, level of education, source of livelihood, occupation and economic sector in which the respondent works, the socio-economic group to which he belongs, and the type and size of the family unit. A special study will be made of families of mixed nationality. Responses indicating a residence of less than two years will also be analyzed in terms of the respondent's place of origin (USSR 1969b: 638, 643, 649, 655, 657–58, 661, 666).

Perhaps the greatest significance of the nationality data extracted from the 1970 census will be what they reveal about the relative size of the Great Russians and thus about fertility differentials in various areas of the Soviet Union. In this respect, the most important problem confronting the Soviet regime is that for some years now the largely Muslim population in Central Asia has been growing faster than the Great Russian population. According to 1968 figures, the crude birth rate was about 2.5 times greater in Central Asia than in the Russian Republic (for example, the rate was 37.3 per 1,000 in the Tadzhik SSR as opposed to 14.2 in the RSFSR). Paralleling this trend, and largely as a result of it, the proportion of Great Russians in the total population of the USSR has been on the decline over the past decade. The first results of the Soviet census gave a preliminary view of how these differential birth rates and migration affected the various republics. The total population of the country had increased from 208,827,000 in 1959 to 241,-748,000 in 1970, or by 16 percent. However, the difference between the Great Russian center and the Soviet Asian periphery was by a ratio of approximately one to four: the intercensal increase was by 11 percent in the Russian Republic, 45 percent in Uzbekistan, 40 percent in Kazakhstan, 42 percent in Kirgizia, 46 percent in Tadzhikistan, and 42 percent in Turkmenistan (*Izvestia*, April 19, 1970). If these trends continue, the Great Russians will at one point no longer constitute a majority of the national population. When I talked with Soviet demographers in Moscow and Kiev in September 1969, they emphatically denied the existence of this problem, but they obviously did not want to pursue the subject. An early indication of Soviet concern may possibly be found in the fact that the first postwar demographic research unit established in the USSR was located not in Moscow but in the Central Asian city of Tashkent.

So far, the regime's response to this problem has been rooted in the hope that gradual urbanization and modernization in the Central Asian republics would decrease their birth rate. If an appreciable slowdown is not achieved soon, the regime will be confronted with some difficult decisions. If the central government were to encourage birth control in Central Asia, it would risk both domestic and international repercussions, since such a policy would arouse resentment not only in the areas affected but in other countries with a similar culture. Therefore such an approach will probably be avoided if at all possible. As an alternative, Moscow might bring strong pressures on the republic governments to adopt and enforce their own birth-control programs. On the other hand, an argument could be made against the long-range wisdom of discouraging population growth in Soviet Central Asia: it shares a long border with China, and its peoples are already greatly outnumbered by their Chinese neighbors. Since there is nothing Moscow can do that will significantly alter the over-all Soviet-Chinese population ratio (which can currently be estimated at 242 to 833 million), this argument may not carry too much weight. The regime could, however, step up its efforts to populate the area through internal migration. In any event, all of these considerations underscore the importance of the nationality data collected in the census, since the trends they reveal may be crucial in shaping policy decisions.

Questions 9 and 10 will yield important data on the pattern and level of education in the Soviet Union. In particular, they will provide information with which to measure the progress made toward achieving the proclaimed goal of ten years of schooling for all citizens. It is interesting to note that a question posed in 1959 on literacy was omitted from the 1970 schedule. The rates tabulated on the basis of this question were somewhat loaded in that they pertained only to the portion of the population aged 9 to 49; obviously they would have been lower if those over 50 had been included. Nonetheless, these rates registered enormous progress toward the eradication of illiteracy and—given the fact that many of the elderly of 1959 would now be dead— the omission of this question in 1970 seems quite reasonable.

Item 11, the last in the basic schedule, was the first question dealing directly with economic and occupational characteristics. It was mainly designed as the basis for a preliminary statistical allocation of the population into economically active and inactive categories. In subsequent analyses many more details on Soviet economic life will be garnered from the responses to Questions 12 through 15, as well as from the special questionnaire related to persons employed in households and in private subsidiary agriculture.

Of the questions put to the sample, Items 12 and 13 will provide data for an analysis of how the labor force is distributed among the different branches of the national economy and—within these branches—among 70 separate kinds of production units or institutions. The labor force will also be classified by 49 major occupational groups and some 325 specific occupations (including 120 types of employment that exist across the board in all the branches of the national economy). The information solicited in Question 13 on the former occupation of pensioners will probably be analyzed with age data to help determine potential labor reserves.

The 14th question is new and important. In the first place, it will reveal details about levels of employment in seasonal industry. It will also provide the information necessary to explain the discrepancy between the census count of the *total* number of persons in the labor force (including full-time and temporary jobholders) and the TsSU's annual compilation of the *average* number of persons employed, a figure which is adjusted downward to account for temporary jobholders and seasonal employment (cf. Feshbach 1962). These data are also the first statistics available in many years which could be used, if the authorities so choose, to examine unemployment in the Soviet Union. Since 1930, when the Stalin regime suddenly decreed an end to the registration of unemployment, the official attitude has been that none existed. Thus, despite the obvious presence of frictional, structural, and technological unemployment (cf. Feshbach 1966), studies of the phenomenon have been taboo. It would be very interesting to know whether any such study is contemplated; none has been announced.

Question 15 will supply the TsSU with data on the distribution of the population according to socio-economic category, again to be correlated with data on distribution according to branch of the economy, occupation, level of education, geographical location, and so forth.

With respect to those employed solely in private agriculture (90 percent of whom were women at the time of the 1959 census), the data obtained from Question 15 will be supplemented by the information provided in the special questionnaire. Thus, it will be possible to analyze this population group in terms of age, education, source of livelihood, former occupation, number of years since the last job held, number and age of children under 16, and conditions under which work in the socialized economy would become feasible—again in order to analyze potential labor reserves. All but one of these tabulations are being undertaken for the first time.

Also new are the projected studies of migration to be based on answers to Questions 16 through 18. These questions are important as a means of determining sources of labor supply and the rate of labor turnover. Question 16 will permit analysts to determine the total number, the proportion by nationality (in combination with Question 7), and the year that migrants arrived in a given area. The size of migration flows between different republics, *oblasts*, economic regions, cities, and rural areas will be calculated on the basis of Item 17. Finally, the reasons for migration—as given in Question 18—will be analyzed, probably in the main for the light they can shed on labor incentives. These migration data are crucially related to the economic problem of promoting development in the labor-deficit areas beyond the Urals and the strategic necessity of expanding settlement along the Sino-Soviet border.

UTILITY OF THE 1970 CENSUS

The 11-year interval since the last census may create methodological problems in the use and interpretation of published data. While the TsSU has many unreleased data by single year of age, much of the 1959 material available to the public was tabulated only on the basis of 5-year age intervals. Whatever the format and detail of the materials published from the 1970 census, the opportunity has been lost for a simple comparison of the 5-year age groups of 1959 with exactly the same groups a decade later.

A number of important questions are ignored in the census. For example, nowhere was a question posed on income or earnings, or on the critical question of Soviet housing conditions and facilities. Nor was any effort made to collect fertility data for use in population projections. Omissions like these mark the Soviet census as a relatively limited instrument of inquiry as compared—for instance—to the U. S. census of 1970. There are many other differences in the way censuses are conducted and their results are used in the two countries. As one indication, the published results of the Soviet Union's 1959 census filled only 2,830 pages in all, those of the United States 1960 census 138,000 pages. It has been reported that the TsSU prepared hundreds of additional collections of data for use by particular internal institutions, but not for release to the public. When I asked P. G. Podiachikh, the head of the census-taking administration of TsSU, about the possibility of obtaining a full set of the 1959 census volumes, he made it clear that they were not available. There would have been insufficient demand, he said, to cover the costs of printing all census data for public consumption.

Whatever its shortcomings, the 1970 census represents the first thorough-going effort to collect Soviet population data since 1926, and it ought to produce some fascinating results. It is more sophisticated than past Soviet censuses in that sampling has been used for the first time, and a wide range of new data has been projected for tabulation. The following list summarizes the new tables that have been promised:

1. Population by nationality, analyzed with data on source of livelihood.

2. Characteristics of the family, as determined by number of children, total number in the family, social group, nationality, level of education of the parents, and other factors.

3. Number of persons in the able-bodied ages engaged in household or private agricultural activities, tabulated in combinations of level of education and age, source of livelihood and age, former occupation and number of years since employed, former occupation and age, and conditions under which work in the socialized economy would become feasible.

4. Number of pensioners and their former occupation.

5. Number of persons who worked an incomplete year in 1969.

6. Length of residence in a given place, by age and social group.

7. Number of persons residing in a given place less than two years, by sex, former place of residence (republic and *oblast*), nationality, and age.

8. Reasons for changing place of residence.

9. Reasons for absence from permanent place of residence.

10. Commuting time between home and place of work or study for urban workers, employees, and students.

Needless to say, an enormous amount of work is involved in preparing the whole range of standard census data as well as all these new tabulations. The TsSU plans to process the census data in several stages, reflecting a logical order of priority (Kolpakov 1969: 57). Preliminary figures have been announced, giving the population count for the USSR as a whole and for the various republics, *oblasts, krais,* and a number of cities. By July 30, 1970, data from the special questionnaire on persons working in households and private agriculture were supposed to be prepared. By the end of 1970, population statistics were to be correlated with data on age, sex, nationality, native language, educational attainment and enrollment, family composition, and source of livelihood. The rest of the tabulation program is to be carried out with respect to all 8,889 administrative units of the USSR (down to and including the *raion* level) during 1971 and 1972. The publication of final results in sixteen volumes is supposed to be completed in the first half of 1973; present plans are for eight subject volumes.

Census taking, a serious business in all countries, is of special significance in a country that relies on economic planning. For the Soviet authorities, the 1970 census will establish basic parameters with respect to population characteristics and labor resources that can help in shaping future plans. For outside observers, the census results will be a source of important knowledge about the social and economic conditions prevailing in the Soviet Union.

References

BRACKETT, JAMES W. 1962. "Demographic Trends and Population Policy in the Soviet Union," in Joint Economic Committee of the U. S. Congress, *Dimensions of Soviet Economic Power.* Washington, D. C.: U. S. Government Printing Office.

CONQUEST, ROBERT. 1968. *The Great Terror.* London: Macmillan.

FESHBACH, MURRAY. 1962. *The Soviet Statistical System: Labor Force Record-keeping and Reporting since 1957.* U. S. Bureau of the Census, International

Population Statistics Reports, Series P-90, No. 17. Washington, D. C.: U. S. Government Printing Office.

———. 1966. "Manpower in the USSR: A Survey of Recent Trends and Prospects," in Joint Economic Committee of the U. S. Congress, *New Directions in the Soviet Economy*, Part III. Washington, D. C.: U. S. Government Printing Office.

KOLPAKOV, B. T. 1969. *Vsesoiuznaia perepis naseleniia 1970 goda* [All-Union Census of Population, 1970]. Moscow.

LEEDY, FREDERICK A. 1969. "The 1970 Soviet Census of Population: Content, Organization, and Processing," in American Statistical Association, *Proceedings of the Social Statistics Section, 1969*, Washington, D. C., pp. 470–473.

LORIMER, FRANK. 1946. *The Population of the Soviet Union: History and Prospects*. Geneva: League of Nations.

PODIACHIKH, P. G. 1969. "On the Methodological and Organizational Questions of the 1970 All-Union Census of Population," in Central Statistical Administration of the USSR, *Vsesoiuznoe soveshchanie statistikov, 22–26 aprelia 1968 g., stenograficheskii otchet* [All-Union Conference of Statisticians, April 22–26, 1968, Stenographic Report]. Moscow: Statistika, pp. 173–214, 616–689.

———. 1970. "The Program of Processing the Results of the 1970 All-Union Census of Population," *Vestnik Statistiki*, No. 2, 23–33.

USSR. CENTRAL STATISTICAL ADMINISTRATION. 1963. *Narodnoe khoziaistvo SSSR v 1962 godu, statisticheskii yezhegodnik* [The National Economy of the USSR in 1962, A Statistical Yearbook]. Moscow: Statistika.

———. ———. 1969a. *Vsesoiuznaia perepis naseleniia—vsenarodnoe delo* [All-Union Census of Population—A National Matter]. Moscow: Statistika.

———. ———. 1969b. *Vsesoiuznoe soveshchanie statistikov, 22–26 aprelia 1968 g., stenograficheskii otchet* [All-Union Conference of Statisticians, April 22–26, 1968, Stenographic Report]. Moscow: Statistika, pp. 616–689.

U. S. BUREAU OF THE CENSUS. 1968. *Statistical Abstract of the United States, 1968*, 89th ed. Washington, D. C.: U. S. Government Printing Office.

The 1970 census in the United States was subjected to more criticism— and more irresponsible criticism—than any prior count (cf. Petersen 1972). The issues that made headlines were the alleged invasion of privacy, but the actual changes were the continuing professional effort to collect data of higher quality and greater use to the nation, with even less of a bother to the enumerated population than previously. Some of the recent work toward these ends is described in the following paper.

Joseph Waksberg, an employee of the U. S. Census Bureau since 1940, has been chief of its Statistical Methods Division since 1963. In this post, he is responsible for setting and appraising sampling methods, survey procedures, and research conducted to improve the Bureau's methodology. He is author or co-author of a number of technical reports issued by the Bureau, and of journal articles on various aspects of population statistics.

Leon Pritzker, the co-author of this paper, is presently director of the marketing information services group of Anheuser-Busch, Inc. Until 1967 he was also an employee of the U. S. Census Bureau, acting in his last post as chief of the Response Research Branch, Statistical Research Division.

CHANGES IN CENSUS METHODS

Joseph Waksberg and Leon Pritzker

During the last thirty years or so, the U. S. Census Bureau has instituted substantial changes in the methods of enumeration, the application of survey methods to new subject-matter areas, and an extensive program of research and development. Most of the changes in data collection developed from intensive work on the theory and practical applications of finite-population sampling. Sampling theory provided a philosophy, a set of criteria applicable to many problems of survey and census methodology, models, and techniques. All of this has had a profound influence on current methods of census taking.

The sampling philosophy and criteria first produced methods of optimizing sample designs. Later this approach was generalized, leading to attempts to optimize survey designs in a much broader context, and thus to a profound change in attitudes regarding both the role of sampling and the relation of sampling errors to other errors in the census. Starting in 1940 and with increasing emphasis in subsequent censuses, the entire range of activities was examined to determine logically the sources of errors or other inaccuracies in the census in order to minimize, given a total budget, the impact of all errors combined.

Before 1940, the emphasis had been to produce the most accurate census possible, with "accuracy" more or less limited to data processing. Inordinate amounts of money and effort were spent to reduce clerical tabulation errors, for these were the ones whose impact could most easily be seen. Starting with the 1940 census, the Bureau began to question whether an improvement in accuracy was worth the additional cost. Balancing the costs of different levels of accuracy against those of wrong decisions resulting from errors in statistics imitated the type of thinking fundamental to modern sampling. Over the same period knowledge grew on how data-processing errors are related to other sources of inaccuracy in the censuses, and thus on how to realize a methodology that minimized the total effect of all sources of error.

From new developments in sampling theory and methods, new research

SOURCE: Adapted and abridged from the *Journal of the American Statistical Association*, **64** (1969), 1141–49, with permission of the authors and the journal.

was undertaken to investigate methodological problems in census taking. The fact that a small, well designed, and well administered sample can yield more accurate measurements than one on a much larger scale suggested the use of the former as a check on the latter. In 1937, a sample survey was first used to evaluate a complete registration of the unemployed. Systematic applications to censuses started with the 1945 Census of Agriculture and continued with the 1947 Census of Manufactures and the 1948 Census of Business. The scope of such research was considerably expanded for the 1950 Census of Population, Housing, and Agriculture; and in more recent censuses studies have been continued on approximately the same scale.

Traditionally, census taking has been equated with counting. For example, the accuracy of the number of establishments was a dominant factor in the censuses of industry and trade conducted by the Bureau of the Census. Subsequent research showed, however, that too high a price was paid for unneeded accuracy on that small proportion of farms and business firms that required excessive resources for counting, that were economically insignificant, or that in many cases perhaps should not even have been defined as businesses. The most important goal of such economic censuses is how to obtain accurate measures of economic aggregates as industrial production, retail sales, agricultural production, and the like. Following this changed view, a canvass is made not of a presumably complete list of establishments but of a sample. The Census of Agriculture is the latest to incorporate this new methodology; until recently it was regarded as essentially a demographic census, in which the counts of farms and of farmers, though their accuracy was admittedly limited, were to be given high priority.

A fundamental goal of a demographic census, on the other hand, is still an accurate count. Much of the census history of the past generation entailed the recognition of how inaccurate enumerations had been, and how difficult it is to count the entire population.

Using an analysis of variance and measurements of the components involved, one can produce methods for assessing nonsampling error. During the last fifteen years, models have been established to classify and evaluate errors in censuses and thus to provide the inputs needed to minimize the total mean-square error of census statistics.

One classification of nonsampling errors is between the enumerator's and the respondent's (and communication between the two). The lack of accuracy in many important statistics was largely due either to enumerators' systematic errors or the respondents' ignorance or unwillingness to reply. For statistics on small areas, each covered by only a few enumerators or in some cases only one, a major source of error may be that these individuals introduce idiosyncratic but consistent errors into the process. One of the most important achievements has been to develop models in which these individual biases are viewed as between-enumerator variances and thus much more measurable.

The primary purpose of a census is to produce small-area statistics. For the nation as a whole and even for its large subdivisions, complete censuses are unnecessary. On most subjects sample surveys of such areas can produce data at least as accurate and in most cases more so. The purpose of many of the procedures recently introduced has been to reduce the enumerator's influence on the final results. This reform has affected both the coverage and the content of the censuses.

Respondents' errors can be classified between those that appear to be random and those that appear to be systematic and biasing. Generally random response errors of individuals have only a minor over-all effect on census statistics, although such errors may be more significant in measuring relations, especially among dependent variables. Until now, the major effort has been to control and reduce systematic errors and in demographic censuses to improve coverage by better selection, training, and control of interviewers.

DEMOGRAPHIC CENSUSES

The 1930 Population and Housing Census can be viewed as the last of the old style. Changes in methodology made since then have often resulted from the research and evaluation programs, as can be seen from a list of the major developments:

Sampling. The 1940 census was the first in which sampling was used to collect data and prepare some of the tabulations. In 1950 its use was extended, but such items as labor force, occupation and industry, citizenship, and place of birth were retained on a 100-percent basis, because it was believed both that these items required the great accuracy attainable only from the whole population, and that dependence on sampling for traditional census items should await additional experience. In the 1960 census the restrictions on the use of sampling were almost completely removed: except for items virtually required to define the population and housing items needed for block statistics, all were collected on a sample basis. The same policy was followed in 1970.

Three factors extended the use of sampling: (1) The 1950 evaluation program—in particular the match of figures from the census and Current Population Surveys and the several studies of variance in responses—indicated that, for most census statistics of a census tract or larger area, a moderate sampling error would affect the total mean-square error only slightly. In other words, since for most items errors based on simple response or enumerator variance and biases were already fairly large, a sampling error would not reduce the quality even in small areas. (2) With the use of sampling, data of essentially equivalent accuracy could be collected at lower costs and with a shorter time between collection and publication of results. The economies made it possible both to reduce the budget and to improve field methods and controls in order to improve the quality of the data collected. (3) The sampling procedures worked reasonably well. Biases in sample selection were not great enough seriously to affect most uses of the data.

Self-enumeration. Through 1950, an enumerator read the census questions to one respondent in each household and recorded the replies. In 1960, many householders were given forms to fill out at their leisure; the enumerator examined the completed questionnaire and asked only those questions omitted by the respondent. Only when householders had neglected to fill out the questionnaire at all did the enumerator conduct a complete interview. A similar self-enumeration was used for the 1970 census.

The heavy reliance on self-enumeration grew out of the studies of variance among enumerators in 1950 and 1960 and some experimental procedures in preparing and implementing the 1950 census. According to these analyses, the behavior of enumerators largely contributed to the variance in certain characteristics for small areas, for most enumerators introduce certain types of more or less consistent errors. The findings of the 1960 study confirmed the expectation that indeed self-enumeration sharply reduced both enumerators' errors and, in all likelihood, bias and random-response variance.

Coverage Improved through Mailing Lists. The 1960 evaluation also indicated that the enumerators generally could not provide an adequate coverage of residences. Experiments suggested that mail carriers knew the households on their routes well enough to improve previously compiled lists. This and an improved self-enumeration system led to the mail-out, mail-back census used in about 60 percent of the country in 1970. A mailing list developed partly from existing sources and partly by census enumerators was checked and updated by the post office. Questionnaires were mailed to this corrected list with a request that they be filled in and mailed to a census district office, where the schedules were edited by a field staff. When items were omitted, enumerators sought the missing information, if possible, by telephone. Personal visits were made to addresses from which no replies came.

The advantages of this procedure include: extension of self-enumeration, greater flexibility and accuracy in geographical coding, a smaller number of enumerators needed, the possibility of concentrating on difficult areas, the elimination of the bias that is possible when the enumerators select a sample.

That perhaps 3 percent of the population was missed in the 1960 census (and somewhat higher proportions in earlier censuses) is now well known. Typically this undercount has been concentrated in certain population groups and probably in certain geographic areas, such as inner-city poverty sections of the large metropolitan areas. An evaluation of the coverage indicated that although the mail system would help improve it generally, it would not resolve these particular difficulties. Consequently, new procedures were developed for 1970: confidence of the community was sought by working with neighborhood groups; the enumerators assigned to such areas were more intensively trained and closely supervised; and a special check was made of those who moved during the census period.

Geographic Detail.   A striking change introduced in 1970 was the identification of "block faces" (street segments within blocks), which made it possible to produce statistics for many more small areas than previously. A file was built up containing the beginning and ending house numbers on either side of every block, an odd-even designation for the house-number range, and codes for street name, block number, and geographic coordinates. Since the file is also on computer tape, each address on the list can be automatically coded to its block face and simultaneously assigned to all the larger areas of which the particular block face is a part. Many communities would like to use the address coding guide in a number of ways, apart from exploiting the 1970 census more fully, and copies of the guide were sold at cost.

Electronic Equipment.   A few years after finite-sampling theory began to be used, electronic equipment became available. It has affected census techniques in three different ways:

1. Electronic equipment, most obviously, increased the efficiency of processing data by speeding up the operation, reducing costs, and increasing accuracy. Thus, most of the laborious editing and coding once performed by clerks is now done by computers. Slow and, by modern standards, inefficient tabulating machines have been replaced by the computer; and slow, costly, and inaccurate key punching has been largely replaced by electronic reading devices.

2. Two more sophisticated methods of data processing possible only with a computer have been introduced. In the statistical estimation of both samples of censuses and sample surveys, complex but improved procedures became practical with the advent of computers. The same was true of editing to eliminate inconsistencies or blanks in census entries, classifying responses, and in coding (classification). The use of a computer made it possible to program more elaborate relations and also improve the accuracy of clerical editing and coding.

3. Improved selection of samples is possible both for sampling in the censuses and for post-enumeration surveys, for which the census constitutes a major part of the sampling frame. These techniques were first used with economic surveys, though the indications are that after the 1970 census more extensive demographic applications will be made.

The first commercial electronic computer, Univac I, was developed for the Census Bureau to process some of the 1950 census. By 1960, the processing of the entire enumeration was built around electronic equipment. The computer was used not only for tabulations but also for editing, imputation for nonresponse, and sample estimation. Electronic scanning equipment was developed for the input, in order to eliminate the costly and error-prone key-punching operation. The scanning device is called Fosdic, an acronym for Film Optical Sensing Device for Input to Computers.

This machine can "read" information from a microfilm copy of an appropriately designed and marked schedule and transfer it to magnetic tape for processing by computers.

In 1970 essentially the same system was based on more sophisticated computers and Fosdics. The respondents filled out Fosdic questionnaires directly, rather than the more conventional schedules used in 1960. In 1960, the tables were reproduced by offset printing from computer print-outs—a rapid and inexpensive method but with a final product of rather poor appearance. With a new electronic machine, Linotron, built by a private company for the U. S. Government Printing Office, a cathode-ray photo-typesetting process yields a product equivalent in versatility and quality to fine printing.

Methods of Delivering Data.   Through 1950, the results of the censuses were essentially a set of published volumes. The computer made possible three new methods of delivering data, all of which were utilized in 1960. (1) Some types of summary results were made available on computer tape, as well as in published form. (2) It was easier and cheaper to prepare special tables on request. (3) All of the reported data for a 1-in-1,000 sample of the population were put on tapes, which (after appropriate steps to protect confidentiality) were made available to users at cost, as a base for their own analyses. These innovations were extended in 1970.

Evaluation and Research.   Symbolic of the changes over the past decades is a tacit acceptance that research and development are essential parts of census methodology, to which a reasonable proportion of the total budget should be assigned. Many if not most of the current procedures used in censuses are a direct outgrowth of lessons learned in evaluation and experimental programs. Not all problems have been recognized or solved, and research and development are properly a continual part of censuses.

Reference

PETERSEN, WILLIAM. 1972. "Forbidden Knowledge," in Saad Z. Nagi and Ronald G. Corwin, eds., *Social Contexts of Research*. New York: Wiley.

4 AGE AND SEX

In the history of population theories and doctrines that Nathan Keyfitz reviewed, the reader will recall, the topic was generally the whole population—its relation to the food supply, whether it was at the optimum level, and so on. Most demographic analyses begin, on the contrary, by dividing up the total population into appropriate parts that can be compared for their rates of mortality, fertility, migration, and so on. As in many other disciplines, population theory has developed almost independently, neither much influencing empirical studies nor being much influenced by them.

The categories that any analyst uses depend, apart from what data are available, on which he believes will divide the population into significantly different subunits. Three typical classifications are exemplified in this and the following two chapters—by age and sex, by subnation, and by residence. Of the three, the first is in several respects the most fundamental. Whether families in the lower class have more children or higher death rates is subject to social conditions that can change (and have changed radically); but the relation between age and fecundity, or the difference in death rates specific by age and sex, is rooted in physiology. All cultures assign different roles to males and females, and to children, youth, adults, and the aged. Because of this universal relevance, data on age and sex are included whenever

114

demographic records are gathered and are generally fairly accurate (but see p. 81).

One of the most interesting recent developments concerning age structure pertains to its relation to the decline in mortality. If proportionately fewer die at young ages, more live to older ages and the median age of the population rises—or so one would suppose. That common sense is in this instance not a good guide is the theme of the next paper.

Its author, Ansley J. Coale, is one of the country's most distinguished economist-demographers, professor of economics at Princeton University and director of its Office of Population Research. He has been chairman of the Committee on Social Aspects of Technological Change of the Social Science Research Council (1950–51), president of the Population Association of America (1967–68), and a technical advisor on population to the U. S. Bureau of the Census (1965 to date). Among the ten books he is associated with, the most influential perhaps is one co-authored with Edgar M. Hoover —Population Growth and Economic Development in Low-Income Countries *(Princeton University Press, 1958), which was one of the first significant attempts to measure the economic benefits of reducing the fertility of an underdeveloped country. His several dozen scholarly papers reflect his major interests in formal demography and economic policy.*

HOW A POPULATION AGES OR GROWS YOUNGER

Ansley J. Coale

When we speak of the age of a population we refer to the age of its members, and to be precise we should use the term *age distribution* of a population—how many persons there are at each age—rather than the age of a population. The only way a single age can be given for a group of persons is by using some sort of average. A *young* population, then, is one that contains a large proportion of young persons, and has a low average age, while an *old* population has a high average age and a large proportion of old people.

The ages of various national populations in the world today are very different, and in many countries the present age distribution differs markedly from the past.

The oldest populations are found in Northwestern Europe. Around 1960 in France, England, and Sweden, for example, 12 percent of the population was over 65, and half of the population in these countries was over 33, 36, and 37, respectively. The youngest populations are found in the underdeveloped countries—those that have not incorporated modern industrial technology in their economies—the populations of Asia, Africa, and Latin America. Half of the population of Pakistan was under 18 years, of the Congo under 20 years, and of Brazil under 19 years. The proportion over 65 in Brazil was less than one-fourth that in France. The proportion of children under 15 was twice as great in Pakistan as in England. Paradoxically, the oldest nations—China, India, and Egypt—have very young populations.

The highly industrialized countries all have older populations than the underdeveloped countries, and also older populations than they did fifty to a hundred years ago. Since 1900 the median age rose in England from 24 to 36, in the United States from 23 to 30, in Japan from 23 to 26, and in Russia from 21 to 27. In the underdeveloped countries, however, the age distributions changed only slightly, and they have, if anything, become slightly younger. In Taiwan, for example, the median age declined from 21 to 18 since 1915.

What accounts for these differences and these trends in the age distribution of population? One obvious factor to consider is migration. A famous spa has an old population because old people come there for the cure, and university towns like Princeton have young populations because young people come there to study. But the age distribution of most national populations is not much affected by migration, especially today when almost everywhere international migration is restricted.

Whether a national population is young or old is mainly determined by the number of children women bear. When women bear many children, the population is young; when they bear few, the population is old.

The effect of fertility on the age distribution is clearest when a population continuously subject to high fertility is compared to one continuously subject to low fertility. The high-fertility population has a larger proportion of children relative to adults of parental age as a direct consequence of the greater frequency of births. Moreover, by virtue of high fertility a generation ago, today's parents are numerous relative to *their* parents, and hence the proportion of old people is small. Conversely, the population experiencing a prolonged period of low fertility has few children relative to its current parents, who in turn are not numerous relative to *their* parents. Prolonged high fertility produces a large proportion of children, and a small proportion of the aged—a population with a low average age. On the other hand, prolonged low fertility produces a small proportion of children and a large proportion of the aged—a high average age.

It is the small number of children born per woman that explains the high average age now found in industrialized Western Europe, and the high birth rate of the underdeveloped countries that accounts for their young populations. The increase in average age and the swollen proportion of old people in the industrialized countries are the product of the history of falling birth rates that all such countries have experienced.

Most of us would probably guess that populations have become older because the death rate has been reduced, and hence people live longer on the average. Just what is the role of mortality in determining the age distribution of a population? The answer is surprising: mortality affects the age distribution much less than does fertility, and in the opposite direction from what most of us would think. Prolongation of life by reducing death rates has the perverse effect of making the population somewhat younger. Consider the effect of the reduction in death rates in the United States, where the average duration of life has risen from about 45 years under the mortality conditions of 1900 to about 70 years today. Had the risks of death prevailing in 1900 continued unchanged, and the other variables—rates of immigration, and rates of childbearing per mother—followed the course they actually did, the average age of the population today would be greater than it is: the proportion of children would be less and the proportion of persons over 65 would be greater than they are. The reduction of the death rate has produced, in other words, a younger American population.

These statements seem scarcely credible.

Does not a reduction in the death rate increase the average age at death? Are there not more old people as a result of reduced mortality than there would be with the former high death rates? How then can it be said that a reduction in the death rate makes a population younger?

It is true that as death rates fall, the average age at which people die is increased. But the average age of a population is the average age of living persons, not their average age at death. It is also true, as we all immediately realize, that as death rates fall the number of old persons in a population increases. What we do not so readily realize is that reduced mortality increases the number of *young* persons as well. More persons survive from birth to ages 1, 10, 20, and 40, as well as more living to old age. Because more persons survive to be parents, more births occur.

The reason that the reduced death rates, which prolong man's life, make the population younger is that typical improvements in health and medicine produce the greatest increases in survival among the young rather than the old.

There is one kind of reduction in death rates that would not affect the age distribution of the population at all, that would lead to the same proportion of population at every age as if mortality had not changed. This particular form of reduced mortality is one that increases the chance of surviving one year by a certain amount—say, 0.1 percent—at every age. The result would be one-tenth of a percent more persons at age 1, 5, 10, 60, and 80—at every age—than there would have been had death rates been unaltered. Because there would be 0.1 percent more parents, there would also be 0.1 percent more births. Therefore the next year's population would be 0.1 percent larger than it would otherwise have been, but the proportion of children, of young adults, of the middle-aged, and of the aged would not be altered—there would be 0.1 percent more of each.

Reductions in mortality of this singular sort that would not affect the age of the population at all are not found in actual human experience. However, there has been a tendency for persons at all ages to share some of the increased chances of survival, and the effect of reduced death rates on the age distribution has consequently been small—much smaller than the effect of reduced birth rates, in countries where both fertility and mortality have changed markedly.

As the average duration of life has risen from lower levels to 65 or 70 years, the most conspicuous advances in survival seem always to have occurred in infancy and early childhood. It is for this reason that reduced mortality has had the effect of producing a younger population, although the effect has usually been obscured by the much more powerful force of a falling birth rate that has occurred at the same time. Thus the population of the United States has actually become *older* since 1900, because of falling fertility; but falling mortality (with its tendency to produce a younger population) has prevented it from becoming older still.

Not all increases in length of life result in a younger population. The countries with the greatest average duration of life have by now about exhausted the possibility of increasing survivorship in a way that makes for a younger population. In Sweden today 95 percent survive from birth to age 30, compared to 67 percent in 1870. At best, survival to age 30 in Sweden could approach 100 percent. No important increase in population at younger ages would result. If there are further major gains in the chances of prolonged life in Sweden, they must occur at older ages; and if they occur, they will make the population older.

Every individual inexorably gets older as time passes. How old he gets depends on how long he avoids death. President Eisenhower remarked after his retirement that he was glad to be old, because at his age, if he were not old, he would be dead.

Populations, on the other hand, can get older or younger. They get older primarily as the result of declining fertility, and younger primarily as the result of rising fertility.

The most highly industrialized countries have all experienced a decline of fertility of about 50 percent since their preindustrial phase, and they all have older populations than they used to have. In France and the United States, for example, the number of children each woman bore declined for more than a century, reaching a minimum just before the Second World War. In each country during this period the population became progressively older. In fact, the "aging" of the population continued for a time after fertility had passed its minimum. Between 1800 and 1950 the median age of the French population rose from 25 to 35 years, and in the United States in the same interval the median age increased from 16 to 30. In both countries there has been a substantial recovery in fertility during the past 25 years from the low point reached in the 1930s. This rise in fertility produced the first decrease in median age recorded in the statistics of either nation. Between 1950 and 1960 the median age in France fell from 35 to 33, and in the United States from 30.2 to 29.6.

This reversal in the trend toward an older population in the United States has been accompanied by a more pronounced reversal in the way proportions of children were changing. The long-term decline in fertility in the United States meant that the proportion of children to adults steadily shrank from about .85 children (under 15) per adult (15 and over) in 1800 to .33 per adult in 1940. By 1960 the proportion had rebounded to .45 children per adult. In fact, the increase in the *number* of children in the population between 1950 and 1960—more than 15 million—was greater than the increase between 1900 and 1950.

The abrupt reversal of the long-term trend toward an older population has meant the first increase in the relative burden of child dependency in the history of the United States. The very productive American economy can certainly afford to support this burden, but it has not been painless. The extremely rapid increase in the number of children in the 1950s required the construction of many new schools and the training of many teachers. In some communities, where foresight, willingness to pay increased taxes, or resources were inadequate, schools have been overcrowded and the quality of instruction has suffered.

The countries that have not undergone intensive industrialization have experienced no major changes in fertility, no trends of sustained decline and recovery such as occurred in France and the United States. Rather they have experienced a largely unbroken sequence of high birth rates. There has been in consequence little change in the age composition of underdeveloped areas. All have 40 percent or more under age 15, only 2 to 4 percent over 65, and a median age of 20 years or less.

The age distributions of the industrialized countries on the one hand and of the preindustrial countries on the other are ironically mismatched with what each sort of country seems best equipped to accommodate. In Pakistan or Mexico nearly one person of every two a visitor might encounter would be a child, and only two or three of every hundred would be old (over 65); while in England only one in four would be a child and about one in eight would be old. In the industrialized countries, where the proportion of the aged is so large, the importance of the family in the predominantly urban environment has diminished, and consequently the role of respected old patriarch or matriarch has nearly vanished. The wealthy industrial countries can readily afford to support a sizable component of old people but have not in fact always done so adequately. The aging of their populations has been accompanied by a weakening or a disappearance of the traditional claims of the aged on their descendants for material support and, perhaps more tragically, by a weakening or disappearance of a recognized and accepted position for old people in the family. In the underdeveloped countries, on the other hand, the relatively few old people are accorded traditional respect and whatever economic support their families have to offer, and hence the aged are less subject to special economic and social deprivation.

Because of extremely young age distributions, adults in the impoverished underdeveloped countries must support a disproportionately large dependent-child population—twice as great a burden of dependency per adult in the working ages of 15 to 65 as in typical industrialized countries—a burden these poor countries can scarcely afford. The enormous proportion of children makes it extraordinarily difficult, where incomes are extremely low, to provide adequate shelter, nourishment, and education for the young. Moreover, the preindustrial countries can expect no relief from dependency as a result of the spectacular drop in death rates now occurring. Unless fertility declines, this drop in mortality will only make the populations younger, adding to the already extreme burden of dependent children.

In sum, it is the industrialized countries that, better able to afford a high burden of child dependency, have only half the proportion of children found in underdeveloped areas, and that, having abandoned the institutions giving a meaningful role to the aged, have four times the proportion of the elderly found in preindustrial countries.

In almost all Western countries and for the entire modern period, age-specific death rates have been lower for females than for males. The reasons are in part physiological (Madigan 1957), in part that medical advances in obstetrics and in treating cancers particularly associated with females have been greater than in the control, say, of the cardiovascular ailments that kill off proportionately more men. But from the point of view of a sociologist, the most interesting causal factor is the different patterns of life in modern industrial societies that are associated with the two sexes. In at least some underdeveloped economies, the lower status of women results in a higher female death rate, and it is amazing that there is also one Western population of which this has been so in modern times.

Ireland has been a demographic anomaly for a century or more, with the only major famine to afflict a Western nation in modern times, the highest rate of emigration, the highest age at marriage, and the highest rate along several other dimensions. Excellent monographs have analyzed particular aspects of Ireland's population, but until now, strangely, no one has written an over-all analysis. Robert E. Kennedy, Jr., has now filled in this puzzling gap with a book that will appear about the same time as this one. It links the population anomalies to each other and to Ireland's social system.

The following paper is partly based on one chapter of that book. Ireland's aberrant pattern of mortality, Kennedy shows, is related both to the country's family structure and to its better known fertility and emigration. Professor Kennedy is on the faculty of the University of Minnesota, where he has also served as chairman of the Minnesota Center for Population Studies, which is initiating research and family-planning services in Latin America and Africa.

THE SOCIAL STATUS OF THE SEXES AND THEIR RELATIVE MORTALITY IN IRELAND

ROBERT E. KENNEDY, JR.

That female longevity in the 20th century almost always exceeds male has become one of the most widely accepted generalizations in the social sciences. But before 1900 on a worldwide basis it probably was not unusual for males to have higher longevity, and the present pattern of lower female mortality at every age became typical in the West only after the 1920s (Stolnitz 1956: 22–25). This paper will use the Irish experience over the last century or so to illustrate the change from higher female mortality at some ages to lower female mortality at every age, and to propose that the greater preferential treatment given males in the past was a major factor explaining the trend.

Systematic studies to explain the relative mortality of the sexes are rare, probably because it is difficult to distinguish biological from environmental factors. Perhaps one of the best attempts to hold environmental factors constant is Madigan's study (1957) of the mortality experience of persons with essentially the same life styles—teaching Catholic monks and nuns. For this select population Madigan found that the female advantage in mortality persisted. The unusually high sex ratios of Ceylon, India, and Pakistan are primarily due to excess female mortality according to El-Badry (1969), and these mortality differences result from not only maternal mortality but also the preferential treatment given to males at almost all ages. The widening gap between the sexes in the mortality rates of adults in Western nations during the past several decades apparently has had an

SOURCE: Written specially for this volume. Portions of this article are taken from Robert E. Kennedy, Jr., *Irish Emigration, Marriage, and Fertility.* University of California Press, copyright 1972 by the Regents of the University of California.

environmental factor as a major cause: the greater increase in cigarette consumption among males (Preston 1970).

There is also evidence that females should enjoy lower rates of mortality, since males have higher mortality during fetal life (Shapiro *et al.* 1968: 43) and also in a number of nonhuman species (Dublin *et al.* 1949: 129). The greater physical soundness of females has been attributed to genetic causes, specifically the fact that the male possesses only one x-chromosome while the female possesses two (Herdan 1952). If females have greater longevity for biological reasons, the impact of social or environmental factors would be to widen or narrow the gap. Customs important enough to influence mortality rates should be readily apparent to both societal members and outside observers. In Ireland, such customs are more characteristic of rural than urban areas, and were more prevalent before the Second World War than today.

SOCIAL CUSTOMS

It has been said that Ireland is divided by a boundary even more pernicious than that between the North and the South—the boundary between the sexes (Ussher 1954). Arensberg and Kimball (1961: 202–3) described the situation as it existed in County Clare in 1932:

> Men and women are much more often to be seen in the company of members of their own sex than otherwise, except in the house itself. They go to mass, to town, or to sportive gatherings with companions of their own sex. Till recently and even now in remote districts, a conventional peasant woman always kept several paces behind her man, even if they were walking somewhere together.

To walk behind the male was symbolic of the female's inferior position generally in Irish rural society at that time. Women and children did not eat their meals until after the men and older boys had had their fill (*ibid.*: 35–37), a practice which systematically made the more nutritious food and larger helpings available to the favored sex. That males got the better food and more of it was apparently also the case among the urban working classes. In Sean O'Casey's play, *The Shadow of a Gunman* (1966: 115), set in Dublin of 1920, a married couple were described: "He is a man of 45, but looks relatively much younger than Mrs. Grigson. . . . He has all the appearance of being well fed; and, in fact, he gets most of the nourishment, Mrs. Grigson getting just enough to give her strength to do the necessary work of the household." The exploitation of females by Dublin males in the early 1920s suggested the title of O'Casey's *Juno and the Paycock* (1966: 13–14):

Shovel! Ah, then, me boyo, you'd do far more work with a knife an' fork than ever you'll do with a shovel! . . . Your poor wife slavin' to keep the bit in your mouth, and you gallivantin' about all the day like a paycock!

The subordination of daughters in some Irish families was gross. Although things had changed considerably by the late 1950s, an observer (McNabb 1964: 230–31) still described the status of teenage girls in the rural areas of Limerick in the following way:

When a daughter reaches 16, if she remains on the farm she must do a full day's work, and too often her life is one of unrelieved drudgery. . . . [Girls] are favored neither by father nor mother and accepted only on sufferance. This is, perhaps, too strong a conclusion, and it would be better to say they are loved but not thought of any great importance. In general, the girl is subservient to all other members of the family and shares no confidences with either her parents or her brothers. Her only right is to a dowry if she marries with her parents' consent.

In contrast, the son in the Irish family system was generally given preferential treatment. Sons were subordinate to their father but above everyone else in the household in the way their mother treated them. In both rural and urban areas and among all social classes, daughters were expected to provide their brothers with special service and comforts. As a 26-year-old Dublin woman told an observer (Humphreys 1966: 162–63) in the early 1950s, speaking in front of her mother and brothers (who agreed with her comments):

If I am sitting in the easy chair there and Matt or Charlie come home, I am expected to get up and give them the chair. They just say "Pardon me" and up I get. . . . There is no use fighting against it. I used to, but I soon found out which way the wind blew—we have to wait on the boys from sole to crown. . . . Mammy is just a slave to them, a willing slave, and we are expected to be, too. And that is general. That's the common attitude.

Two practices prevalent in rural areas especially favored males in the allocation of vital resources. On many Irish farms the income from the sale of animals and cash crops was kept by the husband, who was under no obligation even to tell his wife how much he had. He was bound by custom to provide for his wife and family, but only after looking after his own personal needs and those of the farm and livestock (Arensberg and Kimball 1961: 47–48). Under this system the wife and children were liable to suffer if the husband overindulged in drink and gambling, or if he was willing to sacrifice his family's welfare in order to purchase more land or livestock. As in eating priorities, the wife and children would probably be supported by leftovers, with the sons getting the largest share.

The second rural practice favoring males was in the division of labor. Generally men took care of the fields and the animals when they were in the fields, while women were responsible for feeding the animals when they were in the barn, milking the cows and processing the milk, and taking care of the vegetable garden, in addition to the usual duties of cooking, housework, and child care. Whether the initial division of labor was equal or not (by the latter half of the 19th century only a small proportion of Irish agricultural land was tilled, most of it being in pasture), eventually women were expected to help do men's work, but men would be ridiculed for helping with the women's work. Women were usually called out into the fields during turf cutting, during the planting, cultivation, and lifting of potatoes, and during haymaking time when the pitching, raking, and building some of the haycocks were left to the women (ibid.: 33–50).

The situation of females in urban areas was much better, at least with regard to family income and expected workload. According to Humphreys (1966: 234–36), the Dublin family of the early 1950s was a partnership in which both spouses agreed how to spend their income, and many wives actually were responsible for the money. Very few married women were employed outside their home; at each census between 1926 and 1966, only 5 to 6 percent of married women were working (Ireland 1926: Vol. V, Part II, 5; 1936: Vol. V, Part II, 5; 1946: Vol. V, Part II, 5; 1961: Vol. V, 5; 1966: Vol. V, 9). Their workload differed considerably by residence: the urban housewife was expected only to keep house, cook, and care for her husband and children; but the rural wife, in addition to these normal duties as a mother and wife, did much on the farm that was not classified as work outside the home.

In short, males were the favored sex in Irish society, and in rural areas they controlled many of the resources needed for good health. The mortality statistics show how such customs may have influenced the death rate of the sexes.

MORTALITY PATTERNS

Perhaps the most direct indication of the relative mortality of the sexes in Ireland can be seen by comparing the life expectancy by sex in that country with the English and American experience. The general level of mortality was similar in the three countries, with the greatest longevity often recorded in Ireland. Among males, for example, life expectancy at birth was greater in Ireland than in England and Wales at least from 1871 to 1926, and greater in Ireland than in the United States between 1901 and 1911, and then again in 1961 (Table 1). But when life expectancies by sex within nations are compared, the Irish pattern is distinct from the English or the American. While females had greater longevity in all three countries, and while the female advantage gradually increased after the

Table 1. Excess of Female over Male Life Expectation at Birth in Years, Ireland, the United States, and England and Wales, 1870–72 to 1960–62

APPROXIMATE PERIOD [a]	IRELAND			ENGLAND AND WALES			UNITED STATES [b]		
	MALE	FEMALE	FEMALE EXCESS	MALE	FEMALE	FEMALE EXCESS	MALE	FEMALE	FEMALE EXCESS
1870–72	49.6	50.9	1.3	41.4	44.6	3.2	n.a.	n.a.	n.a.
1880–82	49.4	49.9	0.5	43.7	47.2	3.5	n.a.	n.a.	n.a.
1890–92	49.1	49.2	0.1	44.1	47.8	3.7	n.a.	n.a.	n.a.
1900–02	49.3	49.6	0.3	48.5	52.4	3.9	48.2	51.1	2.9
1910–12	53.6	54.1	0.5	51.5	55.4	3.9	50.2	53.6	3.4
1925–27	57.4	57.9	0.5	55.6	59.6	4.0	57.8	60.6	2.8
1935–37	58.2	59.6	1.4	60.2	64.4	4.2	60.6	64.6	4.0
1945–47	60.5	62.4	1.9	66.4	71.5	4.7	65.1	70.3	5.2
1960–62	68.1	71.9	3.8	68.0	73.9	5.9	67.5	74.4	6.9

n.a. Data not available.

[a] Specific periods were Ireland—1870–72, 1881–83, 1890–92, 1900–02, 1910–12, 1925–27, 1935–37, 1945–47, 1960–62; United States—1900–02, 1909–11, 1920–29, 1930–39, 1946, 1960; England and Wales—1871–80, 1881–90, 1891–1900, 1901–10, 1910–12, 1920–22, 1937, 1950–52, 1961–63.

[b] White population in reporting areas.

SOURCES: *Censuses of Population of Ireland, 1946 and 1951,* "General Report," Table 51, p. 68; Ireland, *Commission on Emigration and Other Population Problems, 1948–1954,* Statistical Appendix, Table 23, p. 311; *Statistical Abstract of Ireland, 1965,* Table 27, p. 37; *Statistical Abstract of the United States, 1965,* Table 59, p. 53; England and Wales, *Annual Abstract of Statistics, 1964,* Table 36, p. 38; Louis I. Dublin et al., *Length of Life: A Study of the Life Table,* rev. ed. (New York: Ronald Press, 1949), Table 17, p. 60.

1920s in all three, the gap between the sexes was much smaller in Ireland than in the other two nations. Females had life expectancies from 2.8 to 5.2 years longer than the male in England and Wales between 1870 and 1946, and in the United States between 1900 and 1946. But in Ireland the female advantage was only from 0.1 to 0.5 years between 1881 and 1926, and at no time between 1870 and 1947 was the difference greater than 2 years.

The relatively narrow gap between the sexes in life expectancy in Ireland should be less characteristic of Irish urban areas than the nation as a whole, if our presentation of Irish customs has been correct. Life tables for Irish urban areas became available in 1935–37, and from that time up to the most recent life table (1960–62), the urban areas showed female life expectancies from 3.7 to 5.3 years greater than male (Table 2). The actual

Table 2. Expectation of Life at Birth, by Sex and Urban Residence, Ireland, 1935–37 to 1960–62

	TOTAL POPULATION			URBAN POPULATION		
PERIOD	FEMALE	MALE	FEMALE EXCESS	FEMALE	MALE	FEMALE EXCESS
1935–37	59.6	58.2	1.4	57.0	53.1	3.9
1940–42	61.0	59.0	2.0	58.4	54.4	4.0
1945–47	62.4	60.5	1.9	60.5	56.8	3.7
1950–52	67.1	64.5	2.6	66.7	62.3	4.4
1960–62	71.9	68.1	3.8	71.8	66.5	5.3

SOURCES: Ireland, *Commission on Emigration and Other Population Problems, 1948–1954*, Tables 78, 81, pp. 106–108; *Statistical Abstract of Ireland, 1950*, Tables 13, 14, pp. 17, 18; *1953*, Tables 17, 18, pp. 28, 29; *1964*, Tables 27, 28, pp. 37, 38; *1968*, Tables 27, 28, pp. 37, 38.

difference between rural and urban areas is understated in the table, of course, since the figures for the entire nation include the urban sector. I have been able to find life tables for the rural Irish population for only two periods, 1935–37 and 1831–41. In the latter case, the life tables were calculated from data in the 1841 census on the over one million deaths that had taken place in the 32 counties during the prior ten years. Although a century apart in time and quite different in total life expectancies, the mortality patterns by sex and rural-urban residence were similar (Table 3). Even though the life expectancies of both sexes were lower in the urban areas, the female advantage over the male in longevity was greater in urban than in rural areas. Between Dublin and rural areas in 1831–41, the differential was 5 years; in 1935–37 the differential between urban and rural areas was 3.4 years. One can reasonably speculate that the female advantage was larger in Dublin than in the smaller civic districts during 1831–41 because

Table 3. Expectation of Life at Birth, by Sex and Rural-Urban
Residence, Ireland, 1831–41 and 1935–37

PERIOD AND AREA	FEMALE	MALE	FEMALE EXCESS
1831–41:			
Dublin	28	24	4
Civic districts	24	24	0
Rural districts	29	30	−1
1935–37:			
All areas	59.6	58.2	1.4
Urban areas	57.0	53.1	3.9
Rural areas	61.0	60.5	0.5

SOURCE: *Census of Ireland, 1841*, "Report," pp. lxxx–lxxxii; Ireland, *Commission on Emigration and Other Population Problems, 1948–1954*, Tables 79, 81, pp. 106, 108.

Irish rural customs were more pervasive in the smaller towns and villages than in the more industrial and anglicized capital.

Life expectancy at birth does not show differences by age, which the subordinate status of both rural and urban daughters would lead us to expect. The 1831–41 and 1931 data permit such a comparison. The mortality data from the 1841 census by age, sex, and rural-urban residence are probably marred by differences in the underreporting of deaths and other errors in the various subcategories, but the general pattern is both striking and similar to that presented by the reliable 1931 data (Table 4). If we consider only those subcategories in which female death rates *exceeded* the male, the greater relative disadvantage of rural females is apparent at both time periods at almost all ages except for children under 5. In 1931 the excess of female deaths in *rural* areas was highest among girls aged 10 to 14 years and women aged 25 to 44 years, the most frequent time of childbearing. In both periods, the greatest excess for urban females was among girls aged about 10 to 14 years, a time of life when virtually all were living at home with their parents and brothers. Excess mortality among urban females over 35 did not appear during either period—a pattern consistent with the reported rural-urban difference in work loads expected of older women.

The long-term trends in relative Irish mortality by age and sex between 1864 and 1967 are given in Table 5. With the possible exception of the first several years after the compulsory registration of vital statistics began in 1864, there is little reason to suppose that the underregistration of deaths differed by sex. Some male-dominated societies show a greater underregistration of female deaths, but if this happened in Ireland during the 1860s

Table 4. Estimated Average Annual Death Rates by Age, Sex, and Rural-Urban Residence, 1831–41 (32 Counties) and 1931 (26 Counties)

PERIOD AND AGE GROUP	DEATHS PER 10,000 OF THE SPECIFIED AGE AND SEX				FEMALE DEATH RATES AS A PERCENTAGE OF MALE	
	RURAL AREAS		URBAN AREAS			
	MALES	FEMALES	MALES	FEMALES	RURAL	URBAN
1831–41						
5 and under	371	364	417	414	98	99
6–10	73	80	96	105	110	109
11–15	46	56	49	61	122	124
16–25	156	153	169	171	98	101
26–35	141	165	204	205	117	100
36–45	160	181	274	254	113	93
46–55	225	218	342	295	97	89
56–65	384	408	475	450	106	95
66–75	509	512	578	540	100	93
1931						
Under 5	162	142	341	279	88	82
5–9	20	18	36	26	90	72
10–14	14	18	20	23	128	115
15–19	26	29	34	37	112	109
20–24	39	42	48	48	108	100
25–34	43	54	52	57	126	110
35–44	53	67	88	78	126	89
45–54	93	104	178	132	112	74
55–64	238	238	373	317	100	85
65 and over	746	693	878	773	93	88
All ages	139	143	160	149	103	93

SOURCES: *Census of Ireland, 1841,* "Report," p. lxxxiv; Saorstat Eireann, *Annual Report of the Registrar General, 1931,* Table 19, p. 29.

and early 1870s the recorded statistics would understate the actual excess of female mortality.

The most dramatic feature of the data is the sudden improvement in females' relative mortality between the 1940s and the 1950s. Part of the change among older adults could have been due to a greater increase in cigarette consumption among males (Preston 1970). But since the gap between the sexes widened in every age group, and especially among persons aged 10 to 34 years, more general environmental factors are probable. One would be rapid urbanization: the proportion living in towns of 1,500 or more increased from 39 percent in 1946 to 49 percent in 1966, compared with the increase from 22 to 39 percent during the 95 years

Table 5. Female Age-Specific Average Annual Death Rates as a Percentage of Male, Selected Age Groups, Ireland, 1864–70 to 1961–67

	AGE GROUP							
PERIOD	UNDER 5	5–9	10–14	15–19	20–24	25–34	35–44	55–64
1864–1870	90	102	112	96	79	92	95	95
1871–1880	91	106	120	102	83	91	90	95
1881–1890	90	109	129	115	89	96	96	98
1891–1900	89	109	134	122	92	93	96	101
1901–1910	88	113	140	123	95	92	99	101
1911–1920	88	114	129	112	94	94	98	98
1921–1930	86	104	120	115	98	105	105	98
1931–1940	84	101	113	111	108	113	105	94
1941–1950	81	89	109	109	111	113	100	86
1951–1960	77	87	85	77	83	87	91	73
1961–1967	79	79	73	50	54	72	77	62

SOURCE: Calculated from: Ireland, *Report on Vital Statistics, 1967*, Table 9, p. 11.

before 1946 (Ireland 1926: Vol. X, 15; 1936: Vol. IX, 14; 1946 and 1951: *General Report*, 24–25; 1961: Vol. I, 140–141; 1966: Vol. I, xvi, 11). As larger proportions of the total population lived in urban areas, the female advantage there was reflected in a widening gap between the sexes.

After the Second World War, the lot of the rural female should have improved enough to narrow the rural-urban difference between life styles. The proportion of private rural dwellings with electricity rose from a negligible figure in 1946 to 71 percent in 1961 (Ireland 1961: Vol. VI, 121–22). The many important labor-saving devices that became available with electricity reduced both the amount of physical effort required of rural females and possibly also the length of their working day. These were, for example, water pumps, electric kitchen ranges, electric irons, and water heaters. Electricity also brought first radio and then, during the 1960s, television; between 1945 and 1966 the number of persons per radio-television license declined from 17 to 5.26 in the nation as a whole, and from 32 to 5.5 in the rural province of Connacht (Ireland 1950: 183; 1967: 321). The importance of television in inculcating different values is indicated by the fact that in Ireland about half of all broadcasting time is given to imported programs (Ireland 1967: 322). Irish farm women were made familiar with different life styles, including in particular images of the higher status enjoyed by American and English women.

From the recent, more "modern" patterns of mortality by sex, one can judge the impact of environmental factors on the mortality ratios of earlier periods. Among persons under 5, for example, the recent ratios are not very different from those of fifty or even a hundred years ago, in spite of great reductions in infant and childhood mortality. That since the 1920s female rates in this age group fell relatively little compared with male suggests that infants and small children probably were given similar care regardless of sex also before the 1920s.

The effect of sex roles on the mortality ratio appeared suddenly after early childhood, and was most salient among those aged 10 to 19. The reasons for the rise in the ratios among teenagers after the 1870s, and among older women between 1921 and 1950, are a matter for speculation. There may have been selective migration of healthier rural females, but I am not aware of any data with which one could test this hypothesis. One could suppose that, on the contrary, healthy rural females, better able to cope with the physical demands made on them, would have had less reason to emigrate than their less fit sisters. If female deaths were underregistered during the first few years of compulsory registration of vital statistics in the 1860s and early 1870s, part of the subsequent increase in the female mortality recorded would have been due to more accurate statistics. Land laws were eventually revised so that no more money was needed to purchase a holding than one had been paying for rent, with the cost of the legal transfer paid out of public funds (Beckett 1966: 407). But the decade of greatest transfer of land ownership was also the one of highest excess female mortality among young girls, when the death rate of females aged 10 to 14 was 40 percent higher than that of males. Could there have been other expenses associated with land ownership, which some of the more land-hungry farmers paid with money taken from the support of their families? The rise in relative female mortality among older persons a decade or so later may have been due, at least in part, to the aging of this cohort. The males of this generation perhaps felt less obliged to share their incomes with their wives, who, if they did not choose to migrate to urban areas, had grown accustomed to getting very little.

The change in Ireland's mortality ratio in several age groups can be highlighted by an international comparison of causes of death by age and sex. Although there may have been some differences in diagnostic procedures between England and Wales and Ireland, on the one hand, and the United States, on the other, the pattern is clear. In the early 1950s, maternal mortality was more than three times as high in Ireland as in either the United States or England and Wales, but by the mid-1960s all three countries had similarly low levels. This rapid decline in Irish maternal mortality paralleled the sudden fall in Ireland's mortality ratios during the same period.

But maternal mortality may indicate not only the relative status of females in Ireland but also the later age at marriage and larger average family size of the Irish. Thus, the patterns of cause of death by sex, both before and after the childbearing period, probably are more reliable indicators of the relative status of the sexes. To reduce marginal examples, I took only those causes of death that in Ireland in 1951 resulted in at least one more female death than male per 100,000 persons of the same age and sex. Among those aged 5 to 14 in the early 1950s, mortality from infectious and parasitic diseases was much greater for Irish females than for both Irish males and both sexes in the United States and in England (Table 6). From two causes the female rates were higher than the male in England, and from one in the United States, but the differences were small, of an entirely different order than the excess mortality in Ireland. If the lack of a clearly defined cause of death indicates relatively poorer care before death, then the greater number of Irish female than male deaths in this category also illustrates the preferential treatment given to males.

That Irish females age more rapidly than males was noted in descriptions of the relative social status of the sexes, and it also shows up in the international comparisons of causes of death among persons aged 45 to 64 (Table 7). Among older persons the death rates from anemias and certain disorders of the nervous and circulatory systems were higher among Irish females than males, while the reverse was true among Americans. Although English females did have higher rates than English males for some causes of death, the differences generally were smaller than for the Irish. The only cause of death for which both American and English ratios were higher than the Irish was diabetes mellitus.

CONCLUSION

The mortality statistics of Ireland support the impression given by descriptions of Irish life that sons received preferential treatment both in rural and urban areas, and that in rural areas males of all ages beyond early childhood were favored in the allocation of vital resources. The gap in expectation of life was narrower in rural than in urban areas; for both rural and urban residents the female disadvantage was greatest among those aged 10 to 19; and in rural areas excess female mortality extended into late middle age. The recent decline in the ratio of female to male death rates probably was associated with increased urbanization, modernization brought about by rural electrification, and improvements in medicine and public health, which through the reduction in such causes as maternal mortality more often benefited females than males. Until the late 1940s, however, the less adequate female diet in many Irish families probably contributed to the females' lower resistance to certain infectious and parasitic diseases; and malnutrition and fatigue resulting from continued heavy workloads also probably explain why rural Irish females aged more rapidly than males. Similarly, the higher death rates in the United States from tuberculosis, pneumonia, and influenza among rural than urban females have been attributed to the supposition that the harder working life of

Table 6. Deaths per 100,000 Persons of the Same Sex and Aged 5 to 14, by Specified Causes, Ireland (1951), United States (1955), and England and Wales (1955)

CAUSE OF DEATH	DEATH RATES						FEMALE DEATH RATES AS A PERCENTAGE OF MALE		
	IRELAND		UNITED STATES		ENGLAND AND WALES		IRELAND	UNITED STATES	ENGLAND AND WALES
	FEMALE	MALE	FEMALE	MALE	FEMALE	MALE			
Tuberculosis of the respiratory system	4.5	0.7	0.1	0.1	0.3	0.1	640	100	300
Rheumatic fever	4.1	1.4	1.0	1.0	0.9	0.4	290	100	220
Ill defined and unknown	3.8	2.2	0.4	0.7	0.0	0.0	170	60	100
Miscellaneous infectious and parasitic diseases	2.6	1.1	1.0	1.1	0.7	0.8	240	90	90
Chronic rheumatic heart disease	1.9	0.7	0.2	0.1	0.4	0.5	270	200	80
Scarlet fever and streptococcal sore throat	1.9	0.7	0.1	0.1	0.1	0.1	270	100	100
All causes	70.0	76.8	38.0	58.4	34.2	47.1	91	65	72

SOURCE: United Nations, *Demographic Yearbook, 1957*, Table 17, pp. 494, 508, 516.

Table 7. Deaths per 100,000 Persons of the Same Sex and Aged 45 to 64, by Specified Causes, Ireland (1951), United States (1955), and England and Wales (1955)

CAUSE OF DEATH	IRELAND		UNITED STATES		ENGLAND AND WALES		FEMALE DEATH RATES AS A PERCENTAGE OF MALE		
	FEMALE	MALE	FEMALE	MALE	FEMALE	MALE	IRELAND	UNITED STATES	ENGLAND AND WALES
Vascular lesions affecting central nervous system	142.0	98.1	95.5	110.3	109.6	111.2	145	87	99
Hypertension without mention of heart	31.1	23.7	6.4	8.5	11.8	17.5	131	76	67
Chronic rheumatic heart disease	22.2	17.5	24.1	25.5	37.4	23.8	127	95	157
Anemias	19.4	12.3	1.4	1.7	3.1	2.1	158	82	148
Diabetes mellitus	13.4	9.9	26.1	18.5	8.2	4.5	135	141	182
Rheumatic fever	3.5	2.1	0.6	1.0	0.5	0.5	167	60	100
All causes	1,206.1	1,527.1	837.5	1,534.1	768.2	1,353.5	79	55	57

SOURCE: United Nations, *Demographic Yearbook, 1957*, Table 17, pp. 494, 508, 516.

rural housewives resulted in greater fatigue and lower resistance. There is also evidence that fatigue resulting from continuous hard physical labor, especially after 40 years of age, contributes to premature death (Dublin *et al.* 1949: 78, 233).

The Irish case illustrates well how male dominance is associated with relatively high female mortality, a linkage that before the 20th century may have been common in some European societies (Stolnitz 1956: 23–25). Ireland has been unusual in that social customs sustaining male dominance persisted into the mid-20th century.

References

ARENSBERG, C. M., and S. T. KIMBALL. 1961. *Family and Community in Ireland.* Gloucester, Mass.: Peter Smith.

BECKETT, J. C. 1966. *The Making of Modern Ireland: 1603–1923.* London: Faber and Faber.

DUBLIN, LOUIS I., A. J. LOTKA, and MORTIMER SPIEGELMAN. 1949. *Length of Life: A Study of the Life Table,* rev. ed. New York: Ronald Press.

EL-BADRY, M. A. 1969. "Higher Female than Male Mortality in Some Countries of South Asia: A Digest," *Journal of the American Statistical Association,* **64,** 1234–1244.

HERDAN, G. 1952. "Causes of Excess Male Mortality in Man," *Acta Genetica et Statistica Medica,* **3,** 351–375.

HUMPHREYS, A. J. 1966. *New Dubliners: Urbanization and the Irish Family.* London: Routledge and Kegan Paul.

IRELAND.1926. *Census of Population.* V, Part II; X.

———. 1928. *Agricultural Statistics, 1847–1926.* "Report and Tables."

———. 1936. *Census of Population.* V, Part II; IX.

———. 1946. *Census of Population.* V, Part II.

———. 1946 and 1951. *Census of Population.* "General Report."

———. 1950. *Statistical Abstract.*

———. 1961. *Census of Population.* I; V; VI.

———. 1966. *Census of Population.* I; V.

———. 1967. *Statistical Abstract.*

MADIGAN, FRANCIS C. 1957. "Are Sex Mortality Differentials Biologically Caused?" *Milbank Memorial Fund Quarterly,* **35,** 202–223.

McNABB, PATRICK. 1964. "Social Structure," in Jeremiah Newman, ed., *The Limerick Rural Survey, 1958–1964.* Tipperary: Muintir Na Tire Rural Publications.

O'CASEY, SEAN. 1966. *Three Plays.* London: Macmillan.

PRESTON, S. H. 1970. "An International Comparison of Excess in the Death Rates of Older Males," *Population Studies,* **24,** 5–20.

SHAPIRO, SAM, EDWARD R. SCHLESINGER, and ROBERT E. L. NESBITT, JR. 1968. *Infant, Perinatal, Maternal, and Childhood Mortality in the United States.* Cambridge, Mass.: Harvard University Press.

STOLNITZ, GEORGE J. 1956. "A Century of International Mortality Trends: II," *Population Studies,* **10,** 17–42.

UNITED NATIONS. 1957. *Demographic Yearbook.* New York.
————. 1967. *Demographic Yearbook.* New York.
USSHER, ARLAND. 1954. "The Boundary Between the Sexes," in J. A. O'Brien, ed., *The Vanishing Irish.* London: W. H. Allen.

The discrimination against women in Ireland is distinctive only in its degree. To some extent this is a worldwide phenomenon. In the United States, the Civil Rights Act of 1964 was the first federal legislation that prohibited employers, trade unions, and employment agencies from discriminating on the basis of sex. It is no longer legal to refuse to hire a woman for a job she can do, to pay her less for the same work, "to limit, segregate, or classify employees in such a way as to deprive any individual of employment opportunities or otherwise adversely affect the employee's status." Broad as this language is, the courts have interpreted it even more broadly. A mother of seven preschool-age children was denied a job in a factory; the Supreme Court ruled unanimously that employers cannot refuse to hire women with small children while accepting men in the same situation. Fifty female employees of Newsweek *threatened to file suit unless the job of writer was opened to them; the magazine gave in before the case went to court. An Air Force captain successfully opposed a regulation that no servicewoman could have personal custody of a child for more than one month a year. In the first sex-discrimination case filed by the Justice Department, against the Libbey-Owens-Ford Company, the corporation agreed to abandon its policy of hiring women only for two low-level tasks. Such cases attract attention in part because they are exceptional; the routine pattern remains essentially the same as before 1964.*

How much can one law affect the "sex labeling" of jobs, as the author of the next paper aptly terms the ingrained "natural" association of men or women with particular occupations? The data on which the article was based are from before the law was passed, but the analysis is indicative of probable future trends. So long as marriage is more important to females than to males, will not most women sacrifice their own careers to their husbands', to their home duties, to their children? In any case, apart from an activist minority, do most women want to give up the relative placidity of housework or low-level outside occupations and accept the more competitive, highly responsible occupations now mostly reserved for men? In short, will the family change fundamentally, with all that such an alteration would imply for fertility, because of the somewhat lessened discrimination in extrafamilial activities?

Valerie Kincade Oppenheimer, though young in her profession, has made herself an expert on such questions. She wrote her dissertation at the University of California in Berkeley on the female labor force (Oppenheimer

1970), and in 1966–67 she undertook postdoctoral research on a similar topic at the Population Investigation Committee of the London School of Economics. Currently, with a three-year grant from the Russell Sage Foundation, she is doing an analysis of female labor-force data from the 1970 census, while also a research sociologist at the University of California at Los Angeles.

THE SEX LABELING OF JOBS

VALERIE KINCADE OPPENHEIMER

How did what can be termed female jobs in the United States develop and why do they persist? Before answering these questions, it is necessary to determine (1) the range of jobs held predominantly by females and (2) the extent to which female workers are concentrated in these jobs (cf. Oppenheimer 1970).

Of the total female labor force in 1900 and 1960 (as well as in the intervening censal years), about half was concentrated in occupations in which 70 percent or more of the workers were women. Important in this list were lower-level professionals (such as nurses and teachers), clerks, private household workers, operatives in the clothing and textile industries, and such service workers as waitresses, practical nurses, and hospital attendants. Notably absent were major occupational groups like managers, farmers, craftsmen and foremen, and laborers. Women's greater opportunities in 1960 are indicated by the larger number of occupations that were at least 70 percent female and the declining importance of private household and factory work. But of the seventeen occupations that had been 70 percent female in 1900, fourteen remained so in 1960, though with a greatly diminished combined weight. Women also became increasingly important in a few occupations, such as bookkeeping, as well as in some others not even separately listed in the 1900 census, such as office-machine operators or attendants in physicians' and dentists' offices.

This census list of "female" occupations is, of course, an imperfect indicator of the jobs that females actually held. With a limited number of occupational categories, the census schedule sometimes combines occupations held predominantly by one sex or the other. For example, in 1950 half of the joint classification of barbers, beauticians, and manicurists were women; but when hairdressers and cosmetologists were reclassified into a separate category, this proved to be 92 percent female. The fact that industry as well as occupation is important raises a similar problem. For

SOURCE: Abridged slightly from *Industrial Relations,* 7 (1968), 219–234, with permission of the author and the journal.

example, although women constituted 67 percent of the assemblers in electrical machinery, equipment, and supplies in 1960, they were only 16 percent of the assemblers in motor vehicles and motor-vehicle equipment. The summary statement that women made up 44 percent of *all* assemblers, then, hides more than it reveals. Occupational data are especially inadequate for very general categories like "sales workers, n.e.c." (not elsewhere classified) or "clerical workers, n.e.c.," in which a sizable proportion of female workers were to be found. The female density in these groups was not high (59 percent of the clerical workers, n.e.c., and 40 percent of the sales workers, n.e.c.), but if the industrial breakdown of these two occupational groups is examined, about half the workers prove to be in industries where at least 70 percent of the workers in these occupations were female. There is also intra-industry variability in the sex labeling of jobs—for example, regional differences in the proportion of women working as laundry and dry-cleaning operatives and as textile spinners, or differences among various firms within a single occupation. Such differences are obscured by industrywide averages —and no finer breakdowns are available.

With the more recent censuses it is practically impossible—and with earlier censuses completely out of the question—to take into simultaneous account such factors as occupation, industry, region, and type of work organization. Thus, one cannot really subject any propositions about sex labeling to a rigorous test, and any theory purporting to show that certain characteristics of an occupation lead to the use of female rather than male labor is vulnerable.

CHEAP LABOR THAT IS AVAILABLE AND SKILLED

Keeping these difficulties in mind, let us try to outline some of the factors in the development and persistence of the sexual division of labor outside the home. Cheapness plus availability have typified female labor (National Manpower Council 1957: 86–109, 220–44; Abbott 1910: 305–14; Lebergott 1964: 126–27; U. S. Women's Bureau 1963: 5ff; McNulty 1967). This combination has encouraged the use of women in many jobs—such as, to cite a prime example, elementary school teaching (Woody 1929: 460–518; Abbott 1910: 119–20). In the 19th and early 20th centuries, many school districts— particularly rural ones—could or would not pay wages attractive to male teachers. On the other hand, few other nonmanual occupations were open to women of middle-class status or aspiration, many of whom were therefore available for teaching. It does not appear that women *displaced* men in teaching—though they may have *replaced* those who responded to the many opportunities available to native males.

Another example of the combination of cheapness and availability is semiskilled factory work.

The ease with which any man could become a freeholder and the superior chances of success in agriculture made it difficult to find men who were willing to work in manufacturing establishments. . . . Moreover, as a question of national economy, fear was expressed regarding the possible injury to our agricultural interests if much labor were diverted from the land. Manufactures, if they were to be established, must not, it was emphatically said, be built up at the expense of agriculture. . . . The establishment of the factory system . . . substantially meant, with us, the creation of new work, and made imperative a large increase in our wage-earning population (Abbott 1910: 48–49).

While men were reluctant to enter factories, women were in plentiful supply as their employment in agriculture was limited (*ibid.*: 55ff; Lebergott 1964). From its earliest days, they formed a major source of labor in the cotton industry, which in turn has been one major reservoir of operative jobs for American women.

Another combination decisive in the sex labeling of jobs is cheapness plus skill. Elementary teaching, for example, requires a fairly high level of education but is usually poorly paid. Other similar occupations are illustrated in Table 1, which shows data from the 1960 census. These occupations were selected as not only predominantly female but also with an average educational attainment greater than for the male labor force as a whole. In spite of this greater educational attainment, however, both the male and female workers in these occupations had a lower income than the average male worker. Thus, the more educated labor in several female occupations is not compensated by a proportionately higher income. Fully 71 percent of women in the professional and technical category, 98 percent of those in clerical occupations, and about 42 percent of all female workers were found in such occupations. Furthermore, the women's education is not a gratuitous accompaniment of the job but characteristic of the demand itself. Even 25 years ago, over 90 percent of employees in both New Haven and Charlotte preferred clerical workers with at least a high-school education (Noland and Bakke 1949: 194–95). In general, industrialization has produced a continuously growing demand for workers with a fairly high level of general education plus some special skills, with a resultant chronic (except in periods of depression) shortage of "middle-quality" labor. Occupations in a poorer position to compete for middle-quality labor—secretarial work or elementary teaching, for example—use low-paid, educated females. To substitute males would require either a rise in the price paid or a decline in the quality, or both. Only compelling reasons would change the sex composition of female occupations of this type.

SEX-LINKED CHARACTERISTICS

One reason that employers demand either male or female labor is their desire for traits linked to one sex or the other. Skill in spinning, weaving,

Table 1. Relative Income and Educational Standing of Selected [a] Female Occupations, United States, 1960

| | RATIO OF OCCUPATION TO TOTAL MALE LABOR FORCE | | | |
| | MEDIAN SCHOOL YEARS COMPLETED | | MEDIAN INCOME IN 1959 | |
OCCUPATION	MALE	FEMALE	MALE	FEMALE
Total	1.00	1.09	1.00	0.59
Professional workers				
Dancers and dancing teachers	1.12	1.12	0.83	0.61
Dietitians and nutritionists	1.14	1.19	0.76	0.68
Librarians	1.50	1.46	1.01	0.77
Musicians and music teachers	1.34	1.33	1.03	0.29
Nurses	1.17	1.19	0.84	0.71
Recreation and group workers	1.36	1.32	1.00	0.78
Social and welfare workers	1.49	1.48	1.04	0.87
Religious workers	1.47	1.21	0.77	0.49
Elementary teachers	1.53	1.48	1.03	0.85
Teachers, n.e.c.[b]	1.48	1.45	1.10	0.74
Therapists and healers	1.48	1.45	0.97	0.83
Clerical workers				
Library attendants and assistants	1.23	1.18	0.55	0.54
Attendants in physicians' and dentists' offices	1.12	1.12	0.68	0.53
Bank tellers	1.14	1.12	0.84	0.63
Bookkeepers	1.14	1.12	0.89	0.64
File clerks	1.12	1.10	0.75	0.59
Office-machine operators	1.13	1.12	0.96	0.68
Payroll and timekeeping clerks	1.13	1.12	1.00	0.73
Receptionists	1.13	1.13	0.77	0.57
Secretaries	1.15	1.14	1.05	0.71
Stenographers	1.14	1.14	1.02	0.70
Typists	1.13	1.13	0.80	0.64
Telephone operators	1.11	1.10	1.07	0.67
Cashiers	1.08	1.08	0.78	0.53
Clerical workers, n.e.c.[b]	1.12	1.12	0.99	0.66
Sales workers				
Demonstrators	1.08	1.09	[c]	0.50
Hucksters and peddlers	0.92	1.09	0.82	0.16

[a] Includes all occupations in which at least 51 percent of the workers were female and in which the median of school years completed was more than 11.1, the median for the total male experienced civilian labor force.

[b] Not elsewhere classified.

[c] Base not large enough to compute a median.

SOURCE: U. S. Census of Population, 1960: Occupational Characteristics, Subject Report PC(2)–7A, Tables 9 and 28.

and sewing, for example, was traditionally associated with the female role, and two of the major early industries were cotton and clothing. Women frequently had some experience in spinning and weaving before they entered the cotton mill; and the clothing industry, since it started to develop before the invention of the sewing machine in 1850, at first depended on hand sewing (Abott 1910: 215–45). The point is not that such characteristics are in fact inherent traits of males or females but that employers believe one sex has the edge in some important respect.

Most jobs entailing much physical strength are automatically labeled male. In New Haven and Charlotte, for example, about 90 percent of employers preferred men for common laboring jobs and about 75 percent required them; women were preferred only for cleaning jobs (Noland and Bakke 1949: 184–85). Many employers believe women to have a greater manual dexterity and greater patience. Thus, "firms manufacturing small delicate electronic units emphasize the importance of finger dexterity and patience in making precise measurements with small instruments and usually consider women better qualified than men for such jobs" (U. S. Women's Bureau 1962: 3). Employers in New Haven and Charlotte felt that women are "less likely to be dissatisfied with jobs which are repetitive or monotonous and for which pay is relatively low," such as, as one example, clerical positions (Noland and Bakke 1949: 25–26, 65).

Finally, sheer feminine (and masculine too, I presume) appeal is considered an important factor at times. For example, in a 1960 study for the National Office Management Association, about 28 percent of the 2,000 companies surveyed stated that sex appeal is one important qualification in hiring receptionists, switchboard operators, secretaries, and stenographers (Ginder 1961; National Manpower Council 1957: 104).

Since women's participation in the labor force is often intermittent, jobs requiring on-the-job training entail a greater risk for the employer who hires females. It is not that jobs favorable to the employment of women require no skills, but that these skills can be attained before employment. As the principal example, most female white-collar occupations require a fairly high level of general education and some specialized skills, both of which the woman brings with her to the job. To be a secretary, school-teacher, librarian, nurse, or laboratory technician, one needs some schooling plus some specific training; and since most of the requisite skills can be obtained in advance, supplementary training for a particular job is worthwhile even for a relatively temporary employee. Under such circumstances, women are less risky employees.

TRADITION

Once there is a sex label on a job, tradition is likely to keep it there. Those who made the family's clothes at home did so in the factories, those who nursed the sick at home did so in the hospitals, those who took care of their own houses were domestics. Even today, a high proportion of working women are in traditionally feminine occupations. For example, in a firm that the U. S. Women's Bureau (1962: 8) examined:

> The electronic technicians . . . declared that women would be very readily hired if they were qualified—but no women have ever applied for such a job. The obstacle of traditional thinking appears to affect some employers as well as some women. . . . Employers in the local area almost always specified men on their job orders for technicians. However, placement officers at that office noted that employers seemed to be willing to hire women when they were referred. It had apparently not occurred to some employers that women might be available for such work.

The National Manpower Council (1957: 88–89) also emphasized the importance of tradition:

> The distinctions between "men's" and "women's" jobs appear to be particularly sharp in certain manufacturing fields. In professional, service, and sales work, jobs are often closed to women because it is taken for granted that they should be held by men. It is believed that, if women are placed in such jobs, they are likely to produce negative reactions not only among male supervisors, fellow employees, and customers, but also in the public at large.

MIXED WORK GROUPS AND FEMALE SUPERVISORS

The difficulties involved in having work groups made up of both men and women and the problems—real or presumed—involved with having women in supervisory positions tend to keep the sex composition of a job homogeneous. Since both sexes have been trained from youth not to compete, neither knows how to behave when male and female workers are on an equal level. If a woman is introduced into a male work group, "the necessary adaptations to her presence appear excessive to everyone concerned, including immediate changes in verbal habits, dress, and comportment, and potential changes in the organization of the group." If enough women are introduced to balance the sex ratio, the sexes often form two groups, which may be quite hostile to each other (Caplow 1954: 237ff). Employers may not be able to recruit a man for a "woman's" job unless it is obvious that he is given some extra privileges. "Especially in factories . . . men will avoid jobs they regard as 'women's.' These are usually the jobs in which a high proportion of the workers, generally over 60 percent, are women" (National Manpower Council 1957: 90–91).

If men and women competed fully with each other, one obvious result might be more women in supervisory positions. However, a fairly widespread belief holds it best not to have female supervisors. For example, 74 percent of the New Haven employers and 83 percent of those in Charlotte preferred men for administrative and executive positions (Noland and Bakke 1949: 184–85). Men are thought to be better able to deal with men—that is, most clients, other management people, suppliers, and so on; and as supervisors, men command more respect, even from women. Most of the employers interviewed in the 1950s and in 1960 "maintained that women as well as men generally prefer male supervisors. It was asserted that women are more likely to accept instructions from a man than from a woman" (National Manpower Council 1957: 106).

One reason which has been suggested for the difficulties in using women in supervisory positions is that women generally have a lower status than men, and frictions arise when lower-status individuals try to originate action for those of higher status. "In our society most men grow up to be comfortable in a relationship in which they originate for women and to be uneasy, if not more seriously disturbed, when the originations go in the other direction" (Whyte 1949; cf. Caplow 1954: 238ff). A study of the restaurant business found, for example, that the several complementary roles—waitress-counterman and waitress-barman—necessitated all sorts of devices to insulate the man from the waitress so that she could not give him direct orders.

In sum, since employers and workers alike frequently believe that female supervisors are not as effective as male, supervisory and executive jobs are often reserved for men.

CAREER CONTINUITY AND MOTIVATION

Continuity in a job can be important in order to acquire or maintain skills, to establish seniority, or to prove one's loyalty to an organization. An individual may need to be continuously employed in one firm for some years before advancement, especially to an executive level, is available to him. Even more important than continuity within one firm is an uninterrupted involvement in an occupation, industry, or profession, whether to keep up in a rapidly changing field or not to lose ground in institutionalized apprenticeship systems.

Since women's participation in the labor force is usually intermittent, they are obviously seriously handicapped. Those with professional or managerial aspirations often cannot get necessary on-the-job training or promotions because employers feel that it is not worth the risk. One reason employers did not want to have women in executive positions was that "it is desirable that this group shall have as little turnover as possible. Too many women are likely to marry and leave the job" (Noland and Bakke 1949: 80, 94–95; cf. National Manpower Council 1957: 105).

Many female workers are secondary breadwinners, a situation that both reinforces wage discrimination and seriously weakens the commitment to work and a career. Even a man motivated mainly to improve his family's welfare is, for that reason, more committed than a woman to his work; in his case, familial and work commitments pull together. The time, energy, and interest devoted to women's occupational aspirations are usually seen as competing with the welfare of the family. As a result, women often do not want to rise from file clerk, say, to executive, where the responsibilities become too onerous. Nor do many want to go through professional training as time-consuming and difficult as medicine, law, and college teaching require.

This lack of career goals is illustrated in three surveys of female college graduates: a Woman's Bureau survey of the class of 1957, a study by Alice Rossi of a sample three years after graduation, and a national sample of the class of 1964. While most of the women in the 1957 study were working or planned to work at some point in their lives, only 18 percent (14 percent of the married) planned to have a career (U. S. Women's Bureau 1959: 41, 44). Alice Rossi (1965) reports on the replies to one of her questions:

"An American woman can be very successful in a variety of ways. Which of the following would you most like to be yourself?" The most frequent answers were to be the mother of several accomplished children and to be the wife of a prominent man.

In the 1964 study, while few (8 percent) preferred to be just housewives, only 20 percent said they wanted to combine family and career and only 12 percent thought this a realistic expectation. And they were probably right, for only 8 percent of the male graduates wanted their wives to combine family and career.

Regardless of the actual level of female motivation, that employers believe women have lower career aspirations affects hiring and promotion policies.

Women were described as usually less willing than men to make sacrifices required to secure the training which would qualify them for advancement. Frequently, it was reported, they are even unwilling to take advantage of chances for immediate promotion. It was suggested that this lack of interest and initiative could be both a cause and an effect of women's restricted opportunities in the working world (National Manpower Council 1957: 94, 104ff).

A related factor is that many professional and managerial careers require geographical mobility. A married woman, whose husband's career usually has priority, may have to leave a good job to accompany him or she may have to stay put when her best job opportunities are elsewhere.

SUMMARY

Three major female professions—nursing, teaching, and librarianship—depend on skilled but cheap labor in fairly large quantities; they are traditionally female occupations; most of the requisite training is acquired before employment; and career or geographical continuity is not essential. Diligence and a certain devotion to the job are required, but long-range commitments and extensive sacrifices of time and energy are not. Such employment seldom puts the worker in a supervisory position over male employees, and when nurses, for example, initiate action for patients, the authority to do so derives from the attending physician. The characteristics of the female professions, in short, encourage the employment of women.

The predominantly male professions—law, medicine, dentistry, architecture, university teaching and administration, and the clergy, among others—are so by tradition. They demand great investments of time, energy, and devotion; extensive and often difficult schooling, a life of overtime work; and the freedom to move or not to move. Managerial occupations demand the same features except for extensive education—although increasingly a BA is a minimum requirement and some graduate work in business administration meets with considerable favor.

Clerical work requires cheap but fairly well educated labor, with training achieved mainly before entry into the labor market. The work demands characteristics supposedly more typical of women—manual dexterity plus a tolerance for monotonous tasks. Here also a strong commitment is unnecessary; geographical mobility or high motivation is not important, but if the ultimate goal is to rise into a managerial position, continuity may be essential. Many salesmen have to travel and usually women, especially married women, are not willing or able to leave their families.

Among manual jobs, most craft occupations are traditionally male, and control over recruitment keeps them that way. When both men and women are in operative occupations, they are not the same ones; women are concentrated in the lower-paid jobs. The presumed male (strength) or female (manual dexterity) characteristics may be important factors in sex labeling, as well as the avoidance of women in supervisory positions over men.

In sum, what is surprising is not that men and women usually compete in separate labor markets, but that one kind of labor is ever substituted for the other.

References

ABBOTT, EDITH. 1910. *Women in Industry.* New York: Appleton.

CAPLOW, THEODORE. 1954. *The Sociology of Work.* Minneapolis: University of Minnesota Press.

FICHTER, JOSEPH H. 1967a. "Career Expectations of Negro Women Graduates," *Monthly Labor Review,* **90,** 36–42.

————. 1967b. *Graduates of Predominantly Negro Colleges—Class of 1964*. U. S. Public Health Service, Publication No. 1571. Washington, D. C.: U. S. Government Printing Office.

GINDER, CHARLES E. 1961. "Factors of Sex in Office Employment," *Office Executive*, 36, 10–13.

KAPLAN, DAVID L., and M. CLAIRE CASEY. 1958. *Occupational Trends in the United States, 1900 to 1950*. U. S. Bureau of the Census, Working Paper No. 5. Washington, D. C.: U. S. Government Printing Office.

LEBERGOTT, STANLEY. 1964. *Manpower in Economic Growth*. New York: McGraw-Hill.

MCNULTY, DONALD J. 1967. "Differences in Pay between Men and Women Workers," *Monthly Labor Review*, 90, 40–43.

NATIONAL MANPOWER COUNCIL. 1957. *Womanpower*. New York: Columbia University Press.

NOLAND, E. W., and E. W. BAKKE. 1949. *Workers Wanted: A Study of Employers' Hiring Policies, Preferences, and Practices in New Haven and Charlotte*. New York: Harper's.

OPPENHEIMER, VALERIE KINCADE. 1970. *The Female Labor Force in the United States: Demographic and Economic Factors Governing Its Growth and Changing Composition*. Institute of International Studies, Population Monograph No. 5. Berkeley: University of California.

ROSSI, ALICE S. 1965. "Women in Science: Why So Few?" *Science*, 48, 1196–1202.

SMUTS, ROBERT W. 1959. *Women and Work in America*. New York: Columbia University Press.

U. S. Bureau of the Census. 1963a. *Census of Population, 1960: Characteristics of the Population*. Vol. I, Part 1. Washington, D. C.: U. S. Government Printing Office.

————. 1963b. *Census of the Population, 1960: Occupation by Industry*. Report PC(2)–7C. Washington, D. C.: U. S. Government Printing Office.

U. S. WOMEN'S BUREAU. 1959. *First Jobs of College Women*. Bulletin 268. Washington, D. C.: U. S. Government Printing Office.

————. 1962. *Careers for Women as Technicians*. Bulletin 282. Washington, D. C.: U. S. Government Printing Office.

————. 1963. *Economic Indicators Relating to Equal Pay*. Pamphlet 9. Washingington, D. C.: U. S. Government Printing Office.

WHYTE, WILLIAM F. 1949. "The Social Structure of the Restaurant," *American Journal of Sociology*, 54, 302–310.

WILLIAMS, JOSEPHINE. 1946. "Patients and Prejudice: Lay Attitudes toward Women Physicians," *American Journal of Sociology*, 51, 283–287.

WOODY, THOMAS. 1929. *A History of Women's Education in the United States*, Vol. 1. New York: Science Press.

5 SUBNATIONS

Populations are typically classified by age and sex, as exemplified in the papers included in the last chapter, and by residence, which will be discussed in the next one. Other classifications vary greatly, and it is convenient to divide them into two generic types, following the analogy of the achieved and the ascribed status of a person. To measure the movement of an individual up the social ladder, or of a nation toward full economic development and cultural modernity, analysts generally use one or another index of social class—mainly occupation, but also such related characteristics as education and income. In contrast, some classifications are defined by criteria that are (or are perceived to be) more or less immutable—race, origin, national stock, language, citizenship, religion, region (in the sense of a cultural rather than a political division), and so on. As the contrary of social class, I have proposed that the most appropriate term for the second generic type, analogous to ascribed status, is subnation. *Except for their smaller size, subnations have the main features that we associate with nationality: an actual or putative biological descent from common forebears, a common territory, an easier communication inside than outside the group, a sentimental identification with insiders and thus a relative hostility toward out-*

siders. As with nations, not all subnations need show every distinguishing characteristic.

In several different respects, the most significant of the subnations in the United States is the Negro tenth. Two well trained demographers have concentrated on the analysis of Negroes, and their works represent some of the best studies of this interesting topic now available. They have co-operated as co-authors of the next paper.

Reynolds Farley, who received his doctoral degree from the University of Chicago in 1964, is an associate professor of sociology at the University of Michigan and an associate director of its Population Studies Center. Almost every one of his dozen articles is on Negro population trends, and his book on the subject, Growth of the Black Population: A Study of Demographic Trends *(Chicago: Markham, 1970), is the best over-all analysis.*

After receiving his doctorate from Harvard in 1960, Karl E. Taeuber worked with the Biometry Branch of the National Cancer Institute (1959–61), as research associate of the Population Research and Training Center of the University of Chicago (1961–63), and as social scientist at the Rand Corporation (1969–70). He is presently chairman of the department of sociology at the University of Wisconsin. His two books and several dozen articles almost all relate to either of his two professional interests—internal migration and the Negro population.

The paper that Professors Farley and Taeuber wrote together is a dispassionate discussion of a highly emotional topic, based on careful compilation of data from a large number of census publications and analyzed with measures that Karl and Alma Taeuber themselves devised in an earlier work. Certainly one could not ask for a better statement on desegregation trends during the early 1960s. However, the situation of Negroes changes so rapidly that the paper's conclusions may be out of date. According to preliminary findings from the 1970 census, an average of 85,000 Negro parents moved with their children to formerly white suburbs in each year since 1964, making up a total of more than 800,000 such migrants during the whole intercensal period. These figures are still small relative to the enormous white out-migration from central cities, but it appears from the preliminary data that the Negro migration to suburbs is rising rapidly and that the growth of Negro populations in the central cities is slowing down (New York Times, July 12, 1970). Whether these apparent patterns do develop or not, the change does not detract from the solid worth of Farley and Taeuber's paper, both as an analysis of the period it covers and as an example of the methodology that might be used in analyzing later statistics.

POPULATION TRENDS AND RESIDENTIAL SEGREGATION SINCE 1960

REYNOLDS FARLEY AND KARL E. TAEUBER

According to an editorial in the *Washington Post* (December 28, 1966), "A great tide of migration is segregating American life, as most of us live it, faster than all of our laws can desegregate it." A national concern with civil rights developed in the late 1950s in part as a response to the problems engendered by momentous demographic change, but the change itself was largely unrecognized. The 1960 census eventually produced evidence of the absolute loss of white population and gain of Negro population in many large central cities (Schnore 1965: 255). In many cities, there was net out-migration of whites, particularly young adults, but the natural increase prevented decline in total numbers and masked the magnitude of change. Over the same period, Negro population was increasing rapidly not only in New York and Chicago, but in Los Angeles, Syracuse, Boston, Milwaukee, and most other large cities.

The 1960 census provided the most recent reliable basis for a detailed assessment of population trends. Fortunately, the Bureau of the Census from time to time conducts special censuses in various cities. Some are taken at the request and expense of local areas which need current data; some are conducted to pretest census methodologies; and some are conducted under congressional mandate (for example, the Voting Rights Act of 1965). Until the full results of the 1970 census become available, these special censuses provide the best available information about population change, migration patterns, and trends in residential segregation since 1960.

We have assembled data for all thirteen cities in which a special enumeration conducted after 1960 reported a total population of at least 100,000 and a Negro population of at least 9,000, and for which the 1960 and later census-tract grids are reasonably comparable (U. S. Bureau of the Census 1961, 1964–67). These cities, their populations, and their growth rates are shown in Table 1.

POPULATION CHANGE AND MIGRATION PATTERNS

Of the thirteen cities, seven experienced a decline in total population, by as much as 10 percent in Providence and Buffalo. In each city the Negro population grew more rapidly or—in the case of Shreveport—decreased less rapidly than the white population. As a consequence the percentage of

SOURCE: Reprinted from *Science*, **159** (March 1, 1968), 953–56, with permission of the authors and the journal. Copyright 1968 by the American Association for the Advancement of Science.

Table 1. Population Change and Racial Composition, Thirteen American Cities, 1960 to Mid-1960s

CITY	DATE OF SPECIAL CENSUS	TOTAL POPULATION (THOUSANDS)		PERCENTAGE CHANGE 1960 TO MID-1960s		PERCENTAGE NEGROES	
		1960	MID-1960s	NON-NEGRO	NEGRO	1960	MID-1960s
Buffalo	April 18, 1966	535	481	−13.5	15.7	13.2	17.0
Providence	October 1, 1965	208	187	−11.9	24.5	5.4	7.4
Rochester	October 1, 1964	319	306	−7.1	34.6	7.4	10.4
Cleveland	April 1, 1965	876	811	−14.7	10.2	28.6	34.1
Des Moines [a]	April 28, 1966	209	206	−1.5	6.3	4.9	5.3
Evansville [a]	October 20, 1966	142	143	0.4	6.2	6.6	6.9
Fort Wayne	January 24, 1967	155	160	0.2	39.8	7.5	10.2
Greensboro	January 25, 1966	120	132	8.8	13.9	25.8	26.7
Louisville [a]	May 14, 1964	391	387	−3.0	11.7	17.9	20.2
Memphis [a]	March 27, 1967	491	497	−6.8	14.8	37.6	42.6
Raleigh	January 25, 1966	94	105	12.2	12.7	23.4	23.4
Shreveport [a]	June 15, 1966	158	147	−9.1	−2.2	33.1	34.7
Sacramento [a]	October 9, 1964	189	192	−0.8	29.7	6.5	8.3

[a] Areas annexed after 1960 are excluded.

Negroes rose after 1960, in the southern cities and in Sacramento as well as in the northern cities.

National sample surveys conducted by the Bureau of the Census (1966: 1) document on an aggregate basis the prevalence of the demographic change observed in the thirteen cities:

In the first six years of the 1960s, the Negro population in large cities increased by more than 2 million while the white population in the same areas decreased by 1 million. The survey of March 1966 confirms that, to an increasing extent, Negroes are living in metropolitan areas and, within these areas, in the central cities. Between 1960 and 1966, the Negro population living in metropolitan areas increased by 21 percent, from 12,198,000 to 14,790,000, and almost all of this increase occurred within central cities. The white population living in metropolitan areas increased by 9 percent, from 99,688,000 to 108,983,000, and all of this metropolitan increase occurred outside central cities.

Special census tabulations, like those from the decennial census, show the population by age, sex, and color. From these data estimates of net migration were calculated. As a first step, survival ratios from a national life table for 1962 were applied to the 1960 population of each city (specifically for age, sex, and color) to estimate its population at the special census date (U. S. National Center for Health Statistics 1964). This estimated population was then compared to the population enumerated by the special census and the difference represented net migration (Table 2). Except for Sacramento, at least 94 percent of the nonwhites in each city were Negroes.

From eleven of the thirteen cities there was a substantial net out-migration of whites in the post-1960 period. Cleveland lost 110,000 people, or 18 percent of the white population, over five years; Buffalo 15 percent over six years; and Shreveport, Memphis, and Providence more than 10 percent over five to seven years.

Migration losses were proportionately greatest among whites aged 20 to 29 at the start of the period. Those aged 30 to 39 also had high migration losses, and children under 10 moved with their parents. For eight cities there was a net migration balance into the city among whites aged 10 to 19. These results are consistent with other migration data indicating a continued attraction of central cities to young adults, but a marked out-movement during the family-expansion stage of the life cycle (Shryock 1964: 424). In all cities there was a net out-migration of older whites, with no evidence of a move back to the city among those whose children are grown.

Migration patterns for nonwhites were diverse. Among those aged 20 to 29 in 1960, the seeming pattern was the typical net out-migration from southern cities and net in-migration to northern cities. But there is no simple summary of other age groups. In some northern cities with large Negro populations (Buffalo and Cleveland), net migration during the early 1960s

Table 2. Estimated Net Migration, by Color and Age, Thirteen American Cities, 1960 to Mid-1960s

| CITY AND COLOR | NET MIGRA-TION | NET MIGRATION PER 100 PERSONS IN AGE GROUP IN 1960 | | | | | | |
		TOTAL	0–9	10–19	20–29	30–39	40–49	50–64	65+
Buffalo									
White	−68,565	−15	−19	−9	−26	−16	−11	−12	−13
Nonwhite	+574	+1	+3	0	+6	+1	−6	−2	−7
Providence									
White	−24,292	−12	−19	+3	−31	−17	−11	−8	−8
Nonwhite	+1,125	+9	+13	+23	+13	+2	−1	+5	a
Rochester									
White	−22,477	−8	−12	+8	−19	−14	−9	−8	−16
Nonwhite	+4,210	+17	+12	+29	+23	+10	+3	+3	a
Cleveland									
White	−110,893	−18	−33	−5	−38	−32	−19	−18	−20
Nonwhite	+1,878	+1	+3	+3	+4	−5	−2	+2	−3
Des Moines									
White	−12,973	−7	−12	+6	−17	−11	−5	−4	−2
Nonwhite	−306	−3	+1	−9	−3	−1	−1	−2	a
Evansville									
White	−6,824	−5	−7	−7	−4	−5	−5	2	−5
Nonwhite	−363	−4	+1	−24	a	+1	−2	+26	a
Fort Wayne									
White	−9,311	−6	−11	+8	−15	−10	−7	−5	−6
Nonwhite	+1,806	+15	+16	+29	+19	+7	+3	a	a
Greensboro									
White	+941	+1	−1	+15	0	−2	−5	−6	−4
Nonwhite	+954	+3	+6	+26	−24	+1	−14	−1	a
Louisville									
White	−23,030	−7	−14	+3	−20	−11	−5	−4	−2
Nonwhite	+2,483	+4	+4	+9	+5	+3	+5	+6	−2
Memphis									
White	−35,991	−12	−20	+4	−22	−16	−11	−7	−5
Nonwhite	+2,266	+1	+4	−5	−10	0	−3	+7	−7
Raleigh									
White	+3,875	+5	0	+39	−27	−2	−4	−6	−5
Nonwhite	+1,333	+6	+5	+23	−6	+3	+1	+4	a
Shreveport									
White	−13,351	−13	−21	−6	−23	−16	−11	−4	−1
Nonwhite	−9,420	−17	−18	−26	−24	−16	−14	+1	−11
Sacramento [b]									
White	−5,264	−3	−4	+1	−11	+2	−1	−4	−6

[a] Rate not calculated because denominator is less than 1,000.

[b] No migration rates for nonwhites were calculated for Sacramento since 40 percent of the nonwhites in this city were Orientals.

was slight. In northern cities with smaller Negro populations, net migration was sometimes large (Rochester and Providence) and sometimes small or negative (Des Moines and Evansville). Some southern cities had a net gain of Negro population through migration (Greensboro, Memphis, Louisville, and Raleigh), but some lost (Shreveport). The early 1960s may represent a transitional period in Negro migration. As Negro migrants seek out a variety of urban destinations, the earlier pattern of movement from southern cities to a few large northern cities may no longer be dominant (Taeuber and Taeuber 1965a).

Growth of the Negro population does not depend on a continued in-migration of Negroes. Negro populations in most cities include many women in the childbearing ages and many more about to enter these ages. Not only do white populations have a significant out-migration, but their older age structures are less conducive to high rates of natural increase. For instance, in Providence in 1965 the median age of whites was 35 years, of Negroes 19 years. In Buffalo in 1966 the median age of whites was 35 years, of Negroes 21 years. In Rochester in 1965, 17 percent of the whites, but 44 percent of the Negroes, were under age 15. Differential natural increase and white out-migration from cities are sufficient for continued increases in Negro percentages regardless of the pace of Negro migration to cities.

TRENDS IN RESIDENTIAL SEGREGATION

The growing Negro populations in many cities have expanded into housing outside the previously established Negro census tracts. These are small areas, containing on the average about 4,000 persons, for which basic census data are tabulated. In Buffalo, for example, in 1960 most Negroes lived in a belt of tracts extending south and west of downtown. By 1966 this belt had grown to include several more tracts. Almost all of Cleveland's Negroes, in both 1960 and 1965, lived east of the Cuyahoga River in a broad belt stretching from downtown to the city limits. Local estimates indicate the development of several predominantly Negro residential areas in the eastern suburbs (Regional Church Planning Office 1965). Few Negroes lived on the other side of downtown: according to the 1965 special census, of the 300,000 Clevelanders west of the Cuyahoga more than 99 percent were white.

The other cities lacked such extensive established Negro areas in 1960, but solidly Negro residential areas have developed. In Rochester, areas southwest and immediately north of the central business district became increasingly Negro. In Providence, Negroes replaced whites in tracts in the Federal Hill area and south of downtown along the Providence River. In each of the thirteen cities the development and spread of predominantly Negro residential areas can be traced.

It is also possible to use these data to calculate summary indices of residential segregation. In contrast to the detailed descriptions of Negro residential patterns obtained from maps, such indices facilitate comparisons among cities and through time.

Using city block data for a large number of American cities, the Taeubers (1965b) assessed trends in residential segregation from 1940 to 1960. In cities of all sizes and in every part of the country, Negroes and whites were found to be residentially segregated. From 1940 to 1950, when the housing market was very tight, existing patterns were maintained and additional whites and Negroes were housed in a highly segregated pattern. Residential segregation generally increased. During the 1950s there was an increased availability of housing. A multiple-regression analysis for 69 cities relating changes in segregation to changes in other characteristics suggested that in many northern cities "the growing Negro populations, together with the demand for improved housing created by the improving economic status of Negroes, were able to counteract and in many cases to overcome the historical trend toward increasing residential segregation. In southern cities Negro population growth was slower and economic gains were less. The long-term trend toward increasing segregation slowed but was not reversed" (Taeuber 1965).

The Taeubers' measure of segregation (1965b) was the dissimilarity index, calculated from city-block data on the number of housing units occupied by whites and nonwhites. For assessment of post-1960 trends, we shall use the dissimilarity index calculated from census-tract data on the number of Negroes and non-Negroes. Because the size of the index depends on the areal units from which it is calculated, the indices shown here are not directly comparable with the Taeubers'. Calculation of the index requires percentage distributions of Negroes and of non-Negroes in all the census tracts of a city. The index is one-half the sum of absolute differences between the two percentage distributions. The numerical value of the index indicates the minimum percentage of Negroes (or of non-Negroes) whose census tract of residence would have to be changed to obtain an areally homogeneous distribution of the two groups. A value of 100 indicates complete segregation; of zero, no segregation.

Dissimilarity indices for the thirteen cities in 1960 and at the special census dates are shown in the first two columns of Table 3. The differences indicate a pattern of increasing residential segregation. Only in Fort Wayne and Sacramento did Negroes and non-Negroes become less segregated from one another during the early 1960s.

The thirteen cities are not a random sample, and we cannot claim to show that residential segregation in American cities is generally increasing. But these results together with those for 1940–60 together constitute strong evidence that the pervasive pattern of residential segregation has not been significantly breached. Whether the temporal trend for a particular city has been up, down, or fluctuating, the magnitude of the change has usually

Table 3. Indices of Residential Segregation, Thirteen American Cities,
1960 and Mid-1960s

| | DISSIMILARITY INDEX | | REPLACEMENT INDEX | | HOMOGENEITY INDEX | | | |
| | | | | | NEGRO | | NON-NEGRO | |
CITY	1960	MID-1960s	1960	MID-1960s	1960	MID-1960s	1960	MID-1960s
Buffalo	84.5	85.1	19.4	24.0	65	74	95	95
Providence	64.2	70.3	6.6	9.6	23	30	96	94
Rochester	76.7	79.3	10.5	14.8	44	53	96	95
Cleveland	85.2	87.2	34.8	39.2	81	86	92	92
Des Moines	76.7	77.3	7.1	7.8	35	40	97	97
Evansville	76.9	80.5	9.5	10.3	54	61	97	97
Fort Wayne	79.8	79.2	11.1	14.5	38	52	95	95
Greensboro	83.8	89.1	32.1	34.9	83	88	94	96
Louisville	78.6	81.2	23.1	26.2	68	73	93	93
Memphis	79.3	83.7	37.2	40.2	79	86	88	89
Raleigh [a]	75.0	78.0	26.9	28.0	72	74	92	93
Shreveport	82.5	85.1	36.5	38.6	81	85	90	92
Sacramento	58.2	57.2	7.1	8.7	24	29	95	94

[a] Indices were calculated from data for 19 tracts lying entirely within the city and 11 tracts lying across the city boundary.

been small. Stability in segregation patterns has been maintained despite massive demographic transformation, marked advances in Negro economic welfare, urban renewal and other clearance and resettlement programs, considerable undoubling of living quarters and diminished crowding, high vacancy rates in many of the worst slums, and an array of federal, state, and local antidiscrimination laws and regulations.

The analysis of census data points to stability in segregation patterns, with some preponderance recently of small increases in a segregation index. How can these results be reconciled with the rapidly increasing segregation perceived by most civil-rights groups and many other observers? Such observers are likely to be looking at something more than simply the patterns of housing segregation. Composite indices can combine measures of the proportion Negro with measures of residential segregation. Because the two components are not highly correlated, the Taeubers (1965b: 195) argued against use of such an index for comparisons between cities. Nevertheless, we believe there may be heuristic value in two composite indices among the many that have been proposed. These are well formulated to represent the magnitude, respectively, of the desegregation and the segregation problem.

DESEGREGATION AND SEGREGATION

By the desegregation problem, we mean the proportion of the population that would have to be moved to effect complete residential desegregation. The index of dissimilarity gives a superficial answer, specifying the desegregation problem on the assumption that persons of only one race are to be moved, from areas in which they are overrepresented to areas of underrepresentation. Moving persons of only one race would depopulate many areas and require substantial additional housing in others. More realistic is a series of exchanges of white and Negro households, accomplishing desegregation while maintaining existing housing stock. The minimum percentage of the total population that would be moved by such a procedure is given by the so-called replacement index

$$2q(1-q)D$$

where q is the proportion Negro in the total population and D is the index of dissimilarity (Walker *et al.* 1967: 5).

By the segregation problem, we mean the tendency of residential segregation to create racial homogeneity among neighborhood contacts (on the street and in stores, schools, and other neighborhood facilities). For an objective, census-based measure of this type of phenomenon, it is necessary to assume that contacts within an area (census tract, city block, school district) are made at random among the resident population. For a Negro chosen at random from the city's population, the probability of residing in tract i is n_i/N, where n_i is the number of Negroes in tract i and N is the total number of Negroes in the city. The probability that another individual randomly chosen from tract i is also a Negro is $\frac{n_i - 1}{t_i - 1}$ where t_i is the total population in tract i. For convenience, this term may be approximated by n_i/t_i. If we take the joint probability of the two events, sum over tracts, and express the result in percentage scale (Bell 1954), we have

$$(100/N)\Sigma n_i{}^2/t_i$$

This index may also be interpreted as the average percentage Negro in census tracts, weighted by the number of Negroes in the tract. From the Coleman report (1966: 21), some evidence may be adduced for the proposition that the educational achievement of Negro pupils is the less, the higher the percentage of Negroes in their schools. More generally, the social-psychological consequences of residential segregation might be hypothesized to be some function of the average Negro percentage encountered by Negroes in their neighborhoods. It is in this sense that the index may be regarded as measuring the segregation problem. We designate it the Negro homogeneity index.

The dissimilarity and replacement indices are racially symmetrical. Negroes and non-Negroes are equally segregated from each other. The homogeneity index is racially specific. The average Negro percentage encountered by Negroes may differ from the average white percentage encountered by whites (the white homogeneity index).

The replacement and homogeneity indices (Table 3), in contrast to the dissimilarity index, have a wide range in magnitude. This reflects the wide range in values of q (the proportion Negro) and the additional variance introduced by the squared terms appearing in each composite index. The replacement and Negro homogeneity indices are highly correlated. Both indices increased for each of the thirteen cities between 1960 and the later date. For most cities, both segregation (D) and proportion Negro (q) increased, but the relative increase was small in the former compared to the latter. Trends in the composite indices are largely determined by trends in the Negro proportion.

To summarize: We examined special census data for thirteen cities to assess trends in population, migration, and residential segregation from 1960 to the mid-1960s. In these cities, the demographic trends of the 1950s are continuing. There is a net out-migration of white population, and in several cities a decline in total population. Negro population is growing rapidly, but increasingly by a natural increase rather than net in-migration. The concentration of whites in the suburbs and Negroes in the central cities is continuing. Within the cities, indices of racial residential segregation generally increased. The combination of small increases in residential segregation and large increases in the Negro percentage has greatly intensified the magnitude of the problems of segregation and desegregation of neighborhoods, local institutions, and schools.

References

BELL, WENDELL. 1954. "A Probability Model for the Measurement of Ecological Segregation," *Social Forces*, **32**, 357–364.

COLEMAN, JAMES S., ERNEST Q. CAMPBELL, and A. M. Mood. 1966. *Equality of Educational Opportunity*. Washington, D. C.: U. S. Government Printing Office.

REGIONAL CHURCH PLANNING OFFICE. 1965. "Changes in the Nonwhite Population," *Newsletter*, No. 21. Cleveland.

SCHNORE, LEO F. 1965. *The Urban Scene*. New York: Free Press.

SHRYOCK, HENRY S., JR. 1964. *Population Mobility within the United States*. Chicago: Community and Family Study Center, University of Chicago.

TAEUBER, KARL E. 1965. "Residential Segregation," *Scientific American*, **213**, 12–19.

———, and ALMA F. TAEUBER. 1965a. "The Changing Character of Negro Migration," *American Journal of Sociology*, **70**, 429–441.

———, and ———. 1965b. *Negroes in Cities*. Chicago: Aldine.

UNITED STATES. BUREAU OF THE CENSUS. 1961. *Census of Population, 1960,* PHC(1), Parts 21, 28, 39, 45, 49, 57, 83, 89, 122, 124, 127, 129, and 143. Washington, D. C.: U. S. Government Printing Office.

———. ———. 1964–67. *Current Population Reports,* Series P-28, Nos. 1376, 1377, 1386, 1390, 1393, 1411, 1413, 1430, 1431, 1435, 1441, 1446, and 1453. Washington, D. C.: U. S. Government Printing Office.

———. ———. 1966. *Current Population Reports,* Series P-20, No. 157. Washington, D. C.: U. S. Government Printing Office.

———. NATIONAL CENTER FOR HEALTH STATISTICS. 1964. *Vital Statistics of the United States, 1962,* Vol. II, Section 5. Washington, D. C.: U. S. Government Printing Office.

WALKER, DOLLIE R., ARTHUR L. STINCHCOMBE, and MARY S. McDILL. 1967. *School Desegregation in Baltimore,* Final report. Baltimore: Johns Hopkins Center for the Study of Social Organization of Schools.

Though neither is stated explicitly, one could read two underlying assumptions into the paper of Professors Farley and Taeuber, and it is worth looking at both of these postulates. The first is that the residence pattern of Negroes is a resultant of two opposed forces—"segregation," the expression of white prejudice, and "desegregation," the efforts of official agencies to overcome that prejudice. There is certainly much truth to this view, but there is also a third factor, which might be termed "congregation," or the preference of persons of any subnation—including Negroes—to live among their conationals. Though it would generally be extremely difficult to distinguish between segregation and congregation empirically, it is important to maintain the difference between the concepts. It may be that the rise of black nationalism during the early 1960s affected the residence patterns of Negroes both directly and indirectly, both by emphasizing pride in black neighborhoods and by excluding whites from those neighborhoods. Whether this was a factor is an empirical question, and not one that should be eliminated in advance from an analysis.

The second implicit point concerns the effect of white prejudice, which is once again a social reality but not as absolute as it is sometimes represented. The next article, "Inequality and Opportunity," constitutes an attempt to deal with this question on the basis of solid statistical data. In short, if a person fails to move up in the United States, to what degree is it due to his own lacks, to what degree to other factors? The paper was delivered originally as a presidential address to the Population Association of America.

Otis Dudley Duncan, the author, is a professor of sociology at the University of Michigan and an associate director of its Population Studies Center. He is one of the most prolific and most influential of American demographers, the author or editor of sixteen books and several dozen scholarly papers. Among these one should mention in particular The American Occupational Structure *(with Peter M. Blau; Wiley, 1967), which is in some respects a larger version of this article. His current research is on how one can construct social indicators by replicating earlier sociological surveys.*

INEQUALITY AND OPPORTUNITY

OTIS DUDLEY DUNCAN

Let me begin with definitions of the terms appearing in the title. *Inequality* refers to the dispersion of the distribution over a population of any of the rewards and status distinctions conferred by a society on its members —such as income, wealth, level of living, leisure, prestige, recognition, power, authority, skill, information, civil liberties, welfare, or life chances. Only some of these items have been so quantified that we can compute an actual measure of inequality, and for even fewer of them do we have replicated measurements taken periodically. According to Herman Miller's analysis (1966: chap 1), there has been no trend toward either increasing or decreasing inequality in the distribution of income during the past two decades, although there may well have been some reduction in income inequality between 1929 and the end of the Second World War. Incidentally, the failure of that trend to continue was correctly forecast by Joseph J. Spengler (1953). We have no time series, as we have for income, on the concentration—that is, inequality—of the distribution of power in American society. The lack of such measurements has not prevented the formation of strong opinions on the subject by commentators and social critics.

Opportunity refers to the probability of finding one's self at a high, medium, or low position on any of the scales of status or reward just mentioned, insofar as that probability is a function of the circumstances of birth and rearing in a given family of orientation, locality, region, cultural or ethnic group, or social milieu. Restriction of opportunity is synonymous with social stratification, the essence of which is the intergenerational transmission of differences in status, whether of greater or lesser degree.

Stratification, therefore, could be lessened in two ways: first, by reduction in inequality itself—as in the lowering of Gini's coefficient, defined for the Lorenz curve of income distribution—for in this case there is less difference in status to be transmitted between generations; and, secondly, by decreasing the magnitude of the regression (or other appropriate measure of relation) of filial on paternal status, such as a reduction of the degree

SOURCE: Reprinted from *Population Index*, **35** (1969), 361–366, with permission of the author and the Population Association of America.

to which the schooling of members of a birth cohort depends on the race, rural-urban residence, and schooling of their parents.

The measurement of opportunity is complicated by the factor of growth, which produces a rise in the mean level of achieved status over time, between generations, and in successive cohorts. American white men born in 1900–04 received an average of 9.4 years of schooling, as compared with 7.4 received by their fathers, a difference of 2.0 years. For those born in 1930–34, the corresponding figures were 12.0 and 8.7, producing an intergenerational difference of 3.3 years (B. Duncan 1965: 43). This may have been a cohort for which the intergenerational difference was near the peak for all cohorts born in the 20th century, inasmuch as the acceleration of educational attainment for cohorts born in the first third of the century will be echoed in an acceleration in the attainment of the parents of those born in the succeeding third.

However one may project the long-run trend for the future, it is clear that all our measurements for the past are affected by upward mean shifts. The consequence is that intergenerational status comparisons generally reveal a greater prevalence of upward, than of downward, mobility. An estimate for 1962 is that 25 percent of men aged 25 to 64 had experienced long-distance upward mobility, while another 25 percent underwent short-distance movement up the occupational scale. Some 28 percent were at very nearly the same occupational levels as their fathers, while only 15 percent had undergone short-distance downward mobility and 7 percent long-distance movement down the scale (Blau and Duncan 1967: Table 4.5). Thus, fully 50 percent of the population clearly experienced upward mobility while only 22 percent clearly experienced downward mobility. Yet the high prevalence of upward mobility in this population does not gainsay the reality of stratification, that is, restriction of opportunity. One way to express it is by means of the regression coefficient of 0.4, which measures the degree to which the son's status depends on the father's. Another way is to display origin-specific destination probabilities. For example, one's chances of being a professional worker, if one's father was so classified, were seven times as great as they were if one's father was a laborer: 41 percent versus 6 percent (U. S. Bureau of the Census 1964: Table 1).

Such findings on the extent of intergenerational mobility and the degree of intergenerational status transmission do not have a self-evident interpretation, either from the standpoint of their explanation or from that of their consequences.

We should probably not wish to attribute the entirety of the correlation between son's and father's status to social stratification, that is, to restriction of opportunity. For one thing, there is substantial evidence that intelligence, as we now measure it, has a rather high heritability (Jensen 1967). Knowing this, one might be inclined to explain the intergenerational correlation in status achievement by parent-offspring resemblance in intelligence. Although this topic is shrouded in uncertainty, we do not have to rely wholly on conjecture. A rudimentary multivariate causal model provides a rough quantification of the respective influences of ability and parental status on level of occupational achievement (O. D. Duncan 1968a). The model shows their influences to be somewhat overlapping but preponderantly distinct. Meritocracy, therefore, is widespread in the American population, inasmuch as ability does count, irrespective of family background. Restriction of opportunity is likewise widespread, inasmuch as level of social origin has an influence, irrespective of ability. That both statements are true is a complication of social reality as well as of analysis. Analysts who are intolerant of ambiguity may join the ideologists, for whom questions have clear and decisive answers.

Interpretation of the facts on social mobility from the standpoint of consequences must be a bit more speculative. Given both the sizable intergenerational correlation of statuses and the intergenerational upward mean shift in status, a man's achievement can well be limited or restricted by his social origin, while yet placing him at a level rather higher than that of his origin. How he may experience this subjectively is imponderable. Certainly it is curious that an effort to measure "subjective achievement" produced correlations with objective measures of income, occupational status, and educational attainment no higher than about .4 or .5 (O. D. Duncan 1969a: Tables 1, 2). Respondents clearly do not apply to themselves with ruthless consistency the scales of success or failure implicit in a social grading of roles. Or, perhaps, they adjust their status aspirations after the fact. This much we can say with some confidence: the variable, social mobility, has proved to be a less portentous factor in the formation of intergroup attitudes and in the determination of differential fertility than had been anticipated (Hodge and Treiman 1966; Blau and Duncan 1967: chap. 11).

As the concepts have been elucidated here, inequality is static, opportunity dynamic. Cross-sectional distributions serve to index degrees of inequality at a point in time, and the comparison of distributions for different points in time provides a starting point for the diagnosis of trend. Sources of inequality can be evaluated to a limited degree by the standard demographic techniques of decomposition. The paradigmatic studies by Dorothy S. Brady (1965), by A. J. Jaffe and R. O. Carleton (1954), and by Herman Miller (1966: chap. 6) suggest the advisability of decomposition by birth cohorts followed by systematic comparison of inter- and intracohort changes in distribution. Annual population surveys could provide much more grist for this analytical mill, were the importance of the cohort strategy more fully appreciated.

The decomposition of changes in inequality, however, is only a step toward dynamic analysis. The notion of opportunity invites us to view social stratification as a process, one characterized by a number of causal parameters that can, in principle, be estimated. Research inspired by this point of view will not necessarily lead to a standard, compact set of simple indices, but rather to a succession of more carefully specified and elaborated models. Such work will have a decreasing degree of resemblance to classic demographic analysis, but will put increasingly rigorous challenges to our systems for compiling demographic information.

The most egregious restrictions on opportunity in American society are those associated with race. It is important to understand that what is at stake here is the intergenerational transmission of liability to discrimination on the basis of race, and only secondarily the transmission of the generally low socio-economic status of the parental generation in the black population. An illustrative result for young adult men will convey the point, although the specific magnitudes are subject to uncertainty (O. D. Duncan 1969b). In 1964, the earnings of Negro men aged 25 to 34 were about 55 percent as great as those of white men of the same age. The dollar gap amounted to some $3,000. Of this gap 18 percent could be attributed to the disadvantageous social origins of Negro men, indexed by the educational and occupational levels of the heads of the families in which they grew up. An additional 3 percent was due to the racial differential in size of families of orientation. Some 22 percent of the gap not already accounted for arose from differences in the realized mental abilities of white and Negro children, as revealed in standard tests. Apart from differences in family size and socio-economic level, and apart from differences in mental test scores, length of schooling accounted for 2 percent of the income differential. Another 12 percent turned on the differences between white and Negro men in the occupations followed, net of the factors of education, mental ability, number of siblings, and social origins. Altogether, the calculation accounts for some four-sevenths of the income gap. The remaining 43 percent is due to the fact that Negro men in the same kinds of occupations, with the same amount of schooling, with equal mental ability, having come from families of the same size and socio-economic position, had annual earnings only three-fourths as high as those of white men with the stated average characteristics of the Negro men.

To repeat, only 21 percent of the $3,000 income gap could be explained by the Negroes' disadvantage with respect to social origins and size of family of orientation. The remaining components reflected a cumulation of disabilities specific to racial status. An implication is that no amount of attention in public policies and programs to any single disability—whether intellectual, educational, or occupational—could by itself eliminate the greater part of the gap. Compensation for the legacy of past discrimination, in the absence of marked change in the pattern of current discrimination, could reduce the gap by only one-fifth. On the other hand, the elimination of discrimination in the current situation, while leaving Negroes handicapped with respect to the residue from disabilities experienced in the past, would produce a situation in which such a residue would move rapidly toward zero in succeeding generations (Lieberson and Fuguitt 1967). The society need not hesitate to eliminate racial stratification on the supposition that such good work will be undone by a putative "culture of poverty."

Just as we lack firm trend data on many aspects of social inequality, so it proves difficult to establish firm estimates of the trend in opportunity. My reading of the evidence is that there almost certainly has been no increasing rigidification of the social structure of the kind that was once anticipated on the basis of such developments as the closing of the frontier, the diminution of immigration, the lessening of fertility differentials, and the decline in the role of independent entrepreneurship. Observations on both educational and occupational mobility are consistent with the supposition that opportunity—defined as above, in abstraction from the fact of growth—has remained about constant in terms of secular trend over the period since the First World War (O. D. Duncan 1965; 1968b).

This summary describes findings which, I fancy, are "value-free" in the sense that their acceptance into a body of verified understandings about social stratification should depend on their correspondence to reality and not on the values of the scientists who developed them. But a value-free science need not be produced by value-free scientists. The motivation for our research in this field is presumably a widely shared concern with such values as a belief in human dignity and a desire for social arrangements that will encourage realization of human potentialities. The scientist as such is no expert in the formulation and appreciation of values, but he may be of service in indicating how different values can interact to give rise to ambiguity in attitudes toward social problems.

Equalitarian values in one or another version are widely held in our society. In the light of these values, many critics find cause for dissatisfaction in the current performance of our social system. Two complementary objectives of deliberate social change may be distinguished: the enhancement of opportunity and the reduction of inequality.

Some consequences or prerequisites of increased opportunity should be observed. Movement toward parity of the circumstances under which persons develop is a movement toward a situation in which the capacities and dispositions with which they are born account for an increasing share of the variation in their achieved statuses. For, as Frederick Osborn (1968: 103) has pointed out, "trends toward the equalization of educational opportunity" will have the result that "hereditary ability wherever found will have a better chance to show itself." Project such a trend to its limit, and you end up with the pure meritocracy, depicted by Michael Young (1961) as a social system with its own peculiar ways of denying satisfaction to human impulses and its own institutional vulnerabilities. Another implication is that to reduce stratification presupposes the neutralization of the acquired advantages that a fortunate family might wish to pass along to its offspring, as well as the elimination of the disadvantages the less fortunate family might otherwise confer on its children. A substantial equalization of opportunity may well require an intervention much more far-reaching than we have yet seen on the part of the society and of the state into the processes of nurture and early socialization, hitherto almost monopolized by the family. I do not comment on the relative importance of the values of equal opportunity and family solidarity; I merely note their incompatibility in an ultimate sense (Eckland 1967).

On the strategy of reducing inequality, as distinct from giving everyone the same opportunity to enjoy success—or failure—we need to know more about status and reward as incentives. If rewards are made independent of performance—that is, if failure is abolished—need we worry about the source of motivation for achievement? Or does the solution lie not in the abolition of failure—or success—but in its redefinition? Are there, in other words, rewards that can be distributed to the accomplished without diminishing the supply of alternative rewards available for distribution to the less accomplished?

One does not have to be a prophet to foresee that our present passion for demographic and economic growth will some day be superseded by a concern for population quality and ecological balance. When this inevitable adaptation is effected—inevitable, that is, barring the catastrophe that will forestall all adaptation—perhaps it will seem more natural to espouse a hierarchy of values in which our assessment of men will not depend so heavily on their ability to "get ahead."

References

BLAU, PETER M., and OTIS DUDLEY DUNCAN. 1967. *The American Occupational Structure.* New York: Wiley.

BRADY, DOROTHY S. 1965. *Age and Income Distribution.* Research Report No. 8, U. S. Social Security Administration, Division of Research and Statistics. Washington, D. C.

DUNCAN, BEVERLY. 1965. *Family Factors and School Dropout: 1920–1960.* Final Report, Cooperative Project No. 2258, U. S. Office of Education. Ann Arbor: University of Michigan.

DUNCAN, OTIS DUDLEY. 1965. "The Trend of Occupational Mobility in the United States," *American Sociological Review,* 30, 491–498.

———. 1968a. "Ability and Achievement," *Eugenics Quarterly,* 15, 1–11.

———. 1968b. "Social Stratification and Mobility: Problems in the Measurement of Trend," in Eleanor B. Sheldon and Wilbert E. Moore, eds., *Indicators of Social Change: Concepts and Measurements.* New York: Russell Sage Foundation.

———. 1969a. "Contingencies in Constructing Causal Models," in Edgar F. Borgatta, ed., *Sociological Methodology, 1969.* San Francisco: Jossey-Bass.

———. 1969b. "Inheritance of Poverty or Inheritance of Race?" in Daniel P. Moynihan, ed., *On Understanding Poverty: Perspectives from the Social Sciences.* New York: Basic Books.

ECKLAND, BRUCE K. 1967. "Genetics and Sociology: A Reconsideration," *American Sociological Review*, 32, 173–194.

HODGE, ROBERT W., and DONALD J. TREIMAN. 1966. "Occupational Mobility and Attitudes toward Negroes," *American Sociological Review*, 31, 93–102.

JAFFE, A. J., and R. O. Carleton. 1954. *Occupational Mobility in the United States, 1930–1960*. New York: King's Crown Press.

JENSEN, ARTHUR R. 1967. "Estimation of the Limits of Heritability of Traits by Comparison of Monozygotic and Dizygotic Twins," *Proceedings of the National Academy of Sciences*, 58, 149–156.

LIEBERSON, STANLEY, and GLENN V. FUGUITT. 1967. "Negro-White Occupational Differences in the Absence of Discrimination," *American Journal of Sociology*, 73, 188–200.

MILLER, HERMAN P. 1966. *Income Distribution in the United States*. Washington, D. C.: U. S. Government Printing Office.

OSBORN, FREDERICK. 1968. *The Future of Human Heredity*. New York: Weybright and Talley.

SPENGLER, JOSEPH J. 1953. "Changes in Income Distribution and Social Stratification: A Note," *American Journal of Sociology*, 59, 247–259.

U. S. BUREAU OF THE CENSUS. 1964. "Lifetime Occupational Mobility of Adult Males: March 1962." *Current Population Reports*, Series P-23, *Technical Studies*, No. 11.

YOUNG, MICHAEL. 1961. *The Rise of the Meritocracy: 1870–2033*. Harmondsworth: Penguin Books.

An important proportion of the population of the world's countries is made up of a particular type of subnation—refugees. How to define this category, how many exist, what their conditions of life may be—these and similar questions are generally embedded in the same political disputes that generated the original movement and established the refugee settlements. Most demographers, therefore, have preferred to pass over this type of migration as beyond the possibility of impartial scholarly analysis. Yet the numbers involved—well over 10 million the world over (not including almost that number of East Pakistanis in India), and generally growing from year to year—are too great to ignore, and the impediments to analysis are no greater than in many other emotion-laden problems that sociologists and demographers study in depth.

The following article, on Palestinian refugees, is by James A. Michener, who hardly needs an introduction to any literate American. According to his own account of his life, he left home at age 14 and for a number of years lived like a hobo, working intermittently as a sports columnist, an amusement-park spotter, and an actor on the Chautauqua circuit. Feeling a need for some formal education, Michener entered Swarthmore College on a scholarship. After graduation he spent two years in Europe, studying painting in Siena, doing research in the British Museum, collecting rare songs in the Hebrides, and working as a chart corrector on a Mediterranean coal carrier. Back in the United States, he was a college teacher for a number of years and then became a textbook editor at Macmillan. His writing career took a jump when, following his war service in the Pacific, he wrote Tales of the South Pacific, *which won the Pulitzer Prize in 1947. Since then he has written extensively, both fiction and nonfiction. His latest works are a factual account of the background to the student riots at Kent State University and a novel,* The Drifters, *about alienated youth and its worldwide search for a hedonistic life style.*

WHAT TO DO ABOUT THE PALESTINIAN REFUGEES

JAMES A. MICHENER

The civil war in Jordan, like the hijacking and destruction of four international airliners by Palestinian refugees following the Maoist line, grew out of the fact that after 22 years the world has failed to find a solution to one of its thorniest problems: how to provide justice for the Palestinian refugee. Is it possible for the American observer to isolate the truth in this inflammable situation? What follows is as free from special pleading as it can be made.

Who are the Arab refugees? They fall into two groups. The first comprises those Arabs who for two years prior to 1948 lived in that part of British Palestine which subsequently became Israel. In the course of the 1948 Israeli war for independence, they left their homes and became refugees. Twenty-two years later they are still living in refugee camps in four nations which share common boundaries with Israel: Egypt, Jordan, Syria, Lebanon.

The second group comprises those Arabs who prior to 1967 lived in lands which Israel occupied in the Six-Day War of 1967. This group is less significant than the former in that the solution of their problem is simpler. Any reasonable peace treaty that will be worked out between the Arab states and Israel will provide for the immediate return of these refugees to their homes. In the vast majority of cases, the homes would lie in lands reverting to Arab rule. Israel has stated that she is eager to accomplish this as promptly as possible, for no one wishes to retain these refugees in camp a day longer than necessary. But when their problem is solved, the 1948 group still remains homeless.

Could the refugee problem have been avoided? Ironically, the UN Partition Plan for Palestine, adopted November 29, 1947, took into account the

SOURCE: Abridged from the *New York Times Magazine*, September 27, 1970, by permission of William Morris Agency, Inc., on behalf of the author. © 1970 by Marjay Productions, Inc.

desirability of insuring a homeland for the Palestinians. The plan was generous in concept, and if it had been accepted by the Arab states, the boundaries which Israel ultimately occupied would have been much reduced. Jews would have been restricted to areas that were already predominantly Jewish and, most important, the Palestinians would have held in 1947 more than what they can reasonably hope to attain in 1970. On the other hand, it was not unreasonable for the Palestinians to cry, "Who has the authority to *give* us anything? All of Palestine belongs to us and we'll take it all." So the Arabs went to war and in the resulting peace settlement the Palestinians lost everything that had been awarded them, a portion going to Israel, the bulk to Transjordan. Today, among the fanatical groups, the all-or-nothing philosophy still prevails, but among most Arabs it is generally recognized that the best the Palestinians can attain is an approximation of what they already held in 1947.

How many refugees were there originally? This is a crucial problem on which experts do not agree. As to the 1948 refugees, we have only one figure which is agreed upon: when the last accurate estimate was made in 1967—the Arab states have refused to allow an official census lest they lose UNRWA funds—the total population of the camps was 1,317,749 persons. The vital question is: How many of these came from Palestine in 1948?

Some years ago, I studied every available document on this subject and concluded that the total could not have been more than 600,000. Jewish scholars who have worked on the problem longer than I have come up with the figure 539,000. In 1970, a group of impartial Quakers from America, Canada and England stated: "There were approximately 750,000 Arab refugees who left their homes just before, during, or after the war of 1948."

There is no historical evidence whatever to support the argument that Palestine in 1948 sustained a population from which 1,317,749 could have been extracted. Growth from natural causes in the intervening years could have accounted for some of this increase, but much of it must have come from the insertion into the camps of persons who were not legitimate refugees. Anyone seeking to handle this problem intelligently must first decide how many refugees there were in the 1948 period.

In 1967, about 357,000 Arabs fled from such places as the West Bank of the Jordan, the Gaza Strip, the Sinai, and the Golan Heights. This is the group that everyone agrees should be repatriated as quickly as possible. In addition, there were 217,000 Arabs who were already refugees from the 1948 war and whose camps were overrun. Like mournful sheep they were driven from one set of intolerable conditions to another. They are among the world's most pitiful people.

Did they flee or were they expelled? This is a bitterly contested question, and because I once thought it important I spent two years trying to unravel it. Jews claim that in 1948, when it appeared that the Arabs would win easily, Arab leaders then broadcast appeals to the Arab population of Palestine to flee their homes, clutter up the roads and make Jewish control of the area impossible. Impartial English sources have always supported this contention, as do the verbal histories of the period. For example, *The Economist* of London reported in its issue of October 2, 1948, "There is but little doubt that by far the most potent factor was the announcement made over the air by the Arab High Committee urging all Arabs in Haifa to quit. It was clearly intimated that those Arabs who remained in Haifa would be regarded as renegades." The British police chief reported, "Every effort is being made by the Jews to persuade the Arab population to stay and carry on with their normal lives, to get their shops and businesses open and to be assured that their lives and interests be safe." And Glubb Pasha, a distinguished British general of Jordanian forces, said simply, in an article in a British newspaper, "The Arab civil population panicked and fled ignominiously."

Arabs, however, claim that no such broadcasts were made, that stories of Arab leaders demanding that Arabs flee the area were fabrications circulated to damage the reputation of the Grand Mufti of Jerusalem, and that any Arab who fled Palestine did so because he was kicked out by the Jews. They argue that Arabs fled in terror from a massacre which the Jews had perpetrated at the village of Deir Yassin on April 9, 1948, and were thus war refugees in the accepted sense of that term. Israelis reply that the hideous accident of Deir Yassin, in which somewhere between 250 and 1,000 Arabs were slain by irregular Jewish troops not under control of the Israeli Army, happened when villagers refused, through confusion, to utilize a broad escape route that had been set up for them. Israelis have apologized endlessly for this blemish on their record and relate it to four comparable massacres of Jews in which Arabs did not provide escape routes.

This difference of opinion over what had caused the flight used to seem more significant to me than it now does. "If the Arabs fled willingly, in response to a miscalculated military order, they surrendered any moral right to their former holdings," I reasoned, "but if they were forced out by the Jews they were indeed refugees and now retain title to their former possessions." I now believe that this distinction is irrelevant and divisive. The only moral issue which need concern us is that refugees are rotting in camps when they should be living productive lives elsewhere. In their present condition they constitute a threat to world peace, and trying to allocate responsibility for their initial flight is unproductive.

Recent studies support the view that trying to pinpoint responsibility would get us nowhere.

Dan Kurzman, an American Jew with impressive credentials as a former correspondent for the *Washington Post*, states in his independent study of the period, *Genesis 1948*, that he was unable to find any proof that the Arab leadership had ordered its people to evacuate Palestine, and the Quaker committee previously referred to concluded in early 1970, "From research materials available and from direct discussions with many persons who were on the scene, it is our considered judgment that most of those who fled did so out of the perfectly human tendency to panic in the face of warfare and to flee from the fighting."

Are any of the refugee camps located in Israel? No. When the 1948 war ended, it was discovered that some 200,000 Palestinian Arabs had refused to flee. When given a choice, they elected to live within the Jewish state. They prospered and are now among the most fortunate Arabs in the Middle East, insofar as economics, education, and health services are concerned. They dominate large cities like Nazareth; when I lived in Haifa, I patronized both an Arab restaurant, because the food was superior, and an Arab store, because the owners, Elza and Said Suidan, were such a delightful couple. By natural increase this original body of Arabs has now grown to 300,800, and while they do not enjoy untrammeled freedom or equality—even Israelis admit, "It'll be a long time before there's an Arab commander-in-chief of the Israeli Army"—they do maintain their own political parties and elect members to the Knesset. In two wars they have refrained from forming a fifth column. The contrast between how the Arab states handled incoming refugees and how Israel handled those who stayed behind is conspicuous.

Are there Jewish refugees? Yes, a great many. Yemen, Egypt, Iraq, Syria, and Morocco, to name only a few Arab countries, have expelled large portions of their Jewish populations, often without allowing them to carry any property with them. The total of such refugees, depending upon definitions, could run as high as 475,000. The wealth left behind by these Jewish refugees was considerable and it is not illogical to ask that this total be deducted from whatever debt a peace conference decides is owed by Israel to the Arab refugees. But whether an honest calculation of either of these debts is now possible remains doubtful.

Various protagonists have tried to differentiate between the Arab and the Jewish refugees. Arabs point out that Israel needed the immigrants to populate an empty land, required them as labor in a burgeoning industry, and in effect based Israel's developing economy on them. They were thus an asset rather than a hindrance, so that the Arab states in giving Israel this needed population were conferring a boon which more than offset individual Jewish losses. Israelis argue that whereas the Arab refugees left of their own accord during a war which the Arabs started, the Jewish refugees were kicked out by their host countries in time of peace, and whereas the Arab states made no effort to absorb their newcomers, Israel made every effort to welcome theirs.

I consider all such arguments irrelevant and nonproductive. What we are faced with is the pragmatic fact of two million refugees, Arab and Jewish, and the making of just decisions relating to them.

How have the refugees been supported? It is not widely known that for the past two decades the United States taxpayer has largely supported this isolated, undigested, tragic group of people. Officially they have been under

the protection of UNWRA, whose budget has come 66 percent and sometimes almost totally from the United States. Since 1948 we have contributed
more than $471,618,000 to the perpetuation of this festering thorn in the life
of both Arab and Jew.

A bitter irony of the situation is that the refugees hate the United States,
which has supported them for 22 years, and love Russia, which has contributed nothing to their upkeep.

How have the refugees lived? As I have said, miserably. I was able to
visit three of the camps and saw a sickening parade of families in which
father, mother, and all the children had known nothing but this slovenly
existence. There is nothing in the United States to compare with the worst
sections of such a camp. There were, it is true, other more favored corners,
where life was about as good as in one of America's worst prison camps. That
these camps have not spawned a plethora of criminals is amazing; that they
have produced the Fedayeen, bent on revenge, is not surprising.

*Have other nations ever absorbed refugee populations of comparable
size?* In the aftermath of the First World War, more than a million and a
half refugees floated about Europe. This was when Fridtjof Nansen, the
Norwegian polar explorer and winner of the Nobel peace prize, performed
his marvelous mission of finding homes for all. In the ugly Greek-Turkish
War of 1921–22, 1,400,000 Greeks were forced out of Asia Minor and were
quickly, though perhaps unwillingly, absorbed by homeland Greece with a
minimum of disruption. In the Second World War, refugees numbered more
than 13 million, with most of them being ultimately absorbed. It is sometimes overlooked that Japan, much less able to accommodate additional citizens than the Arab states, nevertheless absorbed in 1945, as a consequence of
her defeat in the Second World War, 6,289,000 refugees from Manchuria,
China, Korea, and Southeast Asia. More spectacular was the exchange of
populations between India and Pakistan following independence in 1947,
when 15 million changed countries.

I remember living in Karachi when penniless Moslem refugees from India
flooded all civic areas. Tent cities proliferated and destitute families lived
in doorways. Pakistan, nearly bankrupt, had no possibility of finding homes
for these millions, but it did. India performed a similar miracle. In comparison with most other nations, the Arab performance was grudging.

On the other hand, John B. Wolf, professor of history at New York State
University, in a finely reasoned article in *Current History*, argues, "Any
cursory investigation which concludes that a large number of refugees can
be settled within states contiguous with Israel is inaccurate." He points out
the interesting fact that Lebanon's constitution requires that the president
come from the largest religious sect—in 1970 Christian, by a minuscule
margin—and that a sudden influx of Moslem refugees would upset the
balance and even threaten civil war. Syria's precarious balance between
various Leftist and Centrist groups contending for dominance inhibited her

from making place for a group of unpredictable refugees. That Egypt is pitifully overcrowded may account for why even yet she refuses to grant citizenship to refugees who arrived in 1948. As for Jordan, Wolf says, "Ironically, King Hussein, whose country was the only state to give the refugees citizenship *en bloc,* finds the future of his dynasty contingent on a final solution to their problem." As if to prove Wolf's argument, Palestinians in 1970 came close to declaring war on Jordan, expressed their contempt for the Bedouin armies of the king, held Amman in a state of siege, and four times tried to assassinate Hussein.

Distance and Culture. The Arab refugee who fled the lake-side city of Tiberias in 1948 had to travel 8 miles before he reached his Arab refuge. From Safed it was 9 miles to the border. From Haifa, which had been the home of many Arabs, it was only 40 miles to Arab land. Arabs who fled Jerusalem walked about eight city blocks to their new homes. From the major population center in Jaffa it was 14 miles to safety.

These short distances mean two things. To travel from one's homeland in Palestine to one's new home in one of the host countries required no radical adjustment in either space or culture. In this respect it was one of the simplest exchanges of population in history, and not to be compared with the plight of 200,000 Hungarians who fled their country in 1956 for places like Venezuela, Australia, and New Jersey. A man from Elizabethton, Tenn., who emigrates to Los Angeles travels 2,314 miles and enters a wildly new cultural pattern. The Dutchman who had to leave Java and go home to Amsterdam, never having seen it before, made a journey in space and culture that was shocking in the magnitude of its changes. The Arab refugee had it comparatively easy.

On the other hand, it was this very proximity to the scene of one's childhood that inflamed the imaginations of the refugees and kept them burning for the past 22 years. An Arab in the camp at Jericho, if he had fled from the Jewish section of Jerusalem, could have walked back to his former home in four hours, had he been allowed to do so.

Which of the refugees want to return to their homes? Those few wealthy Arabs who scurried out of Palestine before the war erupted were able to establish themselves in neighboring lands. They are now like Irishmen in Boston and Swedes in Minnesota. They affirm that they wish to return to the homeland but would be appalled if they were forced to do so. That they would like to recover parcels of land that had once belonged to them there can be no question, but in general they are quiescent.

Moderately well-to-do Arabs who lost homes, or farms, or favorable situations in society have a real complaint. They have been deprived of property which was justly theirs and they yearn to recover it. They are not numerous, but they represent some of the finest elements in Arab life and occupy a strong moral position.

The average Arab who fled was neither well-to-do nor a pauper. He suffered the loss of what possessions he had accumulated, and the ensuing dislocation has been a hardship to him. One must not believe at face value, however, the fervent claims of such families as they recall nostalgically a style of living they had never known. It has been calculated that if all the Arab millionaires who claim to have lived in Haifa in 1947 had actually lived there it would have been a city wealthier than Paris, more ornate than Versailles.

There remains the largest group of refugees, those that had little in Palestine and resembled their kin across the border who had little in Jordan, or Syria, or Egypt. Sometimes these people lie about their lost wealth; more often they tell the truth. They want to return because they loved where they lived, and perhaps their loss is the greatest of all.

The outside observer has got to be impressed with the deep sincerity of refugee literature as it expresses the longing for return. Nasir ad-Din an-Nashashibi, in his novel, *Return Ticket*, gives this picture of a refugee father speaking of his love for the scenes of his youth:

> Every year I shall say to my little son: We shall return, my son, and you will be with me; we shall return to our land and walk there barefoot. We'll remove our shoes so that we may feel the holiness of the ground beneath us. We'll blend our souls with its air and earth. . . . We'll turn here and there to trace our lives.
>
> Where are they? Here with this village square, with this mosque's minaret, with the beloved field, the desolate wall, with the remains of a tottering fence and a building whose traces have been erased. Here are our lives. Each grain of sand teaches us about our life. Do you remember Jaffa and its delightful shore, Haifa and its lofty mountain, Beth Shean and the fields of crops and fruits, Nazareth and the Christian's bells, Acre and the memory of Al-Jazzar, Ibrahim Pasha, Napoleon and the fortress, the streets of Jerusalem, my dear Jerusalem, Tiberias and its peaceful shore with the golden wave, Majdal and the remnant of my kin in its land?

Reliable figures are not available, but it is generally believed that if repatriation with some chance of recovering former possessions were made available, not more than 200,000 Arabs would want to go back to Israel, but no one knows. Israel fears that the host governments would find ways of forcing all 1,317,749 back to constitute an unabsorbable Arab minority.

Do the Arabs own Palestine? This is an irrelevant question, almost an idiotic one, and it is just as irrelevant to ask, "Do the Jews own Palestine?" The prehistoric owners of the land seem to have been a proto-Semitic race known to Bible readers as Canaanites, and it can be said fairly firmly that neither Jew nor Arab has ever *owned* Palestine by unbroken right of inheritance. Jews occupied the land for 2,800 years before the first Arab appeared, were expelled from most of it by the Romans, filtered back, were killed off again by the Crusaders, filtered back again to live in commendable harmony with Arab-Moslem neighbors, first under Turkish rule and after 1918 under

British. Minor difficulties began to develop in the late 1800s, when heavy Jewish settlement threatened Arab interests, and materialized in the pre-1948 era, when it became obvious that the postwar influx of Jews had given them commanding industrial, educational, and governmental advantages.

It is positively ridiculous to say that in the abstract either Arab or Jew owns Palestine. If exclusive consideration is given to priority and longevity of claim, the land is Jewish. If continuity from 636 A.D. through 1947 is the criterion, the Arabs own it. If military victory against a coalition of Arab states which ignored the United Nations plan for the area is determinative, the Jews won the land in 1948, and ratified their claim in the 1956 and 1967 wars. I would prefer to think that the only "owners" were the ancient Canaanites, all subsequent visitors being interlopers who, through energy, love for soil, good government, religious intensity, or military capacity, have earned a right to occupy what part of it they needed, sharing the rest with their neighbors. I have studied this question for nearly twenty years and can come to no other conclusion. To me historical arguments have become senseless, for they can be used to prove anything in this area; if pressed, I could make as logical a case for Turkish "ownership" as for any other, and my conclusions would be totally irrelevant.

I have grown especially impatient with Jewish arguments that Israel was never an Arab land, and, more specifically, never under the governance of Palestinians who now seek to recover it. This reasoning is based on the undeniable but irrelevant fact that in the long years from 636 A.D., when Moslems first occupied the area, down to 1918, when the British captured it from Turkey, it was always ruled by outsiders, often non-Arab, and never by those Palestinian Arabs who lived on the land. On the other hand, it is informative to point out that there has never been a Palestinian nation, and that the establishment of one, which might be justified as a working solution, would set a historical precedent.

The result of the foregoing reasoning is obvious. Arabs and Jews are obligated to work out some sensible system of occupancy that will be fair to each, just as Protestants and Catholics are required to do in Ireland, the French and the English in Canada, and the blacks and whites in the United States. History frequently presents nations with pragmatic contradictions which must be resolved. It is prudent to solve them in regard to the facts of history, but not in slavish submission to them.

What alternative solutions are possible? Arabs maintain that Israel is obligated to give every one of the 1,317,749 refugees a free choice between returning to Israel or resettling normally in Arab countries, the cost of such resettlement to be borne by Israel. In addition, each refugee would receive cash compensation for actual losses incurred in 1948. World opinion and common sense support this claim.

Has Israel ever agreed in principle to the payment of reparations? Yes, consistently. I have talked with literally thousands of Israelis and almost without exception they have confessed to the existence of a moral problem. Jews in other countries have done the same. It has been widely proposed that Jewry throughout the world would take up a collection for the paying of reparations to the dispossessed Arabs, and numerous non-Jewish agencies have indicated that they would contribute to the fund, for this would be a small price to pay for peace.

Has Israel ever agreed in principle to total repatriation? No. Her position is this. Since Israel's population is only 2,841,000, of whom 300,800 are already Moslems, the forced incorporation of an additional 1,317,749 Moslems would mean that out of a 4,158,749 total population 39 percent would be Arabs, and the character of the country would be radically altered. "Israel would cease to be Israel," a member of the Knesset told me. "We would become a second Cyprus, where Greek fights Turk into the foreseeable future. Do the nations of the world seriously want us to create such a state, prey to every kind of disruption?" Nasser himself said, "If Arabs return to Israel, Israel will cease to exist."

There seems little likelihood that Israel would ever agree to accept the return of every Arab who wished to come back, even though Arab experts have confided that from their studies they believe that no more than 10 percent would wish to do so. This would mean only 150,000 returnees, a number which would seem to be manageable. On the other hand, Israel has given limited proof of her willingness to accept some refugees by establishing periods during which refugees with strong family ties in Israel have been free to return. About 40,000 have availed themselves of this opportunity.

Acknowledging the force of world opinion, Israel would probably now be willing to increase the number of 1948 refugees it would accept. The refugees from the 1967 war pose a much less serious problem and one that ought to be easily solved.

If there is in Israel a general agreement on reparations and repatriation, why has something not been done? Up to now Israel has held that the refugee problem could be discussed and settled only within the context of a total peace treaty for the Middle East. Arabs contend that the question of reparations and repatriation must be settled before peace can even be discussed. On these immovable rocks of contrasting interpretation all attempts to settle the problem have foundered.

Have international solutions ever been suggested? In 1952 the United Nations passed a resolution calling for the establishment of a fund of $250 million, to be raised by voluntary contributions from member states, for "relief and reintegration." The plan failed when the Arab states, perhaps justifiably, felt that for them to accept was tantamount to sweeping a moral problem under the rug of the world's conscience. For the same reason an ambitious plan by American leaders to provide $300 million for resettlement and $500 million for developing the natural resources of the host countries failed. In 1955 the Arab governments rejected Eric Johnston's $200-million project to develop Jordan Valley because it would have reduced by as many as 250,000 the number of refugees in Jordan. The Arabs need not be considered venal in refusing such plans; like the Israelis, they want to see the refugee problem handled as part of an over-all settlement and feel that if they give way in this detail, they weaken their general case.

In attempting to reach an adjudication of this impasse, negotiators should keep in mind the moving words of Egypt's foreign minister, Mahmoud Riad, who late in 1967 said, "It is erroneous on the part of some to believe that the problem of the people of Palestine can be solved exclusively from a humanitarian point of view. It also cannot be considered simply as a tragedy similar to an earthquate or an epidemic which fate causes to fall upon a certain people. The question is a national and political one and must be dealt with on that basis." The humanitarian aspect of this problem is clear-cut and is agreed upon by all. What we seek now are acceptable political accommodations.

It was to this purpose that Abba Eban on July 24, 1970, proposed an "urgent international conference on Arab refugees to work out a five-year plan for a settlement of the problem." He made the striking proposal that "this conference can be called in advance of actual peace negotiations," and called for the establishment of "an open communal border with Jordan, providing her with duty-free access to the Mediterranean," an innovation which would permit all residents of what used to be Palestine to move about with comparative freedom.

Bibliography

GELLHORN, MARTHA. 1967. "Palestinian Refugees," *Manchester Guardian* (July 24, 26, 28).

HARARI, MAURICE. 1962. *Government and Politics of the Middle East*. Englewood Cliffs, N. J.: Prentice-Hall.

ISRAEL. MINISTRY FOR FOREIGN AFFAIRS, INFORMATION DIVISION. 1970. *Facts about Israel, 1970*. Edited by Misha Louvish and Mordekhai Nurock. [Jerusalem].

KANEV, ITZHAK. 1968. *The Arab Refugees and Research on Their Real Number*. Tel Aviv: Economic and Social Research Institute.

KERR, MALCOLM H. 1968. *The Middle East Conflict*. Headline Series, No. 191. New York: Foreign Policy Association.

KURZMAN, DAN. 1970. *Genesis 1948*. New York: Random House.

LOVE, KENNETH. 1969. *Suez: The Twice-Fought War*. New York: McGraw-Hill.

MEZERIK, AVRAHM G. 1958. "Arab Refugees in the Middle East," *International Review Service*, Vol. 4, No. 44. New York.

———. 1962. "Arab-Israel Conflict and the United Nations," *International Review Service*, Vol. 8, No. 73. New York.

———. 1969. "Arab-Israel Conflict and the UN," *International Review Service*, Vol. 14, No. 101. New York.

Middle East Journal. 1968–70. "Chronology, Arab-Israeli Conflict," various issues.

PINNER, WALTER. 1967. *The Legend of the Arab Refugees: A Critical Study of UNRWA's Reports and Statistics*. Tel Aviv: Economic and Social Research Institute.

SANUA, VICTOR D. 1970. "The National Character of the Arabs and Its Effect on the Middle East Conflict." Paper presented at the meeting of the American Psychological Association, Miami, Florida.

SYRKIN, MARIE. 1966. "The Arab Refugees, A Zionist View," *Commentary*, **41**, 23–30.

THOMPSON, CAROL L., ed. 1970. "The Middle East," *Current History*, Vol. 58, No. 341 (January), entire issue.

UNITED NATIONS. GENERAL ASSEMBLY. 1970. "Resolutions Regarding Assistance to Palestine Refugees (19 November 1948—10 December 1969)." New York.

————. RELIEF AND WORKS AGENCY FOR PALESTINE. 1969. *Refugees in the Near East, 1 July 1968—30 June 1969*. New York.

————. ————. 1962. "A Brief History of UNRWA, 1950–62," No. 1. "Summary Data on Assistance to the Palestine Refugees (December 1948—31 December 1962)," No. 2. "The UNRWA Education and Training Programme (1950–1962)," No. 3. "The UNRWA Health Programme, 1950–62," No. 4. "UNRWA Experience with Works Projects and Self-Support Programmes: An Historical Summary (1950–1962)," No. 5. "The Problem of the Rectification of the UNRWA Relief Rolls (1950–1962)," No. 6. Beirut: UNRWA Information Papers.

WOLF, JOHN B. 1967. "The Arab Refugee Problem," *Current History*, **53**, 352–357.

————. 1970. "The Palestinian Resistance Movement." Unpublished manuscript.

6 CLASSIFICATION BY RESIDENCE

The rural-urban differentiation is at once one of the most important and perhaps the most unwieldy of those used in social analysis. The industrialization of Western countries' economies and the modernization of their cultures were invariably accompanied by a mammoth urban increase, but it is doubtful whether the growth of cities in today's underdeveloped nations typically connotes the same trend. And any attempt to compare urbanization between countries or over time is extraordinarily difficult because of the great variation and continual change in key definitions.

The range of possible articles in this area is very wide, and the selection has been limited to three first-rate papers on important but generally neglected topics. The first is on "metropolitan dominance," a concept that has seldom been defined unambiguously. One index that Charles Galpin used in his very early studies, for example, was the range of a metropolitan newspaper's distribution; but it is certainly also true that the Chicago Tribune, *to take a prime example, was shaped considerably by the necessity of catering to its large proportion of small-town and rural readers. More fundamentally, most of those who direct national or regional affairs from New York, Washington, Chicago, or Los Angeles were not born in those metropolitan centers;*

the instruments of dominance are located there, but those who wield them have often been brought up in small towns, whose point of view they seldom quite abandon. The next paper, which examines some other limits to metropolitan dominance in two quite different settings, contributes significantly to urban theory.

Its author, Richard M. Morse, is a professor of history at Yale University and has been chairman of its Council on Latin American Studies. In 1970–71 he was a fellow at the Center for Advanced Study in the Behavioral Sciences and a visiting professor at Stanford University. He is the author of two books on Brazilian history and of two dozen articles on Latin American urbanization and urban history, on which he is the leading expert writing in English or, so far as I know, in any language. For one familiar with sociological writings, his analyses are especially impressive, for he combines the historical depth one would expect from one in his discipline with an incisive use of sociological concepts.

THE LIMITS OF METROPOLITAN DOMINANCE IN CONTEMPORARY LATIN AMERICA

RICHARD M. MORSE

This paper is concerned with the transmission of change or innovation from larger to smaller urban centers in Latin America, and it attempts to determine limits within which the relation between such centers can usefully be conceived as one of unidirectional influence.

We should recognize at the outset that an extreme version of the "internal colonialism" argument might hold that the large Latin American city is *not* primarily a transmission belt for social and economic change and that its more central function is to maintain small towns and rural areas in subordination. Indeed, Martins's study (1969) of São Paulo's Paraíba valley purports to show that even when technological change does selectively penetrate an agricultural zone, "colonial" relationships may make industrialized enterprises less profitable than traditional labor-intensive farming.

For most observers, however, the analysis of internal domination does not preclude acceptance of the view that a large metropolis is a point of origin, or relay from abroad, of advanced technology, rationalist orientation to production, educational innovation, fads, fashions, and styles. So natural is it to assume metropolitan radiation that we must stretch our minds a bit to envision the contrary possibility, that is, a small- to large-town,

SOURCE: Paper presented at the 39th Congress of Americanists, Lima, Peru, August 1970. Reprinted with the author's permission.

or a rural-to-urban, flow of influence or innovation. One instance is Gilberto Freyre's account (1961) of the influence of rural social patterns and architectural style on Brazilian cities of the early 19th century. During the same period the United States offers a different kind of example. Here industrialization and technological innovation were incubated outside the large, commercially prosperous urban centers; industry came to the cities only after the expansion of urban possibilities for complementarity in the factors of production (Pred 1966).

For contemporary Latin America, however, researchers seem generally to endorse Redfield's conclusion for Yucatan (1941: 14)—namely, that social change originates in principal cities, in this case Mérida, and emanates with diminishing impact to successively smaller centers: the municipal seat, peasant village, tribal village. Redfield's corollary to this thesis was that the city's price for transmitting social change to smaller communities is a reverse flow of "ambitious young men" and "successful merchants and planters" (1941: 21). A generation later tears are still shed over the urban siphon effect: "Large cities receive young, intelligent, dynamic immigrants; small towns lose their best people, who are replaced by peasants without training or capital" (McGreevey 1968: 218). Leeds (1969: 62) holds that internal migration causes persons to be "sorted out and distributed along the hierarchy" on a gradient of increasing skill and urban experience. And from their research on Monterrey, Mexico, Browning and Feindt (1968) suggest that migrant groups are arrayed along three ascending plateaus of a socio-economic continuum whose up curve correlates with length of urban residence.

Thus, while Redfield's static construct of the folk-urban continuum has fallen into disrepute, its dynamic corollaries (radiation of modernizing influences from large to small urban centers; flow of more skilled or dynamic migrants from small to large centers) appear still to enjoy respectability. Perhaps we must either accept Redfield's whole package or else re-examine the widely researched though seemingly self-evident proposition that migrants with urban skills gravitate more naturally and adapt more readily to large urban centers. The question may be more than academic in view of the fact that cityward migrations in Latin America are becoming less selective for education, occupation, and urban background.

The issue becomes clearer once we confront a certain ambiguity attaching to common notions about large Latin American cities. To planners and developers the metropolis seems a cockpit of modernization, a growth pole, an arena for economic rationalization, a specialized society where positions are increasingly distributed by merit rather than ascriptive criteria. On the other hand, sociologists and anthropologists such as Juan Carlos Argulla, Manoel Tosta Berlinck, Fernando Henrique Cardoso, Bertram Hutchinson, Anthony Leeds, Lisa Redfield Peattie, and others find that urban societies are embedded in larger national societies and exhibit citified versions of more generalized systems of domination and clientage. Analysts of urban development in contemporary Latin America are obliged to reconcile these two perspectives.

Such a formulation of the matter has obvious implications for the study of internal migration and for the conventional view of the big-city siphon effect. Interesting in this connection is Casimir's study (1967) of inter- and intragenerational mobility in two towns of the Brazilian Northeast (Juàzeiro, population 28,000, and Petrolina, population 21,000); it suggests that in-migrants may be quicker than natives to seize on job opportunities and that out-migration of natives to larger cities may partly signify their being edged out by more aggressive groups. For Latin America in general an ECLA study (1969: 110) notes that "medium landholders, who formerly composed the upper classes of provincial towns and cities, are being increasingly displaced toward the big cities, often leaving their lands to groups on the rise." In big-city labor markets "dynamic" arrivals may even be at a discount. Cali industrialists prefer "docile" workers from the impoverished minifundios of Nariño to the less deferential, more proletarianized workers from Caldas and Antioquia, who are "less given to submission and are better informed as to the value of their labor" (Valencia 1965: 46).

The evidence frequently given for the talent drain is that out-migrants from small towns have above-average schooling for communities of origin, a finding established for Peru, Chile, Colombia, Guatemala, and elsewhere (Alers and Appelbaum 1968; Herrick 1965; Adams 1969; Roberts 1970). The inference that such migration represents a "loss" for home towns assumes that the out-migrants' education is pertinent to local needs and that their services are in demand. Margulis's study (1968: 144–46) of towns and villages in La Rioja, Argentina, however, indicates a probably more typical case. Local education "does not correspond to the economic needs of the region of origin" and serves rather "as a means of socialization for future out-migrants." Community leaders accept migration as a long-standing, inevitable process and regard schooling as a way of preparing Riojanos for city life. Although leaders deplore regional economic stagnation, they blame it on external factors and devote their energies to preserving the *status quo*. "Rooted in cultural stereotypes, their attitude toward education is parternalist and charitable. The schooling imparted separates the individual from roles oriented to the local economy and prepares him for urban roles." In the rural zone of Córdoba province, Critto (1969: 346) observes, the urban middle-class orientation of school curricula is such that the "failure of children in school, a most frequent occurrence, signifies the victory of community integration." Similarly in highland Peru:

The school acts as an organism to promote emigration. Teachers tell the young that on the coast there are secondary schools, work, industries, ministries, etc. The need to work or to keep studying obliges them to leave, and the attraction of

Lima arouses expectations in them by the demonstration effect of the capital (Montoya 1967: 104; see also Lowder 1970: 27–30).

Wolfe (1967; also ECLA 1969: 177–206) indicates that such cases are typical. He observes that Latin American elites have, by default, relegated responsibility for public school curricula to urban middle-class cadres of teachers, functionaries, and planners; that schooling kindles vague aspirations that cannot be satisfied in rural settings; and that youths must go to larger towns for postprimary education. Griffin's assumption that "the most valuable human resources of the [Peruvian] countryside are lost to the urban areas" (1969: 63) is therefore in partial contradiction to his assertion that Spanish American schools provide "literary, legal, and humanistic training— at the expense of instruction in science, mathematics, and applied technology" (1969: 101).

Large cities do not so much drain off talent and enterprise from towns, perhaps, as provide a structural complement to small-town attitudes and institutions. For the "education" of prospective migrants consists not in imparting skills and trades for which there is a big-city market—a service which French towns rendered for 19th-century Paris (Chevalier 1950)— but in communicating a general outlook and set of expectancies and in making youths dysfunctional for local occupation.[1] To urge upon Latin America the model of the stolid bourgeois town of Flaubert's France or the more dynamic "covenanted" town of the United States is a bit like thrusting on it the legendary model of the entrepreneurial middle class. In fact the analogy is close. For just as some observers suggest that the Latin American middle classes may become polarized either toward patronal identification or toward proletarization (Graciarena 1967: 201–3), so one might loosely say that certain towns stand a chance to become "small cities," given a happy conjunction of "external" factors, while many face a destiny of stagnation and impoverishment (Wolfe 1966: 39; Tricart 1964: 243–44; ECLA 1969: 98–100).

The failure, then, of large urban centers to transmit generous doses of change or development to smaller ones is not adequately explained by the hypothesis that cities are drawing off the more skilled and ambitious components of the small-town labor force. Nor, as Cardoso and Faletto (1969) demonstrate, is it adequately explained by the external-dependency thesis, which postulates links of colonial control descending from world financial and political centers to Latin American metropolises and, through them, to rural outposts. What we require is a delineation of institutional structure and process *specific* to Latin American societies which will help account for the seeming passivity or inertia of metropolitan hinterlands.

[1] Centralized education planning may "rationalize" this pattern. Herrick (1965: 37) reports that Chilean vocational schools are concentrated in towns outside Santiago which provide no market for their graduates—with obvious effects on migration.

An obvious strategy for our purpose is comparative analysis. The comparison developed in the following paragraphs is between two small towns, one in Mexico and one in France, and rests on the findings of community studies by Díaz (1966) and Anderson and Anderson (1966). Each town is located at the periphery of a metropolis, which leaves little doubt as to the origin and force of "metropolitan influence." The Catholic, seigneurial traditions of French civilization make the French town more commensurable for our purposes than a United States town, and in some ways more suggestive. The Mexican town with its Indian traditions, conservatism, and religiosity is certainly not "typical" of all of Latin America. Yet to the extent that one can identify broad similarities of institutional process in that large and diverse region, the Mexican town seems considerably less alien to them than does the French.

The French town of Wissous lies ten miles from Paris (1962 population, 2,780,000) and the Mexican town of Tonalá ten miles from Guadalajara (1960 population, 737,000), Mexico's second-largest city, a state capital and historic administrative, commercial, and educational center. Wissous is an age-old agricultural village, probably of Celtic origin although the earliest documentation dates from 1090; the modern town (population 2,500), described as very self-contained, still registers the weight of tradition in its appearance and tempo. Tonalá (population 5,400), also an ancient farming center, was a tribal capital when the Spaniards reached it in 1530. Findings on each town, summarized in Table 1, reveal differences of kind not ascribable merely to divergences of cultural style and economic level, nor even to the more powerful metropolitan orbit of Paris.

The explanation for the differential response of Tonalá and Wissous to bombardment by big-city pressures lies deep in the social order. The Mexican town "is not the village that chose progress; it is a town to which few things have happened" (Díaz 1966: 211). New careers followed by townsmen "do not function for communicating the urban culture to Tonalá." Tonaltecans do not "take on city ways or city values as a result of the visits of the prodigal sons" (216). The industrial growth of Guadalajara since the Second World War has not caused Tonalá to respond "as a separate unit through all the stages of development from a peasant community through an industrial town." Its fate is probably mere physical engulfment by the city (220). Wissous, on the other hand, has witnessed a "silent revolution," in response not to legal changes but to "an evolutionary development, a spread outward" from the metropolis that has caused social structure to change "generically from that of a farming village to that of an urban-industrial suburb" (Anderson and Anderson 1966: 261–62).

To quantify this disparity one might design research to identify the number and social location of change-prone or achievement-oriented persons in each community. Such studies, however, are more documentary than explanatory; furthermore, they construe motivations along polar coordinates,

Table 1. A Comparison of Small Towns: Tonalá (Mexico) and Wissous (France)

TONALÁ	WISSOUS

Government

Administrative structure reflects Spanish traditions. Limited municipal autonomy; town budget only $480. Mayor removable by state governor. Federal or state control of water supply, schools, antimalaria program, *ejido* organization, Court of First Instance, health center. Town officials maintain only elementary services, cannot initiate urban renewal. "As long as Tonaltecans depend upon the [good character and civility] . . . of outsiders and of powerful politicians, they will not develop the prerequisites for corporate action" (27–28, 105–15).

Revolutionary law of 1789 provided "well developed rational-legal organization." Mayor is "the hinge between local and national government," has police authority and appointive power as local head of national bureaucracy, represents elected municipal council, supervises "all communal establishments and undertakings." Local government assisted by 15 commissions and committees, which include outside experts and interest groups (135–48).

Marriage

Institutionalized "bride stealing" reinforces dominance-submission in marriage, antagonisms between affinal groups, in-group character of *cuarteles* (neighborhoods) (54–66).

"Choice of spouse is at the initiative of the young couple, and only informal pressures may be employed to influence their decision." Marriage a "bilateral contract" benefiting both parties, may involve a "property contract which can be explicit and written." Fathers may take aggressive political action in a family association (174–77).

Social Classes

Most villagers classifiable within "lowest groups of the social ladder; a few families might be considered lower middle class." Dichotomy between manual and nonmanual workers. Bourgeoisie of storekeepers, graziers, landowners, grain dealers, two priests, a pharmacist, a factory owner; bourgeois models of behavior are "pre-Revolutionary patrons and hacendados." The mass are "convinced they are 'the poor' "; largest group are potters, others are farm and factory workers. The innovator or upwardly mobile is "a laughable rather than a respected figure" (94–99, 213).

Small upper-middle class of businessmen, factory managers, professional people—mostly newcomers. Older inhabitants distributed in middle-middle class of medium-hold farmers and merchants; lower-middle class of smallholders, shopkeepers, artisans, established field hands; small upper-lower class of field laborers; small lower-lower class of underemployed field hands. Lower classes swelled by unskilled immigrant factory hands (232–34).

Table 1. (Cont.)

TONALÁ	WISSOUS
Religion	
Guadalajara more important to Tonaltecans as ecclesiastical than as administrative center. Recent priest reorganized neighborhood religious festivals to eliminate personal violence. Religious associations are the only corporate groups. Town is pro-clerical, suspicious of "atheistic, socialist" government politicians (32, 115–16, 129).	Priest "an ineffective leader apart from purely religious functions." Church participation "emotionally and intellectually dead at the end of the 18th century. No doubt it had been so for a long time" (164–66).
Agriculture	
Low productivity, poor technology and information, bad organization caused by "amoral familism." Corn, beans, squash produced for family consumption, some peanuts and corn for market. Peripheral chicken farms owned by outsiders (192–97).	"Generally, the Wissous farmer has always been ready to offer new products according to market demands." Close relation to Paris market. Economic cooperation not based on kinship. Cooperative granaries and insurance companies, apprentice training, technological improvement programs. Most farmers above average in possession of cars, utilities, luxuries (184–91).
Business and Industry	
Pottery-making a household industry; no attempt to maximize output or efficiency; economic rewards subordinated to personal respect; resistance to assembly-line and cooperative methods. Pottery-making regarded as *destino*, not vocation. Uneasiness over contractual, businesslike social relationships. Guadalajara entrepreneurs see Tonalá as poor investment site, though one shirt factory attracted there by "sweatshop" wages, low taxes, lack of government supervision. Exchange not impersonal and market-oriented but imbedded in social relationships (38–41, 162–89, 199–206).	Modest industrialization (five manufacturing firms). Much commuting to Paris factory jobs. Town becoming an "agglomeration of strangers." Trades and industries controlled by national organs; government agencies set standards and prices, collect taxes, supervise industrial management. Workers unionized. Family no longer basic unit of production (111–12, 193–96).

SOURCES: Díaz 1966; Anderson and Anderson 1966 (page references in parentheses).

not in cultural clusters. The two studies in question go far beyond quantification, just as they go beyond the familiar dichotomy into communities dominated by diffuse primary groups and by rationalistic secondary groups.

In Tonalá religious associations are the only corporate groups and are perceived as having purely ritual functions. "They are not the nuclei around which to form mutual loan funds, marketing cooperatives, or civic organizations." The infrequent case of corporate action for a civic purpose (for example, to get electric power restored) is a dramatic, easily organized, one-time action which solicits outsiders to make decisions and supply remedies. Local leaders are restricted to administrative, not innovative, action. Factionalism is *ad hoc* and situation-oriented. Even kinship does not support social action because families, like the larger society, are composed of "a series of separate, divided roles hierarchically arranged." An individual's life is governed by external duties, not internal norms. Each person maintains an idiosyncratic set of dyadic relationships, with crosscutting allegiances that preclude definition of group boundaries (Díaz 1966: 123–37).[2]

The case of Wissous reveals how misleading it can be to classify Tonalá as a "traditional" society. One may argue indeed that Wissousians value "tradition" more positively than do Tonaltecans, that in appreciable measure the "silent revolution" of Wissous has occurred not under the banner of economic progress, social justice, and democracy, but as the outcome of strategies shrewdly designed to *rework* and *preserve* traditional values, privileges, and institutions in the face of metropolitan pressures. After identifying some forty associations in Wissous (for education, sports and youth, neighborhood development, religion, family, merchants, farmers, veterans, and workers) the Andersons find (1966: 197–230, 243–44) not that they supersede or cut across age-old groupings of community proper, church, family, shop, and farm, but that they comprise a *replicate social structure* "based upon and devoted to the special interests of each of these groups." A central conclusion is that factional associations do not so much hasten the disintegration of the small, traditional, urbanizing community as "reinforce and adapt traditional institutions by providing a rational-legal, hierarchical structure for the older groups." As a result class lines, although important on the national scene, are "no longer meaningful [locally] as part of the social structure of institutionalized groups."

The Tonalá-Wissous contrast, then, is best construed not as a tradition-prone versus a change-prone society, but as two societies wedded to traditional identities and forms of social action. Both communities, that is, prefer preservation of identity to modernization, but the French community har-

---

[2] Foster's notions of the "dyadic contract" (1967: 212–43) and the "image of limited good" (1967: 122–52) are important clues to understanding Latin American urban as well as village societies. Silberstein (1969), for example, finds dyadic analysis fruitful for the Rio *favela*.

bors "antibodies" to modernism that foster the reworking and reinforcement of traditional structures, thus engendering "development." It would seem, then, that "developers" in Latin America might take a leaf from the psychoanalyst and, contrary to current practice, give priority to questions of identity over those of change.[3] As Santos (1969: 46) insists:

The object of development theory cannot be to describe the course of a society which one does not really understand toward a society which will never be. In other words the object of development theory must consist in the study of the *laws of development* of the societies we wish to understand.

The case of Tonalá reinforces our earlier assertion that the apparent stagnancy of many small settlements in Latin America is not adequately explained by unidirectional core-periphery models of internal domination or colonialism. Forces of centralization and control must be understood as part of nationwide patterns of social process and institutional morphology. The task of the regional, social, or economic planner in Latin America is not so much to chart the lines of metropolitan influence and control over hinterlands and to devise strategies for ameliorating their impact as it is to explore ways in which the metropolis may *come to terms with* the small town, and with the history, culture, and institutional inheritance in which both participate. The metropolis is as much prisoner as master of a depressed hinterland.

References

ADAMS, DALE W. 1969. "Rural Migration and Agricultural Development in Colombia," *Economic Development and Cultural Change,* 17, 527–539.

ALERS, J. OSCAR, and RICHARD P. APPELBAUM. 1968. "La migración en el Perú: Un inventario de proposiciones," *Estudios de Población y Desarrollo* (Lima), 1, 1–43.

ANDERSON, ROBERT T., and BARBARA GALLATIN ANDERSON. 1966. *Bus Stop for Paris: The Transformation of a French Village.* New York: Doubleday.

BROWNING, HARLEY L., and WALTROUT FEINDT. 1968. "Diferencias entre la población nativa y la migrante en Monterrey," *Demografía y Economía,* 2, 183–205.

CARDOSO, FERNANDO HENRIQUE, and ENZO FALETTO. 1969. *Dependencia y desarrollo en América Latina.* Mexico: Siglo Veintiuno.

CASIMIR, JEAN. 1967. "Duas cidades no nordeste do Brasil: Sua estrutura social e sua importância para a planificação econômica regional," *América Latina,* 10, 3–48.

[3] Some of the best known small-town studies miss this point. Redfield's confusion about his "village that chose progress" becomes explicit when in the closing paragraph he observes that the people of Chan Kom *"have no choice* but to go forward with technology" (1950: 178; italics supplied). Harris's claims for the "urbanness" of Minas Velhas rest largely on attitudinal, not psychological or structural features of the society (1956: 274–89).

CHEVALIER, LOUIS. 1950. *La formation de la population parisienne au XIXe siècle.* Paris: Presses Universitaires de France.

CRITTO, ADOLFO. 1969. "Análisis del campo y la ciudad, después de la migración campo-ciudad en Córdoba," in Jorge E. Hardoy and Richard P. Schaedel, eds., *The Urbanization Process in America from Its Origins to the Present Day,* Buenos Aires: Instituto Torcuato Di Tella.

DÍAZ, MAY N. 1966. *Tonalá: Conservatism, Responsibility, and Authority in a Mexican Town.* Berkeley: University of California Press.

ECONOMIC COMMISSION FOR LATIN AMERICA. 1969. *El cambio social y la política de desarrollo social en América Latina.* New York: United Nations.

FOSTER, GEORGE M. 1967. *Tzintzuntzan: Mexican Peasants in a Changing World.* Boston: Little, Brown.

FREYRE, GILBERTO. 1961. *Sobrados e mucambos,* 3rd ed., 2 Vols. Rio de Janeiro: José Olympio.

GRACIARENA, JORGE. 1967. *Poder y clases sociales en el desarrollo de América Latina.* Buenos Aires: Paidos.

GRIFFIN, KEITH. 1969. *Underdevelopment in Spanish America: An Interpretation.* London: George Allen and Unwin.

HARRIS, MARVIN. 1956. *Town and Country in Brazil.* New York: Columbia University Press.

HERRICK, BRUCE H. 1965. *Urban Migration and Economic Development in Chile.* Cambridge, Mass.: M.I.T. Press.

LEEDS, ANTHONY. 1969. "The Significant Variables Determining the Character of Squatter Settlements," *América Latina,* 12, 44–86.

LOWDER, STELLA. 1970. "Lima's Population Growth and the Consequences for Peru." University of Liverpool, Centre for Latin American Studies, Monograph 2, pp. 21–34.

MARGULIS, MARIO. 1968. *Migración y marginalidad en la sociedad argentina.* Buenos Aires: Paidos.

MARTINS, JOSÉ DE SOUZA. 1969. "Modernização agrária e industrialização no Brasil," *América Latina,* 12, 3–16.

MCGREEVEY, WILLIAM. 1968. "Causas de la migración interna en Colombia," in Centro de Estudios sobre Desarrollo Económico, *Empleo y Desempleo en Colombia,* Bogotá: Universidad de los Andes.

MONTOYA ROJAS, RODRIGO. 1967. "La migración interna en el Perú: Un caso concreto," *América Latina,* 10, 83–108.

PRED, ALLAN R. 1966. *The Spatial Dynamics of U. S. Urban-Industrial Growth, 1800–1914: Interpretive and Theoretical Essays.* Cambridge, Mass.: M.I.T. Press.

REDFIELD, ROBERT. 1941. *The Folk Culture of Yucatan.* Chicago: University of Chicago Press.

———. 1950. *A Village That Chose Progress: Chan Kom Revisited.* Chicago: University of Chicago Press.

ROBERTS, BRYAN R. 1970. "Migration and Population Growth in Guatemala City: Implications for Social and Economic Development." University of Liverpool, Centre for Latin American Studies, Monograph 2, pp. 7–20.

SANTOS, THEOTÔNIO DOS. 1969. "Le Crise de la théorie du développement et les relations de dépendance en Amérique Latine," *L'Homme et la Société*, 12, 43–68.

SILBERSTEIN, PAUL. 1969. "Favela Living: Personal Solution to Larger Problems," *América Latina*, 12, 183–200.

TRICART, JEAN. 1964. "Un ejemplo del desequilibrio ciudad campo en una economía en vía de desarrollo: El Salvador," *Cuadernos Latinoamericanos de Economía Humana*, 5, 229–255.

VALENCIA, ENRIQUE. 1965. *Cali: Estudio de los aspectos sociales de su urbanización e industrialización*. Economic Commission for Latin America, Social Affairs Division, E/LACCY/BP/L.6, November 29. New York: United Nations.

WOLFE, MARSHALL. 1966. "Rural Settlement Patterns and Social Change in Latin America," *Latin American Research Review*, 1, 5–50.

———. 1967. "Educación, estructuras sociales y desarrollo en América Latina," *América Latina*, 10, 15–42.

In the narrow view of a demographer, the most interesting difference between rural and urban populations is of course how the two residential settings affect fertility and mortality. In the early-modern West, cities generally set brakes to population increase. For so long as public health and sanitation were still rudimentary, the mere congestion in urban centers typically raised their death rates above those in the countryside. And as far back as records go, the urban birth rate was almost invariably well below the rural one. Thus, when larger proportions of the rapidly increasing populations of underdeveloped countries started to move to metropolitan centers, some analysts saw this trend as the forerunner to the deceleration demanded by social and economic policy makers. But the mass control of some of the main infectious diseases, which has been the proximate cause of the rapid population growth in such nations, operates well anywhere; the difference in mortality by rural-urban residence is usually slight, and sometimes favors the city dwellers. More surprising, successive studies of particular countries have shown that in some instances (at first presumed to be anomalous) urban fertility is not below that in the villages. Two of these were by the author of the next paper, on India (Robinson 1961) and on Mexico (Robinson and Robinson 1960). The paper chosen here is valuable in part because it sums up some of these earlier studies and suggests a general revision of the earlier theory; see also, in this respect, the article on Egypt by Abu-Lughod (1964).

Warren C. Robinson is a professor of economics at Pennsylvania State University. He has been a consultant or adviser to the Pakistan Institute of Development Economics, the Government of Pakistan's National Research Institute for Family Planning, the population service of the U. S. Agency for International Development, and—in this country—the National Planning Association and the Outdoor Recreation Resources Review Commission. His several dozen papers range over a number of topics but are concentrated on the relation between population growth and economic policy in under-developed areas.

URBANIZATION AND FERTILITY: THE NON-WESTERN EXPERIENCE

WARREN C. ROBINSON

Nearly all commentators on the less developed areas stress the importance of urban growth and its economic, social, and also demographic implications. Urbanization is at once a cause and an effect of the break-up of the old agricultural societies and a symptom of what may ultimately become urban-industrial societies in the Western pattern. To demographers one of its most important features is its possible impact on fertility and the population growth in these nations.

In the West, the decline of fertility seems to have originated primarily in cities and to have spread from the urban foci into the rural hinterland. It is possible that in the less developed countries, likewise, urbanization may eventually have a profound influence upon population growth. The possibility must be taken into account in the consideration of the general economic and social implications of urbanization (United Nations 1957: 123).

This paper is an empirical investigation of the relation between urbanization and fertility in the less developed nations.

CONVENTIONAL VIEWS AND THE RECENT EVIDENCE

The existence of a rural-urban fertility differential must certainly rank as one of the most widely validated and accepted generalizations in Western demography, demonstrated for virtually every country in the European sphere of settlement. The difference has varied among countries and from region to region within countries, but urban fertility 30 percent or more below rural fertility can be described as common (for example, Bogue 1959: 306). The reasons for the lower urban fertility also seem clear enough. Warren Thompson (1935: 166–69) lists, among other factors, such things as the negative economic value of children in the city, the parents' desire

SOURCE: Reprinted from the *Milbank Memorial Fund Quarterly,* 4 (1963), 291–308, with permission of the author and the Fund.

for social and personal pleasure, and the relatively easy access to contraception and abortion.

Various researchers have satisfied themselves that the urban-rural fertility differentials are to be found also among non-Western populations of less developed nations. Writing some years ago on the basis of a survey of many parts of the globe, Jaffe (1942) concluded rather sweepingly:

> Urban-rural differential fertility is far more widespread than was originally thought. Not only does it exist today in the European nations and in those lands whose population is predominantly of European descent, but it is also found among the populations of Latin American countries, . . . Asiatic populations, . . . Moslems in Palestine, the native Negroes and the Asiatics in South Africa, and the nonwhite group . . . in the United States [cf. Tietze 1958].

Studies in depth of particular countries—including India and Pakistan (Davis 1951: chap. 10), Mexico (Moore 1951: 219ff), Puerto Rico (Combs and Davis 1951), Malaya (Smith 1952: 52ff), Ceylon (Huyck 1945), and Japan (Taeuber 1958: 256ff)—all appeared to support this conclusion. The United Nations (1953a: 15) was undoubtedly expressing the consensus when it stated:

> There are adequate statistical data to demonstrate that fertility is lower in urban industrial countries than in agricultural countries, and that it is lower in urban than in rural parts of the same country, whether the country is industrially advanced or not [cf. United Nations 1953b: 78ff].

By and large such generalizations have gone unchallenged. The occasional exceptions to the general rule have been seen as curiosities, explicable in terms of some unique local circumstance—for example, in Egypt (Kiser 1944; El-Badry 1956). In fact, the lower urban fertility has been so uncritically accepted that very few appear to have asked why such differentials should exist in the less developed nations. Even in their large cities contraception was virtually unknown; such family planning as was practiced affected only a small proportion of the population and certainly was not sufficient to explain observed rural-urban differentials in fertility ratios of 30 to 40 percent. Why, then, did these differentials exist?

In the past, an almost total lack of reliable data has hampered demographic investigations of the less developed regions. The spate of censuses in the 1950s cast more light than ever before on the special demographic problems of these countries.

Table 1 presents nineteen urban and rural fertility ratios for non-Western countries, calculated from censuses taken in the 1950–60 decade. Some interesting contrasts are revealed. In five cases the urban fertility ratios were actually above the rural; in three, there were virtually no differences; in four, the urban rates were lower by 15 percent or less; in two they were

Table 1. Urban and Rural Fertility Ratios, Selected Non-Western Populations, 1950–60

	INFANTS AGED 0 TO 4 PER 1,000 FEMALES AGED 15 TO 49		URBAN AS A PERCENT OF RURAL
	URBAN	RURAL	
Algeria (1954) [a]	894	845	105.8
Brazil (1960)	430	778	55.3
British North Borneo (1951) [b]	706	579	121.9
Burma (1953) [c]	156	146	107.0
Ceylon (1953)	549	672	81.7
Chile (1952)	451	709	63.6
Cuba (1953)	375	729	51.4
India (1951)	598	626	96.0
Iran (1956) [d]	134	147	91.0
Jamaica (1953) [e]	366	622	58.8
Libya (1954) [f]	582	679	85.7
Malaya (1957) [g]	844	800	105.5
Mauritius (1952) [h]	524	580	90.3
Morocco (1952)	508	791	64.2
Nepal (1952/54) [i]	423	440	96.1
Nigeria (1952) [j]	1,958	1,184	165.4
Pakistan (1951) [k]	1,169	1,195	97.8
Sudan (1955/56) [l]	717	808	88.7
Union of South Africa (1951) [m]	453	654	69.3

[a] Algiers agglomeration compared with the rest of the Algiers Department.

[b] Sandakan Town compared with the rest of British North Borneo.

[c] Infants aged 0 to 1 per 1,000 females aged 16 to 45; Rangoon City compared with three adjoining rural districts.

[d] Infants aged 0 to 1 per 1,000 females aged 15 to 44; Tehran City compared with the rest of Tehran Province.

[e] Kingston and the urban part of St. Andrew compared with the rest of Jamaica.

[f] Tripoli compared with the rest of Libya.

[g] Singapore compared with the rest of Malaya.

[h] Port Louis District compared with the rest of Mauritius.

[i] Urban and rural Katmandu District compared.

[j] Infants and children aged 0 to 7 per 1,000 females aged 15 to 60; rural and urban Ibadan District compared.

[k] Infants and children aged 0 to 9 per 1,000 females aged 10 to 39; four urban municipalities in East Bengal compared with all East Bengal.

[l] Infants and children aged 0 to 4 per 1,000 "females over puberty, not past child-bearing"; Khartoum Town compared with the rest of Khartoum Province.

[m] "Natives" only.

SOURCES: National census reports of the respective countries.

lower by 30 percent or less; and in the remaining five cases they were lower by more than 30 percent, including one by nearly 50 percent. Now, the age data on which all these ratios were based are subject to considerable error in reporting and enumeration. The nineteen countries are not, in any statistical sense, representative of all less developed areas. Nevertheless, the data certainly must shake one's faith in the comfortable assertions concerning urban-rural fertility differentials. Instead of uniformity, there is a spectrum.

Only a handful of these countries have rural-urban age distributions available over an extended period. To detect any trends present, the data were broken into three decennial periods, 1931–40, 1941–50, and 1951–60. In all cases, there was a negative correlation between national fertility ratios and the percentages of the population classified as urban, but the values of the coefficients fell, being respectively —.62, —.21, and —.15. (Only the first of these is significant at $p = .05$.) Presumably the degree of association between urbanization and fertility ratios has been decreasing with the passage of time.

Studies in depth of several populations for which urban and rural fertility ratios can be computed over the same three decades also lead to this conclusion. For example, Mexico changed from 33 percent urban in 1930 to 43 percent in 1950, yet its fertility ratio rose from 575 to 626. During this period urban fertility increased and the fairly large differentials narrowed (Robinson and Robinson 1960). Similar trends are observable in India and elsewhere (Robinson 1961).

Thus, it is possible to reconcile the results shown in Table 1 with the conclusions reached by the earlier investigators: the fairly strong relation between fertility ratios and urbanization before the Second World War changed into a much more moderate one. Explaining this apparent trend requires a bit of ingenuity.

INFANT MORTALITY AND MARITAL PATTERNS

As in Table 1, nearly all studies of differential fertility in the less developed nations are based on the fertility (or child-woman) ratio. This measure, the number of children aged 0 to 4 per 1,000 females aged 15 to 49, is used when data are available from a census but not from birth registrations—the typical situation in the less developed nations.

This index is plainly a makeshift, designed to furnish a measurement of fertility when birth statistics are lacking. It is derived entirely from the data by age in one census. Though the child-woman ratio is useful chiefly because of this fact, it demands caution for the same reason. Instead of births, the ratio is based on the survivors of previous births; it includes the survivors of births during the five years preceding the census, and unavoidably includes the effects of infant and childhood mortality during this period (Barclay 1958: 172).

It is a common supposition that infants and children have higher risks of mortality in the urban agglomerations of less developed areas than in their rural districts (for example, UNESCO 1958: 34–35). However, it is extremely difficult to test this thesis, since registration data on births and infant deaths are typically not available. Nevertheless, for particular cities and countries some comparisons can be made (Table 2). In the 1930–39 decade, only one city was below its national average of infant mortality; three others showed virtually no difference; and the other nine all had rates above the nations, in five instances by 35 percent or more. But by the 1950–59 decade only four cities remained higher than their national average, and only one of these by as much as 20 percent; five cities were virtually identical; and four were below their national averages. Where the city rate was below the national rate in 1930–39, it fell even further by 1950–59; where there was no difference in 1930–39, one developed by 1950–59; where the city rate started out above the entire country, either the pattern was reversed or the difference was sharply diminished by the end of the period. Only Georgetown, British Guiana, and Colombo, Ceylon, ran counter to this trend, and in both these cases with a moderate and fluctuating change.

Thus, differences in infant mortality ran exactly counter to those in the fertility ratio. As the relative level of urban infant mortality fell, that of urban fertility ratios rose. In both cases, earlier urban-rural differentials have been narrowing.

Marriage patterns also differ by rural-urban residence. A lower percentage of urban females are married at nearly all ages. When a comparison is made using the marital fertility ratio (that is, children aged 0 to 4 per 1,000 *married* females aged 15 to 49) instead of the fertility ratio, the usual effect is to reduce somewhat the apparent rural-urban differences (for example, United Nations 1953b: 95).

INFANT MORTALITY, URBANIZATION, AND PERCENT MARRIED

The relative effect on the fertility ratio of each of three factors—urbanization, infant mortality, and percentage married—was tested with forty-four observations of less developed countries in the period 1930–60 (Table 3). These data were then analyzed with three separate correlations: for the entire period, for 1930–44, and for 1945–60 (Table 4). By a simple correlation, there is a negative association between the fertility ratio and percent urban, a strongly positive one between infant mortality and percent urban, and, in the later period, a significant negative one between percent urban and percent married. Holding constant the effect of these other two independent variables (X_2 and X_4) drastically alters the relation between the fertility ratio and percent urban. In the earlier period, the greater the urbanization the higher the fertility ratio; but in the later period there is virtually no relation at all.

Table 2. Average Infant Mortality Rates, Selected Non-Western Countries and Their Major Cities, 1930–39, 1940–49, and 1950–59

	INFANT DEATHS PER 1,000 LIVE BIRTHS			CITY RATE AS PERCENT OF NATIONAL RATE		
	1930–39	1940–49	1950–59	1930–39	1940–49	1950–59
Latin America						
British Guiana	139.6	99.2	72.2			
Georgetown	131.9	88.6	88.4	94.5	89.3	122.4
Argentina	98.5	79.7	63.8			
Buenos Aires	55.8	40.1	33.3	56.6	50.3	52.2
Colombia	141.0	147.1	109.5			
Bogotá	192.9	162.9	104.0	136.8	110.7	95.0
Mexico	131.4	112.0	85.7			
Mexico City	151.5	142.3	84.8	115.3	127.1	99.0
Uruguay	96.7	81.1	64.5			
Montevideo	99.9	63.8	43.1	103.3	78.7	66.8
El Salvador	132.3	108.3	79.8			
San Salvador	196.9	135.9	90.0	148.8	125.5	112.8
Asia						
Ceylon	173.9	122.6	73.9			
Colombo	171.8	133.6	83.3	98.8	109.0	112.7
India	169.0	150.0	110.0			
Bombay	247.6	189.9	121.8	146.5	126.6	110.7
Philippines	147.5	96.0	100.1			
Manila	146.2	143.2	65.6	99.1	149.2	65.5
Thailand	95.9	91.0	61.5			
Bangkok	164.4	126.4	61.7	171.4	138.9	100.3
Malaya	156.6	100.5	83.3			
Singapore	186.1	145.9	57.6	118.8	145.2	69.1
Africa						
Algeria	86.0	96.4	92.0			
Algiers	145.0	138.0	97.8	168.6	143.2	106.3
Egypt	162.8	152.7	166.1			
Cairo	198.8	205.7	166.4	122.1	134.7	100.2

SOURCES: United Nations, *Demographic Yearbook, 1951*, Table 19, pp. 328ff; *Demographic Yearbook, 1959*, Table 28, pp. 596ff. World Health Organization, *Annual Epidemiological and Vital Statistics, 1939–1946*, Part I, Table 46, pp. 83ff; *Annual Epidemiological and Vital Statistics, 1947–1949*, Part I, Table 23, pp. 137ff; *Annual Epidemiological and Vital Statistics, 1950*, Part I, Table 4, pp. 28ff; *Annual Epidemiological and Vital Statistics, 1954*, Part I, Table 35, p. 396. Issues of the annual public health, vital statistics, or other reports of the following territories: Aden, Antigua, Leeward Islands, Argentina, Bahamas Islands, St. Lucia, St. Christopher-Nevis, St. Vincent, Dominica, Mozambique, Sarawak, Algeria, Venezuela, British Guiana, Ghana, Hong Kong, Burma, Barbados, Bermuda, British Honduras, North Borneo, Ceylon.

Table 3. Fertility Ratios and Related Factors, Selected Countries of Asia, Africa, and Latin America, 1930–60

	DATE	FER-TILITY RATIO [a]	INFANT MORTALITY RATE [b]	PERCENT URBAN [c]	PERCENT MARRIED [d]
1930–45					
Egypt	1937	547	163.7	25.1	86.3
Mauritius	1944	479	148.6	28.5	73.6
Jamaica	1943	475	105.6	18.2	50.7
Mexico	1940	580	127.6	35.1	70.6
Puerto Rico	1940	606	122.6	30.3	68.6
Chile	1930	528	221.1	49.4	56.8
	1940	480	234.1	52.4	57.6
Colombia	1938	628	146.7	29.1	46.3
Venezuela	1941	593	129.6	39.3	31.7
Hong Kong	1931	354	574.0	88.4	81.0
India	1931	629	179.1	11.1	96.4
Palestine	1931	823	161.5	43.4	83.7
1946–60					
Algeria	1948	633	99.7	23.6	82.8
	1954	743	85.3	22.9	83.4
Egypt	1947	546	146.6	30.1	85.1
Mauritius	1952	742	110.1	34.9	82.0
Costa Rica	1950	686	93.1	33.5	61.4
El Salvador	1950	623	96.8	36.5	59.0
Barbados	1946	422	163.5	39.6	52.0
British Honduras	1946	508	134.4	55.8	62.8
Bermuda	1950	490	42.3	11.6	68.6
Guatemala	1950	695	110.1	25.0	69.2
Nicaragua	1950	650	92.4	34.9	57.8
Panama	1950	695	55.9	36.0	64.4
Puerto Rico	1950	725	73.9	40.5	72.7
Argentina	1947	423	79.7	62.5	57.3
Brazil	1950	653	171.0	36.2	64.3
British Guiana	1946	565	112.3	27.6	69.4
Chile	1952	517	153.5	60.2	62.7
Colombia	1951	691	130.7	38.0	59.8
Ecuador	1950	705	123.1	28.5	66.0
Paraguay	1950	694	63.2	34.6	53.1
Venezuela	1950	711	94.0	53.8	56.8
Ceylon	1946	543	133.6	15.4	78.8
	1953	810	80.1	15.3	78.5
India	1951	549	130.0	17.3	93.6
Malaya	1947	565	94.5	26.5	86.9

Table 3. (Cont.)

	DATE	FER-TILITY RATIO[a]	INFANT MORTALITY RATE[b]	PERCENT URBAN[c]	PERCENT MARRIED[d]
North Borneo	1951	579	117.0	13.4	83.5
Sarawak	1947	572	75.0	10.8	82.6
Singapore	1947	532	174.3	72.5	76.9
	1957	844	51.2	63.1	62.5
Thailand	1947	626	95.2	9.9	76.4
Fiji Islands	1956	832	47.5	18.3	77.7
Western Samoa	1956	901	41.3	18.7	62.9

[a] Children aged 0 to 4 per 1,000 females aged 15 to 49.
[b] Deaths before the first birthday per 1,000 live births.
[c] According to the nations' definitions of *urban*, which vary considerably.
[d] Percentage of females aged 15 and over who have ever married.

SOURCES: As in Table 2; also United Nations *Demographic Yearbook, 1949–50,* Table 5, pp. 168ff; *1954,* Table 7, pp. 236ff; *1958,* Table 6, pp. 138ff; *1959,* Table 8, pp. 195ff; *1960,* Table 9, 373ff.

No simple correlation existed between the percentage of females married and either the dependent variable (X_1) or the other independent variables, apart from the negative correlation, already noted, with percent urban in the later period. Holding constant the effect of infant mortality and percent urban produces a fairly high positive correlation in the earlier period between the fertility ratio and percent married, but the relation apparently weakened over time.

Infant mortality showed a consistently high negative correlation with the fertility ratio and a high positive correlation with percent urban, especially in the earlier period. Holding constant the effect of the other independent variables (X_3 and X_4) increases the correlation between infant mortality and fertility ratio in the earlier period, and lowers it slightly in the later. For the whole period the multiple correlation of the fertility ratio and all three independent variables (percent urban, infant mortality, and percent married) was only slightly higher than that with infant mortality alone.

From this analysis of the separate and joint effects of the three factors likely to cause differences in the fertility ratios, the infant mortaliy rate appears to be the most important. The seemingly strong association between percent urban and fertility ratios in the earlier period is actually one between infant mortality and fertility ratios. The correlations between infant mortality and urbanization, and apparently between urbanization and fertility ratios, weakened over time. Percent married and percent urban showed an increasingly negative correlation.

Table 4. Simple, Multiple, and Partial Coefficients
between Fertility Ratios and Three Related Factors,
Selected Less Developed Countries, 1930–44,
1945–60, and 1930–60

	1930–44	1945–60	1930–60
r_{12}	−.57 [a]	−.53 [a]	−.53 [b]
r_{13}	−.42	−.17	−.26
r_{14}	+.12	−.02	+.07
r_{23}	+.86 [b]	+.29	+.54 [b]
r_{24}	+.27	+.07	+.11
r_{34}	−.03	−.51 [b]	−.31 [a]
$r_{1.234}$			+.55 [b]
$r_{12.34}$	−.63 [a]	−.50 [b]	−.50 [b]
$r_{13.24}$	+.43	+.01	+.10
$r_{14.23}$	+.51	+.03	+.18
$N =$	12	32	44

[a] Significant at $p = .05$.
[b] Significant at $p = .01$.
$X_1 =$ Fertility ratio (infants and children aged 0 to 4 per 1,000 females aged 15 to 49).
$X_2 =$ Infant mortality rate (deaths at age 0 per 1,000 live births).
$X_3 =$ Percent urban (various definitions).
$X_4 =$ Percent married (females aged 15 and over who were ever married).

These data must be interpreted cautiously. It is likely, in particular, that the accuracy of the infant mortality rates varied from country to country and over time. But only a massive and one-sided accumulation of such inaccuracies could negate totally the rather strong associations shown. The statistical pattern makes good sense and fits in with other evidence bearing on the topic.

To summarize, rural-urban fertility ratios are not uniformly differentiated. In about half the cases, urban fertility is below rural; in others there are no apparent differences; and in still others urban fertility appears to be higher than rural. An adjustment for the biased data on infant mortality contained in fertility ratios makes it possible to interpret this diversity. In one group of countries, fertility ratios show differences that in all probability reflect differences in infant mortality. In another group of countries, where urban-rural differences in infant mortality are small, virtually no differences in fertility ratio are observed. In a third group of countries, what may be called a genuine urban-rural fertility differential has developed because urban females marry at higher ages.

The faulty data on infant mortality contained in the fertility ratio may also explain the apparent conflict between this survey and the earlier results of Jaffe, Tietze, and others. If several decades ago urban infant mortality was generally higher than rural, and if these differentials have been narrowing over time, lower urban fertility ratios would have been more prevalent at the earlier period. This may also explain the apparent rise in urban fertility which has puzzled some observers (see, for example, United Nations 1953a: 16).

The absence of a substantial gap in rural-urban fertility is another indication that urbanization in Asia and Africa is proceeding differently from the past urbanization of the West.

Many cities in Asia and the Far East, in contrast with Western cities, often retain strong village characteristics or those of an agglomeration of villages. . . . Although a rather small elite indigenous population [has] the same characteristics as urban residents in the West, the mass of many Asian cities is resident in village agglomerations and tend to retain "folk" characteristics. The characteristics of the urban residents, identified with such dichotomies or continua as "folk-urban," "rural-urban," or "community-society," do not hold for the mass of residents in many Asian cities (UNESCO 1958: 34–35).

References

ABU-LUGHOD, JANET. 1964. "Urban-Rural Differences as a Function of the Demographic Transition: Egyptian Data and an Analytical Model," *American Journal of Sociology,* **69,** 476–490.

BARCLAY, GEORGE W. 1958. *Techniques of Population Analysis.* New York: Wiley.

BOGUE, DONALD J. 1959. *The Population of the United States.* Glencoe, Ill.: Free Press.

COMBS, J. W., and KINGSLEY DAVIS. 1951. "Differential Fertility in Puerto Rico," *Population Studies,* **5,** 104–116.

DAVIS, KINGSLEY. 1951. *The Population of India and Pakistan.* Princeton, N. J.: Princeton University Press.

EL-BADRY, M. A. 1956. "Some Aspects of Fertility in Egypt," *Milbank Memorial Fund Quarterly,* **34,** 23–43.

HUYCK, EARL. 1945. "Differential Fertility in Ceylon," *Population Bulletin* (United Nations), **4,** 21–29.

JAFFE, A. J. 1942. "Urbanization and Fertility," *American Journal of Sociology,* **48,** 48–60.

KISER, CLYDE V. 1944. "The Demographic Position of Egypt," in Milbank Memorial Fund, *Demographic Studies of Selected Areas of Rapid Growth.* New York.

MOORE, WILBERT. 1951. *Industrialization and Labor.* Ithaca, N. Y.: Cornell University Press.

ROBINSON, WARREN C. 1961. "Urban-Rural Differences in Indian Fertility," *Population Studies,* **14,** 218–234.

———— and ELIZABETH H. ROBINSON. 1960. "Rural-Urban Fertility Differentials in Mexico," *American Sociological Review,* **25**, 77–81.

SMITH, T. E. 1952. *Population Growth in Malaya.* London: Oxford University Press.

TAEUBER, IRENE B. 1958. *The Population of Japan.* Princeton, N. J.: Princeton University Press.

THOMPSON, WARREN S. 1935. *Population Problems,* 2nd ed. New York: McGraw-Hill.

TIETZE, CHRISTOPHER. 1958. "Human Fertility in Latin America," *Annals of the American Academy of Political and Social Science,* **316**, 84–93.

UNESCO. 1958. *Urbanization in Asia and the Far East,* edited by Philip M. Hauser. New York.

UNITED NATIONS. 1953a. *Demographic Yearbook, 1952.* New York.

————. 1953b. *The Determinants and Consequences of Population Trends.* Population Bulletin No. 17. New York.

————. 1957. *Report on the World Social Situation.* New York.

The distinction that Robinson made with respect to fertility is both important in itself and also indicative of much deeper differences between Western cities (whether present-day or at an earlier stage of industrialization) and those in underdeveloped countries. Most of these latter nations acquired their independence in the post-1945 years, and they are generally ruled from capitals that were creations of the former imperial powers.

The new capitals of Asia have been faced with a drastically new set of conditions overnight, and . . . the resultant anomalies have been much the same for each of them. With the exception of Delhi, all of them (Karachi, Colombo, Rangoon, Bangkok, Kuala Lumpur, Singapore, Djakarta, and Manila) were essentially or wholly foreign creations. Delhi . . . has been the capital of India only since 1911; until then the capital was Calcutta, which was as much a foreign creation as any of the others. . . . The new cities became the largest in each country, in most cases the only real cities, because they served all or nearly all of the commercial functions for the new kind of economy which the foreigners developed in differing degrees all over the country, superimposed on an economy which remained agrarian and largely precommercial (Murphey 1957).

In short, the rural-urban difference in the newly independent nations is greater than in the West because it includes as a half-hidden element a residual hostility between native patriotism and the seat of prior imperial rule.

The following paper focuses on this pattern in the cities of Negro Africa. Its author, Professor Arnold L. Epstein, is the head of the department of anthropology, Australian National University, having taught earlier at the University of Manchester. He was engaged in field work in Northern Rhodesia (presently Zambia) during 1950–56, for most of this period as a re-

search officer of the Rhodes Livingstone Institute in Lusaka. His work among the Tolai people of New Britain resulted in a volume titled Matupit: Land, Politics and Change *(Berkeley: University of California Press, 1969). He also edited a book called* The Craft of Social Anthropology *(London: Tavistock, 1968).*

URBANIZATION AND SOCIAL CHANGE IN AFRICA

A. L. EPSTEIN

The achievement of political independence in so many African countries and their emergence into nationhood are spectacular and dramatic expressions of the great contemporary upheaval of society throughout the continent. Among the many factors contributing to these developments has been the growth of large modern towns and cities, in themselves both a striking index of change and a stimulus to further change. The importance of the towns in social change has been noted by students of African affairs. Thus Hodgkin, a political scientist, commented (1956: 18) that "it is above all in these new urban societies that the characteristic institutions and ideas of African nationalism are born and grow to maturity." Hodgkin remarked the parallels between urban growth in Africa today and that in England in the early phases of the Industrial Revolution. Gluckman (1960: 56–57), from a more specifically anthropological point of view, wrote in somewhat similar terms:

Modern industrial towns have everywhere produced specific types of associations arising from the needs of urban life. . . . We must expect these associations inevitably to develop in Africa. . . . An African townsman is a townsman, an African miner is a miner.

Hodgkin and Gluckman marked a big advance in thinking about these problems by their emphasis on the positive features and functions of urban life. Yet, as our knowledge of African urbanism accumulates, it also becomes clear that such formulations may do less than justice to the complexity of the phenomena, and can lead to an obscuring of certain important problems calling for analysis. Thus, for example, the connection that Hodgkin postulates between the growth of towns and the rise of African nationalism seems, on the face of it, straightforward and indisputable. On the other hand, we must face the fact that the countries of tropical Africa where nationalism has been most advanced have sometimes had very small pro-

SOURCE: Abridged from *Current Anthropology*, 8 (1967), 275–295, with permission of the author and the journal.

portionate numbers engaged in wage labor, surely a primary mark of modern urban life. Clearly, urbanization in modern Africa has gone hand in hand with a number of other processes—industrialization, Westernization, the growth of settler communities, and so forth—all of which have to be kept analytically distinct if we are to make valid generalizations.

Consideration of Gluckman's position also points up the increasing need for sharper and more varied conceptual tools. Thus if, as he has argued, every African is "detribalized" as soon as he leaves his tribal area to come to town, what meaning is to be given to the term *urbanization* itself, and how can we decide whether one African or one population is more "urbanized" than another? It is of course true, as Gluckman remarks, that the man who comes to town finds himself involved in different kinds of grouping from those which obtained in the village; he also earns his livelihood in a different way and comes under different authorities. But none of this can tell us anything of what Mitchell and Shaul (1963) have called "the degree of commitment to urban residence," still less of the connection between urban commitment and the development of new patterns of behavior and sets of values and attitudes. For example, in a study of power and prestige among urban Africans (Mitchell and Epstein 1957), the respondents were divided into three categories according to the period they had resided in town: (1) under 2 years; (2) between 3 and 7 years; and (3) 8 years and over. The data showed that urban court members were ranked higher by respondents in the second category than by those in the first or the third. In short, urbanization, in at least one of its dimensions, involves a process of growth and change.

A further difficulty of Gluckman's formulation is that while it correctly invites us to set our studies of African urbanization in the context of studies of urban life elsewhere, it does not enable us to handle so readily the problem of variation in urban social systems. As studies of modern urban Africa accumulate, it becomes increasingly plain that in a number of important respects the West African situation differs markedly from that obtaining in South and Central Africa (see, for example, Banton 1966). While it is possible to detect certain general patterns in African urbanization, the deeper understanding of this phenomenon and its role in social change requires not only that we pay closer attention to the problem of variation but that this diversity be handled within a single conceptual framework.

What, then, are we to understand by *urbanization?* In an immediate sense, it refers, of course, to living in towns as against living in rural settlements, and it is on this basis that simple, quantitative indices of urbanization are sometimes constructed: for example, the proportion of a population resident in towns of a given population size at a given moment. Such indices are useful for certain limited purposes, for example, as a measure of demographic change, but in other respects the results they give are not always very helpful, particularly in the African context. What, for instance, is to be made of a measure which is based on the number of cities with a population of 100,000 or more and gives Nigeria an index of urbanization of 4.3, whereas Zambia, whose Copperbelt constitutes a large, modern industrial and urban complex, does not even register (see Appendix in Almond and Coleman 1960)? There are parts of Nigeria where Africans have lived traditionally in large, densely populated settlements, but where the contemporary drift to the towns has been relatively slight. A number of Yoruba towns, for example, have populations in excess of 100,000 but between 1921 and 1952 Yoruba country had the lowest rate of urban growth in Nigeria, and the population of these cities remained fairly homogeneous (Coleman 1958: 75). In Zambia, by contrast, during this same period about 250,000 Africans came from every part of the country and beyond to live and work in the towns of the Copperbelt. It seems more meaningful to me, therefore, to regard urbanization as involving a process of movement and change; its essence is that it creates the possibility of discontinuity with some pre-existing set of conditions. This may be contrasted with urbanism, which is the way of life in the towns themselves. In this way it may be possible to speak, for example, of Yoruba urbanism without necessarily implying Yoruba urbanization, though it is clear that this process too is now occurring on an increasing scale (Schwab 1966). It follows also that urbanization cannot be treated as a unidimensional phenomenon: it has demographic, social-structural, and cultural aspects, each of which poses separate analytical problems, but which also have to be studied in their interrelations.

THE DETERMINANTS OF URBAN SOCIAL STRUCTURE

Many writers nowadays remind us that towns were known in Africa long before the onset of the modern period, particularly in West, and parts of Central, Africa. Many of the famous urban centers of the past have declined, however, and those that have remained important have done so only by undergoing a transformation. The towns with which we are chiefly concerned, then, are new, and in most cases have seen their most rapid growth in the decade or two following the Second World War. During this period the population of many centers more than doubled. Unlike the traditional towns and cities, these new centers are the product of colonialism: as Dresch (quoted in Balandier 1956: 497) puts it, "they are towns built up around the mine, tends to develop a markedly paternalistic regime great importance in stamping the towns with a number of general characteristics: great racial and ethnic diversity, accompanied by wide differences between the groups in economic and social status, technical skills, and way of life. In general terms, the dichotomy of rich and poor has correlated closely with that of white and black, between whom a third "color group" of Asians or Levantines has frequently intervened.

These contrasts and divisions within the community are at once reflected in the physical layout of the town. The physical separation of the races and of ethnic groups finds its most rigid expression in the principle of apartheid in the Union of South Africa, but the tendency for African urban dwellers to be housed on their own separate estates was almost universal in pre-independence days. Pons (1969) notes how the location of the African areas contributed to their "suburban" or dormitory character: from early morning until the night curfew which prohibited African entry to the "European town" and European entry to the African areas, there was much movement between the two. The African area (*centre extra-coutumier* or "municipal location") has indeed some affinities with a suburb in a Western city, but its legal status is quite different. Moreover, the effect of social convention and administration has been to set a barrier round the location and thus effectively to exclude the residents from full participation in the life of the town and the enjoyment of its amenities. Africans in what is now Zambia used to sum it up succinctly: tarred roads always stop at the entrance to the location. In the countries of West Africa, physical segregation was not built into the legal code, but the social pattern has often been broadly similar. In some cases, indeed, the town includes a number of areas that belong to different ethnic or tribal communities. Thus in Monrovia, the capital of Liberia, the Vai, the Kru, and the Bassa each corporately owns and administers its own area (Fraenkel 1964: 52).

However, the "colonial experience" itself has not been uniform, and other variables which touch more immediately the process of urbanization and the system of social relations that build up within the town need to be brought into the analysis: (1) the "industrial structure," that is, the organizational framework through which the town seeks to achieve those economic aims and purposes that brought it into existence, or give it its present importance; (2) the "civic structure," which derives from the policies and practices of its administration; and (3) the "demographic imperative" (Mitchell 1959), which affects in a variety of ways the social composition of the town and the degree of urban commitment.

The important differences I noted earlier between the patterns of West African urbanization and those further to the south derive in the main from differences in "industrial structure." The wealth of many of the West African countries has been based on various cash crops: palm oil, cocoa, or peanuts. Hence, as Hodgkin has remarked (1956: 78), many of the larger towns have been relatively feeble as production centers and have developed rather as centers of import and export and, increasingly, of administration. This, I suggest, immediately gives them a character that contrasts sharply with that of more purely industrial towns. In my own work on the Copperbelt, I have drawn attention to the different ways in which urban associations and the patterns of political leadership develop in a mine township as compared with a municipality (Epstein 1958; 1961). The company town, built up around the mine, tends to develop a markedly paternalistic regime providing for and controlling most aspects of the social life of the workers and their families. By contrast, the commercial township, with its hundreds of small firms offering many different forms of employment, is much more diversified in its structure, and its people tend to develop a more independent outlook. Interesting confirmation of this view is to be found in Powdermaker's study (1962) of the impact of mass communications in Luanshya, where Africans in the municipal location bought many more magazines and newspapers and read much more widely than their fellows in the mines. It is in the ports and great commercial centers rather than around the mines that variegated interest groups may be expected to emerge and political associations and trade unions to develop and flourish. It is not enough, then, to regard modern urban centers in Africa simply as towns: if we are to understand the systems of social relations developing within them and their implications for social or political change, we have to think of them too in terms of industrial structure—as administrative centers, as marketplaces, as seaports or rail junctions, and as centers of production, or as various combinations of these.

Towns differ not only in the patterns of their economic activities, but also in the institutions and practices through which they are governed. Thus, stabilization was the policy favored in the Belgian Congo, and its result was the development of the *centre extra-coutumier,* a self-contained residential and administrative unit under the close supervision of a European administrative officer, within which Africans could establish a stable family life in their own homes. The situation that obtained in Stanleyville, where a team of investigators found they had a convenient sampling frame available because all dwelling compounds were officially recorded by number (Pons 1956: 244), contrasts sharply with that in Lagos, where the fieldworker's task was more difficult, partly because the records were inadequate, partly because the household itself was so puzzling to define. Marris notes (1961: vii) that people who shared the same room might be unrelated and live entirely independent lives; on the other hand, a wife might live several streets away from her husband, though she would cook for him every day and depend upon him for support.

Such differences of policy and practice in regard to the housing of African urban dwellers are usually the expression of basic differences in the approach to urban administration. Other such differences appear in policy in regard to the acquisition of land rights within the township area; in the presence or absence of measures for "influx control"; in the different forms of machinery of urban local government; and in the extent to which Africans participate in civic affairs or in the administration of justice. An interesting illustration of the latter point is to be found in the part played by "tribal" authorities in urban administration in different places. In some cases, for example, the system of local administration has been built up around the principle of tribal representation. In Freetown, Sierra Leone, tribal headmen were officially recognized and played an important part in maintaining law and order (Banton 1957), while on the Copperbelt tribal elders fulfilled similar functions. Moreover, on the Copperbelt and in other towns of Northern Rhodesia, as well as in the *centres extra-coutumiers* of the Belgian Congo, African urban courts had been established by government where disputes (mainly matrimonial) involving Africans could be settled in accordance with African customary law. By contrast, in Dar-es-Salaam there was no urban court, and the magistrates' courts interfered in such matters hardly at all (Leslie 1963: 220).

If the forms of local administration are an important source of variation between towns, then we can classify the towns of Africa by the positions they occupy along a continuum defined in terms of civic structure. At one end of such a scale would be the towns and cities of the Union of South Africa, where the civic structure is marked by segregated housing areas and a tightly administered policy of influx control. At the other end would be the situation of relative laissez-faire that seems characteristic of West Africa. The towns and cities of West Africa have commonly grown up around the sites of long-established indigenous settlements, and many features of the old towns have been incorporated in the new (Lloyd 1959). Often, indeed, they are syntheses of villages in which each village, though absorbed in the growing town, has preserved its identity (Hodgkin 1956: 72). Clearly such centers have a much more organic character than those in which African town dwellers are required to live in municipal locations or mine compounds. It follows that in the West African countries there has been a much less rigid approach to matters of urban administration: not only is there less direct control over housing and housing conditions, but there is not that same insistence on maintaining public standards of hygiene and sanitation that is one of the hallmarks of the settler-dominated city to the south. Between these two extremes was the former Belgian Congo, where, as we have seen, theoretically "tight" urban administration went hand in hand with a policy of urban stabilization. While a new bourgeoisie was not produced on the West African model, men no longer able or willing to seek wage employment (and also divorced women and elderly widows) were able to support themselves in the town and did not have to return to the village, as in South Africa or Zambia.

A classification of African towns from the standpoint of their "industrial structure" does not coincide completely with that based on civic structure; at a number of points, the industrial classification appears to cut across the other, which was mainly an expression of the settler-nonsettler cleavage. For example, it is my impression that in (Southern) Rhodesia, whose main cities have been manufacturing rather than marketing centers, more scope has been allowed to African business enterprise. A number of Africans in Salisbury and Bulawayo have emerged as wealthy businessmen and storekeepers. Many of these seem to have been associated with the African nationalist movement, but it may not be without significance that African merchants in Rhodesia have been noticeably more "accommodationist" (Coleman 1960: 273), and the nationalist movement itself, at least until quite recently, less militant than elsewhere.

Southall (1961: 6) has distinguished two types of town: the old, established, slowly growing town, found mostly in West Africa, Tanganyika (Tanzania), and Uganda; and the new town of mushroom growth, primarily found in the Union of South Africa, the Rhodesias, Kenya, and the Belgian Congo. Examination of the data from the standpoints of industrial and civic structure leads to a refinement of Southall's categories; it counteracts any tendency to view urbanization too simplistically, for example in terms of broad contrasts between geographical regions; and it raises issues for further inquiry.

The third factor is the demographic: imbalances occur when rural people seek work in towns. Typically, the structure of the urban population is marked by an excess of men over women and an over-all predominance of those aged 20 to 40. These factors relate to the patterns of migration and to the continuing relations between the town and the areas from which it draws its labor supply.

The drift to the towns is the universal concomitant of early industrialization, but the way in which it occurs is not everywhere the same. In 19th-century England, for example, the expansion of the industrial towns was achieved by the flow of labor from the smaller rural places in their immediate hinterland. In Africa a few instances of progressive migration have been reported (see, for example, Doucy and Feldheim 1956), but in the main urbanization has proceeded, not by a series of stages, but by a sharp leap from small village to distant urban center, from *kisendji*, the ancient way of life of the tribe, to *kizungu*, the civilized way of life of the towns (Pons 1956: 250). But if in Africa the transition to the town has been somewhat sharper, paradoxically, the break with the village has been less radical. The new African urban laborer remained bound by social, political, and even religious ties to his kinsmen in the rural areas so that, as Mitchell observes (1961: 232), it is the circulation of labor rather than its migration which has become characteristic. In this context physical distance becomes important, the response to urban living among different groups being related, at least in part, to the ease with which they can return to their rural homes. So in the East African seaport of Dar-es-Salaam, whose main sources of labor are not too remote, the agricultural seasons still have immediacy, since "indebtedness is relieved for many by a capital sum accruing from the rice harvest in June-July, mainly from fields in their home districts" (Leslie 1963: 7). Similarly, the fact that East London in South Africa is able to meet most of its labor requirements from the reserves of the Ciskei and Transkei, which lie on its very doorstep, accounts for the relative tribal and linguistic homogeneity of its African population (Reader 1961). More important, the ease with which large numbers of East London laborers are able to move back and forth between town and country at weekends puts the Xhosa migrant in a very different position from that, say, of the "Blantyre" in Johannesburg, who, some thousands of miles from his home in Malawi, is necessarily less amenable to the pressures of incapsulation. There is also the question of the *situation* of the home area, giving rise to what Leslie has called "the community of the route." Leslie describes how, when Dar-es-Salaam was a very small town and most of the in-migrants came by foot, the earliest entrants naturally set down their loads at the first opportunity, on the side of town nearest to the direction of their coming. As others followed them and went to the address of those already there, and then "hived off" and built themselves houses nearby, there was a perceptible polarization of tribes, each group tending to inhabit the quarter nearest its place of origin.

THE SOCIAL STRUCTURE OF THE TOWN

Wirth (1938) has offered a sociological definition of the city as a relatively large, dense, and permanent settlement of heterogeneous individuals, and from these postulates has sought to deduce its major identifying characteristics. Urban social relations are dominated, in this view, by the cash nexus and the labor market, and contacts in the city tend to be impersonal, superficial, transitory, and segmental. Diversification allows for a greater variability in personal behavior; as primary groups decline in significance, there is a corresponding emphasis on formal procedures of social control and on the development of associations. The towns of modern Africa satisfy the criteria of Wirth's definition of the city, and there is much in his analysis which has an immediate relevance to African urbanism. Indeed, many of those who have written of the African towns in terms of their poverty, the breakdown of family life, the rise of prostitution, juvenile delinquency and crime, and the problems of psychic maladjustment are describing phenomena that are fully accounted for in Wirth's theory. Nevertheless, the picture is curiously lopsided and leaves out of account many of the more positive features of urban life. The Africans who flock into the urban centers are not isolates in a "world of brutal indifference where it occurs to no man to honor another with so much as a glance" (Engels 1950: 24). Quite to the contrary, what is so universally striking about the life of African towns is its ebullience and gusto, its camaraderie, and the casual ease with which social contacts are established (Wilson and Mafeje 1963; Sampson 1956; Ekwensi 1954). Nor is this simply a reflection of "the peculiar *humaneness* in African social relations" of which African intellectuals frequently speak (Worsley 1964: 127). The point is that the African who comes to town rarely arrives as a complete stranger.

Every African urban dweller tends to be involved in a complex network of social relations, composed of ties with neighbors, work mates, friends, and acquaintances. At the core of the network, however, are those who are readily fitted into the elastic categories of kinship provided by a classificatory system of terminology and those who count as fellow-tribesmen (Epstein 1961). These ties clearly introduce an element of stability into an extremely fluid situation: they link together large numbers of individuals not only within the one town, but between one town and another, and between town and country. More than this, they provide the basis for a more elaborate scheme of organizing social relationships in the new environment. I refer here to what has been variously termed "urban tribalism" (Mitchell 1956; Epstein 1958), "supertribalism" (Rouch 1956), or "ethnicity" (Wallerstein 1960). As Mitchell has so clearly demonstrated, the "tribalism" that is so prevalent a feature of African urbanism is a phenomenon of a quite different order from the "tribalism" of the rural areas: in the latter it refers to a particular kind of social regimen in which social relationships are organized within a distinctive structural and cultural framework; in the former the tribe is no longer an organized political and social unit, but serves rather as a means of classifying a heterogeneous urban population into a limited number of meaningful social categories.

Tribal associations have sometimes been spoken of as an adaptive mechanism, easing the adjustment of migrants to the strange surroundings of the town. Thus, according to Little (1957: 593), the association facilitates this adjustment by substituting for the extended group of kinsmen a grouping based upon common interest which is capable of serving many of the same needs. Support for this view is perhaps to be found in the fact that where a particular tribe is dominant in the town, or enjoys a special relation to it, as in the case of the Ganda in Kampala, its members are unlikely to form a separate tribal association (cf. Leslie 1963: 40).

All these various forms of organization have their basis in tribalism, but it is clear that they cannot be adequately understood as simple manifestations of the "tribal principle." As the towns have grown, their African populations have been increasingly diversified in terms of occupation, formal education, and style of life. This does not necessarily imply the emergence within the towns of a class structure on the Western model. On the other hand, a number of studies do attest to the development of systems of social stratification defined in terms of status groups in the Weberian sense (Xydias 1956; Mitchell and Epstein 1959; Schwab 1961). However, the vast majority of recent in-migrants to towns are not "joiners," and it seems to me to be an obscuring of the sociological issues to argue, as Little has done (1965: 24), that the growth of voluntary associations represents the newly arrived migrants' response to urban conditions, "a spontaneous adjustment to their environment." I would argue rather that tribal associations have to be understood in their relation to associations of other types and to the over-all status system that has developed within the community.

RELATIONS BETWEEN TOWNS

In addition to the circulation of population between town and country characteristic of contemporary Africa, there is also considerable movement between towns. For example, Mitchell (1953) has shown that newcomers to the Copperbelt move about a good deal in the first five years of their residence, and then settle down in one town. This raises at once important questions about the spatial distribution of urban centers within a country, the relations that develop between them, and the implications that variation in these regards has for social change, particularly in the political field. According to Coleman (1960: 273), many countries of Africa are, in effect, "one-city states," and the single major city, also the territorial capital, often dominates such a country's political life. Coleman develops the argument that this circumstance permits concentration of political activity in one place and thus facilitates the mobilization of political strength. By contrast, in those countries having two or more major cities, such as Zambia (Lusaka vs. the Copperbelt), Rhodesia (Bulawayo vs. Salisbury), or the Congo (Leopoldville vs. Elizabethville), African political leadership has been dispersed, if not competitive, and it has been far more difficult to organize a comprehensive nationalist party on a territorial basis. This argument has considerable merits, but it seems to me that what is important is not so much the number of different foci of interest, but how the different centers are involved with one another. Zambia and the Congo present an interesting contrast: The Congo centers were not only physically distant from one another, but their industrial structures were also quite different and they tended to draw their African populations from quite different areas. In short, there appears to have been little convergence between them, and it would be interesting to know what kind of communication took place between the major Congo cities. By comparison, though towns of the Copperbelt frequently had concentrations of particular tribes, in the main all the principal urban centers drew on the same territorial population. The number of the towns and their close physical proximity to one another meant that they stood out in opposition to one another *as towns*. Each in time developed its own subtle distinctiveness, so that it used to be said, for example, that some of the Copperbelt towns had characteristic styles of drumming and dress. Opposition between the towns was expressed through the football league and other forms of competition. In short, for an understanding of the role of urbanization in developing new sets of identities, a key question would seem to be to what extent the growth of towns gives rise to a system of crosscutting ties and allegiances.

TOWN, COUNTRY, AND NATION

Another aspect of urbanization is a "feed-back" process, the influence of town on country and the implications of urban growth for social change. Wilson (1941–42) has analyzed brilliantly the concomitants of a system of migrant labor, showing how instead of stimulating an agricultural revolution in the reserves to match the industrial revolution in the towns, it led to rural deterioration. Circulation of population between town and country did something to ameliorate these conditions, since a certain amount of wealth did filter back in this way to the tribal areas. Circulation of the population was, as Wilson noted, "the keystone of the unstable arch of present-day Northern Rhodesia economy."

The towns are the locus of the new civilization: here are to be found new concentrations of economic and political power, and the new avenues of communications along which the influences of the towns may reach out into the countryside in varied and subtle ways. The important questions to be asked here are therefore: What are the relations of town and country? More specifically, since we are concerned with countries most of which have only recently attained nationhood, what implications do the varying features of urban social systems have for national integration?

Two assumptions commonly underlie much discussion of this aspect of urbanization: (1) that towns inevitably act as instruments of social transformation and (2) that change is uniformly in the same direction and of the same character. Both seem to derive from the fact that the model of urban-rural relations has frequently been constructed around the response of a single tribe or area, which was deemed to be typical. Sometimes, far from transforming the countryside, the pull of the towns becomes, paradoxically, a means by which the traditional system in the reserves is perpetuated. Here rural-urban relations are in a state of relatively stable equilibrium. Thus amongst the Pedi and other South African groups, where land is critically short, the export of surplus manpower to the towns does not merely prevent the disintegration of the rural social system; it positively reinforces that system (Sansom 1965). The network of rural ties is maintained in the towns, where kinsmen and others assist one another in getting jobs, frequently with the same firm, and finding accommodation. Moreover, individuals who achieve influential positions in the towns can translate them into positions of prestige within the tribal system when eventually they return home.

The response, then, of different groups to the pull of the towns is not uniform. Some groups, for example, the Ila of Zambia or the Masai of Kenya, have (for reasons which are still imperfectly understood) consistently rejected town life. The responses of others have been conditioned by features of the indigenous culture and social structure, or even in some cases by special constitutional arrangements, such as those once enjoyed by the Barotse of Zambia (which from time to time created difficulties between the Barotse and other tribes in the towns). Such differences are reflected in different patterns of incorporation into the life of the town. In Lunsar, Sierra Leone, for example, the traditionally slave-owning and Muslimized Fulbe (Fula) seek to minimize their involvement with other groups, and they do this by avoiding manual occupations or others which would involve status inferiority: they work as tailors, petty traders, and the like (Butcher 1965).

Unless we take into account the different constellations of rural-urban relations, we cannot hope to understand the significance that ethnicity comes to assume in the wider political field. Wallerstein (1960) argues that ethnicity serves to aid national integration in a number of ways. Yet if the towns are new focal points of integration, they are also a fertile source of conflict, so that ethnicity may come to play an important part in shaping, in some cases perhaps even dominating, the character of national politics. Thus, it has been said of the Congo that ethnic nationalisms were born in the large urban centers, where Congolese of different origins, speaking different languages, intermingled. These contacts, far from "bringing their hearts close together," only made them more conscious of their differences and strengthened their feelings of mutual alienation (van Wing, quoted in Lemarchand (1964: 99). The converse of this proposition is illustrated in Stanleyville, where the ethnic diversity of its population was the main reason for its conspicuous indifference to the appeals of ethnic nationalism. There were, as one of Lemarchand's African informants observed, too many tribes in Stanleyville, and none of them had any striking predominance.

The differential response to, and participation in, the life of the town among the tribes may also be an expression of different regional interests. For example, Mitchell and I have shown that while "tribalism" is a primary category of social interaction among Africans in the towns of the Copperbelt, the tribal nexus is frequently crosscut by membership in trade unions, staff associations, and other bodies. On the other hand, there are some groups which do not appear to become involved in the urban "melting pot," a notable instance being the Ila of the Southern Province of Zambia. When emergence of different political parties expresses the diversity of regional interests rather than more purely ideological differences, there may be much less room for the operation of crosscutting ties. Presumably these factors weigh heavily on political leaders striving to create a new nation: perhaps from this point of view they may contribute something to our understanding of the emergence of one-party states in Africa and of the opposition in some parts between the new national leadership and the tribal chiefs.

Viewed against the background of tribal life, urban existence involves changes—what Mitchell (1966) has recently suggested we should call "situational" as distinct from "processive" or historical change—in almost every department of social life: in family and kinship relations, in types of association and grouping and forms of leadership, in the use of leisure, and in patterns of speech (Epstein 1959). Indeed, given the common technological base of modern urban society, claims such as that "the social structure of urban Africans is increasingly tending . . . to approximate more closely to Western institutions" (Hellmann 1956: 743) might appear at first sight as self-evident. However, the processes of urban social growth in Africa are not automatic or predetermined. African urbanism, as I have repeatedly stressed, is not characterized by uniformity, and Hellmann's delineation of the South African situation has clearly less immediate relevance to West Africa. Moreover, as Hellmann herself argued on an earlier occasion (1937: 432), the Africans are not a supine people, and their incorporation into the wage-earning economy of the towns has not involved the complete submergence of their indigenous culture. Mitchell (1965) shows how Africans in Salisbury continue to interpret their experience of personal misfortune in the urban world in terms of categories and assumptions that have their roots in tribal culture and society. I would argue from this that in the study of urban social relations we need to pay attention to content as well as to form. For example, the African trade-union leader may be expected to have much in common with his English counterpart; to be successful, he must be able to organize, to hold and sway an audience, and to negotiate. The character of his leadership will also be shaped, however, by his own conception of his role and the expectations that his followers have of him, and these may be very different from those of a typical British trade unionist. Thus, for many Africans on the Copperbelt the union leader takes on many of the attributes of the tribal chief and is expected to behave like one in certain contexts. African urban institutions, even when most closely fashioned on an alien model, do not become a mere mirror image of the prototype; they become infused with elements that derive from African tribal culture. Urbanization and Westernization often go closely together in modern Africa, but analytically they must not be confused. It was this point that presumably Hodgkin had in mind when he spoke of the capacity of African townsmen to create a new indigenous civilization.

References

ALMOND, GABRIEL, and JAMES S. COLEMAN, eds. 1960. *The Politics of the Developing Areas.* Princeton, N. J.: Princeton University Press.

BALANDIER, GEORGES. 1956. "Urbanism in West and Central Africa: The Scope and Aims of Research," in Forde 1956.

BANTON, MICHAEL. 1957. *West African City.* London: Oxford University Press.

———. 1966. "Social Alignment and Identity in a West African City," in Hilda Kuper, ed., *Urbanization and Migration in West Africa.* Berkeley: University of California Press.

BUTCHER, D. 1965. "The Role of the Fulbe in the Economic and Social Life of Lunsar, Sierra Leone." Unpublished doctoral dissertation, University of Edinburgh.

COLEMAN, JAMES S. 1958. *Nigeria: Background to Nationalism.* Berkeley: University of California Press.

————. 1960. "The Politics of Sub-Saharan Africa," in Almond and Coleman 1960.

DOUCY, ARTHUR, and PIERRE FELDHEIM. 1956. "Some Effects of Industrialization in Two Districts of Equatoria Province (Belgian Congo)," in Forde 1956.

EKWENSI, CYPRIAN. 1954. *People of the City.* London: Andrew Dakers.

ENGELS, FREDERICK. 1950 (1845). *The Condition of the Working Class in England in 1844.* London: Allen & Unwin.

EPSTEIN, A. L. 1958. *Politics in an Urban African Community.* Manchester: Manchester University Press.

————. 1959. "Linguistic Innovation and Culture on the Copperbelt," *Southwestern Journal of Anthropology,* 15, 235–253.

————. 1961. "The Network and Urban Social Organization," *Rhodes-Livingstone Journal,* 29, 29–62.

FORDE, C. DARYLL, ed. 1956. *Social Implications of Industrialization and Urbanization in Africa South of the Sahara.* Paris: UNESCO.

FRAENKEL, MERRAN. 1964. *Tribe and Class in Monrovia.* London: Oxford University Press.

GLUCKMAN, MAX. 1960. "Tribalism in Modern British Central Africa," *Cahiers d'Etudes Africaines,* 1, 55–70.

HELLMANN, ELLEN. 1937. "The Native in the Towns," in Isaac Schapera, ed., *The Bantu-Speaking Tribes of South Africa.* London: Routledge.

————. 1956. "The Development of Social Groupings among Urban Africans in the Union of South Africa," in Forde 1956.

HODGKIN, THOMAS. 1956. *Nationalism in Colonial Africa.* London: Muller.

LEMARCHAND, RENÉ. 1964. *Political Awakening in the Congo.* Berkeley: University of California Press.

LESLIE, J. A. K. 1963. *A Social Survey of Dar-es-Salaam.* London: Oxford University Press.

LITTLE, KENNETH. 1957. "The Role of Voluntary Associations in West African Urbanization," *American Anthropologist,* 59, 579–596.

————. 1965. *West African Urbanization.* Cambridge: Cambridge University Press.

LLOYD, PETER C. 1959. "The Yoruba Town Today," *Sociological Review,* 7, 45–63.

MARRIS, PETER. 1961. *Family and Social Change in an African City.* London: Routledge & Kegan Paul.

MITCHELL, J. CLYDE. 1953. "A Note on the Urbanization of Africans on the Copperbelt," *Rhodes-Livingstone Journal,* 12, 20–27.

————. 1956. *The Kalela Dance.* Rhodes-Livingstone Paper 27.

————. 1959. "The Study of African Urban Social Structure." Unpublished paper for CCTA Conference on Housing and Urbanization, Nairobi.

————. 1961. "Wage Labour and African Population Movements in Central Africa," in K. M. Barbour and R. M. Prothero, eds., *Essays on African Population.* London: Routledge & Kegan Paul.

————. 1965. "The Meaning of Misfortune for Urban Africans," in Meyer Fortes and Germaine Dieterlen, eds., *African Systems of Thought*. London: Oxford University Press.

————. 1966. "Theoretical Orientations in African Urban Studies," in Michael Banton, ed., *The Social Anthropology of Complex Societies*. London: Tavistock.

————, and A. L. EPSTEIN. 1957. "Power and Prestige among Africans in Northern Rhodesia: An Experiment," *Southern Rhodesian Journal of Science*, **45**, 13–26.

————, and ————. 1959. "Occupational Prestige and Social Status among Urban Africans in Northern Rhodesia," *Africa*, **29**, 22–39.

————, and J. R. H. SHAUL. 1963. "An Approach to the Measurement of Commitment to Urban Residence." Paper presented to the Second Central African Scientific and Medical Congress, Lusaka.

MURPHEY, RHOADS. 1957. "New Capitals of Asia," *Economic Development and Cultural Change*, **5**, 216–243.

PONS, V. G. 1956. "The Growth of Stanleyville and the Composition of Its African Population," in Forde 1956.

————. 1969. *Stanleyville: An African Urban Community under Belgian Administration*. London: Oxford University Press.

POWDERMAKER, HORTENSE. 1962. *Copper Town: Changing Africa*. New York: Harper & Row.

READER, D. H. 1961. *The Black Man's Portion*. Cape Town: Oxford University Press.

ROUCH, JEAN. 1956. "Migration on the Gold Coast," *Journal de la Société des Africanistes*, **26**, 33–196.

SAMPSON, ANTHONY. 1956. *Drum: A Venture into the New Africa*. London: Collins.

SANSOM, B. 1965. "The Social System of the Pedi." Unpublished paper.

SCHWAB, WILLIAM B. 1961. "Social Stratification in Gwelo," in Aidan W. Southall, ed., *Social Change in Modern Africa*. London: Oxford University Press.

————. 1966. "Oshogbo—an Urban Community?" in Hilda Kuper, ed., *Urbaniza- and Migration in West Africa*. Berkeley: University of California Press.

SOUTHALL, AIDAN W. 1961. "Introductory Summary," in Southall, ed., *Social Change in Modern Africa*. London: Oxford University Press.

WALLERSTEIN, I. 1960. "Ethnicity and National Integration in West Africa," *Cahiers d'Etudes Africaines*, **3**, 129–139.

WATSON, WILLIAM. 1958. *Tribal Cohesion in a Money Economy*. Manchester: Manchester University Press.

WILSON, GODFREY. 1941–42. *The Economics of Detribalization*. Rhodes-Livingstone Papers 5 and 6.

WILSON, MONICA, and ARCHIE MAFEJE. 1963. *Langa: A Study of Social Groups in an African Township*. Cape Town: Oxford University Press.

WIRTH, LOUIS. 1938. "Urbanism as a Way of Life," *American Journal of Sociology*, **44**, 1–24.

WORSLEY, PETER. 1964. *The Third World*. London: Weidenfeld & Nicholson.

XYDIAS, NELLY. 1956. "Social Effects of Urbanization in Stanleyville, Belgian Congo," in Forde 1956.

7 MIGRATION

The differentiation between the urban and rural sectors of any population develops in large part, as was noted in the last chapter, through internal migration. The variation among country people is constantly reduced by the fact that some of them—those who are least suited to rural life or, in their own estimate, most likely to succeed in the city—leave, and by their departure reinforce the separation between town and country. In most nations this continual movement is very difficult to study. In the United States, even a jurisdiction like California, where net migration until recently constituted the greater part of population increase, depends on a potpourri of statistics from which to estimate the numbers arriving and barely attempts to guess at their characteristics. Such difficulties become all but insurmountable in a comparative study of the internal migration in several countries, for whether a person is recorded as a migrant depends less on his behavior than on the more or less arbitrary definitions used by various data-collecting agencies.

A partial solution to this problem of comparability is offered in the following article, by Larry H. Long. After receiving his doctorate in sociology from the University of Texas (1969), he engaged in postdoctoral

*studies in demography at the University of Pennsylvania (1969–70). He is
currently a demographer with the U. S. Bureau of the Census.*

ON MEASURING GEOGRAPHIC MOBILITY

LARRY H. LONG

It has long been felt that there is more geographic mobility within the
United States than in almost any other country in the world, but we lack
statistical data to test this hypothesis and to tell by how much countries differ,
if they do. According to Henry Shryock (1964: 116):

> One frequently reads statements in popular publications, or even in the litera-
> ture of social science, that Americans are the most mobile people in the world
> and that they are more mobile now than ever before in their history. Actually
> statistics do not exist to prove or disprove these statements.

In the last few years, however, statistics that can be used to answer these
questions have become available. This article presents data from recent
censuses and national sample surveys in the United States, Canada, Great
Britain, and Japan to show how these statistics might be used to answer
this question.

The well known problem is how to control for the effect of administrative units of vastly different size and shape that various countries use
to define migration. Most major works on internal migration (for example,
Lee *et al.* 1957; Shryock 1964; Taeuber *et al.* 1968; and United Nations 1970)
give examples of how the choice of units influences the observed rate of
migration, and Kulldorff (1955) and Thomlinson (1961) have derived
mathematical techniques that under special circumstances allow for the size
and shape of an area. The general issues in "statistical geography" were
summarized a few years ago by Duncan *et al.* (1961: 7), who observed that
in analyses based on national data for units of irregular size and shape, "it
is not always possible to effect a suitable standardization. Inter-area comparison of internal migration rates is a case in point." Thus, "students of
internal migration for the most part have had to content themselves with
making informal allowance for the noncomparability of migration rates
arising from differences in the size and shape of areal units."

Since no adequate solution to the problem is in sight, an alternative is
to ignore migration-defining areas altogether and to consider *all* moves.
Rates of residential mobility—that is, the probability of changing one's

SOURCE: Reprinted from the *Journal of the American Statistical Association,* **65** (1970),
1195–1203, with permission of the author and the journal.

house or usual address during an interval of one or five years—provide an unambiguous index of total geographic movement that is independent of particular administrative units and is therefore applicable in all countries. Such statistics became available for the first time in the 1961 censuses of Canada and of Great Britain and the 1960 census of Japan, which can be compared with the abundant data on residential mobility in the United States.

As can be expected, minor differences in census practices prevent perfect comparability. In the rates to be presented, whenever possible the numerator was defined as total number of movers (including movers from abroad), and the denominator as the total resident population included in the census or sample. In the case of Britain, however, the denominator constitutes persons reporting on duration of residence, and there is thus a slight upward bias in Britain's rates. Also, there is a slight downward bias in the Canadian data, which exclude persons not living in private households.

GENERAL INTERNATIONAL COMPARISONS

The basic data are presented in Tables 1 and 2. Table 1 gives five-year residential mobility rates by age and sex for the United States, Canada, England and Wales, and Scotland. Table 2 gives one-year rates by age and sex for the United States, England and Wales, Scotland, and Japan. Patterns by age are not a primary consideration in this article, and the age breakdowns shown are simply the most comparable for all these countries.

Over-all rates for the United States and Canada are similar, and both are clearly higher than those elsewhere. During the five-year interval, 36 to 37 percent of the population of Great Britain changed their addresses, compared with over 45 percent of Canada and about 50 percent of the United States. During the one year, about 20 percent in the United States moved, compared with around 11 percent in Britain and 8 percent in Japan. Thus, by both measures, the United States had the highest rates of residential mobility, and Britain's rates were significantly lower than those for Canada and the United States.

The length of the interval makes a significant difference in comparing nations. The rates for the United States and Britain, thus, differ more for the shorter interval: for the five-year interval the British rate is 72 to 73 percent of the United States rate, but only 57 percent for the one-year interval. This suggests that proportionately more Americans than British moved several times during the five years, as is also shown by the fact that the ratio of one-year to five-year rates is 0.41 for the United States but only 0.31 for Britain.

If persons changed their residence according to the current age-specific rates in each of these countries, how many times would they move during their lifetime? This can be calculated by adapting standard demographic

Table 1. Percentage of Population Residentially Mobile ᵃ during Five Years Prior to the Census by Age and Sex, United States (1960), Canada (1960), England and Wales (1961), and Scotland (1961)

AGE CATEGORY	UNITED STATES		CANADA		ENGLAND AND WALES		SCOTLAND	
	MALES	FEMALES	MALES	FEMALES	MALES	FEMALES	MALES	FEMALES
5–14	52.3	52.5	43.6	43.6	37.5	37.4	38.7	39.3
15–24	59.7	65.4	44.5	55.7	39.1	49.3	37.0	46.7
25–44	63.4	57.8	60.1	55.6	51.9	47.1	52.0	47.7
45–64	36.6	34.2	32.7	32.4	24.1	23.4	24.1	23.1
65+	29.3	30.4	26.1	28.6	22.4	24.2	22.2	23.3
All ages 5+	50.9	49.4	45.1	45.8	36.8	36.0	36.9	36.3

ᵃ All persons who changed their residence, including those who moved from abroad and those who moved and failed to report to their place of prior residence.

sources: U. S. Bureau of the Census, U. S. Census of Population, 1960: Vol. I. Characteristics of the Population, Part 1, U. S. Summary, Table 164. Canada, Dominion Bureau of Statistics, Census of Canada, 1961: General Characteristics of Migrant and Non-Migrant Population, Table 1. Great Britain, General Register Office, Census, 1961, England and Wales: Migration Tables, Table 2; Census, 1961, Scotland: Internal Migration, Table 2.

Table 2. Percentage of Population Residentially Mobile [a] during Twelve Months circa 1960, by Age and Sex, United States (1960–61), England and Wales (1960–61), Scotland (1960–61), and Japan (1959–60)

AGE CATEGORY	UNITED STATES		ENGLAND AND WALES		SCOTLAND	
	MALES	FEMALES	MALES	FEMALES	MALES	FEMALES
1–4	29.7	30.3	20.6	20.5	16.9	16.6
5–13	18.6	18.7				
5–14			9.6	9.7	9.3	9.3
14–24	27.6	32.7				
15–24			17.5	21.6	15.1	19.2
25–44	25.7	21.3	15.8	13.2	14.6	12.4
45–64	12.4	12.0	6.6	6.5	6.4	6.1
65+	9.6	9.6	6.5	7.0	6.5	6.6
All ages 1+	20.9	20.3	12.0	11.6	11.2	10.8

AGE CATEGORY	JAPAN	
	MALES	FEMALES
1–14	4.5	4.5
15–19	15.5	13.6
20–24	18.4	17.9
25–29	16.8	14.3
30–39	9.7	6.8
40–49	5.5	3.9
50–59	4.0	3.1
60–69	2.6	3.0
70–79	2.2	2.3
80+	2.0	2.3
	8.7	7.4

a All persons who changed their residence, including those who moved from abroad and those who moved and failed to report their place of prior residence.

SOURCES: As given in Table 1 for England and Wales and Scotland. U. S. Bureau of the Census, Current Population Reports, "Mobility of the Population of the United States, March 1960 to March 1961," Series P-20, No. 118, August 1962. Japan, Bureau of Statistics, Population Census of Japan, 1960, Ten Percent Sample Tabulations, Part 1: Marital Status and Migration, Table 2.

techniques to residential mobility data (Wilber 1963). To calculate the expected number of moves an individual makes during his lifetime from data for a one-year period, one makes two assumptions: (1) during the interval each mover moved only once, and (2) persons reporting the same address at the beginning and end of the interval did not move at any time during the interval. The product of the age-specific probability of moving and the appropriate L_x value from a life table yields the expected number of moves at age x. The sum of the values for each age x and for all later ages—that is, the total expected number of moves during and after each age x—is then divided by the population alive at the beginning of each age x—that is, the l_x column of a life table. The result is interpreted as the expected number of moves an individual at age x makes during his remaining lifetime or, more precisely, the expected number of years with moves.

The results of these calculations are shown in Table 3. A 1961 life table

Table 3. Expected Number of Moves per Person during Remaining Lifetime, United States, England and Wales, and Japan, circa 1960

UNITED STATES		ENGLAND AND WALES		JAPAN	
AGE CATEGORY	MOVES PER PERSON [a]	AGE CATEGORY	MOVES PER PERSON [a]	AGE CATEGORY	MOVES PER PERSON [a]
1–4	13.64	1–4	8.35	1–4	4.90
5–19	12.53	5–14	7.57	15–19	4.31
20–24	9.81	15–24	6.64	20–24	3.60
25–29	7.68	25–44	4.73	25–29	2.72
30–34	6.00	45–64	1.98	30–39	1.96
35–44	4.86	65+	0.99	40–49	1.17
45–64	3.29			50–59	0.75
65–74	1.40			60–69	0.46
75+	0.87			70–79	0.28
				80+	0.14

[a] That is, expected moves per person in the age interval and at all later ages.

SOURCES: As for Table 2, plus U. S. Public Health Service, National Vital Statistics Division, *Vital Statistics of the United States, 1961:* Vol. 2, *Mortality,* Part A, 2–7.

for the United States was used to calculate the expected number of moves an American would make in his lifetime according to levels of residential mobility prevailing around 1960–61 in the United States, in England and Wales, and in Japan. Thus, a person aged one year would move 13.64 times over the course of an American's lifetime, 8.35 times according to the rates for England and Wales, and 4.90 times according to the Japanese rates. At age 35 a person moving according to United States rates could expect about as many additional moves as at age 25 according to English rates, and at age one according to Japanese rates. In other words, an American at approximately the midpoint of his life would anticipate about as many additional moves as he would make in his entire lifetime according to Japanese rates.

These quite large differences suggest an American style of life adapted to residential mobility. Either the rates in Table 2 or the expected moves per person in Table 3 can be used as a basis for saying that around 1960 residential mobility in Great Britain was less than 60 percent, and in Japan less than 40 percent, of that in the United States.

So far as can be observed from the broad age breakdowns, the rates in all the countries are high for young children and persons in their late teens and twenties, and rather steadily decline thereafter. In Japan the curve peaks more at the young-adult ages than in the other countries. For both time intervals, males had higher rates than females in all countries except Canada. In all the countries females had higher rates at ages over 65 and, except for Japan, at ages 15 to 24. The higher rate for females at ages over 65 is due to the fact that many wives outlive their husbands and then change their address.

ARE THE APPARENT DIFFERENCES "REAL"?

The question here is not what factors might explain the observed differences but rather what differences we want to explain.

For the five-year period, differences between the United States and Canada are insignificant; the slightly higher rate for the United States is probably due to the fact that these data, but not the Canadian, included persons not in private households. Since most of those living in hotels, boarding houses, military barracks, and the like are males who move frequently, the difference in sampling affects the sex ratio of migrants as well as their number (see Table 1).

The data seem to reveal three levels of residential mobility—in North America generally, in Great Britain, and in Japan. Such a conclusion is not necessarily invalid, but it is incomplete. We ought to allow for the fact that these nations have different proportions of their labor force in agriculture, since farmers have very low rates of residential mobility (Table 4). With this correction there are not three levels of residential mobility but only two. Again the United States and Canada have about the same rate, but the difference between Japan and Britain disappears. It would appear, therefore, that Japan as a whole has a lower rate than Britain because of the larger percentage of its population in agriculture. For nonagricultural males the British rate is still about 59 percent, but the Japanese rate about 66 percent, of the United States rate. These differences among the nonagricultural labor forces are significant, to be explained in terms of the social-structural features of the four countries.

The conclusion that there are only two levels of residential mobility—

Table 4. Percentage of Employed Males Residentially Mobile, by Broad Occupational Class, United States, Canada, Japan, and England and Wales, circa 1960

	RESIDENTIAL MOBILITY RATE		MALE LABOR FORCE
	FIVE-YEAR	ONE-YEAR	OUTSIDE AGRICUL-
COUNTRY AND CATEGORY	PERIOD	PERIOD	TURE (PERCENT)
United States			91.8
Employed males	50.8	19.9	
Male labor force outside agriculture	52.4	20.4	
Canada			87.5
Employed males	49.0	n.a.	
Male labor force outside agriculture	53.0	n.a.	
Japan			74.1
Employed males	n.a.	10.3	
Male labor force outside agriculture	n.a.	13.4	
England and Wales			94.8
Employed males	37.6	11.9	
Male labor force outside agriculture	38.0	12.1	

n.a. No data available.

SOURCES: U. S. Bureau of the Census, *Current Population Reports*, "Mobility of the Population of the United States, March 1960 to March 1961," Series P-20, No. 118, August 1962; *U. S. Census of Population, 1960: Migration for States and State Economic Areas*, Table 9. Canada, Dominion Bureau of Statistics, *Census of Canada, 1961: Migrant and Non-Migrant Population in the Labour Force*, Table J7. Japan, Bureau of Statistics, *Population Census of Japan, Migration*, Vol. 2, Part 2, Table 4. Great Britain, General Register Office, *Census, 1961, England and Wales: Migration Tables*, Table 2.

one for North America and another for Britain and Japan—was based on a five-year mobility interval in the first two countries and a one-year interval in the second. Over one year the United States may have somewhat more movement within areas than Canada, though not necessarily more movement between local areas (Canada 1967; United States 1962). According to the 1961 census, 52.3 percent of Canadian *households* had been in their dwelling for less than five years, a figure even higher than the 45 percent of *persons* the same census listed as living at different addresses in 1956 and 1961. It is also higher than the five-year rate for the United States. But in Canada the percentage of households with a duration of residence of less than one year was only 15.3—noticeably lower than the 20 percent of the population that moves each year in the United States. Thus, there may still be three levels of residential mobility over a one-year period—with the United States having a slightly higher rate than Canada, and Britain and

Japan having the same lower rate, when the percentage of the population in agriculture is taken into account.

In sum, this article has ranked four industrial countries by the geographic mobility of their populations. The differences depend in part on the length of the mobility interval. The best available measure is a period rate of residential mobility, a kind of least common denominator applicable in all countries, which circumvents the problem of evaluating moves between local administrative areas of different size and shape. Presently only the four countries discussed in this article present these statistics. The same information is apparently available in the Swedish population registers for perhaps the past 200 years, but has not been tabulated (Hägerstrand 1963; Wendel 1957).

References

CANADA. DOMINION BUREAU OF STATISTICS. 1967. "Geographic Mobility in Canada, October 1964–October 1965," *Special Labour Force Studies*, No. 4, by May Nickson.

DUNCAN, OTIS DUDLEY, RAY P. CUZZORT, and BEVERLY DUNCAN. 1961. *Statistical Geography*. Glencoe, Ill.: Free Press.

HÄGERSTRAND, TORSTEN. 1963. "Geographic Measurements of Migration, Swedish Data," in Jean Sutter, ed., *Human Displacements, Measurement and Methodological Aspects*. Paris: Hachette.

KULLDORFF, GUNNAR. 1955. *Migration Probabilities*. Lund Studies in Geography, Series B, No. 14. Lund: Gleerup.

LEE, EVERETT S., ANN RATNER MILLER, CAROL P. BRAINERD, and RICHARD A. EASTERLIN. 1957. *Population Redistribution and Economic Growth, United States, 1870–1950*, Vol. 1: *Methodological Considerations and Reference Tables*. Philadelphia: American Philosophical Society.

SHRYOCK, HENRY S., JR. 1964. *Population Mobility within the United States*. Chicago: Community and Family Study Center, University of Chicago.

TAEUBER, KARL E., LEONARD CHIAZZE, JR., and WILLIAM HAENSZEL. 1968. *Migration in the United States: An Analysis of Residence Histories*. Public Health Monograph No. 77. Washington, D. C.: U. S. Government Printing Office.

THOMLINSON, RALPH. 1961. "A Model for Migration Analysis," *Journal of the American Statistical Association*, 56, 675–686.

UNITED NATIONS. 1970. *Methods of Measuring Internal Migration*. Population Studies, Manual VI. New York.

UNITED STATES. BUREAU OF THE CENSUS. 1962. "Mobility of the Population of the United States, March 1960 to March 1961," *Current Population Reports*, Series P-20, No. 118. Washington, D. C.: U. S. Government Printing Office.

WENDEL, BERTIL. 1957. "Regional Aspects of Internal Migration and Mobility in Sweden, 1946–50," in David Hannerberg, Torsten Hägerstrand, and Bruno Odeving, eds., *Migration in Sweden*. Lund Studies in Geography, Series B, No. 13. Lund: Gleerup.

WILBER, GEORGE W. 1963. "Migration Expectancy in the United States," *Journal of the American Statistical Association*, 58, 444–453.

That American analysts of international migration have concentrated so narrowly on their own country is not merely an indication of ethocentrism, for in terms of numbers the United States has been the most important receiving country in the modern era. Nevertheless the study of international migration has acquired a certain parochial flavor, and the three pieces that follow were deliberately chosen to supplement this too narrow range.

For most norteamericanos South America is Spanish (or, in Brazil, Portuguese) in language and culture. It is my impression that even social scientists are seldom aware of the large components in these populations of German, Italian, Russian Jewish, African, Japanese, and other subnations, most of which have retained a far greater distinctive cohesion than their counterparts to the north. Most of the immigrants to the United States fitted into a society whose basic structure had been set before their arrival. In contrast, modern Argentina was largely a creation of the mass immigration, which overwhelmed both the native population and its pre-industrial culture. As the next paper argues, immigration is thus a much more important factor in the history of Argentina, in spite of the fact that many more Europeans went to the United States.

The author, Gino Germani, is the Monroe Gutman Professor of Latin American Affairs in the department of sociology at Harvard University. Born in Italy, he emigrated to Argentina and then to the United States, thus living out some of the themes analyzed in this article. As professor of sociology at the University of Buenos Aires (1946–62) and director of its Institute of Sociology (1955–64) and of the Center for Comparative Sociology (1964–66), Germani was largely responsible for introducing modern methods of social analysis to that country and, indeed, to Latin America as a whole. Of his ten books, nine are in Spanish, and most of these are on the same topics analyzed in the paper: Argentina's social and political structure and how it was transformed by mass immigration.

MASS IMMIGRATION AND MODERNIZATION IN ARGENTINA

GINO GERMANI

Contemporary Argentina cannot be understood without a thorough analysis of the role of immigration, which both powerfully stimulated the country's modernization and caused a substantial economic, social, and political realignment of the population. In no other country did the proportion of adult foreigners reach the level in Argentina, where for more than

SOURCE: Reprinted in an abridged version with the author's permission from *Studies in Comparative International Development*, Vol. 2, No. 11 (1966).

sixty years aliens constituted around 70 percent of the capital city's adult population and almost 50 percent of that in the heavily populated and economically important provinces.

Immigration resulted from a conscious policy to replace the social structure inherited from colonial society with one inspired by the advanced West. This plan had three parts: (1) mass immigration; (2) universal and compulsory education; and (3) the importation of capital, development of modern forms of agriculture and livestock breeding, and heavy investment in social capital, especially railroads. Immigration was intended both to populate an immense sparsely settled territory and to modify the population's composition.

To understand these aims, one must recall the rationale of the elites that conceived and carried out the nation's reorganization. The revolution for national independence had been led by an elite inspired by the 18th-century Enlightenment. This small number of creoles, mostly of the upper class in Buenos Aires and a few other cities, contrasted sharply with the traditionalist majority of the population, whether urban or rural. Because of their lack of a mass base, the Independence elite could not establish a modern state, and it took years of anarchy and autocracy for them to see that a prerequisite was a change in Argentina's social structure and human composition. Their intent then became to modify the "national character," to "Europeanize" the Argentine population, to produce a "regeneration of the races," in Sarmiento's expression; physically to bring Europe to America, in the well known formulation of Alberdi.

A CENTURY OF FOREIGN IMMIGRATION

One of the first changes introduced by the new regime in 1810 was to open the country to foreigners, thus eliminating the strict isolation the Spaniards had enforced in their colony. The governments of the following two decades tried to attract immigrants, but unsuccessfully; and the Rosas dictatorship practically re-established the old colonial barrier against foreigners. After the downfall of the autocracy, the promotion of immigration became a formal state function according to the 1853 Constitution. For nearly seventy years thereafter, Europeans arrived in Argentina in a continual stream, interrupted only by the economic crisis of the 1890s and the First World War.

Of the nearly 60 million Europeans who emigrated overseas, Argentina received some 11 percent, a much smaller proportion than went to the United States, but considerably larger than to any other immigration country (Isaac 1947: 62). Moreover, in contrast to the 6.5 million foreigners who arrived between 1856 and 1930, the local population was only an estimated 1.2 million in 1856. For many decades, in many important sectors of the population, the foreign-born outnumbered the natives. After around 1930, also in response to Argentina's industrial development, another stream of immigration was added from other South American countries, especially Bolivia, Paraguay, and Chile (Germani 1961).

As in other receiving countries, some of the immigrants to Argentina returned to their native lands or left for other destinations. Unfortunately, the statistics do not distinguish between permanent and transitory migrants. Net overseas immigration can be estimated as the difference between total departures and total arrivals of European passengers traveling second or third class (Table 1). Most overseas emigrants to South America, especially

Table 1. Estimated Net Overseas Immigration to
Argentina, 1857–1965

PERIOD	NET IMMIGRATION (−000)
1857–1860	11
1861–1870	77
1871–1880	85
1881–1890	638
1891–1900	320
1901–1910	1,120
1911–1920	269
1921–1930	878
1931–1940	73
1941–1950	386
1951–1960	316
1961–1965	206

SOURCES: Alessandro Bunge, "Ochenta y cinco," *Revista de Economía Argentina,* 1944; and information provided by the Dirección Nacional de Estadísticas y Censos.

in the period under discussion, wanted only to save enough money to return to their native villages and buy land (Romero 1956b: 176; Sarmiento 1900, 5: xxxvi, 73). Thus, the remigrants were probably of two types—those unable to adjust to social, economic, and personal conditions, and those who had earned the money they desired.

Almost half of the immigrants were Italian, and a third were Spanish—followed by Polish, Russians, French, and Germans (Table 2). Italian immigration dominated almost the whole period. A sizable Polish immigration began in the decade following the First World War and continued up to 1940. Russian immigration was high around the turn of the century and again following 1918. In these same periods the immigration from Germany and Eastern Europe included a large proportion of Jews.

Table 2. Percentage Distribution of Net Overseas Immigration to Argentina
by Nationality, 1857–1958

PERIOD	TOTAL	ITALIAN	SPANISH	POLISH	OTHERS
1857–1860	100	17	21		62
1861–1870	100	65	21		14
1871–1880	100	44	29		27
1881–1890	100	57	21		22
1891–1900	100	62	18		20
1901–1910	100	45	45		10
1911–1920	100	12	68		20
1921–1930	100	42	26	13	19
1931–1940	100	33		58	9
1941–1950	100	66	29	4	1
1951–1958	100	58	34		8
1857–1958	100	46	33	4	17

SOURCES: Alessandro Bunge, "Ochenta y cinco," *Revista de Economía Argentina,* 1944;
and information provided by the Dirección Nacional de Estadísticas y Censos.

THE DEMOGRAPHIC IMPACT OF IMMIGRATION

A number of demographers have challenged the common-sense notion
that immigration always effects an increase in the receiving population
(Isaac 1947: chap. 4). In the United States, for instance, a "substitution
theory" was widely accepted (Spengler 1958). Indeed, the effects of immigration can be quite complex, but nobody has contested its importance in
a sparsely populated country like Argentina. Its population grew from a
little more than 1.7 million in 1869 to more than 20 million in 1960, or by
almost twelve times in ninety years.

According to Mortara's estimate (1947), immigrants and their children
contributed more to Argentina's population than the natural increase of
the natives (see Table 3). In this sense Argentina represents an extreme
case, even compared with the United States or other Latin American states.
During the period 1869–1959, while the population of another important
receiving country like Brazil grew six times, Argentina's grew more than
ten times. Chile, where immigration was practically nonexistent, took 110
years to increase by less than four times. Without immigration, the population of Argentina in 1940 would have been 6.1 million instead of over 13
million.

About 90 percent of the foreigners settled in the Buenos Aires metropolitan area and the central provinces of the country, which together make
up no more than a third of the nation's territory. This concentration was
intensified by the fact that, especially after 1914, most immigrants went to

Table 3. Components of Population Growth, Major Immigration Countries
of the Americas, 1841–1940

COUNTRY	NATURAL INCREASE OF NATIVES		IMMIGRATION		NATURAL INCREASE OF IMMIGRANTS	
	MILLIONS	PERCENT	MILLIONS	PERCENT	MILLIONS	PERCENT
Argentina	5.2	41.9	3.6	29.0	3.6	29.0
United States	67.7	59.1	25.0	21.8	21.8	19.0
Canada	8.0	78.4	1.0	9.8	1.2	11.8
Brazil	28.6	81.0	3.3	9.4	3.4	9.6
Total, North and South America	163.0	70.9	36.0	15.6	31.0	13.5

SOURCE: Giorgio Mortara, "Pesquisas sobre populaçoes americanas," *Estudos Brasileiros de Demografía,* Monograph No. 3, 1947.

the cities, so that by 1960 68 percent lived in the large urban centers. Since over 71 percent of the immigrants were male, and about 65 percent aged between 20 and 60 (Willcox 1929, 1: 540), their proportion in certain key sectors of the population increased even faster throughout the period of mass immigration. The effects of immigration on the labor force began to lessen only after 1930; by 1960 two-thirds of the foreigners were more than 40, and nearly one-third over 60 (Table 4).

Table 4. Sex Ratio and Age Composition of Sectors of the Population,
Argentina, 1869–1960

CENSUS YEAR	MALES PER 100 FEMALES			PERCENT AGED 14–64		
	TOTAL	NATIVE	FOREIGN-BORN	TOTAL	NATIVE	FOREIGN-BORN
1869	106	94	251	56.5		
1895	112	90	173	57.9	48.6	85.0
1914	116	98	171	61.4	50.3	87.4
1947	105	100	138	65.2	61.9	83.7
1960	101	99	110	63.0[a]	61.3[a]	75.0[a]

[a] Based on a sample survey.

SOURCES: Argentine censuses.

IMPACT ON THE ECONOMIC AND SOCIAL STRUCTURE

The effect of immigration on Argentina's economic growth can hardly be overstated. Immigrant labor helped to occupy the unexploited land and develop agricultural production, which transformed Argentina from an importer in 1870 to one of the world's principal exporters; to build a railroad system, public works, and housing; to expand the commercial and service sectors; and to begin industrial development. The stratification system and many traditional social values were also greatly affected by the overwhelming mass of foreigners; the new type that replaced the old creole stock has not yet been clearly defined, but its predominance is beyond question.

Immigrants' participation in the economy varied greatly from one sector to another, depending on their original skills and the country's social-economic structure at the time of their arrival. Most immigrants came from the poorer strata of their native lands. Up to 1890, more than 70 percent were peasants, but this proportion decreased sharply in following years. Up to the middle of the 20th century, about 41 percent were peasants, 23 percent unskilled workers, and about 36 percent skilled in various manual or nonmanual vocations. Even those from a peasant background seldom went to the rural areas, but rather to the cities to work in industry or the service sector.

Throughout the country's history property had been largely concentrated among a relatively small number of families. One of the declared aims of mass immigration, to settle Europeans in the almost empty rural areas, was realized to a certain extent, but far less than if the latifundium had not been the predominant type of holding during the whole period of mass immigration. On the *estancias* (cattle ranches) the immigrants' participation was very low; the expansion and modernization of this activity were undertaken by the big Argentine landowners, and most of the laborers were also native. Commercial companies subdivided some land and organized "colonies," often making a good deal of money through what amounted to selfish speculation. Many owners of vast properties in the more favored areas preferred, however, to exploit their land by renting to tenants rather than by outright sale. The system often favored large units not only for cattle breeding but also for extensive farming. As land became increasingly valuable, it was less accessible to immigrants, very few of whom acquired a rural property after 1900. Those who rented land not only were blocked from ownership but frequently were displaced from one area to another (Gori 1958: 84). Since only a minority of the European peasants could base themselves in the countryside with a stable land ownership, most who remained in Argentina finally settled in the cities.

Although the data are fragmentary (Table 5), they illustrate foreigners' participation at different levels of the three economic sectors. In 1914, only 10 percent of the landowners, and 22 percent of the cattle-ranch owners, were immigrants. The proportion of foreign-born approximated the national average only in the heterogeneous census category lumping together administrators, managers, and renters. In the secondary and tertiary sectors, on

Table 5. Percentage Foreign-born in Designated Occupational Categories, Argentina, 1895 and 1914

OCCUPATIONAL CATEGORY	1895	1914
Primary sector		
All landed-property owners [a]		10
Owners of *estancias*		22
Renters of *estancias*		34
Managers [b] of *estancias*		44
Managers [b] of agricultural properties		57
Secondary sector		
Owners of industrial firms	81	66
Manual and white-collar workers in industry	60	50
Tertiary sector		
Owners of commercial firms	74	74
Manual and white-collar workers in commerce	57	53
Liberal professions	53	45
Public administration	30	18
Artisans and related workers	18	27
Workers in business administration	63	51
Domestic servants	25	38

[a] Excluding the city of Buenos Aires.
[b] Including owners and renters.

SOURCES: Population and special censuses of Argentina, 1895 and 1914.

the contrary, immigrants dominated the new occupations emerging with Argentina's transformation: the entrepreneurs, managers, and workers in the industrial and commercial fields at the root of modernization. As early as 1895, 80 percent of industry was in the hands of foreigners; the proportion was lower among salaried personnel but always above the national average. Much of the subsequent industrialization was directly linked to agriculture and cattle breeding. Such activities as the processing of meat and other perishable goods, which were the only "large-scale" industries of the time, constituted 40 percent of industrial production. The export of their products paid for the imported consumer goods that the landed elite and the upper middle class bought. Most of the other industrial firms produced inexpensive, low-quality goods for the lower strata. Although these firms, mostly quite small, supplied two-thirds of the internal consumer market, they were not a key factor in the national economy (Dorfman 1942: 16–22; Germani 1955: 130).

With the rapid growth of population and the general expansion of the economy, the internal market also increased greatly, stimulating the rise of many industrial and commercial firms and the growth of public services.

By 1895, the population was 37 percent urban; by 1914, it had passed the halfway mark. At the same time, the two-stratum social structure of the mid-19th century was replaced by a much more complex one. The middle strata, less than 11 percent of the population in 1869, increased to 25 percent in 1895 and to more than 30 percent in 1914. Of this emerging middle class, the proportion of foreign-born was larger than of the total labor force, especially in industry, commerce, and services (Table 6). These imprecise

Table 6. Percentage Foreign-born by Occupational Strata, Argentina, 1895–1960

OCCUPATIONAL STRATA	1895[a]	1914[a]	1960[b]
Middle strata			
Primary sector	43	45	16
Secondary and tertiary sectors	59	51	16
Lower strata			
Primary sector	25	35	15
Secondary and tertiary sectors	39	48	15

[a] Computed from an unpublished reclassification of the 1895 and 1914 censuses, prepared for the Institute of Sociology, University of Buenos Aires, by Ruth Sautú and Susana Torrado.
[b] Estimates based on a sample survey in the 1960 census.

estimates illustrate with another set of data how important immigrants were in modernizing the social structure. In the Buenos Aires metropolitan area and the littoral provinces, the modernization was more or less completed between 1870 and 1910.

With the rise of a substantial middle class, there emerged also a modern urban proletariat, also predominantly of foreign origin. The terms *middle class* and *urban proletariat* do not relate to occupation alone but also to attitudes, ideologies, aspirations, and self-identification. In politics the transition was expressed in the rise of middle-class parties and of proletarian protest movements. Though antagonists within the urban-industrial setting, the middle classes and the proletariat were united in their joint association with the country's modernization. Both were opposed by the landed elite, who pressed increasingly to maintain an economic structure favorable to their interests. They wanted to continue the economy's orientation toward the production and export of primary products and thus, in other respects, to curtail the modernization that they themselves had initiated. The subsequent history of the country followed from this threefold opposition— economic, geographical, and ethnic—between the native elite and rural working classes based on primary production in the country's hinterland and, on the other hand, the foreign-born urban middle classes and the proletariat based on industry and commerce in the capital and the provinces contiguous to it.

One of the important factors shaping this historical process was social mobility. The landowning elite was not an entirely closed class; its origins were fairly recent, and a few "new" families were able to reach the upper social level. But such opportunities were narrow compared with those offered in the economy's burgeoning sectors. When immigrants were admitted to the country, one of the questions put to them concerned their occupation. Over the whole period of mass immigration, from 1857 to 1924, 92.1 percent classified themselves as laborers, whether skilled, unskilled, or casual (Argentina 1925). The new middle class, so heavily recruited from these immigrants, were thus mainly of lower-class origin. Between 1895 and 1914, no less than two-thirds of middle-class persons either were sons of manual workers or had begun their own occupational careers from that level (Germani 1964). Social mobility, the norm in the central area of Argentina, changed the attitudes and ideologies of those experiencing it.

THE ECONOMIC-POLITICAL ASSIMILATION
OF THE FOREIGN POPULATION

The relation between natives and foreign-born in Argentina was unlike that in any of the other immigration countries during the mass exodus from Europe. Even the United States, though it received more immigrants in absolute numbers, was relatively less affected (Table 7). There the maximum percentage of foreign-born, 14.7 in 1910, thereafter fell steadily to 5.4 in 1960. In Argentina, the foreign-born went from more than a quarter of the population in the 1890s to nearly 30 percent just before the First World War, staying as high as 23 percent until 1930. In 1960 the percentage was still 13, or not quite the highest proportion ever reached in the United States. These extraordinary figures merely suggest the immigrants' impact on Argentine society, for—as we have noted—their concentration in important sectors of the economy and society was even greater. In the city of Buenos Aires, to take the key example, the foreign-born comprised two-thirds to three-quarters of the population during the 60 years following 1869.

In most studies of assimilation, there is a tacit assumption that the receiving society is large enough in population size, as well as strong enough in institutional development, to absorb the newcomers. But what if the receiving country starts with a small number of people and a relatively permeable social structure, and if the newcomers both are greater in number and become associated with greater social-economic power?

A crucial question in analyzing the adaptation of immigrants is the degree to which they constitute a unitary group. In Argentina they were neither nationally nor culturally homogeneous, but the Italians constituted

Table 7. Population and Percent Foreign-born,
Argentina and the United States, 1810–1960

CENSUS YEAR	TOTAL POPULATION (MILLIONS)		PERCENT FOREIGN-BORN	
	ARGENTINA	UNITED STATES	ARGENTINA	UNITED STATES
1810	0.4	7.2	n.a.	11.1
1850	1.3	23.2	n.a.	9.5
1870	1.7ᵃ	39.8	12.1ᵃ	14.1
1890	n.a.	62.9	n.a.	14.6
1895	4.0		n.a.	
1900	n.a.	76.0	n.a.	13.6
1910	n.a.	92.0	n.a.	14.7
1914	7.9		29.9	
1920	8.8	105.7	24.0	13.2
1930	11.7	122.8	23.5	11.6
1950	17.0	150.7	15.8	6.8
1960	20.0	178.5	12.8	5.4

n.a. No data available.
ᵃ 1869 census.

SOURCES: Brinley Thomas, ed., *Economics of International Migration* (London: Macmillan, 1958), p. 136. Francisco de Aparicio and Horacio Difrieri, eds., *La Argentina, Suma de Geografía* (Buenos Aires: Peuser, 1961), p. 94. Dirección Nacional de Estadísticas y Censos, *Boletín,* various years.

at least one extremely large foreign nationality. Probably few identified with their countries of origin, since many immigrants derived from backward or traditionalist cultures; but that did not mean that they saw Argentine culture as superior and therefore worthy of imitation. Their emigration was a rupture with their past, a release from tradition. Even if they started with the intention only to make money, so as to return to their native village and buy land, their very attempts to carry out this purpose led them to abandon it. They were now "mobilized," and the change was irreversible. Unconsciously and unwillingly, the immigrants were the bearers of modernization (Sarmiento 1900, 5: 229–30).

After the deluge of immigrants was over, there was still an Argentina: the country did not lose its identity. Old and new had been fused into a transformed country, still responding to the mass 19th-century influx. Where the immigrants settled, the native social types and social structure were partly destroyed, to be replaced by a new type and a new structure, not yet well defined.

The mass of the old rural population had adapted to the colonial setting and taken on characteristically Spanish traits. The gaucho, later the subject of a national myth, was a kind of peon on horseback. A casual laborer, with neither a home nor a permanent job, the gaucho moved freely across the limitless pampas, depending only on his horsemanship and his courage. His manly ideal had no place for regularity, frugality, foresight, rational calculation; he did not aspire to own land or to rise in the social scale (Martínez Estrada 1948, 1: 237–92; Gori 1958; 1952). Undoubtedly most of these traits were shared by the actual peons, who made up the majority of the native population. And insofar as the master of the *estancia* showed the same personal courage, physical strength, and deft horsemanship, he thereby acquired his peons' personal loyalty. The material culture, based on the production of livestock, was both technically and socially primitive. Agriculture and sedentary work of any kind were considered to be inferior; regular, goal-directed work was despised. There was little feeling of national identity among the rural population or, probably, the lower urban strata; loyalty was mainly local, personified in the *caudillo*, or political-military strongman.

This was the style of pre-immigration Argentine life. The foreigners brought new attitudes toward agriculture, saving, economic life, and mobility aspirations; even on the pampas they showed a much greater flexibility and creativity than the local population (Sarmiento 1900, 5: 64ff). Under the impact of immigration, old cultural patterns dissolved. Objects of great material and symbolic value, in particular the horse, lost all importance: clothes, tools, vehicles, food, housing, furniture, and forms of leisure were all profoundly transformed or totally replaced. Far from trying to adapt his European culture to the local scene, the typical immigrant, especially the Swiss or German, "tried to reaffirm it through the training of his children at home and in school. As the representative of law, he preferred his country's consulate to the formal representatives of Argentine authority, which he had to accept even though he distrusted them." Generally the immigrant spoke and read newspapers in his native language, maintained organizations to reinforce ties with the fatherland. In the early years of the mass immigration, some agricultural colonies chose their own local authorities, which in isolated sites were like alien fortresses in the middle of the Argentine nation (Gori 1952).

Though the cities lacked this isolation, particularly in Buenos Aires nationalities were sometimes segregated ecologically. Whether in the countryside or an urban center, a settlement of immigrants was termed a *colony*, and each strove to establish a highly organized community with its own newspapers, schools, hospitals, and various voluntary associations, all reinforcing ties to the home country (Table 8). Acting through such associations, some foreign governments were able to generate patriotism *after* the migration—for example, of Italians or Spanish, who had initially little identification with their country of origin. Based largely on nostalgia, their "retrospective patriotism," as Sarmiento (1900, 5: 76) termed it, developed most among the elite of each foreign nationality. That it generally remained

Table 8. Voluntary Associations, by Nationality of Their Membership,
Argentina, 1914

NATIONALITY OF MAJORITY OF MEMBERSHIP	NUMBER OF ASSOCIATIONS		PERCENTAGE OF BASE POPULATION ENROLLED AS MEMBERS	
	BUENOS AIRES CITY	REST OF COUNTRY	BUENOS AIRES CITY	REST OF COUNTRY
Native Argentine	19	153	10.4	2.1
One foreign nationality	97	752	14.5	15.1
Several foreign nationalities (including workers' centers)	98	83	19.7	1.4

SOURCE: Third national census of Argentina.

weak among the mass of immigrants was an important factor in the survival of Argentine national identity.

At first these voluntary associations provided services—education, sanitary facilities, mass media, and the like—otherwise unavailable to most of the Argentine population. Later, when Argentine institutions, whether public or private, provided the same range of services, the purpose of the nationality associations was more clearly to maintain the fatherland's language and traditions and thus to provide a locus for values different from the "submissive" or "authoritarian" types prevalent among the natives. The working-class elite among many nationalities found a leadership role in the associations, as in the later protest movements. In fact, however, the associations also became a means by which immigrants integrated into Argentine society, and that may well have been one reason for their popularity. In contrast, Argentine internal migrants a half century later participated only slightly in the voluntary associations established in the cities, and this fact contributed to their social disorganization and thus helped block their ready assimilation to urban life (Germani 1961).

In Sarmiento's arresting phrase (1900, 5: 101), Argentina was seen as a "republic of foreigners," who were served by nationals performing such unprofitable and burdensome tasks as keeping order, defending the territory, administering justice, and thus preserving the immigrants' rights and privileges. Even the Italians, who eventually proved to be the most assimilable, seemed to threaten national independence; for their large numbers and high concentration were reinforced by powerful organizations and the attitude of the Italian government, which under the rule of *jus sanguinis* viewed every person of Italian descent as its subject. The Argentine elite was caught in a continual dilemma; opposed to the foreign schools or other attempts to create alien communities, it also continued to foster immigration as the prerequisite to the country's modernization.

One of the proclaimed aims of immigration was to provide a stable base for a functioning democracy. Under the Constitution, naturalization required only two years' residence and a simple procedure, but hardly any foreigners took advantage of it. Up to 1914 only a fraction of one percent of foreign-born residents were naturalized, and in 1947 these still comprised only 7.2 percent. Citizenship was not a prerequisite to any positions in the civil service or even, in some circumstances, to suffrage in local elections. On the other hand, although naturalization gave to the new citizens all political rights—with the exception of being elected president of the republic—few of them participated in politics or were interested in it. They came from countries where political participation was low, and the electoral system in Argentina at the end of the 19th century, although formally based on universal suffrage, operated so as to minimize effective participation (as also in advanced European countries at that time). Elections generally took place in an atmosphere of indifference. The landed elite, reluctant to share its power through genuine universal suffrage, yielded only when the cities' middle and working classes had organized enough power outside of the formal political structure to impose a change.

Typical of the early parapolitical organizations were the so-called Political Centers for Foreigners (Gori 1952), which were based on foreign nationality rather than existing Argentine parties and thus aroused fear and indignation. But the "workers' circles" and other working-class organizations, international in composition and cosmopolitan in ideology, were not looked on with greater favor. Immigrants were excluded from the country's political life (either voluntarily or because of the ambivalent attitude of the elite), and when they organized on their own, whether by nationality or by social class, they were repressed by severe laws and systematic police persecution. This repression, however, was a response not to their foreign origin, but to their protest movements (mostly anarchist), which were perceived as a threat to the social order. The elite wanted to populate the desert, but without the necessary reforms in the agrarian structure. They wanted to integrate the immigrants into the body politic, but without sharing their traditionally exclusive power.

COMPONENTS OF ASSIMILATION

The usual lack of political participation is only one facet of the more general relation between Argentina's native and foreign-born populations. This can be analyzed by dividing "assimilation" into component elements of *adjustment, participation, acculturation,* and *identification* (Eisenstadt 1954: chap. 1). Systematic research is still in the future, and much of what can be offered is speculative.

Adjustment refers to the performance of the individual immigrant in his various new roles. Success is measured by whether he can participate without excessive psychological stress. The high cost of the mass immigration may be indicated by the substantial proportion of returnees, due to the facts that land could seldom be purchased, that life in both rural areas and the cities was hard. Documents abound in descriptions of immigrants' poverty and suffering, but it is also true that many acquired a degree of social and economic well-being they could not have hoped for at home. If, as some suppose, family life had been poorly organized among the lower strata in the countryside, immigration helped to establish legitimacy as the norm (cf. Taylor 1948: chap. 13).

Participation, the first social dimension, is a collective view by the receiving society. Participation can be usefully analyzed along three dimensions: *extent,* by which new roles are contrasted with continuing old ones; *efficiency,* as measured by the receiving institutions; and *reception,* or the degree to which the host country accepts immigrants. It is usual that foreigners' participation varies from one sphere of activity to another. In the economic sector the immigrants' participation was high, for it was stimulated not only by their initial need but by the prospect of upward mobility. About 40 percent of the marriages by immigrants from 1890 to 1910 were outside their nationalities, often to native women (Savorgnan 1957). The participation of immigrants in Argentina's intellectual and artistic life helped develop its typical cosmopolitan character, which nationalists on the Right and Left have often denounced as a block to "authentic" national consciousness (cf. Hernández Arregui 1957; 1960). Though immigrants were blocked from participation in national politics, this was not true of their sons. The proportion of second-generation foreigners among legislators in the two houses, only 38 percent in 1889, rose to 55 percent by 1916 (Cantón and Arruñada 1960). Thereafter the proportion fluctuated with the political fortunes of the middle class, rising with its access to power, falling when the "oligarchy" returned in the coup of 1930, and rising again after 1945 (Imaz 1964: 9). In the military and the Church, the second generation also were important. From roughly 1940 to 1965, more than three-quarters of the generals and admirals and of the bishops were of immigrant origin (*ibid.:* 60, 175).

In spite of these integrative forces, Argentina seemed—at least up to around 1914—to be composed of juxtaposed segments, each of which claimed its members' loyalty. But as time passed it became evident that, for most of the foreign stock, ethnic segregation was limited to certain sectors, which did not affect the universalist norms governing society as a whole. When the second generation joined the voluntary associations their parents had founded, these organizations lost some of their specific ethnicity; for example, after the virtual cessation of immigration around 1930, the language of most of the associations changed to Spanish. Over the same period the importance of ecological segregation lessened considerably. In some of the urban slums, each *conventillo* (a building of one or two stories with rooms, usually one to a family, constructed around a central courtyard) had a genuine integrative force, which was strengthened as the second generation moved both up the social scale and out of the slums.

During the transitional stage, the segregated sectors, even while preserving the cultural traditions of the various homelands, nonetheless facilitated social integration. Some carry-over of alien cultures was entirely compatible with general assimilation, especially in a country relatively free of antagonistic tensions. Argentina has some anti-Semitism, but not more than such other Western countries as the United States or France. When specifically asked about Jews, about 22 percent of a random sample of family heads in the Buenos Aires metropolitan area replied with an anti-Semitic response (Germani 1962); and in the same survey only 4.4 percent of the respondents gave anti-Italian answers, only 3.5 percent anti-Spanish. Hostility to English or North Americans was considerably greater, but this reflected a political orientation more than ethnic prejudice.

Acculturation, or the immigrants' absorption into the host country's cultural patterns, was obviously fostered by the foreign stock's increasingly greater participation in Argentine institutions. Acculturation can vary from relatively superficial new learning to a deep penetration into the personalities of the newcomers or their children. Invariably it affects the receiving culture as well as the immigrants.

The sizable literature of impressionistic essays that attempt to characterize a society born of mass immigration is not matched by scientific studies. In the composite culture that is emerging, contributions particularly of the Italian and the Spanish elements are recognizable, even if substantially modified in this new context. In most of the larger cities the Italian influence is to be seen in language, gestures, food, and many customs. The Spanish influence, no less strong, is less visible because it is easily confused with creole elements. Some popular products of this fusion, like the tango, have become important symbols of the new Argentina. The fact that immigrants' children often moved up into another social class facilitated their adaptation to Argentine culture. Among the second generation, the languages of their immigrant parents have all but disappeared, except to the degree that they have become familiar to the whole population.

Assimilation was aided, of course, by the break in immigration around 1930. At the time of the 1947 census, the foreign stock comprised slightly less than half of the country's population, though in Buenos Aires it was still almost 70 percent (Table 9). Data are not available to make a direct comparison with later censuses, and the other two columns of the table pertain only to portions of the capital's population. In 1947 just under a quarter of the foreign-born were over 60, just under three-quarters over 40. Born into Argentine society, as it were, as young men and women, the immi-

Table 9. Percentage Distribution by Nativity, Argentina
and Buenos Aires, 1947 and 1961

| | CENSUS POPULATION, 1947 | | BUENOS AIRES METROPOLITAN AREA, 1961 | |
NATIONAL ORIGIN	ARGENTINA	BUENOS AIRES CITY	FAMILY HEADS	POPULATION AGED 18+
Native of native parents	53.3	30.9	25.2	33.1
Foreign stock				
Native of foreign-born or mixed parents	31.1	41.1	39.3	39.3
Foreign-born	15.6	28.0	35.5	27.6
Total	100.0	100.0	100.0	100.0

SOURCES: 1947 census; "Stratification and Mobility in Buenos Aires," unpublished paper of the Instituto de Sociología, University of Buenos Aires.

grants as a group aged very rapidly once the flow from Europe was cut off.

Identification, the last component of assimilation, refers to the substitution of a new identity for the prior one with the immigrants' home country, to the intensity of this new identity, and to its effect on attitudes and behavior. Data were collected on these elements of assimilation in a 1961 survey of the foreign stock in the Buenos Aires metropolitan area. Table 10 compares Italians and Spaniards (both first and second generations) of three levels of socio-economic status (a composite index of occupation, education, income, and consumption level). Italians, particularly of the highest status, have assimilated more, however paradoxical this may be in a country whose language is Spanish. But on the whole both nationalities have fitted in well. Practically no one of either nationality wanted to return to his homeland, and only a minority participated in foreign associations or associated predominantly with foreign friends.

It would seem that Argentina has been rather successful in capturing the immigrants' loyalty and integrating them into a part of the general society. This view has often been challenged, however, not only at the height of the mass immigration, but also in recent years. In the words of a prominent Argentine historian, the country's society is still a "hybrid mass, formed by creole and foreign elements coexisting without the predominance of either" (Romero 1956a: 62). A nostalgia for the ethnically homogeneous creole society of the past is typical not only of Right nationalists but of such liberal intellectuals as Alberto Erro, Jorge Luis Borges, and Eduardo Mallea. The lack of a genuine community has been blamed for the political insta-

Table 10. Percent Replying Affirmatively to Questions Indicating Relative
Assimilation into Argentine Society, by Socio-economic Status,
Italian and Spanish Population Aged 18 Years and Over,
Buenos Aires Metropolitan Area, 1961

	SOCIO-ECONOMIC STATUS		
INDICATOR AND NATIONALITY	HIGH	MEDIUM	LOW
Feel closer to Argentina than to home country:			
Italians	48.6	48.7	46.8
Spanish	28.9	46.4	51.3
Not affiliated with any foreign association:			
Italians	88.9	95.7	95.3
Spanish	75.0	86.3	89.5
Do not wish to return permanently to native land:			
Italians	94.4	91.7	93.2
Spanish	83.5	92.7	94.5
Closest friends are Argentinians, or Argentinians and foreigners in same proportion:			
Italians	100.0	89.5	86.1
Spanish	78.6	91.7	88.2
No communication with persons in home country:			
Italians	34.3	46.1	47.6
Spanish	13.8	40.1	51.0
Never experienced discrimination:			
Italians	94.3	92.2	94.9
Spanish	96.6	96.0	93.9
Never or seldom read in native language:			
Italians	80.0	71.9	88.9
No preference for films or theater in own language:			
Italians	21.4	54.1	49.7
Speak only Spanish, or Spanish and own language in the same proportion, when at home:			
Italians	92.9	67.6	39.2
Number of respondents:			
Italians	20	274	335
Spanish	33	228	257

SOURCES: Francis Korn, "Algunos aspectos de la asimilación de inmigrantes en Buenos Aires"; "Stratification and Mobility in Buenos Aires." Unpublished papers of the Instituto de Sociología, University of Buenos Aires.

bility since 1930, the economic stagnation of the 1950s and early 1960s, and the fragmentation of many institutions. The argument does not stand up to detailed analysis. Argentina's social and economic troubles have other causes, even if in part they express the pains of national integration. As against the risks incurred in so rapid an integration of so many foreigners, the present situation must be viewed with optimism. But as against the history of the past homogeneous culture, the same situation evokes less optimism. The problem is primarily time, a condition that impedes even the most efficient assimilation.

References

ARGENTINA. MINISTRY OF AGRICULTURE. 1925. *Resumen estadístico del movimiento migratorio.* Buenos Aires.

CANTÓN, DARÍO, and MABEL ARRUÑADA. 1960. "Orígenes sociales de los legisladores," unpublished paper of the Instituto de Sociología, University of Buenos Aires.

DORFMAN, ADOLFO. 1942. *Evolución industrial Argentina.* Buenos Aires: Losada.

EISENSTADT, S. N. 1954. *Absorption of Immigrants.* London: Routledge and Kegan Paul.

GERMANI, GINO. 1955. *Estructura social de la Argentina.* Buenos Aires: Raigal.

———. 1961. "Inquiry into the Social Effects of Urbanization in a Working-class Sector of Greater Buenos Aires," in Philip M. Hauser, ed., *Urbanization in Latin America.* Paris: UNESCO.

———. 1962. "Antisemitismo ideológico y antisemitismo tradicional," *Comentarios,* No. 34.

———. 1964. "La movilidad social en la Argentina," Appendix, Reinhard Bendix and Seymour M. Lipset, eds., *La movilidad social en la sociedad industrial.* Buenos Aires: Eudeba.

GORI, GASTÓN. 1952. *La pampa sin gaucho.* Buenos Aires: Raigal.

———. 1958. *El pan nuestro.* Buenos Aires: Raigal.

HERNÁNDEZ ARREGUI, JUAN JOSÉ. 1957. *Imperialismo y cultura.* Buenos Aires: Amerindia.

———. 1960. *La formación de la conciencia national.* Buenos Aires.

IMAZ, JOSÉ LUIS DE. 1964. *Los que mandan.* Buenos Aires: Eudeba.

ISAAC, JULIUS. 1947. *Economics of Migration.* New York: Oxford University Press.

MARTÍNEZ ESTRADA, EZEQUIEL. 1948. *Muerte y transfiguración de Martín Fierro.* Mexico: Fondo de Cultura Económica.

MORTARA, GIORGIO. 1947. "Pesquisas sobre populaçoes americanas," *Estudos Brasileiros de Demografía,* Monograph No. 3. Rio de Janeiro: Fundação Getulio Vargas.

ROMERO, JOSÉ LUIS. 1956a. *Argentina: Imágenas y perspectivas.* Buenos Aires: Raigal.

———. 1956b. *Las ideas políticas en Argentina.* Mexico: Fondo de Cultura Económica.

SARMIENTO, DOMINGO F. 1900. *Condición del extranjero en América.* In *Obras completas,* Vol. 5. Buenos Aires: A. B. Sarmiento.

SAVORGNAN, FRANCO. 1957. "Homogamía en los inmigrantes en Buenos Aires," *Boletín del Instituto Etnico Nacional.*

SPENGLER, JOSEPH J. 1958. "Effects Produced in Receiving Countries by Pre-1939 Immigration," in Brinley Thomas, ed., *Economics of International Migration.* London: Macmillan.

TAYLOR, CARL C. 1948. *Rural Life in Argentina*. Baton Rouge: Louisiana State University Press.

WILLCOX, WALTER F., ed. 1929. *International Migrations*, 2 Vol. New York: National Bureau of Economic Research.

One of the points that Professor Germani makes is that the impact of an immigration on the receiving country must be measured by comparing the size of the two populations. This is even more pertinent concerning some other countries of immigration, in particular Israel. And it is also why a number of West European nations have been disturbed by influxes quite small relative to the mass overseas movements of the 19th century. It is particularly interesting to look at the recent intra-European migration in terms of its effect on Switzerland, whose famous amity has been based, in fact, on a rather precarious balance among its several language and religious groups.

Kurt B. Mayer, the author of the next paper, is professor of sociology at the University of Bern and director of its Institute of Sociology. Previously he had been associated for many years with Brown University, where he taught from 1950 to 1966; during his six years as chairman of the department of sociology there, he helped develop it into one of the better centers of demographic training and research. Dr. Mayer's publications, in addition to earlier works on the population of Switzerland (Mayer 1952; 1957), have reflected his interest in social theory and class structure.

POSTWAR IMMIGRATION AND SWITZERLAND'S DEMOGRAPHIC AND SOCIAL STRUCTURE

KURT B. MAYER

Since the end of the Second World War, Switzerland has experienced an unprecedentedly large and unanticipated influx of immigrants. Swiss authorities had feared that the rapid demobilization of the Swiss army might result in serious unemployment, but the postwar boom has continued with only minor fluctuations. Neutral Switzerland had been spared the ravages of war, and Swiss industries have been able to participate fully in the rapid expansion of the West European economy. Confronted with a serious manpower shortage, the Swiss authorities relaxed the immigration

SOURCE: Based in part on "The Impact of Postwar Immigration on the Demographic and Social Structure of Switzerland," *Demography*, 3 (1966), 68–89, which has been abridged and brought up to date with new data. Reprinted by permission of the author and the journal.

barriers and issued work permits to foreign nationals, whose number increased rapidly from 50,000 in 1946 to a maximum of 721,000 in 1964, thereafter declining slightly to 660,000 in 1970.

In a small country, so sizable an influx of aliens must affect the growth and composition of the population. Switzerland's difficulties are compounded by its linguistic and religious diversity. Cultural and political equilibrium among the four language groups and the three major religions has rested on an underlying demographic balance, practically undisturbed for over a century. Once before, around the turn of the 20th century, Switzerland had undergone a mass immigration. By 1914, aliens made up more than 15 percent of the country's population, a greater proportion than in any other European country at the time. But the First World War abruptly reversed the migratory flow; and after peace came, Switzerland required those newly admitted to obtain work permits, which were regulated according to fluctuations in the labor market. Aliens who had been settled before 1914 were permitted to come back, but very few who first entered the country after the war were granted the right to immigrate permanently. They were tolerated only for limited periods, and their number was systematically reduced again during the depression of the 1930s. The net effect was that the number of aliens in Switzerland declined from 552,000 in 1910 to 223,000 in 1941, of whom 114,000 were in the labor force.

This massive immigration had aroused considerable anxiety, for the many resident nationals of Switzerland's large and powerful neighbors seemingly constituted a grave potential danger. Apprehensions about "the alien problem," which agitated Swiss public opinion for several decades, subsided only after large-scale immigration was past. Now once again the public is concerned about how the "foreign inundation" will affect Swiss culture, and authorities express alarm at the increasing dependence of the Swiss economy on foreign manpower.

THE DIMENSIONS OF THE INFLUX

Presently Switzerland distinguishes four categories of foreign workers:
1. "Border crossers"; that is, workers who maintain their residence abroad while commuting daily to a job in Switzerland.
2. Seasonal workers, who receive permits up to a maximum of ten months, renewable on condition that the worker leave the country at the end of each period and leave his family abroad.
3. Workers with permits for year-round employment, valid for one year and renewable. After ten years of uninterrupted residence, nationals of most countries may request the right of permanent establishment.
4. Aliens with the right to remain permanently, who may participate in the labor force on the same basis as Swiss citizens.

These categories were established as part of several changes of postwar policy. At first the Swiss authorities tried to keep the influx of foreign workers temporary and revocable. But as Swiss industry expanded year after year, it became evident that the need for large numbers of workers was becoming permanent, even that the reservoir of foreign workers was not inexhaustible. In order to compete with other European countries actively recruiting the remaining labor supply, Switzerland had to liberalize its rules and to renew work permits indefinitely. From 1959 to 1964 the number of aliens with work permits doubled (Table 1).

Table 1. Aliens in the Labor Force, by Category, Switzerland, 1955–70

YEAR	ALIENS WITH WORK PERMITS [a]				PERMANENT RESIDENTS [b]
	YEAR-ROUND	SEASONAL	BORDER CROSSER	TOTAL	
1955			30,292	271,149	
1956	181,100	108,092	36,873	326,065	
1957	215,368	120,641	41,088	377,097	
1958	220,735	105,099	37,557	363,391	
1959	215,809	114,056	34,913	364,778	
1960	256,519	139,538	39,413	435,476	71,000
1961	332,364	173,459	42,489	548,312	
1962	405,713	194,110	44,883	644,706	
1963	441,765	201,348	46,900	690,013	
1964	465,366	206,305	49,230	720,901	
1965	446,493	184,235	45,600	676,328	104,000
1966	435,979	164,569	48,000	648,548	117,000
1967	435,931	153,514	58,637	648,082	131,750
1968	440,912	144,081	63,062	648,055	146,141
1969	442,687	149,201	67,341	659,229	158,298
1970	429,956	154,732	74,797	659,485	182,898

[a] In August of each year.
[b] In December of each year.

SOURCES: Switzerland, Bundesamt für Industrie, Gewerbe und Arbeit, "Bestand der kontrollpflichtigen ausländischen Arbeitskräfte Ende August 1970," *Die Volkswirtschaft*, 43 (October 1970). Switzerland, Eidgenössische Fremdenpolizei, "Entwicklung und Bestand der ausländischen Wohnbevölkerung 1969," *Die Volkswirtschaft*, 43 (April 1970).

This massive increase renewed the earlier apprehension. After the rapid economic growth of the 1950s, strains on the country's productive capacity in the 1960s generated the beginnings of a serious inflation. The influx of foreigners was blamed for the housing shortage, the lack of teachers, the overcrowding of hospitals, and other inconveniences. In 1963, the Swiss government began a series of measures intended to halt the influx. Employers were generally permitted to hire additional foreigners only if this did not increase the total work force of their plants. Seriatim the restrictions were tightened over the next year, and these measures (with the concomitant anti-inflationary restrictions on credit and building) have apparently slowed down the rate of the alien influx considerably, without, however, bringing it to a full stop (see Table 1).

At this point an agreement with Italy, which continued the earlier policy of liberalizing immigration, was submitted to the Swiss Parliament. The agreement symbolized the end of the illusion of a provisional foreign labor force. To many Swiss, the liberalized conditions under which Italian workers could bring in their families meant that an ever increasing number of aliens would aggravate the already serious problems. After intense debate and some delay, the agreement was ratified. But in 1965, in response to the inflamed public opinion and strong parliamentary pressures, the government imposed further restrictions, designed not only to limit the influx but to reduce the number of foreign workers already present in the country. The number of seasonal construction workers admitted for the 1965 season was cut by 10 percent and restricted to a maximum of 145,000. All enterprises employing more than ten foreign workers had to reduce their foreign labor force by 10 percent in two steps. No foreigner was permitted to change his job during his first year in Switzerland. All aliens required advance permission before entering the country. This last regulation, in force immediately after the war, had fallen into abeyance as the manpower shortage increased; each spring thousands of foreigners, mainly Italians, entered the country ostensibly as tourists, and received work permits after their actual arrival.

These stringent measures were partially effective. By August of 1965 the total number of foreigners with work permits had dropped by 6 percent from its all-time high. But meanwhile the permanently established foreign workers had increased from 71,000 in 1960 to 104,000 in 1965, so that aliens still constituted about a quarter of the Swiss labor force. Each year, therefore, the government imposed additional reductions on the number of foreigners permitted to work in each plant, ranging from 5 percent in 1966 to 2 percent in 1969. Thus, the 659,000 aliens with work permits in August 1969 were 2.5 percent fewer than in 1965. But during this period the number of permanently established foreign workers rose again by more than half to 158,000 (see Table 1). Moreover, the number of aliens not in the labor force also increased from 269,000 in 1965 to 369,000 in 1969. Despite all the government's efforts, the total number of aliens residing in Switzerland increased from 825,000 in December 1965 to 991,000 in December 1969 (Switzerland 1970: Tables 9–10).

The widespread misgivings about the "foreign inundation" subsided but never really disappeared. It was proposed to amend the federal constitution so as to limit the proportion of aliens to 10 percent of the country's population; then, in a more radical version, to 10 percent of the population of every canton except Geneva. In 1970, the second proposed amendment was defeated by only 654,600 to 557,700 votes; it might have passed had not the government adopted more stringent immigration restrictions three months earlier. The prior system of setting limits on the foreign personnel employed by each individual plant has now been replaced by a global ceiling covering the country as a whole. In recent years about 75,000 to 80,000 foreign workers have left Switzerland annually, and under the new rules only a fraction may be replaced by new immigrants. Federal authorities will set this quota annually and allocate a portion to each canton. For 1970 it was put at only 40,000, in order to offset increased labor-force participation by foreign women and youth already living in Switzerland. The new system is intended to ensure that henceforth the total numbers of both resident foreigners and the aliens in the labor force can be stabilized. The abolition of the ceilings on individual plants also responded to the justified criticism that this regulation had produced rigidities in the economic structure by favoring marginal firms. A useful byproduct of the new system, which will be warmly welcomed by demographers, is that the new central register of aliens will provide more accurate immigration statistics.

The aims of the Swiss government largely coincided with those of many foreign workers, especially the Italians, who generally wanted to work in Switzerland only until they could find satisfactory employment at home (Braun 1970: 473ff). This population, consisting primarily of unskilled young men and women, either single or separated from their dependents, was what *The Economist* (April 24, 1965) called it: a foreign army camping in the country without putting down roots.

Partly as a consequence of these regulations, the occupational structure of foreign labor changed radically since the mid-1950s (Table 2). The pro-

Table 2. Percentage Distribution of Aliens with Work Permits, by Major Occupational Group, Switzerland, 1956–70

MAJOR OCCUPATIONAL GROUP	AUGUST 1956	AUGUST 1964	AUGUST 1970
Construction, stone, and glass	28.0	31.6	27.8
Metals and machinery	12.7	19.2	19.0
Hotels and restaurants	15.6	10.5	11.5
Textiles and clothing	9.0	11.3	10.1
Professions and arts	3.0	4.2	5.6
Commerce	1.2	3.9	5.2
Private households	11.6	3.4	3.7
Food, beverages, and tobacco	2.7	3.5	3.4
Agriculture	10.5	2.5	2.2
Other occupations	5.7	9.9	11.5
Total	100.0	100.0	100.0

SOURCE: Switzerland, Bundesamt für Industrie, Gewerbe und Arbeit, "Bestand der kontrollpflichtigen ausländischen Arbeitskräfte Ende August 1970," *Die Volkswirtschaft*, **43** (April 1970), 556.

portion declined of those engaged in such low-paying, low-status occupations as in hotels and restaurants, domestic service, and agriculture. On the other hand, employment in metals and machinery, professions, arts and commerce, which together accounted for only 17 percent in 1956, rose to 30 percent in 1970. Parallel with this upgrading, the rate of turnover slowed down considerably: the proportion of foreign workers with year-round permits who resided uninterruptedly in Switzerland for several years changed dramatically from the 1950s to 1969 (Table 3). Substantial numbers of

Table 3. Percentage Distribution of Alien Workers with
Year-Round Permits, by Length of Stay,
Switzerland, 1955–69

DATE	LESS THAN 3 YEARS	3 YEARS OR MORE	5 YEARS OR MORE
October 1955	75	25	11
February 1959	75	25	11
December 1969	44	56	42

SOURCE: Switzerland, Eidgenössische Fremdenpolizei, "Entwicklung und Bestand der ausländischen Wohnbevölkerung 1969," *Die Volkswirtschaft*, 43 (April 1970), 157.

family members are joining foreign workers; in 1969, for instance, 7,000 wives and 13,000 children immigrated. Finally, the number of aliens in the labor force who have been granted the right of permanent establishment rose from 4,000 in 1959 to 9,000 in 1964 and 18,000 in 1969; it will increase yet more sharply in 1970–74 because of the large immigration ten years earlier (Switzerland 1970).

In sum, the government's tighter measures of control cut the influx and reduced the foreign work force to some extent. But the same regulations helped raise its average level, lengthen the alien workers' average stay in the country, and in fact move the remaining aliens closer to full participation in the society. Several hundred thousand foreigners have to be permanently incorporated into the Swiss population; in demographic fact, a sizable portion of the "temporary" immigrants has become a part of the Swiss population and already affects its economic and cultural composition.

CITIZENS AND ALIENS COMPARED

Full assimilation in Swiss society is difficult. Even children of foreign nationals, though born and brought up in Switzerland, remain political aliens unless they acquire Swiss nationality either through naturalization or, in the case of women, through marriage to a Swiss citizen. But the partial assimilation we have noted is evident when demographic, economic, and cultural characteristics are compared. As one would expect, the transitional group of permanent resident aliens falls between the more recent immigrants and Swiss citizens. Thus, according to the 1960 census, both the citizens and the resident aliens had sex ratios under 100, whereas aliens with temporary permits had the very high ratio of 143.8, reflecting the male preponderance typical of international migrants. Similarly, most immigrants were young, particularly those with only temporary permits (Table 4). The vividly

Table 4. Percentage Distribution of Citizens and Aliens
by Age, Switzerland, 1960

AGE GROUP	SWISS CITIZENS	PERMANENT RESIDENT ALIENS	ALIENS WITH TEMPORARY PERMITS
Under 20	32.6	26.3	20.0
20–39	25.7	20.9	66.9
40–64	30.9	34.1	12.0
65 and over	10.8	18.7	1.1

SOURCE: *Eidgenössiche Volkszählung, 1960.*

etched aging of the permanent resident aliens was a consequence of the precipitate decline in their fertility during and after the war of 1914–18, not significantly countered by the post-1945 "baby boom" that, among citizens, considerably offset this aging. Aliens with temporary permits had the smallest proportion of persons under 20 years of age, for with their imbalanced sex ratio and marital status their fertility was low. Among Swiss citizens, females were surplus at all ages except the youngest, and the disparity increased with age. This sex-age pattern (typical of all West European countries) is due partly to overseas emigration of males and partly to the differences by sex in life expectation. Aliens with temporary permits, on the contrary, had a heavy surplus of males in the middle range of 20 to 64 years, with more females only in the small group aged 65 and over. Among resident aliens the relation between the sexes was much better balanced, again except for the highest age group.

The surplus of alien males in the most marriageable ages could be seen as offsetting the low sex ratio among the citizens, thus improving Swiss girls' chances of finding a husband. In fact, Swiss girls are much more reluctant to marry aliens than are men, in part because immigrants are generally of lower classes. By Swiss mores a native girl may not marry down, a native man may. To try to make a "good match" is considered legitimate for all girls, and one reason foreign females seek employment in Switzerland is to catch a husband. Marriage to a Swiss male is the readiest means of acquiring citizenship: compared to the 51,500 alien women who became citizens by this route during the 1951–60 decade, only 21,100 aliens of both sexes were naturalized. Thus, the many Swiss men who marry foreign brides are deplored not merely by eligible Swiss girls but by the more narrow-minded patriots, who view this "foreign infiltration" as a circumvention of the rigid barriers to naturalization. In view of the inevitable necessity of assimiliating many foreign residents, the fact that marriage has provided a short-cut to assimilation for female aliens should be applauded rather than deplored.

THE NATIONALITY OF ALIENS

The bulk of immigration traditionally originated in the four neighboring countries, in fact in provinces abutting on Swiss frontiers. Prior to 1914, migration to Switzerland was essentially part of the rural-urban movement characteristic of all Western Europe. International boundaries were no barrier, for political restrictions were absent and Switzerland and its neighbors were culturally akin. Both internal and international migration was a response to differences in economic opportunity. When untrammeled migration ended, immigrants still came overwhelmingly from nearby regions of the neighboring countries.

Recently, however, the prolonged economic boom caused growing manpower shortages not only in Switzerland but also in Germany, France, Belgium, and the Netherlands. As a result, Switzerland has had to compete with the rest of Western Europe, importing workers from new areas. Italy was the source of virtually all immigrants in the immediate postwar years, and of two-thirds of the foreign workers up to the mid-1960s. Although the Italians still furnish more than half of the foreign work force, their number declined appreciably from 474,000 (or 66 percent of those with work permits) in 1964 to 372,000 (or 56 percent) in 1970 (Table 5). Over the same period the immigration of Spaniards increased rapidly, and other contingents came from the Balkans: at the end of 1969, 21,000 Yugoslavs, 10,000 Turks, and 9,000 Greeks resided in the country (Switzerland 1970: 162). Evidently the great cultural differences of migrants from such distant countries pose major obstacles to their assimilation.

Moreover, the migratory flow from Italy has undergone a similar shift. In the immediate postwar period, 95 to 96 percent of the Italian immigrants came from the North. Today the Italian government has made strong efforts to channel requests for workers to the underdeveloped South in order to encourage their emigration. By the mid-1960s, according to first-time work contracts certified by the Italian embassy in Berne, only 26 percent came from the North, 14 percent from Central Italy, and 60 percent from the South, now the major labor reservoir in Italy. Because of the greater cultural gap, Southern Italians experience greater difficulties in accommodating to Swiss conditions. If the length of stay is held constant,

Table 5. Distribution of Aliens with Work Permits by Nationality,
Switzerland, 1956–70

COUNTRY OF ORIGIN	AUGUST 1956		AUGUST 1964		AUGUST 1970	
	NUMBER	PERCENT	NUMBER	PERCENT	NUMBER	PERCENT
Germany	69,200	21.2	78,550	10.9	52,975	8.0
France	9,028	2.8	24,012	3.3	41,846	6.3
Italy	206,860	63.4	474,340	65.8	371,814	56.4
Austria	33,915	10.4	27,715	3.8	19,920	3.0
Spain	7,064	2.7	82,230	11.5	112,636	17.1
Other			33,964	4.7	60,654	9.2
Total	326,065	100.0	720,901	100.0	659,485	100.0

SOURCE: Switzerland, Bundesamt für Industrie, Gewerbe und Arbeit, "Bestand der kontrollpflichtigen ausländischen Arbeitskräfte Ende August 1970," *Die Volkswirtschaft*, 43 (October 1970), 557.

fewer Southern Italians express the desire to remain permanently (Braun 1970: chap. 10).

The stream of immigrants has always been to specific regions of Switzerland. In 1960, half of all aliens resided in only four of the twenty-five cantons —Zurich, Geneva, Vaud, and Berne; and nearly a third were concentrated in Zurich and Geneva alone. German and Austrian nationals were primarily in German-speaking areas; but the Italians, apart from some concentration in the only Italian-speaking canton, Ticino, had spread out over German and French Switzerland. The single canton with the highest proportion of all aliens (21 percent in 1960) has long been Zurich, which is cosmopolitan and highly industrialized. It attracts not only Germans and Austrians but one out of five Italians and one out of seven Spaniards and Americans. Only the French prefer Basel among the German-speaking cantons, since it borders directly on the French province of Alsace, and especially Geneva, which is almost completely surrounded by the French territory that makes up its natural hinterland. Geneva has always been the canton where foreign nationals constitute the largest proportion of the total population (22 percent in 1960, even 40 percent in 1910). The seat of many international organizations and a renowned tourist center, Geneva provides economic opportunities to foreign residents from many countries.

THE CULTURAL PLURALISM OF SWITZERLAND

Switzerland's famous harmony was related to the stable proportions of the major language and religious groups, which persisted with only minor variation for well over a century (Mayer 1952: chap. 8). Differences in fertility and mortality would have resulted in a greater ascendancy of the German language, but these were partly offset by the fact that more German speakers migrated to French regions than French speakers to German regions. Since each of the four languages (German, French, Italian, and Romansh) is the only official one in its territory, there is a rapid acculturation among migrants from other regions or abroad and especially among their children, who use only the region's official language in school. This linguistic equilibrium was reinforced by a persistent balance between the two main religions—56 to 59 percent of the total population were Protestants and 41 to 42 percent Catholics. Moreover, since the divisions by language and by religion cut across each other, linguistic and religious pluralism tended to reinforce each other.

The proportion of Italian speakers among foreigners, which prior to 1945 ranged between a quarter and a third, by 1960 had become 60 percent of all aliens with temporary permits (Table 6). This sudden increase of

Table 6. Percentage Distribution of the Population by Language, Switzerland, 1850–1960

YEAR	GERMAN	FRENCH	ITALIAN	ROMANSH	OTHER
Total population					
1850	70.2	22.6	5.4	1.8	0.0
1880	71.3	21.4	5.7	1.4	0.2
1910	69.1	21.1	8.1	1.1	0.6
1941	72.6	20.7	5.2	1.1	0.4
1950	72.1	20.3	5.9	1.0	0.7
1960	69.3	18.9	9.5	0.9	1.4
Swiss citizens					
1910	72.7	22.1	3.9	1.2	0.1
1941	73.9	20.9	3.9	1.1	0.2
1950	74.1	20.6	4.0	1.1	0.2
1960	74.4	20.2	4.1	1.0	0.3
Aliens					
1910	48.6	15.3	32.1	0.2	3.8
1941	49.1	18.1	27.7	0.4	4.7
1950	40.1	15.7	36.2	0.3	7.7
1960					
Total	27.5	7.8	54.1	0.1	10.5
Permanent residents	42.2	18.7	33.8	0.4	4.9
With temporary permits	23.0	4.5	60.3	0.0	12.2

SOURCE: *Eidgenössische Volkszählungen.*

Italian speakers has hampered communication, but not irremediably. Living in a country that depends on tourism and foreign trade, the Swiss have traditionally been adept at learning languages; and as one of the country's four national languages, Italian is somewhat familiar to many Swiss, who have learned at least enough to communicate in work situations and casual contacts. Industrial managements have assigned Italian workers to foremen who can speak their language. Shopkeepers and sales people have also been willing to learn enough Italian to accommodate customers. Although in 1960 only 7 percent of the residents of German-speaking Zurich declared Italian as their mother tongue, all streetcar signs are translated into Italian. In many communities schools offer special language classes for Italian children, and evening courses for adults are given not only by schools but also by many of the large plants that employ foreign workers.

Immigrants in any case eventually adapt their language pattern, and the second generation no longer uses the native tongue of its parents. Thus, the long-run effects of immigration can be gauged not so much from the nationality of immigrants as from their distribution among the country's four language areas (Table 7). The influx of immigrants has canceled the earlier balancing effects of internal migration. Paradoxically, the heavy influx of Italians, which has reduced German speakers to the lowest proportion in Swiss history, will in the long run have the contrary effect; for all aliens who reside in the German-language area will eventually reinforce the demographic ascendancy of German over the Latin languages. French will continue its proportional decline, while Italian will recede from its temporary upsurge and eventually return to its historical position. Romansh—an ancient Latin tongue that has survived since Roman times in a few valleys of the Grisons canton—is threatened with extinction. Despite strenuous efforts to save it (in 1938, a constitutional amendment adopted by popular referendum elevated Romansh to the dignity of a fourth national language), the prospects for its survival are dim.

Obviously, these projections are conjectural. Most aliens enumerated in the 1960 census held temporary permits, and no one knows how many of them will settle permanently. But present indications are that their influx will reinforce the fertility differentials favoring German over the other national languages. These impending changes are not likely to be dramatic. The major national languages are spoken in compact, clearly defined areas, whose boundaries are very unlikely to be changed by immigrants spread widely over a large number of communities—the more so since the Italian-speaking zone is cut off from the rest of Switzerland by high mountains. No heavy concentrations of Italian speakers exist on the German side of these mountains, and their influx will not expand the Italian-language territory.

The effects of immigration on the religious equilibrium are likely to be greater, since migrants do not usually abandon their religion as easily as they do their mother tongue. In the past differences between Catholics and

Table 7. Distribution of the Population by Civil Status, Language Area,
and Language Spoken, Switzerland, 1960

| | NUMBER OF SPEAKERS (−000) | | | | | |
LANGUAGE AREA	GERMAN	FRENCH	ITALIAN	ROMANSH	OTHER	TOTAL
Swiss citizens						
German	3,451	79	34	19	9	3,592
French	131	898	12	1	3	1,045
Italian	16	3	152	1		172
Romansh	6			29		35
Total	3,604	980	198	50	12	4,844
Permanent resident aliens						
German	54	2	19		4	79
French	3	23	10		3	39
Italian	1		17			18
Romansh						
Total	58	25	46	0	7	136
Aliens with temporary permits						
German	89	3	192		25	309
French	11	17	59		28	115
Italian	2		17		1	20
Romansh	1		2			3
Total	103	20	270	0	54	447

SOURCE: *Eidgenössische Volkszählung, 1960.*

Protestants generated prolonged dissension and often violent internal strife, finally overcome only in the middle of the 19th century, after political liberalism was established (Mayer 1952: chap. 8).

Census data on religious affiliation have been available separately for citizens and aliens only since 1900 (Table 8). The proportion of Protestants among Swiss citizens has been declining slowly but steadily throughout the past 60 years; that of Catholics has been rising, due partly to the naturalization of Catholic aliens, but mostly to fertility differentials (Mayer 1957). Catholics, who have always constituted at least two-thirds of aliens, reached a new high of 80 percent, while the proportion of Protestant aliens fell to an all-time low of 16 percent. In 1960, for the first time since census data on religion became available in 1837, the established proportions of Protestants and Catholics changed. As the centuries-old balance ends, it remains to be

Table 8. Percentage Distribution of the Population by Religion,
Switzerland, 1860–1960

YEAR	PROTESTANTS	CATHOLICS	JEWS	OTHERS
Total population				
1860	58.9	40.7	0.4	
1880	58.5	40.8	0.3	0.4
1900	57.8	41.6	0.4	0.2
1910	56.1	42.5	0.5	0.9
1941	57.6	41.1	0.5	0.8
1950	56.3	42.2	0.4	1.1
1960	52.7	45.9	0.4	1.0
Swiss citizens				
1900	61.6	38.0	0.2	0.2
1910	61.4	37.8	0.2	0.6
1941	59.3	39.7	0.3	1.1
1950	58.5	40.3	0.2	1.0
1960	57.1	41.9	0.2	0.8
Aliens				
1900	28.5	68.9	1.9	0.7
1910	25.8	69.5	2.2	2.5
1941	27.2	66.4	4.1	3.1
1950	22.4	71.5	2.9	3.2
1960				
Total	16.1	79.7	1.4	2.8
Permanent residents	22.2	72.6	2.4	2.6
With temporary permits	14.3	81.7	1.1	2.9

SOURCE: *Eidgenössische Volkszählungen.*

seen whether the shift will erode the hard-won religious toleration, one of the hallmarks of modern Swiss pluralism.

Considerable optimism derives from the fact that both internal and international migrations have resulted in strongly mixing the religious elements in the various cantons and cities. However, many more Catholics have migrated to Protestant areas than vice versa. Such strongly Protestant cantons as Zurich and Vaud now contain substantial Catholic minorities, and in 1960 the residents of even the Reformation cities Zurich and Geneva were, respectively, 36 and 47 percent Catholic. On the other hand, most of the former purely Catholic cantons are still so (Mayer 1952: Tables 57, 59) except the few that have become industrialized, like highly industrial Solothurn, where the proportion of Protestants rose from 9 percent in 1837 to 39 percent in 1960. It would appear that Swiss democracy is well prepared to absorb the substantial changes in religious balance.

SUMMARY

On the assumption that the demand for foreign workers would be temporary, Switzerland tried to hire a labor force that could be easily dispensed
with if economic conditions deteriorated. Thus, the occupational characteristics of the more recent immigrants differed sharply from those of both
Swiss citizens and permanent resident aliens. Since small owner-operated
farms dominate Swiss agriculture, proportionately more citizens than aliens
are in farming occupations, even though aliens made up two-fifths of all
hired farmhands in 1960. Most aliens worked in manufacturing and construction, where the proportion of Swiss citizens was less than one-half.

Implicit in such a differential distribution by industry are great differences in social status. Postwar immigrants are heavily proletarian; in 1960,
89 percent of the gainfully occupied aliens with temporary work permits
were manual wage earners (including domestic servants), compared with
58 percent of the permanent resident aliens and only 43 percent of the Swiss
citizens. The most menial jobs have been left to the recent immigrants, and
increasingly citizens have moved from manual to white-collar employment.
Between 1960 and 1964, while total factory employment increased by
110,000, the number of factory workers with Swiss citizenship declined by
24,000. That natives are raised up the occupational ladder by immigrants
entering below them occurred also in the United States and other major
immigration countries, and it is now taking place in other West European
countries that import foreign labor. But Switzerland is unique in the degree
of its dependence on foreign manpower. Far from being expendable, as had
been imagined, most of the foreigners now have become indispensable; if
they suddenly went home, their departure would bring serious economic
dislocations. Even now, production in some industries is regularly disrupted at Christmas time, when the Italian workers take off to spend the
holidays with their families.

Initially Switzerland gained from the importation of foreign manpower
in rapid economic growth at relatively low wages and high profits, but these
benefits were increasingly outweighed by an excessive strain on the country's
productive capacity and strong inflationary pressures. While in the early
postwar years the cost of living rose more slowly in Switzerland than in
most other countries, after 1959 the increase was about 4 percent a year,
weakening Switzerland's competitive position in the world market. With
low-cost imported labor easily available, marginal firms have been able to
survive and thus to retard technological progress. This is a dangerous development in a country lacking natural resources that depends on its export
industries.

Somewhat belatedly, Switzerland has realized that it must halt the influx
and even reduce the number of foreign workers already in the country.
The necessary effort of Swiss firms to alleviate the manpower shortage with

labor-saving devices can only partly succeed, since these are not mass-production industries. Hundreds of thousands of low-status immigrants will have to be retained for a long time, and many of them will have to be permanently incorporated into the delicately balanced population. Almost inadvertently Switzerland has impaled itself upon the horns of a dilemma. Economic prosperity depends on a large body of foreigners, whose continued presence inevitably changes the country's cherished social structure. Indeed, these changes may be less drastic than an alarmed Swiss public opinion fears. But there is no doubt that the Swiss must try much harder to assimilate as many of the foreigners as possible if they are to extricate themselves honorably from this dilemma.

References

BRAUN, RUDOLF. 1970. *Soziokulturelle Probleme der Eingliederung italienischer Arbeitskräfte in der Schweiz.* Erlenbach/Zürich: Eugen Rentsch.

MAYER, KURT B. 1952. *The Population of Switzerland.* New York: Columbia University Press.

———. 1957. "Recent Demographic Developments in Switzerland," *Social Research,* **24,** 331–353.

SWITZERLAND. EIDGENÖSSISCHE FREMDENPOLIZEI. 1970. "Entwicklung und Bestand der ausländischen Wohnbevölkerung 1969," *Die Volkswirtschaft,* **43** (April).

The convention recommended by the United Nations and followed by a number of countries is that one year's residence shall differentiate a visit abroad from a "permanent" migration. The consequence of this patently arbitrary distinction is that international movements of a shorter duration are typically passed over in the scholarly analyses of international migrations (but see, for example, Schmitt 1968; Williams and Zelinsky 1970). Yet, as the following paper plausibly argues, many of the cultural and economic effects of international movements apply almost as much to tourism as to migrations of a year or more.

Its author, Somerset R. Waters, is president of Child & Waters, Inc., a New York management-consulting firm that specializes in research on travel, transportation, and recreation. Mr. Waters is chairman of the development-planning council of Discover America Travel Organizations, past president of the Travel Research Association, and a past consultant to the President's Industry-Government Travel Task Force. He has written widely analyzing the travel industry; and his work has been recognized with, among other citations, Ordre de Mérite Touristique *from the French government and the Research Award Citation from the Travel Research Association.*

THE AMERICAN TOURIST

SOMERSET R. WATERS

During the year 1970 some 24 million American travelers departed from the United States and spent a record-breaking $6 billion in visiting other lands. With their incomes at an all-time high and steadily rising, with new jet planes able to reach any point on the globe in 24 hours, with longer vacations, earlier retirements, and the stimulation of a tidal wave of advertisements and travel publications, these American tourists are ranging from Kyoto to Katmandu, enjoying the wondrous sights and pleasures of planet earth.

The gladdest moment in human life, methinks [said Sir Richard Burton, in 1857], is the departure upon a distant journey. Shaking off with one mighty effort the fetters of habit, the leaden weight of routine, the cloak of many cares, the slavery of home, man feels once more happy. The blood flows with the fast circulation of childhood. Excitement lends unwonted vigor to the muscle, and the sudden sense of freedom adds a cubit to the mental stature. A journey, in fact, appeals to imagination, to memory, to hope—the sister Graces of our mortal being.

These millions of Americans enjoying their "gladdest moments" have brought new prosperity to a number of foreign nations, caused the provision of new transportation and communication links to remote cities and islands, changed international eating and drinking habits, and introduced new hotels, new products, new styles of dress, and a host of other innovations throughout the world.

Perhaps history will show that in the mid-20th century tourism exceeded all other influences on economic, cultural, and social behavior. Within ten years international travelers from all countries will probably be spending more than $60 billion per year in touring the destinations of their choice. Of this total world expenditure, the United States will be spending about $12 billion, excluding international fares to carriers. This vast outpouring of $60 billion tourist dollars—twenty times as large as today's United States foreign-aid program—will have a major role in determining the rate of development in many underdeveloped nations, will cause major shifts in the gold holdings of the industrial countries, and can influence the pattern of international trade for a wide range of consumer products, first introduced into the home market by the returning tourist.

The spending of this projected $60 billion of tourist dollars will cause economic activity in the receiving countries far in excess of the original

SOURCE: Slightly abridged from *Annals of the American Academy of Political and Social Science,* **368** (1966), 109–118, with permission of the journal and the author, who brought the figures up to date.

tourist expenditures. As those in the travel business who receive these imported dollars pay wages and buy supplies, the imported dollar turns over again and again. For each new dollar injected into the economy, at least two dollars of total purchases will be made. On this basis a truer figure for the world's international travel business, in terms of economic activity in 1976, will be more than $120 billion caused by the spending of international tourists.

The magnitude of the projected outpouring of overseas visitors and their spending will undoubtedly impose changes on the host countries, and it will dump a staggering new economic problem into the laps of the ministers of finance of the major tourist-exporting nations. In the United States, for example, our gold holdings today are at a 34-year low and are steadily diminishing. With a deficit in our balance of payments of $4.7 billion in 1970, tourist spending of $6 billion a year for foreign travel caused considerable concern.

Foreign travel also has a delayed action on our balance of payments by increasing imports in the years following the trip. Travel introduces the American to new foods, drinks, and manufactured products. These new tastes increase our imports. For example, freshly baked French bread in considerable quantity is now shipped daily by air freight from Paris to the United States as the result of the tourist's discovery of the great difference between the American and the French product.

If the present rate of growth of international travel spending continues, within ten years American travelers will be taking $12 billion per year out of this country. Economists who study the travel market, however, predict an even higher spending pattern for the next decade for the following reasons:

1. In the mid-1960s American foreign-travel expenditure per capita was much lower than in many other countries—$11.6 as compared to Canada $34.2, Germany $21.2, Scandinavia $24.4, Australia and New Zealand $12.3, United Kingdom $13.5. In fact, there were twenty other countries with a higher per-capita spending for the pleasures of foreign travel.

2. The probability that a family will travel abroad increases sharply as family income passes the $10,000 mark. It has been predicted that by 1975 the average personal income per household in the United States should exceed $11,300 and the number of families of two or more persons with real purchasing power of over $10,000 should exceed 28 million.

3. Interest in international travel increases with education. The rapid increase in number of college graduates in the United States indicates a broadening market for foreign travel.

4. International travel is dominated by two large groups: (a) young people before marriage or before the birth of the first child and (b) middle-aged people before retirement. The numbers in both of these groups are growing rapidly. They will have higher incomes and more leisure time, and

will be exposed to an ever increasing volume of travel-promotional material.

5. Air fares to foreign destinations continue to decrease.

AMERICA AND THE TOURISM BOOM

The keeper of world travel statistics, the International Union of Official Travel Organizations (IUOTO) in Geneva, estimates that international travel receipts increased to $17.4 billion in 1970 from $15.3 billion the year before. This vital segment of international trade was created as the result of an estimated 168 million foreign tourist arrivals in 1970. World foreign-travel expenditures, according to IUOTO, were increasing at an average annual rate of approximately 12 percent for the past twenty years. During the period 1950–70, thus, tourism increased twice as fast as national incomes, which were growing at 6 percent a year.

Another study charting changes during the 1958–63 period showed world tourism expenditures increasing by 75 percent, industrial production by 44 percent, and world trade in manufactures by 45 percent. To countries with rapidly rising populations and in urgent need of new sources of foreign exchange, catering to this mass of free-spending visitors offers an intriguing opportunity. In the words of a tourist official in one of our Southern states, "One Yankee tourist equals one bale of cotton—and he's only half as hard to pick."

Another great appeal of tourism to the international economic planner is its relative stability in a world of continuing shifts and changes. New Zealand may lose much of its British market for butter if Britain joins the European Common Market. Australia may suffer a loss in wool exports if changing weather conditions produce an unexpected drought. A drop in the price of sugar may injure a Caribbean island. Africa's increase in the production of coffee may create suffering in a Central American country. But income from tourism is relatively stable on a constantly upward curve. Each country has natural attractions, and sightseeing can be sold over and over again without depletion of the original resources.

Of the $17.4 billion representing worldwide international tourism earnings in 1970, the United States contributed $4 billion (excluding approximately $2 billion in fares paid to carriers). Although it would appear that almost one out of every five dollars spent for international travel was an American dollar, the influence of the American traveler, for better or worse, was much greater than would appear from these figures. Of the $17.4 billion total tourism earnings of all countries, approximately $10.7 billion represented European earnings, mostly generated by frequent short trips of Germans into Switzerland, Belgians into France, French into Spain, and the like. The United States is the top source of tourists for such faraway places as India, Hong Kong, Japan, Egypt, Turkey, Iran, and Greece. Of course, in Canada, Mexico, and the Caribbean islands the predominance of Americans is overwhelming. As a consequence of this worldwide dispersion of American travelers, there is a special sort of tourist world designed primarily to cater to American tastes. In recent years the development of new hotels, new restaurants, and new sightseeing services, the training of guides, the selection of souvenirs, the design of aircraft and airports, the printing of guidebooks, and the creation of entertainments have for the most part been with an eye to attracting the American visitor.

Most American overseas travelers still visit the famous capital cities. London, Rome, Paris, Madrid, Athens, Cairo, Tokyo, Hong Kong, and Mexico City continue to be highly popular destinations. For the more venturesome tourist, the jet plane plus the availability of a rental car or small taxi aircraft provides an easy escape. He can now sample the life in the most remote regions of the world with unbelievable ease and swiftness. A New York travel agent offers "first-class tours to Samarkand, Bukhara, Tashkent, Alma-Ata, and Baku." Government tourist offices are active in Sierra Leone, Nigeria, Kuwait, Ethiopia, Gabon, Nepal, Macao, Afghanistan, and almost any other spot on earth that catches the traveler's fancy. The Pacific area has captured a fast growing share of the American tourist market: Japan, Taiwan, New Zealand, Australia, Fiji, Tahiti, and Samoa are expanding hotel facilities, building airports, and increasing airline services. The East European countries, including Russia, Poland, Hungary, Czechoslovakia, Bulgaria, and Rumania, have made a determined effort to create and promote a modern tourist industry. Vast hotel-building programs are now under way in these countries. Russia offers trans-Atlantic service by ship and air carriers. Since few Russian tourists have been crossing the ocean, it is obvious that these new services are designed primarily to attract American and Canadian visitors. The largest hotel chain in Europe is Bulgaria's Balkantourist, offering 27,000 rooms.

THE AMERICAN TOURIST—A SOPHISTICATED TRAVELER

Because of the great economic importance of the American tourist to so many countries of the world, he has been interviewed, studied, analyzed, and subjected to every investigative technique available to practitioners of modern market research. We know who he is, where he lives, his income, his age, his educational background, what he reads, his likes and dislikes. But he retains one mystery. To date, no one has been able to explain what turned him into an international traveler in the first place. The travel industry is *not* made up of a mass of people taking a once-in-a-lifetime trip. Its clients constitute a relatively small segment of our population. Most of the members of this little group take many trips. The average American tourist is a sophisticated traveler. He has seen a lot of the popular tourist spots in the world and intends to see many more. He is a collector of places. His appetite increases as his collection grows.

The American public seems to be sharply divided between those who enjoy foreign travel and those who cannot be persuaded to leave the United States. In 1970 about 2.5 percent of the country's population traveled to "overseas" destinations (excluding Hawaii and Puerto Rico). No one can give a satisfactory explanation of the difference between, for example, two high-income neighbors, with similar educational backgrounds, similar homes, similar family responsibilities—yet one that travels and one that does not. It is known that if the nontraveler can be persuaded to take his first foreign trip, then the chances are high that he will continue with other trips.

This outstanding characteristic—the fact that the tourist is a repeat visitor—reappears in every travel survey. But in other respects the average American tourist changes as his destination changes. In Canada he is likely to appear with his family, sightseeing in the family car; or he may be a hunter, a fisherman, or a skier. In Mexico he may be a day visitor enjoying the honky-tonk atmosphere of the many border towns, or he may be a serious tourist traveling deep into the country to visit Mexico City, Cuernavaca, Taxco, Acapulco, or the fabulous Mayan ruins on the Yucatan peninsula.

Visitors to Europe (according to airline statistics) were getting younger: 20 percent under 25 years as compared to 11 percent in 1956. American tourists spent a median of about four weeks abroad compared with six in 1956. Men outnumbered women by 55 to 45 percent, though among those traveling to Europe for pleasure, women made up 60 percent.

The tourist pattern in the Caribbean followed the changes noted in Europe. Tourists were getting younger and taking shorter trips. Increasing four times faster than all other age groups, adults under 25 years accounted for 18 percent of the American travelers, with females outnumbering males by 60 to 40 percent. In other age groups the men constituted 51 percent. Only 57 percent spent more than one week in the Caribbean, as compared to 77 percent in 1956. While in Europe the tourist visited a number of different cities in different countries, in the Caribbean he generally visited only one or two islands.

In South America the trend toward younger travelers was less dramatic, increasing from 11 to 14 percent since 1956 for the under-25 age group. Women accounted for only 29 percent of the Americans in South American flights. Visitors to the Pacific and Asia were considerably older, with a larger percentage of retired people than in other parts of the world. Airlines in the Pacific introduced special low-cost promotional fares, and the expected boom in travel will have major repercussions in the economies of such countries as Japan, New Zealand, Australia, Fiji, the Philippines, and Taiwan.

One surprising side-effect of the worldwide boom in tourism has been a parallel dramatic increase in local appreciation of native culture. Whenever tourism becomes important in the local economy, there is a noticeable increase in interest in native arts and crafts. Tourism brings new appreciation and interest in the indigenous music and dance. It encourages the restoration of ancient monuments and archeological treasures. It provides a reason for the preservation of historic buildings and the creation of museums. It brings about revivals of ancient festivals and the general appreciation of local folklore.

This desire to attract tourists has provided a strong economic incentive to both private and public organizations to preserve and keep alive examples of traditional local culture. In many countries large government appropriations are now being provided for the first time to restore and preserve the cultural heritage. The spending of public funds is justified as necessary to encourage tourism as part of a national program to increase foreign-exchange earnings.

This cultural renaissance is taking place all the way from the village level to the top councils of national governments. The United States foreign-aid programs and the United Nations technical-assistance missions recognize this important relation between the preservation of local cultures and economic growth through tourism. With a modest amount of help, the native craftsman practicing a dying art finds a new demand for his product and then employs young apprentices, thus teaching his trade to a new generation in order to fulfill the increased demand from tourists.

WHO GETS THE FUTURE TOURIST?

Looking ahead ten years, when international tourism spending will probably exceed $60 billion per year, this new economic phenomenon might be considered a vast nongovernmental foreign-aid program. It could provide one of the keys to open the gates of economic opportunity for many developing nations now striving for new sources of foreign exchange; and we as a nation, in the interests of our own security, have a reason to encourage such development.

Unfortunately, the present trends in tourist travel do not favor the developing nations. The share of world tourism receipts captured by the industrial nations is increasing. About 80 percent of the world tourist receipts go to the developed nations, and only about 20 percent to the underdeveloped. What are the chances of changing this trend? Is it realistic for the developing nations to hope to attract a much larger number of American tourists in the coming decade? Among a number of barriers that inhibit travel by Americans to the developing nations, probably the greatest is danger to health. This is seldom mentioned in travel-industry circles. It does not appear on the agendas of international meetings of tourist officials. Little research has been conducted on the incidence of sickness among tourists visiting the developing nations.

One disease, the common "tourist diarrhea," is probably the outstanding cause of fear of travel in the less developed nations. To date medical science has failed to identify the specific agent that causes so much worry and discomfort to international travelers. It is suggested that a well financed medical research program aimed at identifying the cause and determining the proper drugs or inoculations to protect the traveler against *"turista"* (or "Montezuma's Revenge") is one of the most practical paths to assisting the economies of the developing nations.

The lack of modern hotels and other facilities necessary for tourists is a major barrier which usually can only be overcome in the developing countries by either direct government investment in needed facilities or government provision of low-interest loans and other incentives to private organizations. In countries with limited capital, it is often difficult to make a political decision to give priority to building a luxury hotel for the use of foreigners ahead of building factories, roads, or public utilities so badly needed by the local population. The inability to compete with the industrial nations in advertising and publicity is another problem, which stems from the reluctance of political bodies to finance such programs and the inability of government officials to administer wisely the expenditure of promotional funds when they are allocated for such purposes. The other great barrier is the lack of trained specialists to serve in government agencies and in private organizations to plan and execute the many tasks required in developing a successful tourist industry. There is a need for educational institutions to provide training in this relatively new field of international commerce.

On the other hand, there is a bright side to the position of the developing nations in the competition to gain a larger share of worldwide tourist spending. These newer nations have the sunny climate which makes possible year-round travel. They do not lack natural wonders and exotic sightseeing attractions. Labor is plentiful and cheap—a key element in a service industry. The experienced traveler is always in search of a new destination. Air fares are decreasing. And, finally, there is the example of a list of underdeveloped countries that successfully made the transition from isolation to popular tourist destinations: among others, Puerto Rico, the Bahamas, Jamaica, Mexico, Spain, Greece, India, Jordan, Egypt, Yugoslavia, and Thailand have set a pattern which can be followed.

Thus, it may be that the American tourist, aided by a growing number of tourists from other industrial nations, may provide one of the most useful keys to opening the door to a richer, more peaceful life for the roughly one half of the world's population living in a hundred countries now classified as underdeveloped.

References

SCHMITT, ROBERT C. 1968. "Travel, Tourism, and Migration," *Demography,* 5, 306–310.

WILLIAMS, ANTHONY V., and WILBUR ZELINSKY. 1970. "On Some Patterns in International Tourist Flows," *Economic Geography,* 46, 549–567.

8 HEALTH AND MORTALITY

With the decline of infectious diseases as a cause of death, other causes became proportionately—in some cases even absolutely—more significant. Among these the most important is that congeries classified as cardiovascular ailments or, in popular language, heart disease. This is not, of course, a communicable disease but the deterioration of a vital organ because of some combination of the patient's genetic inheritance and style of life. Though cardiologists differ on many other points, they agree that one important contributing factor is overweight, and thus diet. But what a typical person eats is only remotely related to the medical advice he is given; it depends rather on ethnic cuisines, income level, social mobility (in the United States, at any rate, some mobile women see to it that they remain slim), and personal habits (which some psychiatrists have linked to neuroses).

The following article is a fascinating attempt to analyze from the point of view of health care some of the factors in overweight and obesity. The senior author, Robert G. Burnight, received his doctorate from the University of Pennsylvania. He is a professor of sociology at the University of North Carolina (Chapel Hill). For several years he has been serving with the center for population and social research of Mahidol University in Bangkok. He has published two monographs on Thailand, one on family planning and the other on its census. His many other publications are on the population of Connecticut (where he taught for a number of years), internal migration and urbanization, and morbidity.

Parker G. Marden, the co-author, received his doctorate from Brown University in 1966. He is presently associate professor of sociology at Cornell University, program associate in its international population program, and codirector of its training program in comprehensive health planning. His scholarly papers are on historical demography and—especially—the social correlates of disease and health care in underdeveloped nations.

SOCIAL CORRELATES OF WEIGHT IN AN AGING POPULATION

ROBERT G. BURNIGHT AND PARKER G. MARDEN

Evidence is accumulating which shows an association between health problems and overweight (U. S. Public Health Service 1966). Accordingly, warnings against obesity have become an important part of the physician's practice of preventive medicine. Despite the general acceptance of such cautions, however, the amount of social and epidemiological research concerning weight differences has been limited (Goldner 1956). The purpose of this study is to explore certain dimensions of this problem in an urban population that is approaching old age.

The data are drawn from a longitudinal study of a probability sample of 605 white, married couples living in Providence, R. I., on May 1, 1962, in which the husband was 60 to 64 years of age (cf. Burnight 1965). A goal of this study is to investigate the important changes in health that occur during the seventh decade of life. The probability of developing a chronic disease or a disability that requires confinement, or of dying, increases throughout this period. The implications of weight differences take on new meaning, since being overweight and the possibility of becoming ill come into closer juxtaposition. Although a weight condition may interfere with good health at any age, it becomes increasingly relevant to many types of diseases in older age groups.

Few other analyses have been undertaken concerning this question. In 1965, findings were published of an investigation of the relation between obesity and several social factors in a sample population in the Midtown Manhattan Study (Goldblatt *et al.* 1965; Moore *et al.* 1962). The authors could report only one other study which examined weight condition as a

SOURCE: Reprinted from the *Milbank Memorial Fund Quarterly*, **45** (1967), 75–92, with the permission of the authors and the Fund.

social phenomenon rather than as a random and individual occurrence (Pflanz 1962–63).

DEVELOPMENT OF THE WEIGHT VARIABLE

A person's weight relative to that of others can be measured in many ways. Perhaps the soundest procedures are clinical, such as the estimation of body fat from specific gravity (Brozek and Keys 1953), or the measurement of folds of skin and subcutaneous fat (Edwards and Whyte 1962). But measures that involve determining the weight of the body in air and under water or applying calipers to various parts of the body—and even the comparatively innocuous procedure of directly weighing and measuring people —are inappropriate to household-interview studies. Thus, a measure had to be developed from the objective information which an individual can provide: his height and weight.[1] Such information was obtained from all but four of the 1,210 respondents (605 couples) in the Providence study population at the time of interview in 1962.

Given the need to use self-reported figures, the soundest procedure would be to compare the person's height and weight with the "desirable" height-weight tables developed in medico-actuarial studies for the various age groups (Society of Actuaries 1959). However, such figures take into consideration another factor that is unobtainable in large surveys—body build. An alternative procedure represents a reasonable compromise. In the absence of detailed information on desirable weight by height and age that does not include body build, the general recommendation of physicians and others concerned with this problem is that persons should maintain their weight at the level of ages 20 to 24 (Metropolitan Life 1959). Therefore, the present weight of the respondents in the Providence survey was measured relative to the average weights of persons of their height and sex aged 20 to 24 (Table 1).[2] Of course, members of the study population were actually in their twenties four decades ago. But a comparison of the height-weight tables presently in use with one for the early 1920s—when members of the study population were themselves 20 years old—shows a remarkable agreement. Second, the respondents' reported weights at age 20 were also recorded

---

[1] Such self-reporting imposes certain limitations on the study. But, as the Midtown Manhattan Study authors indicated in their report, the errors of respondents in reporting their weight is in the direction of the mean. Thus, some persons who are either overweight or underweight may be mistakenly included in the "normal" weight grouping, thereby understating relations that are present (cf. Moore *et al.* 1962).

[2] Use of the average weights at ages 20 to 24 as a standard presents one problem. A person for whom a desirable weight would be 160 pounds at age 20 might well be obese some 40 years later without gaining a pound, since "maintenance" of constant weight with advancing years obscures the critical change in the muscle-fat ratio relative to the progressive reduction in lean body mass (see Pomeranze 1957). Fortunately, this fact can lead to greater confidence in whatever definite results are obtained, since it will cause some of the existing relation to be hidden or understated.

Table 1. "Desirable" Weight and Average Weight in the Early 1920s,
Persons 20 to 24 Years Old, by Height and Sex

MEN			WOMEN		
HEIGHT (IN.)	"DESIRABLE" WEIGHT [a]	AVERAGE WEIGHT IN THE 1920s [b]	HEIGHT (IN.)	"DESIRABLE" WEIGHT [a]	AVERAGE WEIGHT IN THE 1920s [b]
62	128	124	58	102	108
63	132	128	59	105	109
64	136	132	60	108	113
65	139	136	61	112	116
66	142	141	62	115	119
67	145	144	63	118	122
68	149	149	64	121	125
69	153	154	65	125	128
70	157	157	66	129	132
71	161	161	67	132	135
72	166	165	68	136	139
73	170	169	69	140	142
74	174	174	70	144	145
75	178	178	71	149	149
76	181	183	72	154	154

[a] Metropolitan Life Insurance Company, *Statistical Bulletin*, 40 (November–December 1959).

[b] T. D. Wood, *Personal Health Standard and Scale* (New York: Columbia University Teachers College, 1923).

in the 1962 interview and the correlation could be computed between (1) the deviation of the individual's present weight from his desirable weight—the measure used in this study—and (2) the actual weight change that he had undergone over the forty years. The correlation coefficients were .712 for males and .797 for females, indicating that the measure reflects actual trends. Both sets of comparisons demonstrate that the use of weight at ages 20 to 24 is a fair standard for desirable weight and appropriate for this research.

For this analysis, four categories of weight condition were employed: (1) individuals within 15 pounds of their desirable weight were classified as normal; (2) those more than 15 pounds below their desirable weight were classified as thin; (3) those between 16 and 35 pounds over their desirable weight were categorized as overweight; and (4) those more than 35 pounds in excess of their desirable weight were identified as obese. By this classification, 60 percent of all respondents were above normal weight and more than one of every four was obese (Table 2).

Table 2. Weight Condition in an Aging Population, by Sex

	MALES		FEMALES		TOTAL	
	NUMBER	PERCENT	NUMBER	PERCENT	NUMBER	PERCENT
Thin	30	5.0	6	1.0	36	3.0
Normal	262	43.3	183	30.4	445	36.9
Overweight	200	33.0	197	32.8	397	32.9
Obese	113	18.7	215	35.8	328	27.2
Total	605	100.0	601	100.0	1,206	100.0

$\chi^2 = 61.8$. p $<$ .05.

SOCIAL FACTORS ASSOCIATED WITH WEIGHT DIFFERENCES

In the Providence study population, more than twice as many women as men were classified as obese and as overweight. Furthermore, of the 215 women categorized as obese, 18 (or 8.4 percent) were 100 pounds or more over their desirable weight, but only 3 of the 113 obese males (or 2.7 percent). Conversely, at the lower end of the obese category, 57.5 percent of the men and only 39.1 percent of the women were between 36 and 50 pounds over their desirable weight. Not only was obesity more prevalent among women, but the males so categorized were generally closer to their desirable weight than females.

Although interpretation must be qualified by the small number of cases, five times as many males as females were classified as thin—15 or more pounds below desirable weight. Since analyses such as the Framingham Study have shown that weight loss (crudely reflected here as thinness) is closely associated with ill health,[3] it is revealing that 26 percent of all males in the Providence study had had one or more serious chronic illnesses,[4] as compared with only 17 percent of the females.

Differentials in weight by other social characteristics may have great meaning for one sex and not for the other. Analysis of the relation between socio-economic status [5] and weight condition is especially illustrative (Table 3). Among males, and especially among females, obesity was most prevalent

[3] Personal communication from William B. Kannel, Director of the Framingham Heart Study.

[4] Serious chronic illnesses are those considered to threaten life: malignant neoplasms, cerebrovascular accidents, heart disease, vascular disease, and cirrhosis of the liver.

[5] The measure used to determine socio-economic status was an index based on occupation, education, and income as developed and employed by the U. S. Bureau of the Census (1962). Women were categorized according to the socio-economic status of their husbands.

Table 3. Weight Condition in an Aging Population, by Sex
and Socio-economic Status

SEX AND WEIGHT CLASS	SOCIO-ECONOMIC STATUS [a]						TOTAL	
	LOW		MEDIUM		HIGH			
	NUM- BER	PER- CENT	NUM- BER	PER- CENT	NUM- BER	PER- CENT	NUM- BER	PER- CENT
Males								
Thin	12	5.9	17	6.1	1	0.8	30	5.0
Normal	80	39.6	113	40.5	69	55.7	262	43.3
Overweight	64	31.7	99	35.5	37	29.8	200	33.0
Obese	46	22.8	50	17.9	17	13.7	113	18.7
Total	202	100.0	279	100.0	124	100.0	605	100.0
$\chi^2 = 15.5.\ p < .05.$								
Females								
Thin	1	0.5	3	1.1	2	1.6	6	1.0
Normal	47	23.4	79	28.5	57	46.4	183	30.4
Overweight	61	30.3	87	31.4	49	39.8	197	32.8
Obese	92	45.8	108	39.0	15	12.2	215	35.8
Total	201	100.0	277	100.0	123	100.0	601	100.0
$\chi^2 = 42.8.\ p < .05.$								

[a] U. S. Bureau of the Census, *Methodology and Sources of Socio-economic Status,* Technical Paper Series, Working Paper No. 15 (Washington, D. C.: U. S. Government Printing Office, 1962). Status was classified by the following scores: low, 1–33; medium, 34–66; and high, 67–99.

among those in the lowest category. Women of high socio-economic status, though infrequently obese (12.2 percent as compared to 35.8 percent of all females studied), were often overweight.

Prevalence of obesity and overweight appears to be related to generation in the United States (Table 4). In general, these two pathologies decreased with the length of time that respondents and their families had been in this country, with differences, again, between males and females. Not only was the relation stronger (and statistically significant) for women, but the point at which the differences appeared also varied. In the case of the males, the major difference was between the native-born of native parents and the other two groupings, while the difference for females was most noticeable between the foreign-born and the two native-born categories.

Since socio-economic status and generation in the United States may be closely related, it was important to determine whether the inverse relation between obesity and nativity was independent of status. In general, differences by nativity disappear when socio-economic status is held constant (Table 5). The few exceptional instances are worthy of note. The proportion of women, but not of men, in the upper socio-economic status identified as obese or overweight dropped sharply as length of residence in the United States (as measured by generation) increased.

Table 4. Weight Condition in an Aging Population, by Sex and Nativity

SEX AND WEIGHT CLASS	NATIVE-BORN OF NATIVE PARENTS		NATIVE-BORN OF FOREIGN PARENTS		FOREIGN-BORN		TOTAL	
	NUM-BER	PER-CENT	NUM-BER	PER-CENT	NUM-BER	PER-CENT	NUM-BER	PER-CENT
Males								
Thin	9	7.8	12	4.9	8	3.3	29	4.8
Normal	55	47.8	100	41.1	106	43.3	261	43.3
Overweight	33	28.7	83	34.2	84	34.3	200	33.2
Obese	18	15.7	48	19.8	47	19.1	113	18.7
Total	115	100.0	243	100.0	245	100.0	603	100.0

$\chi^2 = 5.8$, not significant.

SEX AND WEIGHT CLASS	NUM-BER	PER-CENT	NUM-BER	PER-CENT	NUM-BER	PER-CENT	NUM-BER	PER-CENT
Females								
Thin	3	2.3	2	0.7	1	0.6	6	1.0
Normal	48	37.2	100	32.6	35	21.2	183	30.4
Overweight	35	27.2	99	32.2	63	38.2	197	32.8
Obese	43	33.3	106	34.5	66	40.0	215	35.8
Total	129	100.0	307	100.0	165	100.0	601	100.0

$\chi^2 = 13.8. \ p < .05.$

Two other social variables, religion and ethnicity, were combined into five categories: Italian Catholic, Irish Catholic, other Catholic, Protestant, and Jewish (Table 6). The important differentials by religion and ethnicity, again, were less pronounced among males than females. Obesity was much more prevalent among Italian Catholics, both men and women, than any other group. Catholic women in general were disproportionately obese in comparison to Protestant and Jewish women, but not Catholic men. Although the differences were somewhat offset by a higher proportion classified as overweight, Jewish women were much less frequently obese.

Because religion-ethnicity and socio-economic status may be closely related, their combined effect on weight was assessed (Table 7). In the case of females, the relation between obesity and religion-ethnicity nearly vanished in the low socio-economic status. The prevalence of obesity in each of the three low-status Catholic groupings was nearly identical and only the small number of Jewish women deviated sharply from that figure. But, as above, the low proportion of obesity among the Jewish women was offset by a very high proportion (71.4 percent) overweight. In the middle and high socio-economic categories, the relation between religion-ethnicity and weight

Table 5. Percentage Distribution of Weight Condition in an Aging Population, by Sex, Nativity, and Socio-economic Status

SEX AND WEIGHT CLASS	NATIVE-BORN OF NATIVE PARENTS			NATIVE-BORN OF FOREIGN PARENTS			FOREIGN-BORN		
	LOW	MEDIUM	HIGH	LOW	MEDIUM	HIGH	LOW	MEDIUM	HIGH
Males									
Thin	10.7	12.0	0.0	1.8	8.3	0.0	5.9	0.0	3.2
Normal	42.9	42.0	59.5	38.2	36.8	54.5	39.8	44.2	53.1
Overweight	25.0	28.0	32.4	36.4	35.3	29.1	31.4	40.0	28.1
Obese	21.4	18.0	8.1	23.6	19.6	16.4	22.9	15.8	15.6
Total	100.0	100.0	100.0	100.0	100.0	100.0	100.0	100.0	100.0
Number	(28)	(50)	(37)	(55)	(133)	(55)	(118)	(95)	(32)
Females									
Thin	3.5	1.8	2.3	0.0	1.3	0.0	0.0	0.0	5.6
Normal	31.0	21.4	61.4	25.0	33.1	42.6	18.8	23.9	22.2
Overweight	13.8	33.9	27.3	28.3	29.2	45.9	38.7	34.3	50.0
Obese	51.7	42.9	9.0	46.7	36.4	11.5	42.5	41.8	22.2
Total	100.0	100.0	100.0	100.0	100.0	100.0	100.0	100.0	100.0
Number	(29)	(56)	(44)	(92)	(154)	(61)	(80)	(67)	(18)

Table 6. Weight Condition in an Aging Population, by Sex and Religion-Ethnicity

SEX AND WEIGHT CLASS	ITALIAN CATHOLIC		IRISH CATHOLIC		OTHER CATHOLIC		PROTESTANT		JEWISH		TOTAL	
	NUMBER	PERCENT	NUMBER	PERCENT	NUMBER	PERCENT	NUMBER	PERCENT	NUMBER	PERCENT	NUMBER	PERCENT
Males												
Thin	3	1.5	7	6.5	12	11.9	6	5.6	2	2.5	30	5.0
Normal	72	35.8	49	45.8	45	44.5	54	50.4	39	48.1	259	43.4
Overweight	78	38.8	35	32.7	29	28.7	31	29.0	25	30.9	198	33.2
Obese	48	23.9	16	15.0	15	14.9	16	15.0	15	18.5	110	18.4
Total	201	100.0	107	100.0	101	100.0	107	100.0	81	100.0	597	100.0
$\chi^2 = 29.1.\ p < .05.$												
Females												
Thin	0	0.0	3	3.3	1	0.8	2	1.8	0	0.0	6	1.0
Normal	32	17.8	31	33.7	44	33.8	44	38.9	32	40.5	183	30.8
Overweight	56	31.1	23	25.0	43	33.1	39	34.5	35	44.3	196	33.0
Obese	92	51.1	35	38.0	42	32.3	28	24.8	12	15.2	209	35.2
Total	180	100.0	92	100.0	130	100.0	113	100.0	79	100.0	594	100.0
$\chi^2 = 54.4.\ p < .05.$												

Table 7. Percentage Distribution of Weight Condition in an Aging Population, by Sex, Religion-Ethnicity, and Socio-economic Status

SEX AND WEIGHT CLASS	ITALIAN CATHOLIC			IRISH CATHOLIC			OTHER CATHOLIC			PROTESTANT			JEWISH		
	LOW	ME-DIUM	HIGH	LOW	ME-DIUM	HIGH	LOW	ME-DIUM	HIGH	LOW	ME-DIUM	HIGH	LOW	ME-DIUM	HIGH
Males															
Thin	2.8	0.0	0.0	4.3	9.4	0.0	8.5	16.0	0.0	15.4	2.4	2.5	14.3	2.7	0.0
Normal	34.6	33.3	56.3	56.5	40.6	50.0	42.9	41.1	70.0	34.6	48.8	62.5	57.1	45.9	48.6
Overweight	35.5	44.9	31.3	26.1	32.8	40.0	34.3	28.6	10.0	30.8	31.7	25.0	0.0	35.2	32.5
Obese	27.1	21.8	12.4	13.1	17.2	10.0	14.3	14.3	20.0	19.2	17.1	10.0	28.6	16.2	18.9
Total	100.0	100.0	100.0	100.0	100.0	100.0	100.0	100.0	100.0	100.0	100.0	100.0	100.0	100.0	100.0
Number	(107)	(78)	(16)	(23)	(64)	(20)	(35)	(56)	(10)	(26)	(41)	(40)	(7)	(37)	(37)
Females															
Thin	0.0	0.0	0.0	5.9	1.7	5.9	0.0	1.4	0.0	0.0	2.1	2.6	0.0	0.0	0.0
Normal	22.1	6.8	29.4	29.4	31.0	47.1	25.6	37.0	42.9	26.9	27.1	61.5	14.3	45.9	40.0
Overweight	29.8	28.8	47.1	17.6	25.9	29.4	25.6	34.2	50.0	38.5	35.4	30.8	71.4	35.2	48.6
Obese	48.1	64.4	23.5	47.1	41.4	17.6	48.8	27.4	7.1	34.6	35.4	5.1	14.3	18.9	11.4
Total	100.0	100.0	100.0	100.0	100.0	100.0	100.0	100.0	100.0	100.0	100.0	100.0	100.0	100.0	100.0
Number	(104)	(59)	(17)	(17)	(58)	(17)	(43)	(73)	(14)	(26)	(48)	(39)	(7)	(37)	(35)

returned: Italian women were relatively more obese than other women, but less so in the upper socio-economic grouping.

Among low-status males the greatest prevalence of obesity was among Italians and Jews (although the small number in the latter group makes interpretation difficult). The highest prevalence of obesity among men in the middle group was also found among the Italians, and, as with the women, the relation between religion-ethnicity and weight largely disappeared among those of high socio-economic status.

SUMMARY AND INTERPRETATIONS

A very high incidence of obesity and overweight was discovered in the population under study—more than 50 percent of the men and 60 percent of the women were above the normal weight for their age. The differences in weight, moreover, were not randomly distributed. As the Midtown Manhattan Study's authors observed, obesity may always be unhealthy, but it may not always be viewed as abnormal in such subgroups as persons of low socio-economic status or of Italian background (Goldblatt *et al.* 1965). As most discussions of the etiology of obesity have focused upon the individual, this conclusion should not be treated lightly.

More specific findings include: (1) Substantial differences existed in weight condition by sex. More males than females were classified as thin, possibly reflecting differences in health; and, more significantly, more than twice as many women as men were obese. (2) Important socio-economic differences were found. Compared with the 54 percent of the men and 76 percent of the women in the low socio-economic grouping who were either overweight or obese, the percentages for men and women of high status were 44 and 53, respectively. The differences were more marked for females than for males. (3) With socio-economic status controlled, the relation between weight condition and nativity disappeared except among persons of high status. (4) With the same control for socio-economic status, the relation between weight and religion-ethnicity varied. Among women, overweight and obesity were highly prevalent in the low socio-economic grouping regardless of religion-ethnicity, but low-status Italian males were much more frequently above normal weight, and among both males and females, the highest prevalence of obesity and overweight in the middle grouping was also among Italians. The relation between religion-ethnicity and weight disappeared among those of high socio-economic status.

These results are similar to those presented in the Midtown Manhattan Study despite differences in study population, ethnicity, and research design. Weight differentials by socio-economic status were found in both studies, although the earlier research did not analyze this variable so completely. Both analyses uncovered differences in the prevalence of weight conditions by sex, but the direction of this relation differed between the two studies.

The prevalence of obesity was greater among females in this research and greater among males in the Midtown Manhattan Study. Comparisons are marred by the different methods used to identify weight condition,[6] and part of the variation may be due to the age composition of the study populations: the Providence study involved an elderly population, while the respondents in Manhattan ranged from 20 to 59 years. Obesity among females may be a condition that occurs later in life.

In a nation where the popular culture emphasizes slimness as a desirable attribute of females, pressure to conform may increase with closer proximity to the upper class, where the norm is most strongly held, and increasing exposure to these values with length of generation in the United States may lead to its readier adoption (Goldblatt *et al.* 1965). Our analysis indicates that this interpretation requires some modification. The prevalence of obesity among Italian Catholics, even when social class is controlled, suggests that ethnic cuisines are important as well. The Italian-American's diet has a high caloric and fat content (Joffe 1943; Stout *et al.* 1964), and some members of this ethnic group still believe that obesity provides protection from certain diseases (Joffe 1943). Apparently their cuisine was balanced by an orientation to slimness among Italian Catholics of high socio-economic status, who were not more obese than other religious-ethnic groups of the same status. On the other hand, the very high incidence of obesity among all women of low status may mask any ethnic factor.

The message of this study centers upon the word *epidemiological*. McMahon *et al.* (1960: 3) distinguish descriptive from analytic epidemiology:

Epidemiology is the study of the distribution and determinants of disease prevalence in man. Two main areas are indicated in the definition. These are the study of the *distribution* of disease (descriptive epidemiology) and the search for the *determinants* of the noted distribution (analytic epidemiology).

This study, an example of the former, has noted (1) the prevalence of obesity in an aging population, (2) the nonrandom distribution of weight differences, and (3) some of the differentials in weight between subgroups of the population. With such information, the work of analytic epidemiology should begin by asking persons of different ages about their value orientations concerning weight, assessing their diet, and analyzing weight changes and the ages at which they occurred.

---

[6] The height-weight index employed by the Midtown Manhattan Study was based on broad categories for both height and weight uniformly applied to both males and females, thus creating great differences in the identification of obesity. For example, if the Midtown Manhattan Study's height-weight index had been applied to the Providence population, obesity could have ranged from 14 to 30 percent over the desirable weight, depending upon an individual's height. Measuring the deviation of an individual's present weight from the "desirable" weight for persons of the same sex and his exact height eliminated that problem.

References

BROZEK, JOSEPH, and ANCEL KEYS. 1953. "Relative Body Weight, Age and Fatness," *Geriatrics*, 8, 70–74.

BURNIGHT, ROBERT G. 1965. "Chronic Morbidity and the Socio-economic Characteristics of Older Urban Males," *Milbank Memorial Fund Quarterly*, 43, 311–322.

EDWARDS, K. D. G., and H. M. WHYTE. 1962. "The Simple Measurement of Obesity," *Clinical Science*, 22, 347–352.

GOLDBLATT, PHILLIP B., MARY E. MOORE, and ALBERT J. STUNKARD. 1965. "Social Factors in Obesity," *Journal of the American Medical Association*, 192, 1039–1044.

GOLDNER, MARTIN G. 1956. "Obesity and Its Relation to Disease," *New York State Journal of Medicine*, 56, 2063–2069.

HATHAWAY, MILLICENT L., and ELSIE D. FOARD. 1960. *Heights and Weights of Adults in the United States*. Home Economics Research Report No. 10. Washington, D. C.: U. S. Department of Agriculture.

JOFFE, NATALIE. 1943. "Food Habits of Selected Subcultures in the United States," *Bulletin of the National Research Council*, 108, 98ff.

McMAHON, BRIAN, THOMAS F. PUGH, and JOHANNES IPSEN. 1960. *Epidemiologic Methods*. Boston: Little, Brown.

METROPOLITAN LIFE INSURANCE CO. 1959. *Statistical Bulletin*, Vol. 40.

MOORE, MARY E., ALBERT J. STUNKARD, and LEO SROLE. 1962. "Obesity, Social Class, and Mental Illness," *Journal of the American Medical Association*, 181, 962–966.

PFLANZ, M. 1962–63. "Medizinische-soziologische Aspekte der Fettsucht," *Psyche*, 16, 575–591.

POMERANZE, JULIUS. 1957. "Obesity as a Health Factor in Geriatric Patients," *Geriatrics*, 12, 481–484.

SOCIETY OF ACTUARIES. 1959. *Build and Blood Pressure Study*. Washington, D. C.

STOUT, CLARKE, et al. 1964. "Unusually Low Incidence of Death from Myocardial Infarction: Study of an Italian American Community in Pennsylvania," *Journal of the American Medical Association*, 188, 845–849.

U. S. BUREAU OF THE CENSUS. 1962. *Methodology and Sources of Socio-economic Status*. Technical Paper Series, Working Paper No. 15. Washington, D. C.

U. S. PUBLIC HEALTH SERVICE. 1966. *Obesity and Health*. Washington, D. C.: U. S. Government Printing Office.

Even professionals in health care (one might say, especially physicians) usually underestimate the contribution that statisticians have made to the vast improvement of death control. And in the future this contribution could be even greater, for the dominant characteristic of the presently important causes of death is their complex etiology: the cause is not a single germ that can be isolated and, in the most favorable cases, neutralized, but a complex of medical-social factors that can be understood even preliminarily only through a multivariate analysis. But statisticians need data to work with, and what they are given is very often incomplete, inaccurate, and—the point of the next paper—inappropriate. The discussion is about medical statistics in Britain, but with only minor changes it could have been about almost any country in the West.

The author, E. D. Acheson, studied medicine at the Universities of Oxford and London. Presently dean of medicine and professor of clinical epidemiology at the Southampton University Medical School, he was formerly medical director of the Oxford Record Linkage Study and, during a visit to the United States, chief of the division of geographic epidemiology at the Veterans Administration in Washington, D. C. He edited a recent international symposium at Oxford—Record Linkage in Medicine (Edinburgh and London: E. & S. Livingstone, 1968)—which discusses in greater detail some of the same points analyzed in this paper.

SOME REMARKS ON CONTEMPORARY BRITISH MEDICAL STATISTICS

E. D. ACHESON

The first report on mortality published by the Registrar General was issued in 1838. It would be difficult to exaggerate the influence of the regular annual analyses of the three events—birth, death, and marriage—which have appeared over the succeeding 130 years. The death tabulations have been invaluable, providing almost the only data about the long-term fluctuations in the frequency of the more serious diseases, assisting in the formulating of hypotheses, and influencing and compelling public health legislation. In their current fully developed form, together with the decennial supplements, I believe they are unsurpassed in any country.

But times have changed. Table 1, in which material taken from William Farr's report of 1838 is compared with that from a recent year, provides a glimpse of the problems of a different age. At that time one-sixth of all deaths in England and Wales were ascribed to five diseases: typhus, scarlet fever, smallpox, measles, and whooping cough; and if tuberculosis was added, the figure became one-third. The brevity of the dominant diseases was such, their concentration in space and time was such, that one doctor could observe and one piece of paper report the circumstances not only of death but of exposure to the causative factor. My theme will be to examine whether British official medical statistics have changed with the times.

SOURCE: Reprinted with minor editorial revisions from the *Journal of the Royal Statistical Society,* Series A, Vol. **131**, Part 1 (1968), pp. 9–12, with permission of the author and the secretary of the Society.

Table 1. Deaths from Selected Causes, 1838
(England) and 1963 (England and Wales)

CAUSE OF DEATH	1838	1963
Fever		
Typhus	24,577	37
Scarlet fever		
Smallpox	16,268	0
Measles	6,514	127
Whooping cough	9,107	36
Consumption	59,015	5,026
All the above	115,491	5,226
All causes	342,529	572,868

Of all the changes which have occurred since the current system of national medical statistics was developed, four are particularly relevant to this topic. The first is the radical difference in the time scale of evolution of the dominant diseases; in bronchitis, coronary disease, many cancers, and peptic ulcer we are concerned with years or decades, not days or weeks. The second is the increased appreciation that familial factors are important in health and disease, with respect not only to genetics but to the family in the sociological sense. The third is the increased complexity of the organization of medicine and of the preventive and therapeutic measures which can be taken. And the fourth is the increase in population movement.

These trends are large and are likely to continue. They bring with them important new needs. I have selected four of these. The first need is for data about the incidence of illness which is neither rapidly fatal nor the subject of statutory notification. In England the first official attempt to meet this need came with the setting up of the Hospital In-patient Enquiry in 1949 (MacKay 1951). This obtains, on a countrywide scale, basic data about every tenth discharge from a hospital. Many criticisms can be leveled at this survey. As the abstracts are not identified, it is impossible to distinguish between a person discharged and readmitted several times in a year and several different persons discharged once. This inflates morbidity rates, reduces fatality rates, and biases in an unpredictable manner distributions of duration of stay. Moreover, as the sample is of discharges and not persons, it is impossible even to define cohorts of persons for a longitudinal study.

The Hospital Activity Analysis, which is to replace the Enquiry, calls for abstracting data concerning 100 percent of the hospital in-patient spells of treatment (Benjamin 1965). Unfortunately, it has many of the deficiencies of its predecessor. The identification data recorded will be meaningless outside the individual hospital, and it will be impossible, therefore, to collate the material with the subsequent or previous experience of the person concerned.

This leads me to the second need, which is facility in following samples of persons in spite of their movement about the country—for example, in collating information about a person's successive hospital admissions with data about his subsequent death, or information about exposure to occupational hazards or drugs with information about subsequent illnesses. It is not generally recognized how much medical statistical research is impeded by the difficulties in obtaining the most elementary follow-up data.

But there is a further need under this heading for an entirely new type of statistical table—new, that is, in the sense that it would be published regularly on a national scale. For want of a better term I shall call these *personal longitudinal statistics;* by this term I mean statistics in which the unit is the person, not the event, and with which the correlation of two or more events separated in time is easily possible. I envisage, for example, the regular publication of survival rates, re-operation rates, re-admission rates, which are not limited to the experience of patients within a particular hospital but trace their course wherever they are re-admitted or wherever they should die in a defined period of time; the publication also of rates of return to work according to condition and type of treatment; also classifications of persons in terms of the total costs incurred on their behalf within not only the health service but the wider context of the whole welfare service.

These statistical needs, as well as the need for regular information about families, require a fundamental change in the organization of British medical statistics. In a nutshell, the change must be from the statistics of events (whether the event be a birth, death, admission, attendance, or a claim for benefit) to the statistics of persons and of families.

Ideas, like diseases, have latent periods during which they appear to lie dormant. The first explicit statement I have found of the advantages of "personal longitudinal statistics" is in the Report of the Committee on the Preparation of Army Medical Statistics, published in 1861, of which Farr was the principal author. We have it again in the Dawson Report of 1920, and from Dr. Percy Stocks in 1944. The term *record linkage* was coined 21 years ago by H. L. Dunn (1946), the American demographer, to denote the bringing together of birth, marriage, and death records in a series of personal cumulative files. The idea of a national file of families as an effective means of studying fertility over the complete reproductive cycle was proposed by the Statistics Committee of the Royal Commission on Population (1950). None of these ideas has been turned into practice, principally because the technical means have only recently become available.

Record linkage has now come of age. Three international scientific gatherings have discussed the topic in as many months. The Medical Research Council has officially endorsed a national system of medical-record linkage, involving the assembly of vital records and hospital in-patient data into a series of personal cumulative files. Such a system, it has stated, could be founded on existing practices, and "the advantages of such a scheme are so manifold as to outweigh the difficulties of its implementation."

What then are the difficulties? Most persons working in this field would agree that the lack of neither equipment nor techniques is any longer critical. Nor, in my view, is the basic difficulty cost: the largest item of cost, preparing the data, is already met (or shortly will be) in connection with the Hospital Activity Analysis and the registration of vital events.

The real difficulty is political and is a result of the fact that record linkage brings together data about persons across departmental boundaries. It is interested in the whole cake, not the departmental slice. As Bothwell has said, "The person is the unit, not the branch of the health service." Nor, I would add, is the Health Service itself necessarily the unit; we may wish to accumulate with health data related to welfare and education. Unfortunately, the departments and authorities concerned with health matters consider it no part of their business to modify their procedures in order to assist the collation of their data with those of another department. Each takes a departmental view, which means a defensive view against change even when this may be in the general interest.

Opinion in different countries varies on this point, but in Britain we limit the data we collate to those bearing on medical matters. Perhaps, indeed, information about judicial and tax matters should be accumulated separately. For my own part, I hope to see a single system of personal information from which statistics could be derived embracing the closely related topics of health, sickness, education, and welfare, regularly enriched by data on population samples.

In practice, the most important single prerequisite is to adopt one personal filing number by all agencies concerned. At the moment, alas, the departmental barricades are up and the trenches are manned. Someone must reconcile their views—or, to put it less politely, knock their heads together in the general interest! Undoubtedly such changes will need capital expenditure; but, as in the case of standardizing the railway gauges between the states of Australia, not to spend this money may be a false economy. Recently, the United States armed services and the hospital system of the Veterans Administration sacrificed their own filing and identity numbers and adopted social security numbers for all personal records.

There is a view that a system of linked medical records must await the millennium when each hospital and clinic has its computer installation. This is not true. The objectives that have been proposed can be met in stages, and the first stage, to plan for a cumulative national index of hospital morbidity and mortality data on a quarterly batch-processing basis, could begin without delay. To have such an index in two sequences—by name and by diagnosis, carrying simply date, hospital file reference, and elementary social data—would be a considerable advance, and the same material could be used to provide some unique statistical tables.

To conclude, British official medical statistics have not changed with the times and are still based on a system devised 130 years ago. Two fundamental changes are needed: first, the unit of study should be altered from the event to the person and family; and, second, the scope should be enlarged to embrace not only medicine but education and possibly welfare as well.

References

BENJAMIN, BERNARD. 1965. "Hospital Activity Analysis," *Hospital,* **61,** 221ff.

DAWSON, L. 1920 (reprinted 1950). "Future Provision of Medical and Allied Services." Great Britain, Consultative Council, *Interim Report,* Cmd. 693. London: Her Majesty's Stationery Office.

DUNN, HALBERT L. 1946. "Record Linkage," *American Journal of Public Health,* **36,** 1412–1416.

FARR, WILLIAM. 1861. "Report on Medical Statistics." Great Britain, Army, *Report on the Preparation of Army Statistics, &c. and the First Annual Report of the Statistical Branch of the Army Medical Department,* No. 366, Vol. 37, pp. 455ff. London.

GREAT BRITAIN. REGISTRAR GENERAL. 1839. *Annual Report of Births, Deaths and Marriages.* London.

————. ————. 1965. *Statistical Review of England and Wales, 1963.* Part I: *Tables, Medical.* London: Her Majesty's Stationery Office.

————. ROYAL COMMISSION ON POPULATION. 1950. *Papers,* Vol. 2. London: Her Majesty's Stationery Office.

MACKAY, D. 1951. "Hospital Morbidity Statistics." Great Britain, General Register Office, *Studies on Medical and Population Subjects,* No. 4. London: Her Majesty's Stationery Office.

STOCKS, PERCY. 1944. "The Measurement of Morbidity," *Proceedings of the Royal Society of Medicine,* **37,** 593–608.

Since writing this article in 1968, Professor Acheson has changed his opinion about the scope of the records that should be included in any linked system involving medical records. He now feels that medical records (that is, recorded information about the health and sickness of identifiable persons) should be kept separate from other types of personal records and, where possible, should be filed by means of a different personal number. Even so, the paper represents an interesting statement of the problem.

From both the articles included so far in this chapter (as well as dozens of others that one might recommend), one gets the impression that control over early death has improved greatly and that the constant research and expanding services are bound to cut the world's mortality still further. Many of the writings on health care are pervaded by this general mood of optimism, a faith that whatever problems we face will respond no less to our efforts to solve them than the seemingly insuperable ones of the past. It is well to recall occasionally that, in contrast to the well marked advance, there has been a serious deterioration in some respects. In the United States morbidity and deaths closely associated with social disorganization have sometimes increased dangerously—homicides, drug addiction, and so on. A decade ago it was thought that antibiotics would wipe out venereal disease, which a federal official now characterizes as "pandemic"—that is, epidemic throughout the population. Elsewhere in the world the combination of congestion and primitive sanitation constitutes a constant invitation to disaster; in 1969–70 a cholera epidemic spread from its traditional center in East Pakistan with novel, air-based speed across portions of the Soviet Union and the Mediterranean basin, reaching parts of Africa never before affected.

On a world scale the most serious setback is that in India and Communist China (and, on a lesser scale, in other underdeveloped areas) modern medical science is being partly supplanted by native homeopathy. The ruling elites of all postcolonial nations are enthusiastic about Western technology, but they also try to enhance their legitimacy by building links to certain portions of the precolonial culture. Medicine has been one of the most beneficial elements of modernization, but it was also typically dispensed through Christian missions, which according to the present ideology were an integral part of Western imperialism.

When the government of British India supported the dissemination of modern medicine, the traditional practitioners organized in defence of Ayurveda, which the Indian National Congress, the most powerful nationalist body, linked to its general demand for independence. The Kuomintang government of China, similarly, founded an Institute for National Medicine, which included several of the party's important leaders on the board of directors. In both countries the manifest lacks of traditional therapy were explained as a deterioration from the classical lore, brought about by ignorant quacks. The national pride in the country's past has been symbolized by the names given the various schools. What Indian physicians called "scientific" or "modern" medicine, the Ayurvedists called "allopathy," or medical practices that seek to combat disease by attacking only its symptoms. In China, Hsi I (Western medicine) contrasted with Chung I (Chinese medicine), which by the end of the 1920s became Kuo I (National medicine). In the struggle over the issue that developed after India achieved its independence, supporters of Ayurveda in the Congress Party ranged from Deputy Prime Minister Morarji Desai on the far Right to former Home Minister Gulzarilal Nanda on the socialist Left (cf. pp. 397–98). During the years 1948–63, the government instituted five major investigating committees, which brought *up* a series of conflicting recommendations. *By and large the traditionalists have lost the battle to enlist the government fully on their side and have moved to independent measures to revive Ayurveda as the country's sole medicine (Croizier 1970).*

In Communist China, on the contrary, nativist medicine has won out.

At liberation it was noted that this form of medicine had been of great service during the foreign and civil wars and that, neither feudal nor reactionary, it was above all the medicine of the people. In view of this it was restored to official esteem in 1949 (Huard and Wong 1968: 184).

In 1954 the two groups of medical practitioners were fused into the Chinese Medical Association, through which physicians trained in the Western tradition were inculcated with the ancient lore. "The mastery of two such dissimilar forms of thought is no easy matter" (ibid.: 187).

One important practice of Chung I is acupuncture, or the insertion of needles of varying thickness into designated points of the body deeply enough to induce a mild trauma.

It is difficult to draw up a list of diseases curable by acupuncture; one should rather speak simply of patients who have been cured by the method and who are numerous throughout the Chinese world. The diseases concerned include malaria, schistosomiasis [infestation with blood flukes], bacillary dysentery, cholera, appendicitis, pulmonary tuberculosis, poliomyelitis [a viral disease characterized by fever, body pain, and vomiting], encephalitis B [epidemic inflammation of the brain, but with no involvement of the cranial nerve], deaf-mutism, arterial hypertension, enuresis [bed wetting], disturbances of the lacteal secretion [that is, the secretion of milk from the breast], tetanus, dysmenorrhea [painful menstruation], rheumatism, neuralgia, etc. (ibid.: 214).

The following two articles, one of which is about acupuncture, are from recent issues of China's Medicine, an official organ of the Chinese Medical Association (comparable, say, to a foreign-language edition of the Journal of the American Medical Association). The magazine is published by the Foreign Languages Press in Peking.

References

CROIZIER, RALPH C. 1970. "Medicine, Modernization, and Cultural Crisis in China and India," *Comparative Studies in Society and History*, 12, 275–291.

HUARD, PIERRE, and MING WONG. 1968. *Chinese Medicine*. New York: McGraw-Hill.

SUCCESSFUL OPERATION UNDER THE GUIDANCE OF MAO TSE-TUNG'S THOUGHT

DEPARTMENT OF SURGERY, SHANGHAI CHILDREN'S HOSPITAL

Do away with superstition and emancipate the mind.

MAO TSE-TUNG

The patient, a 4-year-old orphan girl, had become lame because of a gradually enlarging mass in her left buttock. She was admitted to our hospital for treatment in June 1967. On examination, a large oval mass measuring 30 by 20 by 15 cm was palpated in the left buttock. A diagnosis of angio-lymphangioma [a tumor involving both lymph and blood vessels] was made. Surgeons of our department and those consulted from a tumor hospital had little confidence of surgical success for this case. Considering such factors as the age of the patient, the size of the deep-rooted tumor and its extensive base, the necessarily large operative wound and unavoidable surgical trauma, and the hot weather which would be conducive to postoperative infection, they suggested that the operation be postponed until autumn.

During the following two months, the tumor increased in size considerably, and the patient began to run a high fever. In spite of intensive antibiotic therapy (penicillin, tetracycline, erythromycin, streptomycin, and chloramphenicol), repeated blood transfusion, and other symptomatic treatment for 14 days, her general condition worsened.

Confronted with this desperate situation, should we adhere to conservative therapy and see the child die? At this crucial moment, some bourgeois "experts" and "academic authorities" in our department stood aside and folded their arms over their chests and shook their heads incessantly. A few comrades among us also lacked conviction and questioned whether or not they would permit one of their own children to run the risk of the operation. However, the great majority of our medical personnel were of the opinion that although the condition of the patient was indeed critical, so long as we put Mao Tse-tung's thought in command, got rid of all the pessimistic, passive ideas in our minds, and made every effort to overcome the difficulties, we could certainly succeed in rescuing the patient by operation. In order to first arm our minds, we began to study Chairman Mao's teachings of "Be resolute, fear no sacrifice and surmount every difficulty to win victory" and "Man has constantly to sum up experience and go on discovering, inventing, creating, and advancing." During this study, a contrast was made between the past and the present. It is only through the wise leadership of our great leader Chairman Mao and the superiority of our socialist society, that this

SOURCE: Abridged from *China's Medicine*, No. 9 (September 1968), pp. 545–548.

child could come to the hospital for treatment. Finally under the direction of Chairman Mao's teachings, a general agreement was reached to perform the operation without delay.

Breaking away from the outmoded conventional idea that no operation should be performed in the presence of infection, young doctors took the lead in analyzing every aspect of the patient's condition to prepare our plan of procedure. This made all see even more clearly that without prompt surgery, the child was sure to die from the severe infection of the tumor, while, on the contrary, with sufficient supportive treatment and under the protection of large doses of antibiotics, complete excision of all the tumor tissue could ensure her life. With these precise problems in mind, we studied the following teachings of Chairman Mao: "Fight no battle unprepared; fight no battle you are not sure of winning." In the light of these instructions, a meeting of the entire medical personnel and workers of the surgical department was held, at which all the relevant problems were discussed as fully as possible. Afterward, preparations were made against operative intolerance, against profuse hemorrhage, against damage to the sciatic nerve, and for management of the operative wound. As a result of our adequate preparedness, the operation was performed without mishap. The patient soon recovered and was discharged. Upon dismissal she was in excellent condition.

The successful treatment of this difficult case was obviously a victory of Mao Tse-tung's thought over the counterrevolutionary revisionist line pushed by China's Khrushchev [not otherwise identified]. Only by arming our minds with Mao Tse-tung's thought and using proletarian politics to command our work can we emancipate our minds from the spiritual fetters long imposed on us by the bourgeois "experts" and "academic authorities" and from all outmoded conventions and regulations, and thus go on inventing, creating, and advancing.

With boundless love and respect for, boundless loyalty to and faith in our great leader Chairman Mao, we changed our patient's name to Wen Li [gentle-sharp, referring to the successful operation], which symbolizes the great victory of the great proletarian cultural revolution and of Mao Tse-tung's thought.

BE RED VANGUARDS TO IMPLEMENT CHAIRMAN MAO'S REVOLUTIONARY MEDICAL AND HEALTH LINE

A PLA MEDICAL TEAM FOR HELPING AGRICULTURE

The sole purpose of this army is to stand firmly with the Chinese people and to serve them wholeheartedly.

MAO TSE-TUNG

SOURCE: Abridged from *China's Medicine*, No. 6 (June 1968), pp. 339–346.

In active response to Chairman Mao's great call to the Chinese People's Liberation Army to help the broad masses of the Left, our medical team of nine army doctors and health workers went to the Taipingshao area of Kuandian County, Liaoning Province, in March 1967, to work among the former poor and lower-middle peasants. In about one year we successfully treated 410 cases of deaf-mutism, 26 cases of blindness, 24 cases of paralysis, 250 cases of chronic bronchitis, and over 3,200 cases of miscellaneous commonly seen diseases. At the same time, we trained more than 70 part-time health workers for the people's commune from among the commune members themselves.

Apart from our medical and training work, which made the broad masses of the former poor and lower-middle peasants fully aware of Chairman Mao's great concern for them, we also did our best to propagate Mao Tse-tung's thought so as to make them healthy both physically and ideologically. During our stay in the countryside in the past year, the year in which the unparalleled great proletarian cultural revolution won decisive victory, we underwent steeling and tempering and greatly heightened our class consciousness, amidst the storms of class struggle between the revolutionary line represented by Chairman Mao and the reactionary line represented by China's Khrushchev. When attending a meeting in Peking, our representatives, together with many activists in the study of Chairman Mao's works from other units, had the honor of being received and reviewed by our great leader Chairman Mao, the red sun in our hearts. This was the biggest happiness, the greatest encouragement, the deepest education for all of us. We pledged ourselves to be ever loyal to Chairman Mao's proletarian revolutionary line and to serve the people wholeheartedly all our lives.

When on our arrival at Taipingshao we were assigned farm work, we were overjoyed, considering it a splendid opportunity to win fresh merits in defending Chairman Mao's revolutionary line. But as more and more people requested treatment, the leaders of our unit decided to organize us into a mobile medical team to attend the sick among the former poor and lower-middle peasants as our main task and enjoined us to repeatedly study Chairman Mao's "three constantly read articles" (Serve the People, In Memory of Norman Bethune, and The Foolish Old Man Who Removed the Mountains) and the meaning of Chairman Mao's policy of "taking firm hold of revolution and promoting production." After studies and discussions we recognized that in the countryside the former poor and lower-middle peasants who constitute the vast majority of the peasant masses want to carry out fully Chairman Mao's policy of "taking firm hold of revolution and promoting production." Thus to cure even one patient among them means an addition to the total fighting strength of the proletarian revolutionaries in defending Chairman Mao's revolutionary line.

TREATMENT OF DISEASES BY ACUPUNCTURE

Sincerely desiring to better serve the people and carry out Chairman Mao's instructions entirely and thoroughly, we turned to Chairman Mao's teachings for direction. Chairman Mao taught us that traditional Chinese medicine is a great treasury and that efforts should be made to develop it. Under the guidance of Chairman Mao's teachings, we started to learn acupuncture, which is easy to perform and inexpensive and has long been proved to be effective in many diseases. The slogan of our acupuncture class was, "Follow Doctor Norman Bethune's example and work for the happiness of the people." We treated our course of study as a practical test of our ability to destroy self-interest and promote public interest. Everyone in the class was a pupil as well as a "patient." With acupuncture point charts as guides we practiced insertion of a needle on our own and on each other's bodies so as to help ourselves memorize all the acupuncture points and master the technique. Through a period of hard training, we soon learned to work independently. First we used acupuncture in treating some minor ailments and then we tackled more obstinate and chronic diseases. Because the effect of acupuncture on many diseases is remarkable and rapid, the confidence of the masses was greatly strengthened. Even among ourselves, some of our comrades who had been doubtful of its efficacy began to change their minds.

Our success with acupuncture brought us more and more patients, even cases of deaf-mutism, blindness, and paralysis. These diseases, as is well known, are difficult to cure. In fact, many of the patients had had treatment in city hospitals but to no purpose. We went into a bitter ideological struggle with ourselves. The pressure of the circumstances was great; we lacked both experience and necessary modern equipment, but we were continually reminded how the deaf-mutes eagerly hoped to be able to shout, "Long live Chairman Mao!" and how the blind earnestly wanted to be able to read Chairman Mao's works. The greatest misfortune for the former poor and lower-middle peasants afflicted with deaf-mutism or blindness was that, living in the great era of Mao Tse-tung and having a boundless love for him, they were unable to hear Chairman Mao's voice, read his red books, and shout, "Long live Chairman Mao!" However, in all the materials we probed the treatment of such diseases as deaf-mutism, blindness, and paralysis by acupuncture was either not touched upon or was considered to be less effective or even ineffective.

According to some authors, in the treatment of deaf-mutism by acupuncture the depth of stimulation at point *tingming* should never go beyond the range of 3–5 *fen*. This led us to consider the possibility that their failure might be because the needle was not inserted deep enough. Hence we decided to defy all old conventions and rules and tentatively practice deeper insertion of the needle on our bodies. We first advanced it to a depth of 5–6 *fen* and then step by step until 2.5 *cun* was reached. At this depth the required sore, distensive sensation—the indication of effectiveness—was fulfilled.

Illustrative Case. The patient, aged 18 years, suffered from congenital deaf-mutism and could hear only loud thunder. Following only ten treatments with deep stimulation he was able to hear the ticking sound of a watch, shout "Long live Chairman Mao!" and speak a few words.

Based on our experience with deaf-mutism, we thought that in acupuncture therapy for cataract the desirable depth of stimulation might also be more than the 3–5 *fen* given in the textbooks. But at what depth the best result could be attained without causing undesirable side-effects could only be clarified through practice. With the help of a mirror, health worker Chen Ji-qin took the initiative to experiment on himself, but he had no sooner inserted the needle at the medial angle of one eye than he had to withdraw it because of excruciating pain. Then the glorious images of the revolutionary martyrs who had given their lives for our happiness today flashed across his mind, and he took upon himself to resume the experiment. As he was engaged in this struggle with himself, he recalled Chairman Mao's words, "Utter devotion to others without any thought of self," and thought of all the blind revolutionaries who needed treatment so that they could actively participate in the struggle for seizing power from the handful of capitalists in the Party during the great proletarian cultural revolution. Spurred into further action with even greater determination, he encouraged himself by reciting Chairman Mao's instruction, "Be resolute, fear no sacrifice and surmount every difficulty to win victory," and continued his experiment. After carrying out a series of experiments in this way, health worker Chen at last learned to treat cataract by acupuncture.

In November last year, health worker Chen Ji-qin and several other comrades were sent to a mine near Fushun to help with the medical work among the miners and the peasants living nearby. One day the mine's hospital sent for Comrade Chen to take part in a consultation upon a difficult case. The patient, a worker, was unable to move his four limbs. He had acute myelitis [inflammation of the bone marrow] and had been treated accordingly. The condition was entirely new to Comrade Chen and at the consultation he could do nothing but sit and listen. Greatly moved by this and inspired by the spirit of Doctor Norman Bethune, Comrade Chen plucked up his courage and suggested the use of acupuncture, which he had found effective in poliomyelitis [a viral disease characterized by fever, body pain, and vomiting] and hemiplegia [paralysis of one side of the body]. The results were quite remarkable. The patient was able to move his right leg after the first treatment and after the second he could flex and extend all four extremities. Two days later he came to receive treatment on crutches. He was completely recovered after only ten days of treatment.

Although during the past year, while doing medical work among the former poor and lower-middle peasants we also propagated Mao Tse-tung's thought among them, we did not understand clearly which work was more important. Then, one day as we were leaving a village after a routine visit and were bidding farewell to many commune members, an old woman rushed forward, with tears in her eyes, and said, "Doctors, you have cured my disease; you are my saviors!" This remark of hers gave us much food for thought. We realized that we had not done our work of disseminating Mao Tse-tung's thought well. Who led us onto the road of today's happiness? Who pointed out to the people of the whole country the road leading to liberation? Our great leader Chairman Mao! Chairman Mao is the savior of the people of China. Without Mao Tse-tung's thought we could have accomplished nothing. All our successes were attributable to Chairman Mao, to the Party, and to Mao Tse-tung's thought. But in the course of our work and daily contact with the masses, we must have, intentionally or otherwise, arrogated to ourselves the successes that came our way.

9

THE ANALYSIS OF FERTILITY

Because it has recently become a social and political issue, fertility is the dominant topic of demographic research; and the composition of this book follows the lead of the discipline. More papers are offered under this heading than any other, some in this chapter (those that mainly attempt to analyze fertility) and others in the next (which is devoted to population policy).

The first paper is on how the social environment affects the physiological ability to have children. This was an important issue in the 19th century, when many believed that the smaller families of city dwellers were due not to the deliberate restriction of conception but to biological impairments resulting from an unhealthful environment. This view was almost entirely abandoned but has recently reappeared (see pp. 10–12, 50–51), though with very few empirical studies relating to the human species. Certainly this article, though it is too unpretentious to resolve the question of whether overcrowding and stress reduce man's ability to reproduce, is suggestive.

It was written jointly by three physicians, members of the staff at the Clinic of Gynecology and Obstetrics in Sarajevo, where Dr. Aleksandar D. Milojković is the head of the Department of Surgery. He has two degrees beyond the M.D., with a master's thesis on "Current Studies of the Causes of Male Sterility" and a doctoral dissertation on "The Problem of Unwanted Pregnancy." He is president of the Bosnia–Herzegovina Association of Gynecology and Obstetrics, a member of the Federal Council of Family Planning. He has published some 43 articles in gynecology and obstetrics, participated in international meetings in eight European countries, attended courses in Paris and Stockholm. Dr. Serćo F. Šimić, an assistant professor in the same department since 1968, is the author of a monograph on celioscopy [examination of the cavity adjoining the Fallopian tubes] in gynecology, as well as 46 papers on gynecology and obstetrics. Dr. Mehmed S. Džumhur, an assistant in the same clinic, is also head of the Department of Sterility and Endocrinology. His main interests have been in genital tuberculosis, sterility, and family planning; and he is presently working on a doctoral dissertation, "Problems of Family Planning in Rural Areas of Bosnia and Herzegovina."

MIGRATION AND PLACE OF WORK AS A CAUSE OF MALE STERILITY

ALEKSANDAR D. MILOJKOVIĆ, SERĆO F. ŠIMIĆ, AND MEHMED S. DŽUMHUR

In a sterile marriage, male infertility, whether absolute or relative, is often an important cause. According to various authors, this is the factor in 20 to 60 percent of all cases or in 56 percent of those in Yugoslavia.

During the past three years we have examined 1,200 males involved in sterile marriages. Contrary to the usual finding that such patients are usually intellectuals, our records showed that most were manual workers (Table 1).

Table 1. Distribution of Male Patients for Infertility by Occupational Category, Sarajevo, Yugoslavia, 1963–66

OCCUPATIONAL CATEGORY	NUMBER	PERCENT
Professionals and employees	463	38.6
Students	17	1.4
Manual workers	702	58.5
Farmers	18	1.5
Total	1,200	100.0

SOURCE: Reprinted from Björn Westin and Nils Wiqvist, eds., Fifth World Congress on Fertility and Sterility, *Proceedings*, Amsterdam: Excerpta Medica Foundation, 1967, pp. 828–829, with permission of the authors.

In our search for the etiology of our patients' sterility, we found diseases that might have caused a disturbance of spermatogenesis—such as parotitis [mumps], various infections, cryptorchidism [a failure of the testes to descend normally], gonorrhea, epididymitis [an inflammation of the testicle], and the like—in only 135 cases, or 8.9 percent. Like other researchers, we could not determine the causes of sterility in most of the patients. However, we made a very interesting observation in comparing disturbances of spermatogenesis between manual workers and white-collar employees or professionals.

Patients suffering from disturbances of spermatogenesis were classified into three types: those lacking any spermatozoa in the semen (azoospermia) and those with severe or mild cases of oligospermia (a relative scarcity of spermatozoa). Manual workers currently active in production were divided into two groups, according to whether they had been working in this occupation for up to three years or more. A comparison of these two categories with professionals and employees is given in Table 2.

Table 2. Percentage Distribution among Male Patients for Infertility by Type of Ailment and Occupational Category, Sarajevo, Yugoslavia, 1963–66

| | | MANUAL WORKERS | |
AILMENT	PROFESSIONALS AND EMPLOYEES	WORKING FOR UP TO 3 YEARS	WORKING FOR 3 YEARS OR MORE
Azoospermia	15.8	16.4	16.0
Severe oligospermia	12.9	42.3	29.9
Mild oligospermia	14.3	29.0	9.1
Total	43.0	87.7	55.0
Number of patients	(463)	(500)	(202)

The range of percentages for professionals and employees would correspond to the average scale of disturbances of spermatogenesis anywhere in Europe. The percentages for workers in their present occupation up to three years, however, are extraordinarily high, and we do not know of any similar data from anywhere in the world.

Note that the findings on azoospermia are almost identical for all three categories. We believe that these proportions of absolute sterility are caused by some illness which resulted in a total and permanent halt in the production of spermatozoids. Note also that the proportions of oligospermia among white-collar employees and manual workers who had worked for more than three years are almost identical. The great difference is between either of these categories and those workers in their occupations for less than three years. The Pearsonian correlation between the incidence of the ailment and the length of work is highly significant, with $p < 0.0001$.

We believe that these young workers, who had no clinical reason for a disturbed spermatogenesis, were suffering from stress during the less than three years of adaptation to their new situation. In their villages before they started working in industry, they had lived at a slower pace, with less noise and stress. Most of them now attend extra courses, with a consequent additional psychic burden. It is well known and experimentally proved that noise and stress cause great changes in gametogenesis. The clamor so familiar in the everyday life of today's cities causes functional and morphological changes in the workers' organism and, through the hypothalamus and neutral copulas, affects the pituitary gland, that regulator of the genital sphere. Under such circumstances, the organism reacts either by a complete adaptation or by falling ill. Since we found no signs of a disturbed endocrine system in our patients, we believe that they had not yet adapted sufficiently to their new way of life.

In summary, workers who had changed their place of residence and started to work in completely new surroundings showed a significantly greater incidence of disturbed spermatogenesis than either professional and white-collar employees or manual workers who had been in their occupations for longer than three years. We can regard this sterility as a transitory half-adaptation of the organism to migration, which will disappear either with a change in the place of work or through a complete adaptation to the new way of life.

Whether or not the conditions of modern life have in some instances cut down fecundity, as the last paper suggests, the overwhelmingly greater part of the reduction of the birth rate during the modern era has certainly been the consequence of human will. This will is shaped, of course, by the physical and social environment; and it is always tempting to draw general inferences from the seeming relation between a single factor and a radical, even if temporary, alteration in life's circumstances. Literary works from James Barrie's The Admirable Crichton *to Elinor Glyn's* Three Weeks *have examined the slight remnants of social conventions when protagonists are temporarily isolated from society's sanctions. According to a story that supposedly started with Census Bureau personnel, the aberrantly high fertility of a Midwestern town was finally explained only by a personal visit to the site, where the investigator was awakened each night of his stay by trains being shuttled from one line to another. The following article is a short analysis of a parallel myth.*

The author, Dr. J. Richard Udry, is professor of sociology and of maternal and child health at the University of North Carolina and associate director of the Carolina Population Center. His several dozen scholarly papers have concentrated on the social-medical analysis of fertility differentials.

THE EFFECT OF THE GREAT BLACKOUT OF 1965 ON BIRTHS IN NEW YORK CITY

J. RICHARD UDRY

Electric power went out in New York City and much of the Northeast in the late afternoon November 9, 1965, and stayed out for up to ten hours. On Wednesday, November 10, 1965, the *New York Times* carried a banner headline on page one, "POWER FAILURE SNARLS NORTHEAST; 800,000 ARE CAUGHT IN SUBWAYS HERE; AUTOS TIED UP, CITY GROPES IN DARK." Light and power first went out at 5:27 P.M. in New York City, and power in all areas was back on at 4:00 A.M.

On Wednesday, August 10, 1966, also in the *Times,* a page-one midsection headline announced, "BIRTHS UP 9 MONTHS AFTER THE BLACKOUT." Under the signature of Martin Tolchin, the following story appeared.

A sharp increase in births has been reported by several large hospitals here, 9 months after the 1965 blackout.

Mount Sinai Hospital, which averages 11 births daily, had 28 births on Monday. This was a record for the hospital; its previous one-day high was 18. At Bellevue there were 29 new babies in the nursery yesterday, compared with 11 a week ago and an average of 20.

Columbia Presbyterian averages 11 births daily and had 15 Monday; St. Vincent's averages 7 and had 10; Brookdale averages 10 and had 13; and Coney Island averages 5 and had 8. However, New York and Brooklyn Jewish hospitals reported that their number of births was normal. . . .

There were 16 babies at Mount Sinai yesterday, 13 at Columbia Presbyterian, and 10 at St. Vincent's, all above average. The number of births was reported normal in Nassau and Suffolk counties, many of whose commuters were stranded in the city November 9; in Newark and Jersey City, which were not affected; and in hospitals in Albany, Rochester, New Haven, and Providence, where the lights went on in mid-evening.

Sociologists and obstetricians were requested to comment on the reported event. One sociologist was quoted as saying, "The lights went out and people were left to interact with one another." Others said that the disruption in routine caused by the blackout and the absence of television might have contributed to the phenomenon. Christopher Tietze was more cautious in his opinion: "I am

SOURCE: Reprinted from *Demography,* 7 (1970), 325–327, with the permission of the author and the Population Association of America, which owns the copyright.

skeptical until I see the data from the entire city. There can be daily fluctuations in individual hospitals that can be misleading. If it should be true, I would think it is because people may have had trouble finding their accustomed contraceptives or just because it was dark" (Tolchin 1966).

The effect of the blackout on birth rates is a relatively easy matter to determine. Through the cooperation of Carl Erhardt and the New York City Health Department, I obtained the number of births for each calendar day for the years 1961 through 1966. I took November 10, 1965, as the date of conception for the blackout babies, and assumed that the average gestational length was 280 days, counting from the last menstrual period, and therefore about 267 or 266 days from conception. From a distribution of gestational ages at birth derived from vital statistics (U. S. Public Health Service 1966), it was estimated that more than 90 percent of the births conceived on November 10 would have been born between June 27 and August 14. I reasoned that if there was an unusual number of conceptions on November 10, then the period between June 27 and August 14, 1966, would contain a greater percentage of the year's births than that contained by the same period in other years.

Table 1 presents the percentage of the year's births occurring per week

Table 1. Births Occurring in New York City from June 29 to August 16, 1961–66

| YEAR | MEAN BIRTHS PER— | | PERCENT OF YEAR'S TOTAL BIRTHS | NUMBER OF BIRTHS ON 267TH DAY |
	DAY	WEEK		
1961	478.7	3,350.6	13.9	475
1962	467.2	3,270.1	13.9	497
1963	476.2	3,333.7	13.9	431
1964 [a]	470.2	3,291.3	13.9	406
1965	457.7	3,203.7	14.1	468
1966	434.5	3,041.6	13.9	431

[a] June 28 to August 15.

SOURCE: Unpublished tabulations furnished by the New York City Department of Health.

from June 27 through August 14 for the years 1961 through 1966. It can be seen that 1966 is not an unusual year in this comparison. For those who still imagine that all babies conceived on a given date are also born on an exact date 267 days later, Table 1 presents the number of births and proportion of the year's births born on the date corresponding to 267 days after the blackout, also for the years 1961 through 1966. This number of births is not at all remarkable for 1966 when compared to the previous five years. Figure 1 presents the critical data graphically. The unshaded area is

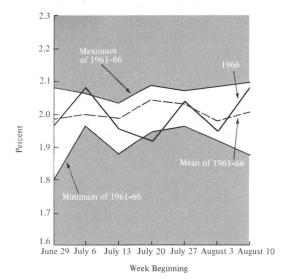

Figure 1. Percentage of Year's Births during Designated Weeks, 1961–66

the limits of variation for the years 1961–65 in percent of the year's births occurring in each of the critical weeks. The dotted line gives the average percent of the year's births occurring in each of these weeks for 1961–65. The solid line is the percent of the year's births for each of these weeks for 1966.

For no week is the value significantly above average for the previous five years. We therefore cannot conclude from the data presented here that the great blackout of 1965 produced any significant increase (or decrease) in the number of conceptions.

Let us not imagine that a simple statistical analysis such as this will lay to rest the myth of blackout babies. Nine months after the Great Snow of 1967 in Chicago, hospitals reported that they were preparing their facilities for an avalanche of "snow babies." It is evidently pleasing to many people to fantasy that when people are trapped by some immobilizing event which deprives them of their usual activities, most will turn to copulation.

References

TOLCHIN, MARTIN. 1966. "Births Up Nine Months after Blackout," *The New York Times* (August 10), p. 1.

U. S. PUBLIC HEALTH SERVICE. NATIONAL CENTER FOR HEALTH STATISTICS. 1966. *Vital Statistics of the United States, 1965.* Vol. I: *Natality.* Tables 1–42, 1–46.

High or low fertility is generally associated, of course, not with any single factor but with that vast and complex conglomerate that we term economic development and cultural modernization. All industrial nations with a modern culture have birth rates well below 30 per 1,000 population; they differ mainly in when and how this low level was realized. In the next paper, this association between modernization and the small family is analyzed in some detail.

The article's author, Norman B. Ryder, is professor of sociology and faculty research associate at the Office of Population Research, Princeton University. Before moving to this position in 1971, he had been Thorstein Veblen Professor of Sociology, University of Wisconsin, and director of its Center for Demography and Ecology. He was editor of the American Sociology Review *(1966–69), and when this volume appears he will be president of the Population Association of America. As one of America's best known analysts of natality, Dr. Ryder has pioneered in the application of mathematical models to this subject. With Professor Charles F. Westoff of Princeton, he is a codirector of the National Fertility Study, a federally sponsored investigation of the reproductive behavior of American wives, and co-author of* Reproduction in the United States: 1965 *(Princeton University Press, 1971).*

THE CHARACTER OF MODERN FERTILITY

NORMAN B. RYDER

During the past 150 years, all presently urbanized and industrialized countries have experienced a transition from a relatively high to a relatively low fertility pattern. Differences among these nations have been a consequence primarily of the dates when fertility started to fall, which in turn largely reflected the modernization of the country. The general character of the socio-economic development has prescribed a single modern fertility at a low level.

This essay describes the movements of demographic indices during this transition, outlines the modes of fertility regulation responsible for these changes, develops an argument concerning the etiology of transition, and speculates on the future of modern fertility (cf. Davis 1963; Freedman 1961–62, 1963).

THE BIRTH RATE

A crude birth rate of 30 per 1,000 dichotomizes fertility levels conveniently between high and low. The nations of the world today are sorted

SOURCE: Reprinted from the *Annals of the American Academy of Political and Social Science,* **369** (1967), 26–36, with permission of the author and the Academy.

into two clusters: the less developed nations with rates well above 30, and the more developed ones with rates well below 30. The data in this paper concern 28 modern nations, selected by the criteria of low fertility, substantial population size, and good information covering a reasonable span of time. If the notable omissions—Argentina, Greece, Israel, and Uruguay—had been included, nothing would have had to be changed appreciably by what is known of fertility movements in these four countries.

The 28 nations are listed in Table 1, showing the decade in which the

Table 1. Decade of Transition to Low Fertility, 28 Selected Countries

1830s:	France
1840s:	Ireland
1880s:	Switzerland, Belgium
1890s:	Sweden, Denmark, England and Wales, Scotland, Australia, New Zealand
1900s:	Netherlands, Norway, Germany, United States
1910s:	Canada, Finland, Austria, Hungary, Czechoslovakia
1920s:	Italy, Spain, Portugal
1930s:	Poland, Bulgaria, Rumania
1940s:	Soviet Union
1950s:	Yugoslavia, Japan

birth rate of each passed permanently below the value of 30. The birth rates of all declined, but the particular paths toward low fertility have differed in various ways. They did not begin their decline from a common high level: birth rates were much higher in Eastern than in Western Europe. Nor did they experience the same tempo of transition: the more recently the nation embarked on decline, the more rapidly the birth rate fell. Thus, Japan accomplished in a few years what it had taken England many decades to do.

The data are adequate to permit a detailed appraisal of movements since 1900 by two convenient measures for the 28 nations: the median birth rate (which divides the countries in half when they are listed in order of their birth rates) and its interquartile deviation (the range of values required to bracket the middle half of the same ordered list).

Two major changes are manifest from Table 2. The median has declined continuously (by more than 40 percent since 1900) except at the ends of the two world wars and a trough during the depression. Second, the dispersion among the countries rose to a peak in the middle of the period and has since declined steadily, again except for the war years. It appears also that almost every nation experienced a small rise following its major decline, although the disturbing effects of the depression and the Second World War often obscure the slight revival.

Table 2. Median Crude Birth Rates and
Interquartile Deviations, 28 Selected Countries,
1900–65

PERIOD	MEDIAN	INTERQUARTILE DEVIATION
1900–04	31.7	6.7
1905–09	31.0	6.3
1910–14	28.9	8.4
1915–19	24.0	6.4
1920–24	26.0	9.1
1925–29	23.0	11.3
1930–34	19.7	10.9
1935–39	19.4	7.3
1940–44	20.4	4.2
1945–49	22.4	5.7
1950–54	21.6	6.4
1955–59	18.8	5.9
1960–64	18.4	4.6
1965	18.3	2.6

In 1965, no country considered "modern" had a birth rate as high as 23; in 1900, only France was (a little) below this figure. The diverse paths followed by individual nations—no less could be expected of societies with widely variant traditions and with differential exposure to war, revolution, and migration—led to a surprising equality. The concave shape of the series for the interquartile deviation is what would be expected from the fact that nations successively transferred from higher to lower fertility.

REFINEMENTS OF THE BIRTH RATE

The crude birth rate may distort fertility variations because its level depends in part on the numbers of women in each childbearing age relative to the total population. The refined index customarily used is the gross reproduction rate (Table 3). With two high and two low exceptions, these are now concentrated within some 20 percent of the mean value of 1.30. Thus, the conclusion that the fertility of these countries is highly similar holds after introducing a control for differences in age distributions.

The gross reproduction rate corrects some false impressions derived from birth-rate variations. In the United States between the late 1930s and the early 1960s, for example, the birth rate rose by 21 percent, but the gross reproduction rate by 58 percent. Change in the age distribution was responsible for the difference. Because fertility was low in most countries during the 1930s, their birth rates today are artificially depressed by age distribu-

Table 3. Estimated Gross Reproduction Rates,
28 Selected Countries, 1965

1.80–1.89:	Ireland
1.70–1.79:	New Zealand
1.60–1.69:	
1.50–1.59:	Canada
1.40–1.49:	Netherlands, Australia, United States, Scotland, Norway, Portugal, France
1.30–1.39:	England and Wales, Spain, Denmark, Austria
1.20–1.29:	Belgium, Italy, Yugoslavia, Finland, Switzerland, Sweden
1.10–1.19:	West Germany, Czechoslovakia, Poland, Soviet Union
1.00–1.09:	Japan, Bulgaria
0.90–0.99:	
0.80–0.89:	Rumania, Hungary

tions temporarily unfavorable to childbearing. But those countries which did not achieve low fertility until after the war have an age distribution favorable to childbearing. Thus, Japan's birth rate is the same as that of England and Wales, yet Japan's gross reproduction rate is 30 percent lower.

The age distribution can be misshaped in ways that depress the birth rate by war mortality (the Soviet Union is the outstanding contemporary case) and by emigration. Despite Ireland's high gross reproduction rate, its birth rate is moderate, in large part because more than half of each cohort of Irish babies leave their homeland before completing their reproductive span. This is one effective if perverse way of restricting population growth.

The gross reproduction rate is also technically flawed in that, whenever there is a trend toward earlier childbearing, it registers more fertility from year to year than the participant couples experience during their lifetimes. Since just such a trend has characterized most modern nations recently, many of the fertility levels recorded in Table 3 are spuriously high; for 20 years American fertility was distorted upward by the trend toward earlier childbearing. Now that trend has ended, the spurious surplus has vanished, and the gross reproduction rate has consequently declined (Ryder 1958). We must exercise due circumspection when tempted to infer from year-to-year movements of fertility the advent of new family values, new birth-control techniques, or other fundamental changes.

MODES OF FERTILITY REGULATION

Fertility reduction must be by reduction of the probability of intercourse, of conception if intercourse occurs, or of birth if conception occurs. It is presumed, on admittedly sketchy evidence, that fertility throughout Europe was once as high as it is now in the still underdeveloped nations, because of the early and nearly universal marriage and the high marital fertility. Then, some 500 years ago, marriage patterns in Western Europe changed toward a rather high age at marriage and low proportions eventually marrying (Hajnal 1965). The consequence for this region was a moderately high birth rate (about 35), the level at which Western (but not Eastern) European nations entered the modern demographic era. In the past 150 years, the predominant transformation has been a decline in marital fertility, beginning in France and a little later in the United States, and now pervasive in the modern world. Although the data do not permit confident assertion, the modern nations now appear to be embarked on a fourth phase, to a combination of low marital fertility with high nuptiality, again beginning in France and a little later in the United States. This is part of the explanation for the recent small rise in fertility in most modern societies. The sequence in Western Europe and its overseas heirs, in summary, has been:

High nuptiality and high marital fertility
Low nuptiality and high marital fertility
Low nuptiality and low marital fertility
High nuptiality and low marital fertility

Apparently, the nations of Eastern Europe (but not Japan and probably not the Soviet Union) have cut the sequence by omitting the two intermediate stages.

Patterns of age at marriage relative to fertility levels are most diverse, probably because the evolution is not everywhere complete and because societies have made different choices in their drive toward lower fertility. Gross reproduction rates are relatively high in New Zealand (with high nuptiality) and in the Netherlands (with low nuptiality); gross reproduction rates are relatively low in Japan (with low nuptiality) and in Bulgaria (with high nuptiality). But the predominant tendency seems to be convergence toward the early marriage of nearly everybody, and the careful regulation of subsequent childbearing. The important exceptions are Ireland, Spain, and Portugal, characterized by a tardy economic development combined with influential Catholicism.

It is so well known that the predominant mode of fertility regulation is contraception that until recently demographers have ignored the importance of the alternatives of nuptiality control and abortion. Information about the means used to restrain marital fertility has been fragmentary and anecdotal, but it is generally agreed that efficacious procedures (such as *coitus interruptus*) have long been known and used by most if not all populations. In explaining the historical decline in marital fertility, much less weight is given to the technical improvement of means (such as the condom and diaphragm) than to the increased employment of these and other means.

As a supplement or alternative to contraception, abortion has probably been significant always and everywhere, despite its danger and moral oppro-brium. Because it has been illegal, its influence on variations in fertility is unknown. In the past two decades, abortion has been legalized in a number of countries characterized by insufficient and inefficient contraception and a high incidence of illegal abortions. Japan, the Soviet Union, and subse-quently all countries of Eastern Europe except East Germany and Albania have permitted abortion on socio-economic grounds. As legal abortions rose, birth rates dropped rapidly; the lowest fertility in the world today is among these countries. Though the controls introduced with legalization have reduced the health risks appreciably, abortion is an expensive alternative to contraception, and we may expect a persistent effort to shift to it from abortion.

The decline in the fertility of modernizing nations has everywhere been intentional and not, for instance, the outcome of the working of mysterious biological forces. And except for the recent provisions legalizing abortion —which facilitate individual intent—the reproductive decisions have been made by couples rather than by governments or religious bodies. Indeed, the transition has taken place despite the persistent efforts by such agencies to thwart the general will.

Why did couples in every country experiencing modernization sys-tematically reduce the numbers of babies they were bringing into the world? Despite a broad agreement on the general socio-cultural factors involved, demographers remain intellectually dissatisfied, for the complex of inter-dependent elements is far too diffuse to permit a confident specification of the necessary (let alone the sufficient) conditions for modern fertility regu-lation. What follows is a preliminary attempt to identify what seem to me to be the basic components of the explanation.

HIGH-FERTILITY NORMS

Every society maintains fertility norms, standardized solutions to the problems of sex and procreation. By explicit and implicit rewards and punishments, the society indoctrinates its members to conform with these norms, which channel individuals' behavior by criteria based on group interests, rather than the desire, however strong, of the persons concerned. And yet to say that a society has high fertility because it has high-fertility norms, which channel individuals' behavior by criteria based on group fertility was once high because it was the tradition to have many babies, but now rationality dictates a small family. It would be a crude misreading of social history to interpret the decline of fertility as a straightforward consequence of the growth of intelligence and understanding, or of the rise of materialism; no orientation could be more materialistic than that essential to a subsistence economy.

The fact is that high-fertility norms prevailed because they were rational means toward ends, given the conditions of high mortality and the family farm as the basis of productive organization. High fertility was mandatory for societal survival and desirable for the leaders of the kinship group. So long as human labor was the principal source of energy, offspring were necessary as helpers in the fields, as defenders against attacking tribes, and as sources of security in their parents' later years. Children were raised frugally and put to work early. From the family's viewpoint, they were essential productive assets.

In underdeveloped areas, couples have many births not precisely because they want them, but because the groups to which they are responsible want them and secure them by enforcing high-fertility norms. The fundamental clue to fertility decline is not the introduction of rationality, but change in the goals toward which rational acts are directed: the ends of the family have been replaced by those of the individual.

In peasant societies, marriage is characteristically arranged at a very early age, and the young couple incorporated within the larger kin unit. Since in this economic context extra labor is important, the couple are enjoined to produce children for the greater good of the group as a whole. But in the European family type that developed some 500 years ago, the independent nuclear family was the norm, with each couple responsible for the support of its own children. Accordingly, marriage had to be delayed until these responsibilities could be met. Since the parents controlled access to the land, they decided also the time of marriage. Thus, the system provided control over the relation between population and resources. Moreover, since agriculture was typically labor-extensive, there was a lower demand at the margin for additional labor than in peasant societies (Ryder 1959).

The West European system set the stage for modern fertility by counterposing the interests of parents and children, and the interests of one sibling and another, at the time of movement from family of orientation to family of procreation. The specific pressures on these structural strains were mortality decline and urban economic development. High levels of fertility had been required to produce small numbers surviving to adulthood, because spouses were likely to die prematurely and the incidence of infant and child mortality was high. Mortality decline produced the large family for the first time. Its size grew both in numbers and in years: the labor force on the family farm was increased, often beyond the efficient utilization of the extra hands; with more years to live, the parents postponed passing on the property to the children, thus raising the age of marriage; and more siblings survived to adulthood, so that each had a smaller share of the patrimony.

At the same time as mortality decline was putting pressure on the relations between parent and child and between sibling and sibling, the growth of urban industry and the opening of the new world provided alternative employment opportunities. Migration to European cities and to the cities and farmlands of America rose to major proportions. In consequence, the bearing and rearing of children became much less rewarding for the parents who stayed on the farm, spatial and social distance grew between families of orientation and procreation, and the postponement of marriage could be circumvented. Under these circumstances there may even have been some rise in fertility for the time being, at least in some parts of Europe.

Then the crucial normative transformation occurred. Society institutionalized the rights of the individual *vis-à-vis* the family and thus helped build the citizenry appropriate to a modern economy. Three developments were pertinent in creating a low-fertility climate: legislation prohibiting child labor and prescribing the education of children, and the establishment of a higher status for women. Large families had been the outcome of the great inequality between the generations and between the sexes. Children were no longer mass-produced once they were withdrawn from the farm and the factory and put into school.

When the focus of work organization was transferred from the rural family to the urban society, the cost of raising children rose because necessities cost more, the preparation of children for urban jobs is more expensive, and the child's income once he takes a job belongs to him and not to his parents. Moreover, since the urban woman can seek satisfactions elsewhere than in motherhood, her influence on reproductive decisions increases—and the burdens of bearing and rearing children have always fallen more directly and heavily on women.

Thus, the locus of authority has moved away from the family toward the individual and toward the formal organizations characteristic of the modern state. The society has replaced the family as the instrument of education, the avenue of employment, and the source of social security for the individual. Parents no longer dispense the worthwhile things of life and the rights and responsibilities of power; the new contract is directly between each individual and his society, for in many ways the individual's interests coordinate with those of the modern economy. Strong family relationships, on the contrary, are incompatible with the rational allocation of human resources. And the more scope a society provides for individual initiative and responsibility, the more likely is a low level of fertility.

The role of formal public instruction is suggested approximately by the fact that the decline of illiteracy has everywhere accompanied the decline of fertility. The educational system gives the individual an alternative source of new normative orientations and expands his vision beyond the local community. With education children can exploit new economic opportunities, and the process increases the expense to the parents. Education makes continued mortality decline more likely, and gives more individuals access to the efficient contraception with which to attain new reproductive goals. Children are separated from their parents for most of their pre-adult life, and girls and boys are treated with approximate equality. Education is the cutting edge of the modern world; the school is the arena within which the new contract between individual and society is made.

THE BASIS FOR MODERN FERTILITY

Throughout the modern world there is now a remarkable demographic consensus. Marriage is at a rather early age, and the couple proceed to have a small number of children at regulated intervals. Both celibacy and voluntary infertility are highly improbable; and, at the other extreme, the large family is an anachronism. The range in fertility among modern nations depends essentially on whether the proportion of couples who have three children is greater or less than that with two children.

Since the new interests of both the individual and society have resulted in a decline of the family, how can one explain the continuation of adequate reproduction? Though the family's functions are much narrower than they once were, the remnant is not only valuable but essential. It may be that the family is no longer an important production unit (although the housewife has an array of capital equipment for the provision of services), but it continues to distribute the products of the economy. More to the point, the family has become specialized as a producer of non-economic goods. The end of the individual's service to his family's interests has not applied in reverse. There is no present substitute for the family as the instrument of socialization. The family provides stable, diffuse, and unquestioning support for the individual whenever he returns from the competitive, impersonal environment of modern occupational and educational life. The family is an oasis for the replenishment of the individual psyche. Thus, if the family does not provide the person with what he or she expects and requires, the common solution is divorce. The demographic structure required to maintain the individual's emotional equilibrium is difficult to specify, but it would not seem to demand more than a few children. Perhaps it is pertinent to the modern family's social-psychological balance that most parents desire one child of each sex.

Obviously the society has a vital interest in the reproduction of citizens, as necessary for societal survival. Positive sanctions encourage marriage and childbearing, and negative sanctions penalize the sterile and the celibate. Explicitly, since the bearing, rearing, and educating of children are too expensive for the individual couple, society subsidizes the family through family allowances, tax exemptions, and facilities for health and education; it assumes the responsibility for employment, for protection and defense, and for security throughout the low points of life. Without such aids, children would be a luxury beyond the reach of most couples. Society's ability to influence the reproductivity of its citizens is essential to its future: the difference between two children and three, however inconsequential for the couple concerned, may be of overwhelming import for social and economic progress.

The effect of religion on contemporary fertility is difficult to assess. Notwithstanding the cleavage in contraceptive doctrine, Catholic and non-Catholic populations differ little in their birth rates—though Catholics are more likely to control nuptiality in striving for the common objective of low fertility. In some nations, religious leaders have supported legislation that has slowed somewhat the dissemination of contraceptive knowledge and means. Yet perhaps the major effect religion has had on the pace of fertility decline has been indirect, through modifying the choice among the alternative modes of regulation, through support for the family's authority over the individual, and through the implications for economic development in the support of traditional virtues. Similarly, ideological orientations have generally had little effect on population. Modernizing stimuli have had the same demographic responses in socialist as in capitalist societies. The politico-economic structure affects reproduction indirectly, through the pace of economic development and the scope the individual is given to pursue his well-being.

SPECULATIONS ON THE FUTURE

It appears unlikely that the average fertility in these 28 modern nations will change much. The trend toward similarity will probably continue: those countries with the lowest birth rates will not tolerate a subreplacement level —at least no country yet has; and those with high birth rates and low per-capita income (Spain, Portugal, and Ireland) should show further declines as economic development continues.

Modern contraception has become available only in the 1960s. The intra-uterine device and the oral contraceptive are "modern" in the sense that they are the first to separate contraception from sexual intercourse. Fertility decline has recently been observed in those countries, largely the English-speaking nations, where oral contraception is beginning to be used extensively. Although the required analysis is incomplete, there is reason to believe that the principal impact of oral contraception has been to permit couples to delay the births of their children—a type of behavior that reduces the birth rate without changing completed family size. Knowledge about family planning is most comprehensive for the United States. Here, although most pregnancies are unplanned, they are typically failures only of timing. The excess fertility that modern contraceptives could eliminate is small with respect to the total population, though not for the most deprived classes.

The most likely consequence of contraceptive innovations is that absti-nence (in the form of delayed marriage) and abortion will be abandoned. More efficient contraception will probably cause the most decline in nations where there is now the greatest discrepancy between the numbers of children intended and achieved. Improvement of regulatory means does not imply a fertility decline, but rather a lesser gap between reproductive intent and achievement. Unfortunately, we cannot tell which are reflected in current international differences in marital fertility.

It is well known that the world's richer nations have a much lower fertility than the poorer ones, and that the rising per-capita income consequent from economic development has been associated with fertility decline. But within the group of modern nations there is today no relation between the level of development and fertility. It seems probable that the more developed nations can effectively realize their somewhat higher reproductive goals, and that the less developed nations are less efficient in achieving somewhat lower reproductive goals. In that case, a direct relation between fertility and income should be established as the more effective fertility regulation reduces the gap between intentions and achievements.

It would seem that a rise in per-capita income would be associated with one in fertility. But rising fertility means a higher rate of population growth, and thus a sacrifice of irreplaceable resources universally regarded as essentials of the good life. It is difficult to believe that a successful society would permit demographic despoliation to continue; it is equally difficult to contemplate the precise ways in which reproductive restraint could be achieved, given the disparity in perspective between the individuals who make reproductive decisions and the social aggregate exposed to the consequences. In any case, with the improved ability to determine fertility, the response to instability in the environment will be more sensitive. Fertility fluctuations are likely to be of greater amplitude and with more embarrassing consequences than in the recent past. Strait is the gate and narrow is the way between too much and too little fertility. There may well be few that find it.

References

DAVIS, KINGSLEY. 1963. "The Theory of Change and Response in Modern Demographic History," *Population Index*, **29**, 345–366.

FREEDMAN, RONALD. 1961–62. "The Sociology of Human Fertility," *Current Sociology*, **10/11**, 35–68.

———. 1963. "Norms for Family Size in Underdeveloped Areas," *Proceedings of the Royal Society*, Series B, **159**, 220–245.

HAJNAL, JOHN. 1965. "European Marriage Patterns in Perspective," in D. V. Glass and D. E. C. Eversley, eds., *Population in History*. London: Edward Arnold.

RYDER, NORMAN B. 1958. "The Reproductive Renaissance North of the Rio Grande," *Annals of the American Academy of Political and Social Science*, **316**, 18–24.

———. 1959. "Fertility," in Philip M. Hauser and Otis Dudley Duncan, eds., *The Study of Population*. Chicago: University of Chicago Press.

That all modern industrial nations have a lower fertility than those with a traditional culture and a peasant economy is true, but demographers do not agree that the causal relation is as direct as it might seem from the last article. It is necessary, first of all, to distinguish the end-product from the transitional process. The fact, similarly, that all modern industrial nations are highly urban is no longer interpreted to mean that cities, per se, act as

instruments of modernization and industrialization (cf. pp. 188–98). In the
following paper, the author examines both sides of the question and reaches
the conclusion—in surprising contrast to the conventional wisdom of the
demographic transition—that the main initial impetus of a transformation
to modern-industrial status is to raise a country's birth rate. If this is true, and
there is some supportive evidence more recent than that presented in the
paper, it means that the struggle of underdeveloped nations to achieve eco-
nomic-cultural parity with the West is even more difficult than it had been
depicted. For not only does the typically rapid growth of population impede
economic development, but such development as is nevertheless achieved
tends to raise the birth rate still more.

The author of the paper, David M. Heer, is an associate professor of
demography at the Harvard School of Public Health. He is the author of two
books and the editor of two others. The main themes in his three dozen
scholarly papers are the differential analysis of fertility and its policy
implications.

ECONOMIC DEVELOPMENT AND FERTILITY

DAVID M. HEER

Two schools of population theorists have developed contrasting views
concerning the effect of economic development on fertility. The first school,
which contends that economic development has an inhibiting effect on
fertility, has been perhaps the predominant view in recent years, expressed
most succinctly in the theory of the demographic transition as set forth by
Warren S. Thompson (1946: 22–35), C. P. Blacker (1947), Kingsley Davis
(1949: 603–8), Frank Notestein (1953), and others. According to this theory,
a nation manifests characteristic types of demographic process dependent
on its stage of industrialization and, by implication, on its level of economic
development.

For example, Warren Thompson and Kingsley Davis divide the nations
of the world into three classes. Class I nations are highly industrialized,
have low fertility and mortality, and show little or no population growth.
Class II nations are beginning the process of industrialization, have declining but still high fertility, rapidly declining mortality, and, on balance, a
high rate of population growth. Class III nations, not yet industrialized, have
both high mortality and at most only a moderate population growth.

The theory of the demographic transition, which was popularized soon
after the Second World War, is congruent with the generally inverse association between fertility level and degree of industrialization among nations

SOURCE: Abridged from *Demography*, 3 (1966), 423–444, with permission of the author
and the Population Association of America, which owns the copyright.

today. The theory is also congruent with the facts that currently industrialized nations all have lower fertility than before their industrialization; that in most nations during recent years, the social classes with the highest incomes have had lower fertility than those with lower incomes (cf. Freedman 1963: 95–97). From this last association, one can argue that, as the income of the lower classes rises, their future fertility will conform to the current fertility of the higher classes.

A second school of thought, of which Malthus was perhaps the foremost representative, has contended that economic development promotes fertility. Malthus believed that an increase in the demand for labor increased the proportion of persons marrying, reduced the average age at marriage, and increased fertility (Malthus 1914, 1: 167, 277–78; 2: 27–28, 132, 140, 230–31). Presumably his views were colored by what he conceived to be recent fertility trends during England's industrial revolution. Later critics of Malthus's views have generally attributed the acceleration in population growth exclusively to lowered mortality. However, recently several historical demographers have produced evidence indicating that fertility may well have increased during England's period of industrial development in the early 19th century (Krause 1957; Habukkuk 1953) and that a similar increase may have occurred in the Netherlands during its period of commercial development in the late 17th and 18th centuries (Petersen 1966).

The link between fertility increase and economic development has been supported also by studies showing the association of birth and marriage rates with business cycles. In the United States during the period 1919–37, with an appropriate time lag, marriages and births of each parity increased when business conditions improved and declined when business fell off (Galbraith and Thomas 1941). Dudley Kirk (1942) arrived at similar conclusions for Germany during the 1920s. Other researchers have worked with data from other countries, and in all cases the results have shown a positive correlation between birth and marriage rates and the business cycles (cf. Freedman 1963: 108).

In a recent study (1962), Easterlin has considered the influence on fertility not only of general business conditions but also of the demand for labor from persons of reproductive age relative to that from those past the period of having children. One of the prime factors sustaining the American baby boom, he suggested, was that during the 1950s very high wages and salaries were paid to the persons aged 20 to 29: because of the small number of babies born during the depression, the supply of new entrants to the labor force was abnormally low when demand for labor was high; and those entering the labor force in the 1950s, exceptionally well educated in comparison with older age groups, had a competitive advantage in employment.

In another study, W. Stys (1957) has shown that the average completed family of Polish peasant women born during the latter half of the 19th century varied directly with the size of their farm. The average number of births per mother ranged from 3.9 among landless peasants to 9.1 on farms of more than seven hectares. The variation in fertility resulted mostly from differences in the mother's age at marriage, but births per year of marriage were also slightly higher among women living on the larger farms.

A study by Gordon DeJong (1965) also implies that an increase in economic status leads to higher fertility. He put to respondents in the Southern Appalachian region three questions concerning the ideal number of children today: (1) for a "well-off" couple, (2) for the average young couple, and (3) for a couple "not well off." They set the ideals, respectively, at 4.02, 2.79, and 1.5 children, implying that respondents of each social class would increase their fertility as their economic circumstances improved and would reduce it if their income declined.

STATEMENT OF HYPOTHESIS

These two contrasting views concerning the effect of economic development on fertility demand reconciliation. However, few have attempted to do this. One of the findings from an earlier study (Heer and Turner 1965) concerns the relation between fertility, economic level, and change in economic level. For 318 local areas in 18 Latin American nations that had a census around 1950, we correlated the child-woman ratio with eight other variables, six of which measured various correlates of the level of economic development: local and national proportions urban, local and national proportions literate, and local and national proportions of the labor force in agriculture. By a multiple-regression analysis, the six variables taken together correlated positively with level of economic development and inversely with fertility.

From the differences between actual fertility in each local area and that predicted by the correlates of economic development, it seemed that nations with unusually great advances in per-capita economic level included most of the areas with higher than expected fertility, and that nations whose recent increase in per-capita income had been slow included most of the areas with lower than predicted fertility. A more rigorous test confirmed this conjecture, and we concluded:

Serious consideration must be given the hypothesis that a rapid increase in the level of economic development tends, *ceteris paribus,* to lead to higher fertility. Of course, the other factors are never equal. What appears to happen can be stated as follows. An increase in the level of economic development leads to an increase in fertility as married couples become more optimistic concerning their future economic status. On the other hand, the increase in the level of economic development then sets in motion other forces, such as increased knowledge and use of birth control and increases in net economic cost of children, which tend to reduce fertility. In the long run, the forces depressing fertility tend to be stronger than the forces increasing fertility unless the increase in per-capita income continues at a high rate. Thus many, if not most, nations exhibit the classic pattern of fertility decline with advancing industrialization.

At the time this was written, we were unaware of two other studies, both of which came to the conclusion that, controlling for other variables, fertility is directly rather than inversely associated with per-capita income. For a sample of 30 nations, including both developed and underdeveloped, Weintraub (1962) obtained a partial-correlation coefficient of .25 between the crude birth rate and per-capita income. Adelman (1963) studied the effect on the fertility of women in each of seven 5-year age groups of several independent variables: per-capita income, an index of education, the percent of labor force employed outside of agriculture, and population density. For each of the seven age groups, the regression coefficient of per-capita income on fertility was positive, and the regression coefficients of the other three variables on fertility were all negative.

Weintraub's and Adelman's studies give considerable support to the hypothesis that the direct effect of economic development is to increase rather than decrease fertility. If this hypothesis is valid, the fact that fertility over the long run has declined in all industrial societies as their income advanced must then be explained by an inverse association between fertility and such other factors as may be positively related to income (cf. Freedman 1961–62; United Nations 1965: 134–51).

Among these is the level of education, which usually rises with an increase in economic level. A higher educational level, in turn, increases the flow of communications of all types (Schramm 1964: 20–57), including those specifically concerned with the technology and consequences of birth control. If we assume that in any society some women have had as many children as they wish, the more women who know about birth control the more will practice it and the lower will be that society's fertility. A higher level of education, moreover, usually increases the proportion of adolescents and young adults attending school, probably raising the average age at marriage and thus reducing fertility. Hence, holding constant the nation's economic well-being, we should expect a nation's level of education to vary inversely with its fertility.

As a second factor, a usual consequence of improving a nation's economic level is a decline in mortality at young ages, as Adelman's study has shown. Because under conditions of constant fertility a lower infant and childhood mortality increases the cost of supporting a family, it may stimulate a change to smaller families. One should note that a general decline in mortality is usually greater at younger than at older ages (United Nations 1956: 26–27).

In any society where a substantial proportion of mothers breast-feed their children, a high rate of infant mortality results in increased fertility. For during the mother's lactation her fecundity is greatly reduced (Potter 1963).

Dr. Laila Sh. El Hamamsy, head of the Social Research Center of the American University in Cairo, advanced a third reason why high infant and childhood mortality should be positively correlated with elevated fertility. In her view, with such a high death rate, parents do not invest as much emotional energy in any of their children, since the pain of bereavement would be proportional to the amount of such an investment. And the more devotion to any one child, the less is left for other children. Therefore, the expenditure of large amounts of energy in any one child should lead to a wish for fewer children. Thus, reduced rates of infant and childhood mortality, by encouraging intensive emotional involvement with each child, should reduce fertility.

With a high rate of infant and childhood mortality, finally, women may bear more children on the average than they desire as surviving family members. For with a high average childhood mortality, the variance in the proportion of children in each family who die will also be high. On the other hand, with very low infant and childhood mortality, women can assume that all their children will survive to maturity.

Other institutional changes may reduce fertility. For example, the elderly rely increasingly on pensions from governments and business corporations rather than on sustenance from kin. Under the traditional system parents tend to have enough children so that at least one son will be alive when the couple has reached old age (Morrison 1956). Under an impersonal system of old-age insurance, this motivation for children is lacking.

Another frequent concomitant of economic development is an increased rate of social mobility. Most studies of this factor have focused on whether socially mobile persons have lower fertility than nonmobile persons—a level of analysis irrelevant to whether societal differences in social mobility influences fertility. (The use of individual data where aggregate data are appropriate has been termed the atomistic fallacy; cf. Riley 1963: 706–7.) A change in a society's rate of mobility might influence the fertility of both mobile and nonmobile, for such a change would supposedly be associated with a fading of traditional and hereditary rankings and, hence, with a compensatory use of conspicuous consumption to demonstrate high status. Greater consumption necessitates a diversion of funds from such other expenditures as raising a large family (Freedman 1961–62: 60). As Banks (1954) noted, the high standard of living that the middle class of England considered necessary in the late Victorian period led to its success in reducing the number of children.

Still another relevant change often accompanying economic development is that the net economic cost of children (that is, the gross expenditures involved in bearing and rearing children minus the return they themselves bring into the family) increases relative to that of commodities parents might buy in place of children (Becker 1960). As the economic well-being of a society rises, child labor becomes less frequent and the period of education, and thus of dependency, becomes greater.

Nations with a relatively large recent increase in economic development would show, *ceteris paribus*, a relatively high fertility. Many persons in a rapidly developing country might not yet have developed a taste for the new consumption articles available to them because of their new wealth. Rather, they might continue to buy more familiar articles, including the "consumption" of more children.

TEST OF THE HYPOTHESIS

According to the theory, to repeat, the direct effect of a society's increased economic well-being is to increase its fertility, but because of various indirect effects an increase in economic level in fact decreases fertility. One may therefore predict that the zero-order correlation between economic well-being and fertility is inverse but that the partial association, holding constant the indirect effects of an improved economic well-being, is positive. Further, a higher well-being should increase the educational level and decrease infant and childhood mortality. Therefore, holding other relevant variables constant, the partial association between well-being and education should be positive and that between well-being and infant-childhood mortality negative. Since a high level of education and a low infant-childhood mortality may be taken as necessary conditions for low fertility, the partial correlation between educational level and fertility should be negative and that between infant-childhood mortality and fertility positive.

A rise in economic well-being may also increase reliance on impersonal organizations rather than on kin for sustenance of the elderly, may increase social mobility, and may raise the net economic cost of children relative to consumer commodities. Each of these changes supposedly depresses fertility, but none of them is easily measured. A test of this part of the theory will not be attempted here.

This study is based on a cross-sectional analysis of all nations in the world for which relevant data were available. A total of 41 nations are included, a somewhat larger number than the 37 in Adelman's study or the 30 in Weintraub's. The data of this study, like those of Weintraub and Adelman, refer to the early years of the 1950 decade. Almost without exception, data are taken from United Nation publications.

Fertility was measured by the general fertility rate for males (number of births divided by the male population 15 to 54 years old) for the year 1953. This somewhat unconventional measure was considered more appropriate than the commonly used rates. The denominator of the crude birth rate, of course, includes more than that portion of the population capable of conceiving a child. And certain of the nations, in particular the USSR, had a very large excess of women over men in the reproductive ages. In such cases, male rather than female fertility is probably a more accurate indicator of what the fertility level would be, given a normal sex ratio.

The level of economic development was measured by estimated average income per capita of the population aged 15 to 64, rather than the total population, as in both Weintraub and Adelman. Between two nations with an equal average income per wage earner, the one with the lower fertility will have the higher income per capita of the total population. Hence, with the other index of economic well-being there is a spurious tendency for high income to be associated statistically with low fertility.

The level of education was measured by newspaper circulation per 1,000 population aged 15 and over in 1952, 1953, or 1954. For her index of education, Adelman averaged literacy and newspaper circulation per capita. But according to my hypothesis, literacy is relevant only insofar as it is associated either with communication flow or with school attendance among young adults, neither of which is reflected by literacy as well as by newspaper circulation. The denominator in the rate, the population aged 15 and over, was based on the reasonable assumptions that 15 years mark the beginning of both reading newspapers and any effect on fertility.

The operational measure of infant and childhood mortality was simply the mortality of infants under one. Ansley J. Coale has informed me that mortality at older ages of childhood correlates so highly with infant mortality that it can be ignored.

Two additional variables were included as controls. Population density in 1953 was included because Adelman and Grauman (1965) showed that it may have an important partial association with fertility. The percentage increase in per-capita energy consumption from 1937 to 1953, considered to be a good index of the recent change in economic development, was included because it was presumed that the indirect effects of an economic advance conducive to reduced fertility took place somewhat later than the improved economic well-being itself. However, apart from newspaper circulation and infant mortality, no measures were available for these indirect effects.

The study tests two models concerning the determinants of fertility, an additive one in the form $Y = a + b_1x_1 + b_2x_2 + \ldots + b_nx_n$ and a multiplicative one in the form $Y = a(x_1^{b_1})(x_2^{b_2})(x_3^{b_3}) \ldots (x_n^{b_n})$. Weintraub's study used the former and Adelman's the latter, which she found gave a better fit than the additive model. Neither Weintraub nor Adelman examined the adequacy of prediction for individual nations. Analyzing the residuals from the regression equation gives one the opportunity of examining what additional factors may also be important in determining cross-national differences in fertility.

RESULTS

The values of each variable for each nation are presented in Table 1. The matrix of zero-order coefficients is presented in Table 2: Part A

Table 1. Indices of Fertility and of Five Variables Assumed by Hypothesis to be Associated with Fertility, 41 Nations, c. 1953

NATION	FERTILITY BIRTHS PER 1,000 MALES AGED 15–54 X_1	PRODUCTIVITY NET NATIONAL PRODUCT PER CAPITA AGED 15–64 ($) X_2	LITERACY NEWSPAPERS CIRCULATION PER 1,000 PERSONS AGED 15+ [e] X_3	INFANT MORTALITY INFANT DEATHS PER 1,000 BIRTHS X_4	POPULATION DENSITY PERSONS PER SQUARE KILOMETER X_5	INDUSTRIALIZATION INCREASE IN PER-CAPITA ENERGY CONSUMPTION, 1937–53 (%) X_6
Argentina	84.2	708	144	63.4	6.6	31
Australia	80.6	1,489	578	23.3	1.1	49
Austria	58.5	561	278	49.9	83.0	66
Belgian Congo	140.6 [a]	127	3	148.0 [a]	5.2	200
Belgium	58.9	1,189	487	41.9	287.7	−9 [f]
Canada	104.1	2,144	360	35.6	1.5	47
Ceylon	136.8	194	63	71.2	126.4	50
Chile	133.1	613	126	112.4	8.7	31
Colombia	157.5 [b]	460	99	111.0	10.6	150
Denmark	66.3	1,172	515	27.2	101.5	25
Dominican Republic	165.8	304	43	74.2	48.3	200
Ecuador	191.8 [c]	278	87	115.8	12.8	200
Egypt	159.2	204	40	145.8	22.0	62
Finland	83.0	1,069	387	34.2	12.3	41
France	68.2	1,131	311	41.9	78.0	4
West Germany	59.0	752	340	46.4	197.8	−5
Greece	64.6	334	97	45.3	59.2	50
Guatemala	201.2	289	47	102.8	28.1	100
Honduras	168.8	271	34	64.0	13.3	−12
Hungary	78.5	407	167	70.8	103.1	114

Iceland	109.3	1,329	663	19.0	1.5	43
Ireland	79.7	679	333	39.4	42.0	3
Italy	63.7	474	145	58.4	158.0	32
Jamaica	138.2	310	63	64.1	135.6	188
Japan	81.1	313	536	48.9	234.5	4
Luxemburg	52.8	1,264	555	42.3	116.4	−9 f
Malaya	176.2	581	89	83.4	42.7	−5
Mexico	184.4	401	32	95.2	14.3	48
Netherlands	81.6	805	355	22.2	312.2	24
New Zealand	95.5	1,656	515	25.7	7.6	35
Norway	67.8	1,140	529	22.0	10.4	37
Peru	148.2 d	227	72	98.2	7.0	131
Portugal	85.7	313	90	95.5	92.8	33
Puerto Rico	145.0	813	120	62.8	247.7	237
Sweden	55.4	1,448	642	18.7	15.9	48
Switzerland	61.4	1,519	393	29.8	118.1	31
Thailand	120.2	140	7	64.9	38.0	300
USSR	100.0	766	322	68.0	8.5	92
United Kingdom	57.6	1,178	796	27.6	208.4	9
United States	91.8	2,959	494	27.8	17.1	35
Venezuela	176.0 d	975	112	67.9	6.2	337

a Weighted average of figures for white and native populations. b Baptized births only. c Excludes live births of children dying within 24 hours. d Excludes births to jungle Indians. e Population and circulation data were not always from the same year. f Belgium and Luxemburg combined.

SOURCES: Base population on which rates were calculated: United Nations, *Demographic Yearbook, 1954 and 1961* (New York, 1955 and 1962). Births: United Nations, *Demographic Yearbook, 1960* (New York, 1961). Net national product, for Hungary and USSR: Simon Kuznets, *Six Lectures on Economic Growth* (Glencoe, Ill.: Fress Press, 1959), p. 20; for all other countries: United Nations, "Per-capita National Produce of 55 Countries, 1952–54," *Statistical Papers*, Series E, No. 4 (New York, 1957). Newspaper circulation: United Nations, *Demographic Yearbook, 1953, 1954, and 1955* (New York, 1954, 1955, and 1956). Infant mortality: United Nations, *Demographic Yearbook, 1962* (New York, 1963). Population density: United Nations, *Demographic Yearbook, 1954* (New York, 1955). Energy consumption: United Nations, *Statistical Yearbook, 1955 and 1956* (New York, 1956 and 1957).

Table 2. Matrix of Zero-Order Correlation Coefficients

	X_2	X_3	X_4	X_5	X_6
A. Additive model					
X_1	−0.4417	−0.6851	0.7031	−0.3794	0.5467
X_2		0.7111	−0.6642	−0.0607	−0.3207
X_3			−0.7761	0.2150	−0.5160
X_4				−0.2795	0.4109
X_5					−0.1993
B. Multiplicative model					
X_1	−0.5270	−0.6617	0.6801	−0.3654	0.5547
X_2		0.8460	−0.7735	−0.1380	−0.4151
X_3			−0.7747	0.0868	−0.5760
X_4				−0.0192	0.4323
X_5					−0.2214

X_1 = Births per 1,000 males 15 to 54 years old.
X_2 = Net national product per capita aged 15 to 64.
X_3 = Newspaper circulation per 1,000 aged 15 and over.
X_4 = Infant deaths per 1,000 births.
X_5 = Persons per square kilometer.
X_6 = Percentage increase in per-capita energy consumption, 1937–53.

presents the actual values of each variable (appropriate for the additive model), and Part B the natural logs of these values (appropriate for the multiplicative model).

The results of the multiple-regression and correlation analysis with fertility as the dependent variable are presented in Table 3, Part A for the additive model and Part B for the multiplicative. To determine which of several independent variables has the highest association with the dependent variable, one can use either the partial-correlation or the standardized regression coefficient. The square of the partial-correlation coefficient is equal to the incremental variance explained by the given independent variable divided by the variance left unexplained by the previous variables. The standardized regression coefficient is equal to the change in the dependent variable associated with a unit change in a given independent variable when both independent and dependent variables are expressed in the form of standard scores. Usually, but not invariably, the rank order of the several partial-correlation coefficients will be identical to the rank order of their corresponding standardized regression coefficients.

Table 4 presents the results of the multiple-regression and correlation analysis for each of the two models with economic development as the dependent variable, Table 5 with newspaper circulation as the dependent variable, Table 6 with infant mortality as the dependent variable, Table 7 with population density as the dependent variable, and Table 8 with per-

Table 3. Results of the Multiple-Regression Analysis with Male Fertility as the Dependent Variable

VARIABLE	PARTIAL-CORRELATION COEFFICIENT	t RATIO FOR PARTIAL-CORRELATION COEFFICIENT (35 D.F.)	STANDARD-IZED REGRESSION COEFFICIENT (β COEFFI-CIENT)	REGRESSION COEFFICIENT (B COEFFI-CIENT)
A. Additive model				
X_2	0.1020	0.6065	0.0996	0.0075
X_3	0.2384	−1.4520	−0.2811	−0.0579
X_4	0.3690	2.3490	0.4153	0.5511
X_5	−0.2131	−1.2907	−0.1504	−0.0791
X_6	0.3082	1.9169	0.2329	12.2787
	$R_{1.23456} = .7911$		$F_{(5, 35)} = 11.7104$	
	$R^2_{1.23456} = .6259$			
B. Multiplicative model				
X_2	0.0371	0.2197	0.0487	0.0202
X_3	−0.1440	−0.8609	−0.2005	−0.0678
X_4	0.4240	2.7695	0.4748	0.3443
X_5	−0.3995	−2.5785	−0.2901	−0.0788
X_6	0.2447	1.4928	0.1900	0.1875
	$R_{1.23456} = .8008$		$F_{(5, 35)} = 12.5107$	
	$R^2_{1.23456} = .6412$			

X_2 = Net national product per capita aged 15 to 64.
X_3 = Newspaper circulation per 1,000 aged 15 and over.
X_4 = Infant deaths per 1,000 births.
X_5 = Persons per square kilometer.
X_6 = Percentage increase in per-capita energy consumption, 1937–53.

capita increase in energy consumption as the dependent variable. Table 9 presents for each model the actual fertility for each nation, the fertility predicted by the regression equation, and the difference between actual and expected fertility.

How well do these results support the hypothesis of this study? Multiple-regression and correlation analysis, of course, does not by itself reveal anything concerning causation. To make causal inferences, one needs not only statistical association but a basis to decide whether the association is a spurious result of a third variable or variables, and whether the association occurs because variable *A* causes variable *B*, variable *B* causes variable *A*, or both variables mutually interact.

According to my theory, the direct and indirect effects of economic development, taken together, cause fertility to decline. This part of the hypothesis receives support in the zero-order correlation of —.442 between fertility and economic development (—.527 correlation between the natural logs). Logically, one could say that the association results solely from the fact that high fertility impedes economic development. However, if only a small part of the association between fertility and economic development is due to the effect of fertility on development, then the validity of the theory is supported.

The prediction that the direct effect of economic development on fertility is positive receives slight support from the multiple and partial correlations; the partial-correlation coefficient is only .102 in the additive model and .037 in the multiplicative, and the values of t for the partial-correlation coefficients are below the level of significance. Nevertheless, the direct effect of economic level on fertility may be stronger than the partial association would indicate, since high fertility probably has a long-run adverse influence on economic development—a point strongly stressed by Coale and Hoover (1958) and other leading demographer-economists. If the influence of fertility on level of economic development is to produce a negative association between the two variables, and if in fact we find a positive association, then there are grounds for believing that the positive effect of economic level on fertility is greater than that suggested by the partial association between the two variables.

Finally, the prediction that economic development causes several factors that tend to reduce fertility levels is supported in Table 2, which shows strong zero-order associations between economic level and, respectively, newspaper circulation and infant mortality. Since the partial associations between economic level and these two variables are also high (Table 4), the associations may not be spurious. But do the associations exist because economic level causes changes in newspaper circulation and infant mortality, or vice versa? On the one hand, a high rate of communication flow may, as Schramm (1964) has suggested, be an important cause of economic development. On the other hand, a high level of newspaper circulation no doubt depends on high average education, which, in turn, depends on a large expenditure for education. Thus, at least part of the association may be due to the effect of economic level on newspaper circulation.

One might argue that part of the relation between infant mortality and economic development is spurious: infant mortality is strongly related to adult mortality and morbidity, and high morbidity at adult ages impedes economic development. On the other hand, public-health facilities obviously cost money (though sometimes relative little money for large improvements in infant mortality), and hence at least part of the association is doubtless due to the effect of economic development on infant mortality.

How much do increased education and decreased infant-childhood mor-

Table 4. Results of the Multiple-Regression Analysis with Net National Product per Capita Aged 15 to 64 as the Dependent Variable

VARIABLE	PARTIAL-CORRELATION COEFFICIENT	t RATIO FOR PARTIAL-CORRELATION COEFFICIENT (35 D.F.)	STANDARDIZED REGRESSION COEFFICIENT (β COEFFICIENT)	REGRESSION COEFFICIENT (B COEFFICIENT)
A. Additive model				
X_1	0.1020	0.6065	0.1044	1.3876
X_3	0.4412	2.9083	0.5327	1.4575
X_4	−0.3450	−2.1744	−0.3975	−7.0092
X_5	−0.3382	−2.1263	−0.2444	−1.7084
X_6	0.0151	0.0893	0.0117	8.1819

$$R_{2.13456} = .7796 \qquad F_{(5,\,35)} = 10.8488$$
$$R^2_{2.13456} = .6078$$

VARIABLE	PARTIAL-CORRELATION COEFFICIENT	t RATIO FOR PARTIAL-CORRELATION COEFFICIENT (35 D.F.)	STANDARDIZED REGRESSION COEFFICIENT (β COEFFICIENT)	REGRESSION COEFFICIENT (B COEFFICIENT)
B. Multiplicative model				
X_1	0.0371	0.2197	0.0282	0.0526
X_3	0.6495	5.0539	0.6884	0.4335
X_4	−0.3327	−2.0875	−0.2837	−0.3829
X_5	−0.3298	−2.0666	−0.1822	−0.0922
X_6	0.0812	0.4817	0.0480	0.0881

$$R_{2.13456} = .8900 \qquad F_{(5,\,35)} = 26.6726$$
$$R^2_{2.13456} = .7921$$

X_1 = Births per 1,000 males 15 to 54 years old.
X_3 = Newspaper circulation per 1,000 aged 15 and over.
X_4 = Infant deaths per 1,000 births.
X_5 = Persons per square kilometer.
X_6 = Percentage increase in per-capita energy consumption, 1937–53.

tality reduce fertility? Both Parts A and B of Table 3 show partial associations, as expected. The associations, especially those between infant mortality and fertility, are probably not spurious. However, could variations in fertility cause variations in newspaper circulation and in infant mortality, rather than vice versa? Conceivably adults with many children have less time to read, and mothers of many children may spend less attention and money on each of them. Both of these arguments are plausible, as are also the arguments outlined earlier why newspaper circulation and infant mortality should affect fertility. Thus, it seems plausible that these associations reflect cause-effect relations in both directions.

Table 5. Results of the Multiple-Regression Analysis with Newspaper
Circulation as the Dependent Variable

VARIABLE	PARTIAL-CORRELATION COEFFICIENT	t RATIO FOR PARTIAL-CORRELATION COEFFICIENT (35 D.F.)	STANDARD-IZED REGRESSION COEFFICIENT (β COEFFICIENT)	REGRESSION COEFFICIENT (B COEFFICIENT)
A. Additive model				
X_1	−0.2384	−1.4520	−0.2021	−0.9817
X_2	0.4412	2.9083	0.3654	0.1335
X_4	−0.3330	−2.0895	−0.3178	−2.0481
X_5	0.0699	0.4147	0.0418	0.1069
X_6	−0.2332	−1.4186	−0.1494	−38.2544
	$R_{3.12456} = .8550$		$F_{(5, 35)} = 19.0242$	
	$R^2_{3.12456} = .7310$			
B. Multiplicative model				
X_1	−0.1440	−0.8609	−0.1034	−0.3058
X_2	0.6495	5.0539	0.6129	0.9733
X_4	−0.1881	−1.1333	−0.1513	−0.3244
X_5	0.1748	1.0503	0.0911	0.0732
X_6	−0.3203	−2.0002	−0.1786	−0.5213
	$R_{3.12456} = .9027$		$F_{(5, 35)} = 30.8227$	
	$R^2_{3.12456} = .8149$			

X_1 = Births per 1,000 males 15 to 54 years old.
X_2 = Net national product per capita aged 15 to 64.
X_4 = Infant deaths per 1,000 births.
X_5 = Persons per square kilometer.
X_6 = Percentage increase in per-capita energy consumption, 1937–53.

The data neither prove nor refute my theory of the relation between economic development and fertility. Further research on small areas within nations may test the theory further.

As in Adelman's analysis, population density proved to have an important inverse association with fertility. One possible reason is that density affects the net cost of children relative to consumer commodities. It is appropriate to provide children with a large living space—which has a cost roughly proportional, *ceteris paribus,* to population density. It is plausible, also, that high fertility increases population density. Hence, once again, the association probably reflects a cause-effect relation in both directions.

The increase in per-capita energy consumption showed, as predicted, a

Table 6. Results of Multiple-Regression Analysis with Infant Mortality
as the Dependent Variable

VARIABLE	PARTIAL-CORRELATION COEFFICIENT	t RATIO FOR PARTIAL-CORRELATION COEFFICIENT (35 D.F.)	STANDARD-IZED REGRESSION COEFFICIENT (β COEFFICIENT)	REGRESSION COEFFICIENT (B COEFFICIENT)
A. Additive model				
X_1	0.3690	2.3490	0.3279	0.2471
X_2	−0.3450	−2.1744	−0.2994	−0.0170
X_3	−0.3330	−2.0895	−0.3490	−0.0542
X_5	−0.1779	−1.0696	−0.1116	−0.0442
X_6	−0.0994	−0.5908	−0.0667	−2.6508

$$R_{4.12356} = .8394 \qquad F_{(5, 35)} = 16.6998$$
$$R^2_{4.12356} = .7046$$

VARIABLE	PARTIAL-CORRELATION COEFFICIENT	t RATIO	STANDARDIZED	REGRESSION
B. Multiplicative model				
X_1	0.4240	2.7695	0.3786	0.5221
X_2	−0.3327	−2.0875	−0.3903	−0.2891
X_3	−0.1881	−1.1333	−0.2339	−0.1091
X_5	0.1121	0.6674	0.0727	0.0272
X_6	−0.0842	−0.5002	−0.0584	−0.0795

$$R_{4.12356} = .8449 \qquad F_{(5, 35)} = 17.4702$$
$$R^2_{4.12356} = .7139$$

X_1 = Births per 1,000 males 15 to 54 years old.
X_2 = Net national product per capita aged 15 to 64.
X_3 = Newspaper circulation per 1,000 aged 15 and over.
X_5 = Persons per square kilometer.
X_6 = Percentage increase in per-capita energy consumption, 1937–53.

positive partial association with fertility. Obviously, fertility in 1953 could not directly effect an increase in energy consumption from 1937 to 1953. However, fertility in 1953 is highly associated with that in 1937, which might well have influenced the subsequent change in energy consumption. In the main, nevertheless, the high fertility would have reduced any subsequent increase in the economic level and hence in per-capita energy consumption. Therefore, the association would represent the average of two countervailing effects, but with the influence of increase in per-capita energy consumption on fertility greater than the indicated correlation.

In terms of proportion of total variance that each explains, there is little to choose between the two models. The additive model explains 62.6 percent

Table 7. Results of the Multiple-Regression Analysis with Population
Density as the Dependent Variable

VARIABLE	PARTIAL-CORRELATION COEFFICIENT	t RATIO FOR PARTIAL-CORRELATION COEFFICIENT (35 D.F.)	STANDARD-IZED REGRESSION COEFFICIENT (β COEFFICIENT)	REGRESSION COEFFICIENT (B COEFFICIENT)
A. Additive model				
X_1	−0.2131	−1.2907	−0.3020	−0.5742
X_2	−0.3382	−2.1263	−0.4681	−0.0670
X_3	0.0699	0.4147	0.1168	0.0457
X_4	−0.1779	−1.0696	−0.2837	−0.7156
X_6	−0.0070	−0.0415	−0.0075	−0.7519
	$R_{5.12346} = .4989$		$F_{(5, 35)} = 2.3200$	
	$R^2_{5.12346} = .2489$			
B. Multiplicative model				
X_1	−0.3995	−2.5785	−0.5503	−2.0248
X_2	−0.3298	−2.0666	−0.5967	−1.1792
X_3	0.1748	1.0503	0.3352	0.4171
X_4	0.1121	0.6674	0.1729	0.4613
X_6	−0.0426	−0.2521	−0.0455	−0.1654
	$R_{5.12346} = .5651$		$F_{(5, 35)} = 3.2833$	
	$R^2_{5.12346} = .3193$			

X_1 = Births per 1,000 males 15 to 54 years old.
X_2 = Net national product per capita aged 15 to 64.
X_3 = Newspaper circulation per 1,000 aged 15 and over.
X_4 = Infant deaths per 1,000 births.
X_6 = Percentage increase in per-capita energy consumption, 1937–53.

of the total variance in fertility, the multiplicative one 64.1 percent. From Parts A and B of Table 9, one can see that in general the multiplicative model better predicts the fertility of European nations, the additive model that of underdeveloped nations.

What in general were the differences between the fertility predicted for each nation and its actual fertility? By the prediction of both equations, 22 nations should have had a higher fertility than that observed and 19 nations a lower one. Fertility in the Belgian Congo was very much overpredicted by both equations, probably because many women there have been made sterile by venereal disease. There is a high correlation between the incidence of venereal disease in the country's various provinces, the percent of women

Table 8. Results of Multiple-Regression Analysis with Percentage Increase in Per-Capita Energy Consumption as the Dependent Variable

VARIABLE	PARTIAL-CORRELATION COEFFICIENT	t RATIO FOR PARTIAL-CORRELATION COEFFICIENT (35 D.F.)	STANDARD-IZED REGRESSION COEFFICIENT (β COEFFICIENT)	REGRESSION COEFFICIENT (B COEFFICIENT)
A. Additive model				
X_1	0.3082	1.9169	0.4078	0.0077
X_2	0.0151	0.0893	0.0195	0.0000
X_3	−0.2332	−1.4186	−0.3639	−0.0014
X_4	−0.0994	−0.5908	−0.1480	−0.0037
X_5	−0.0070	−0.0415	−0.0065	−0.0001
	$R_{6.12345} = .5873$ $R^2_{6.12345} = .3450$		$F_{(5,\,35)} = 3.6866$	
B. Multiplicative model				
X_1	0.2447	1.4928	0.3151	0.3192
X_2	0.0812	0.4817	0.1373	0.0747
X_3	−0.3203	−2.0002	−0.5743	−0.1968
X_4	−0.0842	−0.5002	−0.1215	−0.0893
X_5	−0.0426	−0.2521	−0.0398	−0.0110
	$R_{6.12345} = .6363$ $R^2_{6.12345} = .4049$		$F_{(5,\,35)} = 4.7625$	

X_1 = Births per 1,000 males 15 to 54 years old.
X_2 = Net national product per capita aged 15 to 64.
X_3 = Newspaper circulation per 1,000 aged 15 and over.
X_4 = Infant deaths per 1,000 births.
X_5 = Persons per square kilometer.

who are childless, and the fertility rate (Romaniuk 1963). Moreover, fertility there may have undergone a recent substantial increase, from a crude birth rate of 34 per 1,000 in 1953 to one of 43 in 1956–57. According to the second survey, in many provinces there had been a substantial recent decline in the proportion of childless women.

The reason for the overprediction of fertility in Thailand is probably that the actual figure used for that nation, based on the reported crude birth rate of 31 per 1,000, was erroneous. By a United Nations estimate, Thailand's crude birth rate during the 1950–55 period, based on a reverse-survival calculation from the population aged 5 to 9 as enumerated in the 1960 census, was 46 per 1,000 (United Nations 1965: 51).

Table 9. Difference between Actual Male Fertility and That Predicted by Regression Equation

NATION	ACTUAL	ESTI-MATED	DIFFER-ENCE	ACTUAL	ESTI-MATED	DIFFER-ENCE
A. Additive model				B. Multiplicative model		
Argentina	84.2	115.9	−31.7	84.2	117.1	−32.9
Australia	80.6	77.2	3.4	80.6	90.8	−10.2
Austria	58.5	97.9	−39.4	58.5	87.7	−29.2
Belgian Congo	140.6	187.2	−46.6	140.6	231.9	−91.3
Belgium	58.9	60.7	− 1.8	58.9	65.7	− 6.8
Canada	104.1	101.2	2.9	104.1	106.6	− 2.5
Ceylon	136.8	113.9	22.9	136.8	101.2	35.6
Chile	133.1	143.1	−10.0	133.1	140.2	− 7.1
Colombia	157.5	157.2	0.3	157.5	156.5	1.0
Denmark	66.3	69.7	− 3.4	66.3	65.0	1.3
Dominican Republic	165.8	142.1	23.7	165.8	131.0	34.8
Ecuador	191.8	165.1	26.7	191.8	161.2	30.6
Egypt	159.2	166.2	− 7.0	159.2	155.8	3.4
Finland	83.0	89.3	− 6.3	83.0	86.4	− 3.4
France	68.2	88.6	−20.4	68.2	76.9	− 8.7
West Germany	59.0	76.0	−17.0	59.0	71.5	−12.5
Greece	64.6	104.0	−39.4	64.6	90.6	−26.0
Guatemala	201.2	146.9	54.3	201.2	140.7	60.5
Honduras	168.8	113.5	55.3	168.8	110.9	57.9
Hungary	78.5	119.0	−40.5	78.5	104.7	−26.2
Iceland	109.3	68.0	41.3	109.3	81.0	28.3

Ireland	79.7	85.3	− 5.6	79.7	77.5	2.2
Italy	63.7	99.5	−35.8	63.7	87.7	−24.0
Jamaica	138.2	127.1	11.1	138.2	111.1	27.1
Japan	81.1	60.9	20.2	81.1	69.3	11.8
Luxemburg	52.8	71.1	−18.3	52.8	70.3	−17.5
Malaya	176.2	121.9	54.3	176.2	107.4	68.8
Mexico	184.4	139.9	44.5	184.4	132.6	51.8
Netherlands	81.6	56.7	24.9	81.6	56.2	25.4
New Zealand	95.5	81.2	14.3	95.5	80.0	15.5
Norway	67.8	74.5	− 6.7	67.8	73.3	− 5.5
Peru	148.2	147.9	0.3	148.2	153.3	− 5.1
Portugal	85.7	127.2	−41.5	85.7	110.9	−25.2
Puerto Rico	145.0	124.0	21.0	145.0	106.3	38.7
Sweden	55.4	69.4	−14.0	55.4	67.6	−12.2
Switzerland	61.4	80.3	−18.9	61.4	63.5	− 7.1
Thailand	120.2	151.0	−30.8	120.2	149.1	−28.9
USSR	100.0	115.9	−15.9	100.0	119.8	−19.8
United Kingdom	57.6	43.3	14.3	57.6	58.4	− 0.8
United States	91.8	92.6	− 0.8	91.8	78.5	13.3
Venezuela	176.0	159.9	16.1	176.0	154.8	21.2

There is no simple reason why the actual fertility in Argentina, Austria, Greece, Hungary, and Portugal was much lower than predicted. Of these five nations, four are predominantly Roman Catholic; thus, the Church's stand against "mechanical" contraceptives did not prevent these nations from reaching fertility levels considerably lower than expected from the variables considered here.

According to the additive equation, the following five nations showed the greatest positive difference between actual and expected fertility: Honduras, Guatemala, Malaya, Mexico, and Iceland. According to the multiplicative equation, the five nations with the greatest positive discrepancy were Malaya, Guatemala, Honduras, Mexico, and Puerto Rico. The two lists overlap, with four nations on each. Reasons for the substantial underpredictions, perhaps particularly for Guatemala, Honduras, and Mexico, may be the low reported fertility in the Belgian Congo and Thailand, because of which the equations predict lower fertility for all the other less developed nations.

Iceland and the Netherlands were the only European nations for which fertility was substantially underpredicted—surprisingly, for Iceland has an unusually high ratio of males to females in the reproductive age groups, and the proportion of married men is therefore lower than it might be otherwise. Lincoln Day (1968) has hypothesized that among developed countries, those that are predominantly Protestant but with a substantial Roman Catholic minority will have higher fertility than those almost entirely Roman Catholic. The Netherlands supports this hypothesis (cf. pp. 342–46).

DISCUSSION

If true, these results have several very important policy implications. It may be unwise to rely on uncontrolled economic development to cut down fertility, for economic development, if it is to be effective in reducing fertility, must be accompanied by changes in social structure—changes that in some degree usually accompany industrialization. Most important, nations of equal economic development vary in their populations' health and education, and these variations help determine the variations in fertility. Thus, a government committed to reducing the nation's fertility in order to further economic development should make sure that the budget also includes relatively large allocations for health and education.

I have hypothesized that the major effect of education on fertility may be through an increased flow of communications concerning birth control. What if a specially organized effort is made to increase communications about birth control, ignoring the fact that the general level of communications flow remains very low? Birth-control campaigns in several nations with a low educational level may answer this question.

That infant and childhood mortality greatly affect fertility level is relevant to the controversy over whether public-health programs in under-developed nations are worthwhile. In a chapter of their book *Hungry Nations*, entitled "The Fallacy of Public Health Programs—You Can't Afford the Luxury," the Paddocks (1964: 128–29; cf. Taylor 1965) state:

> When faced realistically, nevertheless, it will be recognized that public health actually damages the economy of a backward nation and definitely delays, if it does not eliminate, hope for a rise in living standards until population control is effectively organized. . . . If product remains constant, then each year the standard of living, the amount of food available per person, is reduced as the number of mouths increases.
> And the cause of population expansion is not a rise in birth rates; it is a decrease in death rates.
> Herein is the fallacy of public health programs; they decrease death rates without curtailing birth rates.

This argument ignores the possibility that death rates do affect birth rates. If in fact a lower infant and childhood mortality is a condition for the eventual reduction of fertility, then the argument is invalid. This study suggests that the vigorous support of public-health programs strongly aids in reducing fertility, even if it means a temporary increase in the rate of population growth (cf. Leibenstein 1957: 250–52). Further research on this topic is obviously needed. The effect of infant and childhood mortality on the success of fertility-control programs can easily be studied experimentally in nations with a variety of both types of policies.

References

ADELMAN, IRMA. 1963. "An Econometric Analysis of Population Growth," *American Economic Review*, 53, 314–339.

BANKS, J. A. 1954. *Prosperity and Parenthood*. London: Routledge & Kegan Paul.

BECKER, GARY S. 1960. "An Economic Analysis of Fertility," in National Bureau of Economic Research, *Demographic and Economic Change in Developed Countries*. Princeton, N. J.: Princeton University Press.

BLACKER, C. P. 1947. "Stages in Population Growth," *Eugenics Review*, 39, 88–102.

COALE, ANSLEY J., and EDGAR M. HOOVER. 1958. *Population Growth and Economic Development in Low-Income Countries*. Princeton, N. J.: Princeton University Press.

DAVIS, KINGSLEY. 1949. *Human Society*. New York: Macmillan.

DAY, LINCOLN H. 1968. "Natality and Ethnocentrism: Some Relationships Suggested by an Analysis of Catholic-Protestant Differentials," *Population Studies*, 22, 27–50.

DEJONG, GORDON. 1965. "Religious Fundamentalism, Socio-economic Status, and Fertility Attitudes in the Southern Appalachians," *Demography*, 2, 540–548.

EASTERLIN, RICHARD. 1962. *The American Baby Boom in Historical Perspective*. New York: National Bureau of Economic Research.

FREEDMAN, RONALD. 1961–62. "The Sociology of Human Fertility," *Current Sociology*, Vol. 10/11, No. 2.

———. 1963. *The Sociology of Human Fertility*. Oxford: Basil Blackwell.

GALBRAITH, VIRGINIA, and DOROTHY S. THOMAS. 1941. "Birth Rates and the Interwar Business Cycles," *Journal of the American Statistical Association*, 36, 465–476.

GRAUMAN, JOHN V. 1965. "Fertility and Population Density: A Macrodemographic Approach." Paper presented at the annual meeting of the Population Association of America.

HABAKKUK, H. J. 1953. "English Population in the Eighteenth Century," *Economic History Review*, 6, 117–133.

HEER, DAVID M., and ELSA S. TURNER. 1965. "Areal Differences in Latin American Fertility," *Population Studies*, 18, 279–292.

KIRK, DUDLEY. 1942. "The Relation of Employment Levels to Births in Germany," *Milbank Memorial Fund Quarterly*, 28, 126–138.

KRAUSE, J. T. 1957. "Some Implication of Recent Work in Historical Demography," *Comparative Studies in Society and History*, 1, 164–188.

KUZNETS, SIMON. 1959. *Six Lectures on Economic Growth*. Glencoe, Ill.: Free Press.

LEIBENSTEIN, HARVEY. 1957. *Economic Backwardness and Economic Growth*. New York: Wiley.

MALTHUS, THOMAS R. 1914. *An Essay on Population*. New York: E. P. Dutton.

MORRISON, WILLIAM A. 1956. "Attitudes of Males toward Family Planning in a Western Indian Village," *Milbank Memorial Fund Quarterly*, 34, 262–286.

NOTESTEIN, FRANK W. 1953. "The Economics of Population and Food Supplies," in Eighth International Conference of Agricultural Economists, *Proceedings*. London: Oxford University Press.

PADDOCK, WILLIAM and PAUL. 1964. *Hungry Nations*. Boston: Little, Brown.

PETERSEN, WILLIAM. 1966. "The Demographic Transition in the Netherlands," *American Sociological Review*, 25, 334–347.

POTTER, ROBERT G., JR. 1963. "Birth Intervals: Structure and Change," *Population Studies*, 17, 155–166.

RILEY, MATILDA WHITE. 1963. *Sociological Research*. Vol. 1: *A Case Approach*. New York: Harcourt, Brace & World.

ROMANIUK, A. 1963. "Fécondité et stérilité des femmes congolaises," in International Population Conference (New York, 1961), *Proceedings*, 2, 109–117. London: International Union for the Scientific Study of Population.

SCHRAMM, WILBUR. 1964. *Mass Media and National Development*. Stanford: Stanford University Press.

STYS, W. 1957. "The Influence of Economic Conditions on the Fertility of Peasant Women," *Population Studies*, 11, 136–148.

TAYLOR, CARL E. 1965. "Health and Population," *Foreign Affairs*, 43, 475–486.

THOMPSON, WARREN S. 1946. *Population and Peace in the Pacific*. Chicago: University of Chicago Press.

UNITED NATIONS. 1956. *The Aging of Populations and Its Economic and Social Implications*. New York.

————. 1957. "Per-capita National Product of 55 Countries—1952–54," *Statistical Papers*, Series E, No. 4. New York.

————. 1965. *Population Bulletin*, No. 7, 1963. New York.

WEINTRAUB, ROBERT. 1962. "The Birth Rate and Economic Development: An Empirical Study," *Econometrica*, **40**, 812–817.

At one time even sociologists and political scientists used to refer to the transformation of underdeveloped areas as "economic development," but it has become obvious—as indicated in the papers of both Ryder and Heer— that much more is involved in "modernization" than a change in the economy. In particular, norms affecting the level of the birth rate operate first of all within the family, which is only distantly associated with the economic structure. In some cultures the nuclear family is embedded in a larger kin group, in others relatively isolated; what difference does the type of organization make with respect to natality? This is the subject of the next paper.

Thomas K. Burch, the senior author, joined the Population Council staff in 1970 and is the associate director of its demographic division. Before that he was an associate professor of sociology at Georgetown University and director of the demographic division of the Center for Population Research there. He has been a member of the Papal Commission on Population and Birth Control (1964–66) and of the advisory panel on population and food in developing nations, Policy Planning Council, U. S. Department of State (1966–69). Almost all of his two dozen papers are concerned with the analysis of factors affecting family size.

Murray Gendell, the co-author of the paper, an associate professor of sociology at Georgetown University, succeeded Burch as director of the demographic division of its Center for Population Research. He had received his degree from Columbia University with a dissertation subsequently published as Swedish Working Wives *(1963). His scholarly papers reflect his dominant interest in the institutional determinants of fertility.*

EXTENDED FAMILY STRUCTURE AND FERTILITY: SOME CONCEPTUAL AND METHODOLOGICAL ISSUES

THOMAS K. BURCH AND MURRAY GENDELL

There is a striking contrast between the wide acceptance of the proposition that the extended family encourages high fertility and the scarcity of

SOURCE: Slightly abridged from the *Journal of Marriage and the Family*, 32 (1970), 227–236, with permission of the authors and the journal.

relevant empirical evidence (Clark 1967: 186; Nimkoff and Middleton 1960: 218; Petersen 1961: 353–55, 358, 562–63; Phelps and Henderson 1958: 230; President's Science Advisory Committee 1967: 36; Thomlinson, 1965: 154–55). In his authoritative review of the literature, Freedman (1961–62: 50) could speak of "no more than illustrative evidence," and the additional empirical studies since Freedman's review are also far from adequate. One reason for this inadequacy has been the failure to deal with the conceptual and methodological problems involved in testing the proposition.

The major theoretical discussions of the relations between extended family and fertility are by Lorimer (1954), Davis (1955), and Davis and Blake (1956). They differ in detail but generally their basic theses are sufficiently similar to be summarized together:

1. Both corporate kinship systems, such as clans and organized lineages, and extended-family systems tend to motivate and support early and nearly universal marriage and high marital fertility, and thus high levels of societal fertility. According to Lorimer, the influence of extended families in this direction is neither so strong as that of corporate kinship groups nor necessary; in some situations, he speculates, extended families might even restrict fertility.

2. Extended families are defined as (a) groups of relatives living in the same household or (b) networks of kin living in different households. Davis (1955) speaks more generally of the subordination of the nuclear family to the wider kinship structure, expressed in authority patterns, economic solidarity, and, *often but not always,* joint residence. Kin who do not occupy the same dwelling, however, often live near one another.

3. Societies that emphasize the independent nuclear family, and the related principle that a man is responsible for the support of his wife and children, tend to have low societal fertility. Where contraception is not widely practiced, this low fertility may be effected by late marriage and high proportions never marrying. (This proposition also applies to societies in which the stem family system prevails. This type is not here considered to be an extended residential form, but rather a particular kind of independent nuclear family.)

4. These propositions do not imply that the family system of a society is the only or the most important factor influencing fertility. In some situations, fertility may depend less on the family system than on economic, religious, ecological, or other nonfamilial factors.

5. Family systems can influence societal fertility in various ways. Lorimer (1954) stresses the influence of religious and cultural ideals regarding family strength and continuity, norms which when built into the personality might motivate marriage and reproduction independently of the family context. Davis (1955) gives greater weight to the structural features conducive to early and nearly universal marriage and hence high fertility. Economic solidarity, he argues, permits the children to marry earlier than they could

if they had to support themselves. Furthermore, matri- or patrilocality motivates parents to get their children married in order to establish links with other family lines, expand their own lines, and relieve the household budget of the expense of unmarried children. The spouses are motivated to have many children to strengthen the family line and/or their own status in the household. The realization of high fertility is facilitated by the fact that parents share the burdens of support and childrearing with the others in the household.

Other authors have discussed the issue less systematically and extensively, but some of their comments are worth noting. According to Stycos (1958), there are three qualifications to the view that extended-family patterns cause high fertility. First, extended residential families or joint households may be much less prevalent in nonindustrial societies than their cultural ideals suggest. Second, with declining infant and child mortality, even the classic extended family must recognize a point of diminishing returns—some level of fertility dysfunctional to the extended family itself. Third, women in underdeveloped nations typically do not express a desire for many children, as they presumably should if theory is correct.

Freedman (1961–62: 50–51) speculates that in the past the causal relation between extended families and fertility may have operated in such nations as India, but that modernization may have been sufficient to destroy the association. Also, he asks, will fertility vary by family type within one society in the same way as among societies with differing family systems?

Goode argues that there is no inherent connection between the independent nuclear-family system and low fertility (1963a: 240, 250; 1963b; see also Davis and Blake 1956: 217), for the family size is based on the couple's decision rather than that of a wider kinship group. Hence, it can be high (as on the American frontier) or low (as in an industrial city), depending on circumstances.

EMPIRICAL RESEARCH

The writings of Lorimer and Davis have inspired a number of empirical studies of the relation. Three are summarized here as illustrations.

Nag (1967) presented data obtained in 1960–61 from 3,725 ever-married women living in seven villages of West Bengal, representing several Hindu and Muslim castes. Women were classified by family type according to the following criterion: "All families with more than one ever-married person related to one another [are] joint families, and the rest simple families" (*ibid.:* 160). Many women lived in joint families, so defined, but on the average they bore smaller numbers of children. The pattern was not quite so consistent when age-standardized rates were computed from Nag's data (Pakrasi and Malaker 1967). Then the differentials were reduced within all but one of the three Muslim and all three of the Hindu groups; in one group the differential was reversed (Table 1). The number of cases was small, and many of the differences were of doubtful statistical significance.

Table 1. Age-Standardized Average Number of Children Ever Born per Ever-Married Women Aged 10 or More, by Family Type, Religion, and Caste, Seven Villages of West Bengal, 1960–61

| | SIMPLE FAMILY | | JOINT FAMILY | |
| | CHILDREN PER | NUMBER OF | CHILDREN PER | NUMBER OF |
RELIGION AND CASTE	FAMILY	WOMEN	FAMILY	WOMEN
Hindu				
Brahmin	4.32	64	3.93	113
Satchasi and Ghosh	4.04	125	3.97	160
Other	3.32	107	3.31	105
Muslim				
Sheikh	4.74	147	4.54	98
Non-Sheikh	3.04	1,296	2.76	1,222
Fishermen	2.26	224	2.40	64

SOURCES: Moni Nag, "Family Type and Fertility," *Proceedings of the World Population Conference, 1965* (New York, 1967), Vol. II, Table 1, pp. 162–163; Kanti Pakrasi and Chittaranjan Malaker, "The Relationship between Family Type and Fertility," *Milbank Memorial Fund Quarterly,* 45 (1967), 451–460, Table 1.

In a parallel study by Pakrasi and Malaker (1967), 1,018 married couples in Calcutta were classified as living in simple families (that is, those containing only the couple and their unmarried children) or in joint families (simple families plus one or more relatives). Their criterion for family type was thus less stringent than Nag's and controls were included for duration of marriage and for social class (Table 2). Pakrasi and Malaker also found substantial numbers of women living in "joint families," particularly in marriages of shorter duration, and with a lower cumulative fertility than women in simple families except in the lowest class of "manual laborers, skilled and unskilled." Once again, the number of cases was small. (Previous studies in India yielded approximately the same results: Bebarta 1964; Chidambaram 1967; Driver 1960; Mathen 1962; Poti and Datta 1960; Rele 1963; Surendranathan 1965; United Nations 1961.)

Recent studies from Taiwan present a rather mixed picture of the relation between family type and fertility. According to survey data from Taichung, "living in a nuclear family rather than in a stem or joint family is linked to lower fertility values" (Freedman 1964). Of Taichung women aged 35 to 39, only 23 percent were living in joint or stem families, the rest in nuclear families. Women in that age category hardly differed by family type in the mean number of live births, differed only slightly in the mean number of

Table 2. Average Number of Children Ever Born per Couple,
Standardized for Duration of Marriage, by Social Class
and Family Type, Calcutta, 1956–57

| | SIMPLE FAMILY | | JOINT FAMILY | |
| | CHILDREN PER FAMILY | NUMBER OF COUPLES | CHILDREN PER FAMILY | NUMBER OF COUPLES |
SOCIAL CLASS				
Class I	2.9	107	2.5	131
Class II	3.4	176	3.1	283
Class III	3.5	173	3.8	148

SOURCE: Kanti Pakrasi and Chittaranjan Malaker, "The Relationship between Family Type and Fertility," *Milbank Memorial Fund Quarterly*, **45** (1967), 451–460, Table 3.

children the wife wanted (4.4 in joint, 4.3 in stem, 4.0 in nuclear), but differed substantially in the use of fertility controls, including abortion and sterilization.

According to a Taiwan survey in 1966 (Liu 1967a), age-standardized rates of children ever born to ever-married women aged 15 to 49 barely differed by family type, whether for the whole island, cities, urban townships, or rural townships (Table 3). With the data presented by separate age

Table 3. Age-Standardized Fertility According to Two Indices, by Type of Family, Cities and Townships of Taiwan, 1966

INDEX AND RESIDENCE	NUCLEAR	STEM	JOINT
Own Children under 5 per Ever-Married Woman Aged 15 to 49			
Total	.76	.84	.88
Cities	.67	.79	.87
Urban townships	.82	.84	.85
Rural townships	.88	.90	.93
Children Ever Born per Ever-Married Woman Aged 15 to 49			
Total	3.5	3.7	3.7
Cities	3.2	3.5	3.4
Urban townships	3.6	3.8	3.7
Rural townships	3.9	3.9	4.0
Number of cases	(30,000)	(14,500)	(4,500)

SOURCE: Paul K. C. Liu, "Differential Fertility in Taiwan," in International Union for the Scientific Study of Population, *Contributed Papers* (Sydney Conference, Australia, August 1967), Table 1.

groups, however, older women (40 and over) in nuclear families clearly had a lower cumulative fertility than those in joint families. A different pattern emerged with *own children under 5 years* rather than *children ever born.* By the former measure, fertility to wives aged 15 to 49 was highest in joint families, intermediate in stem families, and lowest in nuclear families. The differences were not large but were consistent by type of area, and the number of cases was large enough to assure statistical significance. However, reversals and inconsistencies were apparent among younger women; and the measure is affected by mortality, which may have differed by family type (Freedman 1964: 24).

What bearing do such studies have on the theory relating family structure and fertility? To answer this question it is necessary to specify precisely both the theory and the methodology and data required to test it. This can be done by considering the following four interrelated sets of problems: (1) the time reference of the theory, (2) the level of analysis, (3) the definition of key variables, and (4) the problems of causation.

TIME REFERENCE OF THE THEORY

Many relevant data that pertain to institutions of the past are now unavailable. It has been suggested, for example, that the stem family of pre-industrial Europe helped account for the fact that the highest fertility there was lower than that in contemporary agrarian societies (Petersen 1961: 358). But knowledge is hardly complete of fertility during that era or of the realities of family structure (including regional differences and time trends). Whatever further research may reveal, there is presently little empirical evidence for the prevailing view.

It is at least possible that studies of contemporary societies are largely irrelevant as tests of the theory, for the modernization of India, Taiwan, and other developing nations may have destroyed or greatly modified traditional family structures, or broken the earlier causal link between family structure and fertility (Freedman 1961–62). This point takes on added force from the fact that almost all developing nations have experienced a substantial decline in mortality, which strongly influences both family structure and fertility (Burch 1970; Collver 1963; Ryder 1955).

In short, the Lorimer-Davis theory that extended-family systems cause high societal fertility may be true but not applicable to the present situation.

LEVELS OF ANALYSIS

One should distinguish between individual and aggregate levels of analysis. At one extreme, the theory concerns societies as units of analysis. Davis (1955), for instance, uses institutional patterns to explain why the fertility level of agrarian societies has continued high despite the substantial declines in mortality. His thesis—that the subordination of the nuclear unit to larger kinship structures encourages the production of many children—implies that neolocal nuclear families will have a lower fertility than comparable units in joint households.

On the other hand, virtually all empirical studies of this topic have been based on the individual woman as the unit of analysis (an exception is Namboodiri 1967). From such studies we can know whether women living in extended families have more children than those living in nuclear or stem families, possibly whether the association is spurious and, if not, what mechanisms are involved. Such research cannot tell us, however, whether fertility differs in societies according to whether extended, stem, or nuclear units prevail. Vice versa, studies based on aggregate units do not necessarily imply any conclusions at the individual level. One reason for this disjunction is that societal fertility is determined not only by the number of children characteristic of a family type but also by the distribution of women of reproductives ages among the various types. Whether industrial societies pose the same dilemma depends on the definition of family type. If the criterion is not merely who lives with whom (in the same household, or perhaps nearby) but includes the nature and degree of kin interaction *irrespective of place of residence*, then the same indeterminacy can exist between levels of analysis among industrial societies with few extended families defined by residence alone.

The inconsistency may run the other way. With no association at the individual level, societal fertility and the predominant type of family structure may be related at the aggregate level in accordance with the theory. In India, for example, this would be so if most women in the reproductive ages lived in joint households and their fertility was no higher than that of women living in nuclear households. The few local studies available, including the two already discussed (Tables 1 and 2), suggest this as a definite possibility.

In short, the meaning of the hypothesized relation differs at the individual and the aggregate level. Discussion of the theory should specify the level(s) at which the relation ostensibly exists, making clear the distinctive methodological requirements of each.

DEFINITION OF KEY VARIABLES

Theories linking the extended family with high fertility also differ, as we have noted, in the meaning given to "extended." Both Lorimer and Davis use two different, though related, criteria: (1) a group of relatives living in the same household and (2) a network of kin involving regular interaction (visiting, authority, mutual aid, and so forth).

In order to ascertain whether the nuclear family in industrial society is as isolated as had been widely believed, analysts of the family increasingly have been studying the amount and type of kin interaction. This line of inquiry has not, to our knowledge, been extended to include the relation of kin interaction to fertility. Many of these studies, moreover, restrict the subject population to kin who do not share the same residence. Since inter-action and co-residence are not mutually exclusive, the essential point with respect to the hypothesis is whether sharing a household with kin changes fertility; if so, it may do so at least in part because within shared households the type of interaction significantly differs, or occurs more frequently or intensely. In Japan, according to Taeuber (1958: 104), "Whatever the ex-ternal relations with the more extended kin group, it is among the small group of people living together that relations are closest and most frequent." Adams (1967) makes a similar point concerning Latin American family systems. Indeed, since many kin live near each other, it might be useful to see whether there are significant variations in fertility and patterns of kin interaction as residential proximity (including co-residence) varies. Studies of kin interaction have not generally been made at the aggregate level, where one could test such assertions as that the interaction and interdependence among related nuclear families are greater in nonindustrial than in industrial societies. Could such a difference account at least partly for the pronounced difference in fertility between these two types of societies?

The co-residence concept is familiar, perhaps mainly because of the convenience of this criterion for census enumerations. There appears, how-ever, to be little agreement on how to define the various family types (Castillo 1967; International Union 1967), sometimes because operational definitions blur the conceptual distinctions. Everyone agrees in calling husband, wife, and their unmarried children the nuclear family. No unanim-ity exists, however, on how to classify variants of this basic structure—for example, couples without children (at all or at home) or children with one parent. Operational definitions frequently ignore or leave implicit these variations, so that it is often unclear what is included in the count of families classified as nuclear. And even if it is clear, the validity of hypotheses may depend on which peripheral types are included and which left out.

Non-nuclear families are defined on the basis of either generational or collateral extension, or both, and there is consequently less agreement on their definition—except perhaps for the stem family, in which only one child may marry and live with his family of procreation. Units that are neither nuclear nor stem are sometimes referred to as extended families. But some "extended" units are based only on collateral extension—for example, two siblings each with a spouse and unmarried children. Other "extended" fami-lies, with both generational and collateral extension, may consist of the head of the household and his spouse, their unmarried children and their married sons or daughters, each with spouse and children. A house with more than three generations does not differ in any practical (in view of the relative infrequency of such cases) or theoretical principle.

It is not clear, however, why the stem family is a separate category. Is the significant criterion that its structure is basically a generational extension? Or is it that, as asserted by Davis and Blake (1956: 216–18), it stresses—in contrast to the extended family—the marital rather than the filial or sibling link? It is true that at least in some European countries the marital bond dominated the stem family, but this was not true in the family ideal of preindustrial Japan. It had a stem structure, but the filial tie was more important than that between husband and wife or brother and brother (Dore 1967: 98). But if the only important consideration is the relative importance of the marital or filial and sibling ties, there is then no reason to distinguish the nuclear and stem types, for presumably—with the Japanese family again as an exception—in both types the marital tie has priority. On the other hand, if the relative importance of marriage is not the only relevant factor, then the type of extension may be significant, possibly reflecting, for instance, variations in authority patterns or social controls in the household.

The additional distinction among extended families that such an analysis would require can be exemplified in the Taiwan studies (Freedman 1964; Liu 1967a), where distinctions among nuclear, stem, and extended families were based on the following definitions:

The nuclear family is composed of husband, wife, and unmarried children. The stem family is composed of the same members as a small family plus one or more parents on either the husband's or wife's side. The joint or extended family is composed of two or more small or joint families united by blood or marriage relationships. The survey explicitly asked whether or not relatives were eating as well as living in the same house. Only those members actually eating together were counted in determining the type of family (Liu 1967b: 57).

The definitions of the nuclear and stem types are unobjectionable, but the broad characterization of extended families blurs the distinction between collateral and generational extension. From these Taiwan studies one cannot ascertain whether, with respect to higher or lower fertility, collateral extension is being compared with generational extension or with a combination of the two types.

Even so, the Taiwan studies are better conceptually than other inquiries. Nag (1967), for example, classified "all families with more than one ever-married person related to another" as joint families, contrasted only to nuclear (called "simple") families. Pakrasi and Malaker (1967) defined the "joint family" as a nuclear family plus at least one additional relative, whether or not (apparently) ever married. Thus, the category "joint family" may include some more accurately classified as "nuclear," not to mention "stem," for which no provision was made. In these cases, fertility differed little between the two types of families and a more rigorous specification of types may not have changed this finding. But greater precision might well have resulted in a different distribution of persons and families according to type of family—a critical datum in studies on the aggregate level.

Among the various measures of fertility, most empirical investigations have used the longitudinal one of cumulative fertility (that is, the number of children ever born), relating it to the type of residential family in which the respondent is *currently* living. However, some of the reproduction may have taken place when the woman was living in a different type of family. Thus, the strongest differential that Liu (1967a) found was with a measure of recent fertility, own children under 5 years of age living in the household, though the cumulative fertility to women under 25 (which is also generally fairly recent) does not clearly differentiate by family type (cf. Nag 1967). Information is needed on the relation between current residence and current fertility, and between cumulative fertility and the woman's residential history.

Another problematic definition is of the "age at marriage." According to Davis and Blake, Lorimer, and other theorists, the extended family affects age at marriage and thus marital fertility as such. Indeed, Davis and Blake derived almost all the effect of family structure on societal fertility from its influence on the intermediate variable of age at marriage. Yet in only one of the studies here reviewed was age of marriage dealt with explicitly: Nag's data showed no relation between current family of residence and age at marriage, age at beginning cohabitation, or age at first birth. It would be helpful to know the age at marriage of women by type of residential family both prior to and after their marriage, and thus to control for age at marriage in any comparisons of fertility by family type. Controlling for current age (as in Liu 1967a) is equivalent to some degree, for if women of a given age in non-nuclear families married younger than their age-mates in nuclear families, they should have a higher cumulative fertility. Since Liu did not find this, presumably they either did not marry earlier, or, having done so, they had a smaller number of children per year of marriage. Only with explicit information on age at marriage could we tell which factor is more important. Pakrasi and Malaker controlled for duration of marriage, but not simultaneously for current age—which may mask variation in cumulative fertility due to different ages at marriage. None of the studies took into account the closely related question of what proportion of women eventually marry and its possible relation to prevailing family structure.

CAUSATION

Causation may sometimes run from fertility to family structure, not simply the reverse. Also, extended-family structure may depress as well as enhance fertility, thus producing less net effect than claimed.

Nag (1967) and Driver (1963: 39) suggested that women in joint households have intercourse less frequently because of the lack of privacy and the pressure by kin to observe periodic taboos on coitus. Stycos (1958) and others suggested that, in some circumstances, the extended family may want its members to have fewer children, and try to motivate them in this direction. In contemporary India couples who do not head the households in which they are living may be pressured out if they have too many children (Rele 1963: 197). Burch (1967: 360) has shown that in Panama the number of non-nuclear relatives of the household head is inversely related to the number of his children in the household. Direct evidence on such possible selective processes is lacking in the studies we have reviewed.

That couples with high fertility may be forced out of joint households implies that a comparison of the fertility by types of households should include a control for relationship to head. Wives of heads, for instance, are apt to have more children than the other female relatives. It would be desirable also to control for movement from one household type to another, taking into account the sequence of moves, as well as the length of time and thus the phase of the life cycle spent in each. For example, a newly married couple may live in the household of the groom's father until the young man can set up his own. Or brothers and their wives and children may live in the same household until their father, the head of the household, dies (Goode, 1963b: 238–47).

SUMMARY

Few studies have been conducted on the relation between family type and level of fertility. To our knowledge, all but one are at the individual level of analysis and define family type by co-residence. At the aggregate level, thus, virtually no empirical evidence exists to test the hypothesis that societies in which extended families predominate have higher fertility. The meager evidence at the individual level provides little support for the hypothesis that women in extended families have more children than those in other residential types. The relation of kin interaction to fertility is unknown. Clearly, the widespread conviction that the extended family is statistically associated with—let alone a contributing cause of—high fertility is not empirically warranted.

Much more empirical inquiry is needed, methodologically more refined than heretofore. It will be essential to distinguish between individual and aggregate levels of analysis and between co-residence and kin interaction, to define more carefully the various types of family structure, to keep the time reference of fertility (current or cumulative) congruent with that of family structure (cross-sectional or longitudinal), to take into account marriage patterns, and to be more alert to the possibility of countercausal forces. Work along these lines may not only settle the question whether and in what sense the extended family encourages high fertility, but add to our knowledge about family dynamics, family structure, and their relations to social and economic structure.

References

ADAMS, RICHARD N. 1967. *The Second Sowing*. San Francisco: Chandler.

BEBARTA, P. C. 1964. "Family Structure and Fertility," *Proceedings of the Indian Science Congress*, 51st and 52nd Sessions, Part III. Calcutta: Indian Science Congress.

BURCH, THOMAS K. 1967. "The Size and Structure of Families," *American Sociological Review*, **32**, 347–363.

———. 1970. "Some Demographic Determinants of Average Household Size: An Analytic Approach," *Demography*, **7**, 61–69.

CASTILLO, GELIA T., et al. 1967. "The Concepts of Nuclear and Extended Family: An Exploration of Empirical Referents." Unpublished paper, University of the Philippines, College of Agriculture, Manila.

CHIDAMBARAM, V. C. 1967. "Fertility in Kerala," in International Union for the Scientific Study of Population, *Contributed Papers* (Sydney Conference), pp. 225–236.

CLARK, COLIN. 1967. *Population Growth and Land Use*. New York: St. Martin's Press.

COLLVER, ANDREW. 1963. "The Family Cycle in India and the United States," *American Sociological Review*, **28**, 86–96.

DAVIS, KINGSLEY. 1955. "Institutional Patterns Favoring High Fertility in Underdeveloped Areas," *Eugenics Quarterly*, **2**, 33–39.

———, and JUDITH BLAKE. 1956. "Social Structure and Fertility: An Analytic Framework," *Economic Development and Cultural Change*, **4**, 211–235.

DORE, R. P. 1967. *City Life in Japan: A Study of a Tokyo Ward*. Berkeley: University of California Press.

DRIVER, E. D. 1960. "Fertility Differentials Among Economic Strata in Central India," *Eugenics Quarterly*, **7**, 77–85.

———. 1963. *Differential Fertility in India*. Princeton, N. J.: Princeton University Press.

FREEDMAN, RONALD. 1961–62. "The Sociology of Human Fertility: A Trend Report and Bibliography," *Current Sociology*, **10/11**, 35–119.

———, et al. 1964. "Fertility and Family Planning in Taiwan: A Case Study of Demographic Transition," *American Journal of Sociology*, **70**, 16–27.

GOODE, WILLIAM J. 1963a. "Industrialization and Family Change," in Bert F. Hoselitz and Wilbert E. Moore, eds., *Industrialization and Society*. Paris: UNESCO.

———. 1963b. *World Revolution and Family Patterns*. New York: Free Press of Glencoe.

INTERNATIONAL UNION FOR THE SCIENTIFIC STUDY OF POPULATION. 1967. "Variables for Comparative Fertility Studies: A Working Paper."

LIU, PAUL K. C. 1967a. "Differential Fertility in Taiwan," in International Union for the Scientific Study of Population, *Contributed Papers* (Sydney Conference), pp. 363–370.

————. 1967b. *The Use of Household Registration Records in Measuring the Fertility Level in Taiwan.* Taipei: Institute of Economics, Academia Sinica.

LORIMER, FRANK. 1954. *Culture and Human Fertility.* Paris: UNESCO.

MATHEN, K. K. 1962. "Preliminary Lessons Learnt from the Rural Population Control Study of Singur," in Clyde Kiser, ed., *Research in Family Planning.* Princeton, N. J.: Princeton University Press.

NAG, MONI. 1967. "Family Type and Fertility," in World Population Conference, *Proceedings, 1965,* Vol. II. New York: United Nations.

NAMBOODIRI, N. KRISHNAN. 1967. "Fertility Differentials in Nonindustrial Societies." Unpublished paper.

NIMKOFF, MEYER E., and RUSSELL MIDDLETON. 1960. "Types of Family and Types of Economy," *American Journal of Sociology,* 46, 215–225.

PAKRASI, KANTI, and CHITTARANJAN MALAKER. 1967. "The Relationship between Family Type and Fertility," *Milbank Memorial Fund Quarterly,* 45, 451–460.

PETERSEN, WILLIAM. 1961. *Population.* New York: Macmillan.

PHELPS, HAROLD, and DAVID HENDERSON. 1958. *Population in Its Human Aspects.* New York: Appleton-Century-Crofts.

POTI, S. J., and S. DATTA. 1960. "Pilot Study on Social Mobility and Differential Fertility," in *Studies in Family Planning.* New Delhi: Government of India, Director General of Health Services.

PRESIDENT'S SCIENCE ADVISORY COMMITTEE. 1967. *The World Food Problem,* Vol. II. Washington, D. C.: U. S. Government Printing Office.

RELE, J. R. 1963. "Fertility Differentials in India: Evidence from a Rural Background," *Milbank Memorial Fund Quarterly,* 41, 183–199.

RYDER, NORMAN. 1955. "The Influence of Declining Mortality on Swedish Reproductivity," in *Current Research in Human Fertility.* New York: Milbank Memorial Fund.

STYCOS, J. MAYONE. 1958. "Some Directions for Research on Fertility Control," *Milbank Memorial Fund Quarterly,* 36, 126–148.

SURENDRANATHAN, N. G. 1965. "Family Organization in Kerala through Ages and Its Effect on Fertility," in R. S. Kurup and K. A. George, eds., *Population Growth in Kerala: Its Implications.* Trivandrum: Bureau of Economics and Statistics.

TAEUBER, IRENE B. 1958. *The Population of Japan.* Princeton, N. J.: Princeton University Press.

THOMLINSON, RALPH. 1965. *Population Dynamics.* New York: Random House.

UNITED NATIONS. 1961. *The Mysore Population Study.* New York.

In the differential analysis of family size, one recurrent comparison is by religion. The differences that show up, however, are seldom really related to religious beliefs as such. In the United States, most studies show that Jews have close to the lowest fertility—except when they are orthodox Jews, who have close to the highest. "Protestants" are too heterogeneous to classify as a single unit, and with respect to family size they also range from very high (Southern fundamentalists) to low (Northern middle class). Even the Roman Catholic Church, which has forbidden the use of the most effective contraceptives, is not unitary, especially in a comparison among several countries. France's marital fertility rate has long been one of the lowest in the world, and Ireland's one of the highest among Western nations. Perhaps the most ardent Catholics are—or used to be—in the Netherlands, for they became a self-conscious minority in a country established in a war against Catholic Spain. Though Dutch Catholics were given equal civil rights as long ago as 1853, some of their leaders still demand "emancipation." The effects of this stance on the church-related welfare agencies is the subject of the next paper.

The author, Dr. Anthon J. van 't Veer, teaches the sociology of administration at the University of Utrecht. He has also been in Utrecht's civil service (1946–60) and was recently elected to its City Council (1969–70).

ROMAN CATHOLIC FERTILITY IN TUDDEREN: AN ANALYSIS OF ONE FACTOR

Anthon J. van 't Veer

In his well known book on the fertility of Dutch Roman Catholics, van Heek (1954: 8; cf. van Heek 1956) posed the following questions, among others:

What factors account for the fact that the over-all fertility of Dutch Catholics is higher than that of non-Catholic groups in the Netherlands?

Do Dutch Catholics observe their Church's moral prescriptions, in particular those pertaining to the control of fertility, differently from Catholics elsewhere?

In answer to the first question, van Heek concluded that in the Netherlands marital fertility differs substantially between Catholics and non-Catholics. This is not, however, exclusively the consequence of religion *per se*, though this does play a very important role that generally is given too little attention.

In reply to the second question, he postulated that the relatively high fertility of Dutch Catholics, as compared with that of Catholics in other countries, is only one of many indications of their greater militancy and more forceful religious élan. Examples of this mental set can be divided into two categories: purely ecclesiastical, marked by A, and social-organizational, marked by B. The stance (1954: 164ff) is to be seen above all in Holland's sterner church organization, A, and in the separate organization of Catholic

SOURCE: Translated by William Petersen from "Het geboorteniveau van de Rooms-Katholieken in het Drostambt Tudderen," *Mens en Maatschappij*, 37 (1962), 24–28, and reprinted with the permission of the author and the journal.

trade unions and other secular associations, *B*. Other manifestations of this mentality include the tendency not to participate actively in non-Catholic international bodies, *B;* the stricter observance of Lenten duties, *A;* the fervent endorsement of large families, *A* and *B;* and the more rigid opposition to the use of contraceptives, *A*.

High evaluation of the large family has been classified as in both categories. When van Heek discussed the influence of religion on fertility (thus, how Catholic moral philosophy affects a stand on the population question), he used the term "religious factor" (see, for example, *ibid.:* 37, 45, 48, 58, 70, 97–98). Holland's relatively high birth rate he cited as partly a consequence of this factor. However, this influence is determined and maintained by the forces that we have divided into two categories, so that we can say that the "religious factor" in fact comprises two components.

In his book van Heek made no attempt to trace which of the two components exercised the greater influence. That would not have been easy, for in the Netherlands ecclesiastical and social Catholicism are closely interwoven. In order to differentiate the causes in such a situation, one would need a kind of social laboratory in which each of the categories could be eliminated in turn. We should thus look for a place where the Church is active but not its subsidiary organizations, or where the organizations are at work but not the Church.

The latter case can now be found in the bailiwick of Tudderen, near the township of Sittard, which was transferred to Dutch jurisdiction on April 23, 1949, as part of the correction of the Dutch-German border. Dutch Catholic social organizations are active in Tudderen, but ecclesiatical authority is exercised *not* by the Netherlands episcopate but by the bishop of Aachen. The area had a population of about 6,300, of whom 1,100 were Dutch. More or less the whole population is Catholic. This is thus not a district made up exclusively of Dutch Catholics, but one in which Dutch Catholic organizations are busy.

Now what happened to Tudderen's fertility? The birth rate, which averaged 19.5 in the period May 1949 to December 1950, rose to 25.0 in 1959, while over the same time the birth rate of contiguous German districts fell from 16.3 to 12.9. Since the populations of both areas are rather small, they respond more quickly to fluctuations in related factors and one can trace cause-effect patterns, therefore, only with the greatest caution. Under these circumstances it seemed desirable to use a moving average as the base of calculations. The rising trend is then unmistakable, as in the birth rates of Tudderen from 1951 to 1959 (see the third column of Table 1).

The comparable German district comprises Saeffelen, Breberen, Schümm, Gangelt, and Birgden, with a total population of about 8,600. Even though these data did not permit the calculation of a moving average, one can certainly posit a decline in fertility or—to be as cautious as possible—in any case no rise.

Table 1. Moving Averages of Marriages, Births, and
High-Parity Births per 1,000 Population,
Tudderen, 1951–59

YEAR	MARRIAGE RATE	BIRTH RATE	RATE OF 2ND AND LATER BIRTHS
1951	12.4	19.3	6.9
1952	12.2	19.4	7.2
1953	11.2	20.7	9.5
1954	10.3	20.1	9.8
1955	10.3	20.8	10.5
1956	10.3	22.8	12.5
1957	9.9	23.2	13.3
1958	9.6	23.9	14.3
1959	8.9	24.5	15.6

About Tudderen's fertility before 1950 the following is known (Coebergh 1952: 74): from September 1939 to October 1946 (that is, the war and immediate postwar period), the birth rate was 14.4; and from November 1946 to April 1949 (that is, during the postwar recovery), it was 14.5. Both these periods, obviously, were marked by abnormal circumstances. If the two decades from 1919 to 1939 can be taken as "normal," the birth rates then were 29.0 in 1919–25 and 23.2 from 1926 to May 1939. The comparable rates in the adjacent townships of the Dutch province of Limburg were, respectively, 37.6 and 31.0, and for the period May 1949 to December 1950 the rate was still 28.1. Under such circumstances, we can hardly interpret Tudderen's higher rates as a "restoration of prewar conditions," but must judge them in relation to the general fertility decline over the prior thirty years.

One might suppose that Tudderen's fertility rose because during the years of the Dutch administration there has been no war and the bailiwick's economic situation has improved. Thus, since there were no losses in military actions and emigration became less significant, one could conclude that more young men remained in the area. Consequently, more young persons may have married, with a rise in the number of births as a natural result. This argument, however, is not entirely tenable. There was indeed an important improvement in the bailiwick's well-being, but the adjacent territory that remained under German jurisdiction is not poverty-stricken. The standard of living has also risen there, even if relatively less. The argument concerning an improved economy and the absence of war applies no less to the present German territory, where presumably more young men ought also to have remained and married. But there the birth rate has not gone up.

There is a second line of argumentation. In spite of the young blood presumably present in Tudderen, nuptiality has fallen. Marriage rates calculated as a moving average declined steadily from 1951 to 1959, as shown in the second column of the table. But it could be that within a year of the ceremony each marriage produced a first-born child. The numerator of the birth rate is made up of these infants plus those of higher parity. But from the table it can be seen that the rise in the birth rate was due primarily to second and subsequent births—that is, to increasing family size. In about one-fifth of new marriages, assuming no control of conception, the birth of the first child—if there is one at all—comes later than during the first year.

If the rise in fertility was not caused by an improved welfare, or by a rise in nuptiality, or by the direct influence of Dutch Catholicism, there remains the influence of the Catholic social organizations that acculturated this new population to the life style of Limburg, the adjacent province of Catholic Netherlands. The organizations that began working in Tudderen found some Catholics there, both natives of Limburg and others, who were already following this life style; and their influence complemented and strengthened the endeavors of the new institutions.

The number of Catholic social organizations presently operating in Tudderen is not modest.

Catholic trade union movement:
  St. Joseph Construction Workers Union
  Roman Catholic Mineworkers Union
Catholic Workers Women's Organization
The Limburg Green Cross (a national health-insurance association, which in Limburg is informally linked to the Catholic Church), engaged in district nursing, courses for mothers, prenatal care, midwives' services, infant care, child care
Catholic Society for the Rehabilitation of Prisoners
St. Joseph Society for Convalescent Care
Mater Amabilis School
Roman Catholic social workers

Omitted from this list, it is interesting to note, are parochial evening classes for adults, teen-agers, and young mothers. The reason is that the Bishop of Aachen, who has jurisdiction over the territory, opposed them; for he reckoned these to be part of his terrain. Apart from a few mass meetings for young people of 15 years and over, the Dutch social organizations have been able to do nothing in this regard.

According to Coebergh (1952: 76), Tudderen's fertility had always been lower than that of the adjoining townships of Limburg. He ascribed this difference to the bailiwick's loss of young emigrants, which was linked to its social-ethical structure. Since Tudderen came under Dutch jurisdiction, it is just this social-ethical structure that may have been altered by the work of the Catholic social organizations.

What conclusions can be drawn from this presentation?

1. One must take into account the fact that what van Heek terms the religious factor is made up of at least two components, one purely ecclesiastical and the other social-organizational.

2. In a situation where the religious factor is exclusively the second component, this can be taken to be responsible for phenomena that van Heek ascribes to the whole factor.

3. Such a case pertains in particular to non-Dutch Catholics under the influence of Dutch Catholic social organizations. One can presume, however, that also in the Netherlands itself the social-organizational component of the religious factor may have a stronger influence on Dutch Catholics than the purely ecclesiastical one.

These conclusions must be regarded as suppositions. This caution is made necessary by the short time that the territory under study has been in this special situation. On the other hand, the suppositions are important enough, also for day-to-day practicalities, to be worth noting here. Nor should this paper be interpreted as a criticism of van Heek's theory, but rather a reinforcement of it. Van Heek himself called his study exploratory and called for further research (1954: 13, 115). The intent of this paper is to indicate the direction of such research that could be most fruitful—namely, a sociological and social-psychological investigation of the differential influence exerted by the two components of the religious factor. One must take into account, of course, the fact that Roman Catholics are made up of several social classes, and it is quite possible that susceptibility to the influence of one or the other component may therefore differ from one place to another.

References

COEBERGH, P. M. 1952. *Het Drostambt Tudderen.* Maastricht.

VAN HEEK, F. 1954. *Het geboorte-niveau der Nederlandse Rooms-Katholieken: Een demografisch-sociologische studie van een geëmancipeerde minderheidsgroep.* Leiden: Stenfert Kroese.

————. 1956. "Roman-Catholicism and Fertility in the Netherlands: Demographic Aspects of Minority Status," *Population Studies,* 10, 125–138.

It is often thought that religious faith is the only belief system that affects attitudes toward family size and thus population growth, but this is certainly not the case throughout the world. Latin America is an especially interesting arena to observe, for there all three of the ideologies most significant for population analysis—Roman Catholicism, several varieties of Communism, and avid nationalism—compete and interact. Ideology in Latin America is the topic of the next paper.

Its author, J. Mayone Stycos, is a professor of sociology at Cornell Uni-

versity, former director of its Latin American Studies Program (1962–66), and presently director of its International Population Program (1962 to date). He has been a consultant for the Agency for International Development (1962–64), a senior consultant on Latin America for the Population Council (1963 to date), a member of the Latin American Science Board of the National Academy of Sciences (1963–65). He is the author or editor of eleven books and numerous articles, almost all of which are concentrated on the topic to which he has devoted most of his professional life—fertility in Latin America, its determinants and consequences, and means of bringing it under control.

IDEOLOGY, FAITH, AND POPULATION GROWTH IN LATIN AMERICA

J. MAYONE STYCOS

The paradox of population in Latin America lies in the culture's inability to organize its immense land area and considerable natural resources for the benefit of a relatively *small* population. Given this inability, which has deep roots in the past, the continent's extremely rapid rates of population growth in recent decades can only be viewed as an expensive luxury. Our task is to see to what extent religious and political ideologies are obscuring the appreciation of this basic fact.

Low-income populations in Latin America have high fertility. Customarily, intellectuals of both North and Latin America attribute this fact to deep-rooted psychological drives for reproduction among the lower classes. This oversimplified and romanticized view unfortunately seems to be gaining a wide audience. Even so normally sober a journalist as James Reston loses control when dealing with the tantalizing concept of *machismo*—an attribute, according to Reston, which stems from the "stubborn vanity and stupidity of the ignorant male in Latin America, . . . [who is] worse than the baboon and worships the cult of virility long after he has forgotten the cult of Christianity. . . . The Latin male is not satisfied with love, he must have life—one new life a year, if possible, in order to prove he is good for something." [1]

The consequences of accepting such theories are not trivial, for the resistance of the baboon to social change is well known. If big families are

SOURCE: Reprinted from Population Reference Bureau, Selection No. 26 (1969), with permission of the author and the Bureau. The paper is also included in J. Mayone Stycos, *Ideology, Faith, and Family Planning in Latin America* (New York: McGraw-Hill, 1971).

[1] *New York Times,* April 9, 1967.

truly desired to prove the virility of men and the femininity of women, then family-planning services are a waste of time and resources. Indeed, this is exactly what some Latin Americans believe. But reputable opinion surveys in Latin America show that most men and women there do not conform to the simple-minded notion of *machismo*. On the average they want only three or four children.

In the absence of public discussion of family planning—and in light of widespread ignorance about the "controllability" of human fertility—we should not expect the attitudes of Latin American women to be intense, well crystallized, and unswerving. But at the same time we can have little doubt that, generally speaking, these women would prefer a moderate family size to a large one.

There are two basic things which can be done with such a latent preference: (1) wait for it to become activated "naturally" as a product of social and economic changes, or (2) reinforce and crystallize it through direct education.

IDEOLOGICAL CONFLICT

A "great debate" is now waging between spokesmen for these two alternatives. In this debate, support for the hypothesis that a demographic transition can be achieved by means of direct educational techniques comes from Donald J. Bogue (1966), who says: "Family-planning research . . . begins with the assumption that by the discovery of new principles we may be able to devise programs that can accomplish the desired results more quickly than would be possible if we waited for the solution along the lines of increased literacy, rising urbanization, improved levels of living, increased contact with technological-cultural change." We should note that Bogue is here not only propounding a theory of social change, but an *ideology*. It is therefore not surprising that his argument collides with at least one other combined theory of social change and ideology—Marxism.

Throughout most modernizing countries, and especially in Latin America, we can distinguish at least three major ideological types—the conservative, the social reformist, and the revolutionary. The conservative puts the *status quo* first and revolution last, reluctantly granting social change second place. The reformer puts social change first and the *status quo* last, with revolution occupying second place. The revolutionary puts revolution first and social change last. He prefers the *status quo* to social change because the latter might stem the revolution, while the former, growing more intolerable, can only precipitate it (Hirschman 1963). What places does population control occupy in this system of values?

Economists are increasingly of the opinion that population control can accelerate economic development by lowering the dependency ratio, reducing the cost of social services, shrinking unemployment, and raising per-capita product. While spreading the benefits of economic development less thin, it should generate economic development through increased savings for investments in capital-producing enterprises. Finally, by alleviating food shortages and other pressures attributable to population increase (such as rural overcrowding and urban migration), population control might ease social tensions. It should be noted that these gains from population control can take place *without* any radical change in the distribution of wealth, ownership of the means of production, and so forth. Quite rationally, therefore, population control should be most valuable to Latin American conservatives, of secondary importance to social reformists, and anathema to revolutionaries. But rational behavior is not a simple matter in Latin American societies.

As usual, the revolutionaries have reacted most consistently, rejecting population control as a palliative designed merely to ease revolutionary pressures and divert attention from the true source of society's ills—the capitalist economic system. More recently, some Marxists have softened their traditional hostility to Malthusian theory, at least to the extent of admitting that population growth can impede economic progress while birth control can alleviate population growth. These Marxists feel that birth control, however, will be a natural response to the revolutionary changes they are promoting. The fact that Communist nations have some of the most efficient birth-control programs in the world while condemning population control is proof that they are not opposed to birth control *per se*, but only to the *ideology* of population control and to its proposed sequence in the development of societies.

The conservatives, who should be most enthusiastic about birth control, are split because of conflicting ideologies and credos. In Latin America the conservatives tend to be the more traditional, orthodox Catholics, who may have moral objections to family planning. They also represent the business world which sees more consumers and cheap labor as the very fuel of industry. Finally, many conservatives are strongly nationalistic. They view their ever more populous nations with pride, and they regard population control as a new attempt by the colonial powers to emasculate Latin American societies. In this vein, the editor of El Salvador's *Diario de Hoy* (June 21, 1963) warns of "the true conspirators against our America, who come with a plan of massive destruction! They plan to destroy the capital of Latin America, to frighten away private investment, to socialize us before we have capitalized, and to block our growth, slashing the wombs of Latin mothers, castrating Latin males, before we have grown sufficiently or taken possession of the vast empty lands of the continent" (cf. Stycos 1965).

In point of fact birth control is making greatest headway among the liberal social reformers, who are becoming convinced that it can speed economic development without jeopardizing the social reforms they espouse. These liberals see birth control as a humane way to reduce abortion and illegitimacy and to increase personal freedom. Since they tend to be nominal Catholics or Leftist activist Catholics, they deem moral-religious considerations to be of secondary importance. Their main worry about family planning is the way the United States sometimes promotes it. The more they are told, by presidents of the United States and others, that five dollars invested in birth control is worth a hundred dollars invested in economic development (cf. p. 382), the more concerned they are that bargain-loving United States will choose the lesser investment. In addition, they are afraid that both American and local conservatives will substitute Lippes loops for agrarian reform.

To sum up these conflicting attitudes toward birth control, we can say that Latin Americans are ideologically divided over its desirability, sequence, and over-all place in the strategy of development.

ATTITUDES OF THE HIERARCHY

There are, furthermore, major differences according to religious faith. Although the Roman Catholic Church has tended toward a simple pronatalist ideology, its main position on birth control is more complex, stemming from its belief in a natural law which prohibits interference with the physiological consequences of the sexual act. In the past I have argued that this official tenet has little bearing on contraceptive practice in Latin America, but the recent Papal encyclical, *Humanae Vitae,* compels a reconsideration of the question. How have Latin American clergymen and laymen reacted to this controversial pronouncement?

Unmoved by the storm of protest among North American and European prelates, the Latin American hierarchy has responded to the encyclical in a relatively mild and orthodox manner, although few leaders were as blasé as the Puerto Rican churchman who announced that "the encyclical should cause neither alarm nor confusion among Catholics." [2] Aside from being a political victory for the Church's conservative wing, the encyclical was well received by those ascetic souls who saw a tidal wave of hedonism sweeping the world. A Costa Rican priest, congratulating the Papal Nuncio, referred to the "unbraked sensualism and hedonism threatening the family and society" and declared that the encyclical had "again saved the world from moral ruin." [3] Even more explicit was Colombia's Monseigneur Valencia Cano, who held that "exhibitionism in all forms is making continence impossible, with the logical *sequelae* of homosexuality and the most aberrant bestiality. . . . These excesses are most evident in the developed countries. . . . The encyclical is a violent but necessary brake to sexual corruption in the western world." [4]

[2] *El Mundo* (San Juan), July 31, 1968.
[3] *La República* (San José), August 3, 1968.
[4] *El Tiempo* (Bogotá), August 8, 1968.

In a number of countries the encyclical was turned against family-planning programs sponsored by the United States. The Archbishop of Tegucigalpa, Monseigneur Hector Enrique Santos, called the Honduras family-planning program "totally immoral" and tending to "develop prostitution," adding, "A foreign government which conditions its aid by programs of this kind is not a friend but an enemy which seeks to reduce us to permanent impotence." [5] In Costa Rica the Archbishop's office observed, "It would be interesting to find out how many thousands of dollars have been invested in Costa Rica in that campaign of disorientation and disrespect for human dignity." [6] The Apostolic Administrator of Colombia referred to United States aid in family planning as "a flagrant violation of the Rights of Man expressed in the United Nations Charter." [7] According to a Cartagena priest, "Any nation accepting such [birth-control] conditions enslaves in man the freest act of nature." [8]

While outright clerical opposition to the encyclical was rarely expressed publicly, two exceptions in Brazil should be mentioned. The Auxiliary Bishop of Porto Alegre and Secretary General of the National Bishops Conference, Dom Ivo Lorscheisder, flatly disagreed with the encyclical and favored the use of the contraceptive pill.[9] Even more spectacular was a large *Jornal do Brasil* headline announcing: "DEBATE AMONG PRIESTS APPROVES PILL 4 TO 1." The debate had taken place among several priests and physicians at the Conference of Brazilian Clergy before an audience of a hundred priests, friars, and secular Catholics. One priest called the text of *Humanae Vitae* totally obsolete. A Benedictine physician, Dom Tito, recommended to those of divided conscience that they "use the pill and practice periodic abstinence, thus giving each side its due." [10]

The debate goes on. Even in that center of conservative Catholicism, Medellín, Colombia, a newspaper reports that "young priests share the opinions of high churchmen in Europe and Canada that the encyclical was not what they had hoped for after the recommendation of the special papal commission," while "older priests stick firmly to the text and point out the grave sin of those who use artificial contraceptives." [11] We may anticipate attempts on the part of the conservative clergy to keep such outspoken views from the public. At the same time, however, other forces are working for an accommodation of conflicting opinions. The Latin American Assembly of the Christian Family Movement, categorizing the encyclical as neither "irreformable nor infallible," saw something new and unusual about it. "For

---

[5] *El Día* (Tegucigalpa), August 19, 1968.
[6] *La República* (San José), July 31, 1968.
[7] *El Espectador* (Bogotá), August 1, 1968.
[8] *Ibid.*, August 8, 1968.
[9] *Jornal do Brasil* (Rio de Janeiro), August 17, 1968.
[10] *Ibid.*, August 10, 1968.
[11] *El Espectador* (Bogotá), July 31, 1968.

the first time," it noted, "an encyclical is presented as a point of departure for subsequent reflection." [12]

REACTIONS OF THE PUBLIC

The ultimate impact of the encyclical will be not in what the Church does, but in what most Latin American Catholics do. It is far too soon to be sure about their response, and no summary analysis is intended here. But some early bits of evidence are available, of interest to those in the United States, Latin America, and elsewhere concerned about the effect of population growth on Latin American standards of living. For a preliminary look at the encyclical's influence, we divide our attention between the middle classes who, by and large, already control their fertility, and the lower classes, who do not.

Middle-class Women. It is not customary in Latin America for middle-class women to preach what they practice, but the encyclical gave them a rare opportunity to do so. Women in professional occupations were particularly sought out by journalists, since they were both newsworthy and articulate.

One of the remarkable conditions brought to light was the willingness of women of the middle and upper classes to speak in public about the birth-control issue. They not only freely discussed contraception but freely disagreed with the Pope. Their openly expressed opinions showed that a revolution had taken place among Catholic women—a revolution which the Church had been instrumental in creating.

In Colombia, *El Tiempo* published the names, occupations, and photographs of its interviewees. The excerpts below reveal the frank and aggressive flavor of the women's responses.[13]

A public-relations expert: The encyclical "seems counterproductive. . . . For years the university-educated classes have been practicing family planning. In my case, in ten years of marriage I have a boy of four and a girl of four months."

A secretary: "Many people will use their own methods and that's what I will do."

An artist: "May the Holy Father, during his visit to an underdeveloped country such as ours, realize the poverty and the demographic problems common to all Latin America."

A radio announcer: "The need not only to plan the family but especially to slow down the demographic explosion is so obvious that it is difficult to explain why the Church made a decision which officializes a latent schism."

Miss Bogotá: "It seems ridiculous that the Church would pronounce against contraception in the way it has. . . . We are in the midst of a

[12] *Ibid.*, August 27, 1968.
[13] *El Tiempo* (Bogotá), August 1, 1968.

terrible population explosion. . . . For people without education it is very difficult to pretend that periodic continence is adequate."

The most fascinating post-encyclical interview was a semiprivate one published in Costa Rica's *La República*. A reporter questioned six professional women in a group, published their names and photographs, but did not attribute any particular quotation to any particular woman.[14] The women were aware of these conditions, and their comments were exceptionally candid. Three examples follow:

"Most women are against the encyclical, but as we're Catholics and part of a Catholic society, it hurts us to speak publicly against it; and in practice we can't accept what is being asked."

"Rhythm is permitted, but what can assure us a normal cycle? The pills. Do we go back to pills to regularize menstruation? That's why the encyclical is extremely difficult to explain. Too drastic!"

"The problem for the priest is tremendous. I'm a good Catholic and go to him when I need advice, but two weeks ago he allowed me to use the pills. Now what? Two weeks ago it wasn't a sin and now it is."

The foregoing surveys are far from being systematic or scientific, nor do they present examples of opinions favorable to the encyclical. I only wish to point out that when professional women are willing to speak out with such intensity and frankness, it means that their freedom from ancient religious and sexual taboos is becoming a reality.

Lower-class Women. What effect will the encyclical have on lower-class Latin American women—when they hear of it, that is? Two weeks after the encyclical was issued, a hundred women attending out-patient clinics in Tegucigalpa, Honduras, were asked whether they had heard about the Pope's new statement. Ninety percent said they had not. On the chance that our sample was biased, we took another survey in 330 lower-income urban homes, most of which had radio sets. Three to four weeks after the announcement of the encyclical, only 20 percent of the women had heard about it. We asked members of this minority whether the encyclical had changed their thinking about family planning. Nine out of ten said no. Finally, we asked them whether the encyclical would change what they were *doing*. Half of them said no, *nobody* said yes, and the rest said they weren't doing anything.

We asked the women to tell us why they did not agree with the encyclical. Some of their answers:

"The Pope does not know the true life of the poor."

"The Pope will not help us to raise our children."

"The real evil is to bring children into the world to suffer, or to die in abortion."

"I am a Catholic but I am also poor, and it hurts to see my children without shoes and naked."

[14] *La República* (San José), August 11, 1968.

Such women could be taught the periodic-continence technique of birth control, but the Latin American clergy and the medical profession engaged in this instruction would have time for little else. In Colombia, where Catholic groups have tried to teach the rhythm method over the past two and a half years, the effort has been considerable and the results meager. The Jesuit University's family-planning clinic at San Ignacio Hospital in Bogotá has held more than 2,900 private consultations and enrolled over 1,870 women in fifteen short courses. What has been the result? A recent report has classified only 133 women as using rhythm (Garcia-Conti 1967). An even more intensive effort to spread the rhythm technique was made at the El Guabal Clinic in Cali. By the end of 1966 the clinic had arranged 2,393 medical consultations, 7,966 home visits or interviews by auxiliary nurses and social workers, and 188 group meetings. The result? Only 188 couples were using rhythm (Jaramillo Gomez and Londoño).

BUYING TIME

While it is too early to weigh the lasting effects of the encyclical, it appears to have had a greater impact on formal population programs than on individual consciences or behavior. Even with respect to family-planning programs, however, it is only a matter of time before public demand will compel governments to supply the necessary services. It may also be only a matter of time before the Roman Catholic Church adjusts to the new facts of life and the Leftists abandon their encouragement of misery as the shortest road to revolution. Timing, moreover, is the thing that population experts and economic planners are most likely to affect.

In Latin America, as in many parts of the world, a slowdown in population growth will advance the rate of economic development. Similarly, an acceleration of economic growth will ultimately slow the population boom. To say that rates of development and population growth are mutually related, however, is not to say that they are equally important. The dampening of population growth is more a means of promoting economic development than an end in itself. Population control will not alone solve the problems of starvation, crime in the streets, and political unrest. It will make the job easier, though, and it will buy the Latin American nations something they very badly need: time.

Unfortunately, as I have tried to show, the problem of Latin American population control is far from simple, surrounded as it is by ideological controversy, questions of religious faith, and suspicions of foreign political domination. In the light of these delicate considerations the internationalization of population-control programs should be given the highest priority. At the present time, North American foreign aid and North American foundations and private international agencies carry the brunt of the burden by default, since international population programs are painfully weak. The

United Nations continues to provide excellent demographic analyses, but it is not equipped to meet the urgent need for population programming. The Organization of American States recognizes the relevance of population trends to economic and social planning, but it cannot offer technical assistance since this is logically the province of the Pan American Health Organization (PAHO), whose program in family planning is weak in organization, staff, and conviction.

Clearly, the population-planning functions of these agencies need to be strengthened. If they cannot be raised to an effective level, then a new population agency, regional or international, must be created and given the funds, staffs, and mandate to do the job. No such agency could set population goals, but it could, on request, help any nation which has defined its own population targets. Thus, if Argentina wished to speed up its rate of population growth, a stronger PAHO or new regional agency would help it to do so. And if Honduras wished to slow down its rate of growth, it, too, would get effective assistance. No Church, no creed, no ideology should stand in the way of this approach to mankind's interests.

References

BOGUE, DONALD J. 1966. "Family Planning Research: An Outline of the Field," in Bernard Berelson *et al.*, eds., *Family Planning and Population Programs*. Chicago: Chicago University Press.

GARCIA-CONTI, FRANCISCO. 1967. "Third Report on the Development of Family Planning Program and Research in the Physiology of Reproduction," mimeographed. Bogotá: Colombian Association of Medical Schools.

Hirschman, Albert O. 1963. *Journeys Toward Progress*. New York: Twentieth Century Fund.

JARAMILLO GOMEZ, MARIO, and JUAN LONDOÑO. 1968. "Primera valoración comparativa de los servicios pilotos de planifición familiar," *Regulación de la Fecundidad* (Bogotá), Vol. 1.

STYCOS, J. MAYONE. 1965. "Opinions of Latin American Intellectuals on Population Problems and Birth Control," *Annals of the American Academy of Political and Social Science*, **360**, 11–26.

One of the commonest methods of analyzing either fertility or mortality, as several of the papers in the book illustrate, is to divide the population into what seem to be appropriate subgroups and compare their specific birth and death rates. Implicit in this commonplace method is a fact that is typically overlooked, or at least not stressed—that the demographic transition constitutes not only a rapid growth of the total population but a differential increase of its several parts. Certainly the variation is not the same as what Herbert Spencer termed the "survival of the fittest" (a phrase that Darwin accepted as "more accurate" than natural selection). Have the altered social conditions affected man's over-all hereditary quality, and if so in what direction? The discussion of this important question is not very often on a high level. A considerable proportion of social scientists magically eliminate all genetic influences by closing their eyes to them; and, on the other side, one school of eugenicists seems to consider nothing else.

The following paper, on the genetic implications of demographic trends, is a calm, reasoned, factually based analysis. The author, Dudley Kirk, holds the Dean and Virginia Morrison Professorship in Population Studies in the Food Research Institute and is a professor in the Department of Sociology at Stanford University. His return to academia in 1967 followed a long and distinguished career with the U. S. Department of State (1947–54) and as director of the demographic division of the Population Council (1954–67). Of his three books, Europe's Population in the Interwar Years *(1946) remains —in spite of its date—perhaps still the best single work on the population of Europe. His several dozen scholarly papers range over a number of demographic topics, with a continuing concern about policy as their principal connecting theme.*

GENETIC IMPLICATIONS OF DEMOGRAPHIC TRENDS

DUDLEY KIRK

The outstanding human biological fact of our time is the rapid multiplication of our species. In this country and most of the Western world, man has freed himself from many of the selective pressures that have kept his numbers down since his beginnings. Now this achievement is spreading to the rest of the world. The result is what is dramatized as the "population explosion." Western populations have undergone a revolution in their vital processes as fundamental as the industrial revolution and modernization in its impact on the individual. The vital revolution (or demographic transition, as it is more academically described) is the transition from wastefully high birth and death rates to the much more efficient lower birth and death rates that now prevail in the more advanced countries. The discussion relates to the United States, but similar developments are occurring in all advanced countries.

In all developed countries, both deaths and births are now largely controlled, on the one hand by mastery of the physical environment and on the other by the voluntary choices of couples on the number of their offspring.

SOURCE: Reprinted with slight editorial modifications from "Patterns of Survival and Reproduction in the United States: Implications for Selection," in National Academy of Sciences, *Proceedings,* 59 (1968), 662–670, with permission of the author.

In mortality, of course, "controlled" means postponed, not eliminated altogether. But postponement beyond the ages of reproduction is equivalent to immortality as a factor in natural selection. Similarly, the reduction in average number of offspring is chiefly the result of millions of couples' voluntary choice to restrict family size. Surveys show that over 90 percent of white couples of proved fertility practice birth control at some time during their married life. This practice is not always efficient, but in terms of statistical averages it is very effective in restricting family size. In 1800, the average American woman passing through her reproductive life had seven children; today she has three or less.

It seems reasonable to suppose that such major changes should have very important genetic effects. In any society natural selection occurs because different genotypes produce different numbers of offspring and because different proportions of offspring survive to the age of reproduction. It follows that differentials in reproduction and survival are important only to the extent that they involve important differences in genotype. I am here discussing not the actual genotypic selection (which is, of course, extraordinarily difficult to measure) but possible selection intensity under different demographic conditions—that is, the opportunity for natural selection.

SURVIVAL

There has been a dramatic reduction in mortality and hence presumably in selection intensity. While the fact is generally understood, the magnitude of the gains is probably not often recognized (Table 1). Only two-thirds of

Table 1. Percentages Surviving to Ages 15, 30, and 45, White Males and Females, by Year of Birth, United States, 1840–1960

YEAR OF BIRTH	AGE 15		AGE 30		AGE 45	
	MALES	FEMALES	MALES	FEMALES	MALES	FEMALES
1840	62.8	66.4	56.2	58.1	48.2	49.4
1880	71.5	73.1	65.7	67.4	58.3	61.1
1920	87.6	89.8	83.4	88.0	79.8	85.8
1960	96.6	97.5	95.1	96.9	92.9	95.9

SOURCE: Paul H. Jacobson, "Cohort Survival for Generations since 1840," *Milbank Memorial Fund Quarterly,* 42 (July 1964), 36–53.

the white females born in 1840 reached age 15 and only about half reached age 45. According to conservative projections, 97.5 percent of the females born in 1960 will live to age 15 and 96 percent to age 45. Females who die before the end of the reproductive years now constitute only about 4 percent, instead of 50 percent as in 1840.

Somewhat less progress has been made in reducing deaths among males. Of male cohorts born in 1960, it is estimated that less than 97 percent will survive to age 15, and about 93 percent to age 45. Furthermore, since male reproductivity generally starts later and continues beyond age 45 with a less abrupt termination than for women, the effect of mortality is greater at these higher ages. Consequently, selection intensity is somewhat greater for males, but still minimal in comparison with the past. Barring major catastrophes, further reduction of selection intensity for both sexes is almost certain, but of course within a narrow range, since it is already so close to zero. The data shown in Table 1, since they relate to the cohort's year of birth, involve projections, especially for those born in 1960. Already by 1965, current life-table values were approximating or had exceeded the projections given in the table.

Most of the force of natural selection is directed at maintaining stability —that is, canceling the maladaptations to the organism's environment that otherwise would occur. Has this "protective" selection been relaxed? Surely it must have. The force of this relaxation is somewhat ameliorated by several factors.

1. The major saving of life has been in the reduction of infectious and epidemic diseases through environmental means. It does not seem that genetically determined resistance to most infectious diseases (to the extent that it exists) is an adaptation of great consequence in modern society. Several of the great epidemic and endemic diseases—smallpox, cholera, plague—were mastered and largely eliminated in the 19th century. Since then, great progress has been made against those remaining: pneumonia and influenza, typhoid fever, tuberculosis, syphilis, diarrhea and enteritis, and the communicable diseases of childhood. Organic diseases are now the great killers—cardiovascular-renal diseases and cancers account for about three-fourths of all deaths. These organic diseases may depend more on genetic inheritance, but they are not so important in earlier life and therefore do not much affect survival to and through the reproductive period (cf. Spiegelman 1964). Largely because other causes have been so reduced, deaths by accident and violence are major causes of death prior to age 45. It is certainly nothing new to have negative selection of persons prone to accident and violence, but unhappily it seems unlikely that fatal automobile accidents will early lead to a genetically superior race of better drivers!

2. Deaths related to specific inherited defects have not been reduced nearly so much as the total. Thus, two-thirds of female deaths and over 60 percent of male deaths up to age 30 are now due to congenital malformations and diseases of early infancy, which often involve immaturity (U. S. Public Health Service 1967a, 2: Part B, Tables 1–4, 1–9). These include an important component of genetic defects, the most serious of which are still being removed from the population through deaths.

3. Were it possible to do so, the survival factor should be computed from

conception rather than from live births. Fetal wastage and stillbirth, especially of the malformed, are still high. The wastage in early pregnancy is believed to be very high, presumably much more important than subsequent fetal wastage and mortality in eliminating gross malformations and genetic anomalies.

It would be unwise to take much comfort from these ameliorative factors. Undoubtedly many persons of genetically weak constitution are now surviving who earlier would have succumbed to disease or to the harsher environment. Furthermore, determined efforts are being made to reduce infant deaths, including those involving genetic defects. It is reasonable to expect that an increasing proportion of individuals having a weak physical constitution and/or carrying deleterious mutations will survive and reproduce. The direction is not at issue; to measure the specific nature and rapidity of the changes is extremely difficult and is beyond the scope of this paper.

On the other hand, environmental gains are more than compensating for any genetic deterioration, as evidenced by the gains in physical stature, by the reductions in morbidity, and by the falling death rates themselves. Even more important, what is deteriorating is our fitness for the physical environment of the past, not that of the present or the future. The genetic qualities required for effective performance in a peasant or pastoral society are presumably very different from those required in our primarily urban and sedentary life. We are losing our adaptability for the former but certainly much less for the life of the present, and perhaps even less for that of the future.

REPRODUCTION

The commonplace that in modern societies natural selection by deaths has been replaced by the social selection of births is faulty in two ways. Selection by number of progeny, just as "natural" as selection by deaths, has usually been the more important element in the past, as it is in the present. Thus Spuhler's comparisons (1962) of selection intensity show that fertility components were more important than mortality in most of the numerous modern and premodern populations he analyzed.

Demographic changes in four areas affect the opportunity for natural selection through differential fertility: (1) mating and marriage, (2) childlessness, (3) number of offspring, and (4) age at childbearing and mean length of generation.

Mating and Marriage. The married state has become more prevalent in the United States over the last two generations, but particularly since 1940. Thus, of all men aged 14 to 44, the percentage currently married increased from 50.5 in 1940 to 61.2 in 1960; of women, from 58.7 in 1940 to 68.9 in 1960 (U. S. Bureau of the Census 1967). This increase was due to three factors: a larger percentage of men and women marry; they marry earlier;

and they spend more of their potentially reproductive years in marriage. To illustrate: in 1966, 95.0 percent of women aged 35 to 44 (that is, in the later years of childbearing) had ever married, as compared with 88.6 percent in 1910 and 91.4 percent in 1940. The median age at first marriage of men fell from 26.1 in 1890 to 22.8 in 1960; that of women from 22.0 in 1890 to 20.3 in 1960. As a consequence of this earlier first marriage, less widowhood, and higher rates of remarriage, more of the reproductive years are now spent in marriage despite a rise in divorce.

Childbearing is not entirely restricted to married couples: illegitimacy in the United States has risen rapidly. Since 1940, the estimated proportion of illegitimate births doubled for whites and increased by over 60 percent for nonwhites. According to national estimates based on statistics of states that report illegitimacy, 3.4 percent of white births and 24.5 percent of nonwhite births were illegitimate in 1964 (U. S. Public Health Service 1967b); and the true figures are doubtless higher. Mating outside of marriage, as well as marriage itself, has increased.

That the potential reservoir of parents has been increasing was in part responsible for the "baby boom." What it means genetically is that a larger percentage than previously of each cohort is exposed to the "risk" of child-bearing, especially through earlier and almost universal marriage. We are "reverting" to the situation prevailing in premodern societies, where marriage and mating are almost universal. Age at marriage is lower in the United States than in most other Western countries, but of course higher than in most premodern societies.

Childlessness.   In the United States there are three reasons why adults fail to have children: biological infecundity, failure to mate or marry, and the practice of birth control. The second and third are unimportant in most premodern societies, including our own at an earlier stage. In the United States a hundred years ago, only a tenth of the women living through the childbearing period were childless. With less marriage and at later ages, and more practice of birth control, 23 percent of women born in 1909 were childless. Now again, with more and earlier marriage, and probably greater success in the medical treatment of sterility, only 7 percent of married women and 12 percent of all women at age 35 are currently childless.

Mortality and childlessness are genetically the same: the persons concerned have no descendants. Combining these effects, about half the women born in 1840 did not participate in the reproduction of the next generation. Now the combined effect is only 15 percent: some 85 percent of each current female cohort not only survives but also produces offspring.

Number of Offspring.   As noted earlier, the average number of children born per woman is much lower than in the earlier years of our history—three or less versus seven. Surviving children per woman are much more comparable in number. While mortality has declined continuously, natality has not followed a continuous decline since the 1930s. After the Second World

War, the average number of children per woman rose from a low of 2.3 (for the female cohort born in 1909) to about 3 for those born in 1940, who have not yet completed their childbearing.

From the point of view of natural selection the variance is more important than the average (see Table 2), for the possible selection intensity of the

Table 2. Percentage Distribution of Offspring by Parity,
Selected Cohorts of Women, United States

| | DATE OF BIRTH OF COHORT | | | EXPECTED DISTRIBU- |
| | COMPLETED FERTILITY | | AT AGE 36 | TION, MARRIED WHITE |
PARITY	1871–75	1909	1928	WOMEN UNDER 40, 1962
0	17	23	11	4
1	16	22	12	7
2	14	22	24	26
3	12	13	22	28
4	10	8	14	21
5	7	4	8	7
6 and over	24	8	9	7
Total	100	100	100	100

SOURCES: Column 2: Wilson H. Grabill, Clyde V. Kiser, and Pascal K. Whelpton, *The Fertility of American Women* (New York: Wiley, 1958), p. 343. Columns 3 and 4: adapted from U. S. National Office of Vital Statistics, *Vital Statistics, Special Report* 51, 1, 1960, Table 2; *Vital Statistics of the United States, 1964,* Table I-19. Column 5: Ronald Freedman, David Goldberg, and Larry Bumpass, "Current Fertility Expectations of Married Couples in the United States, 1963," *Population Index,* 31 (1965), 3-20.

natality component did not fall with the long secular decline in family size. This anomaly is explained by the fact that reduction of the mean number of children does not necessarily reduce the variance, but the contrary. Thus, the index of selection intensity for the fertility component (or the variance in the number of children born divided by the square of the average number born per parent) was 0.710 for women born in 1871–75, who averaged 3.5 children. For women born in 1909 the index was 0.881, with an average of only 2.3 children, the lowest number of any American cohort (Crow 1958). With the recovery of the birth rate after 1940, the index will certainly decline sharply, although the women concerned have not completed their childbearing. There will almost certainly not be much increase at higher parities, which would contribute heavily to variance, since birth rates at the higher reproductive ages are now very low. Finally, if the expectations of married white women under age 40 in 1962 are realized—with 75 percent in the range 2 to 4 (Freedman *et al.* 1965)—the index for this group will decline to 0.26.

Since 1957 the "baby boom" has receded, and the birth rate in 1966 was the lowest for any year since 1936. This relates to changes in the age structure and may or may not portend a reduction in family size. The recent drop certainly is not just the result of the pill; during the 1930s couples were just as successful in birth control with other methods. But the facts that contraceptive methods are becoming easier and more reliable, that family planning is therefore more effective, will probably further restrict the number of high parities.

Parental Age. The intrinsic rate of natural increase is determined not only by the number of children, but also by the length of generation. A couple marrying and having children early have a higher rate of reproduction than one marrying and having the same number of children late. Recent demographic trends have also reduced this source of differential fertility. Not only is marriage earlier, but intervals between marriage and first and subsequent births have been reduced, so that births are increasingly concentrated in the early childbearing years. The average length of the female generation has declined from 28 years in the 1930s to 26 at the present time, with less variance around the mean. The median American woman is married before she is 21, has her first child at that age and her third and last at age 27. The average woman's childbearing period has been reduced to about 7 years.

This concentration of childbearing in young ages and at low parities has a direct genetic influence, since a number of genetic disorders are correlated with age of mother, birth order, and number of children per family. These include new mutations, such as Down's syndrome (mongolism), and genetic factors in combination with environmental factors, such as Rh-erythroblastosis, congenital malformations of the circulatory and nervous systems, cerebral palsy, and so on. Canadian data suggest that older mothers of high parity have twice the incidence of the latter type of disorder, as compared with young mothers of low parity (Newcombe 1964). Reviewing Japan's experience between 1947 and 1960 (that is, earlier childbearing and smaller families), Matsunaga (1966) estimates a reduction by one-third for mongolism, more than half for Rh-erythroblastosis, and on the order of one-tenth for the remaining defects. These data suggest the order of magnitude in gains from concentration of childbearing at lower ages and lower parities. Furthermore, reduction of the number of siblings limits the opportunity for consanguineous marriage and for inbreeding in general, and hence cuts the number of births with defects arising from such marriages.

Differential Fertility. Within the total population discussed so far, there are major differences in reproduction by social, economic, religious, and ethnic characteristics. Historically there were, for example, enormous differences between the urban dweller and farm resident, the uneducated and the college graduate, the professional and the laborer, and so on. These differentials evoked fears that we were "breeding from the bottom," with the least capable producing the most children.

Whatever their earlier significance, socio-economic differentials in fertility have contracted since the Second World War, especially between 1950 and 1960, for such characteristics as rural-urban residence, occupation, income, and education (U. S. Bureau of the Census 1955; 1964). Most elements in the population have shared in the increase in fertility, but especially those with better education, more income, and higher occupation, and this has narrowed the differentials.

To take a single, rather dramatic example: in 1950, white women aged 40 to 44 with less than eight years of schooling who had ever been married had over twice as many children as those with four or more years of college. In 1960, this margin had been cut to 50 percent more, and with current trends it will have declined by 1970 to below 40 percent more. Women of intermediate educational levels fall between these extremes, and because of a general upgrading of education there is now less variance about the mean. Thus, the completed fertility of married women with four or more years of college, only 59 percent of the average for all married women born in 1901–05, rose to 73 percent for women born in 1916–20, and presumably will rise to between 89 and 93 percent for women born in 1926–30. The gap between the most educated and the average is much less than before.

This reduction is not so true of two other fertility differentials—by religion and by race. In this country Catholic fertility has been consistently higher than non-Catholic, and this difference has probably not narrowed in recent years. The genotypic significance of this difference is obscure. In any case, the rapid change in Catholic attitudes about family planning may well result in a convergence in birth rates by religion.

The position of the nonwhite population (chiefly Negro) is quite different from the white. The opportunity for natural selection remains much higher as regards both mortality and natality. Twice as high proportions of Negroes die before reaching age 15 and age 45. Negro women have more children, more widely scattered through the childbearing period, but more Negro women are childless in marriage. The result is greater variance in number of offspring and more opportunity for natural selection. Differential fertility is also much greater: reproduction of urban, educated, and middle-class Negroes is similar to that of whites, whereas that of low-income and rural Negroes is much higher than of whites of comparable socio-economic status. At present the Negro birth rate is declining as the low-fertility elements become a larger part of the whole. The same forces are at work among Negroes as among general population—reduction in mortality, family size, and fertility differentials—but in each case the process has not gone so far. The population has and for some time will have a growing proportion of Negroes—the percentage of nonwhite births increased from 14.4 in 1950 to 15.8 in 1960 and to about 16.9 in 1965 (U. S. Public Health Service 1967a; 1967b).

SUMMARY AND CONCLUSIONS

Demographic trends in the United States are strongly reducing the opportunity for natural selection. This is the result of several convergent elements.

1. The mortality component in selection intensity has been dramatically reduced. There is surely some dysgenic effect, notably from the survival of deleterious mutations, but environmental changes have made some hereditary defects irrelevant, such as susceptibility to diseases that now are curable.

2. A larger proportion of persons in the reproductive ages are married, and hence exposed to the "risk" of childbearing, than a generation ago. There is also less childlessness and perhaps some decrease in physiological sterility. About 85 percent of each white female cohort born now lives to adulthood and participates in the reproduction of the next generation.

3. Since 1940 the average number of children per couple has risen somewhat after the long secular decline in fertility ending in the 1930s. There is a growing concentration of couples with two to four, and especially two or three, children. The variance and hence the opportunity for natural selection through variability in numbers of offspring are much reduced.

4. The average length of generation has fallen and the variance has diminished, owing to the concentration of births to parents in their 20s and early 30s.

5. Differential fertility between socio-economic groups is generally declining. Potential selectivity by residence, occupation, income, and education is thereby diminished. An important exception is race: Negro fertility and mortality are declining, but both are still substantially higher than for whites. The opportunity for natural selection is higher in the Negro population.

There is a growing homogeneity in reproduction. According to the seeming trend of the white population of the United States, the great majority will continue to live to adulthood, marry, and have two or three children. To the extent that this occurs, each generation will be close to a genetic carbon copy of its predecessor, aside from mutations that are absorbed by the genotype.

At the same time, it must be emphasized that present fertility could change rapidly, as it has in the past. Furthermore, the genetic implications could be modified, for example, by an increase in assortative mating, which would rearrange genes without necessarily changing their frequency in the total population. The levels and trends of mortality have been more stable: barring catastrophe, the very low mortality at younger ages will continue. A relaxation of selection intensity of the degree and durability now existing among American and Western peoples has surely never before been experienced by man.

The potential results are not clear and will require far more sophisticated analysis. In the short run, present demographic trends are reducing the incidence of serious congenital anomalies because of the younger average age at childbearing, the lower average parities, and the reduction of consanguineous marriages. And surely medical and environmental correction of genetic defects will far outrun the effects of the deleterious mutations. The longer-run effects depend upon the potential increase in mutational loads and how serious these may prove to be in a rapidly changing environment more and more created by man himself.

References

CROW, JAMES F. 1958. "Some Possibilities for Measuring Selection Intensities in Man," *Human Biology*, **30**, 1–13.

FREEDMAN, RONALD, DAVID GOLDBERG, and LARRY BUMPASS. 1965. "Current Fertility Expectations of Married Couples in the United States, 1963," *Population Index*, **31**, 3–20.

MATSUNAGA, EI. 1966. "Possible Genetic Consequences of Family Planning," *Journal of the American Medical Association*, **198**, 533–540.

NEWCOMBE, H. B. 1964. "Screening for Effects of Maternal Age and Birth Order in a Register of Handicapped Children," *Annals of Human Genetics*, **27**, 367–382.

SPIEGELMAN, MORTIMER. 1964. *Significant Mortality and Morbidity Trends in the United States since 1900*. Bryn Mawr, Pa.: American College of Life Underwriters.

SPUHLER, J. N. 1962. "Empirical Studies on Human Genetics," UN–WHO Seminar on the Use of Vital and Health Statistics for Genetic and Radiation Studies, *Proceedings*. New York: United Nations.

UNITED STATES. BUREAU OF THE CENSUS. 1955. *U. S. Census of Population, 1950:* Special Report P–E, No. 5C, "Fertility." Washington, D. C.: U. S. Government Printing Office.

———. ———. 1964. *U. S. Census of Population, 1960:* Final Report PC(2), Part 3A, "Women by Number of Children Ever Born." Washington, D. C.: U. S. Government Printing Office.

———. ———. 1967. *Current Population Reports*, Series P-20, No. 159. Washington, D. C.: U. S. Government Printing Office.

———. DEPARTMENT OF HEALTH, EDUCATION AND WELFARE. 1965. "White–Nonwhite Differential," *Indicators* (September). Washington, D. C.: U. S. Government Printing Office.

———. PUBLIC HEALTH SERVICE. 1967a. *Vital Statistics of the United States, 1965*. Washington, D. C.: U. S. Government Printing Office.

———. ———. 1967b. *Natality Statistics Analysis, 1964*. Series 21, No. 11. Washington, D. C.: U. S. Government Printing Office.

10 POPULATION POLICY

If Dudley Kirk is correct in his analysis of how the structure of population growth has affected the genetic quality of the human species, then the over-all improvement in the environment has resulted (or, with respect to some variables, may have resulted) in a partial deterioration of the human stock. Policymakers of every nation continue trying to raise the level of living and to reduce the death rate, but the eugenics movement has few adherents anywhere. The next essay poses the question, "Why?" and offers a novel answer.

Its author, Kingsley Davis, is the Ford Professor of Sociology and Comparative Studies at the University of California at Berkeley and director of International Population and Urban Research on that campus. Among his other important posts, he has been president of both the American Sociological Association (1959) and the Population Association of America (1962–63), chairman of Section K and vice-president of the American Association for the Advancement of Science (1963), and United States representative to the UN Population Commission (1954–61). No partial list could do justice to his writings. The books and journal articles on demographic topics are distinguished by Davis's persistent and often pioneering efforts to analyze population phenomena in a sociological context—as in this paper.

366

SOCIOLOGICAL ASPECTS OF GENETIC CONTROL

KINGSLEY DAVIS

The organic world represents a compromise between stability and change. On the one hand, the segregation of the germ cell partially insulates each species from temporary environmental disturbances. On the other hand, random mutations and enduring environmental shifts gradually alter the species through natural selection. A comparable but less recognized reconciliation of stability with change is achieved in human societies. Once it is granted that *Homo sapiens* participates in these two distinct systems of compromise between stability and change, several implications can be drawn. One inference, for example, is that attempts to improve mankind— that is, to thwart stability and maximize desired change—can deal with either system. They can alter the biological capacities and traits of the human organism by artificial selection, or they can reform the culturally transmitted institutions through social movement. Interestingly, only one of these methods—the second—has ever been tried. The genetic approach, though sometimes discussed, has never been used for human beings on a significant scale, despite its success with plants and animals.

We thus come to a puzzling scientific question. Since the two methods of human reform are not mutually exclusive, why is it that only one has been utilized? Each method rests on a distinct and effective principle. Beyond doubt the inherited make-up of a species can be altered by planned intervention. Beyond doubt a social system can be changed by deliberate effort. It follows that any proposed improvement in man's condition could theoretically be pursued by both methods at once with no conflict (unless of course the improvement excludes one or the other method by definition). Not only is there no logical conflict between the two principles of human improvement, but the possibility needs to be faced that, in the long run, they are mutually dependent. Obviously, the two are capable of considerable independent variation. Some social change is possible without genetic change, and probably the reverse is true. There has apparently been little human evolution during the last 30,000 years, a period during which there has been the greatest sociocultural change.

> There has been no increase in brain size since the time of Neanderthal . . . nearly 100,000 years ago! . . . Cro-Magnon man, who entered history about 30,000 years ago, differs physically from modern man no more than do various modern races of man from each other (Mayr 1963: 652–54).

SOURCE: Reprinted in a slightly abridged form from John D. Roslansky, ed., *Genetics and the Future of Man* (Amsterdam: North-Holland Publishing Co., 1967), with the author's permission.

Two peoples as genetically different as the Japanese and the Northwest Europeans now have social systems more like each other than either is like its own prior feudal system. But one would have to be sanguine indeed to maintain that there is no limit to the independent variation of the two principles governing the human species. The evolution of an ever more complicated technology, for example, may reach an eventual plateau due to the limitations of the human brain, both in average and in extreme mental capacity. The genetic damage from nuclear weapons in the next world war may prove so great that present civilization cannot be maintained.

If both genetic control and social reform are potentially effective, and if they are not mutually exclusive, then why has one been used to improve life and the other not? Why, for instance, has the eugenics movement never left the ground? A possible answer is that genetic improvement is a long, slow process, whereas social reform promises quick results. In keeping with what was said above, however, we must remember that the speed of social change is generally exaggerated. A high proportion of what passes for social reform tends to prevent rather than to induce long-run social change. Social-reform efforts are like mutations; most of them are dysfunctional and therefore lethal or short-lived. Since the parts of a society, like an organism, are interlinked, even a successful solution of one social problem often ultimately defeats itself by creating one or more unforeseen and unendurable new problems. On the other hand, the slowness of induced genetic change is commonly exaggerated. Some of the quickest results of scientific breeding are achieved in the first generation (cf. Stern 1960: 650–57), which can hardly be said of most successful social reforms or revolutions. It is therefore not certain that as a general rule social reform is speedier than genetic reform.

Other common explanations can be dismissed as patent rationalizations. It is alleged, for example, that the science of genetics is not sufficiently developed to make genetic control feasible, but animals and plants were successfully bred long before Mendelian genetics was born. Again, it is alleged that human beings cannot agree on the traits they consider desirable. This is true, but they cannot agree on anything; failure to agree does not prevent their stating and enforcing rules that provide social control and stability. Actually, there is more agreement on human traits considered desirable than on many other matters (cf. Carter 1962a: 245–46).

My view is that the main reason why human genetic control has never been seriously tried does not lie in the slowness of genetic change, in the paucity of genetic knowledge, or in the lack of consensus. It lies rather in the stubborn resistance to change inherent in human societies. In other words, eugenics is itself a social movement. Before it can be effective genetically, it has to be effective socially. It has a double barrier to cross, because it combines in a peculiar way the two systems of transmission in the human species. The changes in society that would be required to succeed in a program of human genetic control would be so fundamental that they would tend to dwarf all previous social revolutions. The socially transmitted sentiments and behavior patterns that would have to be disturbed are so deep in the minds of all of us that any imagined escape from them seems either horrible, paradoxical, or ridiculous, because they turn into pure means the things that we conceive to be ultimates.

INTENDED VERSUS UNINTENDED GENETIC CONTROL

Since men live in a sociocultural environment, their genetic make-up is inevitably shaped by the long-run continuities and discontinuities in this environment. Overwhelmingly, however, the effects of sociocultural patterns on heredity are not only unforeseen but also unrecognized. Thus, people are not normally aware of statistical regularities in their mating patterns. When age at marriage is mentioned, they think of the "legal age." When selection of partners is mentioned, they think of their personal tastes and do not realize the trait homogamy and the geographical propinquity that characterize the mating of the population in general. They are reasonably aware of the laws and customs pertaining to marital selection but not of the genetic effects of these norms or of the effects of behavioral regularities existing independently of norms.

So the great bulk of social influences on genetic change have to be sharply distinguished from deliberate genetic control. However, it is precisely these social factors which give rise to most of the problems that make us regard genetic control as desirable. A typical argument for genetic control takes the following form: A given social pattern is resulting in hereditary selection that may prove unfortunate in its consequences; therefore, some special effort must be made—that is, some control measure must be adopted —to alter the pattern in question. Usually the genetic consequences are inferred from the social practice itself, without satisfactory independent evidence (for example, with respect to traits which, like general intelligence, are polygenic in character). But in other instances (for example, the effect of medical successes on the diffusion of single-gene diseases), the biological evidence may be substantial. In any case the arguments for genetic control all rest on the belief that the existing sociocultural environment, either in whole or in part, is resulting in a pattern of genetic selection that is less desirable than could be achieved by deliberate effort.

This view clearly implies that remedial action is possible, despite a common semantic confusion over "the survival of the fittest." By definition, those biological strains that expand their numbers most rapidly are "best adapted" to their environment. Such "fitness," however, does not mean that the strain in question is "most desirable" or that it will prove "most fit" in the future. "Nature" does not compel us to continue a sociocultural environment which, in propping up or correcting the defective phenotype, inadvertently gives survival power to the myopic, stupid, diabetic, deaf, or schizophrenic genotype. In altering the selective system we may wish to be humane (no one wants to deny insulin to the diabetic or forgo correction of pyloric stenosis), but to save the defective and yet pay no attention to their reproduction is shortsighted, because it favors the present generation at the expense of many future ones.

If a part of the social system is bringing about a result felt to be deleterious, then another part (some control apparatus) will have to be created to correct it. But the fact that the deleterious practices form a part of the existing social system indicates that they control the behavior of the very population which presumably is being asked to change them. In India, for example, the forces motivating a parent to marry off his daughters at any cost, regardless of their condition, help to keep defective traits in the gene pool; but since this parental obligation is an integral part of a wider social order, it cannot be changed overnight. The Indian parent will not alter his behavior toward his daughter's marriage simply because of its genetic effect on the population. He is not worried about the gene pool, but about the opinion of his neighbors, relatives, and caste mates; he is concerned with meeting his religious and kinship obligations. In the same way, the obligation of a husband in the United States to prevent his wife from committing adultery—including even opposition to artificial insemination with sperm from a donor—is not likely to be set aside in the interest of genetic improvement.

Too often the obstacle to some recommended social change is thought of as simply an attitude. The remedy is then equally simple—it is to "change people's attitudes" by suitable propaganda, advertising, or education. But, unfortunately, battles are not won by psychological warfare alone. The motivation for conduct is determined by economic interests, social rewards and penalties, political pressures, organic needs, group loyalties, force and the threat of force—all structured in an ongoing and complex social milieu. It follows that no change of attitude will prove possible unless the social and economic conditions causing the attitude are changed.

In the case of genetic control it is clear that the parts of the social system that would have to be changed are especially resistant to alteration. This can be seen when we realize that the social structures most relevant to genetics are those having to do with health and medical practices on the one hand and with marriage and the family on the other. These govern, respectively, the two processes involved in biological selection: mortality and reproduction. In both cases extremely strong motivation is encountered—in the first, because good health and physical survival are at stake; in the second, because the institutions governing sexual expression, pregnancy, and childrearing are involved.

On the medical side, it is precisely the success of the social controls tending to maximize survival that is producing genetic trends that many people find alarming. In India in 1911–21 the death rate was such that only

38 percent of the males born would survive to age 20 (Davis 1951: 240). In the generation of white males born in the United States in 1840, 61 percent survived to age 20, whereas it is estimated that among those born in 1960 over 96 percent will live to that age (Jacobson 1964). In other words, not long ago in human history mortality prior to the age of reproduction was the principal mechanism for positive genetic selection in human populations. The remarkable constitution built up by this selective process forms the rich genetic inheritance that the human species is coasting on at present. Now, however, to all intents and purposes, selection on the basis of differential mortality has been eliminated, because virtually nobody dies before the reproductive period and very few before the end of it. Jacobson estimates that among the white females born in 1960 in the United States, 96 percent will survive to age 45.

The social controls yielding such complete success in nonselectivity are so strong that there appears no possibility whatever of changing them. Most of the state laws of this nation, for example, do not permit abortion even in order to prevent a genetically damaged child from being born; it seems unlikely that permitting death after birth will be tolerated. Instead, we can confidently expect that the proportion of defective phenotypes in the population will continue to rise—because the excess mortality once characterizing such defectives has all but disappeared.

If this conclusion is correct, then the entire burden of eugenic policy is thrown onto the reproductive side. (We are now speaking of selection only. There is, of course, another aspect of eugenic policy, which is that of minimizing radiation and other causes of predominantly deleterious mutations.) Here the formidable system of religious and moral control over sexual and family relations is encountered. An examination of what this means will prove illuminating.

GENETIC CONTROL AND THE FAMILY

Perhaps the most fundamental obstacle to genetic control through deliberate reproductive selection lies in a curious fact. The human species has retained a very primitive mode of social organization with respect to human reproduction. It has retained a system in which people are connected socially by birth (kinship) and in which responsibility for the rearing of children is primarily given to those who biologically engender them. In some ways, indeed, the form that this system takes in modern industrial society is more elementary than it is in primitive communities, for in the latter there is often a highly institutionalized and fictional quality in extended kin relations and frequently a lack of concern with whether or not a child is biologically "one's own."

In industrial societies the elementary unit—the nuclear family, consisting of the reproducing pair (the parents) and their own offspring (the children)

—stands out. It is about as simple as a familial mode of reproduction can be made, and yet it is the means by which the most complex human societies replace themselves. There is a serious question, however, whether it is too frail a vehicle for the duties it is asked to perform. Certainly, under the conditions of an industrial open-class society, it appears to function in a dysgenic way.

In the hunting and gathering economy that prevailed throughout most human history, the cultural apparatus was not elaborate enough to mediate greatly between the individual organism and his physical environment. Since mortality in early life was very high, the burden of genetic selection did not fall very heavily on the reproductive side. But even with respect to reproduction, the family system did a fair job of favorable breeding. It did so primarily by a slight complication of the family unit—namely, polygyny.

There is considerable confusion in ethnographic literature over the meaning of polygyny. The confusion seems mainly to stem from thinking of societies as being synonymous with "a culture," or a set of "customs." By this conception, if the society "allows" polygyny, it is "polygynous." However, the fact that a social system allows something does not make it prevalent, nor does the fact that it does not allow something make it nonexistent. Thus, Latin American countries do not permit polygyny (at least in their official religious and legal machinery), but a significant portion of Latin American men have more than one woman who is bearing their children. We are referring to *de facto* polygyny, regardless of whether or not it is *de jure*. Unfortunately, it is easier to get information on what people in a society say should be done than to get data on what they actually do. But even on an ethical basis Ford and Beach (1951: 108) found that in 84 percent of their sample of 185 societies "men are permitted by custom to have more than one mate at a time." Similarly, Murdock (1949: 28) found in his sample of societies that 193 permitted and encouraged polygyny and only 43 did not. (There is no warrant that I know of for the statement by Mayr [1963: 651] that "most cases of polygyny among contemporary peoples were . . . secondarily derived from a preceding monogamy.") Polygyny persisted with amazing tenacity. It is found in most agrarian societies today, including Latin American countries and virtually the whole of Africa. The practice has meant that the most successful males sired a disproportionately large share of the next generation.

However, as the neolithic revolution spread widely throughout the world, the human species was able to put a much more elaborate cultural technology between itself and the noncultural environment. The selective value of polygyny accordingly changed character. With the domestication of plants and animals, the successful male was not necessarily the keen-eyed and swift hunter, but perhaps the myopic schemer, the social manipulator, and the inheritor of property. Furthermore, the second and third mates (whether wives or concubines) tended to be drawn from the less advantaged economic strata, with unknown effects on genetic selection, if any.

In industrial societies there has doubtless been an increase in plural mating, but the further development of technology—in this case, contraception and abortion—has freed such mating from procreation and hence from genetic significance. Enduring unions involving an otherwise married man and giving rise to children have therefore become rare in advanced countries. How this has come about can be understood in terms of the changing interrelation between the family and the rest of the social order as modern society emerged. With the shift of production from the home to the factory or office, the economic value of the housewife declined. A wife remained financially valuable only if she ceased to be merely a housewife—that is, if she entered the outside labor force; but if she did that, she received remuneration of her own and thus acquired independence. Furthermore, with the opening up of jobs to women on an individual basis, regardless of their marital status, women no longer had to form an enduring sexual union with a man in order to gain an adequate livelihood. Therefore, even when they came from the lower classes, they were not forced to accept a secondary or tertiary marital or concubinal relationship with a male. They could either remain unattached or marry a relatively unsuccessful male and help him out by participating in the labor force. In turn the first wife was more independent and thus less likely to tolerate her husband's taking a second mate. At the same time, the man found that a second wife or concubine had less and less utility to him. She was not productive; the value of her children was virtually nil, again because production had largely shifted from the home and because an education was increasingly required; and sexual gratification was possible without a durable legal commitment to the woman and without her bearing children. For these reasons the marginal utility of a second mate, in relation to the cost and trouble, became negative.

MONOGAMY, DEATH CONTROL, AND FAMILY PLANNING

The closer the economy is to subsistence, the more selective it is from the standpoint of traits adapted to the physical, or noncultural, environment. With the improved control of mortality in the 19th century, the number of living children in the household rose to an unprecedented average. This, together with the increased cost of children and their growing disutility except as playthings and ego surrogates, led to the use of birth control. The result was that the ambitious man and woman, instead of contributing more than their share to the next generation, contributed a lesser share. Their aspirations were higher for themselves and their children, and their knowledge and use of birth control techniques were superior to those of the less successful. The class differences in fertility began to widen noticeably in the latter half of the 19th century in the industrializing countries, reached their greatest spread some time around the turn of the century, depending upon the circumstances of the particular nation, and eventually (most noticeably during the period of the baby boom after the great depression) began to contract (Westoff 1954; Kiser 1960). The class differentials have thus declined in magnitude, and with the shift to lowest levels among the middle strata, the inverse correlation of reproduction with occupational status has become less pronounced. This is particularly true when success within the broad occupational or educational strata is analyzed, for then it is often found that success and fertility are positively correlated (Carter 1962b).

There is no reason to believe that the inverse correlation between fertility and social status will soon completely reverse itself, despite wishful thinking. The reason is that one of the conditions supporting the inverse association is not likely to change—namely, the factor of greater aspiration among those who are in, or rise to, the upper social strata. Even though contraceptive techniques may become so simple that anybody, no matter how inefficient, can control births, it may still remain true that those who count on getting ahead in life, and having their children do so, will on the average have fewer offspring. Furthermore, the family-allowance schemes that many countries now have—for example, Canada, France, Belgium, and Sweden—tend, if they increase fertility at all, to have more effect upon those in poor than on those in good circumstances, because the lower the income the higher the ratio of the child allowance to it. Progressive income taxes, liberal welfare schemes, increased prevalence of premarital conception among juveniles, ease of youthful marriages, quick cure of venereal diseases, and subsidized housing for lower-income groups—all of these characteristics of contemporary society are conducive to a negative relation between socio-economic status and fertility. There are of course factors pushing in the opposite direction. To a certain extent children have become items of conspicuous consumption which the better-off can afford. Also, children are easier to care for if the family can afford to live in spacious suburbs and to withdraw the wife completely from the labor force. No one knows for sure what will happen in the future, but I would expect that approximately the present situation will continue for some time—that is, that reproduction will be highest at the two ends of the socio-economic scale and lowest among those in the middle who are too educated to have children carelessly and too poor to have them abundantly. In the meantime, in the majority of the world still groping toward a modern social system, the class differences in fertility will probably become greater before they become smaller again.

Not only does the small nuclear family, as affected by the rest of industrial society, fail to produce unintended positive genetic selection, but it also militates against policies deliberately aimed at genetic control. This can be seen in the curious polarization of modern life. In most primitive and archaic agrarian systems there is a great deal of economics in household and kinship groups (because these are still productive organizations) and a great deal of companionship in other work groups (because these are stabilized and traditional). In our type of society, however, the economic and professional world is so much involved with rapidly changing technology that work relations are competitive and instable. Any individual must be emotionally prepared to break bonds easily, to start life again in a new neighborhood or community, to deal with a new boss. Even the physical surroundings change so rapidly that attachment to the place where one grew up is attachment to only a memory.

My purpose is not to condemn these societal traits. They are simply the features of societies that have a high level of living. But the traits do clearly throw the burden of strong and continued companionship, of mutual trust and personal dependence, upon the nuclear family. Male friendships tend to be superficial and ephemeral. A man confides his personal feeling to his "girl friend" or his wife, not to his male companions, who are usually his business associates and therefore also his competitors. The husband-wife bond is therefore given tremendous strength. Similarly, the parent-child bond receives strong emphasis as a personal relationship. Children are the only human beings over whom the parents have personal as distinct from economic control, and for the child the parents are ordinarily the only stable personal anchor in a world of changeable relations and procedures.

As a consequence, contemporary society powerfully impels people into marriage and parenthood. "Going steady" at a tender age, a drop in the average age at marriage throughout the industrialized world, and early childbearing are overt manifestations of this impulsion. Inevitably the ethical feeling arises that marriage and procreation are somehow inalienable rights. The personal identity with "one's own child" has the implication (doubtless reinforced by the popularization of genetics) that a child should, if at all possible, be biologically one's own.

Thus we reach a result surprisingly like the past. In the medieval system, or in any traditional agrarian society, the institutional structure was such as to motivate people to marry and to produce many births. The structure reflected past millennia in which any social system that survived had somehow to compensate for a high death rate. But the family and reproduction were so intertwined with the economic and class system that marriage was not necessarily considered an inalienable right of every person regardless of his condition. In medieval Europe a precondition was personal command of the means of support for a wife and family (Russell 1949; 1948: 154–64; Homans 1941: chap. 10).

In backward countries today, with relatively high mortality and high fertility, the size of family varies greatly. For this there are several reasons: there is little or no medical treatment for low fecundity and not much birth limitation. Also, the factors governing mortality tend to strike some families more than others. In advanced countries, however, couples nearly all aim to have *some* children, hence seek treatment for sterility or low fecundity, but they limit their offspring after they have had their desired number, and the desired number tends to be a common standard. Furthermore, since few people die during childhood, the mortality factor is nearly constant as among families.

In a country like the United States, the peculiar and unique benefits of the family are felt to be everybody's birthright. Birth control is taken for granted, but it is not used either to produce only enough children to replace the population or to improve the genetic inheritance or environmental opportunities of the next generation. It is used instead to have as many children as the couple personally want under existing conditions, regardless of future demographic or genetic effects. By this system nearly everybody gets married at a relatively young age when economic conditions permit. In the United States in 1960, the median age for brides at first marriage was 20.1; for grooms, 23.1; and the proportion of women aged 35 to 39 who had ever been married was 94 percent. Furthermore, the degree of standardization in number of children per family has reached a point never before achieved in human history. In 1960 in the United States, among all families with a head aged 35 to 44, nearly half had two or three children under 18 years of age. In the Philippines in 1958, on the other hand, among ever-married women aged 35 to 44, the maximum proportion in any two orders of living children was about 30 percent, which was approximately the proportion having five or six living children. Obviously, to the extent that the variation is not random with respect to genetic factors, one can see how much more selective the system is in underdeveloped as against the highly standardized and culturally successful developed countries.

Given the traits just discussed—the emphasis on the nuclear family as the personal unit in modern society, the feeling that everyone has a right to marry and procreate some children of his own, the insistence that everybody be kept alive at any cost—we see little likelihood of a new positive system of genetic control arising soon in industrialized societies.

Significantly, geneticists and others shy away from the notion of "compulsion" in regard to any restraint on reproduction. There is of course compulsion in *promoting* reproduction. Laws against abortion compel pregnant women to bear a child even against their wishes; laws against birth control forbid couples to acquire contraceptive materials or information or to become sterilized even when they wish to do so; laws against divorce force some couples to stay married against their wishes; laws taxing bachelors and/or using tax money for family allowances compel people at large to favor parenthood. But when compulsion is suggested for wise *limitation* of childbearing, it tends to be rejected out of hand by official policy—sometimes with thundering ecclesiastical denunciation, sometimes with ridicule. When, for example, someone suggests that couples be licensed to bear children, he is generally ridiculed, because the idea runs counter to habitual sentiments. Yet marriage is, in essence, a license to bear children. Its only peculiarity is that it gives an unlimited franchise and it is easier to get than almost any other kind of license—far easier than a driver's license, a beer or a hunting license. About the only sense of restraint ever attached to it is a quantitative one: some people feel that a couple should have no more than the number of children they can support and rear adequately. This, however, is only a "should," with no enforcement contemplated, and many who hold this view would severely limit the means available. Furthermore, there is an equal or greater emphasis on the treatment of sterility, on the ground that every couple should have at least two children. The whole question of reproduction is thus surrounded by a mystique that places it beyond control for collective purposes. If we cannot find ways to avoid the personal tragedies represented by high rates of premarital pregnancy, illegitimate births, ill advised marriages, unwanted children, and venereal disease, we are not likely to find a way to improve, or even save from decay, the genetic constitution of future generations.

To say that a system of eugenic control is *theoretically* possible or conceivable is one thing. To say that it can *actually* be put into practice is another. I reach the conclusion that the existing reproductive institutions, despite some variation, make it unlikely that people will soon start controlling themselves genetically, although such control is theoretically possible. An effective system of eugenic control would involve profound changes in the very web of relations that organizes and expresses the personal lives of moderns. It would overthrow the existing system of emotional rewards and punishments, the present interpretations of reality, the familiar links between the person and social status.

Most people therefore, even when they favor eugenics, do not wish to reform our reproductive institutions for eugenic purposes. At most they want to make only small changes that will leave the basic family system intact. For instance, a familiar proposal is the provision of genetic counseling services, to inform couples of the probabilities of gross genetic defects in their prospective offspring. This would be a humane effort which no more achieves genetic control than the use of contraception for private purposes achieves population control.

IS GENETIC CONTROL SOCIOLOGICALLY POSSIBLE?

My purpose in discussing the sociological obstacles is not to suggest that genetic control is impossible. It is rather to show that human beings are still a long way from such self-control. A species that cannot yet even control its own sheer numbers is obviously not likely to control its genetic constitution. Doubtless something will perhaps be accomplished within the next fifty years by the dissemination of knowledge about specific genetic diseases and their control through genetic counseling and selective birth control. But there seems to be no indication that such limited measures will evolve into a comprehensive scheme for selective human breeding that will substantially raise the average level of genetic capacities in the population or greatly increase the proportion having abilities now defined as superior. This would require such fundamental changes in reproductive institutions and control systems that it appears unlikely as an evolutionary process.

However, social change occurs not only by gradual evolution but also by a saltatory process—revolution. It is possible to imagine a catastrophe so great that it would spark a eugenic transformation in one or more advanced nations. To do so, it would have to be, of course, a genetic crisis, and the only one that suggests itself is one produced by the use of nuclear weapons in a third world war. Such a genetic crisis might well rally public support for a eugenic program which would doubtless ultimately do more for human heredity by selecting against slightly harmful rather than extremely harmful mutants (cf. Kimura 1967). It is likely, too, that the catastrophe would initially reduce and contaminate the resources on which human beings depend, making necessary the most stringent control measures. In the longer run, by decimating the population but allowing most resources to recover rapidly, it would perhaps lower the people-resources ratio and thus stimulate the substitution of technology for manpower. Human societies might thus move to a new level of all-round scientific utilization, with genetic regulation as a single, though crucial, feature. With more science, the necessity of breeding people with greater intellectual capacities, to advance science itself, would become imperative. Thus the scientific control system would become self-reinforcing, carrying genetic improvements to a point hardly dreamed of today.

Once successfully adopted, genetic regulation would tend to persist even when the genetic crisis giving rise to it had passed. The reason would lie partly in the self-reinforcing nature of comprehensive scientific utilization just alluded to. It would also lie in the superiority of a society having genetic control over one not having it. Deliberate genetic control certainly appears to be the "absolute weapon," the most powerful means for survival yet contemplated.

The potential gain from systematic improvement of human inheritance seems enormous. It holds the promise of transforming human society in precisely those ways in which purely cultural change is impotent. It would revolutionize not merely the instrumentalities of life but the proclivities and limitations inherited from our long ancestry of hunters and gatherers, proclivities that are now inappropriate for the complex sociocultural environment in which we try to live. It would reverse the present tendency to eliminate the selective bars against physical defects and mental mediocrity. It would save the species from its lopsided dependence on cultural props for biological inadequacies.

To be sure, genetic regulation, like any other human effort, runs the risk of failure. The artificially created thoroughbreds of the species might prove less viable than the mongrels. But if human effort waited on an absolute guarantee of success, we would never do anything. We already have the scientific means to make considerable improvements in human heredity, even without the biochemical interventions intimated by recent discoveries. The major obstacle to a program of human hereditary improvement is therefore not any lack of genetic science but the resistance inherent in the stability system of existing societies. Just how drastic the changes in productive and political institutions would be is impossible to say, but they would probably be so drastic that most human beings, with minds and motives formed under existing institutions, cannot even tolerate them in theory, much less in practice.

Under the circumstances, we shall probably struggle along with small measures at a time, with the remote possibility that these may eventually evolve into a genetic control system. We shall doubtless increasingly seek to restrain reproduction in those cases in which there is patently a large risk of grossly defective offspring. As more genetic anomalies are discovered, as more tests for heterozygous carriers are discovered, this procedure will grow in importance. The morality of specific techniques of applied genetics—artificial insemination, selective sterilization, ovular transplantation, eugenic abortion, genetic record keeping, genetic testing—will be thunderously debated in theological and Marxian terms dating from past ages. Possibly, within half a century or so, this may add up to a comprehensive program.

If and when it does come, the deliberate alteration of the species for sociological purposes will be a more fateful step than any previously taken by mankind. It will dwarf three of the previous most revolutionary steps: the emergence of speech, the domestication of plants and animals, and the industrial revolution. The reason is simple: whereas these other changes were sociocultural in character and thus subject to the limitations of man's capacities, the new development would be both sociocultural and biological. It would, for the first time, enable man to overcome the sole limit on sociocultural evolution, the limit set by his innate capacities. These capacities would change very slowly, and quite probably in a downhill direction, under present conditions of inadvertent selection. On the other hand, deliberate control, once begun, would soon benefit science and technology, which in turn would facilitate further hereditary improvement, which again would extend science, and so on in a self-reinforcing spiral without limit. In other words, when man has conquered his own biological evolution he will have laid the basis for conquering everything else. The universe will be his, at last.

References

CARTER, CEDRIC O. 1962a. *Human Heredity*. Baltimore: Penguin Books.
———. 1962b. "Changing Patterns of Differential Fertility in Northwest Europe and in North America," *Eugenics Quarterly*, 9, 147–150.
DAVIS, KINGSLEY. 1951. *Population of India and Pakistan*. Princeton, N. J.: Princeton University Press.

FORD, C. S., and E. A. BEACH. 1951. *Patterns of Sexual Behavior.* New York: Harper.

HOMANS, GEORGE C. 1941. *English Villagers of the Thirteenth Century.* Cambridge: Harvard University Press.

JACOBSON, PAUL H. 1964. "Cohort Survival for Generations since 1840," *Milbank Memorial Fund Quarterly,* 42, 36–53.

KIMURA, MOTOO. 1967. "Recent Advances in the Theory of Population Genetics," in World Population Conference (Belgrade, 1965), *Proceedings,* 2, 478–480. New York: United Nations.

KISER, CLYDE V. 1960. "Differential Fertility in the United States," in National Bureau of Economic Research, *Demographic and Economic Change in Developed Countries.* Princeton: N. J.: Princeton University Press.

MAYR, ERNST. 1963. *Animal Species and Evolution.* Cambridge: Harvard University Press.

MURDOCK, GEORGE P. 1949. *Social Structure.* New York: Macmillan.

RUSSELL, JOSIAH C. 1948. *British Medieval Population.* Albuquerque: University of New Mexico Press.

———. 1949. "Demographic Values in the Middle Ages," in George F. Mair, ed., *Studies in Population.* Princeton, N. J.: Princeton University Press.

STERN, CURT. 1960. *Principles of Human Genetics,* 2nd ed. San Francisco: Freeman.

WESTOFF, CHARLES F. 1954. "Differential Fertility in the United States: 1900 to 1952," *American Sociological Review,* 19, 549–561.

The most urgent task, whether or not effective measures are taken to improve man's genetic stock, is to institute controls over his rapidly growing numbers, especially but—in the longer run—not exclusively in underdeveloped areas. In countries like India, Pakistan, Indonesia, and most of Latin America, there is a desperate shortage of investment funds for basic capital goods. Each new birth diverts that much more to consumption by an infant, who of course will not produce anything for years to come. In economic terms, thus, each nonbirth adds to the national economy. Several economists have tried to estimate just how much a country, assuming a particular set of circumstances, benefits from inducing potential parents not *to have a child. Such a model was first developed by Stephen Enke, who over the past decade has continuously refined it in a series of papers, of which the next article is a recent and elegant example.*

Dr. Enke is presently manager of the economic-development programs at TEMPO, General Electric's Center for Advanced Studies, Santa Barbara, Calif. Formerly he was on the faculties of UCLA, Duke, and Yale. He has also been head of the logistic department at the RAND Corporation (1948–58), Deputy Assistant Secretary of Defense for Economics (1965–66), and director of the President's Review of Selective Service Exemptions and Deferments (1969–70). His principal scholarly interests are in economic development, international economics, and defense economics.

BIRTH CONTROL FOR ECONOMIC DEVELOPMENT

STEPHEN ENKE

There is a growing interest in the possibilities of lowering birth rates in order to raise per-capita incomes in many of the less developed countries. Described below is one economic-demographic method of assessing what reduced human fertility might contribute to increased economic development. Justifications of government programs to increase voluntary contraception are also considered.

In less developed countries, one-half or more of annual increases in national output is being "swallowed" by annual increases in population, with income per head rising very slowly. Most of these countries have natural increases of from 2 to 3 percent a year. Hence they are doubling their populations every 35 to 23 years. This results not from rising birth rates but from falling death rates during the past 25 to 40 years—mostly attributable to improved health measures.

Some of their governments have decided that they cannot afford to wait for a spontaneous decline in fertility, resulting perhaps from more education, greater urbanization, and improved living. Instead, a few governments are encouraging voluntary use of contraceptives. The objective is economic development.

Many questions remain. How effective in raising incomes per head is reducing fertility as compared with other investments of resources? Could and should governments of less developed countries encourage voluntary contraception?

INCOME PER HEAD

One measure of successful economic development is a rising income (output) per head of population. It is ordinarily associated with other indicators of increasing welfare such as greater annual investment. Another measure is fewer people living in poverty.

Income (output) per head is a ratio. Governments have sought to raise this ratio by increasing its numerator—investing in factories, dams, highways, and the like—in order to increase the annual national output of goods and services. However, where politically feasible, governments can also raise the ratio of output per head by decreasing the denominator. A comparison of economic effectiveness can be made of changing the denominator and the numerator independently.

In a very simple arithmetic calculation, an imaginary less developed country may be expected, in 1980, to have a national output (V) of $2500

SOURCE: Reprinted from *Science*, **164** (May 16, 1969), 798–802, with permission of the author. Copyright 1969 by the American Association for the Advancement of Science.

million and a population of (P) of 12.5 million for a yearly output per head (V/P) of \$200. The government may decide to spend an extra \$2.5 million a year for ten years starting in 1970 to raise V/P. It can use these funds to increase output (ΔV) or to decrease population (ΔP) from what they would otherwise be. If the significant rate of return on traditional investments is 10 percent annually,[1] an investment of \$25 million from 1970 to 1980 will yield a ΔV in 1980 of \$2.5 million, so that a $\Delta V/V$ is 0.1 percent.

Alternatively, the \$2.5 million per year might have been spent on birth control. If the annual cost of an adult practicing contraception is \$5[2] and the annual fertility of contraceptive users is otherwise typically 0.25 live births, then in 1980 the population (12.5 million) would be 1.25 million smaller than expected. Thus $\Delta P/P$ is 10 percent.

Apparently the amount of money spent each year on birth control can be a hundred times more effective in raising output per head than that spent on traditional productive investments—for $V\Delta P/P\Delta V$ here equals 100. Had the rate of return on investments been 20 percent annually instead of 10 percent, had the annual cost of birth control been \$10 instead of \$5, or had the fertility of contraceptors otherwise been 0.125 instead of 0.25, this superior effectiveness ratio would have been 50 to 1 instead of 100 to 1. Had all three parameters been altered by a factor of two to weaken the argument, the expenditures on birth control would still be 12.5 times more effective.

The explanation is that it costs fewer resources to prevent a birth than to produce a person's share as a consumer of national output. This numerical example was the basis for President Johnson's statement to the United Nations General Assembly in San Francisco that \$5 spent on birth control was worth \$100 used for economic development. Calculations of this kind do not convince everyone, however, for they exclude so many of the economic and demographic interactions that could be expected from reduced fertility.

[1] This 10-percent rate of return is not compounded for two reasons. First, such compounding would imply that income from capital is entirely saved and invested, although it is otherwise assumed that only a small and varying fraction of income in general is saved and invested. Second, in reality investments have a so-called "gestation period," the increment in output not commencing sometimes for several years after the investment of funds begins (for example, construction of factories). For simplicity, and because these two considerations are countervailing, they have been ignored. Their net effect if included would have favored the argument.

[2] Contraceptive pills, wrapped and packaged, are now available to governments for about 25 cents a monthly cycle; distribution probably doubles this cost. Latex condoms wrapped in aluminum foil are available to governments at about \$2.50 in the United States and \$1.25 in Japan per gross. The new plastic condoms may be cheaper. Distribution costs through regular commercial channels could be around \$0.60 per dozen. The intra-uterine device costs about a penny to make and from \$5 to \$10 to insert (by public-health doctors). In India, vasectomies are being performed at a direct cost less than \$10. Direct costs per acceptor-year reflect the mix of methods used and the number of years that a person uses each method. If half of all acceptors use condoms or pills and the other half take intra-uterine devices or vasectomies, over a 5-year period the direct acceptor-year cost is less than \$4.

DEVELOPA: A LESS DEVELOPED COUNTRY

In order to assess the impacts of declining human fertility, a more complete economic-demographic model is needed. Any computer model should include at least the demographic and economic interactions shown in Figure 1.

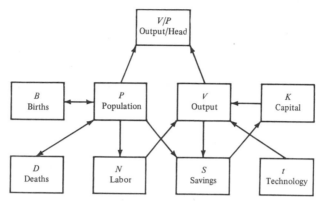

Figure 1. Population and Output per Head

Specifically, the demographics involve projections of rates of mortality and fertility by age and sex, and data on the initial age and sex distribution of the less developed country. Age and sex distributions can be calculated at 5-year intervals. Given the labor-force participation coefficients by age and sex, the available labor force (L) can be computed.

The economics involve a national production function that relates number of employed workers (N), capital stock (K), and improving technology (t) to national output (V). Annual savings that increase K are related positively to V and negatively to P. An increasing K not only raises output per worker but reduces the surplus labor ratio (L/N).

A frequently used national production function is of the type

$$\log V = \log z + n \log N + k \log K + y \log (1 + t)$$

where V, N, and K are defined as above, z converts for units, y is years, and n and k are so-called output elasticities of labor and capital, respectively. Thus, if n is 0.5, a 10-percent increase in N will occasion a 5-percent increase in V. In this formulation t is an annually compounded shift factor that increases the productivity of labor and capital by the same multiplier.

In such a model the demographics affect the economics through a changing age distribution. Declining fertilities reduce the ratio of children (who consume but do not produce) to working adults (who do produce when employed with enough capital). Also, more is saved and invested from a given V when P is smaller (Enke 1968).

Let us consider a nonexistent nation called Developa with the attributes typical of a less developed country which has, in 1970, a population of 10 million and an income per head of $150. The crude birth rate is 44 per 1,000 a year. When this model is used, what are the economic consequences of alternative fertility projections, given various parameters? Only two conditions are considered for fertility: When fertility is high the gross reproduction rate is 3.025 throughout. When fertility is low the gross reproduction rate falls from 3.025 in 1970 to 1.95 in 1985 and 1.48 in 2000. (The crude birth rate falls from 44 to 31 and 26, respectively.) Life expectancy at birth increases slowly from 53.4 years in 1970 to 56.6 in 1985 and 59.0 in 2000.

The consequences of these contrasting projections for fertility over 30 years, starting with 1970 as a common base, are shown for 1985 and 2000 (Table 1).[3] In both cases there is an improvement in output per head because of increasing capital per worker and contributions from improving tech-

Table 1. Declining Fertility for Economic Development

		1985		2000	
ITEM AND UNIT	1970	HIGH FER-TILITY	LOW FER-TILITY	HIGH FER-TILITY	LOW FER-TILITY
P, population (10^6)	10.0	15.9	14.1	25.9	18.1
V, output ($\$10^9$)	1.50	2.92	2.99	6.33	6.43
V/P, income per head ($)	150	183	212	245	354
L, available labor (10^6)	3.86	6.09	6.09	9.77	8.66
N, employed labor (10^6)	3.28	5.41	5.49	9.01	8.26
$L-N/L$ unemployment rate (%)	15.0	11.2	9.8	7.8	4.6
K, capital stock ($\$10^9$)	3.50	6.08	6.39	14.2	16.7
K/N, capital per worker ($)	1,066	1,126	1,165	1,572	2,023
SV, savings from income (%)	6.60	10.3	12.3	14.5	18.1
Earnings per worker ($)	228	270	273	352	389
Return on capital (%)	15.0	16.8	16.4	15.7	13.5
Children/population (%)	40.4	44.5	37.4	51.9	30.6
Dependency ratio [a] (%)	88.8	90.8	68.9	92.8	54.4
Living in "poverty" [b] (10^6)	2.50	2.53	1.45	2.20	1.18

[a] Young plus aged divided by work-age population.
[b] Personal income of less than $75 per year.

[3] In these calculations t is 0.015, n is 0.5, and k is 0.35. That n and k sum to less than unity implies diminishing returns to workers and capital because of land-resource scarcity. Annual savings for investment equal 0.25 V minus $35 P, approximately.

nology—the latter compounding to 1.56 over the 30 years. However, when fertility is high, annual V/P increases only 1.63 times to $245, whereas when fertility is low it increases 2.36 times to $354 by the year 2000.

The number of persons living in "poverty"—defined arbitrarily as the state of being able to afford not more than $75 worth of goods and services a year—hardly changes when fertility is high. Savings from income increases nationally from 6.6 percent in 1970 to 18.1 percent by 2000 when fertility is low. The capital per worker increases from $1,066 to $2,023. Hence in 2000 a worker earns $389 a year with low fertility as against $228 in 1970.

These various estimates are only suggestive. Their exact magnitudes are unimportant. What is significant is that combinations of alternative parameters indicate that declining fertility rates do contribute to economic welfare.[4] The absolute population size does not matter as much as the population growth rate. If a population doubles in 25 years, it does not mean that output will also double in that period. The labor force may double, but not all may be employed as productively if there is not a doubling of capital. Twice as much labor and capital will not double output if there is a scarcity of equally useful land. Were it not for a slow improvement in technology, most rapidly growing populations would be hard put to raise their per-capita incomes (Enke 1963).

Conversely, a slowing rate of population growth accords more economic benefits than a slow growth rate, and hence part of the former's gains cannot last beyond a few decades. As fertility rates decline, the ratio of unproductive children to work-age population declines substantially. With low fertility in Developa, this ratio decreases from 0.83 in 1970 to 0.49 in 2000. With high fertility the ratio rises from 0.83 to 0.87. Fewer children per family give each family member more potential consumption from the same family income. But actual consumption should rise less than the potential consumption. The difference is "released" for investment.

With low fertility Developa can have a population of 18.1 million by the year 2000. Table 2 indicates what would happen if its leaders for some reason wanted this same population sooner, by 1989 instead, and so encouraged a continuation of the high fertility rates of 1970. In 1989 V/P is $197 instead of $354 in 2000, and S/V is 11.5 percent instead of 18.1 percent. A worker's average annual earnings are $287 instead of $389. The ratio of the sum of the young and old dependents to the number in the work-age population is 0.914 instead of 0.554. Technology has had only 19 years instead of 30 years to make its contribution. This comparison at the same population size indicates that a slower population growth favors economic welfare.

[4] Income per head of population slightly exaggerates improvements in economic welfare when it rises because of shifts in age distribution from children to work-age adults. In equivalent consumer units, a child is here 0.75 of a work-age adult. In the low-fertility case the increase in income per equivalent consumer is from $171 in 1970 to $394 in 2000.

Table 2. Unfavorable Economic Results of Fast Population Growth

ITEM AND UNIT	1989: HIGH FERTILITY	2000: LOW FERTILITY
P, population (10^6)	18.1	18.1
V, output ($\$10^9$)	3.57	6.43
V/P, income per head ($\$$)	197	354
L, available labor (10^6)	6.89	8.66
N, employed labor (10^6)	6.22	8.26
$L-N/L$, unemployment rate (%)	9.8	4.6
K, capital stock ($\$10^9$)	7.44	16.7
K/N, capital per worker ($\$$)	1,196	2,023
S/V, savings from income (%)	11.5	18.1
Earnings per worker ($\$$)	287	389
Return on capital (%)	16.8	13.5
Children/population (%)	44.7	30.6
Dependency ratio [a] (%)	91.4	54.4
Living in "poverty" [b] (10^6)	2.37	1.18

[a] Young plus aged divided by work-age population.
[b] Personal income of less than $75 per year.

COSTS AND BENEFITS

The stipulated decline in fertility might be due entirely to increased use of contraceptives. It should then be possible to estimate very approximately, from the reduction in births, the number of women using contraceptives and the cost in resources of their doing so. How do these costs compare with the economic benefits?

It is hazardous to estimate the number of adults who must be using contraceptives in order to achieve a given birth decrement. And the cost per contraceptor a year is sensitive to the mix of methods used—a coil being cheaper than pills after several years, for example. Nevertheless very crude estimates of the cost for contraceptors in Developa, assuming conditions of low fertility, are that in 2000, for instance, there will be 2.8 million contraceptors whose use of contraceptives will cost $14 million.[5]

[5] Suppose the birth decrement is X and the fertility rate is y. Then a first crude approximation of the number of contraceptors is X/y. However, there may have to be three fewer conceptions for each two births, because of abortions and miscarriages. And of every three women of fertile age, only two may be at risk of pregnancy, with the other one being either not exposed to intercourse, sterile, or already pregnant at the time. Given these ratios, these two effects cancel, leaving the X/y relation. Few contraceptive methods are perfectly reliable in practice, and this may raise X/y by 1.1 times. Thus, if y is 0.2, for every one birth less there must be 5.5 women attempting contraception. At $5 per contraceptor a year, the cost of preventing a birth is then $27.50.

Estimating benefits is simpler if there is agreement on how to define them. Contraception results in a smaller population commanding more income per head because national output is little affected. It seems reasonable to ignore persons who would otherwise have been born, had it not been for contraception, and to consider only the living population. Thus, Developa in the year 2000, with low fertility, has a population of 18.1 million and an income per head $109 higher than it would have been without contraception. The economic "benefit," defined as population times positive difference in income per head, in that year is $1.97 billion.

How can benefits and costs be compared? The ratio of benefit to cost in a particular year has little meaning. In the year 2000 it happens to be 146, but the benefits enjoyed in that year were due to previous expenditures, whereas the costs of that same year will bring benefits only afterward. If benefits and costs are accumulated over the 30-year period, which makes a comparison more meaningful, the ratio is 82 to 1. This understates the case, for with no subsequent costs there will be benefits after 2000. Possibly significant to policy makers with short time horizons is that the benefit-cost ratio is already 22 to 1 in the fifth year (1975).

EXTENT OF PROGRAM

Still, Developa's low-fertility policy requires widespread use of contraceptives, so much so that the practicality of such a birth-control program must be questioned (Davis 1967).

The resource costs of the program are comparatively insignificant. From 1970 to 2000, the costs that yield $16.6 billion of benefits are $202 million, or about 0.2 percent of the national income accumulated over 30 years. These costs per head of population range from under 20 cents in the fifth year to slightly over 75 cents in the thirtieth year and average about 50 cents annually. Hence, birth-control programs are not a serious rival for funds. Most less developed countries annually use for economic development resources worth approximately $10 per capita. Even an extensive contraceptive program would leave about 95 percent of development budgets available for traditional spending (Enke 1966).

The real question is not adequacy of funds, or even of specific resources such as paramedics and clinics eventually, but whether enough women and men will voluntarily practice effective contraception. Under a policy of low fertility the gross reproduction rate should decline steadily from 3.025 to half that by 2000. In 1985, 22 percent of the population between 15 and 49 years of age would have to be practicing birth control. In the year 2000 this group would be about 30 percent of the men and women of these ages. These percentages are considerably below comparable estimates for developed countries, but they are far above anything yet achieved in any less developed country.

A less extreme and more attainable program would reduce the gross reproduction rate from 3.025 in 1970 to 2.60 in 1985 and 2.25 in 2000. With this medium fertility V/P by 2000 would be $285, compared to $245 with high fertility and $354 with low fertility. Assuming medium fertility, among women and men aged 15 through 49, the necessary contraceptive users would be approximately 8 percent in 1985 and 16 percent in 2000.

How large a percentage of the relevant population will ever practice contraception voluntarily is unpredictable. Fortunately, no minimum participation is necessary to attain some benefits, for even 5 percent practicing is better than none. And clearly this percentage can be influenced by the government.

This economic-demographic model demonstrates that there are other ways of raising individuals' incomes than by reducing fertility. If families saved and invested slightly over twice the percentage of their incomes than was assumed, the same increases in income per head would be approximated with unchanged fertility. Or, if families would innovate technological improvements a little less than twice as rapidly as supposed, about the same economic gains could be realized without birth control (cf. Kuznets 1967).

However, calculations of the proportionate increases in saving and technology that would give the same income increases per head as fertility reduction have no practical significance. Arithmetical equivalents are not real alternatives in this case. Families will not save and innovate more because they do not have fewer children. If there is any association at all among progeny, savings, and innovation, it is more probably one that favors birth control. One could argue that the sort of family that chooses among alternatives, can discipline itself, and manages its affairs well is likely to have fewer children, invest more savings, and innovate more improvements. Doing one may indirectly induce the others.

GOVERNMENT ENCOURAGEMENT OF CONTRACEPTION

Could and should the government of a less developed country encourage contraceptive use? Any such government could do many things to increase contraception. A government can at least have information and devices available at clinics. But it can also subsidize the retail sale of contraceptives and pay doctors to insert coils and perform vasectomies. It can pay bonuses to married women who remain nonpregnant, to "finders" who bring women to clinics for a coil insertion, and to fecund men or women who volunteer for sterilization. It can also educate and exhort through various advertising media.

A given expenditure that reduces fertility contributes so many times more to raising personal incomes than conventional development investments that a government can afford many activities if it increases the number of contraceptors. If the percentage of adults using contraceptives remains small despite government encouragement, at least something will have been gained. The government must then resort more exclusively to traditional investments for dams, and the like.

Many have objected that promoting birth control is not a proper activity of government, arguing that whether adults do or do not have more children is their affair alone. Yet many governments encourage larger families. Some almost seem to have a policy of compulsory pregnancy and birth, with laws not only against abortion but also against furnishing contraceptive information or devices. Governments also have many programs that incidentally favor larger families—programs such as free schooling, public housing, and military conscription (which takes away the labor of sons).

A government that really wished to be neutral with regard to family size would often have not only to legalize contraceptive distribution but also to offset the incidental encouragement of fertility by social-welfare programs through subsidizing birth control to some extent. Finally, if governments wish to give people more control over their lives, public-health programs should not only reduce the risks of premature death but also the risks of unwanted progeny (cf. Berelson 1966; Demeny 1965; Hauser 1963; Hoover and Perlman 1966; Ohlin 1967; Tietze 1967).

SUMMARY

Most less developed countries have population increases approaching 3 percent a year. Death rates have fallen dramatically in the past several decades, but birth rates remain at around 4 percent. Income per head is rising slowly.

Enough is known about the main parameters to use a demographic-economic computer model in order to assess the effects of declining fertility rates on the various indices of economic welfare in a typical less developed country. Thus, halving in 30 years a gross rate of reproduction of 3.025 results in increasing income per head by 3.0 percent a year, instead of 1.7 percent a year with no fertility change. Halving fertility also results in a third more capital per worker after 30 years.

A large birth-control program might directly cost about $5 a year per acceptor. About 25 percent of the population aged 15 through 49 would have to practice contraception to halve the gross reproduction rate in 30 years. During this period the total cost might be roughly $200 million for a less developed country that started with a population of 10 million. Accumulated benefits could be $16 billion. The ratio of benefit to cost is roughly 80 to 1.

References

BERELSON, BERNARD, *et al.* 1966. *Family Planning and Population Programs.* Chicago: University of Chicago Press.

DAVIS, KINGSLEY. 1967. "Population Policy? Will Current Programs Succeed?" *Science,* 158, 730–739.

DEMENY, PAUL. 1965. "Investment Allocation and Population Growth," *Demography,* 2, 203–232.

ENKE, STEPHEN. 1963. "Population and Development: A General Model," *Quarterly Journal of Economics,* 77, 55–70.

———. 1966. "The Economic Aspects of Slowing Population Growth," *Economics Journal,* 76, 44–56.

———. 1968. *Raising Per Capita Income through Fewer Births.* Santa Barbara, Calif.: General Electric-TEMPO.

HAUSER, PHILIP M. 1963. *The Population Dilemma.* Englewood Cliffs, N. J.: Prentice-Hall.

HOOVER, EDGAR M., and M. PERLMAN. 1966. "Measuring the Effects of Population Control on Economic Development: Pakistan as a Case Study," *Pakistan Development Review,* 6, 545–566.

KUZNETS, SIMON. 1967. "Population and Economic Growth," *Proceedings of the American Philosophical Society,* 111, 170–193.

OHLIN, GORAN. 1967. *Population Control and Economic Development.* Paris: Organization for Economic Cooperation and Development.

TIETZE, CHRISTOPHER. 1967. "Effectiveness, Acceptability, and Safety of Modern Contraceptive Methods," World Population Conference (Belgrade, 1965), *Proceedings,* 2, 305–308. New York: United Nations.

By now most Western economists would agree with the premises underlying Enke's model, and at least some policy makers in underdeveloped countries are coming to the same point of view. But there are still, as Professor Stycos pointed out with respect to Latin America (pp. 347–55), many who adhere to various religious or secular ideologies that define contraception as unnecessary, or evil, or a Yankee plot to commit genocide. The main human block to an effective birth-control program, Stycos holds, is the opposition not of the mass of uneducated peasants but of the intellectual elite. This judgment can be documented for other countries as well, as the following paper on India demonstrates.

The author, T. J. Samuel, is currently senior economist with the Canadian Department of Manpower and Immigration. He also teaches demography at the University of Ottawa and economics at Carleton University, Ottawa. His major interest, the economics of international migration, has been reflected in one monograph on the movement of Canadians to the United States, a number of journal articles, and participation in a longitudinal study of immigrants to Canada.

THE DEVELOPMENT OF INDIA'S POLICY OF POPULATION CONTROL

T. J. SAMUEL

The unfavorable effects of population growth on economic development, and the unlikelihood that the socio-economic factors alone (cf. Samuel 1965) would soon reduce the country's fertility, led the government of India to adopt a policy of population control. However, the evolution of this policy was slow relative to the average annual increase of 7 to 8 million during the 1951–61 decade. The development of India's policy falls into four distinguishable periods, which are discussed in turn.

THE PERIOD OF INDIFFERENCE (BEFORE 1947)

Britain's attitude was at times unfavorable, for generally an increase in India's population was seen as synonymous with increased prosperity, for which the British could claim a large share of credit. During the last quarter of the 19th century, when the British Governor of Bombay was urged "to restrain . . . the inordinate aptitude of the people to increase the population," he replied indignantly that he "would do everything in his power for the increase, and nothing for the diminution of the number of Her Majesty's subjects" (Chandrasekhar 1955: 76). Though this view may not have coincided exactly with that in London, it accurately reflected many local administrators' attitude. Some British officials, it is true, recognized that the annual addition to an already large population was "a cause for alarm rather than for satisfaction" (Hutton 1933: 29). But two years later, when a member of the Council of State moved to institute an effort to popularize contraception, the Home Secretary replied with "a bundle of hypothetical hopes and pious wishes, while the nominated members seemed to regard this serious subject only as a welcome diversion from the boring politics of the day" (Adarkar 1935).

Britain's indifference towards the problem of population and its control in India may have derived from the following: (1) The rate of growth of India's population, though high in the later years of the British administration, was lower than that of several Western countries, including Great Britain itself. (2) Neither the British nor the Indians were "development-conscious" before 1947. (3) Political repercussions of such a policy could have damaged British interests. And (4) there was no precedent anywhere for such a policy. It is hardly surprising that the British government did not think in terms of controlling India's population growth.

SOURCE: Reprinted from the *Milbank Memorial Fund Quarterly*, 44 (1966), 49–67, with permission of the author and the journal.

In contrast, the enlightened section of the Indian public, including some politicians, urged the government to develop such a policy. Discussion of the subject was initiated in 1916 with the book, *The Population Problem in India,* by Pyare Kishan Wattal (India, Health Services, 1959). The Neo-Malthusian League, formed in Madras in 1928, published several "treatises" in the Madras *Birth Control Bulletin* on contraceptive techniques. *Marriage Hygiene,* a journal started in 1936 by Dr. A. P. Pillai, was described by Mrs. Margaret Sanger as "the only scientific journal in the world" devoted to advancing the knowledge of conjugal hygiene (Himes 1963: 124).

Among Indian politicians, Mahatma Gandhi recognized as early as 1925 the "necessity of birth control" (Desai 1959: 43) but firmly believed that abstinence (*brachmacharya*) was the only permissible technique. In 1937, the Congress Party's National Planning Committee recommended limiting the number of children "in the interests of social economy, family happiness, and national planning" (Shah 1937: 6). In his presidential address to the Congress Party the following year, Suhash Chandra Bose emphasized the need for a population-control policy (Sovani 1952).

Some official committees recommended on medical grounds that information on family planning be disseminated. For instance, the Famine Inquiry Commission (India 1945: 432) recommended that the personnel in hospitals and health agencies could undertake family-planning activities "consistent with other duties"—this in a country with a population-doctor ratio above 6,000 to 1. According to the Health Survey and Development Committee (India 1946, 2: 477), "the question of the need for a cautious adjustment between the population and the resources that are available cannot be ignored and should receive serious consideration." Since large-scale emigration was not feasible and increasing production was only a "temporary expedient," it found "birth control through positive means as the only method which is likely to be effective." The committee suggested that the state should provide contraceptive advice—though not, because of their cost, contraceptives.

THE PERIOD OF "NEUTRALITY" (1947–52)

The time was ripe for a birth-control policy when the Congress Party assumed India's administration in 1947. None of the official committees was against family planning; eminent leaders like Gandhi did not oppose it in principle; the educated public wholeheartedly supported it; the National Planning Committee was strongly in favor of it; and the chairman of the National Planning Committee, Jawaharlal Nehru, became the Prime Minister. Even so, the Congress government hesitated to introduce such a program. According to Vera Houghton (1951), secretary of the International Committee on Planned Parenthood, India's Director General of Health Services discussed the possibility when he visited London in 1948; later, the Committee was informed that "the matter is still under consideration." This apathy is often attributed to the government's preoccupation with such problems as rehabilitating the 7.5 million refugees from Pakistan, drafting the new constitution, and developing a workable foreign policy. However, the government could easily have set up a population commission to prepare blueprints for a positive population policy to be implemented later.

On April 11, 1951, four years after independence, a Committee on Population Growth and Family Planning was appointed to work out a policy. A majority urged that the government undertake specific measures for family limitation. Dr. Sushila Nayar, a member of the committee and later Minister of Health, disagreed, for "the state can never control population." On the other hand, Lady Rama Rau demanded "first priority" for population control (Notestein 1951). In August 1951, the government approached the World Health Organization for help in organizing field studies of the rhythm method (India, Health Services 1959: 29). However, this did not mean a commitment to a policy of population control. In the message that Prime Minister Nehru sent to the Third International Conference on Planned Parenthood, held in Bombay in 1952, he stated that though the Planning Commission had made "definite recommendations on the topic of birth control, they had not yet been officially accepted by the government, which, over this important issue, still maintained an attitude of neutrality" (Blacker 1953). In the 1951 census report, R. A. Gopalaswami, the former Registrar General and Census Commissioner for India, pictured India's future if the population continued to grow at the same rate as during the 1941–51 decade (13.2 percent). Defining the term "improvident maternity" as a birth "to a mother who has already given birth to three or more children of whom at least one is alive," he suggested that "the incidence of improvident maternity should be reduced from the present level of over 40 percent to under 5 percent within 15 years" (India, Registrar General 1953a: 218). He recommended that top priority be given to a program of population control.

THE PERIOD OF EXPERIMENTATION (1951–61)

In December 1952, the government of India accepted the First Five-Year Plan, which defined the problem of population control as urgent, allotted 6.5 million rupees for family-planning propaganda and experiments, and set a long-run objective of establishing the population "at a level consistent with requirements of the national economy." Advice was to be given on methods of family limitation "if a doctor feels that a woman patient cannot undergo again the strain of pregnancy and parturition without danger to health" (India, Planning Commission 1952: 522). However, a policy based on purely medical grounds could not be interpreted as population control. Similar policies have been suggested in countries attempting to raise their birth rates.

While the progress reports of the First Five-Year Plan (1951–56) were referring to the family-planning program of "vital" and of "supreme" importance (India, Planning Commission 1953: 111; 1954: 254), as late as September 1955 the government was not sure what it wanted to do with the experimental program. When a member of Parliament asked whether the government intended to accelerate its family-planning efforts, Shrimati Chandrasekhar, the Deputy Minister of Health, replied: "The question is still under consideration" (India, Lok Sabha 1955a, 6: 4,914). Nor did the program pass beyond the experimental stage during the Second Five-Year Plan (1956–61). Three months after its start, Prime Minister Nehru said, "Our government has been helping the program not in a major way, but in experimentation" (Brecher 1963: 203). The allotment in the Second Plan was very small and, more important, a large part of it was not spent (Samuel 1964).

Until the late 1950s family planning was recommended to promote the "health and happiness" of the family by the Famine Inquiry Commission (India 1945), the Health Survey and Development Committee (India 1946), the Committee on Population Growth and Family Planning, and the Planning Commission. Near the end of the Second Plan, one of the National Sample Surveys found that the population of India had been growing at an annual rate of nearly 2 percent, an estimate that was confirmed by the 1961 census. The consequences of so high a rate of growth on economic development (cf. Coale and Hoover 1958) helped the government to shift from medical-health to economic grounds as the basis of its population-control program.

POPULATION CONTROL BEGINS (1961–62)

By 1961–62, population control was accepted as "an essential element in the strategy of development" to achieve a faster rate of economic growth (India, Planning Commission 1960: 675). A Health Survey and Planning Committee was appointed to work out a way of population control from the Third Plan onward. It recommended appointing a minister for population control, extending facilities for voluntary sterilization throughout the country, legalizing abortion, a mass importation and subsidizing of cheap contraceptives, promoting intensive research on fertility control, and providing economic incentives to limit families, as well as disincentives through taxation and social security for parents (Christian Science Monitor, December 2, 1961). Few of these recommendations were acted on.

The reasons why India's population-control policy developed so slowly, thus, can be broken down into the attitude of "neutrality" before 1952, the failure to go beyond an experimental stage before 1961, and the hesitation in enforcing the policy effectively after that date. Establishing an effective policy in a country like India was made more difficult by the population size, the division into castes and subcastes as well as language and religious communities, the hostile attitudes of particularly the rural residents, the widespread illiteracy, and low income. However, neither the multiplicity nor the magnitude of these impediments made a policy less necessary, but the contrary.

The government did not have to expend much effort to persuade the people to accept family limitation in the abstract. The people already favored it, as shown by a large number of attitude surveys conducted all over India (Agarwala 1961–62). However, the lack of opposition to the idea of family limitation is not synonymous with a strong motivation to adopt it.

The slow development of a population-control policy and its ineffectiveness were based also on deep-rooted political, ideological, moral, and international factors. It was once believed that India's economic backwardness was due exclusively to the political domination by Great Britain. By the nationalist leaders' argument, India possessed infinite natural resources, and the only problem was how to exploit them in sufficient quantity to effect a higher standard of living. As Gandhi observed in 1920, "India is today ill equipped for taking care of her population not because she is overpopulated but because she is forced into foreign domination, whose creed is progressive exploitation of her resources" (Tendulkar and Jhaveri 1951, 2: 294). Gandhi's views on this point profoundly influenced many of his followers who later came to power.

For a long time, the relation between economic development and population growth was discussed in terms of the "optimum," so that arguments centered on whether a particular country was "overpopulated" or "underpopulated." As late as 1948, Nehru thought that "India is an underpopulated country. . . . We are overpopulated, if you like, because our productive capacity is low. If we increase our production . . . and if this population is put to work for production, then we are not overpopulated" (Sovani 1952). In emphasizing the need for economic development, Nehru ignored how this was affected by rapid population growth.

Even those who recognized the need to curb population growth were reluctant to admit, much less to advocate, that the state should take an active part. It was believed that since official efforts to control population would inevitably fail, they would constitute a "wastage" of scarce resources. Even if population control was in the interest of both family and nation, those responsible for setting policy assumed that population could be successfully controlled only after the attainment of a higher standard of living. For example, though as early as 1936 Nehru denoted India's population as "overwhelming," he still thought that family planning "required a much higher standard of living for the masses" (Nehru 1936: 444). Sushila Nayar adhered to the same view in 1951, when she recommended that "first priority" be given to "education and improvement of living conditions" (Notestein 1951). If without a higher standard of living a policy to control population was bound to fail, enthusiasm for such a policy was slight.

Some circles maintained, similarly, that "the solution of the problem of population lies not in family planning but in economic development" (India, Registrar General 1953b). Parliament often referred to the assumed negative correlation between the standard of living and fertility. In 1953, Rajkumari Amrit Kaur, then the Health Minister, said, "The moment the standard of life of the people is raised, the birth rate falls" (India, Parliamentary Secretariat 1953, 3: 900–1). India's Planning Commission (1960: 522) believed the same.

In any case, not much could be expected from the increased use of contraceptives. In *The Discovery of India*, Nehru (1946: 566) wrote, "The increasing use of contraceptives and the desire to have small, regulated families may have produced some effect in reducing the birth rate, but it is generally recognized that this has not made any great difference." He cited the example of Catholic Ireland, where in spite of the slight use of contraceptives the birth rate started falling even earlier than in other countries. Fertility, Nehru held, declined by a reduction in fecundity. It has been well established, of course, that the fall in Western birth rates was due *not* to lower fecundity but to the use of contraceptives.

Even some who recognized how serious a problem population growth was did not wholeheartedly support a policy of control, for sooner or later this would result in the use of "artificial" methods of contraception. This peculiar stand was a legacy of Gandhi, for whom "birth control by contraceptives was race suicide" (Tendulkar and Jhaveri 1951, 2: 297). It was on this principle that Amrit Kaur, the Minister of Health in the early 1950s, insisted that the World Health Organization restrict its pilot studies to the rhythm method, since "the Indian government is unwilling to consider any other type of family planning in India" (Stone 1953). In 1951, Sushila Nayar, who succeeded Kaur as Minister of Health, stated emphatically that "the state should not undertake population control through the furtherance of contraceptives" (Notestein 1951). After the experiments in Lodi Colony and Ramanagaram proved that the rhythm method could not succeed in India (Blacker 1955), Amrit Kaur, the Health Minister once again, announced that the government would recommend "appliance as well as non-appliance methods of contraception" (India, Lok Sabha 1956, 2: 2,357). With this decision, the experiment in family planning entered a new phase, which the insistence on rhythm had delayed for more than four years.

Comparisons between India and developed countries regarding governmental attitudes toward population control have impeded the development of India's policy. Since compared to that of other countries India's population was growing more slowly, supposedly the problem was not so pressing. For instance, Nehru pointed out that the growth rate of India's population "is lower than that of many countries of Europe and elsewhere" (India, Information 1957, 3: 96). Such comparison generated a self-complacency in those responsible for the developing policy. When a resolution in Parliament requested the government to control population growth more effectively, the Health Minister replied, "The Government of India is the only government in the world that is even attempting to tackle it on a governmental level" (India, Parliamentary Secretariat 1954, 2: 2,589). Nehru, similarly, was not aware of any other government that had done officially as much for family planning (*Population Review,* January 1959, p. 87).

A vigorous policy would not be supported by all the population. The spiritual heir of Gandhi, Vinoba Bhave, whom the masses held in high esteem and to whom such national leaders as Nehru and Lal Bahadur Shastri paid tribute, observed: "You want me to have fewer children. How dare you say such a thing about my house so teeming with life? . . . Do not believe that we are an overpopulated country" (Hoffman 1961: 6). According to some Marxist-leaning members of Parliament, family planning was "based on the nonsensical neo-Malthusian theory that all social evils are attributable to free and unrestricted fecundity" (India, Lok Sabha 1955a, 5: 5,428). Other members commented that the policy "has been a failure" (*ibid.* 1955b, 7: 730) and has not "produced any practical results," (*ibid.* 1954, 6: 1,271), urged the government to stop "any more waste on this account" (*ibid.,* 6: 650), for "in spite of the family-planning centers all over the country" (*ibid.* 1955b, 7: 730), the birth rate was rising. However, this opposition was feeble and, inside and outside Parliament, supporters of the policy far outnumbered its opponents.

In the late 1950s, when population control was developing from the experimental stage, many of the cabinet members did not favor the development of an effective program. Jawaharlal Nehru, Morarji Desai, V. K. Krishna Menon, and Gulzarilal Nanda, who were also members of the Planning Commission, formed the core of the Cabinet in the late 1950s. Their views on population control are public:

Jawaharlal Nehru.   Despite his belief that the birth rate would decline together with an increase in the level of living, Nehru was not opposed to a policy of birth control. "We produce more and more food, but we also produce more and more babies. I wish we produced fewer children" (McCleary 1953: 79). However, "the question of limiting the family is not the primary question. . . . We have to make economic progress much more rapidly" (Brecher 1963). As late as 1963, he was reported to have said that "a solution of the problem depends on education and somewhat better living conditions—it is no good just getting a pill and making everybody swallow it" (*Overseas Hindustan Times,* October 3, 1963). From 1936 to 1963, Nehru remained ambivalent: not convinced of the need for population control, he assented to a program on a limited scale.

Morarji Desai.   An ascetic and a Gandhian, Desai never spoke openly either for or against birth control. When once Nehru was asked in Parliament whether the Cabinet was unanimous on the question, since Desai had "certain views" on it, Nehru responded that the Finance Minister was prepared to submit to the majority opinion (*Population Review,* January 1959, p. 88). From what little is known about Desai's views on the matter, it can be assumed that at best he approved the goals of the policy but not the methods, at worst he took exception to the policy altogether. However, after he left the Cabinet in late 1963, he was not elected leader of the Congress Party on the death of Nehru or even appointed to the subsequent Cabinet; and this decline in his influence should have helped the development of a more realistic population-control policy.

V. K. Krishna Menon. Former Defense Minister Krishna Menon viewed population control with disfavor (see, for example India, Lok Sabha 1957, 7: 13,451), presumably because of his Marxist leanings. He predicted that the population of India would reach 600 million by the end of this century, adding that "for any thinking person this was not a matter to be regarded as a catastrophe" (*Population Review,* January 1959, p. 88).

Gulzarilal Nanda. As Planning Minister, Nanda sent a message to the Family Planning Day in 1960: "Endeavors to raise the standard of living of the people are being neutralized to an extent by unchecked growth of population" (*Family Planning News,* December 1960). In an address delivered to the Asian Population Conference in New Delhi in December 1963, he somewhat complacently pointed to India as an advocate of population control. It is uncertain with what enthusiasm he in fact supported it.

The views of these key cabinet ministers partly explain why population control did not receive the attention it deserved in the 1950s. Scarce investment resources had to be allocated among many needs, and it was politically unfeasible to divert more resources from conventional types of investment to population control.

In short, the government of India often asserts that a population-control policy has developed slowly and ineffectively mainly because of socio-economic, organizational, administrative, and technical factors. However, another reason has been the government's own ambivalent attitude, which in turn has reflected political, moral, and international ideologies. These factors delayed an experimental program and kept it, when it was finally introduced, in the experimental stage for nearly a decade. After the experimental stage was successfully completed in 1961–62, the policy of population control that emerged still lacked the attention it merited by its importance for India's development.

References

ADARKAR, B. N. 1935. "Birth Control Debate in the Council of State," *Marriage Hygiene,* 1, 423.

AGARWALA, S. N. 1961–62. "Family Planning Attitudes in India," *Family Planning News,* **2,** 279–286; **3,** 17–24.

BLACKER, C. P. 1953. "Comment," *Eugenics Review,* **45,** 42–43.

———. 1955. "The Rhythm Method: Two Indian Experiments," *Eugenics Review,* **47,** 93–106; 163–172.

BRECHER, MICHAEL. 1963. *The New States of Asia.* London: Oxford University Press.

CHANDRASEKHAR, S. 1955. *Population and Planned Parenthood in India.* London: Allen and Unwin.

COALE, ANSLEY J., and EDGAR M. HOOVER. 1958. *Population Growth and Economic Development in Low-Income Countries: A Case Study of India's Prospects.* Princeton, N. J.: Princeton University Press.

DESAI, M. P. 1959. *Population Control: A Modern Shibboleth.* Ahmedabad: Navajivan Publishing House.

HIMES, NORMAN E. 1963. *Medical History of Contraception.* New York: Gamut Press.

HOFFMAN, DANIEL P. 1961. *India's Social Miracle.* Healdsburg, Calif.: Naturegraph Co.

HOUGHTON, VERA. 1951. "Planned Parenthood in India," *Eugenics Review,* **43,** 33–35.

HUTTON, J. H. 1933. "Report," *Census of India, 1931,* Vol. I: "India," Part 1. Delhi: Manager of Publications.

INDIA. FAMINE INQUIRY COMMISSION. 1945. *Final Report.* Madras: Superintendent of Government Press.

———. HEALTH SERVICES, DIRECTOR GENERAL OF. 1959. *Family Planning in India.* Delhi: Government of India.

———. Health Survey and Development Committee. 1946. *Report.* Delhi: Manager of Publications.

———. INFORMATION AND BROADCASTING, MINISTRY OF. 1957. *Jawaharlal Nehru's Speeches.* Delhi: Manager of Publications.

———. LOK SABHA SECRETARIAT. 1954. *Lok Sabha Debates.* 8th Session. New Delhi: Government of India.

———. ———. 1955a. *Lok Sabha Debates,* 10th Session. New Delhi: Government of India.

———. ———. 1955b. *Lok Sabha Debates,* 11th Session. New Delhi: Government of India.

———. ———. 1956. *Lok Sabha Debates,* 12th Session. New Delhi: Government of India.

———. ———. 1957. *Lok Sabha Debates,* 2nd Session. New Delhi: Government of India.

———. PARLIAMENTARY SECRETARIAT. 1953. *Parliamentary Debates,* 4th Session. New Delhi: Government of India.

———. ———. 1954. *Parliamentary Debates,* 6th Session. New Delhi: Government of India.

———. PLANNING COMMISSION. 1952. *First Five-Year Plan.* New Delhi: Government of India.

———. ———. 1953. *Five-Year Plan: Progress Report for 1951–52 and 1952–53.* New Delhi: Government of India.

————. ————. 1954. *Five-Year Plan: Progress Report for 1953–54.* New Delhi: Government of India.

————. ————. 1960. *Third Five-Year Plan.* New Delhi: Government of India.

————. REGISTRAR GENERAL AND CENSUS COMMISSIONER. 1953a. *Census, 1951: Report,* Vol. I, Part 1–A. Delhi: Manager of Publications.

————. ————. 1953b. *Census, 1951: Report on Mysore,* Vol. XIV, Part 1. Bangalore: Government of Mysore.

McCLEARY, G. F. 1953. *The Malthusian Population Theory.* London: Faber and Faber.

NEHRU, JAWAHARLAL. 1936. *An Autobiography.* London: Bodley Head.

————. 1946. *The Discovery of India.* New York: Day.

NOTESTEIN, FRANK W. 1951. "Current Items," *Population Index,* 17, 255.

SAMUEL, T. J. 1964. "Why Family Planning Has Had No Impact," *Economic Weekly,* 16, 1685–88.

————. 1965. "Social Factors Affecting Fertility in India," *Eugenics Review,* 57, 5–15.

SHAH, K. T., ed. 1937. *Population.* Bombay: Vora.

SOVANI, N. V. 1952. "The Problem of Fertility Control in India: Cultural Factors and Development of Policy," in *Approaches to Problems of High Fertility in Agrarian Societies.* New York: Milbank Memorial Fund.

STONE, ABRAHAM. 1953. "Fertility Problems in India," *Fertility and Sterility,* 4, 210–217.

TENDULKAR, D. G., and VITHALBHAI K. JHAVERI. 1951. *Mahatma.* Bombay: Times of India Press.

Whether in India, the United States, or any other country, the debate over birth control has been in part over the larger issue, but usually in greater part over the means by which the desired end of smaller families might be achieved. In particular, abortions (which some analysts believe to be the world's commonest method of birth control) are still illegal in most jurisdictions. A number of countries that lacked adequate contraceptives and consequently suffered from a high incidence of illegal abortions brought the practice within the law (the Soviet Union and, following its example, most East European nations); and in Japan the same circumstances were made more onerous by the extreme overcrowding immediately after the Second World War. Sweden, the most important other nation where therapeutic abortions have been legal for several decades, is exceptional in both respects: effective contraceptives were readily available, and the problem was not population pressure but, if anything, the contrary.

The following paper, on what happened to the children born after applications for abortions had been denied, is interesting for its substance, and it also could be used as a model of research design. The joint authors are both associated with the psychiatric research center of St. Jörgen's Hospital, University of Göteborg, Dr. Hans Forssman as professor of psychiatry and Inga Thuwe as a psychiatric social worker.

120 CHILDREN BORN AFTER THEIR MOTHERS' APPLICATION FOR THERAPEUTIC ABORTION HAD BEEN REFUSED

HANS FORSSMAN AND INGA THUWE

The aim of this study was to determine the mental health, social adjustment, and educational level of children whose mothers had applied for legal abortion on psychiatric grounds and been refused. We compared 120 children born of these pregnancies with a control series of equal size, following all the subjects up to their 21st birthday.

Therapeutic abortion was made legal in Sweden in 1939, and during the years relevant to this study (and still today) it was permissible on the following grounds: (1) when, because of the woman's disease, physical defect, or weakness, the birth of the child would endanger her life or health; (2) when the pregnancy is the result of a felony, such as rape or incest, or intercourse with a girl under 15, or intercourse against the woman's will because she is dependent on the man, or any other gross violation of the woman's freedom of action; (3) when the expected child might inherit from either parent a mental or a severe physical disease or deficiency. On July 1, 1946, the law was broadened to include the following indication: (4) when, in view of the woman's circumstances, it can be assumed that the birth and care of the child will seriously undermine her mental or physical health. This amendment came too late to affect the mothers of our subjects, but the psychiatrists at our hospitals seemingly recommended for or against abortion on essentially the same grounds before and after the new law.

There have been a number of Swedish studies of the two parents involved in abortions (see, for example, Lindberg 1948; Malmfors 1951; Ekblad 1955; Arén and Åmark 1957; Arén 1958; Höök 1963; Schlaug 1952). But little has been written about the third member of the trio—the unwanted child. According to Arén and Åmark (1957), of 162 children born after an authorized abortion had not been performed, 12 were sent to a foster home for permanent care or adoption. Malmfors (1951) reported that 7 out of 85 children born after an application for abortion had been refused were left for adoption. Nothing more was said about the fate of these children, and Arén and Åmark did not check their information in the official registers. Furthermore, both studies were made only three to five years after the children were born, when they were too young to permit any firm conclusion about their mental health or social adjustment. Höök (1963) followed 204 children of her sample until their age averaged eight and a half, by which time 15 had been left for adoption; the rest of her data about children cannot be compared with any of ours. This seems to be all that has been written in

SOURCE: Slightly abridged from *Acta Psychiatrica Scandinavica*, **42** (1966), 71–88, with permission of the authors.

Sweden about the fate of these unwanted children. The Danish author J. B. Nielsen (1960) reported that, of 92 children born after an application for abortion had been refused, 2 were stillborn and 8 were abnormal in some respect. But his children, too, were too young at the time of his study to judge their mental health and social adjustment. As therapeutic abortion has been legal in Sweden only since 1939, it has hardly been possible before now to determine the long-term social and psychiatric consequences to children born after an application for abortion has been refused.

SOURCES OF DATA

The subjects studied came from Göteborg, Sweden's second largest city, with a population of about 280,000 in 1939–42, when the children were born. During those years, the city had only one large general hospital, the Sahlgren Hospital, with a psychiatric department that served as a counseling center for mothers seeking a legal abortion. At the time it was the only agency of this kind in Göteborg. The few cases handled by private practitioners during this period are not included in our population.

Thus, the data for this study pertain to all women living in Göteborg who applied for a therapeutic abortion to the psychiatric department of the Sahlgren Hospital during the years 1939–41, inclusive, and were refused. During these years a total of 197 women submitted 199 applications that were turned down. These do not include any who changed their minds and withdrew their applications. In 188 of the 199 cases, the psychiatrist decided against abortion; in 10 cases, the Medical Board refused to authorize it; and in one case also referred to the Medical Board, the Board authorized the abortion but the obstetrician refused to operate because the pregnancy had proceeded too far. Of the 197 women, 3 could not be traced, leaving 194 women and 196 refused applications. Of the 196 pregnancies, 68 (or 34.7 percent) ended in abortions, many of which undoubtedly were illegal.

Thus, 128 of the pregnancies (representing 126 women) proceeded to term. The result was 134 children, including 6 pairs of twins; 4 of the 134 were stillborn, and 10 died as infants, leaving 120 children, all of whom reached the age of 21 (Table 1).

All but one of the 120 unwanted children were registered in Göteborg when they were born. We chose control subjects for these 119 as follows: When the infant was born in one of the city's maternity hospitals, we took the next child of the same sex born in the same hospital. For the 17 born elsewhere, we took the first child of the same sex registered in the city hospitals on the same day. When the control had died before the age of 21, we replaced it with the next child of the same sex in the same hospital. For control subjects for twins, we took the next pair of twins, same-sexed or bisexed as the case was, born in the same hospital. For the 2 children of twin birth, one whose partner was stillborn and one whose partner had died in infancy, we chose

Table 1. Distribution by Year of Birth and Sex, 120 Children Born
after Their Mothers' Applications for Legal Abortions Had Been
Children, Göteborg, Sweden, 1939–42

YEAR OF BIRTH	BOYS	GIRLS	TOTAL
1939	9	6	15
1940	32	13	45
1941	17	22	39
1942	8	13	21
Total	66	54	120

controls as if the study children had not been twins. For the control of the
child born outside Göteborg, we took the next child of the same sex registered in the book of the same parish. Apart from one control who lived in
another country for six months when she was 18, we were able to follow all
subjects, both study and control, from the time they were born until they
were 21.

From the child-welfare boards in the various districts in which the subjects had lived, we learned whether any of the subjects were in their files
and, if so, why. In the districts where the subjects lived or had lived, we
asked at child-guidance clinics, youth psychiatry centers, mental hospitals,
psychiatric departments of general hospitals, psychiatric out-patient services,
and all rural and urban psychiatric consulting bureaus whether they had
been consulted for a mental deviation or illness in any of the subjects. Since
we could not cover all the private practitioners who might have been consulted, we disregarded anything we happened to hear about private consultations.

Sweden has a central penal register in which are recorded every act of
the authorities restricting the liberty of an individual, whether a sentence
to an adult or juvenile prison or an internment in some other kind of an
institution, every person whose sentence was waived because of legal irre-
sponsibility, fines above a certain minimum or that had been paid as an
alternative to penal servitude, and all cases of conditional sentence. With
special permission, we went through these files for other evidence of the
subjects' antisocial conduct.

We also inquired at all the official temperance boards and social agencies
in the districts where the subjects lived after the age of 16, the age at which
persons are registered in social agencies' records. We inquired about the
subjects' schooling in the various districts in which they had resided. Whenever they went to secondary schools, we inquired there whether they had
undertaken other forms of study, and about any examinations they had
passed. We then determined whether before the age of 21 they had studied

at any university by going through the annual lists of students enrolled at Swedish universities.

In Sweden military service is obligatory for men, but not for women. As a rule men must begin military service the year they become 18, but they can put it off for three or more years for reasons of health or education. When our subjects had done this, we sometimes extended our limit beyond the 21st birthday in this one respect. We inquired at the Swedish Institute of Military Psychology about the fitness group in which the subjects had been classed and, if they had completed their military service, about how well they had performed their duties.

ESTABLISHING DIFFERENCES BETWEEN THE STUDY AND THE CONTROL POPULATIONS

The ages of the populations correspond almost to the day. The greatest difference, in the cases of twins, amounted to 25 days. The unwanted children were born of mothers 30 years old on the average, the control children to mothers of 28 on the average. The difference is significant($0.01 > p > 0.005$).

Using the social-class criteria from the Swedish electoral statistics for the years 1937–40, we grouped the subjects according to the father's occupation at the time, or if the mother was unmarried according to hers. Children adopted by couples neither of whom was their real parent were grouped according to the occupation of the adoptive father at the time. But those adopted by men their mothers married after they were born were grouped according to their mothers' occupation when they were born (Table 2). The

Table 2. Distribution by Parents' Social Group, Unwanted and Control Children, Göteborg, Sweden, 1939–42

	NUMBER		PERCENTAGE		
					POPULATION
	UNWANTED	CONTROL	UNWANTED	CONTROL	OF GÖTEBORG,
SOCIAL GROUP	CHILDREN	CHILDREN	CHILDREN	CHILDREN	1940
I (high)	3	4	2.5	3.3	6.5
II	22	32	18.3	26.7	31.4
III (low)	95	84	79.2	70.0	62.1
Total	120	120	100.0	100.0	100.0

two populations did not differ significantly in this respect (p approximates 0.10); of the pairs consisting of one subject from either series, 77 belonged to the same social group and 43 did not.

We considered that the following circumstances in the subjects' history pointed to an insecure childhood background:

1. Complaints to a child-welfare board about the way the subjects were being treated at home. (Every local authority in Sweden is required to set up a child-welfare board, whose duty it is to see that all children in its district are properly cared for. Until 1960 the boards were required to intervene whenever children under 16 were being exposed to physical or mental harm through cruelty or neglect at home, or in danger of becoming delinquent because of their parents' depravity, negligence, or inability to bring up their children.)

2. Protective care under the custody of a child-welfare board. (If advising or warning the parents had no effect, or if the board decided that it would be a waste of time to try to persuade the parents to mend their ways, the board had the right to take the child away from its parents for protective custody.)

3. Placement in a foster home.

4. Placement in a children's home.

5. Childhood in a broken home; that is, either loss of a parent through divorce or death before the child was 15, or birth out of wedlock not followed by legitimization.

Table 3 shows how many subjects in each population were brought up

Table 3. Indications of an Insecure Childhood, Unwanted and Control Children, Göteborg, Sweden

	NUMBER OF CASES [a]	
INDICATION OF INSECURE CHILDHOOD	UNWANTED CHILDREN	CONTROL CHILDREN
Home reported to children's aid bureaus for unsatisfactory conditions	17	6
Child removed from home by authorities	2	0
Child placed in foster home	19	4
Child placed in children's home	30	10
Parents divorced before child was 15	23⎫	13⎫
Parent(s) died before child was 15	10⎬ 60	5⎬ 22
Child born out of wedlock and never legitimized	27⎭	4⎭

[a] The same child may occur in several of the categories.

under each of these circumstances. Of the unwanted children, 32 (26.7 percent), were born out of wedlock, against only 9 (7.5 percent) of the control children. The difference is highly significant ($p < 0.001$). Of pairs with one from each population, 86 were the same in regard to legitimacy and 34 were not. The parents legitimized 5 of the 32 unwanted children born out of wedlock, as did the parents of 5 of the 9 illegitimately born control children. Of the unwanted children, 8 were adopted by others than their real parents; none of the control subjects were adopted.

According to the criteria set, 72 (60 percent) of the unwanted children had an insecure childhood, as against only 34 (28.3 percent) of the control children. If one disregards the periods in children's homes, many of which were quite short, the figures change to 65 (54.2 percent) against 26 (21.7 percent). In either case, the difference is highly significant ($p < 0.001$).

In short, the children born after an application for abortion had been refused ran a greater risk of insecurity in childhood than did their control subjects.

Since there is more delinquency in cities than in other regions, we determined how many of either population had stayed the whole time in Göteborg, and whether the two groups differed in their tendency to move from place to place. Of the unwanted children, 77 (62.2 percent) stayed in Göteborg until they were 21, compared with 85 (70.8 percent) of the control subjects. Of the unwanted children, 21 (17.5 percent) had lived in three or more local districts, and 19 (15.8 percent) of the control subjects. Thus, there was little difference between the two populations, whether in permanency of residence in Göteborg or in the tendency to move from one district to another. There were 55 pairs of whom both the study and the control subject had lived the whole time in Göteborg.

COMPARISONS BETWEEN THE STUDY
AND THE CONTROL POPULATIONS

Of the unwanted children, 34 (28.3 percent) had received psychiatric care in a clinic or a hospital, compared with 18 (15 percent) control subjects. The difference is probably significant ($0.025 > p > 0.01$). Of the unwanted children, 29 had been under the care of a child psychiatrist, 6 had visited a center for adult psychiatry, and 3 of these had been hospitalized. In contrast, 15 of the control subjects had visited a center for child psychiatry, 4 had been patients at a center for adult psychiatry, and 2 had been hospitalized.

Was it because their mothers had been in contact with psychiatrists before the children were born that so many of the unwanted children were registered at centers for child psychiatry? Having once consulted a psychiatrist, these mothers may have found it easier to do so again, whereas the mothers of the control subjects presumably did not take their children to a psychiatrist unless something was seriously wrong. Similarly, the mothers who had consulted a psychiatrist about abortion might be readier to seek psychiatric advice afterwards both for themselves and for their children. Therefore, we tried to determine how many of the mothers up to the year 1959 had consulted a psychiatrist for matters not directly concerned with the abortion. Of the 57 pairs in which both subject and control had lived in Göteborg continuously, 27 subject mothers had gone to a psychiatric out-patient clinic for complaints not directly related to the abortion, as well as 10 of their children. The corresponding figures for the control series were 9 and 0. It was apparent that the supposed influence of a prior consultation was not well based.

Delinquent acts (not including drunkenness) were reported to child-welfare boards concerning 22 (18.3 percent) of the unwanted subjects, 19 boys and 3 girls, as against 10 (8.3 percent) of the control subjects, 9 boys and 1 girl. The difference is probably significant ($p < 0.05$). After investigation by the board, 3 of the first series and 1 of the second were removed from their homes and placed in protective custody elsewhere, in accordance with the law then in force. One child from each population was sent to a reformatory. The penal register listed the names of 10 of the unwanted children (8.3 percent) and of 3 control subjects (2.5 percent). The difference is not significant ($0.10 > p > 0.05$).

The records of the official temperance boards included the names of 19 of the unwanted children (15.8 percent) and 13 control subjects (10.8 percent) for drunken misconduct. The difference is not significant ($0.50 > p > 0.30$).

Of the unwanted children, 17 (14.2 percent) had received some form of public assistance between the ages of 16 and 21, and 3 of the control subjects (2.5 percent). The difference is significant ($0.005 > p > 0.001$). Only one subject, a boy in the control series, received a disability pension: he was an idiot who was permanently institutionalized.

Included in the category "educationally subnormal" were all uneducable subjects, those taught in special schools for the mentally retarded, those whose last school year was in a special class, and a few subjects with a well documented educational subnormality who were taught in ordinary classes only because no form of special training was available for them. By these criteria, 13 of the unwanted children (10.8 percent) were educationally subnormal, as against 6 of the control subjects (5.0 percent). This difference is not significant ($p = 0.10$). One well documented case of mental retardation occurred in each of the two populations.

Only 17 (14.2 percent) of the unwanted children had had some form of higher education beyond the minimum required by law, as against 40 (33.3 percent) of the control subjects. The difference is highly significant ($p < 0.001$). University entrance examinations had been taken by 8 unwanted and 12 control children; 5 unwanted children and 11 control children had studied at a university. Netiher of these differences is significant.

Since a child's education depends greatly on its parents' social standing, we also compared the schooling in the two populations paired by social groups, with 77 subjects in each series. Of these 77, 10 (13.0 percent) unwanted children had had some form of higher education, against 21 (27.3

percent) control children. That is, as shown also by other analyses of the data, it was not differences in class background that caused the unwanted and control children to acquire more or less education.

Of the 66 males in the original series, 10 (15.2 percent) were judged unfit for military service, either by a pre-induction test or later, as opposed to 4 (6.7 percent) of the control subjects. This is not a significant difference ($0.20 > p > 0.10$). According to our possibly incomplete information, 4 of the study males and 2 of the control subjects were exempted on mental grounds.

Up to the age of 21, as far as we followed our subjects, some differences emerged with regard to marriage and parenthood. Of the unwanted children, 20 (17 women, 3 men) had married before age 21, and 14 of the control subjects (9 women, 5 men). The difference is not significant, either for the sexes combined or for either of them. Two of the females from the study population had divorced before they were 21; none of the control women had done so, and no man from either series.

We restricted our analysis of parenthood to the women, as these were the more reliable figures. Of the 54 women in the study population, 14 had had 19 children before they were 21, 4 out of wedlock; 7 of the 54 female control subjects had had 9 children, 3 out of wedlock. One cannot draw any conclusions from these figures. That the control population included fewer cases of early marriage and parenthood was undoubtedly in part because its members had more education on the average.

Sometimes the same subject was found in more than one of the groups studied here. Thus, a person registered with the authorities for misuse of alcohol was often in the files of child-psychiatry centers as well; a man who has been in a mental hospital was sometimes exempted from military service; an uneducable subject received public assistance; and so on. It is interesting, therefore, to compare the number of subjects with none of the defects studied: 58 (48.3 percent) of the unwanted children, as against 82 (68.3 percent) of the control subjects. The difference is significant ($0.005 > p > 0.001$). Among the 77 in each population paired by social group, 34 unwanted cases (44.2 percent) had no defect, against 54 control cases (70.1 percent). The difference is significant ($0.005 > p > 0.001$).

SUMMARY

The authors examined 120 children born after their mothers had applied for therapeutic abortion on psychiatric grounds and been refused, comparing them with an appropriate control series of the same size. All the subjects studied lived and were followed up to the age of 21. Data were assembled from civil and ecclesiastical registry offices, social agencies, school authorities, military authorities, and all the psychiatric in-patient and out-patient clinics in every place the subjects had lived. It was ascertained how many of each population had been registered for mental ill health, antisocial and criminal actions, drunken misconduct, and different forms of public assistance; concerning the men, how they had fared during their military service; likewise, the marital status, number of children, and school ability and educational level.

Many more of the unwanted than of the control children had not had the advantage of a secure family life during their early years. They were registered more often for psychiatric services, and a few more of them received psychiatric care. They were listed more often for antisocial and criminal behavior, and slightly more often for drunken misconduct. They got public assistance more often than the control subjects. A few more of them were educationally subnormal and far fewer had pursued studies above what the law requires. They were more often exempted from military service. More of the females than in the control series married early and had children early. The differences between the two populations in these respects were often statistically significant, and when they were not significant they always pointed in the same direction: the unwanted children were born into a worse situation than the control children (Table 4).

One probable reason for the differences is that the unwanted children were more often reared in homes disrupted by such factors as birth out of wedlock and the death or divorce of their parents while they were still young. In other words, fewer unwanted children were brought up by both their real parents; as a corollary, more were raised by foster parents or in children's homes, though the latter datum may also have reflected the greater number of complaints to the children's welfare boards about the treatment at home.

The authors conclude that the very fact a woman applies for legal abortion means that the prospective child runs a risk of having to surmount greater social and mental handicaps than its peers, even when the grounds for the application are so slight that it is refused. In their opinion, the legislation on therapeutic termination of pregnancy should also consider the social risks to which the expected child will be exposed.

References

ARÉN, PER. 1958. "Undersökning av 100 nyblivna mödrar med legal abort i anamnesen" [One hundred newly delivered mothers with a history of legal abortion], *Svenska Läkartidningen*, **55**, 505–522.

————, and CURT ÅMARK. 1957. "Prognosen vid beviljad men icke utförd legal abort" [Outcome of therapeutic abortions authorized but not performed], *Svenska Läkurtidningen*, **54**, 3709–3784.

DELCOMYN, KIRSTEN. 1952. "Efterundersøgelse af Kvinder, der har fået Afslag på Anmodning om Abortus provocatus" [Follow-up study of women whose application for therapeutic abortion was refused], *Nordisk Medicin*, **48**, 980.

Table 4. Summary of Important Differences between Unwanted and Control Children, Göteborg, Sweden

CHARACTERISTIC	UNWANTED CHILDREN			CONTROL CHILDREN			SIGNIFICANCE OF DIFFERENCE [a]
	NUMBER IN POPULATION	CHARACTERISTIC PRESENT NUMBER	PERCENT	NUMBER IN POPULATION	CHARACTERISTIC PRESENT NUMBER	PERCENT	
Psychiatric consultation and hospitalization	120	34	28.3	120	18	15.0	*
Registration for delinquency at a children's aid bureau	120	22	18.3	120	10	8.3	*
Registration for crime in the penal register	120	10	8.3	120	3	2.5	—
Registration for drunken misconduct	120	19	15.8	120	13	10.8	—
Public assistance between ages of 16 and 21	120	17	14.2	120	3	2.5	**
Subnormal educability or noneducability	120	13	10.8	120	6	5.0	—
Liberal-arts or professional studies beyond the minimum schooling legally required							
Whole series	120	17	14.2	120	40	33.3	***
Subjects paired by social group	77	10	13.0	77	21	27.3	*
Social group III (low)	95	5	5.3	84	17	20.2	**
Social groups I + II	25	11	44.0	36	28	77.8	*
Exemption from military service	66	10	15.2	66	4	6.7	—

Lack of all defects studied						
Whole series	120	58	48.3	120	82	68.3	**
Social group III (low)	95	40	42.1	84	54	64.3	**
Social groups I + II	25	19	76.0	36	28	77.8	–
Subjects paired by social group	77	34	44.2	77	54	70.1	**
Subjects living all their life in Göteborg	55	20	36.4	55	38	69.1	***
Subjects brought up by both their natural parents	60	33	55.0	98	68	69.4	–

[a] A hyphen (–) indicates no significant difference. A difference that probably is significant ($p > 0.05$) is indicated by one asterisk (*), one that is significant ($p > 0.01$) by two asterisks (**), and one that is highly significant ($p > 0.001$) by three asterisks (***).

EKBLAD, MARTIN. 1955. "Induced Abortion on Psychiatric Grounds," *Acta Psychiatrica Scandinavica*, Supplement 99.

FORSSMAN, HANS, and INGA THUWE. 1960. "En socialpsykiatrisk efterundersökning av 120 barn födda efter avslag på abortframställning" [Mental health and social adjustment of 120 children born after application for a therapeutic abortion had been refused], *Nordisk psykiatrisk Tidsskrift*, 14, 265–279.

HÖÖK, KERSTIN. 1963. "Refused Abortion: A Follow-up Study of 249 Women Whose Applications Were Refused by the National Board of Health in Sweden," *Acta Psychiatrica Scandinavica*, Supplement 168.

HULTGREN, GÖSTA. 1959. "Avslag på ansökan om legal abort" [Application for legal abortion refused], *Nordisk Medicin*, 62, 1182–1185.

Lancet. 1964. "Termination of the Pregnancy on Psychiatric Grounds" (editorial), 7372 (December 12), 1279–1280.

LINDBERG, BENGT J. 1948. "Vad gör den abortsökande kvinnan när psykiatern sagte nej?" [What does the woman do when the psychiatrist says No to her application for abortion?] *Svenska Läkartidningen*, 45, 1381–1391.

MALMFORS, KARIN. 1951. "Den abortsökande kvinnans problem" [Problems of the woman seeking abortion], *Svenska Läkartidningen*, 48, 2445–2468.

NIELSEN, J. B. 1960. "Afgørelser i et Mødrehjelpssamråd og en Efterundersøgelse" [Decisions by a maternity-assistance board and a follow-up study], *Ugeskrift for Læger*, 120, 330–335.

SCHLAUG, RUDOLPH. 1952. "Om de abortsökande kvinnornas män" [The male partners of women applying for therapeutic abortion], *Svenska Läkartidningen*, 49, 849–862.

SVENSK FÖRFATTNINGSSAMLING [SWEDISH CODE OF STATUTES]. 1938. Lag om avbrytande av havandeskap [Law on abortion], No. 318. Stockholm.

SVENSKA SOCIALVÅRDSFÖRBUNDET [SWEDISH SOCIAL WELFARE ASSOCIATION]. 1950. Text till lag om samhällets barnavård och ungdomsskydd [Proposed wording of the law on the official supervision of child welfare and protection of youth]. Stockholm.

SVERIGES OFFICIELLA STATISTIK [OFFICIAL SWEDISH STATISTICS]. 1941. *Riksdagsmannavalen åren 1937–1940* [Government election statistics for 1937–40]. Stockholm.

———. 1959. Allmän hälso- och sjukvård 1957 [Public health and care of the sick in 1957]. Stockholm.

TREDGOLD, R. F. 1964. "Psychiatric Indications for Termination of Pregnancy," *Lancet*, 7372 (December 12), 1251–1254.

UHRUS, KERSTIN. 1964. "Some Aspects of the Swedish Law Governing Termination of Pregnancy," *Lancet*, 7372 (December 12), 1292–1293.

Suppose all nations followed Sweden's example with respect to the control of reproduction, and that effective, safe, and cheap contraceptives and abortions were made available to the whole population virtually on demand. Would the sum of free individual choices by potential parents, no longer hampered by the lack of suitable means, add up to the best over-all fertility as judged in terms of the whole community's interest? In other words, is the laissez-faire market a perfect instrument to achieve the optimum public policy with respect to family size? Perhaps the most forceful affirmative responses to these questions were by a professor long associated with the University of Chicago, Dr. Donald J. Bogue (1964; 1967). The following paper is a no less cogent argument on the other side.

Its author, Philip M. Hauser, is a professor of sociology at the University of Chicago and director there of the Population Research Center and the Chicago Community Inventory. He has been acting director (1949–50) and deputy director (1938–47) of the U. S. Bureau of the Census, United States representative to the UN Population Commission (1947–51), a statistical advisor to the governments of Burma and Thailand, president of the American Sociological Association (1967–68), the American Statistical Association (1962), and the Population Association of America (1950). Several dominant themes run through his numerous publications: the analysis of urbanization in a social-political context, improving the collection and utilization of population statistics, and the rational determination of good social policy.

POPULATION CONTROL: MORE THAN FAMILY PLANNING

Philip M. Hauser

Over the past half-century demographers have demonstrated that contemporary rates of world population growth cannot possibly persist very far into the future. They have also demonstrated that, given a finite globe, a zero rate of population growth must eventually be achieved. In this sense there will be population control. The only questions are whether the control will be imposed by nature or by man, and the methods of control that man can employ. Nature's control would be those outlined by Malthus, including famine and disease. Man's control could be either very undesirable and irrational or rational and relatively desirable. In the first category would be behavior patterns recorded in history, including vice and war, as also mentioned by Malthus. With the hydrogen bomb, war for the first time could become an effective method of population control. Other undesirable forms of control effected by man could include homosexuality (which is never accompanied by a high birth rate) and cannibalism (which would have the beautiful symmetry of population decreasing as food supply increased). Needless to say, I am not advocating any of these irrational and undesirable methods of population control. In light of the objections which

SOURCE: Reprinted from *Journal of Medical Education,* Vol. 44 (1969), Part 2, pp. 20–29, with permission of the author and the Association of American Medical Colleges.

still exist to some of the rational and more desirable methods of control, however, it is in order to contemplate some of these drastic alternatives.

A necessary preliminary to considering methods of population control other than family planning is the delineation of what constitutes family-planning methods. As a preliminary to the latter task it is desirable to distinguish among conception control, fertility control, and population control.

Conception control involves all available methods to prevent conception. This includes a battery of techniques: behavioral, mechanical, chemical, physiological, and surgical. The behavioral methods encompass complete abstention from sex, *coitus interruptus, coitus sublimatus,* and the rhythm method; the mechanical methods include the condom, the diaphragm, and the intra-uterine device; the chemical methods include foam tablets, spermicidal jellies, and the like; the physiological methods include the use of steroids and other possible agents for controlling ovulation, possible anti-zygotic agents, and possible spermicides or other agents to induce male sterility; the surgical methods include ligation and vasectomy. Programs of conception control then, are those that employ one or some combination of these methods designed to prevent conception.

Fertility control has as its objective the prevention of births. Methods to prevent births include, of course, all the methods of conception control and, in addition, abortion—the prevention of births after conception has occurred.

Finally, population control has as its objective the control of the rate of population growth. Population control, therefore, encompasses not only fertility control but the control of the relation between fertility and mortality for the world as a whole and, in addition, control of migration for any of its subdivisions.

The family-planning movement, certainly on the basis of its stated objectives and what it does, is restricted to the control of conception and does not aim at either birth control or population control as defined above. Moreover, the objectives of the family-planning movement are to make available to couples the means whereby, on a voluntary basis, they can achieve the number of children they desire. This number will not necessarily be consistent with the possible objectives of either birth control or population control. In fact, on the basis of the limited data available, the desired number of children reported is uniformly well above the level required to achieve a zero rate of population growth—the rate, given a finite planet, that the world must achieve. The evidence is already at hand that justifies the setting of a zero rate of world population growth as an urgent target—a rate to be achieved as rapidly as possible to avoid the ever increasing cost, human as well as monetary, of any growth at all. This is unquestionably the situation for the world as a whole and, despite national variations, for most of the world's peoples.

The family-planning movement also has as one of its stated objectives the spacing of children. Although this objective is primarily to improve the health of mothers and children, it also may result in decreasing the birth rate, even if the total number of children born per couple is the same, by increasing the length of the generation.

PRESENT STATUS OF FAMILY-PLANNING PROGRAMS

Despite the proliferation and notable progress in family-planning programs in recent years, there is as yet no evidence that by the year 2000 a zero rate of growth can be achieved by the developing nations or by the world as a whole. Moreover, it is doubtful that family-planning programs as presently conducted can even significantly reduce population growth rates during the remainder of this century. These conclusions are based on the following considerations:

1. The world has yet to witness a family-planning program which initiated a decline in fertility in a "traditional society" characterized by mass illiteracy and poverty.

2. The examples of "successful" programs to date (for example, Taiwan, Hong Kong, Singapore, South Korea) are in areas where fertility declines had already set in before the advent of national family-planning policies and programs; and their rising levels of education and per-capita income preclude the extension of their experience to populations still steeped in illiteracy and poverty.

Moreover, by reason of inadequate evaluation of program impact, it is not known just what effect most family-planning movements have had in the attainment even of their own limited objectives. The reasons may be summarized as follows:

1. There are as yet no satisfactory methods of measuring small changes in fertility (or population growth rates) over short periods in the developing areas.

2. There are as yet no experiments in family planning, apart from the possible exception of Taiwan, which have precisely measured the impact of an action program on fertility as differentiated from other forces in the secular trend.

These observations are not to be interpreted to mean that family-planning programs as they are presently conducted have failed or are doomed to failure. Most of the programs have been in effect for only short periods or have only recently reached proportions which can be expected to have a significant impact. Nor do I intend to imply that current family-planning efforts are to be abandoned. On the contrary, there is every reason to expand and intensify present efforts, for by the criterion of the stakes involved, these efforts and the resources devoted to reducing excessive fertility are meager and grossly inadequate. In proposing steps that go beyond present programs, I am calling for experiments designed to backstop present programs and to seek increased effectiveness. Experimental efforts of the types discussed below may lead to basic revisions, or to a supplantation of present programs if these should prove to have less than the desired impact.

ALTERNATIVES TO FAMILY-PLANNING PROGRAMS

The present approach of the family-planning movement may be described as simplistic, well justified perhaps as a first effort by time and cost considerations. It may be characterized as a direct approach based on the "facts" gathered in KAP (knowledge, attitudes, and practice) surveys and the assumption that human behavior is rational. Many of the KAP "facts" in my judgment are erroneous (Hauser 1967: 402–5). Moreover, the assumption that human reproductive behavior is rational has proved of limited value in inducing changes in fertility behavior. Both of these judgments are supported by the gap between the 70 percent or more who respond positively on "interest in learning" about birth control and the relatively small percentages who accept clinic services offered gratis by present action programs—frequently at levels of 7 to 10 percent.

The experience of family-planning programs—together with the results of the major fertility studies, which have accounted for relatively small proportions of the variances in fertility behavior (for example, the "Indianapolis Study," "Growth of American Families," and "Family Growth in Metropolitan America")—suggests an alternative to the present simplistic approach. This derives from basic sociological considerations.

Sociology in general utilizes three frames of reference in the study of the person or the social order: the ecological (which subsumes the demographic), the social-psychological; and the cultural-social. The major fertility studies to date, as well as the rationale of the family-planning movement, have treated fertility behavior as the dependent variable and personal and social-psychological factors as independent variables. Both the fertility studies and the family-planning movement have ignored the role of the cultural and social-organizational aspects of fertility behavior. Durkheim's insistence that the "social fact" is anterior and exterior to the individual in exerting constraints on his behavior may contain the clue to a significant missing ingredient both in fertility research and in family-planning programs. It may be necessary to assume that "fertility behavior is in large measure dependent upon the social milieu, and that changes in fertility behavior necessarily involve social change. Or, put in another way, knowledge of persons' attitudes, values, and motivation cannot be expected to account for differences in fertility behavior out of their cultural context. Consequently, changes in fertility behavior cannot be produced through efforts to change attitudes, values, or motivation, except in the context of changes in the social order" (Hauser 1962: 464–65).

This alternative is at the other end of a continuum ranging from the "rational-behavior" approach to the "social-change" approach. Based on the assumption that people will utilize a family-planning clinic if made available to them with an explanation of the advantages that would thereby accrue to them, the rational-behavior approach is, if successful, clearly preferable because of time and cost considerations. The social-change approach would, *a priori,* involve a much greater input of time and funds, assuming that it is known how to induce social change. Since the rational-behavior approach has thus far fallen considerably short of achieving even limited family-planning objectives, the problem is to determine how far along the continuum it is necessary to move in order to achieve the maximum effect per unit of time and money expended. More specifically, the task is how to expand the base of the birth-control clinic so as to increase the number of acceptors and achieve fertility reduction without undue waste of inputs. A series of possible extensions are considered.

A first extension—one that is actually being employed to some extent in Taiwan and elsewhere—consists in the incorporation of the birth-control clinic into a child and maternal health center. A second extension would embody the maternal and child health center into a comprehensive public-health program. These first steps on the continuum leave the family-planning program in the control of the medical world—the physician and public-health personnel.

A more radical extension would be to incorporate the public-health program (or only the maternal and child health center) into a family-counseling service concerned with all aspects of family life. Such a package was actually proposed to me by a Roman Catholic bishop in the Philippines who wanted to make family-planning methods available in his diocese, and such a combination of elements may constitute an excellent approach in all Catholic cultures. This extension of the present base probably involves a broader leadership than the medical profession can give. Certainly a broader leadership is required if the base is widened further to encompass such programs in education as are appropriate at elementary, secondary, and higher levels as well as in adult-education programs. A final step, which by no means exhausts all the steps possible in broadening the base, is to incorporate all the elements involved into a comprehensive program of social and economic development, reaching from the central government into local agencies, employing a holistic approach to the problem of development of both human resources and social and economic institutions.

Key ideas involved in the testing of alternatives to the present family-planning programs (cf. Hauser 1962) may be briefly recapitulated. Five elements are involved.

1. That the fertility-control program be set up in accordance with the principles of experimental design.

2. That random sampling be appropriately employed so that conclusions reached have maximum extensibility.

3. That the dependent variable be an index of fertility or conception.

4. That the independent variables include "control" variables—social-psychological and cultural factors which cannot be manipulated but can be observed before and after the introduction of the experimental variables.

5. That the experimental variables include those required by a cultural-social approach, five of which are identified: economic, environmental, community action, educational, and medical.

The first three elements require no further elaboration here, but the fourth and fifth do. Both the "control" and "experimental" variables are to be considered as independent. The distinction, arbitrary from the standpoint of experimental design, is justified by operational considerations. The control variables, which cannot be manipulated, constitute a basis for stratifying the population into subgroups to be subjected to the application of the experimental variables. The control variables proposed are of two types, "social-psychological" and "cultural." The former include knowledge, attitudes, action orientation, and personality attributes. The latter include essential elements of the social milieu, as for example a classification of areas into "traditional," "transitional," or "modernized" areas. A second category of cultural variables, which may be termed "subcultural," calls for the identification of significant ethnic or racial groups, economic classes, urban or rural populations, sex and age groupings, and the like.

The proposed experimental variables, which are subject to manipulation, include what may be considered five key dimensions of the milieu—economic development, degree of community action, environmental development, educational facilities and services, and medical facilities and services.

Clearly, resources are not likely to be available to permit the actual manipulation of all of these variables, in the sense that the experiment would incorporate economic development; community action; and educational, environmental, and comprehensive medical programs. But in most developing nations various programs of these types are already under way. What is required is active utilization of ongoing programs as, in effect, "natural" laboratory situations. Thus, while the experiment cannot initiate economic-development programs, appropriate populations can be selected for the experiment; and changes in economic levels, as indicated by income per capita, can be measured over time. Within such a framework the impact of varying dosages of family-planning clinics with varying degrees of a broadened base would make feasible the measurement of program impact—as indicated by effect on fertility or conception.

A schema of the type outlined is not likely to prove feasible in its entirety. However, it is desirable to indicate the role that the demographer can play in contributing to the solution of "the population problem"—his role in research and experimental design and evaluation of programs. Moreover, it is necessary to point to a specific alternative to the present family-planning programs. It may be that the approach proposed on an *a priori* basis would take too long and be too costly. To this, the response is that even what one expects to be a very cheap and quick program will turn out to be even more expensive and time-consuming if it does not achieve the desired results.

It should be emphasized, again, that this argument does not imply that present family-planning programs are worthless or that they are to be abandoned. My recommendation is not to slow down present efforts but rather to invest time and effort in experimenting with alternatives against the possibility that the present approach may prove to be futile. It is much too early to conclude that current efforts will not work. It is also foolhardy to assume that they certainly will work and to make no effort to develop alternative programs.

There can be no disputing the observation that present family-planning programs are generally not designed to permit sound conclusions about their effectiveness. The demographer has not yet been effectively utilized either in the design of family-planning experiments or in the evaluation of their effectiveness. Moreover, there is a lamentable tendency for family-planning administrators to evaluate the effectiveness of their own programs, to the extent that any evaluation at all is done. This is a highly questionable practice. It is equivalent to business firms' auditing their own operations—a practice that has long been in ill repute. Evaluation in principle must be the function of a disinterested outside party and, therefore, so also must be the design of experiment—the equivalent of the design of the firm's accounts. The demographer is the logical auditor of fertility-control programs.

EXTENSION OF PROGRAMS TO FERTILITY CONTROL

The discussion thus far has been restricted to programs consistent with the present objectives of the family-planning movement. These objectives, as has been indicated, do not include the goal of population control. As a first step in this direction, it would be necessary for the family-planning movement to enlarge its objectives from conception control to fertility control, and from enabling couples to achieve the number of children they desire to inducing them to have a number of children consistent with a zero rate of population growth.

To aim at birth control rather than conception control, it is necessary to consider the control of births after conception has occurred, or abortion. Ironically, this method is frowned upon by many cultures, some of which interpret it as a form of homicide, while it is legally sanctioned in other cultures and almost universally practiced. Certainly abortion is the most widely practiced form of birth control, including all methods of conception control.

Abortion has been the chief means in effecting the drastic reduction of the birth rate in postwar Japan and also the substantial reductions in socialist Eastern Europe. In these areas, where abortion is legally sanctioned and performed under good medical conditions, it is less dangerous to women than normal parturition. Abortion is also widely practiced in many areas where it is illegal or regarded as immoral. In such nations, including most of the rest of the world, abortion is generally an underground criminal activity or self-induced by women, with such fearful results as the maiming and death of unknown but substantially large numbers of women. By one informed estimate, there may be as many as 40 million abortions per year in the world, and in some countries abortions exceed the number of live births. In the United States illegal abortions may well exceed a million a year. It is mainly the frightful toll that stimulated current movements to liberalize American abortion laws. Moreover, it is largely because of rising abortions in Latin America that no opposition was voiced to a resolution passed by a 1967 population conference, held in Caracas under the aegis of the Organization of American States, favoring the inclusion of family planning in the family-health programs that ministries of health administer in Latin American countries. It is noteworthy that not even the representatives of the Roman Catholic Church who were present objected to this resolution.

It is clear, of course, that whether to sanction abortion as a means of birth control must be decided by individual nations in terms of their own norms. But the taboos against abortion do not prevent its widespread practice, and the problems generated by underground abortion cannot be ignored. It will be increasingly necessary for nations to face up to the problem. The wide spectrum of safeguards and regulations accompanying legal abortion range from relatively rigid rules, which greatly restrict the number possible, to liberal procedures up to and including "abortion by request" as decided by individual physicians in their professional relations with their patients.

It may be argued that an effective program of conception control would make legal abortion unnecessary as well as undesirable. But until an effective program of conception control is achieved, abortion will continue to be widely practiced. Moreover, even with such a program the need for abortion will continue in cases of conception-control failure: rape, incest, delinquency, or the emergence of critical health, social, or economic problems after conception has occurred. In any case, no matter what the posture of a given country may be to abortion, a complete birth-control program, as distinguished from a conception-control program, is not possible without it.

The second objective of a family-planning program that must be changed to achieve fertility control relates to the number of children. As long as the objective of family planning is to enable couples to achieve the number of children they desire, neither an adequate birth control nor population control is likely to be possible. To achieve fertility and population control commensurate with the need, the objective must be to induce couples to restrict their childbearing to the replacement level—that is, to produce the children in order to achieve a zero rate of growth. To set a target of a replacement level of births does not mean, of course, that all couples would be restricted to that number of children. It would still be possible to have a frequency distribution, with some couples having fewer and others more than the replacement level.

There are several ways by which such an objective can be achieved. In the present economically advanced areas in Europe and Northern America, families are generally less than one child per couple above the replacement level. In the United States, for example, the replacement level is 2.11 children per couple and the size of the actual completed family is less than 3. To achieve a zero rate of growth, the economically advanced nations need only do a little more than they are already doing in restricting family size. In such nations the restriction of family size has been entirely voluntary, apparently a by-product of increased education and higher levels of living. There can be little doubt that a replacement level can be achieved in these areas without the employment of special sanctions or incentives.

In the less developed areas, however, the outlook for purely voluntary control is not similar. Moreover, the price of excessive fertility is much greater to the extent that it obstructs economic development, threatens social unrest and political instability, and endangers world peace. Developing areas, therefore, must consider ways of accelerating fertility decline through sanctions and incentives, in addition to voluntarism. Some experiences are already available, as in the monetary incentives to male sterilization in areas of India. But a comprehensive program of sanctions and incentives, compatible with prevalent norms and human dignity, is still to be developed.

Among the devices to be considered in the development of such a scheme are incentives to defer marriage; payments for childless periods above a given parity—preferably the replacement level; payments for sterilization; old-age pensions (to make sons less necessary for support). Such positive programs are to be preferred to sanctions, which are likely to penalize children as well as parents. When famine, disease, or threats to peace become imminent, however, various compulsory programs may be indicated, since under great population pressure some forms of sanctions may be less harmful than the alternatives. Especially worthy of attention is the development of programs to defer marriage, which may decrease fertility significantly. However, such programs may encounter obstacles at least as stubborn as those limiting the number of contraceptive acceptors, for in both cases basic cultural norms are involved.

To achieve fertility control, then, it is necessary to move beyond present family-planning objectives and include abortion as at least an interim means of birth control under adequate legal and medical safeguards; and as the criterion of good policy to substitute for the desired number of children the replacement level of children. It may also be necessary to develop a system including compulsions, which may be less drastic than alternatives facing the developing areas.

Finally, if population control becomes an explicit objective, the comprehensive policy that is called for includes control of mortality and migration as well as fertility. Moreover, it involves the evaluation of any other social and economic programs that may affect fertility, mortality, or migration—for example, immigration and emigration policies, welfare or health programs. Population policy in this sense embraces social and economic development policy, and appropriately so. For any nation that is seeking to raise levels of living and to induce social and economic development is well advised to incorporate population policies into a holistic approach to such modernization. In most nations this would mean incorporating population programs as essential and integral parts of broad national development programs in a manner not now the case.

CONCLUSIONS

Methods of population control that go beyond family planning require an evaluation of the efficiency of present family-planning programs in the control of fertility and population as well as of conception. Even to consider such alternatives makes it explicit that the objective of the family-planning movement is limited to realizing a voluntary control of family size. It is unlikely that present family-planning programs can achieve either fertility control or population control as these have been defined.

To achieve population control present family-planning programs would have to recognize abortion as supplementary to conception control, adopt the objective of inducing couples to desire a replacement-level number of children, and possibly consider abandoning voluntarism in favor of sanctions and incentives. It can be argued that strategically and tactically the family-planning movement can ill afford to take such positions at this time, and this may well be so. But this does not mean that the implications of the restricted objectives can be ignored. Family planners have refrained from active participation in the campaign to add abortion as another birth-control method, and on the whole wisely, for the movement has invoked enough opposition without assuming this burden, too. But the move to liberalize abortion laws is now gaining momentum and receiving increasing support from family-planning personnel. This is in part because abortion, despite futile efforts to sweep it under a rug, is still the world's most widely used method of limiting fertility. In many countries, where it is illegal, abortion still constitutes a mass maiming and killing of women.

In fact, the family-planning movement has not been able to attain even its present limited objectives. The simplistic approach now being used must expand, and experimental work is needed to develop other approaches in case the present efforts prove to be inadequate. And really to control population growth, comprehensive policy and programs should take into account mortality and international migration as well as fertility—and, on the regional or local level, also internal migration.

Even to meet the limited objectives of family planning, the resources available are pathetically inadequate. To achieve the control of either fertility or population would require, as a first step, resources allocated for these purposes at levels far above those achieved on the international, national, or local level.

References

BOGUE, DONALD J. 1964. "The Demographic Breakthrough: From Projection to Control," *Population Index*, 30, 449–454.

———. 1967. "The End of the Population Explosion," *Public Interest*, No. 7, pp. 11–20.

DAVIS, KINGSLEY. 1967. "Population Policy: Will Current Programs Succeed?" *Science*, 158, 730–739.

HAUSER, PHILIP M. 1962. "On Design for Experiment and Research in Fertility Control," in Clyde V. Kiser, ed., *Research in Family Planning*. Princeton, N. J.: Princeton University Press.

———. 1967. "Family Planning and Population Programs: A Review Article," *Demography*, 4, 397–414.

The question to which the previous paper was addressed is perhaps the most important one today in population policy—too important to let any single statement suffice. In the following exchange the issue is joined between another academic demographer and three senior representatives of agencies deeply involved in policy making.

Judith Blake, the author of the first paper, is chairman of the Department of Demography, University of California at Berkeley. This unique department, which combines training in the pertinent portions of several disciplines—particularly sociology, economics, and biostatistics—was fashioned mainly through her efforts. Since her doctoral dissertation, Family Structure in Jamaica: The Social Context of Reproduction *(Free Press, 1961), she has concentrated on the sociological analysis of fertility, in particular making more use of public-opinion polls than perhaps any other demographer.*

Dr. Oscar Harkavy, the first co-author of the rejoinder, is the program officer in charge of the Ford Foundation's Population Office. He has been active as participant or consultant in a large number of official or quasi-official efforts to set population policy, both here and abroad. Mr. Frederick S. Jaffe is director of the Center for Family Planning Program Development of Planned Parenthood—World Population. He is co-author of three books on family planning, and his two dozen articles or public reports are also concentrated on this topic. The third co-author, Dr. Samuel M. Wishik, is a physician with a supplementary degree in public health. He is presently director of program development and evaluation of the International Institute for the Study of Human Reproduction, Columbia University, as well as professor of public-health practice in the School of Public Health and Administrative Medicine there. He also has served on various advisory committees and national or international agencies in the population field, in particular acting as advisor to Pakistan on its national family-planning program.

While this exchange represents some of the best statements on either side to be found in an extensive literature, the debate was of course not settled. Two additional items are of interest: a new estimate of what proportion of American births are unwanted (Bumpass and Westoff 1970) with a comment (Blake 1971). Note that since the references by the several authors are partly to the same sources, they are given in a single list at the end of the articles.

POPULATION POLICY FOR AMERICANS: IS THE GOVERNMENT BEING MISLED?

JUDITH BLAKE

Pressure on the federal government for "action" to limit population growth in the United States has intensified greatly during the past ten years, and at present such action is virtually unchallenged as an official national goal. Given the goal, the question of means becomes crucial. Here I first evaluate the particular means being advocated and pursued in public policy, then I present alternative ways of possibly achieving the goal.

The prevailing view as to the best means is remarkably unanimous and abundantly documented. It is set forth in the seventeen volumes of congressional hearings so far published on the "population crisis" (U. S. Senate 1965–68); in "The Growth of U. S. Population," a report by the Committee on Population of the National Academy of Sciences (1965); in a statement made by an officer of the Ford Foundation who was asked by the Depart-

SOURCE: Reprinted from *Science*, **164** (May 2, 1969), 522–529, with permission of the author and the journal. Copyright 1969 by the American Association for the Advancement of Science.

ment of Health, Education, and Welfare to make suggestions (Harkavy *et al.* 1967); and in the *Report* of the President's Committee on Population and Family Planning (1968). The essential recommendation throughout is that the government should give highest priority to ghetto-oriented family-planning programs designed to "deliver" birth-control services to the poor and uneducated, among whom, it is claimed, there are at least 5 million women who are "in need" of such federally sponsored birth-control assistance.

By what logic have the proponents of control moved from a concern with population growth to a recommendation favoring highest priority for poverty-oriented birth-control programs? First, they have assumed that fertility is the only component of population growth worthy of government attention. Second, they have taken it for granted that, to reduce fertility, one sponsors birth-control programs ("family planning"). Just why they have made this assumption is not clear, but its logical implication is that population growth is due to births that couples would have preferred to avoid. Furthermore, the reasoning confuses couple control over births with societal control over them (Davis 1967; Blake 1965). Third, the proponents of the new policy have seized on the poor and uneducated for birth-control action because they see this group as the only remaining target for a program of voluntary family planning. The rest of the population is handling its family planning pretty well on its own: over 95 percent of fecund couples in the United States already either use birth-control methods or intend to do so. The poor, on the other hand—at least those who are fecund—have larger families than the advantaged; they not only use birth-control methods less but they use them less effectively. The family-planning movement's notion of "responsible parenthood" carries the implication that family size should be directly, not inversely, related to social and economic advantage, and the poor are seen as constituting the residual slack to be taken up by the movement's efforts.

Why are the poor not conforming to the dictates of responsible parenthood? Given the movement's basic assumptions, there are only two answers: the poor are irresponsible, or they have not had the opportunity. Since present-day leaders would abhor labeling the poor irresponsible, they have chosen to blame lack of opportunity as the cause. Opportunity has been lacking, in their eyes, either because the poor have not been "educated" in family planning or because they have not been "reached" by family-planning services. In either case, as they see it, the poor have been deprived of their "rights" (National Academy 1965: 22). This deprivation has allegedly been due to the prudery and hypocrisy of the affluent, who have overtly tabooed discussion of birth control and dissemination of birth-control materials while, themselves, covertly enjoying the benefits of family planning (Cohen 1966: 2).

So much for the logic underlying recent proposals for controlling population growth in the United States. But what is the evidence on which this argument is based? On what empirical grounds is the government being asked to embark on a high-priority program of providing contraceptive services to the poor? Moreover, what, if any, are some of the important public issues that the suggested policy raises—what are its social and political side effects? And, finally, is such a policy, even if appropriate for the poor and even if relatively unencumbered by public disapproval, relevant to the problem of population growth in America? If demographic curtailment is really the objective, must alternative policies be considered and possibly given highest priority?

Turning to the alleged need for government-sponsored birth-control services, one may ask whether birth control has in fact been a tabooed topic among the middle and upper classes, so that the less advantaged could be said to have suffered "deprivation" and consequently now to require government help. One may then question whether there is a mandate from the poor for the type of federally sponsored service that is now being urged, and whether as many as 5 million women are "in need" of such family-planning assistance.

BIRTH CONTROL A TABOOED TOPIC?

The notion that the American public has only recently become willing to tolerate open discussion of birth control has been assiduously cultivated by congressmen and others concerned with government policy on population. For example, Senator Tydings credited Senators Gruening and Clark and President Johnson with having, almost by themselves, changed American public attitudes toward birth control. In 1966, he read the following statement into the 28 February *Congressional Record* (U. S. Senate 1966: 31):

> The time is ripe for positive action. Ten years ago, even five years ago, this was a politically delicate subject. Today the nation has awakened to the need for government action.
> This change in public attitude has come about through the efforts of men who had the courage to brook the tides of public opinion. Senator Clark is such a man. Senator Gruening is such a man. So is President Johnson. Because of their leadership it is no longer necessary for an elected official to speak with trepidation on this subject.

A year later, Senator Tydings reduced to "3 or 4 years" his estimate of the time required to shift public opinion (U. S. Senate 1965–68—1967: 12). Senator Gruening (1967) maintained that the "ninety-eight distinguished men and women" who testified at the public hearing on Senate bill 1676 were "pioneers" whose "names comprise an important honor roll which historically bears an analogy to other famous lists: the signers of the Declaration of Independence, those who ratified the Constitution of the United States, and others whose names were appended to and made possible some of the great turning points in history." Reasoning from the continued existence of old, and typically unenforced, laws concerning birth control (together with President Eisenhower's famous statement opposing birth control), Stycos (1968) stated:

The public reaction to family planning in the United States has varied between disgust and silent resignation to a necessary evil. At best it was viewed as so delicate and risky that it was a matter of "individual conscience." As such, it was a matter so totally private, so sacred (or profane), that no external agents, and certainly not the state, should have anything to do with it.

Does the evidence support such impressionistic claims? How did the general public regard government sponsorship of birth control long before it became a subject of congressional hearings, a National Academy report, and a Presidential Committee report? Fortunately, a question on this topic appeared in no less than thirteen national polls conducted between 1937 and 1966. As part of a larger project concerned with public knowledge and opinions about demographic topics, I have gathered together the original data cards from these polls, prepared them for computer processing, and analyzed the results. The data are all from Gallup polls and are all from national samples of the white, adult population. Here I concentrate on those under 45—that is, on adults in the childbearing age group.

The data of Table 1 contradict the notion that Americans have only recently ceased to regard birth control as a tabooed topic. As far back as thirty years ago, almost three-quarters of the women questioned in these surveys actively approved having the *government* make birth-control information available to the married. By the early 1960s, 80 percent or more of women approved overcoming legal barriers and allowing "anyone who wants it" to have birth-control information. The figures for men are similar. The question asked in 1964—the one question in recent years that did not mention illegality—brought 86 percent of the women and 89 percent of the men into the category of those who approved having birth-control information available for "anyone who wants it." Furthermore, in judging the level of disapproval, one should bear in mind that the remainder of the respondents, in all of these years, includes from 7 to 15 percent who claim that they have "no opinion" on the subject, not that they "disapprove."

An important difference of opinion corresponds to a difference in religious affiliation. Among non-Catholics (including those who have "no religion" and do not attend church), approval has been considerably higher than among Catholics. Among non-Catholic women, over 80 percent approved as early as 1939, and among non-Catholic men the percentages were approximately the same. The 1964 poll showed that 90 percent of each sex approved. Among Catholics, in recent years about 60 percent have approved,

Table 1. White Americans Aged 21 to 44 Who Held that
Birth-Control Information Should Be Made Available to Those
Who Desire It, by Sex, United States, 1937–64

	MEN		WOMEN	
		TOTAL		TOTAL
YEAR	PERCENT	NUMBER	PERCENT	NUMBER
1937	66	1,038	70	734
1938	67	1,111	72	548
1939	74	1,101	73	630
1940	72	1,127	75	618
1943	67	628	73	866
1945	64	714	70	879
1947	76	353	75	405
1959	78	301	79	394
1961	82	336	81	394
1962	85	288	80	381
1963	78	323	79	373
1964	89	324	86	410

Note: The questions asked of respondents concerning birth control were as follows. In 1937: "Do you favor the birth-control movement?" In 1938, 1939, 1940, 1943, 1945, and 1947: "Would you like to see a government agency [or "government health clinics"] furnish birth-control information to married people who want it?" In 1959, 1961, 1962, and 1963: "In some places in the United States it is not legal to supply birth-control information. How do you feel about this—do you think birth-control information should be available to anyone who wants it, or not?" In 1964: "Do you think birth-control information should be available to anyone who wants it, or not?"

and the question in 1964 that mentioned neither the government nor legality brought opinions of approval from 77 percent of the women and 83 percent of the men.

Clearly, if birth-control information has in fact been unavailable to the poor, the cause has not been a generalized and pervasive attitude of prudery on the part of the American public. Although public officials may have misjudged American opinion (and may have mistakenly assumed that the Catholic Church "spoke for" a majority of Americans, or even for a majority of Catholics), most Americans of an age to be having children did not regard birth control as a subject that should be under a blanket of secrecy and, as far back as the 1930s, evinced a marked willingness to have their government make such information widely available. It seems unlikely, therefore, that poorer sectors of our population were "cut off" from birth-control knowledge primarily because informal channels of communication (the channels through which most people learn about birth control) were blocked by an upper- and middle-class conspiracy of silence.

What has happened, however, is that pressure groups for family planning, like the Catholic hierarchy they have been opposing, have been acting as self-designated spokesmen for "public opinion." By developing a cause as righteous as that of the Catholics (the "rights" of the poor as against the "rights" of a religious group), the family planners have used the American way of influencing official opinion. Now public officials appear to believe that publicly supported birth-control services are what the poor have always wanted and needed, just as, in the past, official opinion acceded to the notion that such services would have been "offensive" to certain groups. Nonetheless, the question remains whether or not publicly supported services are actually appropriate to the attitudes and objectives of the poor and uneducated in matters of reproduction. Is the government responding to a mandate from the poor or to an ill concealed mandate from the well-to-do? If there is no mandate from the poor, the provision of birth-control services may prove a convenience for certain women but is likely to have little effect on the reproductive performance of the poor in general. Let us look at the evidence.

IS THERE A MANDATE FROM THE POOR?

The notion that the poor have larger families than the affluent only because they have less access to birth-control information implies that the poor *desire* families as small as, or smaller than, those of the well-to-do. The poor are simply unable to realize this desire, the argument goes, because of lack of access to birth-control information. The National Academy of Sciences Committee on Population (1965: 10) stated the argument very well:

> The available evidence indicates that low-income families do not want more children than do families with higher incomes, but they have more because they do not have the information or the resources to plan their families effectively according to their own desires.

The committee, however, presented none of the "available evidence" that "low-income families do not want more children than do families with higher incomes." Actually, my data supply evidence that runs counter to the statement quoted above, both with respect to the desired or ideal number of children and with respect to attitudes toward birth control.

I shall begin with the preferred size of family. A number of national polls, conducted over some 25 years, provide data concerning opinions on ideal family size. In addition, I include tabulations of data from two national surveys on fertility (the Growth of American Families studies), conducted in 1955 and 1960 (Freedman *et al.* 1959; Whelpton *et al.* 1966). My detailed analyses of the results of these polls and surveys are given elsewhere (Blake 1966a; 1966b; 1967; 1968) and are only briefly summarized here. Table 2

Table 2. Mean Number of Children Considered "Ideal" by Non-Catholic Women, by Education and Economic Status, United States, 1943–68

DATE	AGE RANGE	HIGHEST GRADE COMPLETED			INCOME OR ECONOMIC STATUS				ALL RESPONDENTS	
		COLLEGE	HIGH SCHOOL	GRADE SCHOOL	1 (HIGH)	2	3	4 (LOW)	MEAN	NUMBER
1943	20–34	2.8	2.6	2.6	2.9	2.7	2.7	2.5	2.7	(1,893)
1952	21+	3.3	3.1	3.6		3.3			3.3	(723)
1955 [a]	18–39	3.1	3.2	3.7	3.2	3.1	3.2	3.5	3.3	(1,905)
1955 [b]	18–39	3.3	3.4	3.9	3.4	3.3	3.4	3.7	3.4	(1,905)
1957	21+	3.4	3.2	3.6		3.3		3.5	3.3	(448)
1959	21+	3.5	3.4	3.9		3.5		3.6	3.5	(472)
1960 [a]	18–39	3.1	3.2	3.5	3.1	3.2	3.3	3.2	3.2	(1,728)
1960 [b]	18–39	3.2	3.4	3.6	3.2	3.3	3.5	3.4	3.4	(1,728)
1963	21+	3.2	3.4	3.5	3.3	3.3	3.5	3.5	3.4	(483)
1966	21+	3.1	3.3	3.7	3.2	3.2	3.4	3.7	3.3	(374)
1967	21+	3.1	3.3	3.4	3.3	3.2	3.1	3.4	3.3	(488)
1968	21+	3.2	3.3	3.7	3.2	3.0	3.4	3.6	3.3	(539)

[a] Minimum ideal (results from coding range answers—"2 or 3," "3 or 4"—to the lower figure).
[b] Maximum ideal (results from coding range answers—"2 or 3," "3 or 4"—to the higher figure).

gives mean values for the family size considered ideal by white, non-Catholic women, according to education and economic status.

The data lend little support to the hypothesis that the poor desire families as small as those desired by the middle and upper classes. Within both the educational and the economic categories, those on the lower rungs not only have larger families than those on the higher rungs (at least in the case of non-Catholics) but say they want larger families and consider them ideal. This differential has existed for as long as information on preferred family size in this country has been available, and it persists. It thus seems extremely hazardous to base a major governmental effort on the notion that, among individuals (white individuals, at least) at the lower social levels, there is a widespread and deeply held desire for families as small as, or smaller than, those desired by the well-to-do. No major survey shows this to be the case.

Not only do persons of lower socio-economic status prefer larger families than the more affluent do, they also generally favor birth control less. Tables 3 and 4 show the percentages of white men and women who expressed approval of birth control in surveys made between 1937 and 1964, by educational level and economic status, respectively.

Looking at the educational differential (Table 3), one finds that, in general, the proportion of those who approve birth control drops precipitately between the college and grade-school levels. As far back as the early 1940s, over 80 percent of women and 75 percent of men with at least some college education approved government action on birth control. By 1964, over 90 percent of both sexes approved. By contrast, only 60 percent of men and women with an elementary school education approved in the 1940s, and, despite a rise in approval, there is still a differential. When non-Catholics alone are considered, the educational difference is even more pronounced in many cases.

Turning to economic or income status (Table 4), one generally finds the same results. The high proportions (close to 100 percent) of women in the highest and next-to-highest economic brackets who, in recent years, have approved birth-control efforts are noteworthy, as is the fact that approximately 80 percent of women in these brackets approved such efforts as far back as the 1930s. On the other hand, men and women in lower income brackets have been slower to approve birth-control policies.

Despite the inverse relation just described, I may have overemphasized the lesser approval of birth-control programs on the part of persons of lower economic and social status. After all, in recent years approval often has been high even among people at the lowest social levels. Among women with only a grade-school education, the percentage of those favoring birth-control programs averaged 73 percent in polls taken between 1959 and 1964; among men at the lowest educational level, the corresponding average was 66 percent. Yet it is undeniably true that, throughout the period for which data

Table 3. White Persons Aged 21 to 44 Who Held that Birth-Control Information Should Be Made Available to Those Who Desire It, by Sex and Last Grade of Schooling Completed, United States, 1943–64

| | MEN | | | | | | WOMEN | | | | | |
| | COLLEGE | | HIGH SCHOOL | | GRADE SCHOOL | | COLLEGE | | HIGH SCHOOL | | GRADE SCHOOL | |
YEAR	PER-CENT	TOTAL NUMBER	PER-CENT	TOTAL NUMBER	PER-CENT	TOTAL NUMBER	PER-CENT	TOTAL NUMBER	PER-CENT	TOTAL NUMBER	PER-CENT	TOTAL NUMBER
1943	75	184	68	284	56	157	82	216	74	442	60	207
1945	74	202	62	360	58	140	83	216	68	434	56	207
1947	91	84	72	199	67	66	81	89	74	228	72	81
1959	88	89	76	163	65	49	91	55	79	279	68	41
1961	88	102	81	188	67	46	84	81	81	265	78	50
1962	91	93	85	171	61	23	84	79	82	258	66	44
1963	86	105	79	178	53	40	81	80	78	251	81	42
1964	92	107	88	188	83	29	94	79	86	293	74	38

Table 4. White Persons Aged 21 to 44 Who Held that Birth-Control Information Should Be Made Available to Those Who Desire It, by Sex and Income Bracket, United States, 1937–64

| | MEN | | | | | | | | WOMEN | | | | | | | |
| | 1 (HIGH) | | 2 | | 3 | | 4 (LOW) | | 1 (HIGH) | | 2 | | 3 | | 4 (LOW) | |
YEAR	PER-CENT	TOTAL NUMBER	PER-CENT	TOTAL NUMBER	PER-CENT	TOTAL NUMBER	PER-CENT	TOTAL NUMBER	PER-CENT	TOTAL NUMBER	PER-CENT	TOTAL NUMBER	PER-CENT	TOTAL NUMBER	PER-CENT	TOTAL NUMBER
1937	78	112	70	406	61	520			67	69	78	293	64	372		
1938	65	125	74	453	62	521			80	51	73	232	70	259		
1939	78	116	75	432	73	553			71	68	77	260	71	302		
1940	79	131	75	443	68	553			80	49	78	258	71	311		
1943	76	80	72	219	62	330			80	90	79	272	68	500		
1945	73	67	66	286	62	352			83	75	77	264	64	531		
1947	86	42	77	123	72	188			92	38	71	119	73	237		
1959	83	101	76	120	73	79			83	139	82	152	72	95		
1961	93	42	85	80	87	103	69	111	88	41	80	97	80	76	81	138
1962	82	45	89	71	86	94	80	74	82	51	80	75	84	110	77	140
1963	88	60	84	79	76	96	61	97	87	67	79	107	79	98	75	100
1964	90	67	87	26	93	82	85	79	96	90	90	87	85	104	78	120

Note: Levels 1 to 4 for the years 1961–64 range from incomes of $10,000 and over down to incomes under $5,000. Prior to 1961, levels 1 to 3 represent "upper," "middle," and "lower" income brackets.

are available, the people who needed birth-control information most, according to recent policy pronouncements, have been precisely the ones who were least in favor of a policy that would make it widely available.

The truth of this conclusion becomes more evident when we move to an analysis of a question asked on the 1966 Gallup poll: Do you think birth-control pills should be made available free to all women on relief who are of childbearing age? This question presents the public with the specific issue that is the focus of current policy—namely, birth control especially for the poor. A summary of the replies to this question is given in Table 5, together

Table 5. White Americans Aged 21 to 44 Who Approved the Free Distribution of Birth-Control Pills to Women on Relief, 1966, Compared with Persons Who Approved Birth Control, 1959–64, by Sex, Education, and Economic Status

	MEN			WOMEN		
	1966		AVERAGE	1966		AVERAGE
CATEGORY	PER-CENT	TOTAL NUMBER	PERCENT 1959–64	PER-CENT	TOTAL NUMBER	PERCENT 1959–64
Total	65	264	82	71	385	81
Highest grade completed						
College	82	98	87	75	197	87
High school	58	142	82	70	392	81
Grade school	38	24	66	59	32	73
Economic status						
1 (high)	79	80	89	70	110	87
2	69	75	84	76	99	82
3	59	65	83	70	91	80
4 (low)	39	41	74	67	76	78

with average percentages of people who, in the five surveys made between 1959 and 1964, replied that they approved birth control generally.

It is clear that the over-all level of approval drops when specific reference to a poverty-oriented birth-control policy is introduced. The decline is from an average of approximately 80 percent for each sex during the period 1959–64 to 65 percent for men and 71 percent for women in 1966. Of most significance, however, is the fact that the largest proportionate drop in approval occurs among members of the "target" groups themselves—the poor and uneducated. In particular, there is a remarkable drop in approval among men at this socio-economic level. There is a 42-percent decline in approval among men who have had only a grade-school education and a 29-percent drop among those with a high-school education. Among the college-educated men the drop in approval is by only 6 percent. The results by income parallel those by education: there is a 47-percent drop for men in the lowest income group but only a 9-percent drop for those in the highest income bracket. Even if the tabulations are restricted to non-Catholics (data that are not presented here), the results are essentially the same.

If the ghetto-oriented birth-control policy urged on the federal government meets with limited public enthusiasm, how does the public view extension of that policy to teen-age girls? This question is of some importance because a notable aspect of the pressure for government-sponsored family-planning programs is advocacy of making birth-control information and materials available at the high-school level.

The Committee on Population of the National Academy of Sciences (1965: 13) urges early education in "family planning" in order to prevent illegitimacy.

Government statistics show that the mothers of approximately 41 percent of the 245,000 babies born illegitimately in the United States every year are women 19 years of age or younger. Thus a large proportion of all illegitimate children are progeny of teen-age mothers. To reduce the number of such children born to teen-age mothers, high-school education in family planning is essential.

Katherine B. Oettinger, Deputy Secretary for Family Planning of the Department of Health, Education, and Welfare (Anon. 1968: 3) importunes us not to "demand the eligibility card of a first pregnancy before we admit vulnerable girls to family planning services." The Harkavy (*et al.* 1967: 29) report states:

Eligibility requirements should be liberal with respect to marital status. Such services should be made available to the unmarried as well as the married. . . . Eligibility requirements should be liberal with respect to the age of unmarried women seeking help. This will undoubtedly pose some problems, but they may not be insurmountable. Some publically supported programs are already facing them (for example, in Baltimore).

Representative Scheuer from New York has berated the federal government for not "bringing family planning into the schools." He has cited the "desperate need for family planning by unmarried 14-, 15-, and 16-year-old girls in school [which] is so transparently evident that it almost boggles the imagination to realize that nothing has been done. Virtually no leadership has come from the federal government" (U. S. Senate 1965–68—1967: 18).

Obviously there is little recognition in these statements that such a policy might engender a negative public response. Yet such a possibility cannot be discounted. The results of the 1966 question "Do you think they [the pills] should be made available to teen-age girls?" suggest that a policy of distributing them to female adolescents may be viewed by the public as involving more complex issues than the mere democratization of "medical"

Table 6. White Americans Who Approved Making Birth-Control Pills Available to Teen-Age Girls, by Religion, Sex, Age Category, Education, and Economic Status, 1966

| | ALL RELIGIONS | | | | NON-CATHOLIC | | | |
| | MEN | | WOMEN | | MEN | | WOMEN | |
CATEGORY	PER-CENT	TOTAL NUM-BER	PER-CENT	TOTAL NUM-BER	PER-CENT	TOTAL NUM-BER	PER-CENT	TOTAL NUM-BER
Age								
Under 30	29	86	17	149	34	65	19	102
30–44	19	172	8	238	20	133	7	169
Highest grade completed								
College	32	98	15	100	36	75	13	71
High school	18	142	9	264	19	110	9	180
Grade school	13	24	11	35	6	17	14	28
Economic status								
1 (high)	33	80	11	113	35	58	11	75
2	20	75	13	105	24	58	14	72
3	19	65	7	94	18	50	5	64
4 (low)	13	41	16	82	15	33	14	66

services (Table 6). In general, a proposal to distribute pills to teen-age girls meets with very little approval. There is more disapproval among women than among men. Even among women under the age of 30, only 17 percent approve; among men in this age group, 29 percent approve. At no age does women's approval reach 20 percent, and in most cases it is below 15 percent. Furthermore, restriction of the results to non-Catholics does not raise the percentages of those who approve the policy. Most noteworthy is the socio-economic gradient among men. Whereas 32 percent of college-educated men approve distribution of pills to young girls, only 13 percent of men with a grade-school education do; 33 percent of men in the highest income bracket approve, but only 13 percent in the lowest bracket.

Clearly, the extension of "family planning" to poor, unmarried teenagers is not regarded simply as "health care." Individuals may approve, in a general way, a wider availability of birth-control information without approving federal expenditure to facilitate a high level of sexual activity by teen-age girls. One suspects that explicit recognition and implied approval of such activity still comes hard to our population, and that it comes hardest to the group most involved in the problems of illegitimacy and premarital conception—namely, the poor and uneducated themselves. The extreme disapproval of a policy of distributing pills to teen-age girls that is found in lower-class groups (particularly among lower-class men) suggests that a double standard of sexual behavior is operative in these groups—a standard that does not allow open toleration of the idea that the ordinary teen-age girl requires the pill, or that a part of her education in junior high school and high school should include instruction in its use.

CAN "5 MILLION WOMEN" BE WRONG?

The most widely publicized argument favoring federal birth-control programs, and apparently the one that elected officials find most persuasive, is the claim that there are approximately "5 million" poor women "in need" of publicly subsidized birth-control help (Harkavy *et al.* 1967: Attachment A, pp. 4–19; Planned Parenthood n.d.). I list below some of the principal assumptions upon which this estimate is based—all of which introduce serious upward biases into the evidence.

1. It is claimed that women at the poverty and near-poverty levels desire families of 3.0 children. While this may be true of nonwhite wives at this economic level, it is not true, as we have seen, of white women, who comprise a major share of the "target" group and who, on the average, desire a number of children closer to 4 (especially if Catholics are included, as they are in the "5 million").

2. It is assumed by the estimators that 82 percent of all poor women aged 15 to 44 are at risk of conception (that is, exposed sexually), in spite of the fact that only 45 percent of poor women in this age group are married and living with their husbands. In arriving at the figure of 82 percent, the estimators assumed that all women in the "married" category (including those who were separated from their husbands and those whose husbands were absent) were sexually exposed regularly, and that half of the women in the "nonmarried" category—that is, single, widowed, and divorced women— were exposed regularly. Information is scarce concerning the sexual behavior of widows and divorced women, but Kinsey's data on premarital coitus leads one to believe that the assumption of 50 percent for single women may be high. Among the women with a grade-school education in Kinsey's sample, 38 percent had had coitus at some time between the ages of 16 and 20, and 26 percent at some time between the ages of 21 and 25. Moreover, as Kinsey emphasizes, these encounters were characteristically sporadic (Kinsey *et al.* 1953: 291, 337).

3. The proportion of sterile women among the poor is assumed to be 13 percent, although the Scripps 1960 "Growth of American Families Study" showed the proportion among white women of grade-school education to be 22 percent (Whelpton *et al.* 1966: 159).

4. No allowance is made for subnormal fecundity, although the Scripps

1960 study (*ibid.*: 159) had indicated that, among women of grade-school education, an additional 10 percent (over and above the 22 percent) were subnormal in their ability to reproduce.

5. It is taken for granted by the estimators that no Catholic women would object on religious grounds to the use of modern methods, and no allowance is made for objection by non-Catholics, on religious or other grounds. In other words, it is assumed that all women "want" the service. Yet, in response to a question concerning the desirability of limiting or spacing pregnancies, 29 percent of the wives with grade-school education who were interviewed in the Scripps 1960 study said they were "against" such limitation or spacing (*ibid.*: 177). Among the Catholic wives with grade-school education, the proportion "against" was 48 percent, although half of these objectors were "for" the rhythm method. Similar objections among the disadvantaged have been revealed by many polls over a long period.

6. Perhaps most important, the estimate of 5 million women "wanting" and "in need of" birth-control information includes not only objectors but women who are already practicing birth control. Hence, in addition to all the other biases, the estimate represents a blanket decision by the estimators that the women require medical attention regarding birth control—particularly that they need the pill and the coil. In the words of the Harkavy (*et al.* 1967: Attachment A, p. 19) report:

> This may be considered a high estimate of the number of women who need to have family-planning services made available to them in public clinics, because some of the couples among the poor and near-poor are able to exercise satisfactory control over their fertility. However, even these couples do not have the same access as the nonpoor to the more effective and acceptable methods of contraception, particularly the pill and the loop. So, simply in order to equalize the access of the poor and the near-poor to modern methods of contraception under medical supervision, it is appropriate to try to make contraceptive services available to all who may need and want them.

Yet the 1960 Scripps study found that, among fecund women of grade-school education, 79 percent used contraceptives (Whelpton *et al.* 1966: 159). The 21 percent who did not included young women who were building families and said they wanted to get pregnant, as well as Catholics who objected to birth control on religious grounds. As for the methods that women currently are using, it seems gratuitous for the federal government to decide that only medically supervised methods—the pill and the coil—are suitable for lower-income couples, and that a mammoth "service" program is therefore required. In fact, the implications of such a decision border on the fantastic—the implications that we should substitute scarce medical and paramedical attention for all contraceptive methods now being used by poor couples.

In sum, the argument supporting a "need" for nationwide, publicly sustained birth-control programs does not stand up under empirical scrutiny. Most fecund lower-class couples now use birth-control methods when they want to prevent pregnancy; in the case of those who do not, the blame cannot simply be laid at the door of the affluent who have kept the subject of birth control under wraps, or of a government that has withheld services. As we have seen, opinion on birth control has been, and is, less favorable among the poor and the less well educated than among the well-to-do. In addition, the poor desire larger families. Although it may be argued that in relation to public welfare birth control has, until recently, been taboo because of the "Catholic vote," most individuals at all social levels have learned about birth control *informally* and without medical attention. Furthermore, the most popular birth-control device, the condom, has long been as available as aspirin or cigarettes, and certainly has been used by men of all social classes. When one bears in mind the fact that the poor have no difficulty in gaining access to illegal narcotics (despite their obvious "unavailability"), and that the affluent had drastically reduced their fertility before present-day contraceptive methods were available, one must recognize and take into account a motivational component in non-use and inefficient use of contraceptives. Indeed, were relative lack of demand on the part of the poor not a principal factor, it would be difficult to explain why such an important "market" for birth-control materials—legal or illegal—would have escaped the attention of enterprising businessmen or bootleggers. In any event, any estimate based on the assumption that all poor women in the reproductive group "want" birth-control information and materials and that virtually all "need" publicly supported services that will provide them—including women with impaired fecundity, women who have sexual intercourse rarely or not at all, women who object on religious grounds, and women who are already using birth-control methods—would seem to be seriously misleading as a guide for our government in its efforts to control population growth.

Moreover, the proposal for government sponsorship takes no account of the possible advantages of alternative means of reaching that part of the "market" that may not be optimally served at present. For example, competitive pricing, better marketing, and a program of advertising could make it possible for many groups in the population who are now being counted as "targets" for government efforts to purchase contraceptives of various kinds. When one bears in mind the fact that an important reason for non-use or lack of access to contraceptives may be some sort of conflict situation (between husband and wife, adolescent child and parent, and so on), it becomes apparent that the impersonal and responsive marketplace is a far better agency for effecting smooth social change than is a far-flung national bureaucracy loaded with well-meaning but often blundering "health work-

ers." The government could doubtless play an initial stimulating and facili-
tating role in relation to private industry, without duplicating, on a welfare
basis, functions that might be more efficiently handled in the marketplace.

WOULD THE POLICY HAVE SIDE EFFECTS?

The possible inadvisability of having the government become a direct
purveyor of birth-control materials to poverty groups becomes more clear
when we consider some of the risks involved in such a course of action.

Even if the goal of reducing family size were completely and widely
accepted by the poorer and less well educated sectors of the population, we
should not assume that the general public would necessarily view a policy
concerned with the means and practice of birth control (in any social group)
as it views ordinary medical care—that is, as being morally neutral and
obviously "desirable." Birth control is related to sexual behavior, and in all
viable societies sexual behavior is regulated by social institutions. It is thus
an oversimplification to think that people will be unmindful of what are, for
them at least, the moral implications of changes in the conditions under
which sexual intercourse is possible, permissible, or likely. An issue such as
the distribution of pills to teen-age girls runs a collision course with norms
about premarital relations for young girls—norms that, in turn, relate to the
saliency of marriage and motherhood as a woman's principal career and to
the consequent need for socially created restrictions on free sexual access if
an important inducement to marriage is not to be lost. Only if viable careers
alternative to marriage existed for women would the lessening of controls
over sexual behavior outside of marriage be unrelated to women's lifetime
opportunities, for such opportunities would be independent of the marriage
market and, *a fortiori*, independent of sexual bargaining. But such independence clearly does not exist. Hence, when the government is told that it will
be resolving a "medical" problem if it makes birth-control pills available to
teenagers, it is being misled into becoming the protagonist in a sociologically
based conflict between short-run feminine impulses and long-run feminine
interests—a conflict that is expressed both in relations between parents and
children and in relations between the sexes. This sociological conflict far
transcends the "medical" issue of whether or not birth-control services
should be made widely available.

Actually, the issue of sexual morality is only one among many potentially
explosive aspects of direct federal involvement in family-planning programs
for the poor. Others come readily to mind, such as the possibility that the
pill and other physiological methods could have long-run, serious side effects,
or that racial organizations could seize on the existence of these programs
as a prime example of "genocide." Eager promoters of the suggested programs tend to brush such problems aside as trivial, but the problems, like

the issue of sexual morality, cannot be wished away, for they are quite patently there (U. S. Senate 1965-68—1967: 62). *All* drug taking involves risks, and it is recognized that many of the specific ones involved in long-term ingestion of the pill may not be discovered for many years. No one today can say that these are less than, equal to, or greater than the normal risks of pregnancy and childbirth. Equally, a class-directed birth-control program, whatever its intent, is open to charges of genocide that are difficult to refute. Such a program cannot fail to appear to single out the disadvantaged as the "goat," all the while implying that the very considerable "planned" fertility of most Americans inexplicably requires no government attention at all.

POPULATION POLICY FOR AMERICANS

It seems clear that the suggested policy of poverty-oriented birth-control programs does not make sense as a welfare measure. It is also true that, as an inhibitor of population growth, it is inconsequential and trivial. It does not touch the principal cause of such growth in the United States—namely, the reproductive behavior of the majority of Americans who, under present conditions, want families of more than three children and thereby generate a growth rate far in excess of that required for population stability. Indeed, for most Americans the "family-planning" approach, concentrating as it does on the distribution of contraceptive materials and services, is irrelevant, because they already know about efficient contraception and are already "planning" their families. It is thus apparent that any policy designed to influence reproductive behavior must not only concern itself with all fecund Americans (rather than just the poor) but must, as well, relate to family-size goals (rather than just to contraceptive means). In addition, such a policy cannot be limited to matters affecting contraception (or even to matters affecting gestation and parturition, such as abortion), but must, additionally, take into account influences on the formation and dissolution of heterosexual unions (Davis and Blake 1956).

What kinds of reproductive policies can be pursued in an effort to reduce long-term population growth? The most important step toward developing such new policies is to recognize and understand the existing ones, for we already have influential and coercive policies regarding reproductive behavior. Furthermore, these existing policies relate not merely to proscriptions (legal or informal) regarding certain means of birth control (like abortion) but also to a definition of reproduction as a primary societal end and to an organization of social roles that draws most of the population into reproductive unions.

The existence of such pronatalist policies becomes apparent when we recall that, among human beings, population replacement would not occur at all were it not for the complex social organization and system of incentives that encourage mating, pregnancy, and the care, support, and rearing of children. These institutional mechanisms are the pronatalist "policies" evolved unconsciously over millennia to give societies a fertility sufficient to offset high mortality. The formation and implementation of antinatalist policies must be based, therefore, on an analysis and modification of the existing pronatalist policies. It follows, as well, that antinatalist policies will not necessarily involve the introduction of coercive measures. In fact, just the opposite is the case. Many of these new policies will entail a *lifting* of pressures *to* reproduce, rather than an *imposition* of pressures *not* to do so. In order to understand this point let us consider briefly our present-day pronatalism.

It is convenient to start with the family, because pronatalism finds its most obvious expression in this social institution. The pronatalism of the family has many manifestations, but among the most influential and universal are two: the standardization of both the male and the female sexual roles in terms of reproductive functions, obligations, and activities, and the standardization of the occupational role of women—half of the population—in bearing and rearing children and carrying out complementary activities. These two "policies" insure that just about everyone will be propelled into reproductive unions, and that half of the population will enter such unions as a "career"— a life's work. Each of the two "policies" is worth considering.

With regard to sex roles, it is generally recognized that potential human variability is greater than is normally permitted *within* each sex category. Existing societies have tended to suppress and extinguish such variability and to standardize sexual roles in ways that imply that all "normal" persons will attain the status of parents. This coercion takes many forms, including one-sided indoctrination in schools, legal barriers and penalties for deviation, and the threats of loneliness, ostracism, and ridicule that are implied in the unavailability of alternatives. Individuals who—by temperament, health, or constitution—do not fit the ideal sex-role pattern are nonetheless coerced into attempting to achieve it, and many of them do achieve it, at least to the extent of having demographic impact by becoming parents.

Therefore, a policy that sought out the ways in which coercion regarding sex roles is at present manifesting itself could find numerous avenues for relieving the coercion and for allowing life styles different from marriage and parenthood to find free and legitimized expression. Such a policy would have an effect on the content of expectations regarding sex roles as presented and enforced in schools, on laws concerning sexual activity between consenting adults, on taxation with respect to marital status and number of children, on residential building policies, and on just about every facet of existence that is now organized so as exclusively to favor and reward a pattern of sex roles based on marriage and parenthood.

As for the occupational roles of women, existing pressures still attempt to make the reproductive and occupational roles coterminous for all women who elect to marry and have children. This rigid structuring of the wife-mother position builds into the entire motivational pattern of women's lives a tendency to want a family of at least moderate size. To understand this point, one must recognize that the desired number of children relates not simply to the wish for a family of a particular size but also to a need for more than one or two children if one is going to enjoy "family life" over a significant portion of one's lifetime. This need is increased rather than lessened by improved life expectancy. Insofar as women focus their energies and emotions on their families, one cannot expect that they will be satisfied to play their only important role for a diminishing fraction of their lives, or that they will readily regard make-work and dead-end jobs as a substitute for "mothering." The notion that most women will "see the error of their ways" and decide to have two-child families is naive, since few healthy and energetic women will be so misguided as to deprive themselves of most of the rewards society has to offer them and choose a situation that allows them neither a life's work outside the home nor one within it. Those who do deprive themselves in this fashion are, in effect, taking the brunt of the still existing maladjustment between the roles of women and the reproductive needs of society. In a society oriented around achievement and accomplishment, such women are exceptionally vulnerable to depression, frustration, and a sense of futility, because they are being blocked from a sense of fulfillment both at home and abroad.

In sum, the problem of inhibiting population growth in the United States cannot be dealt with in terms of "family-planning needs" because this country is well beyond the point of "needing" birth-control methods. Indeed, even the poor seem not to be a last outpost for family-planning attention. If we wish to limit our growth, such a desire implies basic changes in the social organization of reproduction that will make nonmarriage, childlessness, and small (two-child) families far more prevalent than they are now. A new policy, to achieve such ends, can take advantage of the antinatalist tendencies that our present institutions have suppressed. This will involve the lifting of penalties for antinatalist behavior rather than the "creation" of new ways of life. This behavior already exists among us as part of our covert and deviant culture, on the one hand, and our elite and artistic culture, on the other. Such antinatalist tendencies have also found expression in feminism, which has been stifled in the United States by means of systematic legal, educational, and social pressures concerned with women's "obligations" to create and care for children. A fertility-control policy that does not take into account the need to alter the present structure of reproduction in these and other ways merely trivializes the problem of population control and misleads those who have the power to guide our country toward completing the vital revolution.

FAMILY PLANNING AND PUBLIC POLICY: WHO IS MISLEADING WHOM?

OSCAR HARKAVY, FREDERICK S. JAFFE, AND SAMUEL M. WISHIK

Federal policies on family-planning services and population research are currently under review as a result of the report of the President's Committee on Population and Family Planning (1968). Judith Blake's article, "Population Policy for Americans: Is the Government Being Misled?," which is presumably intended to influence this review, contains numerous errors of fact and interpretation which it is important to clarify. To support her position, she knocks down several straw men; ignores the bulk of serious demographic research on United States fertility patterns in the last fifteen years, as well as research on the differential availability of health care and the relative effectiveness of various contraceptive methods; and cites opinion-poll data in a manner that distorts the over-all picture. The article's methodological limitations alone are sufficient to suggest that the question raised in its subtitle may more appropriately be turned around and asked of the article itself.

The article is based on six principal propositions.

1. That the reduction of population growth in the United States—indeed, the achievement of "population stability"—is "virtually unchallenged as an official national goal."

2. That, in pursuit of *this* goal, the "essential recommendation" by official and private groups has been a program of publicly financed family-planning services for the poor.

3. That this program of family planning for the poor will not achieve the goal of population stability.

4. That advocates of this policy contend that the poor have been denied access to family-planning services because of "the prudery and hypocrisy of the affluent."

5. That the poor desire larger families than higher-income couples do and are significantly less inclined to favor birth control.

6. That the estimate of 5 million poor women as the approximate number in need of subsidized family-planning services is exaggerated.

Within the exception of proposition 3, each of these statements is seriously misleading or in error. Let us examine the evidence on each point.

SOURCE: Reprinted from *Science,* **165** (July 25, 1969), 367–373, with permission of the authors and the journal. Copyright 1969 by the American Association for the Advancement of Science.

A CONSENSUS ON POPULATION STABILITY?

If the United States had as a national goal the reduction of its population growth and the achievement of population stability—and if the program of publicly funded family-planning services for those who cannot afford private medical care had been advanced as the principal or only means of achieving population stability—Judith Blake's contention that the government is being misled would have much validity. However, neither proposition is sustained by the evidence.

We have individually and jointly been associated with the evolution of public policy in this field for more than a decade. To our knowledge, there has never been an official policy regarding the virtue or necessity of reducing United States population growth, much less achieving population stability. Nor has there emerged among Americans generally a "virtually unchallenged" consensus on what should constitute an official population policy in the United States.

The clearest statement of official *domestic* policy is contained in President Johnson's Health Message to Congress (1966):

We have a growing concern to foster the integrity of the family and the opportunity for each child. It is essential that all families have access to information and services that will allow freedom to choose the number and spacing of their children within the dictates of individual conscience.

Neither in this or in any other statement did the President cite stabilization of United States growth as the objective of federal policy. Nor has such a goal been articulated by Congress or the federal agencies. Secretary Gardner of the Department of Health, Education, and Welfare (HEW) stated (1966) that the objectives of departmental policy are "to improve the health of the people, to strengthen the integrity of the family, and to provide families the freedom of choice to determine the spacing of their children and the size of their families." Later he reiterated (1968) that "the immediate objective is to extend family-planning services to all those desiring such services who would not otherwise have access to them."

It is clear that the federal program has been advanced, not for population control, but to improve health and reduce the impact of poverty and deprivation.

GOALS OF THE FEDERAL FAMILY-PLANNING POLICY

Given this unambiguous framework for federal policy, it is inexplicable how Blake could arrive at the statement that population limitation has become our national goal and that the "essential recommendation" for reaching *this* goal has been to extend family-planning services to the poor. She attributes this "misleading" recommendation to a report by the National Academy of Sciences (1965), a consultants' review of HEW programs written by us (Harkavy *et al.* 1967), and the report of the President's Committee (1968), despite the fact that each of these reports clearly distinguishes a family-planning program for the poor from an over-all United States population-control program or policy. For example, the National Academy of Sciences report stated explicitly (1965: 6) that population growth in the United States "is caused more by the preference for larger families among those who consciously choose the number of children they have than by high fertility in the impoverished segments of the population. The importance of high fertility among the underprivileged lies not so much in its contribution to the national birth rate as in the difficulties that excessive fertility imposes on the impoverished themselves."

The 1967 HEW review sought to determine how well the department's stated policy was being implemented. It found the department's efforts lagging and recommended higher priority in staff and budget for family-planning services and population-research programs. It also distinguished this effort from an over-all United States population policy and program (Harkavy *et al.* 1967: 23–24):

While study should be given to the present and future implications of the growth of the nation's population as a whole—perhaps through a series of university studies sponsored by a Presidential commission—the federal government should at present focus its *family-planning assistance* on the disadvantaged segments of the population. The great majority of nonpoor American couples have access to competent medical guidance in family planning and are able to control their fertility with remarkable effectiveness. The poor lack such access and have more children than they want. It should be the goal of federal policy to provide the poor with the same opportunity to plan their families that most other Americans have long enjoyed. Public financing of family planning for the disadvantaged is clearly justified for health reasons alone, particularly for its potential influence in reducing current rates of maternal and infant mortality and morbidity. Additionally, there are excellent humanitarian and economic justifications for a major directed program to serve the poor.

The President's committee (1968: 15–16) did not concentrate on family planning alone but made numerous recommendations for short- and long-term programs of domestic and international services, research, and education. Its recommendation on domestic family-planning services was justified, again, not in terms of population control, but as a health and social measure:

Excessive fertility can drive a family into poverty as well as reduce its chances of escaping it. The frequency of maternal deaths, the level of infant mortality, and the number of children who are chronically handicapped are all markedly greater

among the poor than in the rest of the population. One of the most effective measures that could be taken to lower mortality and morbidity rates among mothers
and children would be to help the poor to have the number of children they
desire.

As for immediate programs to reduce further the incidence of unwanted
pregnancy among the rest of the population, the committee recommended
(*ibid.:* 15) expansion of biomedical research for improved contraceptive
techniques and expansion of social research; increased education in population dynamics, sex, and human reproduction; and improved training programs for physicians and other relevant professionals. It stated explicitly
(*ibid.:* 37) that these recommended programs "are only *one* of the important
factors that influence population trends," and called for a Presidential commission on population to, among other things, "assess the social and economic
consequences of population trends in the United States . . . [and] consider
the consequences of alternative population policies" (*ibid.:* 37–38).

These reports only reiterate what has been the basic justification for
publicly funded family-planning services for the poor for more than a
decade. The leaders of the United States family-planning movement have
not advanced this program as a means of achieving population stability,
because it has been evident that the poor and near-poor, who constitute only
about one-quarter of the population, are not the major contributors to
population growth in the United States, despite their higher fertility.

Blake believes the American policy should aim toward a zero rate of
population growth, as is her right. But she has no right to accuse family
planners of misleading the public into believing that the extension of family
planning to the poor would bring about such population stability—a claim
they have never made. Of course, any reduction in births, wanted or unwanted, will result in *less* natural increase and, other things being equal, *less*
population growth. Elimination or reduction of unwanted pregnancies
among the poor and near-poor would thus reduce *somewhat* the rate of
population growth, though not eliminate it entirely (cf. Jaffe and Guttmacher
1968).

PRUDERY—OR POLITICS?

Another straw man erected by Blake is the assertion that denial of birth-
control services to the poor has been attributed by advocates of family planning to the "prudery and hypocrisy of the affluent, who have overtly tabooed
discussion of birth control and dissemination of birth-control materials." As
proof that this has not been the case, she cites opinion polls going back to
1937 showing majority support for making birth-control information available
to those who desire it.

The proof is irrelevant in two major respects. First, the issue is not *information* about birth control, but *availability of services* (a distinction which Blake obscures throughout her article). And second, the operative factor in regard to the poor has not been generalized approval or disapproval, but the policies in regard to provision of contraceptive services of public-health and welfare institutions on which the poor depend for medical care. As she notes, it was evident as long ago as the 1930s that most Americans approved of birth control and practiced it in some form (although it was not until the late 1950s that the mass media began to carry relatively explicit birth-control material). But this public-opinion base did not control the policies of public institutions or the attitudes of political leaders. In most tax-supported hospitals and health departments there were explicit or implicit prohibitions on the prescription of contraceptive methods and materials, and many states had legislative restrictions that were enforced primarily in public agencies. To change these policies required protracted campaigns, which began in the New York municipal hospitals in 1958 (cf. Rock 1963: chap. 11; Guttmacher 1959: chap. 8), continued in Illinois, Maryland, Pennsylvania, and other states in the early 1960s, and culminated in legislative actions in 1965 and 1966 in at least fifteen states and in congressional action in 1967 in the social-security and poverty legislation.

The family-planning movement has not ascribed the denial of birth-control services to the poor to a generalized "taboo" but, rather, has ascribed it to concrete prohibitions on provision of services which stemmed from fear on the part of political leaders of the presumed controversial nature of the subject. The fears were perhaps exaggerated, but nevertheless real. The result was that very few poor women received contraceptive guidance and prescription in tax-supported agencies at times in their lives when it would have been of most importance to them—at the premarital examination and after the birth of a child, for example. It was not until the years 1964–66 that several hundred public hospital and health departments began providing family-planning services, and it was not until 1967 that as much as $10 million in federal funds became available to finance identifiable family-planning programs.

FAMILY SIZE DESIRED BY THE POOR

Judith Blake contends that her data show that the poor desire larger families than the nonpoor. She bases her assertion on responses to opinion polls and ignores the three major national studies conducted since 1955, covering larger and properly structured random samples of the United States population, which have probed these issues in depth. Even when the poll responses are accepted at face value, it is of interest to note that the "larger" family said to be desired by those in the lowest economic status group was larger by as much as 0.4 of a child in only 2 of the 12 years cited.

Also of interest is the fact that Blake treats responses to questions on *ideal* family size as evidence of the number of children the poor *want*. At various points in the text she refers to the data she cites as demonstrating *"desired or ideal"* number of children or *"preferred* family size," or states that the poor "say they *want* larger families" (emphasis added). The dubiousness of this methodology is revealed by the very different treatment of responses on *ideal* and *wanted* family size in the 1955 and 1960 Growth of American Families studies (Freedman *et al.* 1959; Whelpton *et al.* 1966) and in the 1965 National Fertility Study (Ryder and Westoff 1969: 14–16).

In the 1955 study, Freedman and his co-workers stated that the question on ideal family size "was not designed to discover the wife's personal ideal but sought a picture of her more stereotyped impressions on what family size should be" (Freedman *et al.* 1959: 221). "The more realistic question about desired . . . family size," they concluded, "is that regarding the number of children wanted at the time of the interview" (*ibid.*: 224). They found that the stereotyped "ideal" generally was higher than the number wanted. In the 1960 study, Whelpton and his colleagues (1966: 37) came to the same conclusion. In the 1965 study, Ryder and Westoff (1969) expressed "profound reservations" about the usefulness of the "ideal" question and found that it "lacks face validity, . . . is relatively unreliable, and has a small variance."

The poll responses cited by Blake appear to show that *ideal* family size varies inversely, among non-Catholic white women, with education and economic status. Responses to detailed surveys on *wanted* family size, however, either show insignificant differences between lower- and higher-status non-Catholic white respondents or *reverse the direction*. The data for 1960 show no difference in the number of children wanted by highest-status and lowest-status non-Catholic whites, and the data for 1965 show a very small increase in the number wanted by the group with only grade-school education. (The pattern for Catholics was, of course, different.) Other measures of socio-economic status show either no difference in the number of children wanted or, in the case of the measure of income, a smaller number for those with income below $3,000 than for those with income above $10,000 (Table 1).

Judith Blake also uses opinion-poll responses, rather than the results of in-depth studies, to measure approval of birth control in the different socio-economic groups. The result is, again, an overstatement of the differences between the highest and lowest social groups. In Table 2 are given excerpts from findings for 1960 and 1965 on approval of the practice of fertility control (including the rhythm method). The only deviation from the near-universal approval of fertility control is in the group with only grade-school education, which is rapidly becoming a smaller proportion of all American women and is hardly coterminous with the poor and near-poor (U. S. Bureau of the Census 1966). Even in the grade-school group, however, more than four-fifths of white women approved of birth control in both 1960 and 1965—a proportion bettered by nonwhite grade-school women in 1965—and all other groups

Table 1. Number of Children Wanted, by Education, Color or Race, Income, and Occupational Status of Respondents, United States, 1960 and 1965

EDUCATION, INCOME, AND OCCUPATIONAL STATUS	1960 WHITE [a]				1965 [c] WHITE			
	TOTAL	PROTES-TANT	CATHO-LIC	NON-WHITE [b]	TOTAL	NON-CATHO-LIC	CATHO-LIC	NEGRO
Education								
College	3.3	3.1	4.8	2.4	3.22	3.03	3.86	2.70
High school (4 yr.)	3.2	3.0	3.9	2.7	3.21	3.01	3.65	2.89
High school (1–3 yr.)	3.3	3.2	3.6	2.7				
Grade school	3.5	3.1	4.3	3.5				
High school (1–3 yr.) or grade school					3.46	3.30	3.83	3.48
Husband's income [d]								
> $10,000	3.3							
$7,000–9,000	3.2							
$6,000–6,999	3.3							
$5,000–5,999	3.3							
$4,000–4,999	3.4							
$3,000–3,999	3.4							
< $3,000	3.2							
Occupation [e]								
Upper white-collar	3.3							
Lower white-collar	3.3							
Upper blue-collar	3.3							
Lower blue-collar	3.3							
Farm	3.5							
Other	3.0							
Total	3.3	3.1	4.0	2.9	3.29	3.11	3.74	3.21

[a] Pascal K. Whelpton, Arthur A. Campbell, and John E. Patterson, *Fertility and Family Planning in the United States* (Princeton, N. J.: Princeton University Press, 1966), Table 54.

[b] *Ibid.*, Table 189.

[c] Norman B. Ryder and Charles F. Westoff, "Relationships Among Intended, Expected, Desired, and Ideal Family Size," *Population Research* (March 1969), Table 4.

[d] Unpublished data from the 1960 "Growth of American Families Studies," made available by Arthur A. Campbell.

[e] Whelpton *et al., op. cit.,* Table 71.

Table 2. Percentage Distribution of Women Who Favored Fertility Control, by Education and Color of Respondents, United States, 1960 and 1965

	WHITE		NONWHITE	
EDUCATION	1960 [a]	1965 [b]	1960 [b]	1965 [b]
College	97	97	97	94
High school				
4 years	95	97	90	94
1–3 years	93	94	78	90
Grade school	82	82	67	84

[a] Pascal K. Whelpton, Arthur A. Campbell, and John E. Patterson, *Fertility and Family Planning in the United States* (Princeton, N. J.: Princeton University Press, 1966), Table 102.

[b] Charles F. Westoff and Norman B. Ryder, "Recent Trends in Attitudes toward Fertility Control and in the Practice of Contraception in the United States," in Samuel J. Behrman, Leslie Corsa, Jr., and Ronald Freedman, eds., *Fertility and Family Planning: A World View* (Ann Arbor: Michigan University Press, 1969).

were nearly unanimous in their approval. It is extremely difficult, in the face of these data, to conjure up the notion of great hostility to fertility control among the poor and near-poor (Westoff and Ryder 1969).

For purposes of policy determination, the most salient questions relate not to all poor and near-poor persons, but to those who are in their prime childbearing years—that is, less than 30 years old. Presumably it is this group which would be most affected by public programs and whose attitudes policymakers would consider most significant. Data from the 1965 study (Tables 3 and 4) permit direct comparison, for farm and nonfarm women

Table 3. Number of Children Wanted by Wives (both White and Nonwhite) under 30, by Income and Farm Residence of Respondents, United States, 1965

	FAMILY INCOME			
RESIDENCE	$8,000 OR MORE	$6,000–7,999	$4,000–6,999	LESS THAN $4,000
Now living on farm	3.97	3.12	3.25	3.21
Once lived on farm	3.08	3.13	2.99	3.19
Never lived on farm	3.13	3.21	3.12	3.06

SOURCE: Unpublished data from the 1965 National Fertility Study, made available by Charles F. Westoff.

Table 4. Percentage Distribution of Wives (both White and Nonwhite) under 30 Who Had Ever Used, or Expected to Use, Any Form of Contraception, by Income and Farm Residence, United States, 1965

	FAMILY INCOME			
RESIDENCE	$8,000 OR MORE	$6,000– 7,999	$4,000– 6,999	LESS THAN $4,000
Now living on farm	84	100	85	89
Once lived on farm	91	97	95	88
Never lived on farm	95	96	93	92

SOURCE: Unpublished data from the 1965 National Fertility Study, made available by Charles F. Westoff.

below 30 in four income groups, of the number of children wanted and the proportion of women then using, or expecting to use, some form of contraception. The conclusion is clear: younger wives in the "poor" and "near-poor" categories want as few children as wives in higher income groups—or want fewer children than the higher-income wives—and have used or expect to use some form of contraception to a similar degree.

Despite the fact that 70 percent of poor and near-poor women regarded as in need of subsidized family-planning services are white (Varky et al. 1967), Blake frequently terms the recommended federal effort a "ghetto-oriented family-planning program." She also describes the charge of "genocide" which has been leveled by some black militants as "difficult to refute." However, the desire of black couples for smaller families than are desired by whites—and for smaller families than they are now having (Table 5)—was clearly demonstrated in the 1960 study (Whelpton et al. 1966: 38, 41).

Table 5. Number of Children Wanted by Wives (both White and Nonwhite), United States, 1960

	NUMBER OF CHILDREN WANTED		PERCENTAGES WANTING TWO CHILDREN OR LESS	
COLOR	MINI- MUM	MAXI- MUM	MINI- MUM	MAXI- MUM
White	3.1	3.5	41	29
Nonwhite	2.7	3.0	55	46

SOURCE: Pascal K. Whelpton, Arthur A. Campbell, and John E. Patterson, *Fertility and Family Planning in the United States* (Princeton, N. J.: Princeton University Press, 1966), Tables 15 and 16.

Table 6. Desired Family Size, by Race and Fertility-Planning Status,
United States, 1965

DESIRED NUMBER OF CHILDREN	PERCENTAGES OF RESPONDENTS WHO REGARD THEIR FERTILITY AS COMPLETED			PERCENTAGES OF RESPONDENTS WHO DESIRE MORE CHILDREN		
	TOTAL	WHITE	NEGRO	TOTAL	WHITE	NEGRO
0–2	36.2	35.4	44.0	27.1	25.7	41.0
3	23.6	24.5	14.8	28.8	29.2	24.3
4	40.3	40.2	41.2	44.2	45.0	34.8

SOURCE: Norman B. Ryder and Charles F. Westoff, "Relationships among Intended, Expected, Desired, and Ideal Family Size," *Population Research* (March 1969), Table 7.

Substantially the same pattern emerges from the 1965 study (Tables 6 and 7): significantly higher percentages of nonwhites continue to prefer a family of two children or less, and the proportion of nonwhites approving and using, or expecting to use, some method of fertility control is indistinguishable from that of whites, especially in the prime childbearing ages.

Table 7. Percentage Distribution of Women Who Approved of Fertility Control (Including the Rhythm Method) and Were Using or Expected to Use Some Form of Contraceptive, by Age and Color of Respondents, United States, 1965

QUESTION AND COLOR	20–24 YEARS	25–29 YEARS	30–34 YEARS	35–39 YEARS
Approved of fertility control				
White	95	97	95	93
Nonwhite	92	93	90	87
Were using or expected to use contraceptives				
White	94	93	88	84
Nonwhite	96	90	84	71

SOURCE: Charles F. Westoff and Norman B. Ryder, "Recent Trends in Attitudes toward Fertility Control and in the Practice of Contraception in the United States," in Samuel J. Behrman, Leslie Corsa, Jr., and Ronald Freedman, eds., *Fertility and Family Planning: A World View* (Ann Arbor: University of Michigan Press, 1969).

EXCESS FERTILITY

Serious demographic research has thus documented the disappearance of the traditional socio-economic and ethnic differentials in fertility aspirations and in attitudes toward fertility control. "Clearly," as Westoff and Ryder (1969: 394) have stated, "the norm of fertility control has become universal in contemporary America." Yet within this general pattern the studies also reveal that many couples do not achieve the degree of control they wish. Some have more children than they want and can be classified in the "excess fertility" category; others fail to have their children when they want them and are described as "timing failures." More than half of American couples reported one or another type of failure in 1965; 21 percent of all respondents acknowledged that at least one of their children was unwanted (Ryder and Westoff 1969). (This must be regarded as an underestimate, since the questionnaire required that respondents characterize specific children already born as either wanted or unwanted.)

While excess fertility is found among all socio-economic groups, it is more acute among the poor, among nonwhites (the majority of whom are poor or near-poor), and among those with higher parity and less education. In spite of the similarity in family-size preferences in all socio-economic groups, the poor and near-poor had a fertility rate from 1960 to 1965 of 152.5 births per 1,000 women aged 15 to 44, as compared to 98.1 for the nonpoor (Campbell 1968). And in spite of the expressed preference of almost all low-income parents for less than four children, nearly half of the children growing up in poverty in 1966 were members of families with five or more children under 18; moreover, the risk of poverty increased rapidly from 9 percent for one-child families to 42 percent for families with six or more children (Orshansky 1968). In terms of poverty, the most significant demarcation appears to be at the three-child level—the average family size wanted by low-income as well as other American couples: more than one-quarter of all families with four or more children were living in poverty, and four out of ten were poor or near-poor. Their risk of poverty was two and a half times that for families with three children or less (Table 8).

The 1965 National Fertility Study provides data on the percentage of unwanted births for each birth order, ranging from 5.7 percent of first births to 56.7 percent of sixth and higher-order births. Application of these percentages to actual births, by birth order, in the years 1960 to 1965, yields an estimated average of 850,000 unwanted births annually in all socio-economic groups. Combination of these data with Campbell's calculation of differential fertility rates shows that approximately 40 percent of births to poor and near-poor couples were unwanted by one or both parents in the years 1960 to 1965, as compared to 14 percent of births to nonpoor couples (Jaffe and Guttmacher 1968). This result appears to be consistent with the 1960 finding of an inverse relation between education and excess fertility, with 32 percent of white, and 43 percent of nonwhite, grade-school wives reporting more children than they wanted (Whelpton et al. 1966: 364).

Table 8. Relation of Poverty to Size of Family, United States, 1966

NUMBER OF CHILDREN	ALL U. S. FAMILIES (–000)	THE POOR		THE POOR AND NEAR-POOR	
		NUM-BER OF FAMILIES (–000)	PER-CENTAGE OF ALL U. S. FAMILIES	NUM-BER OF FAMILIES (–000)	PER-CENTAGE OF ALL U. S. FAMILIES
1	9,081	843	9.3	1,276	14.1
2	8,491	869	10.2	1,323	15.6
3	5,416	694	12.8	1,152	21.3
Total for parities 1–3	22,988	2,406	10.5	3,751	16.3
4	2,923	543	18.6	904	30.9
5	1,396	387	27.7	593	42.5
6+	1,286	541	42.1	747	58.1
Total for parities 4+	5,605	1,471	26.2	2,244	40.0

SOURCE: *Mollie Orshansky,* "The Shape of Poverty in 1966," *Social Security Bulletin,* 31:3, 3–32.

EQUALIZING ACCESS TO EFFECTIVE METHODS

It is precisely the reduction or elimination of this involuntary disparity between the poor and nonpoor which has been the objective of publicly supported family-planning programs. Given the essentially similar preferences of the two groups concerning family size, programs that equalize access to modern methods of fertility control should also help to equalize the incidence of unwanted pregnancy for the two groups. Blake can regard this as a "fantastic . . . blanket decision" imposed by the family planners only if she ignores (1) the evidence on the type of birth-control methods on which the poor rely, (2) the evidence on the relative effectiveness of different contraceptive methods, and (3) the response of poor persons to organized programs that offer them a complete range of methods.

The data on contraceptive practice cited above measure the combined use of all methods, including those known to be least effective in preventing conception. The cited studies also show that couples of higher socio-economic status who can afford private medical care tend to use the more reliable medical methods, while low-income couples depend more on less reliable, nonmedical methods. Among white Protestants in 1960, for example, half as many wives with a grade-school education as college graduates used the diaphragm and twice as many relied on withdrawal (Whelpton *et al.* 1966:

281). Published and unpublished findings for 1965 on methods employed by whites and nonwhites reveal the same picture. Three times as many non-whites as whites relied on the douche (Westoff n.d.) and on suppositories and twice as many relied on foam (Westoff and Ryder 1967: 2). When the condom is classified among effective methods and rhythm is omitted from the analysis because of the different proportions of whites and nonwhites who are Catholic, we find that half of nonwhite users of contraceptives rely on the least effective methods, as compared to about 30 percent of whites (Westoff n.d.).

These findings are significant in two respects: (1) the methods on which the poor rely most heavily have considerably higher failure rates and thus would lead to a higher incidence of unwanted fertility; and (2) the over-whelming majority of poor persons accept the best methods science has been able to develop when they are given the choice.

The relative rates of failure with the different methods range from 1 to 3 failures per 100 women-years of exposure for pills and IUDs to 35 to 38 failures for rhythm and douche, with the numbers for the condom, the dia-phragm, and withdrawal clustering around 15 (Tietze 1964: Tables 3 and 4).

RESPONSE TO FAMILY-PLANNING PROGRAMS

It is difficult to understand how the greater reliance of the poor on non-medical methods can be attributed to their personal preferences in view of the considerable research demonstrating that the poor have little access to medical care for preventive services (see, for example, Yerby 1966). When access to modern family-planning services offered with energy and dignity has been provided, the response of poor and near-poor persons has been considerable. The number of low-income patients enrolled in organized family-planning services under both public and private auspices has in-creased from about 175,000 in 1960 to 850,000 in 1968, as hospitals and public-health departments have increasingly offered services that provide the new methods not associated with the act of coitus (Jaffe and Guttmacher 1968). In virtually all known programs offering a variety of methods, 85 to 90 percent of low-income patients voluntarily choose either pills or intra-uterine devices (IUDs), the most effective methods currently known.

In 1965, a Chicago study found that three-fourths of patients continued to use the pills regularly 30 months after first coming to the clinic, an astonish-ingly high retention rate for any procedure requiring continuous self-medi-cation (Frank and Tietze 1965; see also Polgar and Cowles 1966; Polgar 1966; Bogue 1966; Perkin 1967).

A carefully planned program which introduced the first subsidized services in New Orleans, begun in 1967, enrolled nearly two-thirds of the target population, three-fourths of whom had not practiced birth control or had used nonprescription methods before attending the clinic. When given a genuine choice, 82 percent chose either pills or IUDs, while only 17 percent selected a nonprescription method (Beasley 1969). In the rural Louisiana parish where this program was first tested, the birth rate among the indigent decreased by 32 percent in the first year after the clinic was opened, as compared to a decrease of only 6 percent in four surrounding control counties where no organized family-planning services were available. The illegitimacy ratio in the county in question dropped from 172 per 1,000 live births in 1966 to 121 in 1967, as compared to an increase in the control counties from 162 to 184 (Beasley and Parrish 1968).

5 MILLION WOMEN

Judith Blake challenges the estimate that there are 5 million poor and near-poor women who comprise the approximate population in need of subsidized family-planning services. This estimate has been arrived at independently by Campbell (1968) and the Planned Parenthood Federation's research department (Varky *et al.* 1967), on the basis of U. S. Census Bureau (1966) tabulations of the characteristics of the poor and near-poor. Campbell estimated a total of 4.6 million, while Planned Parenthood estimated 5.3 million. The difference stems from the use of slightly different assumptions in analyzing the data available for obtaining a "need" figure which defines all women who are (1) poor or near-poor; (2) not currently pregnant or wanting to become pregnant; (3) fecund; and (4) exposed to risk of pregnancy. The differences in the assumptions and results are not regarded as significant at this point, when fewer than 1 million low-income patients are reportedly receiving family-planning services.

There exists, of course, no data base from which to define precisely women who have these listed characteristics. Both estimates have been presented as approximations that reasonably interpret available information. It is important to note that 5 million represents a residual number of potential patients at any given time (Campbell 1968); from the total of about 8 million poor and near-poor women aged 15 to 44, there was subtracted an estimate of those who are sterile, those who are pregnant or seeking to become pregnant (allowance being made for the fact that poor couples say they want three children, on the average), and those who are not exposed to the risk of pregnancy (Table 3). The estimate does involve the policy assumption that all others should have available competent medical advice on regulating fertility—even if they choose to practice the rhythm method, or if they are less than normally fecund, or if they have sexual relations infrequently—since such advice will tend to make their family-planning practice more effective. Whether or not all 5 million women would avail themselves of the opportunity remains to be seen. Until the poor are offered a genuine choice, there is no way to determine how many would actually prefer nonmedical methods. Nor is there any way to judge whether low-income Catholics will voluntarily choose methods officially proscribed by their Church to a degree equaling or possibly exceeding the 53 percent of all Catholics who reported in 1965 that they have already used methods other than the rhythm method (Westoff and Ryder 1967: Table 3).

It is interesting to note that Judith Blake does *not* cite the one factor which might be a significant limitation on these estimates—namely, the proportion of low-income women who have been able to secure competent guidance in fertility control from private physicians. There exists no adequate information on this question, perhaps because most researchers have been singularly uninterested in the *processes* through which fertility control techniques are diffused. Fragmentary data from several state Medicaid programs suggest that, at most, the proportion of poor and near-poor persons receiving family-planning services from private physicians is no higher than 10 percent.

In sum, then, the 5-million estimate has been presented as a reasonable approximation, based on the inadequate data that are available, of those who need subsidized family-planning services and for whom wise social policy would attempt to develop programs.

POPULATION POLICY

Judith Blake's article, hopefully, will stimulate responsible and dispassionate study and discussion of population policy in the United States. The scholarly community has thus far given little attention to this question, leaving the discussion largely to polemicists.

Her message is loud and clear: Our society should not waste its resources on family planning for the poor but should seek ways to restructure the family, reconsider male and female sexual roles, and develop satisfying nonfamilial roles for women, if it is to achieve population stability in the long run. We regard the first part of this proposition as erroneous and misleading. The second part, however, needs thoughtful examination as to its feasibility and the costs and benefits to society. The development of voluntary family planning in the immediate future is in no way antithetical to such realistic consideration of population policy for the long run.

It would be useful if Judith Blake were to develop proposals for specific programs to advance the objective of encouraging women to seek satisfaction in careers outside the home. It would be particularly interesting to see whether those programs do not subsume, as a necessary first step, the extension of effective fertility-control measures to all women who want and need them—which we believe is the immediate objective of federal policy on family planning.

A REPLY

JUDITH BLAKE

In their article Harkavy, Jaffe, and Wishik are, in effect, defending their own effort to influence the federal government regarding population policy. Harkavy and Jaffe are executives with organizations that promote "family planning" (the Ford Foundation and Planned Parenthood), and Wishik is a director of a university-based family-planning program. Their past influence is not only directly visible in their consultants' report criticizing HEW's population program for not pushing family planning more aggressively, but it is indirectly evident in the authors' presence (one, two, or all) on committees and hearings concerning population, each appearing to give "independent" but somehow unanimous advice to government agencies, Congress, and the President (Harkavy *et al.* 1967; President's Committee 1968; U. S. Senate 1965–68). My questioning of the alleged facts and logic supporting their advice, and that of others in the family-planning movement, has led the authors to charge me with statements I never made, nonuse of data that they have carelessly overlooked in my article, and failure to include unpublished materials to which I had no access. More interesting is the fact that the authors, in their haste, have unwittingly given their case away. Although Harkavy, Jaffe, and Wishik appear to believe that they are rebutting my article, their "reply" actually constitutes the first explicit admission by family-planning leaders that their interests in contraception are not, under any circumstances, to be equated with population "planning," population "control," or population "policy." This admission is a milestone in our journey toward a genuine population policy for this country. It makes clear once and for all that "family planning" is simply the very limited instrumental activity of making contraception available to those who want it; it is not population policy.

POPULATION STABILITY AND THE GOALS OF FEDERAL FAMILY-PLANNING POLICY

The authors claim that I have said that "reduction of population growth in the United States—indeed, the achievement of population stability—is virtually unchallenged as an official national goal." In fact, I did not mention population stability in this context. I simply said that "action" to "limit population growth . . . is at present virtually unchallenged as an official national goal." Hence, the authors' criticism concerning "a consensus on

SOURCE: This is published here for the first time. A portion was printed as a letter in *Science,* **165** (September 19, 1969), 1203–1204.

population stability" is entirely beside the point, since I never made a single statement concerning an American consensus on population stability. As for the statement I did make, I think it would be hard to deny that action to limit population growth is at present virtually unchallenged as an official national goal. It was a goal stated by President Johnson (1965), who emphasized the need for "population control" in "all our lands—including this land." In his swearing-in speech as Secretary of Health, Education, and Welfare (1965) John W. Gardner said, "This administration is seeking new ideas and it is certainly not going to discourage any new solutions to the problems of population growth and distribution." The need to limit population growth generally was part of the Republican Party platform (1968: 2132) in the last election. President Nixon's 1969 message to Congress concentrated on the undesirable effects and the mammoth difficulties of future population growth in the United States (*New York Times,* July 19, 1969). Senator Tydings (1969) said that the "aggregate growth [in the United States] represents the most serious long-term aspect of the population problem."

As far as I can see, these official statements (and many more) have gone virtually unchallenged—that is, until the article by Harkavy, Jaffe, and Wishik. Now it appears that "family planners"—at least as represented by these three—do not agree that population limitation is needed. They say, "It is clear that the federal program has been advanced, not for population control, but to improve health and reduce the impact of poverty and deprivation." The confusion as to goals is typical. As I showed in my article, it stems from the fact that the family-planning movement has ridden the coat-tails of "the population problem." The movement follows a pat formula —a formula which appeared in all of the documents I criticized, and which appeared again, a week later, in Senator Tydings's speech (1969) to the Senate introducing Senate bill 2108. The formula starts off with an outline of the terrors of the "population problem" and of population growth. It then suggests "family planning" as a solution. This formula has had a certain naive plausibility in developing countries where little birth control exists. But in the United States the formula's inherent contradictions become apparent. In the United States, by the evidence Harkavy, Jaffe, and Wishik themselves cite (Table 4), just about everyone uses contraception; and yet President Nixon must still concern himself about the major problems posed by our demographic growth. Clearly, family planning is not the answer to population growth.

To what is it the answer? Family planners in the United States have scrambled to find a group that "needed" them. Their erroneously high estimate of the "5 million poor women" provided them with a seemingly plausible target. The formula for the United States thus became: Population growth is a terrible problem in the United States, and the immediate problem is the need for family planning by the "5 million poor women" (Tydings

1969: S.4849). With the logic of this argument challenged, indeed with the very existence of the "5 million women" in question, Harkavy, Jaffe, and Wishik retreat completely. They wash their hands of population growth as a problem, and of population policy. They even ridicule me for a concern with demographic increase. They claim they are solely interested in the improvement of health and the "impact of poverty and deprivation." I agree entirely that the recommendations of family planners have little to do with population control or policy. It is gratifying that family planners themselves now openly admit it.

POLITICS—NOT PRUDERY

The authors' section on "prudery or politics" is based on my own analysis. It was I, not they, who pointed out that lack of government action in the past concerning birth control was influenced by a miscalculation of public opinion (including Catholic opinion) on the part of politicians, and not by public prudery. The public has long been ahead of the politicians on this issue, as my data showed. For this reason, claims that the society kept birth control behind a veil of secrecy are spurious. The authors argue that it is not lack of information, but lack of medical services that has led to relative deprivation for the poor. This is also a specious argument, because it is only very recently that medical attention has figured in an important way in the birth-control picture for couples generally. Most Americans have learned of birth control informally and have used nonmedical methods. Why have the poor and less educated known less and operated less effectively? I have argued that any realistic policy must take into account the facts that they were less motivated, wanted larger families, and approved of birth control less. I did not say that they exhibited "great hostility" toward birth control, but rather that their *relatively* less informed and less aggressive behavior can be accounted for in part by their *relatively* lower motivation. If one does not take this into account, one is overselling and overpromising what a program can do, since what has been lacking is not simply access or materials, but interest and desire as well.

FAMILY-SIZE PREFERENCES

What of the family size desired by the poor? The documents I criticized all claim or imply that the poor and less educated desire families as small as, or smaller than, the more advantaged. This claim obviously helps family planners persuade the government to sponsor birth-control services for the poor. Otherwise, such services would not be welcomed by those who presumably "need" them.

However, I cited data from national samples of American respondents extending over 25 years showing that the claim is not true; among whites, less advantaged individuals prefer somewhat larger families than the well-to-do. The data I cited were principally from polls, but they were *also* from the only two national fertility surveys (Freedman *et al.* 1959; Whelpton *et al.* 1966) presently available in print. These are the data that Harkavy, Jaffe, and Wishik say I ignored. The data from the 1965 national fertility survey have, except for a few articles, not yet been published. The article on family-size preferences from this 1965 survey (Ryder and Westoff 1969), published by the National Institute of Child Health and Human Development, had not yet appeared when I wrote mine. To bring all of these materials to the attention of the government is not destructive; the data are part of the actual picture and cannot be ignored in the formulation of policy. To be sure, the realities make decisions more complex, but wishful thinking as the basis of national policy simply guarantees ultimate failure.

In their attempt to discredit the information I have used on family-size preferences, my three critics merely fall into errors and fallacies of their own making. For example, they cite criticisms of data on "ideal family size for the average American family." But, the polling data I used were not based on a question concerning the "average American family." The question asked of respondents in the Gallup poll was, "What do you consider is the ideal size of family?" The three critics also state that there is "an expressed preference of almost all low-income parents for less than [fewer than?] four children." This claim is preposterous. It apparently results from the authors' confusion over the meaning of *average* number of children preferred, which is fewer than four, in contrast to the *proportion* of respondents preferring a given number. From the data cards from the 1960 Growth of American Families study, I tabulated the answers to the question on "wanted" number of children (a question my criticis prefer to one on "ideal" number) by husband's income. Approximately 40 percent of the women in the category "under $3,000" said they "wanted" four or more children! The authors further claim categorically that Negro couples desire smaller families than do white couples. Actually, data exist only for relatively small and limited samples of Negro couples. This would suggest caution; but caution does not inhibit Harkavy, Jaffe, and Wishik. Table 1 of their own article (giving data from the 1960 and 1965 national fertility studies) shows that their claim is true only for better educated Negroes. Negroes with less education "want" more children than do comparable whites, except, of course, for white Catholics!

Finally, Harkavy, Jaffe, and Wishik stumble into the fallacy of misplaced concreteness concerning the nature of the questions asked on family-size preferences. They try to maintain that a question on number of children "wanted" at the time of interview taps a source that is more "real" than a question on "ideal" family size. It depends on what one wants to know. The question on "ideals" presumably taps a set of evaluations concerning family size. The question on "wanted" children at the moment of interview may well also tap evaluations, but I have come to suspect that, in the United States, it is biased in a way that leads women to understate their family-size desires. According to the 1960 fertility survey, there are almost twice as many American couples who will not achieve the number of children they would like to have (because of sterility or subfecundity) as couples whose last child was "not really wanted" at the time of conception (Whelpton *et al.* 1966: 166–67, 236). Subfecundity and sterility are far more of a personal problem for Americans than is "excess fertility." Thus, the women who scale down their family-size "wants" to their fecundity shortcomings may well outbalance those who raise the number they "want" to correspond to the *de facto* existence of children they would have preferred not to have. In particular, the 1960 study found that disadvantaged couples suffered in higher proportions from sterility and subfecundity than the more advantaged (*ibid.:* 153–54, 158–59). This finding corresponds with census data on childlessness (U. S. Bureau of the Census 1964: Table 37).

Nonetheless, in spite of biases, we typically find a very close correspondence among the answers to a variety of questions—ideal, desired, intended, and so on. The data from the 1965 National Fertility Survey show, among whites, very close agreement: the "ideal" averaged 3.24, the "desired" 3.29, and "intended" 3.16 (Ryder and Westoff 1969). Moreover, as to the social differential in preferences, the data from the 1965 study that Harkavy *et al.* cite show a definite educational differential that is in the same direction as the polling data I have used, in the same direction as is shown by the 1955 and 1960 Growth of American Families studies, and in the same direction as has been found in the studies by Westoff *et al.* (1961: 227–28; Westoff *et al.* 1963: 114) on fertility in the largest metropolitan areas of the United States. For the non-Catholics the average difference is approximately a third of a child. Can one-third of a child be pooh-poohed? The authors think so. In answer I cite a statement from the 1960 fertility study that Harkavy and his colleagues have apparently ignored (Whelpton *et al.* 1966: v):

If married couples in the United States were to have an average of 2.5 births by the time they completed their families, the population would eventually level off and nearly stop growing. However, if couples had only one more child apiece, or 3.5 altogether, the population would double within 40 years.

"IN-DEPTH" QUESTIONS ON BIRTH CONTROL?

The authors also do not wish to accept the results of polls showing that disadvantaged individuals have been proportionally less in favor of making birth-control information available than have been the more advantaged. Harkavy and his co-authors speak of my using "opinion-poll" results as against the results of "in-depth" studies. Such Madison Avenue jargon is difficult to understand, but readers may judge for themselves concerning the question Harkavy, Jaffe, and Wishik prefer. The "in-depth" question on birth control from the 1965 National Fertility Study (Westoff n.d.) that they claim I ignored (the results had, in fact, not been published) ran as follows: "Most married couples do something to limit the number of pregnancies they will have. In general, would you say you are *for* this or *against* this?" Apparently, the three authors believe this question has a special mystique, and that having National Analysts (a commercial firm) conduct a survey (for Ryder and Westoff) has certain magic properties not shared by Gallup's American Institute of Public Opinion. If so, it is interesting that the results of the 1965 question tabulated by social level (Table 2 of the Harkavy article) are essentially the same as the polling data. Both sources show a definite drop in approval among respondents with only a grade-school education.

WHAT IS "EXCESS FERTILITY"?

Faced with serious questions concerning their estimate of "5 million women" who are allegedly "in need" of government assistance in family planning, Harkavy, Jaffe, and Wishik turn to the worn gambit of using data on so-called "excess fertility" as an indicator of "need" for public birth control. Yet the cavalier fashion in which they use the terms "excess fertility" and "unwanted" fertility is a misleading travesty of research on this topic.

These terms were carefully defined when they were first used by the authors of the 1960 Growth of American Families study (Whelpton *et al.* 1966: 235–39). The concept of "excess fertility" was based on answers to a question by female respondents concerning whether they, their husbands, or both "really wanted" another child at the time of the last conception. A woman was classified in the "excess fertility" group if either she, or her husband, or both answered negatively. But, the authors of the 1960 study caution us, among 50 percent of the women in this category, one spouse "really wanted" another child. Taking into account only those cases where *both* spouses did not "really want" another child reduces the proportion in the "excess fertility" group from 17 to 9 percent (*ibid.*: 236).

Moreover, the results concerning "excess fertility" (as defined) cannot be used to justify a birth-control policy designed to reduce "wanted" pregnancies. The authors of the 1960 study emphasize that women who were classified in the "excess fertility" group included a fair share whose attitudes toward having another child were simply ill defined or ambivalent (*ibid.*: 236–37):

The hypothesis that the excess-fertility group tends to include couples whose attitude toward wanting another child was not clearly defined is supported by the fact that many wives who said that they had not "really wanted" another child before the last conception also said in response to Question 65 that if they could have just the number they wanted and then stop, they would have the same number they had and even more.

"VOLUNTARY" USE OF THE PILL?

As a buttress to their claim of a desire by the poor for the most "modern" birth-control methods (methods that Harkavy, Jaffe, and Wishik believe require a federal program to "deliver"), the authors emphasize the "voluntary" choice of the pill by low-income patients in birth-control clinics. Yet, as is widely known, these women are not given such a free choice. They "voluntarily" choose the pill because they are given a one-sided story concerning its safety and the undesirability of other methods. Family planners are pressuring women into a risky course when other contraceptive alternatives are available. This is well illustrated by statements of Senator Gruening's when, emboldened by the Harkavy, Jaffe, and Wishik critique of HEW's population program, he called Dr. Gerald LaVeck (director of the National Institute of Child Health and Human Development) on the mat for his caution in evaluating oral contraceptives (U. S. Senate 1965–68—1967: Part 1, p. 62):

Senator Gruening: Well, we appreciate that it is necessary to have an extended period to demonstrate the safety or lack of safety of any contraceptive, whether it be oral or otherwise. But is there something you can do that will bring immediate action or quicker action than eight years?

Dr. LaVeck: We will have some results soon, but other questions will take many years to answer. In the first place, we need large numbers of women. We must be able to follow them very closely. We must be able to assess their health for a number of years. Some possibly adverse effects may occur many years after the oral contraceptives are used. For this reason, using prospective studies, we anticipate it will take a long time.

Senator Gruening: We have had testimony before this subcommittee from several witnesses that, whatever might be the long-range adverse effects of the pill, women prefer to take their chances. They would risk any possible ill effect rather than become pregnant.

Just what is the nature of the "crisis" that could induce the government to take such an attitude as that voiced by Senator Gruening? Have inquiring scientists no right to question the judgment of foundation executives who put a small improvement in contraceptive effectiveness above risks to health?

5 MILLION WOMEN, OR FEWER THAN 2 MILLION?

Turning to the estimate of the "5 million women" who "want" and are "in need of" family-planning assistance of the type Senator Gruening and Harkavy *et al.* are promoting, I have maintained that this estimate (whether by Campbell or by Planned Parenthood) is grossly overstated. This is because it includes women with fecundity problems, women who object on religious grounds, women who have intercourse rarely or not at all, and women who are already using birth control. It also understates the desired number of children. Campbell himself has said that the estimate is high unless one assumes that all of the women will be transferred to the pill or the coil from whatever method they are using. How exaggerated is the estimate? Re-estimates we have made at Berkeley (based on the same type of tabulations from the Census Bureau as were used by Campbell and by Planned Parenthood) show that, if one takes into account the criticisms I have voiced, the number of women is reduced to substantially *fewer than 2 million*—an estimate, moreover, that is generous in many of its assumptions.

POPULATION POLICY

As for "population policy," Harkavy *et al.* have already admitted "loud and clear" (as they would say) that family planning and population policy are not the same thing. Family planning for the poor is not an alternative to the policy considerations I have raised. It is not even a "first step." It is simply a very limited (if well meaning) welfare measure that will, at best, convenience a relatively small group of women. Understandably, Harkavy *et al.* do not find the complexity of limiting population growth in advanced societies to their taste. It is far easier to believe that a few gadgets will turn the trick, and that only poor women are involved. But the weight of demographic evidence here and abroad indicates that the completion of the vital revolution—the return to the population stability that characterized most of man's history—will require complex change in social and economic organization. In my paper, I suggested some of the directions in which we can look for such changes—directions that involve the partial removal of powerful pressures and incentives inducing people in all walks of life to bear children.

References

ANON. 1968. "Teens Still Pay One-Baby Penalty," *Family Planner*, 2 (September).

BEASLEY, JOSEPH D. 1969. "View from Louisiana," *Family Planning Perspectives*, 1:1 (Spring), 2–15.

———, and V. W. PARRISH. 1968. "Epidemiology and Prevention of Illegitimate Births in the Rural South." Paper presented before the American Public Health Association.

BLAKE, JUDITH. 1965. "Demographic Science and the Redirection of Population Policy," in Mindel C. Sheps and Jeanne Clare Ridley, eds., *Public Health and Population Change: Current Research Issues*. Pittsburgh: University of Pittsburgh Press.

———. 1966a. "Ideal Family Size among White Americans: A Quarter Century's Evidence," *Demography*, 1, 154–173.

———. 1966b. "The Americanization of Catholic Reproductive Ideals," *Population Studies*, 20, 27–43.

———. 1967. "Reproductive Ideals and Educational Attainment among White Americans, 1943–1960," *Population Studies*, 21, 159–174.

———. 1968. "Are Babies Consumer Durables? A Critique of the Economic Theory of Reproductive Motivation," *Population Studies*, 22, 5–25.

———. 1971. "Reproductive Motivation and Population Policy," *BioScience*, 21, 215–220.

BOGUE, DONALD J. 1966. "United States: The Chicago Fertility Control Studies," *Studies in Family Planning*, No. 15. New York: Population Council.

BUMPASS, LARRY, and CHARLES F. WESTOFF. 1970. "The 'Perfect Contraceptive' Population," *Science*, 169, 1177–1182.

CAMPBELL, ARTHUR A. 1968. "The Role of Family Planning in the Reduction of Poverty," *Journal of Marriage and the Family*, 30, 236–245.

COHEN, WILBUR J. 1966. *Family Planning: One Aspect of the Freedom to Choose*. Washington, D. C.: U. S. Government Printing Office.

DAVIS, KINGSLEY. 1967. "Population Policy: Will Current Programs Succeed?," *Science*, 158, 730–739.

———, and JUDITH BLAKE. 1956. "Social Structure and Fertility: An Analytical Framework," *Economic Development and Cultural Change*, 4, 211–235.

FRANK, RICHARD, and CHRISTOPHER TIETZE. 1965. "Acceptance of an Oral Contraceptive Program in a Large Metropolitan Area," *American Journal of Obstetrics and Gynecology*, 93, 122–127.

FREEDMAN, RONALD, PASCAL K. WHELPTON, and ARTHUR A. CAMPBELL. 1959. *Family Planning, Sterility, and Population Growth*. New York: McGraw-Hill.

GARDNER, JOHN W. 1965. Speech at swearing-in ceremony as Secretary of Health, Education, and Welfare. *Congressional Record* (August 18).

———. 1966. "Statement of Policy of the Department of Health, Education and Welfare on Family Planning and Population Programs" (January 24).

———. 1968. "Memorandum to Heads of Operating Agencies on Family Planning Policy" (January 31).

GRUENING, ERNEST. 1967. "What the Federal Government Is Now Doing in the Field of Population Control and What Is Needed" (speech before the U. S. Senate, May 3).

GUTTMACHER, ALAN F. 1959. *Babies by Choice or by Chance*. New York: Doubleday.

HARKAVY, OSCAR, FREDERICK S. JAFFE, and SAMUEL M. WISHIK. 1967. *Implementing DHEW Policy on Family Planning and Population—A Consultant's Report*. Washington, D. C.: U. S. Department of Health, Education, and Welfare.

JAFFE, FREDERICK S., and ALAN F. GUTTMACHER. 1968. "Family Planning Programs in the United States," *Demography*, 5, 910–923.

JOHNSON, LYNDON B. 1965. Statement at the 20th anniversary of the UN (June 25); quoted in the *Congressional Record* (March 14, 1967), p. 6494.

——. 1966. Message to Congress on domestic health and education (March 1).

KINSEY, ALFRED C., WARDELL B. POMEROY, CLYDE E. MARTIN, and PAUL H. GEBHARD. 1953. *Sexual Behavior in the Human Female*. Philadelphia: Saunders.

NATIONAL ACADEMY OF SCIENCES. 1965. "The Growth of the U. S. Population." National Resources Council Publication 1279. Washington, D. C.

ORSHANSKY, MOLLIE. 1968. "The Shape of Poverty in 1966," *Social Security Bulletin*, **31**:3, 3–32.

PERKIN, G. W. 1967. " A Family Planning Unit for Your Hospital?," *Hospital Practice*, **2**:5, 64ff.

PLANNED PARENTHOOD–WORLD POPULATION. n.d. *Five Million Women*. New York.

POLGAR, STEVEN. 1966. "United States: The PPFA Mobile Service Project in New York City," *Studies in Family Planning*, No. 15. New York: Population Council.

——, and W. B. COWLES, eds. 1966. "Public Health Programs in Family Planning," *American Journal of Public Health*, **56** (January), Supplement.

PRESIDENT'S COMMITTEE ON POPULATION AND FAMILY PLANNING. 1968. *Population and Family Planning—The Transition from Concern to Action*. Washington, D. C.: U. S. Government Printing Office.

REPUBLICAN PARTY. 1968. "Platform," *Congressional Quarterly, Weekly Report* (August 9).

ROCK, JOHN C. 1963. *The Time Has Come*. New York: Knopf.

RYDER, NORMAN B., and CHARLES F. WESTOFF. 1968. "Fertility Planning Status of American Women, 1965," *Demography*, **6**, 435–444.

——, and ——. 1969. "Relationships among Intended, Expected, Desired, and Ideal Family Size: United States, 1965," *Population Research* (March). Washington, D. C.: National Institute of Child Health and Human Development.

STYCOS, J. MAYONE. 1968. "American Goals and Family Planning," in F. T. Brayer, ed., *World Population and U. S. Government Policy and Programs*. Washington, D. C.: Georgetown University Press.

TIETZE, CHRISTOPHER. 1964. "Use and Effectiveness of Contraceptive Methods in the United States," in Mary S. Calderone, ed., *Manual of Contraceptive Practices*. Baltimore: Williams & Wilkins.

TYDINGS, JOSEPH D. 1969. "Family Planning: A Basic Human Right" (speech before the U. S. Senate), *Congressional Record* (May 8).

UNITED STATES. BUREAU OF THE CENSUS. 1964. *U. S. Census of Population, 1960*. Subject Reports: "Women by Number of Children Ever Born," Final Report PC(2)–3A. Washington, D. C.: U. S. Government Printing Office.

——. ——. 1966. Special tabulation on the characteristics of women living in poverty and near-poverty.

——. SENATE. 1965–68. Subcommittee on Foreign Aid Expenditures, *Hearings on S.1676*, 17 vols. Washington, D. C.: U. S. Government Printing Office.

——. ——. 1966. Subcommittee on Employment, Manpower, and Poverty, 89th Cong. 2nd Sess., *Hearings on S.2993*. Washington, D. C.: U. S. Government Printing Office.

VARKY, GEORGE, FREDERICK S. JAFFE, STEVEN POLGAR, and RICHARD LINCOLN. 1967. *Five Million Women—Who's Who among Americans in Need of Subsidized Family Planning Services.* New York: Planned Parenthood—World Population.

WESTOFF, CHARLES F. n.d. Unpublished data from the 1965 National Fertility Study.

———, ROBERT G. POTTER, JR., and PHILIP C. SAGI. 1963. *The Third Child: A Study in the Prediction of Fertility.* Princeton, N. J.: Princeton University Press.

———, ———, ———, and ELLIOT G. MISHLER. 1961. *Family Growth in Metropolitan America.* Princeton, N. J.: Princeton University Press.

———, and NORMAN B. RYDER. 1967. "United States: Methods of Fertility Control, 1955, 1960, and 1965," *Studies in Family Planning,* No. 17. New York: Population Council.

———, and ———. 1969. "Recent Trends in Attitudes toward Fertility Control and in the Practice of Contraception in the United States," in Samuel J. Behrman, Leslie Corsa, Jr., and Ronald Freedman, eds., *Fertility and Family Planning: A World View.* Ann Arbor: University of Michigan Press.

WHELPTON, PASCAL K., ARTHUR A. CAMPBELL, and JOHN E. PATTERSON. 1966. *Fertility and Family Planning in the United States.* Princeton, N. J.: Princeton University Press.

YERBY, ALONZO S. 1966. "The Disadvantaged and Health Care," *American Journal of Public Health,* **56**, 5–9.

INDEX

Abbott, Edith, 137–138, 140, 144*b*
abortion, 47, 82, 300–301, 305, 349, 371, 400–412, 414, 419–420, 441
Abu-Lughod, Janet, 187, 197*b*
acculturation, 237–238, 251
Acheson, E. D., 276–280
Actuaries, Society of, 265, 275*b*
acupuncture, 282, 286–288
Adams, Dale W., 179, 185*b*
Adams, Henry, 72, 74*b*
Adams, Richard N., 336, 340*b*
Adarkar, B. N., 391, 398*b*
Adelman, Irma, 310, 312–313, 320, 327*b*
Aden, 193*t*
adjustment, 236
Africa, 116, 197, 198–213, 281, 372
    See also individual countries
Agarwala, S. N., 395, 399*b*
age
    errors in reporting, 81

fertility and, 21–22, 82, 116–120, 298–299, 362, 364, 436*t*
of intellectual pursuits, 36–37
at marriage, 19–20, 30–32, 47, 49, 302, 305, 338, 360, 362, 376, 408
migration and, 116, 227, 246–247
mortality and, 31, 117–120, 121–135
    See also population structure
aggregate analysis, 334–335
agriculture, 59–61, 101, 103, 123–124, 130, 179, 183*t*, 202, 204, 224, 228–230, 232–233
Aird, John S., 86, 95*b*
Albania, 301
Alberdi, Juan, 224
Alers, J. Oscar, 179, 185*b*
Algeria, 190*t*, 193*t*, 194*t*
Almond, Gabriel, 201, 211–212*b*
Åmark, Curt, 401, 409*b*
Anderson, Barbara Gallatin, 181–185, 185*b*

Anderson, Robert T., 181–185, 185b
Antigua, 193t
Aparicio, Francisco de, 232t
Appelbaum, Richard P., 179, 185b
Aquinas, Thomas, 43
Arabs(s), 165–174
Arén, Per, 401, 409b
Arensberg, C. M., 122–124, 134b
Argentina, 179, 182n, 193t, 194t, 223–241,
    240b, 257, 297, 314t, 324t, 326
Argulla, Juan Carlos, 178
Aristotle, 42, 43
Arruñada, Mabel, 236, 240b
Asia, 116, 189, 197, 198
    See also individual countries
assimilation, 231–240
Augustine, 40, 42–43, 47
Australia, 77–85, 85b, 297–300, 314t, 324t
Austria, 249t, 297–300, 314t, 324t, 326
Avery, G. S., 15b
Ayurveda, 281–282

Backer, Julie E., 17, 27b
Bahamas, 193t
Baker, R. H., 10, 14b
Bakke, E. W., 138, 140, 142, 145b
Balandier, Georges, 201, 211b
Banks, J. A., 311, 327b
Banton, Michael, 200, 204, 211b, 213b
Barbados, 193t, 194t
Barbour, K. M., 212b
Barclay, George W., 191, 197b
Barker, Ernest, 42, 65b
Barrie, James, 292
Beach, E. A., 372, 380b
Beaglehole, J. C., 71, 72, 74, 74b
Beasley, Joseph D., 457, 466b
Bebarta, P. C., 332, 340b
Becker, Gary S., 63, 65b, 311, 327b
Beckett, J. C., 130, 134b
Behrman, Samuel J., 451t, 453t, 469b
Belgium, 27, 248, 297–300, 314t, 324t, 374
Bell, Wendell, 155, 156b
Bendix, Reinhard, 240b
Benjamin, Bernard, 277, 280b
Berelson, Bernard, 355b, 389, 389b
Bermuda, 193t, 194t
Bernstein, Eduard, 58
Besant, Annie, 50
Bethune, Norman, 285–287
Bhave, Vinoba, 397
biology, 1–2, 50–51, 54–56, 367
Birdsell, J. B., 5, 14b
birth control, 21, 47, 49–50, 82, 189, 305,
    330, 348, 354–357, 360, 373–374,
    381–389, 391–400, 413–423, 424–
    469
Blacker, C. P., 307, 327b, 393, 396, 399b

Bladen, Vincent W., 61, 65b
Blake, Judith, 63, 65b, 330–331, 337–338,
    340b, 423–443, 444–458, 459–466,
    467b
Blau, Peter M., 158, 159, 160, 163b
Bodin, Jean, 44
Bogue, Donald J., 188, 197b, 348, 355b,
    413, 423b, 456, 467b
Bolivia, 225
Bonar, James, 48, 65b
Borgatta, Edgar F., 163b
Borges, Jorge Luis, 238
Borneo, 190t, 193t, 195t
Bose, Suhash Chandra, 392
Boserup, Ester, 59, 66b
Botero, Giovanni, 44, 66b
Bothwell, Peter, 279
Boulding, Kenneth E., 48, 55, 66b
Bourgeois-Pichat, Jean, 25t, 34, 37b
Brackett, James W., 58–59, 66b, 98, 106b
Bradlaugh, Charles, 50
Brady, Dorothy S., 160, 163b
Braibanti, Ralph J. D., 69b
Brainerd, Carol P., 222b
Braun, Rudolf, 245, 255b
Brazil, 116, 177–179, 185n, 190t, 194t,
    226–227, 351
Brecher, Michael, 394, 397, 399b
British Guiana, 192, 193t, 194t
Brown, Harrison, 54, 61, 66b
Brown, R. Z., 10, 14b
Browning, Harley L., 178, 185b
Brozek, Joseph, 265, 275b
Bulgaria, 297–300
Bumpass, Larry, 361t, 365t, 424, 467b
Bunge, Alessandro, 225t, 226t
Burch, Thomas K., 329–341, 340b
Burma, 190t, 193t, 198
Burnight, Robert G., 263–275, 275b
Burton, Richard, 256
Butcher, D., 210, 212b

Caillot, A. C. Eugène, 71, 72, 73, 74, 74b
Calderone, Mary S., 468b
Calhoun, J. B., 10, 14b
Campbell, Arthur A., 450t, 451t, 452t, 454,
    457, 466, 467b, 469b
Campbell, Ernest Q., 156b
Canada, 19, 215–222, 222b, 227t, 257,
    297–300, 314t, 324t, 362, 374
Cannan, Edwin, 52, 66b
Cano, Valencia, 350
Cantillon, Richard, 46, 48, 66b
Cantón, Darío, 236, 240b
Caplow, Theodore, 141–142, 144b
Cardoso, Fernando Henrique, 178, 180,
    185b
Carleton, R. O., 160, 164b

Carlile, Richard, 50
Carter, Cedric O., 368, 374, 379b
Casey, M. Claire, 145b
Casimir, Jean, 179, 185b
Castillo, Gelia T., 336, 340b
Catholic(ism), 42–43, 121, 181, 183t, 184,
    236, 252–253, 269–274, 300, 326,
    341–346, 347–355, 363, 417, 420,
    427–428, 438–439, 449, 456, 458,
    462
causation, 338–339
census(es), 76–85, 85–96, 96–107, 107–
    113, 148–154, 189–191
    See also U.S. Government, Census, Bu-
    reau of the
Ceylon, 121, 189, 190t, 192, 193t, 194t,
    198, 314t, 324t
Chandrasekhar, Shrimati, 394
Chandrasekhar, Sripati, 391, 399b
Charaka, 49
Chen, Huan-chang, 41, 66b
Chen, Ji-qin, 287
Chevalier, Louis, 180, 186b
Chiazze, Leonard, Jr., 222b
Chidambaram, V. C., 332, 340b
Chile, 179, 180n, 190t, 194t, 225, 226,
    314t, 324t
China (Chinese), 41, 81, 85–96, 103, 116,
    281–288
Chou En-lai, 94
Christian(ity), 42–43, 48–49, 83
    See also Catholic
Christian, J. J., 12, 14b
Cicero, 42
cities, see ecology; fertility, mortality, popu-
    lation—urban-rural
Civil Rights Act, 135
Clark, Colin, 28, 49, 66b, 330, 340b
Clark, Joel Bennett, 426
Clark, W. E. LeGros, 15b
Clavel, A., 73, 74, 74b
Coale, Ansley J., 55, 59–60, 61, 66b, 115–
    120, 313, 318, 327b, 394, 399b
Coebergh, P. M., 344–345, 346b
Cohen, Wilbur J., 467b
Coleman, James S., 155, 156b, 201, 205,
    208, 211–212b
Collver, Andrew, 334, 340b
Colombia, 179, 193t, 194t, 314t, 324t, 350–
    354
Combs, J. W., 189, 197b
communication flow, 310, 313, 314–323
conception control, 414
Condorcet, Marquis de, 47, 50
Confucius, 41
Congo, 116, 203–208, 210, 314t, 322, 324t,
    326
congregation, 157

Conquest, Robert, 98, 106b
Cook, James, 71–73, 74b
Coontz, Sydney H., 47, 61, 66b
co-residence, 335–336
Corsa, Leslie, Jr., 451t, 453t, 469b
Corwin, Ronald G., 113b
Costa Rica, 194t, 350–352
Cowles, W. B., 456, 468b
Critto, Adolfo, 179, 186b
Croizier, Ralph C., 282, 282b
Crow, James F., 361, 365b
Cuba, 190t
culture, 9–10, 372, 440
Cunningham, W. J., 13, 16b
Cuzent, G., 71–72, 74b
Cuzzort, Ray P., 222b
Czechoslovakia, 297–300

Darwin, Charles, 2, 50, 66b, 355–356
Darwin, Francis, 66b
Datta, S., 332, 341b
Davis, Kingsley, 48, 63, 66b, 189, 197b,
    296, 306b, 307, 327b, 330–331,
    334–335, 337–338, 340b, 366–380,
    379b, 387, 390b, 423b, 425, 467b,
    441
Dawson, L., 280b
Day, Lincoln H., 326, 327b
De Bovis, E., 72, 74b
Deevey, Edward S., 1–16, 15b
DeJong, Gordon, 309, 327b
Delcomyn, Kirsten, 409b
delinquency, 407, 409–410
Demeny, Paul, 389, 390b
demographic transition, 63–65, 307–308,
    355, 356
Denmark, 25, 27, 297–300, 314t, 324t, 402
Desai, Morarji P., 281, 392, 397–398, 399b
Desgraz, C., 71, 73, 75–76b
detribalization, 200, 207–208, 210
Developa, 383–389
Díaz, May N., 181–185, 186b
Dieterlen, Germaine, 213b
Difrieri, Horacio, 232t
ad-Din an-Nashashibi, Nasir, 171
disease
    cancers, 120, 122, 267n, 277, 358
    chronic, 131, 132t, 133t, 267n, 277
    congenital, 282, 287, 291, 362
    and fecundity, 289–292
    food-related, 55, 122–123, 264–275
        See also famine
    heart, 120, 263, 267n, 277, 358
    infectious, 85, 132t, 133t, 261–262, 276–
        277, 281, 282, 291, 358
    insect-borne, 55
    neurotic, 406–407
    sterility, 290–292

disease *(Cont.)*
  venereal, 281, 322–323, 374
Dixon, Diana, 41n
Dobbins, James, 41n
Dominican Republic, 193t, 314t, 324t
Dore, R. P., 337, 340b
Dorfman, Adolfo, 229, 240b
Doucy, Arthur, 205, 212b
Drake, Michael, 17, 27b
Dresch, J., 201
Driver, E. D., 332, 338–339, 340b
Dublin, Louis I., 122, 125t, 134b
Duesenberry, James, 63, 66b
Dumont, Arsène, 64–65, 66b
Duncan, Beverly, 159, 163b, 222b
Duncan, Otis Dudley, 64, 66b, 67b, 68b, 157–164, 163b, 215, 222b, 306b
Dunn, Halbert L., 278, 280b
Duplessis-LeGuélinel, G., 37b
Durkheim, Emile, 59, 66b, 416
Džumhur, Mehmed S., 290–292

Easterlin, Richard A., 222b, 308, 327b
Eban, Abba, 174
Eckland, Bruce K., 163, 164b
ecology, 3–14, 50–51, 54–56, 60–61, 201–206, 233, 237
economy (economics), 49, 51–58, 61–63, 84, 381–389
  See also fertility, economic determinants, effects of; population, economic development and
Ecuador, 194t, 314t, 324t
education, 36–37, 84, 101, 103, 137–139, 159, 161–163, 179–180, 224, 234, 257, 303, 310, 313, 363, 407, 409–410, 417, 429–431, 432t, 434t, 435, 436t, 450t, 451t, 454, 455
Edwards, K. D. G., 265, 275b
Egypt, 5, 116, 165, 168, 170, 189, 193t, 194t, 311, 314t, 324t
Ehrlich, Anne H., 54, 66b
Ehrlich, Paul R., 54, 66b
Eisenhower, Dwight D., 118, 427
Eisenstadt, S. N., 235, 240b
Ekblad, Martin, 401, 412b
Ekwensi, Cyprian, 206, 212b
El-Badry, M. A., 121, 134b, 189, 197b
El Hamamsy, Laila Sh., 311
Ellis, William, 74, 74b
El Salvador, 193t, 194t, 349
energy, 314–323
Engels, Frederick, 57, 67b, 206, 212b
England (and Wales), 27, 45, 49, 54, 115–116, 119, 124–126, 130–133, 199, 205, 215, 276–280, 297–300, 308, 311

  See also Great Britain
Enke, Stephen, 380–390, 390b
Enlightenment, 47, 224
epidemiology, 274
Epstein, Arnold L., 198–213, 212b, 213b
Erhardt, Carl, 294
Erro, Alberto, 238
Etablissements Français de l'Océanie, Commissariat des, 72, 74b
eugenics, 356, 366–380
Euler, Leonhard, 45, 67b
Eversley, D. E. C., 306b
Eyriaud des Vergnes, P.-E., 73, 74, 74b

Faletto, Enzo, 180, 185b
family (size)
  allowances, 374
  completed, 22–24, 304, 421
  desired, 331, 347–348, 429–431, 448–454, 461–463, 464–465
  extended, 330, 335–340
  fertility and, 65, 301–304, 312, 329–341
  and genetic control, 371–377
  "ideal," 448–449, 462–463
  joint, 331–334
  mortality and, 32–36, 277
  nuclear, 330–334, 336–337, 371, 373–377
  stability, 162–163, 236
  stem ——, 333–334, 337
  structure, 203, 205–206, 330–340, 371–373
Family Growth in Metropolitan America study, 416
famine, 29, 48, 98
  See also disease, food-related
Farley, Reynolds, 147–157
Farr, William, 276–277, 278, 280b
fecundity, 6–7, 9–14, 290–292, 310, 360, 396, 437–438, 463
Fei Hsiao-t'ung, 94
Feindt, Waltrout, 178, 185b
Feldheim, Pierre, 205, 212b
fertility
  control, 414, 419–421, 441–443, 458
  differential by
    age, 21–23, 82, 116–120, 298–299, 362, 364, 436t
    business cycle, 308
    country, 189–191, 297–299, 313–326
    education, 303, 310, 363, 407
    family type, 65, 301–304, 312, 329–341, 371–373
    genetic quality, 356–357, 359–364, 371–377
    ideology, 346–350, 395
    nationality, 102–103

parity, 361, 364
race, 152, 161, 363
religion, 102–103, 304–305, 326, 342–346, 346–355, 363
social class, 23–24, 62–63, 305, 308–309, 362, 374, 404, 407, 455
social mobility, 63–65, 311
urban-rural residence, 187–197, 303, 306–307, 362
economic determinants of, 61–63, 307
economic effects of, 59–61, 305–306, 318–327, 348–349, 421
excess, 453–455, 464–465
illegitimate, 21–22, 350, 360, 370, 373, 405, 435, 458
long-run decline of, 18–19, 21–24, 27, 296–305, 357, 361–362, 425
marriage rates a factor in, 21–22, 32–33, 42–43, 300, 308
measures of, 45, 191–192, 297–299, 312, 334, 343–344, 384
migration and, 299, 302–303
mortality and, 21, 45, 63–64, 192–197, 302, 308, 310–311, 326–327, 357–359, 384
policy, *see* birth control; population policy
psychological factors affecting, 293–295, 311, 370, 416–418
rise in, 308, 309, 312, 323, 360
urbanism a factor in, 103
See also individual countries; birth control; family; fecundity
Feshbach, Murray, 97–107, 106–107*b*
Feuer, Lewis S., 67*b*
Fichter, Joseph H., 144–145*b*
Fiji Islands, 195*t*
Finland, 297–300, 314*t*, 324*t*
Foard, Elsie D., 275*b*
food chains, 3–6, 51
Ford, C. S., 372, 380*b*
Forde, C. Daryll, 211–213*b*
Forssman, Hans, 400–412, 412*b*
Forster, George, 72, 74*b*
Forster, John Reinold, 72, 75*b*
Fortes, Meyer, 213*b*
Foster, George M., 184*n*, 186*b*
Fourastié, Jean, 28–38
Fraenkel, Merran, 202, 212*b*
France (French), 24–25, 27, 28–38, 46–47, 49, 63–64, 115, 116, 118–119, 181–185, 225, 237, 248–252, 297–300, 314*t*, 324*t*, 374
Francis, Roy G., 2*n*
Frank, Richard, 456, 467*b*
Frederick the Great, 44
Fredericson, Emil, 11, 15*b*

Freedman, Ronald, 296, 306*b*, 308, 310, 311, 328*b*, 330–334, 337, 340*b*, 361*t*, 365*b*, 429, 449, 451*t*, 453*t*, 462, 467*b*, 469*b*
Freyre, Gilberto, 178, 186*b*
Fuguitt, Glenn V., 162, 164*b*

Galbraith, Virginia, 308, 328*b*
Gallup polls, 427, 428*t*, 430*t*, 432–434*t*, 436*t*, 449, 462, 463–464
Galpin, Charles, 176
Gandhi, M. K., 40, 49, 392, 395, 396, 397
Garcia-Conti, Francisco, 354, 355*b*
Gardner, John W., 445, 460, 467*b*
Garnier, Jules, 74, 75*b*
Gautier, Etienne, 29, 37*b*
Gebhard, Paul H., 468*b*
Gellhorn, Martha, 174*b*
Gendell, Murray, 329–341
General Adaptation Syndrome, 11–12
generation(s), 6–7, 33–37, 237–238
George, K. Λ., 341*b*
Germani, Gino, 223–241, 240*b*
Germany (German, s), 25, 225, 233, 248–252, 257, 297–300, 308, 314*t*, 324*t*, 343–345
Ghana, 193*t*
Gille, H., 16
Ginder, Charles E., 140, 145*b*
Gini, Corrado, 158
Glass, David V., 45, 67*b*, 306*b*
Glubb Pasha, 167
Gluckman, Max, 199–200, 212*b*
Glyn, Elinor, 292
Godwin, William, 47, 48, 67*b*
Goldberg, David, 361*t*, 365*b*
Goldblatt, Phillip B., 264, 273–274, 275*b*
Goldner, Martin G., 264, 275*b*
Goode, William J., 65, 67*b*, 331, 339, 340*b*
Gopalaswami, R. A., 393
Gori, Gastón, 228, 233, 235, 240*b*
Goubert, Pierre, 29, 30, 37*b*
Grabill, Wilson H., 361*t*
Graciarena, Jorge, 180, 186*b*
Grauman, John V., 313, 328*b*
Graunt, John, 45
Great Britain, 217–218*t*, 221*t*, 257, 278, 280*b*, 315*t*, 391–392
See also England; Scotland
Greece (Greek, s), 41–42, 169, 248, 297, 314*t*, 324*t*, 326
Griffin, Keith, 180, 186*b*
Growth of American Families studies, 416, 429, 437, 449, 450*t*, 462, 463, 464
Gruening, Ernest, 426, 465, 466, 467*b*
Guatemala, 179, 194*t*, 314*t*, 324*t*, 326
Gurney, M., 11, 15*b*

Guttmacher, Alan F., 447, 448, 454, 456, 467b

Habakkuk, H. J., 308, 328b
Haenszel, William, 222b
Hägerstrand, Torsten, 222, 222b
Hajnal, John, 300, 306b
Halley, Edmund, 45, 67b
Hannerberg, David, 222b
Hansen, Alvin H., 61
Harari, Maurice, 174b
Hardin, Garrett, 66b
Hardoy, Jorge E., 186b
Harkavy, Oscar, 424, 435, 437, 438, 444–458, 459–466, 467b
Harris, Marvin, 185n, 186b
Hathaway, Millicent L., 275b
Hauser, Philip M., 66b, 67b, 240b, 306b, 389, 390b, 413–423, 423b
health, see disease; mortality
Heckscher, Eli, 16
Heer, David M., 307–329, 328b
Hellmann, Ellen, 211, 212b
Henderson, David, 330, 341b
Henry, Louis, 16–27, 29n, 37b
Herdan, G., 122, 134b
Hernández Arregui, Juan José, 236, 240b
Herodotus, 49
Herrick, Bruce H., 179, 180n, 186b
Hicks, John R., 61, 67b
Himes, Norman E., 49–50, 67b, 392, 399b
Hirschman, Albert O., 348, 355b
Ho Ping-ti, 41, 67b
Hodge, Robert W., 160, 164b
Hodgkin, Thomas, 199, 202, 204, 211
Hoffman, Daniel P., 397, 399b
Homans, George C., 375, 380b
Honduras, 193t, 194t, 314t, 324t, 326, 351, 353
Hong Kong, 193t, 415
Höök, Kerstin, 401, 412b
Hoover, Edgar M., 60, 66b, 115, 318, 327b, 389, 390b, 394, 399b
Hoppner, Richard Belgrave, 75b
Hoselitz, Bert F., 46, 67b, 340b
Houghton, Vera, 392, 399b
Huard, Pierre, 282, 282b
Huguenin, Paul, 71–72, 74, 75b
Hultgren, Gösta, 412b
Humanae Vitae, 350–354
Hume, David, 47
Humphreys, A. J., 123–124, 134b
Hungary (ian, s), 58, 170, 297–300, 314t, 324t, 326
Hussein, King, 170
Hutchinson, Bertram, 178
Hutchinson, Edward P., 47, 67b
Hutchinson, G. E., 13, 15b

Hutton, J. H., 391, 399b
Huyck, Earl, 189, 197b

Ibn Khaldun, 43–44
Iceland, 315t, 324t, 326
identification, 238–240
Imaz, José Luis de, 236, 240b
income, 158–159, 161, 257, 305–306, 313, 314–323, 381–389, 452t, 454–455
India(n, s), 9, 42, 116, 121, 164, 169, 187, 189, 190t, 191, 193t, 194t, 198, 281–282, 331–333, 339, 370–371, 382n, 390–400, 399–400b, 421
Indians, American, 5
Indianapolis study, 416
Indonesia, 5, 198
industry, 137–142, 183t, 201–202, 205–207, 225, 229–231, 290–292
Institut National d'Etudes Démographiques, 16, 28, 29n, 37b, 38b
intelligence, 159–161
International Union of Official Travel Organizations, 258
International Union for the Scientific Study of Population, 328b, 333t, 336, 340–341b
Ipsen, Johannes, 275b
Iran, 190t
Iraq, 168
Ireland (Irish), 120–135, 134b, 269–273, 297–300, 305, 315t, 325t, 396
Isaac, Julius, 224, 226, 240b
Islam, 102–103, 210
Israel, 164–174, 174b, 189, 194t, 241, 297
Italy (Italian, s), 25, 27, 225–226, 234, 238–239, 244, 248–252, 269–274, 297–300, 315t, 325t

Jaccard, Pierre, 38b
Jacobson, Paul H., 357t, 371, 380b
Jaffe, A. J., 160, 164b, 189, 197, 197b
Jaffe, Frederick S., 424, 444–458, 459–466, 467b, 469b
Jahn, Gunnar, 17, 27b
Jamaica, 190t, 194t, 315t, 325t
Japan(ese), 81, 116, 169, 189, 215, 297–301, 315t, 325t, 336–337, 362, 368, 382n, 400, 420
Jaramillo Gomez, Mario, 354, 355b
Jarrett, Henry, 66b
Jensen, Arthur R., 159, 164b
Jew(ish, s), 83, 225, 237, 252–253, 269–273, 341
   See also Israel
Jhaveri, Vithalbhai K., 395, 396, 400b
Joffe, Natalie, 274, 275b
Johnson, Lyndon B., 382, 426, 445, 460, 468b

Johnston, Eric, 173–174
Jordan, 165–174
Jouan, René, 73

Kanev, Itzhak, 174b
Kannel, William B., 267n
Kaplan, David L., 145b
Kaur, Rajkumari Amrit, 396
Kautilya, 42
Kennedy, Robert E., Jr., 120–135
Kenya, 205, 209
Kerr, Malcolm H., 174b
Keyfitz, Beatrice, 67b
Keyfitz, Nathan, 40–69, 67b, 114
Keynes, John M., 48, 54, 61, 67b
Keys, Ancel, 265, 275b
Kimball, S. T., 122–124, 134b
Kimura, Motoo, 378, 380b
kin, see family
King, Gregory, 45
King, J. A., 9–10, 11, 15b
King, James, 72, 74b
Kinsey, Alfred C., 437, 468b
Kipling, Rudyard, 39
Kirk, Dudley, 308, 328b, 356–365, 366
Kiser, Clyde V., 189, 197b, 341b, 361t, 374, 380b
Kolpakov, B. T., 99, 106, 107b
Korea, 415
Korn, Francis, 239t
Krause, J. T., 308, 328b
Krishna Menon, V. K., 398
Krusenstern, A. J. von, 73, 75b
Kulldorff, Gunnar, 215, 222b
Kuper, Hilda, 211b, 213b
Kurtén, Björn, 9, 15b
Kurup, R. S., 341b
Kurzman, Dan, 167, 174b
Kuznets, Simon, 61, 67b, 315t, 328b, 388, 390b

labor force, see population, active
Lancet, 412b
Landry, Alphonse, 46, 67b
language(s), 83–84, 101–103, 250–252
Latin America, 60, 116, 177–187, 189, 309–310, 336, 346–355, 372, 420
    See also individual countries
Laurie, E. M. O., 10, 15b
LaVeck, Gerald, 465
Lazarsfeld, Paul F., 66b
Lebanon, 169
Lebergott, Stanley, 137–138, 145b
LeChartier, H., 72, 75b
Lee, Everett S., 215, 222b
Lee, Mabel Ping-hua, 41, 67b
Leeds, Anthony, 178, 186b
Leedy, Frederick A., 97n, 107b

Leeward Islands, 193t
Leibenstein, Harvey, 62–63, 67b, 327, 328b
Lemarchand, René, 210, 212b
Lenin, V. I., 99
Leridon, Françoise, 29n
Lescure, P., 71, 73, 75b
Leslie, J. A. K., 204–207, 212b
Lesson, P., 72, 74, 75b
Li Choh-ming, 86, 95b
Libbey-Owens-Ford Co., 135
Liberia, 202
Libya, 190t
Lieberson, Stanley, 162, 164b
life table, 45, 219
Lincoln, Richard, 469b
Lindberg, Bengt J., 401, 412b
Lindeman, Raymond L., 3, 15b
Lipset, Seymour M., 240b
Little, Kenneth, 207, 212b
Liu, Paul K. C., 333–334, 337–338, 340–341b
Lloyd, Peter C., 204, 212b
Lo Jui-ch'ing, 88
Londoño, Juan, 354, 355b
Long, Harry H., 214–222
longevity, 8–12, 121, 124–128, 358
Lorenz, Max O., 158
Lorimer, Frank, 45, 67b, 98, 107b, 330–331, 335, 338, 341b
Lorscheisder, Ivo, 351
Lotka, A. J., 7, 15b, 134b
Louch, C. D., 12, 15b
Louvish, Misha, 174b
Love, Kenneth, 174b
Lowder, Stella, 180, 186b
Lunde, Robert, 41n
Luther, Martin, 49
Luxemburg, 315t, 325t

Machiavelli, 44
machismo, 347–348
MacKay, D., 277, 280b
Mackenroth, Gerhard, 44, 67b
Madigan, Francis C., 120, 121, 134b
Mafeje, Archie, 206, 213b
Mahdi, Muhsin, 43, 67b
Mair, George F., 380
Malaker, Chittaranjan, 331–333, 337–338, 341b
Malaya, 189, 190t, 193t, 194t, 198, 315t, 325t, 326
Mallea, Eduardo, 238
Malmfors, Karin, 401, 412b
Malthus, Daniel, 47
Malthus, Thomas Robert, 12, 40, 47–50, 51, 54, 56–58, 67b, 308, 328b, 413
Mao Tse-tung, 283–288
Marden, Parker G., 264–275

Margulis, Mario, 179, 186b
Marquesas, 72–75
marriage(s)
  age at, 19–20, 30–32, 47, 49, 302, 305, 338, 360, 362, 376, 408
  duration of, 30–34, 82, 408
  and female work, 142–144, 303
  and fertility, 21–22, 32–33, 42–43, 300, 308
  institution of, 182t, 330
  intermarriage, 236, 247–248
  prevalence of, 299–301, 359–360, 364, 370
  rates, 18–21, 192–197
  second and subsequent, 31–32, 82
  See also family; fertility
Marris, Peter, 203, 212b
Martin, Clyde E., 468b
Martínez Estrada, Ezequiel, 233, 240b
Martins, José de Souza, 177, 186b
Marx, Karl (Marxism), 46, 56–58, 67b, 348–350, 397–398
Mathen, K. K., 332, 341b
Matsunaga, Ei, 362, 365b
Mauritius, 190t, 194t
Mayer, Kurt B., 241–255, 255b
Mayr, Ernst, 367, 372, 380b
McArthur, Norma, 72, 75b
McCleary, G. F., 49, 67b, 397, 400b
McDill, Mary S., 157b
McGreevey, William, 178, 186b
McMahon, Brian, 274, 275b
McNabb, Patrick, 123, 134b
McNeill, William H., 41, 67b
McNicoll, Geoffrey, 41n
McNulty, Donald J., 137, 145b
Medawar, P. B., 15b
Meek, Ronald L., 56, 68b
Mehring, Franz, 58, 68b
mercantilism, 44–46, 58
Metropolitan Life Insurance Co., 265, 266t, 275b
Mexico, 119, 178, 181–185, 187, 189, 191, 193t, 194t, 315t, 325t, 326
Mezerik, Avrahm G., 174b
Michener, James A., 164–175
Middle East Journal, 175b
Middleton, Russell, 330, 341b
migration, internal, 101–102, 104–105, 147–156, 178–181, 200–201, 205–207, 214–222
migration, international, 18–20, 82–83, 223–255, 392
Milbank Memorial Fund, 96b, 197b, 341b, 400b
Mill, John Stuart, 51, 58, 68b
Miller, Ann Ratner, 222b
Miller, Herman P., 158, 160, 164b

Milojković, Aleksandar D., 289–292
Mirabeau, Honoré de, 48
Mishler, Elliot G., 469b
Mitchell, J. Clyde, 200, 202, 205, 207, 210–211, 212–213b
Moheau, M. [Baron de Montyon], 49
Montoya Rojas, Rodrigo, 180, 186b
Mood, A. M., 156b
Moore, Mary E., 264, 265n, 275b
Moore, Wilbert E., 163b, 189, 197b, 340b
Morocco, 168, 190t
Morrison, William A., 311, 328b
Morse, Richard M., 177–187
mortality
  by accidents, violence, 281, 358
  animal, 8–10
  child, 313, 326–327, 331
  differential by
    age, 31, 117–120, 121–135
    country, 124–126, 130–133
    family status, 32–36, 277
    genetic quality, 357–359, 364, 371
    sex, 24–26, 31, 120–135
    urban-rural residence, 126–129, 192–197
  fetal, perinatal, 122, 359
  infant, neonatal, 26–27, 192–197, 313, 314–323, 326–327, 331
  long-run decline of, 18–19, 24–27, 29–37, 45, 121–134, 276–277, 280–281, 334, 357, 371, 381
  senescent, 25–26
  statistics, 45, 276–280
  See also individual countries; disease; famine; fertility; war
Mortara, Giorgio, 226–227, 240b
Moynihan, Daniel P., 163b
Mozambique, 193t
Murdock, George P., 372, 380b
Murphey, Rhoads, 198, 213b
Murray, J. H. P., 77, 85b
Myrdal, Gunnar, 54, 61, 68b

Nag, Moni, 331–332, 337–339, 341b
Nagi, Saad Z., 113b
Namboodiri, N. Krishnan, 335, 341b
Nanda, Gulzarilal, 281, 398
Nansen, Fridtjof, 169
Nasser, Gamal Abdel, 173
National Academy of Sciences, 424, 425, 429, 435, 446, 468b
National Bureau of Economic Research, 65b, 67b, 327b, 380b
National Fertility Study, 449, 451t, 452t, 454, 463, 464
National Manpower Council, 137, 140–143, 145b
National Office Managers Assn., 140

nationality, 101–103, 146, 198–201, 210–211, 246–253, 268–273
naturalization, 235
nature (natural), see biology; ecology
Nayar, Sushila, 393, 395, 396
Negroes, 147–157, 161–162, 189, 360, 363, 440–441, 450t, 451t, 452, 456, 462
Nehru, Jawaharlal, 392–398, 400b
Nelson, Richard R., 48, 68b
Nepal, 190t
Nesbitt, Robert E. L., Jr., 134b
Netherlands, 25–27, 248, 297–300, 315t, 325t, 326, 342–346
New South Wales, Public Library of, 72, 75b
New Zealand, 257, 297–300, 315t, 325t
Newcombe, H. B., 362, 365b
Newman, Jeremiah, 134b
Newsweek, 135
Nicaragua, 194t
Nielsen, J. B., 402, 412b
Nigeria, 190t, 201, 203
Nimkoff, Meyer E., 330, 341b
Nixon, Richard M., 460
Noland, E. W., 138, 140, 142, 145b
Noonan, John T., Jr., 42–43, 68b
Nordmann, P. I., 72, 75b
Norway, 16–27, 297–300, 315t, 325t
Notestein, Frank W., 63, 68b, 307, 328b, 393, 395, 396, 400b
Nurkse, Ragnar, 60, 68b
Nurock, Mordekhai, 174b

O'Casey, Sean, 122–123, 134b
Odeving, Bruno, 222b
Oettinger, Katherine B., 435
Ogburn, William F., 65, 68b
Ohlin, Goran, 60, 68b, 389, 390b
Okun, Bernard, 63, 68b
Oppenheimer, Valerie Kincade, 135–145, 145b
Organization of American States, 420
Orleans, Leo A., 85–96
Orshansky, Mollie, 455t, 468b
Osborn, Frederick, 162, 164b
Overbeek, Johannes, 54, 68b

Paddock, Paul, 327, 328b
Paddock, William, 327, 328b
Pakistan(i, s), 116, 119, 121, 164, 169, 189, 190t, 198, 281, 393
Pakrasi, Kanti, 331–333, 337–338, 341b
Palestine, see Israel
Pan American Health Organization, 355
Pan Ku, 41, 68b
Panama, 194t, 339
Papua and New Guinea, 76–85, 85b
Paraguay, 194t, 225

Parrish, V. W., 457, 466b
participation, 236
Patterson, John E., 450t, 451t, 452t, 469b
Paynter, R. A., 8, 15b
Peacock, Alan T., 48, 68b
Pearl, Raymond, 6, 14, 15b
Perkin, G. W., 456, 468b
Perlman, M., 389, 390b
Peru, 179–180, 315t, 325t
Petersen, William, 17n, 29n, 41n, 47–48, 57, 68b, 107, 113b, 308, 328b, 330, 334, 341b, 342n
Petty, William, 44–66, 68b
Pflanz, M., 265, 275b
Phelps, Harold, 330, 341b
Philippines, 193t, 198, 376, 417
physiocrats, 46, 48
Pillai, A. P., 392
Pinner, Walter, 175b
Pius XII, 43
Place, Francis, 50, 68b
Planned Parenthood-World Population, 437, 457, 459, 466, 468b
Plato, 41–42
Podiachikh, P. G., 97n, 105, 107b
Poland (Poles), 225–226, 297–300, 308–309
Polgar, Steven, 456, 468b, 469b
polygyny, 372–373
Polynesia, 71–76
Pomeranze, Julius, 265n, 275b
Pomeroy, Wardell B., 468b
Pons, V. G., 202–203, 205, 213b
population (growth)
    active, 44, 79–80, 84–85, 100–104, 124, 136–144, 158–163, 200–201, 205–206, 228–231, 245–246, 290–292, 384–386
    animal, 2–14, 50–51, 122, 368
    cohort, 19–20, 45, 160
    composition, 79–81, 146–175, 395
    See also language; nationality; religion
    control, 414, 421–423, 441–443, 444–447, 459–461
    cycle, 12–14, 43–44, 51
    decline, 77, 148–150
    density, 3–5, 7–14, 17, 51, 59, 313, 314–323
    dependent, 60, 119–120, 311, 384–386
    economic development and, 5–6, 56–62, 98–99, 159, 185, 227–231, 242–246, 380–390, 394–395, 421–423
    equilibrium, 2–5, 9–14, 45, 47
    optimum, 40, 42, 52–54, 395
    plant ——, 3–7, 50–51, 368
    policy, 40, 48, 58–59, 366–469
    See also birth control
    principle of, see Malthus

population (growth) *(Cont.)*
  projections, 5–7, 31*t*
  registration, 88–95, 276–280
  resources and, 48, 51–59, 60–61
  statistics, 16–17, 29, 45–46, 71–113, 214,
    242–243, 276–280
  structure, 17–18, 35–36, 60, 81–82, 114–
    145
  theory, 39–69, 114
  urban-rural, 17, 79–80, 96–97, 148–213,
    226–227, 230–231, 451*t*, 452*t*
  world, 6, 60–61
  zero, 61, 414–415, 421–422
  See also individual countries and subna-
    tions; various demographic concepts
    and processes
Porter, David, 73–74, 75*b*
Portugal, 297–300, 305, 315*t*, 325*t*, 326
Poti, S. J., 332, 341*b*
Potter, Robert G., Jr., 310, 328*b*, 469*b*
Powdermaker, Hortense, 203, 213*b*
Praeger, Gordon, 41*n*
Pratt, D. M., 13, 15*b*
Pred, Allan R., 178, 186*b*
prejudice, 157–163
President's Committee on Population and
    Family Planning, 425, 444, 446–
    447, 459, 468*b*
President's Science Advisory Committee,
    330, 341*b*
Pressat, Roland, 38*b*
Preston, S. H., 122, 128, 134*b*
Pritzker, Leon, 108–113
Prothero, R. M., 212*b*
Proudhon, P. J., 49
Puerto Rico, 189, 194*t*, 315*t*, 325*t*, 326, 350
Pugh, Thomas F., 275*b*

Quatrefages, A. de, 71, 73, 75*b*
Quesnay, François, 46, 47, 68*b*

Rau, Rama, 393
al-Razi, Abu Bakr Muhammad, 49
Reader, D. H., 205, 213*b*
record linkage, 278–280
Redfield, Lisa, 178
Redfield, Robert, 178, 185*n*, 186*b*
refugees, 164–174, 393
Regional Church Planning Office, 152, 156*b*
Reinhard, Marcel, 38*b*
Rele, J. R., 332, 339, 341*b*
religion, 83, 252–253, 269–273, 341–346,
    427–428, 431, 435, 436, 437
  See also Catholicism; Christianity; Islam;
    Jews
remigration, 225, 245
Republican Party, 460, 468*b*
Reston, James, 347

Rhodesia, 204, 205, 208, 211
Riad, Mahmoud, 174
Ribourt, Pierre François, 71, 75*b*
Ricardo, David, 56
Ridley, Jeanne Clare, 467*b*
Riley, Matilda White, 311, 328*b*
Roberts, Bryan R., 179, 186*b*
Roberts, Stephen H., 73, 74, 75*b*
Robinson, Elizabeth H., 187, 191, 198*b*
Robinson, Warren C., 187–198, 197–198*b*
Rock, John C., 448, 468*b*
Rollin, Louis, 73, 74, 75*b*
Romaniuk, A., 323, 328*b*
Romansh, 250–252
Romero, José Luis, 225, 238, 240*b*
Rosas, Juan Manuel de, 224
Rosenberg, Morris, 66*b*
Roslansky, John D., 367*n*
Rossi, Alice S., 143, 145*b*
Rouch, Jean, 207, 213*b*
Rumania, 297–300
Russell, Josiah C., 375, 380*b*
Russia, *see* USSR
Ryder, Norman B., 296–306, 306*b*, 329,
    334, 341*b*, 449, 450*t*, 451*t*, 453*t*,
    454, 456, 458, 462, 463, 464, 468*b*,
    469*b*

Sagi, Philip C., 469*b*
St. Christopher-Nevis, 193*t*
St. Lucia, 193*t*
St. Vincent, 193*t*
Saint-Yves, G., 71, 75*b*
Samoa, 195*t*
sampling, 100–102, 108–111, 417–418
Sampson, Anthony, 206, 213*b*
Samuel, T. J., 390–400, 400*b*
Sanger, Margaret, 392
Sansom, B., 209, 213*b*
Santos, Hector Enrique, 351
Santos, Theotônio dos, 185, 187*b*
Sanua, Victor D., 175*b*
Sarawak, 193*t*, 195*t*
Sarmiento, Domingo F., 224, 225, 232–234,
    240*b*
Sasportas, L., 72, 75*b*
Sautú, Ruth, 230*t*
Sauvy, Alfred, 46, 53–54, 57, 68*b*
Savorgnan, Franco, 236, 240*b*
Schaedel, Richard P., 186*b*
Schapera, Isaac, 212*b*
Scheuer, James H., 435
Schlaug, Rudolph, 401, 412*b*
Schlesinger, Edward R., 134*b*
Schmitt, Robert C., 71–76, 255, 262*b*
Schnore, Leo F., 148, 156*b*
Schramm, Wilbur, 310, 318, 328*b*
Schroeder, H., 4

Schultz, Theodore W., 60, 68*b*
Schwab, William B., 201, 207, 213*b*
Scotland, 216–218, 297–300
Scott, J. P., 11, 15*b*
segregation, 147–157
Selye, Hans, 11–12, 15*b*
Seurat, L. G., 72, 75*b*
sex (ratio), 19–21, 104, 120–145, 227, 247–248, 267–274, 303, 312, 326, 432*t*, 434*t*, 436*t*, 440, 442
Shah, K. T., 392, 400*b*
Shapiro, Sam, 122, 134*b*
Shastri, Lal Bahadur, 397
Shaul, J. R. H., 200, 213*b*
Sheldon, Eleanor B., 163*b*
Sheps, Mindel C., 467*b*
Shryock, Henry S., Jr., 150, 156*b*, 215, 222*b*
Sierra Leone, 203–204, 210
Silberstein, Paul, 184*n*, 187*b*
Šimić, Serćo F., 290–292
Singapore, 195*t*, 198, 415
Smith, Adam, 47, 56–57, 61, 69*b*
Smith, T. E., 189, 198*b*
social capillarity, *see* social mobility
social class(es), 182–183*t*, 228–231, 267–273, 429–431, 432*t*, 434*t*, 436*t*, 450*t*
  See also population, active; social mobility
social mobility, 63–65, 142–144, 158–163, 230–231, 236
social reform, 367–369, 417–419
social welfare, 407, 409–410
socialism, 56–59
  See also Marx, Karl; USSR
South Africa, 189, 190*t*, 202, 204, 205–206, 209
Southall, Aidan W., 205, 213*b*
Southwick, C. H., 11, 15*b*
Sovani, N. V., 392, 395, 400*b*
Soviet Union, *see* USSR
Spain (Spaniards), 225–226, 232–233, 238–239, 248–249, 297–300, 305
Spencer, Herbert, 40, 50–51, 69*b*, 355
Spengler, Joseph J., 42, 46, 69*b*, 158, 164*b*, 226, 240*b*
Spiegelman, Mortimer, 134*b*, 358, 365*b*
Spuhler, J. N., 359, 365*b*
Srole, Leo, 275*b*
Stalin, Josef, 58, 98
Stangeland, Charles E., 44, 69*b*
sterility, *see* fecundity
Stern, Curt, 368, 380*b*
Stinchcombe, Arthur L., 157*b*
Stocks, Percy, 280*b*
Stolnitz, George J., 121, 134, 134*b*
Stone, Abraham, 396, 400*b*

Stout, Clarke, 274, 275*b*
Strecker, R. L., 10, 15*b*
Stunkard, Albert J., 275*b*
Stycos, J. Mayone, 331, 339, 341*b*, 346–355, 355*b*, 390, 427, 468*b*
Stys, W., 308, 328*b*
subnation(s), *see* population, composition
Sudan, 190*t*
Suggs, Robert C., 73, 75*b*
Suidan, Elza and Said, 168
Surendranathan, N. G., 332, 341*b*
Süssmilch, Johann Peter, 44, 69*b*
Sutter, Jean, 64, 69*b*, 222*b*
Swann, Nancy L., 68*b*
Sweden (Swedish), 16, 25, 27, 31*t*, 115, 118, 297–300, 315*t*, 325*t*, 374, 400–412, 412*b*
Switzerland (Swiss), 233, 241–255, 255*b*, 297–300, 315*t*, 325*t*
Syria, 165–170
Syrkin, Marie, 175*b*

Ta Ch'en, 94–95
Taeuber, Alma F., 147, 152, 153, 154, 156*b*
Taeuber, Irene B., 63, 69*b*, 92*n*, 95, 96*b*, 189, 198*b*, 336, 341*b*
Taeuber, Karl E., 147–157, 156*b*, 215, 222*b*
Tahiti, 71–72
Taitbout, 71, 75*b*
Taiwan, 116, 332–334, 337, 415, 417
Tanzania, 204, 205–206
Taylor, Carl C., 236, 241*b*
Taylor, Carl E., 327, 328*b*
Teissier, Raoul, 71–72, 73, 74, 75*b*
Tendulkar, D. G., 395, 396, 400*b*
Thailand, 193*t*, 195*t*, 198, 315*t*, 323, 325*t*, 326
Thomas, Brinley, 232*t*, 240*b*
Thomas, Dorothy Swaine, 16, 308, 328*b*
Thomlinson, Ralph, 215, 222*b*, 330, 341*b*
Thompson, Carol L., 175*b*
Thompson, Warren S., 188, 198*b*, 307, 328*b*
Thuwe, Inga, 400–412, 412*b*
T'ien Feng-t'iao, 95
Tietze, Christopher, 189, 197, 198*b*, 293, 389, 390*b*, 456, 467*b*, 468*b*
Tolchin, Martin, 293–294, 295*b*
Tonalá, 181–185
Torrado, Susana, 230*t*
Tosta Berlinck, Manoel, 178
tourism, 255–262
Tredgold, R. F., 412*b*
Treiman, Donald J., 160, 164*b*
Tricart, Jean, 180, 187*b*
Tudderen, 342–346
Turkey (Turks), 169, 248
Turner, Elsa A., 309, 328*b*
Tydings, Joseph D., 426, 460, 468*b*

Udry, J. Richard, 292–295
Uganda, 205
Uhrus, Kerstin, 412b
unemployment, 60, 101, 104, 384–386
USSR, 58–59, 60, 96–107, 107b, 116, 169, 225, 281, 297–301, 312, 315t, 325t, 400
United Kingdom, see Great Britain
United Nations
  Conference on Application of Science, 67b
  Economic Commission for Latin America, 179, 180, 186b, 187b
  UNESCO, 192, 197, 198b, 212b, 240b
  General Assembly, 173, 175b, 341b, 382
  Partition Plan for Palestine, 165, 172
  Population Commission, 76, 99
  Population Division, 31t, 38b, 42, 69b, 135b, 189, 192, 193t, 195t, 197, 198b, 215, 222b, 255, 310, 315t, 323, 328–329b, 332, 341b, 355
  UNRWA, 166, 169, 175b
  Statistical Office, 78, 188, 198b, 315t, 329b
United States (Americans), 5–6, 19, 47, 96–97, 116–119, 124–126, 130–133, 135–144, 168–169, 178, 189, 215, 223, 224, 227t, 231–232, 237, 256–265, 279, 281, 297–300, 305, 315t, 325t, 350–351, 356–365, 371, 376, 382n, 420, 424–469
United States Government
  Census, Bureau of the, 95b, 98, 106–107b, 107–113, 115, 145b, 148–152, 157b, 159, 164b, 217–218t, 221t, 267n, 275b, 359, 362, 365b, 457, 463, 468b
  Health, Education, and Welfare, Dept. of, 365b, 425, 435, 445, 446, 459, 460, 467b
  Joint Economic Committee, Congress, 107b
  National Center for Health Statistics, 150, 157b
  National Institutes of Health, 462, 465
  National Office of Vital Statistics, 361t
  Public Health Service, 145b, 219t, 264, 275b, 294, 295b, 358, 360, 363, 365b
  Senate, 424, 426, 435, 441, 459, 460, 468b
  Social Security Administration, 163b
  Women's Bureau, 137, 140–141, 143, 145b
urbanism (-ization), see ecology; fertility; mortality; population—urban-rural
Urlanis, B. T., 58, 69b
Uruguay, 193t, 297
Ussher, Arland, 122, 135b

Valencia, Enrique, 179, 187b
Valenti, D. I., 58, 69b
Valmary, Pierre, 29, 38b
Vancouver, George, 74, 75b
Van Heek, F., 342–346, 346b
Van 't Veer, Anthon J., 342–346
Van Wing, Joseph, 210
Varky, George, 452, 457, 469b
Venezuela, 193t, 194t, 315t, 325t
Verhulst, Pierre-François, 6
Vernier, C., 71, 75b
Vialatoux, Joseph, 46, 49, 69b
Vincendon-Dumoulin, C. A., 71, 73, 75–76b
Voisin, Hubert, 73, 74, 76b

Waksberg, Joseph, 107–113
Waley, D. P., 66b
Walker, Dollie R., 155, 157b
Wallace, Alfred R., 50
Wallace, Robert, 47
Wallerstein, I., 207, 210, 213b
Wallis, Samuel, 71
Wang Nai-chi, 92n, 95, 96b
Wangersky, P. J., 13, 16b
war, 43–45, 98, 368, 378, 413
Waters, Somerset R., 255–262
Watson, William, 213b
Wattal, Pyare Kishan, 392
Weintraub, Robert, 310, 312–313, 329b
Wendel, Bertil, 222, 222b
Westin, Björn, 290n
Westoff, Charles F., 296, 374, 380b, 424, 449, 450t, 451t, 454, 456, 458, 462, 463, 464, 467b, 468b, 469b
Whelpton, Pascal K., 361t, 429, 437–438, 449, 450t, 451t, 452t, 454, 455, 462, 463, 464, 467b, 469b
Whyte, H. M., 265, 275b
Whyte, William F., 142, 145b
Wilber, George W., 219, 222b
Willcox, Walter F., 227, 241b
Williams, Anthony V., 255, 262b
Williams, Josephine, 145b
Wilson, Godfrey, 209, 213b
Wilson, Monica, 206, 213b
Wilson, William, 74, 76b
Wiqvist, Nils, 290n
Wirth, Louis, 206, 213b
Wishik, Samuel M., 424, 444–458, 459–466, 467b
Wissous, 181–185
Wolf, John B., 169–170, 175b
Wolfe, Marshall, 180, 187b
Wolfers, Edward P., 76–85
Wong, Ming, 282, 282b
Wood, T. D., 266t
Woody, Thomas, 137, 145b

work force, *see* population, active
World Health Organization, 193*t*, 393, 396
Worsley, Peter, 206, 213*b*
Wright, Harold, 54, 69*b*
Wrigley, E. A., 69*b*
Wynne-Edwards, V. C., 51, 69*b*

Xydias, Nelly, 207, 213*b*

Yemen, 168
Yerby, Alonzo S., 456, 469*b*
Young, Michael, 162, 164*b*
Yugoslavia (Yugoslavs), 248, 289–292, 297–300

Zambia, 201–203, 208–210
Zelinsky, Wilbur, 255, 262*b*